Canada's International Policies

Agendas, Alternatives, and Politics

Canada's International Policies

Agendas, Alternatives, and Politics

Brian W. Tomlin, Norman Hillmer,
and Fen Osler Hampson

OXFORD
UNIVERSITY PRESS

OXFORD
UNIVERSITY PRESS

70 Wynford Drive, Don Mills, Ontario M3C 1J9
www.oup.com/ca

Oxford University Press is a department of the University of Oxford.
It furthers the University's objective of excellence in research, scholarship,
and education by publishing worldwide in

Oxford New York
Auckland Cape Town Dar es Salaam Hong Kong Karachi
Kuala Lumpur Madrid Melbourne Mexico City Nairobi
New Delhi Shanghai Taipei Toronto

With offices in
Argentina Austria Brazil Chile Czech Republic France Greece
Guatemala Hungary Italy Japan Poland Portugal Singapore
South Korea Switzerland Thailand Turkey Ukraine Vietnam

Oxford is a trade mark of Oxford University Press
in the UK and in certain other countries

Published in Canada
by Oxford University Press

Copyright © Oxford University Press Canada 2008

The moral rights of the author have been asserted

Database right Oxford University Press (maker)

First published 2008

Library and Archives Canada Cataloguing in Publication

Tomlin, Brian W., 1944–
Canada's international policies : agendas, alternatives and politics / Brian
Tomlin, Norman Hillmer, and Fen Hampson.

Includes bibliographical references and index.
ISBN 978-0-19-542109-5

1. Canada—Foreign relations—1945– —Textbooks.   2. Canada—Politics and
government—Textbooks.   3. Canada—History—1945– —Textbooks.
4. Canada—Military policy—Textbooks.   5. Canada—Relations—Textbooks.
I. Hillmer, Norman, 1942–   II. Hampson, Fen Osler   III. Title.

FC242.T64 2007   327.71009'045   C2007-905908-2
1 2 3 4 – 11 10 09 08

Cover image: Christine Balderas/iStockPhoto

This book is printed on permanent (acid-free) paper ∞.
Printed in Canada

Canada's International Policies: Agendas, Alternatives, and Politics

Preface

This volume arose out of our belief that students of Canadian public policy can know more about the process by which Canada's international policies are formulated and chosen. The existing literature on Canadian foreign policy is effective on the content of policy, but such studies do not fully address how policies are made. We believe that the 'how' of policy making is inextricably linked to the 'what' of policy, and that policy analysis must capture both process and content in order to produce a satisfactory understanding of Canada's international policies.

The literature is apt to be strongest on description and prescription, detailing policies and passing judgement about their adequacy. But why do policy agendas change? What alternatives are considered when policy change is in the wind? Who is involved in making crucial choices among alternatives? What are the dynamics in the process of joining problems to policies? Why do policies shift in certain directions at particular times, and remain unchanged at others? When it does undertake explanation, the literature is frequently lacking in explicit theorizing about the determinants of policy. Individual, domestic-national, and international systemic factors are drawn on to explain policies as needed, but their roles are often not explicated theoretically, and models of policy making are left largely implicit. We set as our task the explanation of policy process and content, and the links between them, including policy continuity and change across an array of policy domains. To this end, we have adopted an explicit evolutionary model of policy making to provide the necessary explanation of events.

For research support in the production of this book, we wish to acknowledge the generosity of the Centre for Trade Policy and Law at Carleton University and the University of Ottawa and of Carleton's Centre for Security and Defence Studies. Colleagues read and commented on aspects of the draft manuscript, and we have incorporated many of their suggestions. We extend our particular thanks to

Stephen Azzi, Daniel Bon, Catherine Bragg, Kenneth Calder, Jasmin Cheung-Gertler, Laura Ritchie Dawson, Greg Donaghy, Michael Dolan, J.L. Granatstein, Hector Mackenzie, Nick Hare, Michael Hart, John Hay, Philippe Lagassé, Richard Newport, Harold von Riekhoff, Roger Sarty, Joel J. Sokolsky, Kevin Spooner, and Susan B. Whitney. Philippe Lagassé assisted with the structure and content of the defence chapters, and Jasmin Cheung-Gertler made the same immense contribution to the sections on politics and the responsibility to protect in the chapters on human security. Rachel Schmidt, Marina Sistovaris, and Darryl Whitehead did able research for the book as it developed over the more than two years it was in the writing. At Oxford University Press, we benefited enormously from the abundant goodwill and thorough professionalism of Phyllis Wilson, Kate Skene, and Dina Theleritis. Pamela Erlichman was a subtle editor of an unwieldy manuscript. Megan Sproule-Jones prepared the index, making expert observations along the way that sometimes saved us from ourselves. We remain exclusively responsible for the content of the analysis and any errors or omissions it may contain.

The challenges of joint authorship on a major project are formidable. The exercise, however, has been a collegial one involving an equal partnership where each member of our writing team brought different strengths to the enterprise. Fen Hampson and Norman Hillmer are especially grateful to Brian Tomlin for introducing the work of John Kingdon to them and for the fine example he provided in drafting the first set of cases for the book. For this reason, we have decided to reverse the normal alphabetical listing of authors in the title formally to acknowledge Brian's key role in the making of the volume.

BWT

NH

FOH

Ottawa

24 May 2007

CHAPTER 1

Canada in International Affairs

Throughout the history of Canada's international relations—be it in the realms of international economics, defence and security, or international development—abrupt and often controversial changes in policy have occurred. The successful negotiation of Canada–US free trade in the mid-1980s, followed by the trilateral North American free trade agreement in the early 1990s, marked a sharp departure in the evolution of Canada's international trade policy. Before then, it had largely developed through multilateral negotiations. Similarly, policies regarding foreign investment shifted from an open door to restrictive review, and back, in little more than a decade. In defence policy, Canada's military structure was reorganized substantially into a unified command in the 1960s, and then was overstretched in the 1990s when international deployments increased after the Cold War and defence expenditures were cut to help pay down the national debt. In development assistance, Canada's policies shifted from a global, humanitarian orientation in the 1960s and 1970s to a more restrictive set of assistance programs in the 1980s and 1990s; and in the latter period, Canadian development assistance suffered substantial cuts in the interests of balancing federal budgets. Finally, in the mid-1990s, Canadian foreign policy was seized with an agenda that was centred on human security, a concept that challenged longstanding norms about the inviolability of state sovereignty in international relations. One product of this shift was Canada's leadership of the Ottawa Process to ban anti-personnel landmines, a policy departure that was as innovative as it was unexpected.

Unlike so many recent books on Canada's international relations that try to explain the continuity of Canada's role and why Canada can—and should— remain an activist power in world affairs, this book does not offer prescriptions. Instead, it is focused on explaining the factors and forces that contribute to policy transformation so that students of Canada's international policies can better understand the how and the why of the policy-making process.

All too often, students are presented with a picture that suggests that policy makers are concerned about reinforcing Canada's place in the world so that the country 'can make a difference'. To be sure, rank, status, and power are important. But these are simply means to an end. Public policy is about making difficult decisions on highly complex issues. This is just as true for international affairs as it is for domestic issues. The agenda that practitioners confront on a daily basis is a crowded—if not congested—one. Different interests, ideas, and concerns jostle and compete for their attention. Why do policy makers settle on the issues and problems they do? Why do prominent problems and agendas sometimes fall by the wayside? Why do some groups and interests get heard and not others? As problems get translated into specific policy proposals, they often become highly politicized, engaging different actors in the political arena. What is the nature of this coupling process? And, most important, what role does leadership play in moving a policy idea forward for action? Even when a visible crisis dominates the policy agenda, policy makers must wrestle with alternative courses of action and make tough choices. Who do they talk to and how do they decide?

In addressing these questions, this book argues that the policy-making process in Canada's international relations is messy and often unpredictable. Policy outcomes are not foreordained as many scholars, especially those who have looked at Canadian foreign policy through the prism of traditional models of international relations, are inclined to suggest. When examined closely, there is far less method and structure to the policy-making process than meets the eye. What is clear is that entrepreneurial leadership plays a critical role in mobilizing supportive constituencies in the public policy arena—in getting problems onto the policy agenda, moving those agendas forward, translating them into viable policy proposals, and steering those proposals through the minefields of the federal bureaucracy and the political arena. A crucial element of such leadership is to seize windows of opportunity to introduce new policy initiatives—a process in which timing is everything.

In advancing the argument that 'policy change matters' and that policy change and innovation are some of the less-well-understood aspects of Canada's international policies, we have chosen to focus on a number of turning points in the history of Canadian international relations. The scope of this study is not confined to diplomacy and politics, what some would describe as the more traditional venues of foreign policy. We look at Canada's international policies across the broad spectrum of international investment, trade, development assistance, defence, and human security. In all five issue-areas, we find key moments or episodes where there has been major, if not profound, change in the course and direction of Canada's international policies.

In selecting these issue-areas for inclusion in our analysis, we wanted to achieve as broad a coverage of international policies as possible, while still setting ourselves a manageable task. Globalization has meant that many policy fields traditionally insulated within national boundaries have become international in scope (Doern, Pal, and Tomlin, 1996), and clearly not all could be included. We are confident that our focus on the trade and investment dimensions of international economics, defence and human security, and international development assistance offers a comprehensive portrait of important aspects of Canada's international policies, and we hope that others will be stimulated to undertake similar analyses of issue-areas not covered here.

The next section of this chapter provides an historical overview of Canada's foreign policy in the period since the end of the Second World War. It outlines in brief the main thrusts of the country's international policies. A discussion, and critique, of some of the standard treatments of Canadian foreign policy follows as background for the approach taken in this volume. The final section of the chapter develops the conceptual and theoretical underpinnings of our model of Canada's international policy-making process and explains how the model is applied in subsequent chapters.

IN FOREIGN FIELDS

The international environment changed markedly after 1945. The United States engaged in the world as it never had, and it replaced Great Britain as Canada's closest ally. A formidable adversary, the Soviet Union (USSR), glowered on the horizon of a Cold War that divided the world into two camps. One was led by the United States and the other by the Soviets, the two 'superpowers' that now dominated international relations. Modern weaponry altered the strategic equation: no one was safe from outside aggression. Canada responded accordingly, taking an activist role in postwar international arrangements such as the United Nations, the multiracial Commonwealth and the North Atlantic Treaty Organization (NATO), the first peacetime alliance in Canadian history. Canadians aligned themselves vigorously with the United States against the Soviet Union and its satellites. The country was a bit player no longer.

It took time for Canada's defence thinking to catch up with its foreign policy. After 1945 the government made deep cuts in army, navy, and air force personnel and scotched the dreams of military planners for robust armed forces and major equipment acquisitions. For 1947–8, the military budget was reduced by $140 million to $240 million, a decision that accorded with a national mood bent on peace. Not until Canada's participation in the Korean War (1950–3) did the Cold War really have an impact on defence spending. The crisis in Korea focused the attention of policy makers and their publics on the threat of Soviet attack on Western nations. The public supported government investment in a robust military, and Canada committed army and air force units to NATO in Europe and anti-submarine capabilities to the alliance's maritime forces. Over the decade of the 1950s, the government consistently devoted a quarter of the national budget to defence. Star

The Suez Crisis of 1956 brought Canada to unaccustomed international prominence. The affair was triggered in that year by Egypt's nationalization of the Suez Canal. The canal was on Egyptian territory, but was controlled by Great Britain and France until it was seized by Eygptian President Nasser in July

1956. A vital waterway, it allowed ships to take a shortcut from Europe through the Mediterranean Sea to the Indian Ocean and the Pacific beyond, avoiding the long trip around the horn of Africa. To reclaim their lost property, the British and French attacked Egypt in late October, with the assistance of Israel. Working feverishly at the United Nations in New York, the Canadian foreign minister, Lester B. Pearson, forged an international consensus behind a solution to the crisis: hostilities would cease; Britain, France, and Israel would depart from Egyptian territory; and a UN peacekeeping force would secure and supervise the peace.

Pearson's crisis diplomacy at the United Nations in 1956 reflected tradition as well as innovation. Canada was out to save its allies, the British and French, even though they would have preferred it if Pearson had stayed out of their business. Their invasion of Egypt made Britain and France international pariahs, not least in the United States, where the Anglo-French action was condemned. Pearson found a way to get Canada's mother countries out of the hole into which they had dug themselves, and to move Britain and the US back on the same track in world affairs—to the comfortable and cooperative place Canadians had always liked its two closest partners to be. The future of the Commonwealth, the club of former British nations that was Canada's longtime diplomatic home, was also at stake; when Pearson damped down the fires at Suez, he removed a grave danger to an institution threatened by divisions between Britain and countries such as India, which regarded Britain's actions against Egypt as an attack on the developing world. At home in Canada, the national mood was split between opponents of what Britain had done at Suez and supporters of its stand against Egypt, many of them recent British immigrants. Pearson's reputation was made, however. He was awarded the Nobel Peace Prize for his Suez negotiations and has been widely regarded ever since as the inventor of UN peacekeeping.

The government in Ottawa sent a substantial contingent to the post-Suez UN peacekeeping force in the Middle East. That was the first of the big UN peacekeeping missions. It was followed by two more major peacekeeping activities under the umbrella of the UN, the first to the Congo in Central Africa from 1960 to 1964 and the second to the Mediterranean island of Cyprus, beginning in 1964. Canada contributed substantially to each. Peacekeeping was worming its way into the national psyche as an endeavour Canadians ought to engage in, and one they were good at; it was a policy practice that would come to define Canada as a peaceable kingdom in a mad world. Yet peacekeeping was an adjunct, never an alternative, to Cold War policies. The vital work of Canadian defence lay in NATO and the North American continent. The greatest value of peacekeeping from the government's perspective was that it served Canada's alliance interests. Members of the Canadian military were reluctant peacekeepers. It was boring, repetitive, and unmilitary, they thought, and a distraction from what really mattered (Hillmer, 2003).

The period immediately after the Second World War was pro-American in Canada and in Canadian policy. Links between the Canadian and American militaries accumulated as they fought the Cold War with equal fervour. Trade with the US grew, and American investment poured into the country, promoted by Liberal governments and their economic czar, C.D. Howe. Surveys of opinion demonstrated that Canadians identified themselves positively with the United States—with its values, its leadership, and its international aims. Substantial parts of the Canadian population looked up to the Americans and believed that Canada's dependence on them was beneficial to the country, a conclusion that was understandable in the dark days of the early Cold War (Hillmer, 2005a: 333).

What Canadians admired, however, they inevitably questioned. In the 1957 election, Conservative leader John Diefenbaker was able to exploit a latent resentment in the body politic against the United States with his attacks on US investment and on the Liberals as a party that had too easily aligned Canada to the US. Diefenbaker had other ideas. He wanted to strengthen the old British tie, and to emphasize the development of Canada's North as a way of differentiating the country from the US. These policy ideas mostly remained ideas only. Diefenbaker as prime minister mounted no systematic campaign to confront American investment in Canada and he scurried away from a rash promise to divert 15 per cent of Canadian trade to Britain.

Prime Minister Diefenbaker (1957–63) proved an assiduous Cold War ally to the US at the beginning of his time in office, signing on, for example, to the North American Air Defence Agreement (NORAD). But relations with the United States deteriorated in the early 1960s and disintegrated during the 1962 Cuban missile crisis, when the prime minister publicly questioned the leadership of President John F. Kennedy. Three months later, the Kennedy administration returned the favour, drawing public attention to Diefenbaker's refusal to follow through on his promise to accept US nuclear weapons in Canada. The government fell, and an election was called. The electorate was again divided, this time between those who believed that Canada must follow through on its Cold War commitments and those who accepted the logic of Diefenbaker's argument that having American nuclear arms in Canada threatened the country's sovereignty and contradicted his government's efforts to encourage nuclear disarmament. The Liberals of Lester B. Pearson won, if narrowly; the former foreign minister was prime minister from April 1963 to April 1968.

Prime Minister Pearson's minister of finance, Walter Gordon, was an economic nationalist with strong ideas about the need to lessen Canadian economic dependence on the US. He was determined to change things, and he did not see the need for extensive consultation on his proposals to change the tax system in order to encourage greater domestic ownership of Canadian firms. But colleagues in government and business leaders were not on his side. Neither was the public. Measures introduced in his first budget to curb American investment and encourage Canadian ownership were quickly abandoned, and he did not—could not—try again in his brief time as Pearson's finance minister from 1963 to 1965. He was seldom in government after that, but he maintained an active presence with his warnings about the hazards of a country that was too dependent on the United States. He became the informal head of a movement that came to be called the New Nationalism, made up of champions of an independent Canada.

In that guise he had an influence on politics that he had not known in government (Azzi, 1999: 167).

A two-decades-long period of Canadian scepticism about the United States began in the mid-1960s, helped by America's Vietnam War, the assassinations of US political figures, eruptions over the rights of African-Americans, corporate scandal, and political corruption. It was easy to think of the United States in those years as a wayward empire, led by irresponsible people who threatened world peace, and to hope that Canada could keep it and them at arm's length (Hillmer, 2006: 64). The public enjoyed government rhetoric directed at the United States and the promise of policies that would enhance the country's independence. Gordon and a growing legion of nationalists, some of them very influential and some with more radical notions about how to win back Canada for Canadians, had a receptive audience. Pearson scarcely noticed, but the next Liberal leader was prepared to meet the nationalists partway.

The Liberal government of Pierre Trudeau (1968–79 and 1980–4) implemented a series of measures to deal with the giant American economic and cultural appetite, and to shore up support in the now-strong nationalist constituency. The 1971 Canada Development Corporation encouraged national ownership of business; the Foreign Investment Review Agency, created in 1974, screened investment from sources outside the country; Petro-Canada was established in 1975 as a publicly owned oil company; and agreements with Europe and Japan were signed in the mid-1970s under a policy known as the Third Option. In 1980, when Trudeau returned to power after nine months of Conservative government, he established the National Energy Program (NEP) to Canadianize the oil and gas industry. Cultural matters did not receive the same attention (Azzi, 2007: 75). Nevertheless, in the early 1970s the Canadian Radio-Television and Telecommunications Commission (CRTC) imposed Canadian content regulations for radio and strengthened the existing content regulations for television. The government also increased funding for the Canadian Film Development Corporation (now Telefilm Canada), and created a program of subsidies for the book publishing industry. In 1976, Parliament ended the tax deduction for advertising in the Canadian editions of *Time* and *Reader's Digest* and on US border television stations.

Trudeau, who always professed to be very suspicious of nationalisms of all varieties, also applied a nationalist prescription to other international policies, in keeping with the quite explicit aim of dislodging Canada from its post-1945 multilateralist moorings. He and his closest political friends were disenchanted with the ancient men who had run foreign policy under the Pearson government. With the tide of Quebec separatism rising and evidence of an errant United States everywhere, the Trudeau Liberals were determined to put Canada—its interests and integrity—first in their thinking and action. Canada, the prime minister stated, was a modest power, and ought not to have pretensions about its place in the world. He also supported a relaxation in the friction between the United States and the Soviet Union, known as détente, as both superpowers eased back from the Cold War. In 1969 the government, without consulting its allies, reduced the Canadian Forces' commitment to defending Europe under the North Atlantic alliance, and downgraded the military and peacekeeping. The government's 1970 statement, *Foreign Policy for Canadians*, put economic growth and national unity to the fore (Government of Canada, 1970). International security commitments receded into the background.

Foreign Policy for Canadians counselled the diversification of diplomacy away from its American, Atlantic, and European preoccupations. Trudeau's Canada extended diplomatic recognition to Communist China in 1970. That was meant as an expression of an independent Canadian stance toward the world, and a clear repudiation of earlier policies that the new prime minister claimed had been neither independent nor fully in the national interest. The country had a lot at stake, said Trudeau, because of trade with China and the importance of good relations with that great sprawling country, populated by nearly a billion people. Canada, he insisted, was a Pacific country (Frolic, 1991: 192). The Soviet Union picked up on the independent thrust in Trudeau's thinking, inviting him to make a state visit, the first by a Canadian head of government. This took place in the spring of 1971. During the trip, Trudeau emphasized the two countries' shared characteristics as northern states and complained about the overwhelming presence of the United States in Canadian life, notably the danger that the Americans posed (in his words) to 'our national identity from a cultural, economic and perhaps even military point of view' (Farr, 1989: 108; Sarty, 1993: 121–3).

Such public expressions of Canada's international policies, though they appealed to the nationalist public mood, conveyed the wrong impression. Canada and the United States were tolerant allies, in the good phrase of historian Greg Donaghy, during the turbulent time from the mid-1960s to the mid-1980s, willing to work through their differences and anxious to keep their partnership under constant renegotiation. The 1965 Auto Pact, introducing managed free trade in the automobile and truck sector of the North American economy, was a far better and more lasting indicator of the bilateral economic partnership than the Foreign Investment Review Agency or the National Energy Program. The Canada–United States squabble in that same year, pitting Prime Minister Pearson against US President Lyndon Johnson over the Canadian's mildly dissenting Vietnam address at Temple University in Philadelphia, grabbed headlines and caught the continuing attention of historians. The speech, however, did not substantially damage the relationship between the two countries (Donaghy, 2002: 13–14).

Nothing, then, got in the way of the ever-upward movement of Canadian–American trade flows, and nothing seriously prevented the close cooperation of the two countries in the prosecution of the Cold War. Pierre Trudeau might ruffle the feathers of the American eagle with provocative oratory about the strengths of Fidel Castro's regime in Cuba or the importance of keeping a balanced view of other Communist governments, but Canada was a North American state, a fact underlined by Cold War necessities. The country was vulnerable to attack as it had not been before the Second World War. It needed its best friend, the United States, and responded correspondingly to American needs. As the hopes for East–West détente faded, the Trudeauites paid more attention to NATO, North American defence, and to the military. In 1983, they agreed to allow the testing of US cruise missiles over Canadian soil, the year that they also opened sectoral free trade discussions with the Ronald Reagan administration in Washington. The Americans never completely forgot the early Trudeau, it is true. His attempt to soften nuclear tensions in his celebrated peace mission of 1983–4 was damaged by the perception, not in the United States alone, that he had not been a consistently faithful Western ally.

The strength of its American alliance gave Canada space to pursue a vigorous internationalism (Hillmer, 2002: 70; 2005b: 33). Trudeau had insisted that he wanted no part of his Pearsonian inheritance, but he came to treasure that mantle, later claiming that the great diplomat had always been his model. After an initial hesitation, his government came around to the idea that peacekeeping was a good idea. He poked fun at the Commonwealth when he went to his first meeting of that group's heads of government; by his last, he was a senior statesman in the organization, helping keep it alive with imaginative and dogged diplomacy. He valued the Commonwealth as a window on the developing world and he spoke a great deal about building bridges between its North and its South. Another avenue to what was then called the Third World was the evolving association of French-language countries, *la francophonie*, where Trudeau could do Good Things while simultaneously combatting the aspirations of Quebec to have an international personality separate from that of Canada.

Foreign Policy for Canadians claimed that the newly created Canadian International Development Agency (CIDA) was an important instrument of foreign policy, and that here was a niche for making a unique national contribution to the world. Canada's Official Development Assistance (ODA) shot up in the early Trudeau era, particularly to francophone Africa, and there was a formal government endorsement of the recommendation of Lester Pearson's Commission on International Development that the aid expenditure of developed countries ought to be 0.7 per cent of their Gross National Product (GNP). Canadian ODA never quite got there, and the period of aid activism was quickly over. The figure rose to 0.53 per cent of GNP by 1975–6, but that proved to be its highest point ever.

When the Conservatives achieved power in 1984, they professed to have very different international policies, and they did. In particular, they put a high premium on 'super relations' with the United States (Hillmer and Granatstein, 2007: 276). No less than Trudeau, however, Prime Minister Brian Mulroney (1984–93) turned out to be a Pearsonian, a fierce believer in international structures and in constructive engagement with the world. As with Trudeau, Mulroney's foreign policy was ultimately driven by events beyond Canada's control rather than preconceived notions about what might constitute a Conservative foreign policy agenda (Michaud and Nossal, 2001: 21–2). And like Pearson and Trudeau before him, Mulroney believed that institutions such as the United Nations and the Commonwealth were places where Canada could make its mark independently of the United States.

Mulroney compiled solid internationalist credentials in his nearly ten years in power, establishing himself as a 'committed multilateralist' (ibid.: 17). The prime minister's activist agenda was clear in his personal diplomacy at the UN, the G7 group of leading industrialized countries, the Commonwealth and *la francophonie*. In 1989 Canada added the Organization of American States (OAS) to its impressive list of international club memberships, and the next year under foreign minister Joe Clark the government began to champion the building of a security architecture in the North Pacific region (ibid.: 17–18). With the Cold War over in the early 1990s, the government pursued 'good governance', a policy framework associated with activist interventions abroad to promote democracy, human rights, the rule of law and the market economy (Cheung-Gertler, 2006a). The intent and impact of these policies are open to debate, but the Conservative record in international affairs from 1984 to 1993 cannot be written off as simply an attempt to snuggle up to the United States.

Two of the Conservative government's most striking initiatives came in areas in which this book specializes—defence and trade. The 1987 defence White Paper outlined a massive reinvestment in the Canadian Forces, and promised a new fleet of nuclear-powered submarines to boot. Canada would do its full part in prosecuting the Cold War and would protect its sovereignty from any threat, including from the United States. But this ambitious plan was dead almost from the moment of arrival, the victim of domestic budget constraints and changing global circumstances as the Cold War ended and the Soviet Union ended with it. A comprehensive free trade agreement with the United States (FTA) was an even bolder concept, and it did not fail, although the negotiations went right up to the final deadline and a federal election had to be fought over their outcome. The 1987 FTA deal confirmed Canada's destiny as a North American state. A North American free trade agreement (NAFTA) was achieved in 1993, taking Mexico into the earlier arrangement and creating a huge continental trade zone to rival that of other regional blocs such as the European Union.

When the Berlin Wall fell in November 1989, and the Cold War began to stumble to its eventual close in the early 1990s, the Conservatives departed from their occasionally promising rhetoric about development. Trade promotion and free markets replaced social justice values and strategic interests as the *raison d'être* of Western aid efforts. ODA during the Mulroney years concentrated on a few relatively advanced and wealthy countries whose governments were deemed worthy development partners. This was all in keeping with the tone of the times. A wave of democratization swept the developing world, new markets opened in Asia and the former Soviet republics, and the United Nations embarked on an ambitious agenda of transitional peacekeeping and peacebuilding in Cambodia, Mozambique, El Salvador, and Guatemala.

Notwithstanding the abandonment of the 1987 defence White Paper, the Mulroney government wanted to make its mark in the post–Cold War 'new world order', a phrase coined by US President George H.W. Bush. In 1991, Canadians fought in the Persian Gulf alongside the Americans to squash Iraq's conquest of neighbouring Kuwait. Among its Canadian proponents, that first Gulf

War represented a victory for international order and the United Nations after the UN's deep Cold War slumber (Rudner, 1991: 268; Welch, 1992: 84). Renewed faith in the world body encouraged the revival in UN-sponsored peacekeeping operations, for which the Mulroney government became a leading advocate. Canadian soldiers served with the UN Iran–Iraq Military Observer Group (UNIMOG) and the UN Transition Assistance Group in Namibia (UNTAG), and civilian personnel joined peacekeepers and monitored elections in Central America.

The spirit of international optimism—the hope for a new order of things in the world—did not last long into the 1990s. Evidence of chaos had emerged in the Balkans, as provinces of the Federal Republic of Yugoslavia (FRY) divided along ethnic, religious, and linguistic lines in a frenzy of violent sectarianism. The conditions of state failure were also apparent in Somalia, where the central government could not deliver basic needs to civilian populations or exert control over warring factions. Violence, mass killings, and displacement in the Balkans and Africa signalled a brand of conflict that would be common after the Cold War: clashes within states between rival groups, including some that were state-sanctioned, which exacted a heavy toll on civilian populations. The United Nations responded to emerging post–Cold War disorders with wider peacekeeping operations challenging the principles of consent, limited use of force, and impartiality that had characterized and defined peacekeeping's first generation after Suez (Bellamy, Williams, and Griffin, 2004). Ottawa enthusiastically supported the UN decision to intervene in the troubled Balkan states; up to 1,200 Canadian peacekeepers were deployed to the UN Protection Force in the Former Yugoslavia (UNPROFOR) in 1992. Within nine months 750 Canadian soldiers were deployed on the UN Operation in Somalia (UNOSOM), the United Nations' first true humanitarian intervention (Tessier and Fortmann, 2001: 120). A military coup overthrowing a democratic government in Haiti then became another occasion for a multilateral response initiated by the activist Mulroney (Gecelovsky and Keating, 2001: 200).

When the Liberals succeeded the Mulroney Conservatives after the October 1993 election, they inherited the Balkan operation and soon contributed a Canadian Forces (CF) contingent to Rwanda. They also inherited a serious economic crisis, with spiralling government debt and budget deficits; the new prime minister, Jean Chrétien (1993–2003), pledged sound government management above all else. The 1994 defence White Paper reinforced the status quo of multipurpose, combat-capable CF with the ability to operate across the full spectrum of potential operations. Yet the government's real objective was to cut costs. The decision to maintain fighting forces was based upon the relative cost-effectiveness of a leaner force over innovative, potentially expensive, alternatives. The military budget shrank by more than 40 per cent from 1987 levels to $9.5 billion in 1995; the CF were cut by more than 10,000 personnel by the end of the century. Paradoxically, the Liberal government at the same time committed CF units to a wide variety of UN and NATO operations, including NATO's 1999 war in Kosovo.

Wider peacekeeping missions in Somalia, the former Yugoslavia, and Rwanda failed to match sufficient resources and political will to good intentions, resulting in the continuation of hostilities and violence against civilians. The death of some 800,000 ethnic Tutsis in the 1994 Rwandan genocide and the 1995 massacre of 7,000 Bosnian Muslims at Srebenica in the former Yugoslavia underscored the inability of the United Nations to put an end to humanitarian crises within nation-states. Using soldiers as peacebuilders where there was little or no peace to build upon, in the words of one Canadian observer, represented a costly and inefficient use of limited government resources (Potter, 1996–7: 30–1). The trend was toward the use of organizations like NATO for this purpose, institutions with muscle to back up their mandate, and an explicit CF policy to foster greater cooperation and interoperability with the US military.

Despite his promise to re-establish the Canadian distance from the US that Mulroney had reduced, Prime Minister Chrétien built up a solid relationship with his American counterpart, President Clinton. The president, indeed, spoke out on Chrétien's behalf for a united Canada during the 1995 independence referendum campaign, when Quebecers voted to remain in the country by only the barest of margins. The highly integrated North American economy was at the centre of Canadian international policy, but the Liberals also tried to diversify trade relationships and engage with emerging markets. Frequently led by Chrétien himself, a series of 'Team Canada' trade and business missions set off around the globe, each event featuring the signing of deals worth billions of dollars with Asia-Pacific and Latin American countries. With debts and deficits at the forefront of the national imagination, the missions reinforced the widespread impression that Chrétien's major priorities were on the economic side of international policy. Ottawa bureaucrats clambered aboard the trade bandwagon (Potter, 1996).

The budget crunch led to cutbacks and depleted morale in the policy domains of defence, development, and diplomacy. Added to the drastic cuts to the defence budget was a 30 per cent reduction in Canada's Official Development Assistance funding, while the Department of Foreign Affairs budget had to weather a 24 per cent cut. Canadians, meanwhile, continued to revel in the country's reputation for good international citizenship, which cuts to ODA and diplomatic representation abroad did little to uphold. A combination of limited resources, a domestic climate of fiscal austerity and continuing Canadian global-mindedness, together with fundamental changes to the international security climate, contributed to a movement away from collective security or defence roles and political receptivity to other visions of security (Ross, 2001: 84). Coming into fashion were less costly alternatives to traditional peace and security roles, the democratization of the foreign policy-making process (Nossal, 1995), and new definitions of the meaning of security that went beyond defence and the military.

This was the context for a powerful advocate of and messenger for a program of 'human security'. Lloyd Axworthy was named minister of foreign affairs in

January 1996. He argued that the interdependence between peoples in a global-ized world had diminished the geographical, social, economic, and political spaces between nation-states. Non-military threats, or problems exacerbated by non-military threats, like transnational disease, human rights violations, resource scarcity, environmental degradation or large-scale migration, were as damaging to international peace and security as the threat posed by arms. Axworthy explained that it was in Canada's national interest, as well as part of its responsibility as a global citizen, to reframe international security in terms of the security of peoples, whether in socioeconomic or physical terms. Among the major achievements of Canada's human security agenda were the conclusion of an international treaty to ban landmines, the campaign for the creation of the International Criminal Court (ICC), and the sponsorship of an international commission of experts to reconcile emerging practices of humanitarian inter-vention with principles of state sovereignty through a 'responsibility to protect' (R2P). Each of these initiatives benefited from Axworthy's understanding of the 'soft-power' influence that derives from effective partnerships between govern-ments and civil society.

   The September 11 terrorist attack on New York and Washington was a cata-clysmic event, shaking the foundations of international security and fundamen-tally altering the policy agendas of great powers and smaller states alike. US-led wars in Afghanistan and Iraq soon followed. Canada stayed out of the 2003 Iraq war, but Canadian soldiers were active from the start in Afghanistan, working alongside American armed forces. Afghanistan became the single largest recipi-ent of Canadian aid (Treasury Board of Canada, 2007), some of which went toward supporting CF contingents for stabilization operations. Canadians might find themselves worrying about the foreign policy directions of President George W. Bush's America, but their governments of both stripes, Liberal and Conserva-tive, were solid supporters of the war on terror that the president unleashed after September 11. The Chrétien, Martin, and Harper governments in this period all worked, with some admitted bumps along the road, to build a strong relation-ship with the United States and to guard Canadian economic security from a 'Fortress America' mentality south of the border. In a prominent example of such thinking, Canada concluded a 2001 Smart Border Accord with the United States, in an effort to bolster continental security and protect access to the Amer-ican market for Canadian manufacturers. By contrast, the state of the environ-ment, an international issue of immense proportions, had little traction with political leaders, despite lively public interest in Canada's commitments under the Kyoto Protocol to the UN Convention on Climate Change.

   National security and the national interest surfaced as the robust themes of early twenty-first-century government statements and speeches. The North American partnership sat high on the government's decision agenda, and so too did the rebuilding of the military. The urgent goal, it was being said, was to res-urrect an international reputation that had been forged after the Second World War and frittered away by leaders who did not or would not grasp Canada's responsibilities to global security.

APPROACHES TO THE STUDY OF CANADIAN FOREIGN POLICY

A traditional, levels-of-analysis framework provides a useful way to conceptual-ize some of the different approaches to the study of Canadian foreign policy that are reflected in many recent significant texts. Like any framework, it is not per-fect, and the categories are certainly not mutually exclusive. But the framework does help place these studies in terms of what shapes the choices of Canadian foreign policy decision makers. It also highlights some of the logical problems associated with these approaches and positions our study within this literature.

In our review of this literature, we find that most studies are not concerned about explaining change in Canada's international relations; rather, they are concerned with explaining patterns of continuity and why Canada consistently acts and views itself as a 'middle power' in international relations. Although many of these studies discuss how the field of international relations is chang-ing, especially with the end of the Cold War and the arrival of what is euphemistically referred to as a 'post-9/11 world', they see few signs that Canada's decision makers have adapted to these new realities. Their view (and critique) of the policy process is that it is inert and constrained by capabilities, political culture, tradition, and domestic politics. Although there is a degree of inertia in any political system, as we argue in this book, the history of Canada's international relations—whether it is in the realm of national security, interna-tional economic policy, or development—is also one of change, in some instances dramatic policy change and innovation that has been controversial and transformational.

There have been pivotal moments in Canada's international relations when old policies have been swept aside and new policies put in their place. Why did the policy agendas change? What were the alternatives that were considered when policy was about to change? Who was involved in making crucial deci-sions? How did such decisions get implemented? What drove the policy agenda forward at these critical moments in history? These are just some of the ques-tions that loom large and remain largely unanswered in much of the literature on Canada's international relations.

A levels-of-analysis approach classifies the determinants of state policies in terms of the individual, the nation-state, or the international system (see Waltz, 1959). At the individual level (level 1), the most important factors that influence policy decisions and choices are the psychological dispositions of leaders, includ-ing their belief systems, personalities, and emotive and cognitive biases. Individ-ual-level explanations typically stress the role of human agency and leadership in the policy-making process. At the national level (level 2), among those vari-ables that influence and shape policy outcomes are the structure and nature of the political system (including institutional relationships among the different branches of government), public opinion, the media, interest groups, political culture, ideology, the structure of the economy, and ethnic group relations. Bureaucratic and organizational behaviours and interests also play into this level of analysis in shaping—as well as helping to explain—policy outcomes.

Systemic-level explanations (level 3) focus on the structure of the international—or sometimes regional—system and how the distribution of power, especially military and economic power, affects the policy choices and behaviours of individual states in the system. The implication here, as Waltz notes, is 'that the freedom of choice of any one state is limited by the actions of all others' (Waltz, 1959: 204). Accordingly, states calibrate their national interests in terms of (1) their own capabilities; and (2) the threats and opportunities they see in their external environment. Interests may also be affected and shaped by the pattern of alliances in the international system and the strategic opportunities presented by changes in the balance of power among great powers (and their alliance partners) in the international system.

So-called *realists* typically stress the importance of power relations at the systemic level in shaping the policy behaviours and preferences of states; that is, level-3 factors are the critical determinants of state behaviour. But *realists* are not the only scholars to stress the importance of the international environment. Some scholars argue that systemwide norms and values are also important to understanding the foreign policy behaviours of states, especially because norms change and new ones emerge. For example, evolving human rights norms in humanitarian and international law have chipped away at traditional ideas about the inviolability of state sovereignty in international relations (see, for example, Keck and Sikkink, 1998; Risse, Ropp, and Sikkink, 1999).

In addition to norms, transnational actors, such as multinational corporations, international non-governmental organizations, and even terrorist groups like al-Qaeda, also operate at the systemic level and clearly have the capacity to affect the policy choice and behaviours of states. So too do financial and capital flows and new forms of communication, such as the Internet. A new body of scholarship suggests that the forces of globalization, which contain many of these elements, are transforming the external environment within which states operate (level-3 effects). These same forces are also transforming national politics and public policy through the mobilization of social groups and interests at the domestic level (level 2) (see, for example, Nye and Donahue, 2000; Nye, 2004).

International organizations are also important systemic actors whose operations affect the environment within which states operate—as arenas for bargaining and negotiation, centres for research and policy formulation, and instruments of collective action. An extensive literature in international relations documents the importance of international institutions in agenda-setting and policy formation.

International relations scholars differ in the emphasis they assign to these three levels to explain state behaviour and policy outcomes. *Realists* believe that the anarchic structure of the international system (that is, level 3) is the central constraint on state behaviour and defines the critical foreign choices that states make for themselves. Because the distribution of state power and resources (military and economic) tends to be unequal in the international system, it may be necessary for states to resort to balancing or bandwagoning strategies to secure their national interests. Most balancing or bandwagoning strategies involve the creation of formal (or informal) military and economic alliances as correctives to the power of large and powerful—especially preponderant—states in the international system.

Whereas *realists* favour alliances and military solutions to achieve international order and promote the security interests of states, *liberals* believe that international institutions are the preferred instruments of international peace and security to counter the anarchical tendencies of a state-based, international system. In the liberal variant of the democratic peace (which dates back to the writings of Immanuel Kant) non-democratic states pose the greatest threat to international peace and security in an anarchic international system; that is, the national character of states (level-2 effects) is fundamental to understanding the basis of international order (see, for example, Russett, 1993).

Realist and *liberal* assumptions about the nature of international relations inform much of the contemporary debate and writing about Canadian foreign policy. At the same time, different analysts have placed different degrees of emphasis on which level of analysis is most germane to understanding the factors and forces that shape Canada's foreign policy. These approaches are summarized in Table 1.1. Admittedly, some of these works are more self-consciously theoretical than others. And in many of these works, description and analysis of the determinants of Canadian foreign policy blend almost seamlessly with policy advice and prescription.

The *liberal* tradition, with its emphasis on middle-power internationalism, represents the dominant stream of Canadian foreign policy analysis. It is reflected in the works of such scholars as John Holmes (1970), Andrew Cooper (1997), Tom Keating (1993), Stephen Clarkson (1968, 2002) and John English and Norman Hillmer (1992). These scholars argue that as a middle-ranked power in the international system, Canada is ill equipped to play great-power politics in international relations. Instead, Canada has generally tended to advance its interests by promoting a rules-based international order through effective diplomacy and its membership in international institutions.

Some of these scholars argue that Canada's middle-power activism diminished toward the end of the last century as a result of growing internal pressures and constraints on Canadian foreign policy (level-2 effects). These included the continuing crisis over Canadian unity, which erupted in the 1970s and resurfaced in the run-up to the referendum on Quebec sovereignty in the 1990s, and Canada's weak economic performance, fiscal deficits, and growing levels of public indebtedness. However, as a result of changing systemic opportunities (level 3), for example, the end of bipolarity with the end of the Cold War, the emergence of a global civil society, and the rise of a whole new set of global threats, such as climate change, population growth, etc., these scholars anticipate a new role for Canada in international affairs.

In one of the notable surveys of Canadian foreign policy, Andrew Cooper argues that 'the overall pattern of Canadian behavior in foreign policy can only be understood against the background of the tensions between the old habits

Table 1.1 Levels of Analysis Used in Understanding Canada's Foreign Policy

Level of Analysis	Author	Key Influences on Policy	Sources of Policy Change and Innovation	Key Focus and Analytic Orientation
Perceptual and cognitive factors (level 1)	David Welch	Personality and belief systems of individual leaders, motivated and unmotivated biases	Policy change occurs when elites seek to avoid actual or impending losses (defined in political and economic terms)	Explaining change in Canadian foreign policy
Subsystemic factors (level 2)	Stephen Clarkson Andrew Cooper John English/ Norman Hillmer John Holmes Don Munton Denis Stairs Jennifer Welsh	National values, culture, and generalized belief systems; public opinion; bureaucratic/ intergovernmental politics and interest group pressures	Policy change is incremental and slow; change only occurs when collective belief systems and values change; change may also be driven by mobilized domestic constituencies and public opinion	Explaining continuity in Canadian foreign policy
Systemic factors (level 3)	John Kirton Kim Nossal	National interests, which are defined by hierarchies of power and influence in the inter-national system, geography, and a country's overall level of military and economic resource endowments	Stability in the international hierarchy of power and interest in the international system constrains policy choices; as hierarchies change, there may be some opportunity for innovation	Explaining continuity in Canadian foreign policy

ingrained in the middle power perspective and the thread of the new directions woven in the transition towards altered ways of thinking and acting'. And he goes on to suggest that 'this interplay between old habits and new directions is played out through the assessment of a number of enduring attitudes and issues built into larger debates about the expression of Canadian foreign policy' (Cooper, 1997: 25).

Cooper's discussion about the determinants of Canadian foreign policy privileges level-2 influences that include political culture, generalized belief systems, and ideology (what he refers to as 'national style', 'old habits', and 'ways of thinking'). Like many scholars, he also stresses the importance of statecraft and diplomacy (that is, level 1 or human agency variables): 'Much of the influence Canada has enjoyed in international affairs over the course of the post-1945 era rested on its diplomatic skills' (ibid.: 35). However, in the post–Cold War era, Cooper argues that Canadian policy is being shaped by new developments in its external environment (level 3): 'In light of the transformation in international politics, Canada has both room for maneuver and a greater margin of safety. . . . Military threats are of less concern in the post–Cold War World. Multilateralism has become more refined and pervasive' (ibid.: 282). Even so, Cooper sees that Canada's main challenge is to reinvent its middle power self in this new world: 'The foreign policy agenda is increasingly crowded, with a widened concept of security and a closer intersection between domestic and international issues. Capacity, at the same time, has been altered through pluralization, globalization, and the requirement for legitimization. Alteration in form and function, however, does not mean a reduction in importance. . . . In a world where bargaining and negotiation have become more pervasive, and where institutions and coalitions increasingly matter . . . so have the opportunities expanded for Canada to perform well on the world stage' (ibid.: 294).

Although Cooper stresses the role of history, and especially the Pearson era in defining Canada's diplomatic vocation, other scholars like John Holmes (1970) and Denis Stairs (2003), attribute it to a *mission civilisatrice* that they argue comes from being a non-imperial power. In addition, Canada's Constitution, which stresses the values of 'peace, order, and good government', has also developed into something of an export commodity in recent years as Canadians have preached the virtues of good governance, human rights, and other homegrown values in international affairs.

The proposition that Canada's cultural and political institutions are ready for export is the central theme in Jennifer Welsh's (2004) popularized (and highly personalized) account of the challenges to Canadian foreign policy in a post-9/11 world. Much like Cooper, Welsh stresses that Canada confronts new challenges not just in its own North American neighbourhood, but also on the global stage with the rise of non-state actors and the multiple challenges posed by the forces of globalization, which are affecting states—poor and rich alike—everywhere. In posing the question—Does Canada want to be like Switzerland, a country she says, 'that places emphasis on being a great place to live, rather than engaging in international activism', or a 'model citizen' of the world that effectively deploys its 'soft power' assets to promote its own unique brand of democracy that is based on federalism and multiculturalism? (Welsh, 2004: 163, 189)—she argues that Canada is hamstrung by a national mythology (level-2 factors) that prevents it from assuming its rightful place in the world. These constraining 'myths' are that (1) Canada is the United States' best friend; and (2) Canada is a 'middle power'. The latter, she believes, is particularly problematic because it 'has focused us on process rather than on substance. It is all about forging consensus and building coalitions—but to what end?' (ibid.: 26).

Welsh's view that Canada's traditional, middle-power internationalism is all about process while shy on substance is not shared by other scholars. As Tom Keating (1993) argues, Canada's commitment to multilateralism has involved a lot more than the practice of working diplomatically with others. It has also involved a strong interest in the content of that order and the development of new norms, principles, and rules, particularly in the areas of human rights, humanitarian law, trade, and security. There are also different variants of inter-nationalism in both public opinion and policy circles. Cranford Pratt (1994–5) observes that Canada's 'humane internationalism'—which stressed Canada's ethical obligation to help the poor in developing countries—was in ascendancy in the 1960s and 1970s; however, it all but yielded to a narrower, self-interested internationalism in the 1980s when cuts to Canada's ODA budget took their toll. Public opinion surveys also document that Canadian attitudes toward 'interna-tionalism' are complex and multidimensional. As Munton and Keating (2001) note, 'Canadians cannot therefore accurately be classified simply as internation-alists or alternatively, as internationalists and isolationists . . . while some types of internationalism are widely supported, others are highly controversial' (ibid.: 546).

While Cooper and Welsh stress the importance of national character or style as the principal determinants of policy, Kim Richard Nossal argues that Canada's foreign policy is born out of the pressures of 'three political environments—international, domestic, and governmental' (1997: 7). There is, however, a decidedly *realist* cast to Nossal's discussion of the international setting in which Canada operates. He argues that the crucial determinant of a state's influence in the international system is its power, which, in turn, is shaped by 'geographic location, economic structure, group dynamics, and capability.' 'All states must rely on power to achieve the one goal that all independent entities . . . univer-sally pursue: the capability to make decisions for themselves' (ibid.: 10). Like many *realists*, Nossal also stresses the importance of the distribution of power among states and whether the system is unipolar, bipolar, or multipolar: 'a state's alignments in international affairs will have a profound influence on its foreign policy. . . . Alliances protect, but they also constrain' (ibid.: 9).

But Nossal is not an unrepentant *realist*. To understand how foreign policy choices are made, he argues, 'we cannot ignore the effect of domestic politics on the international policies of the government in Ottawa' (ibid.: 11). Hence, he suggests that we pay close attention to the relationship between the state and society (level 2) and the kinds of pressures that different interests and groups within society have brought to bear on the political process. At the same time, he also stresses the importance of governmental decision making, including 'the institutional and organizational structures that exist for the making of authoritative decisions, the lines of authority within those institutions, and the political relationships within and between different organizations of government' (ibid.: 13). History, too, is important: 'the weight of historical experience will hang, even if not heavily, in the determination of foreign policy, for there can be no denying or forgetting what has gone before' (ibid.: 15).

In spite of the attention Nossal gives to domestic politics in the making of Canada's foreign policy 'choices', there is less room for choice in his frame of reference than meets the eye. He argues that 'the Canadian government cannot do exactly as it pleases in external policy. . . . The picture that emerges of Canadian power is not that of a foremost nation. Rather, it is of a state that must always be sensitive to the preponderance of power on the North American continent' (ibid.: 85).

As students of policy processes, Cooper and Nossal are concerned about explaining the sources of continuity in Canadian foreign policy and describing the internal and external constraints that impinge on policy makers' choices. Nossal writes: 'Despite the massive changes that have occurred since Confederation both within Canada . . . and internationally . . . Canada's external relations have remained remarkably constant over a period of time, in some cases generations' (ibid.: 14). The subtitle of Cooper's book conveys the same message: *Old Habits and New Directions*. But even if choices are constrained, there are still alternative courses of action and room to make choices. Neither author offers a theory of why, over the course of time, policy makers have eschewed particular policies and courses of action while embracing others. And on those occasions in the past where there has been policy innovation and a dramatic shift in the direction of Canada's international relations, such as when Canada embraced free trade with its North American partners, the emphasis that both authors place on the continuity of Canada's international relations makes it difficult for them to explain why such change occurred when it did. In the competition for different ideas and proposals about how Canada's international affairs should be conducted even in the face of adversity when internal or external constraints loom large, *liberal* and *modified realist* interpretations of Canadian foreign policy cannot explain why specific policy initiatives win out over others, nor do they say much about the content of policy initiatives and formulation, except in very general terms.

A similar difficulty is reflected in John Kirton's (2007) recent textbook on Canadian foreign policy. Kirton sets out to develop a model or theoretical explanation that describes, in general terms, Canada's policies and place in the world. He calls his approach one of 'complex neorealism' because 'it makes observers sensitive to those occasions when Canada acts in a way that departs significantly from the mainstream internationalist or alternative dependence pattern' (Kirton,

2007: 73). Kirton argues that 'order, not anarchy' is the defining feature of international relations in today's world and that this 'orderly world' is produced by 'hegemons or major power concerts.' Furthermore, 'in this orderly world, major powers [like Canada] enjoy surplus capability—capability beyond the margin needed for survival, security, sovereignty, legitimacy, territory, and relative capability.' And this surplus allows these countries to do things in support of their 'national values'. Major—or what he also calls 'principal' powers—also see themselves as having a special role in the maintenance of world order: 'they have systematically induced and accepted a sense of responsibility . . . to create and enforce order in the society of states'—a sense of responsibility that is 'reinforced by the new vulnerability arising in a globalizing world' (ibid.: 82).

Like all structuralist theories of state behaviour, Kirton's theory of complex neorealism has difficulty explaining the origins of these values and why some issues gain the attention and interest of policy practitioners while others do not. When there is 'surplus capability'—to use Kirton's terminology—there are many potential things that governments or foreign ministers can choose to do and many different conceivable 'world order' projects to keep them busy. But this does not explain why some projects come to occupy their attention while others languish or fall by the wayside. And this is even true of multilateral institutions like the United Nations or G8 whose agendas are constantly changing and being pushed and pulled in different directions.

The same difficulty in explaining policy outcomes applies to those who argue that Canada's foreign policy has been in more or less continuous decline since the 1950s and the so-called golden age of Canadian diplomacy (Cohen, 2003). These critics lament not only the loss of diplomatic talent in Canada's foreign service as a result of its recruitment and retention policies, but also the shrinking resource base, particularly in the late 1980s and early 1990s, when Canada's diplomatic, defence, and development budgets were cut to the bone because of the federal government's commitment to fiscal austerity. Even when there is reduced 'surplus capability' there is still the necessity for (and elements of) choice. And even if critics lament the direction in which policies move in hard fiscal times—such as Lloyd Axworthy's human security agenda and his promotion of 'soft power'—arguments about fiscal stringency do not explain why these distinctive policy initiatives emerged when they did.

Theories of foreign policy change often focus on individual-level explanations that discuss the personal belief systems of decision makers and their cognitive, emotional, and evaluative frames of reference. For example, some scholars have argued that both Lester Pearson and Lloyd Axworthy's special brand of 'humanitarian internationalism' had its origins in their shared Methodist background and the United Church's commitment to social activism and civil rights (English, 2001).

One of the most recent and novel psychological treatments of foreign policy decision making is David Welch's study, *Painful Choices: A Theory of Foreign Policy Change* (2005). Welch explores the conditions under which the foreign policies of states are likely to change and argues that the default position is typically one of policy inertia. He argues that elites will only change policy not to secure gains but to avoid painful *actual* or *impending* losses. Change takes place 'when policy fails either repeatedly or catastrophically, or when leaders become convinced that it will imminently do so' (Welch, 2005: 46). The nature of a state's polity matters, too: authoritarian regimes are more likely to change policies than are democratic regimes, which are hidebound by institutional and organizational/bureaucratic inertia. As a consequence, he argues, 'democratic and highly bureaucratic states are less sensitive to small prospects of gain or loss than are autocratic or relatively not bureaucratic states' (ibid.: 47). Dramatic policy change, when it occurs, is therefore more likely to be articulated in the 'language of gains, losses, benefits, successes, failures, constraints, and opportunities' (ibid.: 226).

Among the cases of decision making that Welch explores are Canada's efforts in the twentieth century to negotiate free trade arrangements with the United States. In the case of Canada–US free trade negotiations in the 1980s that were led by Prime Minister Mulroney's government, Welch argues that in spite of the fact that negotiating free trade with the United States 'was, of course, a risky business' and Brian Mulroney 'was not a prime minister inclined to take large risks', free trade was 'framed as a way to avoid the loss of secure market access . . . as offering the prospect of reducing protectionist harassment (avoiding a loss) rather than improving Canadian competitiveness (a gain)' (ibid.: 214–15).

Although individual-level explanations, like Welch's book, are useful to understand how elites arrive at particular decisions, they do not provide a logically complete explanation of policy change and innovation. Because policy decisions in democratic states are made through political organizations and institutions, we have to understand how elite preferences, including the preferences of bureaucratic decision makers, are *collectively* shaped and transformed into new policy, and why, in the course of political bargaining and interest group–based politics some ideas and proposals win out over others. And even if policy choices are ultimately framed in terms of gains and losses and are attended by different degrees of risk, we need to know why certain choices arrived on the desks of decision makers and were framed in the way that they were, while others were excluded or shoved aside.

As our brief review of different approaches to the study of Canadian foreign policy suggests, the challenge of any theory of foreign policy change and innovation is to capture and explain the interplay of different variables across all three levels of analysis—the individual, the state, and the systemic. At the same time, we have to recognize that policy is not simply about interests, culture, and belief systems at levels 1 and 2; it is also about ideas, especially those ideas whose 'time has come'. What explains the arrival of new ideas on the policy scene? Why do certain ideas get traction when they do? In order to answer these questions, we have to look beyond traditional models and understandings of Canadian foreign policy to the public policy literature on policy processes and decision making.

MODELS OF POLICY MAKING

In the public, as opposed to foreign, policy literature, three synthetic models of the policy process have dominated (John, 2003). Paul Sabatier and Hank Jenkins-Smith (1993) focused on networks of actors in policy subsystems to explain policy change. In their model, actors join together in *advocacy coalitions* on the basis of their shared knowledge of a problem and their common interest in pursuing certain solutions (Howlett and Ramesh, 2003: 152). Policy alternatives are contested by competing coalitions, and their relative success is influenced not only by the resources they are able to deploy, but also by their ability to adapt their policy ideas in response to external change, while holding the coalition together.

In their *punctuated equilibrium* model of agenda change, Frank Baumgartner and Bryan Jones (1993) note that policies and agendas, rather than changing gradually over time, actually shift rapidly from one stable point to another. Many policy ideas circulate in policy subsystems, competing for attention, but once a particular idea gets attention, it can expand rapidly. This occurs most frequently in response to external events that disturb the equilibrium of the political system. The equilibrium concept, drawn from evolutionary biology, is a useful metaphor to describe discontinuous change in agendas and policies, but Baumgartner and Jones stop short of adopting an evolutionary model of the policy process (John, 2003: 488).

The third predominant synthetic model is John Kingdon's adaptation of the garbage can model, developed originally by Cohen and colleagues (Cohen, March, and Olsen, 1972).[1] The 'garbage' in the original model consisted of separate streams of problems, solutions, participants, and choice opportunities, and the mixing of garbage to make policy was an ad hoc and haphazard process (Howlett and Ramesh, 2003: 176). Kingdon took this notion of streams of problems and solutions, and added an explicitly political dimension to create an evolutionary account of the policy process. Not only is Kingdon's *multiple streams* model of policy making more comprehensive than either the punctuated equilibrium or advocacy coalition models, it is also capable of subsuming the concepts of punctuated equilibria and advocacy coalitions within its theoretical structure. For these reasons, we have adopted Kingdon's model for our analysis of Canada's international policies. The model is described in more detail as follows.[2]

The Multiple Streams Model

The garbage can model, proposed originally by Cohen and colleagues (1972), was developed to advance our understanding of organizational choice in 'organized anarchies'. In this model, as a choice opportunity arises in an organization, various participants become involved, various problems are introduced into the choice, and various solutions are considered. A choice opportunity, therefore, is 'a garbage can into which various kinds of problems and solutions are dumped by participants as they are generated.'[3] John Kingdon's revised version of this model places more emphasis on the 'organized' than the 'anarchy' in attempting to explain why some issues become prominent on decision agendas and how alternative approaches to issues are identified and chosen.[4] Kingdon (1995: 116) asks us to picture a community of specialists:

> Generating alternatives and proposals in this community resembles a process of biological natural selection. Much as molecules floated around in what biologists call the 'primeval soup' before life came into being, so ideas float around in these communities. Many ideas are possible, much as many molecules would be possible. Ideas become prominent and then fade. There is a long process of 'softening up': ideas are floated, bills introduced, speeches made; proposals are drafted, then amended in response to reaction and floated again. Ideas confront one another (much as molecules bumped into one another) and combine with one another in various ways. The 'soup' changes not only through the appearance of wholly new elements, but even more by the recombination of previously existing elements. While many ideas float around in this policy primeval soup, the ones that last, as in a natural selection system, meet some criteria. Some ideas survive and prosper; some proposals are taken more seriously than others.

As the garbage can is transformed into soup, so Kingdon's model becomes explicitly evolutionary. Ideas evolve in a complex selection process, in which many alternatives are considered as the process moves forward, ideas mutate and recombine, and some survive and flourish. In this evolutionary process, wholly new ideas do not suddenly appear and get adopted; instead, ideas float freely through the soup, while their merits are debated by the community of specialists, who attempt to persuade one another, and advocates of particular solutions act as entrepreneurs, attempting to soften up those who need to be persuaded. In this Darwinian process, some ideas die away and others prosper, as a consensus spreads through the relevant community as a particular idea catches on, a tipping point is passed whereby the idea takes off, and a bandwagon effect secures its adoption.

Kingdon conceives this evolutionary policy process as consisting of three separate streams—problem identification or recognition, policy alternatives generation, and politics—that flow through and around decision structures, largely independent of one another. At certain critical times, the three streams come together, and at that juncture major policy change can occur, when policy windows—defined as opportunities to advocate particular proposals or conceptions of problems—are opened, either by the appearance of compelling problems or by happenings in the political stream. To understand how certain problems surface on the policy agenda, and why a particular policy alternative is selected to address the problem, we need to analyze all three process streams flowing through the policy system.

Agendas Change

It is a fact that governments treat only some conditions as problems, while others go unrecognized, or are deemed unsuitable for government action. As a result, our analysis of international policies must begin by asking how it is that some issues or conditions capture the attention of important people in and around government and obtain a place as problems on the governmental agenda (consisting of issues that are getting attention), while others are ignored. Kingdon (1995: 90) suggests how problems capture the attention of these people: 'Sometimes their attention is affected by a more or less systematic indicator of a problem. At other times, a dramatic event seizes their attention, or feedback from the operation of existing programs suggests that all is not well.' Systematic indicators, especially quantitative ones, can signal the presence of a problem either by their magnitude or because of a change in magnitude. Indicators abound of course, but not all are taken to mean that a problem exists that deserves government action. So it is not that indicators, in and of themselves, are critical to problem definition, but that advocates for particular problems search for indicators to use to bolster their arguments, and sometimes they succeed in making the case.

Problems are not always self-evident from their indicators, however. They often require a push from a focusing event to carry them on to a governmental agenda. Such events call attention to the problem, and may arise from the occurrence of a crisis or other dramatic incident, the existence of a compelling symbol, or out of the personal experiences of a policy maker (Kingdon, 1995: 95). A terrorist attack or a severe recession can make an existing problem suddenly more urgent. Similarly, indicators may bring a problem into view, but a powerful symbol, televised images of refugees in distress for example, can focus the attention of important people. Finally, an individual's personal experience may increase the relevance of a particular problem for them, as when the recognition of a condition reinforces a prior belief in such a way as to transform the condition into a perceived problem.

Even a focusing event may be insufficient to carry an issue to a prominent place on the policy agenda. The probability of this happening will be increased in those situations where government officials receive feedback about the inadequacy of existing policies and programs. Such feedback can come from systematic monitoring, more informally from complaints about conditions, or from the lessons of administrative experience (Kingdon, 1995: 101). In any case, such feedback will indicate that things are not as they should be, reinforcing the perception that a problem exists.

Just as issues may surface as problems on governmental agendas through the effects of indicators, focusing events, and feedback, so too issues can drop off agendas. This may happen because those assigned to deal with the problem believe they have solved it, or that they have addressed the problem, even if it is demonstrably not solved. Even if not solved or addressed, problems may drop off the agenda simply because advocates no longer have the time and resources to keep the issue prominent (Kingdon, 1995: 104).

Ideas Evolve
Kingdon argues that ideas about policy alternatives circulate in communities of specialists scattered through and outside government. Individual ideas in this

stream of policy proposals mutate and recombine in a process of continual refinement until some are ready to enter a serious decision stage as alternative choices. Advocates for particular proposals or ideas are policy entrepreneurs, inside or outside of government, who are defined by their willingness to invest resources (time and energy, and occasionally money) in order to secure a future return (desired policies, satisfaction from participation, or career rewards). These entrepreneurs try to build acceptance for their pet proposals, softening up both the policy community and the larger public by pushing their ideas repeatedly and in many different forums.

If entrepreneurs are successful in communicating their idea in a policy community, then a take-off point may be reached where diffusion occurs rapidly and the idea becomes generally accepted (Kingdon, 1995: 140). This process of creating alternatives for policy makers to consider proceeds independently of the process of problem identification. However, viable alternatives must exist before a problem can secure a solid position on the decision agenda. Even in this circumstance, problems and their alternative solutions exist alongside the political stream, which also exerts influence on the policy process.

Politics Matter

In Kingdon's model, developments in the political stream have their most powerful effects on agendas. The stream is composed of elements related to electoral, partisan, and pressure group considerations of politicians and those who serve them. An important component of the political stream is what Kingdon refers to as the national mood. He maintains that governmental participants' sense of the climate of opinion on an issue—gleaned from mail, media, lobbyists, and polls, among other sources—can provide a fertile ground for certain ideas. Similarly, the component of organized political interests is important to those in government in so far as the interests all point in the same direction, thus providing a powerful impetus to move on that course.

The third major element in the political stream is composed of events within the government itself. Governmental actors affect policy agendas through two major processes, turnover and jurisdiction. According to Kingdon, agendas may change because some of the major participants change. Furthermore, agendas are significantly affected by jurisdictional boundaries, and by turf battles.

The final component in the political stream is consensus building. Unlike the policy stream, where consensus is built through persuasion and diffusion, consensus in the political stream is achieved through bargaining and coalition building among participants in the selection of a course of action. As in the policy stream, however, once adherents of a particular alternative have grown sufficiently in number, then the balance of support will tip overwhelmingly in the direction of that option. The distinction between agendas and alternatives is useful analytically in distinguishing the effects of the various components of the political stream. Kingdon maintains that the mix of the national mood and elections has a strong impact on policy agendas, capable of overwhelming the balance of organized forces. But once a problem is on the decision agenda, then organized forces can be expected to step back in to shape alternatives and outcomes.

Of Policy Windows and Policy Entrepreneurs

At certain times in the policy process, a critical dynamic may occur, when the problem, policy, and politics streams align, providing windows of opportunity for action by policy entrepreneurs, who use the alignment to push forward their preferred agendas or pet solutions. Much of the time, these three streams flow through the policy system on largely independent courses. However, the streams come together at critical times, so that a problem is recognized, a solution is developed and available in the policy community, a political change makes the time right for policy change, and potential constraints are not severe (Kingdon, 1995: 165). This joining of the streams is most likely to occur when a policy window opens, and policy entrepreneurs play a critical role in, what Kingdon calls, the coupling of the streams that occurs at the open window. Typically, a policy window opens because the policy agenda is affected by a change or event in the political stream, or by the emergence of a pressing problem that captures the attention of government officials. Kingdon distinguishes between the governmental agenda, which is the set of subjects to which people in and around government are paying serious attention, and the decision agenda, which consists of a smaller set of items from the governmental agenda that is being actively decided upon. Events in the problem or political streams can, by themselves, structure the governmental agenda, but the probability that an issue will rise on the decision agenda is increased if a policy window opens and all three streams are joined.

Whether a window has, in fact, opened is a matter of perception, and may be a matter of debate, because only a test (successful advocacy) will determine its presence. The test must be done quickly, however, because policy windows may not remain open for long. It only takes the loss of one of the three elements to miss the moment of opportunity: if a problem does not remain sufficiently compelling, a solution is not available, or support is not forthcoming in the political stream, then the issue's place on the decision agenda may be lost and the window will close without action. It follows, then, that when a window opens, policy entrepreneurs have to be ready to take advantage of the opportunity to engineer the coupling of the streams that must occur at the open window. To be effective in doing so, entrepreneurs must have one or more of the following characteristics: a claim to a hearing, either because of their expertise on an issue or their leadership of organized groups; political connections or negotiating skills and the savvy to use them effectively; and persistence and tenacity. The multiple streams model is shown in Figure 1.1.

This model is designed to help us 'find pattern and structure in very complicated, fluid, and seemingly unpredictable phenomena.' However, it is very much a probabilistic model, one that explicitly leaves room for a residual randomness in the way events will unfold in any particular policy episode. In addition, it is historically contingent: the direction of change depends heavily on initial conditions, and events may develop in different ways depending on which way they happen to start. In other words, the model can point to the kinds of structural change and forms of individual action that are likely to affect agendas and

Figure 1.1 A Multiple Streams Model of Policy Making

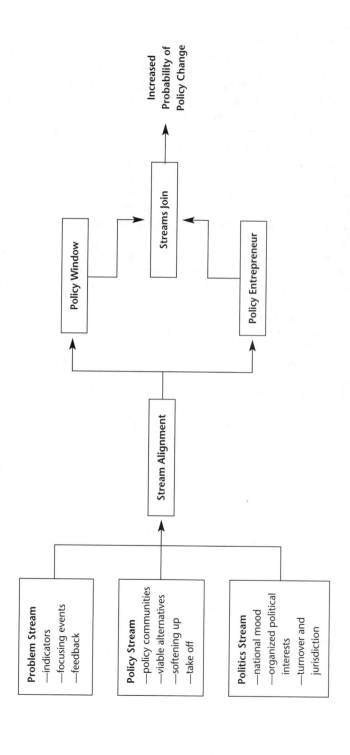

policy choice, but it cannot tell us precisely when those factors will operate to produce particular effects. Nevertheless, it provides a more comprehensive and integrated representation of the policy process than the major alternatives (Kingdon, 1995: 206, 224). Interest group models that focus on competing pressures in the generation and selection of policy alternatives capture important aspects of the political stream, but ignore the important role played by ideas in other parts of the process. Comprehensive-rational models focus on the orderly elements of choice but overlook the larger policy process that is much less tidy, whereas incremental models that accurately capture the evolution of alternatives fail to describe the discontinuous process of agenda change. Kingdon's model, on the other hand, provides us with a comprehensive representation of the enduring streams in the policy process—problems, alternatives, and politics—and alerts us to the critical ingredients—windows of opportunity and the entrepreneurial initiatives that must couple the streams at the openings—that increase the likelihood of policy change.

In the analysis of Canada's international policies that follows, two chapters are devoted to each of our five issue-areas: foreign investment; international trade; international development; national defence; and human security. In the first chapter for each policy area, we describe each of the streams in the policy process, tracking changes in policy agendas, tracing the evolution of policy ideas, and describing changing elements in the stream of politics. The second chapter in each policy area then brings the three streams together, showing how sometimes the streams flowed on separate paths and sometimes they combined to produce change in Canada's international policies. To supplement our analysis of these five policy areas, the final section of the book presents six student-authored case studies of Canada's international policies on a variety of issues in bilateral relationships and multilateral settings.

C H A P T E R   2

Streams in the Investment Policy Process

In this chapter, we describe first the changing policy agenda concerning the role and nature of foreign investment in the Canadian political economy; next, we trace the evolution of alternative policy ideas concerning foreign investment; and finally, we examine the politics of investment policy.[1] Our focus will be on agendas, alternatives, and politics in the period since the end of the Second World War. Chapter 3 will then bring the three streams together in an analysis of continuity and change in Canadian investment policy.

THE INVESTMENT POLICY AGENDA

Canada's uneasy relationship with foreign investment began well enough in the years immediately following the end of the Second World War. At that time government officials, chief among them Clarence Decatur (C.D.) Howe,[2] minister of defence production and of trade and commerce, judged that Canada needed all the investment it could get to finance postwar economic expansion. Therefore, to the extent that there was an investment problem identified on the governmental agenda, it was the shortage of investment capital required by Canada's secondary manufacturing and, especially, resource industries. In a speech given in Boston in 1954, Howe commented approvingly on the increasing foreign participation in Canada's industrial expansion:

> While in the immediate post-war period most of Canada's industrial and resources expansion was financed from Canadian savings, in the more recent period we have had a substantial inflow of foreign capital mainly American. . . . Canada has welcomed the participation of American and other foreign capital in its industrial expansion. In Canada foreign investors are treated the same way as domestic investors.[3]

Even as Howe was voicing his approval, however, agenda change was underway. In 1955, Toronto accountant-consultant Walter Gordon decided to give voice to his growing concern over the acquisition of Canadian enterprises by foreign, largely American, interests (Gordon, 1977: 59). Gordon drafted a paper, intended for publication in the *International Journal*, in which he called for a royal commission on the future direction of the Canadian economy. Gordon's proposal was adopted by the government, and he was named to chair the Royal Commission on Canada's Economic Prospects, established in the spring of 1955.[4]

The commission's staff undertook an ambitious program of research, and the commission solicited briefs from interested groups and conducted nationwide public hearings during the fall and winter of 1955–6. In the process members received considerable feedback about the problem of foreign control of Canadian industries, especially from professional organizations, investment dealers, and organized labour. The debate sparked by the commission hearings, along with substantial press coverage of government statistics published in April 1956 that indicated growing levels of foreign ownership, prompted US Ambassador Douglas Stewart and C.D. Howe to mount a public defence of the role of American capital in Canadian economic development (Azzi, 1999: 42, 44–7). At the same time, that role was coming under intense public scrutiny in connection with the government's plan to provide loan guarantees to an American-controlled private consortium to build a gas pipeline from Alberta to Ontario and Quebec. Opposition parties, objecting to the provision of loan guarantees to an American company, and to the prospect of American ownership of the Canadian pipeline, attempted to block parliamentary approval of the necessary legislation through a filibuster (using extended speeches to delay the vote). The government, with C.D. Howe in the lead, used closure (a vote to end debate) to force a final vote on the legislation, and the government was accused of forcing the Speaker of the House of Commons to reverse a previous ruling in order to shut off debate. The result was a highly publicized uproar in the House, marked by a breakdown in conventional parliamentary decorum that saw Members running into the centre aisle to berate the Speaker. The pipeline episode created 'an intense outburst of anti-American sentiment' (Bliss, 1984: 3), and provided a focusing event in the form of a potent symbol of opposition to Howe's agenda. As indicated in Chapter 1, such events call attention to the problem, and may arise from the occurrence of a crisis or other dramatic incident, the existence of a compelling symbol, or out of the personal experiences of a policy maker.

In his December 1956 preliminary report, Gordon raised foreign investment as a problem that government should deal with, but Howe and his prime minister, Louis St Laurent, chose not to act on the report. When the commission's final report was completed in 1957, it was presented to the newly elected Conservative government of John Diefenbaker, who pointedly ignored it (Smith, 1973: 48). To obtain a place as a problem on the governmental agenda, an issue must capture the attention of important people in and around government, and this usually happens because these people are presented with indicators that a problem exists, or because a focusing event captures their attention, or because they receive feedback suggesting that existing policies are inadequate. Although traces of some of these elements were present for the Gordon Commission, they were insufficient to move foreign ownership onto the agenda. Nevertheless, Gordon had initiated public debate on the issue, flagging a problem related to foreign investment—the degree of economic decision making in the hands of non-residents and the possibility that this could erode political independence. According to Michael Bliss (1984: 3), Gordon injected the foreign ownership question permanently onto the agenda of Canadian politics. Perhaps, but subsequent events suggested that foreign investment was a problem whose time had not yet come.

During the years of Conservative government under John Diefenbaker, from 1957 to 1963, Gordon continued to speak and write about the problematic trend toward non-resident control of Canadian industry that he had defined in his commission report, but few were paying attention. In 1961, he published a book (Gordon, 1961) in which he reviewed the foreign investment problem, but which served mainly as a critique of the Diefenbaker government and a policy guide for the Liberal Party (Smith, 1973: 90). Political change altered the policy agenda in 1963, when the Liberals were elected to a minority government, and Gordon became finance minister, which made him one of the most 'important people in and around government'. In that position he could place the problem of foreign ownership of Canadian resources and companies firmly on the governmental agenda, ensuring that the issue would get serious attention. In addition, with the presentation of his first budget in June 1963, Gordon would ensure that the foreign ownership issue would get on the government's decision agenda, where the question of what to do about the problem would be up for active decision (Kingdon, 1995: 4).

Gordon's effort to deal with the ownership issue in his 1963 budget would not be successful, as described in the following section, and he would ultimately leave the cabinet following the 1965 election. In this period, the foreign investment issue slipped off the governmental agenda, although as a backbencher Gordon continued his advocacy on the problem of foreign ownership, and in 1966 he published another book (Gordon, 1966) setting out his views on the issue. His persistence was paying off, however, and he gained a following in what was forming as the nationalist wing of the Liberal Party. When his supporters succeeded in pressuring Prime Minister Lester Pearson to bring Gordon back into his cabinet in January 1967, Gordon insisted that he would return only if the foreign ownership issue was put back on the governmental agenda. This was accomplished, in a fashion, by appointing a task force of academic economists headed by Melville Watkins from the University of Toronto to study the issue and report to a cabinet committee chaired by Gordon. The eight-member task force received a mandate to study 'the structure of Canadian industry, with special reference to foreign ownership and control' (Smith, 1973: 310), and its analysis focused on the extent of foreign ownership and its impact on the Canadian economy.

The opening sentence of the 1968 task force report set the tone: 'The extent of foreign control of Canadian industry is unique among the industrialized nations of the world.' Something unprecedented was going on in Canada, and two principal problems were seen to derive from this degree of control, namely, that foreign-owned Canadian firms were not economically competitive, by virtue of their branch-plant status, and they, and by extension Canada, were subject to the extraterritorial application of foreign laws and regulations (Beckman, 1984: 16). Whereas Gordon, in his 1957 report, had expressed concern that foreign ownership could somehow undermine economic self-determination, Watkins and his group of economists gave concrete expression to the dangers of excessive foreign ownership, both for the health of Canada's economy and its political autonomy. In making the threat explicit, the Watkins Report, as the document came to be known, provided another step in the incremental process of defining the foreign investment problem and securing its place on the governmental agenda.

Following the election of Pierre Trudeau's Liberal government in 1968, the issue surfaced again. There had been a sharp rise in foreign takeovers in the late 1960s, the public discussion stimulated by the Watkins Report had helped to bring the issue back into the public eye, and a parliamentary inquiry and a couple of high-profile takeover attempts would keep it there. The House of Commons Standing Committee on External Affairs and Defence called for testimony on the state of Canada–US relations, and in 1970 issued a report (known as the Wahn Report after Ian Wahn, the committee chair) that again identified foreign ownership as a problem that threatened Canada's economic development and political autonomy. The committee hearings provided a forum for public feedback to the government about the inadequacy of existing policy, and witnesses pointed to the surge in takeovers that had occurred in the late 1960s as an indication that Canada was facing a serious problem (Smythe, 1994: 183). In 1970, and again in 1971, the cabinet stepped in to prevent the sale of, first, Denison Mines, Canada's largest uranium producer, and then Home Oil, the only major oil producer not under foreign control, to American interests, providing focusing events for the government to ensure that the foreign ownership issue would remain on the governmental agenda (von Riekhoff, Sigler, and Tomlin, 1979: 86). However, the issue was not yet on the decision agenda for action.

That changed in 1969, when the Privy Council Office identified the issue of foreign investment and the control of the economy as a priority problem (Smythe, 1994: 184). To address the problem, the government established another task force, this time chaired by Herb Gray, who like Walter Gordon was a minister without portfolio and an acknowledged nationalist. While these similarities to the Watkins experience were undoubtedly noted by cynics who expected little action, it was also important that this task force was composed of officials from various government departments, rather than academics, and was headed, not by a university economist, but by the prime minister's economic advisor, Joel Bell. The difference was apparent in the mandate given to the task force: whereas Watkins had been asked to study the structure of Canadian industry, with special reference to foreign ownership and control, Bell's group received a more pointed directive: to examine 'domestic control of the national economic environment and the problem of foreign ownership.'[5] Nevertheless, the opening sentence of the 1972 task force report (known as the Gray Report) struck a familiar Watkins refrain: 'The degree of foreign ownership and control of economic activity is already substantially higher in Canada than in any other industrialized country and is continuing to increase.' The problems associated with this level of foreign ownership were also similar to those that had been raised by Watkins: the investment decisions of foreign-controlled firms reflected the laws and priorities of foreign governments, and could limit Canada's industrial development; the dependent Canadian manufacturing operations of foreign corporations were unable to compete internationally; and the truncated activities of Canadian subsidiaries prevented their development into mature business enterprises (Government of Canada, 1972: 5). In sum, foreign ownership was a problem because it impeded Canadian industrial development.

To deal with the problem identified by the task force, the government established the Foreign Investment Review Agency (FIRA) in 1973, as discussed in the following section. With the problem addressed, the foreign investment issue largely disappeared from the decision agenda for several years. Overall levels of foreign investment were dropping in this period, although analysts concluded that the decline was not a result of FIRA's activities (Smythe, 1994: 214), and government attention was focused on the problems of stagflation (a combination of high inflation and high unemployment) and Canadian trade competitiveness. The energy sector, dominated by American-owned firms, was also getting some attention, as high prices and energy shortages in the 1970s made energy security an issue on the governmental agenda. By 1980, the energy sector had become a key government priority, because rising oil and gas prices were producing a revenue windfall for producing provinces and multinational corporations. The problem, from Ottawa's perspective, was that the federal government was not capturing an adequate share of those revenues, which would allow it to assert a federal presence in the confederation (Pammett and Tomlin, 1984: 3), and because multinationals dominated the sector, foreign ownership became part of the problem.

By 1982, however, agenda change was underway again, as Canada and the United States experienced their most severe recession since the 1930s. With the recession came a decline in capital investment, both domestic and foreign, and decreased demand for oil and gas, causing prices for both to drop sharply, with commensurate declines in investment in this important sector. Whereas in 1971 Canada had received 11.5 per cent of world investment flows, by the early 1980s that figure had declined to 3.1 per cent (Smythe, 1994: 224). By 1982, there were indicators aplenty that the economy was in trouble and that investment was in decline, the severity of the recession provided a focusing event that secured the attention of important people in and around government, and there was a chorus of criticism from the business community that existing policies were making the problem worse, and a demand that government do something to fix the situation. For foreign investment, the problem had shifted from too much investment to too little, and solutions would have to focus on attraction rather than regulation and repatriation.

This shift in the definition of the investment policy problem was part of a more general change in Canada's international economic policy agenda in the early 1980s, driven by the severe recession and demands that government do something to deal with its effects. As a result, investment was established as an issue on the government's decision agenda, and then was subsumed as part of the larger trade policy agenda that Canada decided in 1985 to pursue through negotiations with the United States. That process of agenda change is described in Chapter 4, in the section on the trade policy agenda. As a result of the change, investment surfaced again on the governmental agenda, because the US wanted to include investment in the trade negotiations, and when it insisted, the investment issue was back on the government's decision agenda. However, the link with trade issues put the investment problem in a slightly different light. Whereas the problem had been redefined in the early 1980s to address the need for more, not less, investment, the trade link meant that the investment 'problem' would now be to resist American pressure for further liberalization, a throwback to an earlier definition of the problem.

Once this problem had been addressed in the bilateral agreement that was concluded in 1987, and confirmed in a Canadian federal election in 1988, the investment issue largely disappeared once again from the governmental agenda, as implementation of the free trade agreement proceeded. However, the issue unexpectedly surfaced again in 1990 when Mexico proposed the negotiation of a free trade agreement with the United States. Although Prime Minister Mulroney at first indicated that such negotiations would not be of direct interest to Canada, that soon changed when officials in the Department of Industry, Science and Technology, the new home of Investment Canada, pointed out that the US presence in two bilateral free trade agreements on the continent—an American hub with Canadian and Mexican spokes—could lead to a diversion of investment dollars to the United States as the only platform from which to serve all three North American markets (Cameron and Tomlin, 2000: 65). The re-emergence of this investment problem resulted from the focusing event provided by the Mexican decision to negotiate free trade with the United States, and because it was a variant on the investment shortage problem that had been identified in the 1980s, extensive indicators and feedback were unnecessary to move the problem onto the governmental agenda.

With the successful conclusion of the North American free trade agreement (NAFTA), Canada had addressed both sides of its investment problem: ensuring that Canada would remain an attractive investment destination for investors in North American markets; and defining the rights of investors and governments in the treatment of foreign investment. With NAFTA in place by 1994, the government turned to another problem that had been emerging as Canadian firms and subsidiaries expanded their international investments outside Canada. Whereas outward investment was viewed in the 1980s as capital flight—more evidence of Canada's declining status as an attractive investment location—by the 1990s it was accepted as just one more manifestation of the globalization process, necessary for Canadian firms to remain internationally competitive

(Smythe, 1996: 198). The figures on outward investment flows showed a dramatic increase, and corporate Canada, seeing the protections offered to investors in agreements like NAFTA, pressed the government to take action to ensure access for Canadian investors to foreign markets and to protect Canadian investments abroad. It is this new agenda that would occupy governments for the remainder of the 1990s and the first half of the first decade of the new century.

INVESTMENT POLICY ALTERNATIVES

Our focus in this section will be on the evolution of ideas about appropriate policies and policy instruments concerning foreign investment that circulate in communities of specialists inside and outside of government, and on the ways ideas wax and wane, mutate and evolve. As already noted, in the period immediately following the Second World War, a shortage of investment capital was seen as the principal problem facing Canada's economy, and a number of instruments were put in place to encourage investment, without concern for its source. In fact, many policies were explicitly designed to attract foreign investors. For example, accelerated depreciation rates, used to stimulate capital investment, were superior to rates in the US, and as a result provided a further attraction for American investment in Canada (Wolfe, 1978: 10). In addition, an import control policy, instituted in 1947 to address a balance of payments deficit (described in chapter 4), also had the effect of encouraging foreign manufacturers to establish Canadian branch-plants. This open door approach (Bliss, 1984: 3) to foreign investment largely dominated government policy for almost twenty years following the end of World War II.[6]

The first challenge to this accepted wisdom came from Walter Gordon's Royal Commission on Canada's Economic Prospects. In its 1957 report, the commission included a chapter on domestic savings and foreign investment that, while largely positive about the role of foreign investment in the Canadian economy, suggested that it could undermine Canada's economic self-determination (Beckman, 1984: 13). To address this problem, the report did not propose compulsory regulation of foreign investment, but instead suggested several voluntary guidelines, encouraging foreign companies to increase their numbers of Canadian managers and suppliers, disclose financial results for their operations in Canada, place more Canadians on company boards, and sell a greater equity share (20 to 25 per cent) to Canadian buyers (Beckman, 1984: 14; Bliss, 1984: 4). In addition, the commission proposed the use of special depreciation tax incentives and withholding tax penalties to encourage greater Canadian ownership (Azzi, 1999: 52).[7] These recommendations were ignored by the governments of the day.

As indicated previously, when Gordon was appointed finance minister in the Liberal government in April 1963, he brought the foreign investment issue firmly onto the government's decision agenda. He then moved quickly to put in place policies to deal with the problem of excessive foreign ownership that he had defined in his royal commission report. Gordon wanted to include in his first budget measures to restrain foreign investment and encourage the sale of shares in Canadian subsidiaries of foreign companies to Canadians, and he brought a group of outside advisors into his Finance office to help him figure out how to do this, among other things. A key advisor on the foreign investment issue was Geoffrey Conway, an economics Ph.D. student at Harvard University,[8] and a former employee at Gordon's Toronto firm (Smith, 1973: 139). In a letter to Gordon in April 1963, Conway had proposed the use of a transfer tax (of 10 to 15 per cent) on the sale of Canadian companies to restrain takeovers by foreigners, and an increase in the dividend withholding tax for foreign companies and special tax treatment for Canadian firms as a means to regain Canadian ownership (Smith, 1973: 147–8).[9]

Conway's proposals were adopted by Gordon in a series of budget measures aimed at foreign ownership: a 30 per cent tax on the sale of shares of Canadian firms to foreign purchasers (Conway's transfer tax, boosted up); the 15 per cent withholding tax on dividends paid to non-residents was increased to 20 per cent for firms with less than 25 per cent Canadian ownership (Conway's proposal) and reduced to 10 per cent for companies at least one-quarter Canadian-owned (added to discriminate both ways); and companies with 25 per cent Canadian ownership would receive a faster depreciation rate (Conway's special tax treatment). As noted in the previous section, Gordon did not succeed in his efforts to deal with the foreign ownership problem through these budget measures. His proposals were at odds with prevailing thought in the Department of Finance and the Bank of Canada (Smith, 1973: 148), and drew heavy criticism from segments of the business community, inside and outside Canada (Bliss, 1984: 5). Under considerable pressure, he withdrew the 30 per cent takeover tax and the increase in the withholding tax for companies with less than 25 per cent Canadian ownership.

While forced to back down on the budget measures to restrain foreign, and encourage Canadian, ownership, Gordon nevertheless managed to stimulate the next stage in the evolution of ideas about appropriate policies and policy instruments concerning foreign investment when he rejoined the cabinet in 1967 and secured agreement to the appointment of the Watkins task force. As indicated previously, Watkins and his band of economists moved the incremental process of problem definition concerning foreign ownership one step forward with their 1968 report; however, the task force moved back one step in the evolution of policy with its recommendations for action, eschewing the measures to restrain and discriminate against foreign ownership that had appeared in the 1963 Gordon budget, in favour of the approach that had characterized Gordon's 1957 royal commission report, with its greater reliance on persuasion and disclosure. To start, the task force argued that greater monitoring of foreign-owned firms was needed, and proposed the creation of a special agency to gather information, coordinate policies, and promote international guidelines. They also proposed the introduction of new legislation to require financial disclosure by all firms operating in Canada, and block the intrusion of foreign anti-trust and trade prohibition laws into Canada, and the amendment of existing legislation to strengthen competition law and reduce tariffs, this in order to promote

Canadian competitiveness. Finally, the task force picked up on an idea, advanced originally by Walter Gordon in 1961 (Smith, 1973: 90), for a national development corporation to rally domestic capital to replace foreign investment.[10] The idea was first given expression in the 1963 throne speech, when the Liberal government promised to create the Canada Development Corporation, a promise that was repeated in the 1965 throne speech and budget presentation. However, there was substantial opposition to the idea inside and outside government, and appropriate legislation was never enacted. The task force resurrected the Corporation, proposing that it be created to serve as a holding company to mobilize domestic capital and promote Canadian participation in the economy (Beckman, 1984: 17; Bliss, 1984: 7).

Watkins's task force produced a serious analysis of the extent of foreign ownership and its impact on the Canadian economy, and although its recommendations met the same fate as those of Gordon's 1957 report—they were ignored by the government of the day—the Watkins Report was soon established as the foundation document for the discussion of the problem of foreign ownership in Canadian policy communities. That discussion resumed when the Wahn Report repeated some of Watkins's proposals, including the need for a monitoring agency—a Canadian Ownership and Control Bureau, which would assess the performance of foreign companies—but went further in recommending a requirement that 51 per cent of the stock of major subsidiaries be sold to Canadians (Fayerweather, 1974: 172). The committee's recommendations again were ignored by the government, but in any case Gray's task force was in operation by this time.

The 1972 Gray Report continued down the policy path that had been set by Watkins in 1968, one that concentrated on economic performance, rather than Canadian ownership, as had been the focus of Gordon's 1963 budget and Wahn's 1970 report. The key issue for Gray (or, more accurately, for Bell and the other officials on Gray's task force) was ensuring that Canada secured the benefits that were offered by foreign investment, while reducing the negative effects that had been identified as resulting from high levels of foreign ownership. Starting from the premise that some form of government intervention was required, the report raised three possibilities (Beckman, 1984: 19): extend the existing practice of restricting foreign ownership in certain key sectors to include more sectors and industries; establish a mandatory threshold of Canadian ownership for significant firms; or establish a screening process,[11] whereby access would be granted in return for the assurance of benefit to Canada.[12] The report opted for screening, and recommended that significant acquisitions of existing firms (direct takeovers) and the establishment of new firms by foreign interests (greenfield investments) ought to be subject to review, as should major new investments by foreign-based firms already established in Canada (indirect takeovers), but not the operations of these established firms. A separate agency reporting to a minister and cabinet was proposed to undertake the reviews of individual cases.

In a sign that ideas might be evolving, Gordon's long delayed Canada Development Corporation was finally created by the government early in 1971. When

Gray's report was presented to cabinet in July 1971 (but was not released publicly), agreement was reached that a screening mechanism should be established to review significant foreign takeovers, but there was disagreement over the proper scope of review beyond takeovers (Smythe, 1994: 193). The cabinet continued this debate into the autumn, when the report was leaked and published in *Canadian Forum*[13] in November 1971, forcing the government's hand. Gray tabled the report in Parliament in May 1972 and announced the government's intention to introduce legislation to review only direct and indirect takeovers (acquisition of companies with assets in excess of $250,000 or gross revenues in excess of $3 million) through the Department of Industry, Trade and Commerce (Smythe, 1994: 194). Those in favour of a narrow scope had prevailed. However, the government called an election for October 1972 before the legislation was passed.

Following the election, the Gray Report was carried over to the decision agenda of the new government, and revised legislation was introduced in 1973 which differed from the 1972 legislation in two important respects. First, in addition to takeovers, new (greenfield) investments by companies not already established in Canada would be reviewed, as would investment by foreign-based firms already established in Canada when that investment was in a new, unrelated field. This time, proponents of a broader scope for review had carried the day. Second, screening would be conducted by a new federal agency, the Foreign Investment Review Agency (FIRA), operating under the direction of the minister of industry, trade, and commerce (Beckman, 1984: 20; Smythe, 1994: 196). This would ensure a higher profile for the new policy on foreign investment. The legislation was approved in December 1973, and the takeover and new business provisions came into effect in 1974 and 1975, respectively (Donaldson, 1984: 96).

Following the creation of FIRA, as noted previously, the foreign investment issue largely disappeared from the decision agenda, as the government switched to various subsidies and tax incentives to promote research and development and improve export performance for all industries in Canada (Smythe, 1994: 218). On the separate issue of energy security, however, the government's policy response attempted to define a Canadian presence in the American-dominated energy sector, through the creation of Petro-Canada in 1975. This energy initiative is relevant to our analysis of investment policy alternatives because it provided a forecast of future policy directions, and in 1980 the Liberal government moved once again on the investment front. Pierre Trudeau had campaigned on a platform of expanding Canadian control of the economy, and the government set out to make good on this promise through two major industrial policy initiatives, one of which centred on FIRA, while the other focused on the energy sector, with major implications for foreign investment. For the first initiative, the government proposed in 1980 to expand FIRA's powers to allow it to review the performance of existing foreign-owned firms and to assist Canadian companies to buy back foreign-owned firms or to counter foreign bids to take over Canadian firms, proposals that went far beyond the original Gray Report and FIRA's mandate (Smythe, 1994: 227). In the end, cabinet decided not to proceed with these changes.

The second initiative was the National Energy Program (NEP), which was designed to give the federal government more control over energy resources and a greater share of the revenues that were flowing from rising oil prices. When oil prices started their upward movement in 1979–80, senior officials in the Department of Energy, Mines and Resources (EMR) began developing the policy ideas that would form the backbone of the NEP, and they were circulating these ideas in the Ottawa policy community (Foster, 1982: 140), building support for them inside and outside government.[14] The NEP included major changes in the treatment of new and existing foreign investment in the oil and gas sector (Doern, 1984; Doern and Tomlin, 1991: 17). The principal thrust of these changes was to increase Canadian ownership in the sector, in order to reduce outflows of the large amounts of capital that were generated by higher prices, and Petro-Canada was to play a major role in this initiative. The policy instruments adopted were varied and complex, but the general intent was captured in the investment-related objectives that were identified for the Program: 50 per cent Canadian ownership of oil and gas production, Canadian control of a significant number of large firms, and increased federal government ownership in the sector (Smythe, 1994: 240).

The 1982 recession generated new thinking about appropriate policies toward foreign investment. Think-tanks and advisory bodies contributed new ideas to the policy debate, noting that, as a result of the reductions in trade barriers that had been accomplished in the 1973–9 Tokyo Round of multilateral trade negotiations, foreign firms no longer had to create branch-plants to serve the Canadian market, and Canada now had to compete to attract foreign investment to develop new technology and increase industrial competitiveness (Smythe, 1996: 196). The Liberal government adjusted accordingly: FIRA's screening procedures were revised to expedite cases, and threshold definitions for significant investments were raised to reduce the number that would be subject to review; and senior ministers began actively recruiting foreign, including American, investors. Inside FIRA itself, early in 1984 officials were developing recommendations for further changes in the review process that would ease the entry of investment (Saccomani, 1987: 68).

In 1984, the newly elected Conservative government replaced FIRA with Investment Canada, and gave the new agency a mandate to attract foreign investment. Investment Canada would continue to screen foreign investments, but under terms that would significantly reduce the number of cases that were subject to review: thresholds were raised so that only larger direct ($5 million), and very large indirect ($50 million), takeovers would be reviewed, and those reviews would be expedited by administrative reforms; and new investment would get a pass, except when it involved cultural heritage and national identity, which the minister could review at his discretion (Smythe, 1994: 249).[15] It was clear, however, that the principal purpose of the agency was to attract new investment and promote Canada as an investment destination. On the energy front, in 1985 many elements of the NEP were altered substantially to eliminate the provisions to which foreign investors had objected most strenuously, although certain Canadian ownership requirements were retained.

With the Investment Canada transformation, the Conservative government put in place the new prevailing wisdom concerning foreign investment, namely, that it ought to be welcomed, and restrictions should be minimal. There the matter might have rested, at least for a time, but for the decision to negotiate a free trade agreement with the United States, because the investment issue was not closed for the Americans. In its international economic relationships, the US was on a determined course to eliminate all barriers to American investment abroad, a so-called right of establishment, and to secure national treatment for its investors. Regarding Canada, despite Canadian initiatives to liberalize its investment regime, the US wanted to go further, and used the free trade negotiations to do so. The Canada–United States free trade agreement (FTA) extended the principle of national treatment to the establishment of new foreign-owned businesses. It provided for the gradual raising, in four steps, of the Canadian threshold for the review of takeovers from $5 million to $150 million by 1992, meaning that major (in excess of $150 million) acquisitions could continue to be reviewed, but smaller ones would escape scrutiny, and the review of indirect acquisitions would be phased out entirely by 1992. The oil, gas, and uranium sectors were exempted from this relaxation in provisions governing reviews. Finally, the agreement also eliminated investment-related performance requirements that were trade-distorting, including local content, import substitution, and hiring practices (Doern and Tomlin, 1991: 88).

When the investment issue surfaced again with the Mexican invitation to the United States to negotiate free trade, the hub-and-spoke problem had already been addressed by prominent economists in the policy community (Lipsey, 1990; Wonnacott, 1990). Their argument was readily accepted by key officials in the Department of Industry, Science and Technology so that relevant policy communities were agreed that the problem of potential investment diversion should be addressed through a trilateral Canada–Mexico–United States free trade negotiation. However, since the bilateral FTA served as a template for the trilateral negotiations, investment was once again a negotiable issue, and Canada was again under pressure from the US to further liberalize its investment regime.

The final investment provisions of the North American free trade agreement (NAFTA) went considerably beyond the comparable FTA provisions. First, the prohibition on investment-related performance requirements was strengthened in the NAFTA and broadened to include subnational governments. Second, the US was determined to secure protection for American investors against discriminatory treatment during expropriation. In practice, this meant that compensation for expropriation had to be 'prompt, adequate and effective', a US standard developed initially in response to Mexican expropriations of American petroleum interests in the 1930s. This specific language had to be avoided, however, due to Mexican sensibilities, but the agreement uses equivalent language requiring the parties to pay compensation at fair market value without delay. In addition, the US secured agreement to include investor-state arbitration in the investment chapter. The significance of this provision lies in the ability it affords foreign investors to take complaints about a breach of obligations by a NAFTA party to an international arbitration body. This is an important departure from traditional practice whereby only states are capable of bringing international legal proceedings. Finally, the agreement maintained Canada's right to review direct acquisitions by foreign investors that exceed $150 million, and acquisitions in the oil, gas and uranium sectors can be reviewed below this threshold (Cameron and Tomlin, 2000: 40).[16]

The investment provisions of NAFTA became the preferred model for the next stage in the evolution of Canadian foreign investment policy, as the government moved forward on its agenda of ensuring access for, and protecting, Canadian investments abroad. Initiatives in this regard were pursued in both bilateral and multilateral arenas. Bilaterally, Canada began negotiating Foreign Investment Protection Agreements (FIPAs) with a limited number of selected, mainly East European, countries in 1989, seeking investment liberalization and protection commitments on the basis of a model agreement developed under the auspices of the OECD (Organization for Economic Cooperation and Development).[17] Following the conclusion of the agreement with Mexico and the United States, Canada developed a new model, based on the NAFTA investment provisions, and the government initiated a more active program of negotiations, concluding agreements with a total of 24 countries by 2001, and engaging in protracted negotiations with China and India.[18] Canada also participated in a number of multilateral negotiations on investment, but they were unsuccessful.

INVESTMENT POLITICS

Our focus in this section will be on the political forces that drive agendas and ideas concerning the role and nature of foreign direct investment in the Canadian political economy, identifying important shifts in the national mood, the direction of interest group pressures, and significant jurisdictional change and turnover in government. Following the Second World War, the Liberal Party was in power, and C.D. Howe was firmly in control as the 'general manager of the Canadian economy' (Smith, 1973: 27). Howe's influence was the legacy of his role as minister of munitions and supply during the war, when he had substantial control over Canadian industry and the economy, and this carried over into the immediate postwar period, when he wielded considerable power as minister of trade and commerce. His influence was enhanced, however, as a result of the Korean War, when he was also named minister of defence production, with powers similar to those he exercised during World War II (Wolfe, 1978: 11). With Howe in charge, the investment problem was defined in terms of the need for capital, and an open door was seen as the appropriate policy response (Bliss, 1984: 3).

By 1955, others around the cabinet table were chafing under Howe's dominance, and finance minister Walter Harris saw Walter Gordon's proposal for a royal commission on the economy as an opportunity to introduce some new economic ideas into the policy mix, an initiative disdained by Howe (Smith, 1973: 33). While Gordon conducted his commission hearings across the country in 1955–6, public opinion was beginning to swing against foreign investment (Azzi, 1999: 47). Howe's political mismanagement of the trans-Canada pipeline issue was contributing to the swing and was helping to bring about a fundamental shift in partisan and, ultimately, electoral fortunes. With the Liberal government in difficulty, Gordon accelerated the work of the commission by issuing a preliminary report in December 1956, in which he challenged the status quo on foreign investment and proposed 'in moderate terms, a national policy favouring domestic investment'. However, in cabinet, C.D. Howe opposed the report, just as he had opposed the creation of the commission itself, and other ministers were not persuaded by Gordon's arguments (Smith, 1973: 39, 46).

Since the royal commission was established by a government looking for a fresh economic platform, and Gordon was chosen as the prominent Liberal to write it, it is not surprising that the report was not picked up by the minority Conservative government elected in 1957. When Diefenbaker formed a majority government in 1958, the foreign ownership issue largely disappeared from the governmental agenda. Although Diefenbaker had campaigned on a promise to halt the American takeover of Canadian resources and industries (Smith, 1973: 93), his government did not act to fulfill the promise while he held a majority, and his 1962 minority government was preoccupied with monetary and military crises (Newman, 1963: 333), with little thought for foreign investment. However, turnover can be a critical event in the politics stream, and when the Liberals formed a minority government in 1963, Walter Gordon was named minister of finance. The effect on both problem and policy streams was decisive, as he moved the foreign ownership issue onto the decision agenda and proposed his budget measures to deal with the problem.

Gordon's budget measures, and his precipitous retreat from them, cost him dearly in terms of his credibility both inside and outside government, and although he continued as finance minister, Pearson was under pressure from business and banking interests to replace him in the run-up to the 1965 election.[19] When Pearson failed to win a majority in the election that Gordon had urged him to call, Gordon offered to step down as finance minister, and Pearson accepted his resignation. The turnover was significant for investment policy because Pearson chose trade and commerce minister Mitchell Sharp to replace Gordon at Finance, and Robert Winters to replace Sharp in Trade and Commerce, and both had opposed Gordon's efforts to restrict foreign investment. When Gordon resolved in late 1966 to resign his House of Commons seat as well, his supporters in the Liberal caucus brought pressure on Pearson to return Gordon to cabinet. Gordon remained true to his cause, and proposed that he head a cabinet committee to draft a white paper (typically used to lay out a proposed government policy direction) on foreign ownership, and to follow that up with appropriate legislation (Smith, 1973: 257–61, 304, 309). Pearson appointed him minister without portfolio, but instead of a white paper, Gordon got

Watkins and his task force of economists, and the cabinet committee he chaired also included Sharp (but not Winters, who thought so little of the enterprise that he declined an invitation to join). When the Watkins Report was presented to cabinet in January 1968, Winters argued against publication of the report, and Sharp insisted it had no bearing on government policy. With these two key economic ministers opposed, along with senior officials in their departments (Azzi, 1999: 159), the government declined to take a position on the report; Gordon was fortunate to get approval to publish it (Smith, 1973: 346).

While the Watkins Report did not produce the legislation intended by Gordon, it did contribute to the political changes that led to the establishment of Herb Gray's task force, and when Gray tabled his report in Parliament in May 1972, he announced the government's intention to introduce legislation to review takeovers through the Department of Industry, Trade and Commerce (Smythe, 1994: 194). In the cabinet debate over the scope of the review process, as indicated previously, those who wanted a narrow definition prevailed; screening would be limited to takeovers, and already established foreign-based firms would be left alone. However, when the government called an election for October 1972, the legislation died before passage.

Government turnover can be an important event in the politics stream, and although the Liberals were returned to office in the 1972 election, they formed a minority government, dependent on the New Democratic Party for parliamentary support. The foreign investment review legislation was reintroduced, with an expanded scope for review, plus the creation of a new agency to conduct the reviews. Jurisdiction is also important in the politics stream, and in 1972 the Department of Industry, Trade, and Commerce was responsible for the revised legislation, and the new minister, Alastair Gillespie, had been an early proponent of government screening (Fayerweather, 1974: 180). Although officials in the department and its deputy minister, James Grandy, were opposed to restrictions on foreign investment,[20] the department's special advisor on foreign investment, Roberto Gualtieri, had been a member of Gray's task force, had supported the comprehensive screening agency recommended in the Gray Report, and was responsible for drafting the legislation (Saccomani, 1988: 47). Finally, organized interests play a critical role in the politics stream, especially if they are all pointing in the same direction. That was not the case in 1972 when, although the Canadian Chamber of Commerce and other business interest groups weighed in to express their opposition to investment screening, they were countered by the Canadian Labour Congress and the Committee for an Independent Canada, which called for the addition of measures to achieve greater Canadian ownership, while provincial governments were divided (Smythe, 1994: 200).

The minority Liberal government elected in 1972 finally initiated a comprehensive policy concerning foreign investment. In 1974, when FIRA began operations, Trudeau was elected with a renewed majority government, and foreign investment policy largely disappeared from the government's policy radar screen; in 1976, Herb Gray, who had championed the issue, was dropped from Trudeau's cabinet. The Liberal government was defeated in the 1979 election, but after only nine months of Conservative rule, the Liberals were returned to office with a majority government after campaigning on a platform of expanding Canadian control of the economy, by extending the scope of FIRA's mandate to regulate foreign investment and promoting greater Canadian ownership. The major proponent of this new industrial policy was Herb Gray (Clarkson, 1982: 88), who returned to Trudeau's cabinet as minister of industry, trade, and commerce, where in 1980 he ordered his officials to develop proposals to increase FIRA's power to regulate foreign investment and the behaviour of foreign-owned firms. As indicated previously, Gray was unable to secure cabinet approval for the proposals.

The politics surrounding the creation of the National Energy Program went very differently. First, the national mood during the run-up in oil prices in 1979–80 was strongly in favour of increased Canadian ownership in the energy sector and an enhanced role for Petro-Canada (Smythe, 1994: 240). Second, the NEP element of the new industrial strategy was firmly under the jurisdiction of the Department of Energy, Mines and Resources (EMR), and, as noted in the previous section, senior officials in EMR had been developing the ideas underlying the NEP, and were ready to move forward with them. Third, with a new government comes a new minister, and Marc Lalonde was appointed to head EMR. Lalonde was a longstanding Trudeau ally and a strong minister, and he was eager to take on the new agenda. Finally, the government's program was supported by large Canadian oil and gas companies like Dome and Nova, and by the non-producing provinces, especially Ontario. Opposition came from the smaller Canadian firms that made up a majority of the industry, as well as from the foreign, mainly American, firms that dominated the sector (Foster, 1982: 155), and from Alberta.

The politics of foreign investment policy changed dramatically with the onset of the 1982 recession and the election of a Conservative government in 1984. Business lobbies pressured the new government to lead the effort to attract new investment, and immediately following the election, Prime Minister Brian Mulroney travelled to the United States to announce to the Economic Club of New York that 'Canada is open for business again.' When industry minister Sinclair Stevens moved in 1985 to replace FIRA with Investment Canada, there was virtually unanimous support for the move among Canadian business groups, support that was not balanced on this occasion by the views of the Committee for an Independent Canada, which had disbanded in 1981 (Saccomani, 1987: 66). However, the expression of continued public concern over excessive foreign investment in Canada, and strong support for Canadian ownership in the energy sector (Toner, 1984: 241), mitigated against complete liberalization.

As indicated in the section on agenda change, in the mid-1980s foreign investment was subsumed within the larger trade policy agenda that Canada decided to pursue through negotiations with the United States. The changes that occurred in the political stream in that period are described in Chapter 4 in the section on trade politics. Concerning foreign investment, it was the US insistence that investment be part of the bilateral trade negotiations that put the issue back on the government's decision agenda. Although this meant that the always sensitive investment issue would be partially obscured in the complex thicket of trade policy and market access issues that were addressed in the negotiations, the politics of foreign investment were nevertheless problematic for the government. In October 1985, prominent Canadian nationalist Mel Hurtig, concerned over the Mulroney government's open-door approach to foreign investment, gathered a like-minded group of allies in Toronto to establish the Council of Canadians (COC), the evolutionary offspring of Walter Gordon's Committee for an Independent Canada, with a membership that would grow to 14,000 as Canadians debated the free trade question. In April 1987, the COC helped establish the Pro Canada Network (PCN), an anti-free trade umbrella for 30 national organizations and 10 provincial coalitions, with a total affiliated membership of 10 million (Doern and Tomlin, 1991: 210). Although there was an active business coalition supporting free trade, as described in Chapter 4, the COC and PCN gave a highly public voice to the fear that Mulroney was selling out the country, and used the investment issue as evidence. This meant that the government had to handle the investment issue very carefully: in public statements about the negotiations, ministers and officials were reluctant to admit that investment was even on the table; and in the negotiations themselves, the exchange of access for American investors in return for access to American markets could not go so far as to make the tradeoff politically indigestible.

When the investment issue surfaced again in 1990 with Mexico's free trade overture to the United States, not much had changed in the political stream. The Mulroney government was still in office, having been re-elected with a majority after a bruising campaign that had been fought over the Canada–US free trade agreement (FTA), and no major changes in jurisdiction had occurred. In addition, interest groups were still bitterly divided on free trade. Although the election was taken by business groups to have settled the free trade question, opponents denied its legitimacy, arguing that there was no electoral majority in support of the agreement, and that business had bought the election through their unprecedented and illegitimate financing of the campaign (Doern and Tomlin, 1991: 206). Although investment was central to the trilateral negotiations, because of the threat of investment diversion posed by a bilateral Mexican–American agreement, the political considerations that were salient in the policy process were more concerned with the larger issues associated with North American free trade, as had been the case for the FTA, than with the specifics of foreign investment policy; these considerations are discussed in Chapter 4.

When the Liberal government of Jean Chrétien, elected in October 1993, opted to accept and implement the North American free trade agreement that had been negotiated by their Conservative predecessors, it meant that NAFTA's chapter on investment would define Canadian policy toward foreign investment. In 1993, as well, responsibility for attracting foreign investment was transferred from Investment Canada to the Department of Foreign Affairs and International Trade; with few acquisition cases to review, Investment Canada was absorbed into the Department of Industry, and in 1994 ceased to exist as a separate agency. The national mood seemed to have come to terms with the importance of investment, including from American sources; investment policy was now regulated by international treaties, and jurisdiction had been transferred to an outward oriented department with a mission to attract investors to Canada. In these circumstances, government turnover did little more than to confirm the policy status quo. With little left to accomplish on the investment agenda, the government responded to demands from a fairly small community of interests (Smythe, 1996: 199, 205) to make the world safe for Canadian investors, by negotiating bilateral FIPAs (foreign investment protection agreements) and attempting to negotiate comprehensive multilateral agreements.

This chapter has described the changing policy agenda concerning the role and nature of foreign investment in the Canadian political economy since the Second World War. In addition, the evolution of alternative policy ideas concerning foreign investment has been described, with emphasis on identifying the emergence and adaptation of ideas over time. Finally, the chapter has described developments in the stream of politics over this period, identifying important shifts in the national mood, the positions of organized interests at critical junctures, and instances of electoral and jurisdictional change that had the potential to influence agendas and alternatives. In the following chapter, we bring the three streams together in an analysis of continuity and change in Canadian investment policy.

CHAPTER 3

The Evolution of Foreign Investment Policy

In the late nineteenth and early twentieth centuries, the Canadian government adopted a variety of policies that attracted foreign investment to Canada. Particularly important was the National Policy of high tariffs to protect secondary industry, initiated in 1879. The tariffs were designed to protect domestic manufacturing industries, and foreign investment was encouraged in order to establish branch-plants to serve the Canadian market (Dawson, 2004: 5). Foreign capital was also significant in resource development. Over the first half of the twentieth century, a growing proportion of capital inflows came from the United States, and a growing proportion of that capital was in the form of direct, as opposed to portfolio, investment (Bliss, 1984: 2).[1] In sum, Canada had gone out of its way to attract foreign investment, and the slow but steady growth in American equity participation in the Canadian economy that occurred between 1900 and the outbreak of the Second World War had not set off alarm bells. It is at this point, at the end of the war that we pick up the foreign investment story. As the Canadian economy was launched into its postwar economic boom, the streams in the policy process were aligned in such a way that a continuation of the status quo could be expected: the principal problem facing Canada was securing sufficient capital to finance postwar growth; the preferred policy was the open door that had served Canada well for almost 70 years, especially since the source of capital was deemed to be irrelevant to its productive effects; and the politics of the day were dominated by C.D. Howe, the minister of everything (Bliss, 1984: 1), whose influence was expanding along with the economy.

WALTER GORDON'S MISSION

That comfortable status quo was challenged by Walter Gordon, although the challenge began innocently enough. Gordon was well connected to the Liberal government of Louis St Laurent, and in 1955 he was of the view that its economic policies were in need of some fresh thinking. This gave rise to the article he drafted for publication in the *International Journal*, and being a well-connected Liberal, he wanted to ensure that the article would not cause the government embarrassment, so Gordon sent a draft to deputy minister of finance Kenneth Taylor, who shared it with his minister, Walter Harris. Harris saw Gordon's proposal as an opportunity to sidestep C.D. Howe's dominance of the government's economic policy, and he took the royal commission idea to cabinet. Howe saw the commission idea as a challenge to his authority, 'one of the silly tricks of the men he called Junior Leaguers' (Smith, 1973: 33), a group that included Harris. Despite Howe's opposition, Harris carried the cabinet, and persuaded his colleagues to name Gordon to chair the commission (Azzi, 1999: 38).[2]

In light of subsequent developments, it is important to note that the government was doing no more than commissioning a study of the Canadian economy and Canada's economic prospects. If Taylor and Harris actually looked carefully at Gordon's draft article, there would have been nothing on the issue of foreign investment and its impact on Canadian self-determination to suggest where Gordon would go subsequently with his commission report. Although he did argue in the draft for the acquisition of greater Canadian 'financial interest' in resource industries (Azzi, 1999: 37), this was not much of a hint of what was to come later. This may have been deliberate prudence on Gordon's part, since he notes in his memoirs that his draft article was intended to stimulate a debate about 'the sell-out of our resources and business enterprises to Americans and other enterprising foreigners' (Gordon, 1977: 59), and while there were no warnings in the article about a sell-out, that is certainly the direction he took on this issue once the commission was underway. While royal commissions are often lacking in influence, the decision in 1955 to launch the Gordon Commission was important for the evolution of Canadian foreign investment policy, because it touched off a debate in Canada on the issue of foreign ownership and gave Gordon a forum in which to develop his ideas on the problem. The decision was taken, thanks to a particular alignment of an identified problem, an idea, and political considerations: however, the problem identified by Gordon was not foreign ownership, but the need for fresh ideas in a government midway through its second term in office and a party that had been in power for twenty years; the idea for addressing a government grown tired, a royal commission to study the economy, was low risk; and a key minister, while perhaps a junior leaguer, saw the commission as an opportunity to bring some new ideas into a cabinet dominated by Howe.

If Gordon's interest in foreign investment was unclear in his draft article, there was no such ambiguity in his approach to the work of the commission. In directives to staff and in public statements, he indicated that the commission would deal with the issue of foreign, especially American, ownership (Azzi, 1999: 40–1). Research by the commission's staff concluded that the benefits of foreign investment far outweighed any problems it created, problems that could be addressed through general economic policies (Dawson, 2004: 6). When the staff who were working on foreign investment objected to the recommendations for tax incentives and penalties to discourage foreign investment that appeared in Gordon's preliminary report, he ignored their objections and retained the measures in his final report.[3] Clearly, Gordon saw a problem in foreign ownership, and preferred to use voluntary guidelines to change the behaviour of foreign companies and tax changes to encourage Canadian ownership. Others were not convinced, however. When Gordon produced his preliminary report, Howe rejected it, as did officials in his Department of Trade and Commerce, unsurprising for those who were overseeing the status quo. Moreover, officials in the Department of Finance, where the commission originated, making support more likely, were put off by Gordon's haste to produce a preliminary report, and were sceptical of the research and analysis undertaken by the commission to that point. Unlike conditions governing the launch of the commission, there was no fortuitous alignment of the three streams in the reception of its report. Gordon had failed to make a convincing case for the foreign ownership problem, and where no problem exists, no solution is necessary. In any case, political conditions were not right for the adoption of the report: the Liberal government was under fire, and the report's political fate was sealed when its recommendations were picked up by the Conservative opposition, which used them to attack the government for its complacency, catching the commission in the partisan squeeze that made it even less likely that ministers would follow the report's recommendations (Smith, 1973: 38, 44).

If conditions in the politics stream were not right for Walter Gordon's foreign investment agenda in 1956, he could have been forgiven for thinking that things had changed by 1963. The turnover in government had given the Liberals control of Canada's economic policies, and Gordon had been given the finance ministry, with jurisdiction over tax policy, his preferred instrument to discourage foreign, and encourage Canadian, investment. In addition, while finance ministers are usually influential, Gordon 'had a level of influence that few of his predecessors had known' (Azzi, 1999: 95). However, not all was right in the stream of politics. Concerning the national mood, while the Gordon Commission had stimulated growing public opposition to foreign investment, that opposition had begun to subside by 1963, and most Canadians seemed to worry little about the issue (Azzi, 1999: 89). In addition, Gordon would shortly discover that interest group pressures were largely running in one direction, and were opposed to his policies. Nevertheless, turnover and jurisdiction were sufficient political conditions to accelerate the evolutionary process in the problem and policy streams. In the problem stream, Gordon did not need additional indicators, focusing events, or feedback to convince him that there was a problem with foreign investment in Canada; instead, he had previously concluded that the problem was the degree of foreign ownership, and this conviction by a finance minister was sufficient to cause it to be included on the government's decision agenda concerning the economy. As for policy, Gordon had decided in 1956 that new tax measures were needed to address the problem, and return ownership of important sectors of the economy to Canadians, and he had continued to advocate this view in the intervening years.

This accelerated process was unfortunate for Gordon, because he had not yet convinced key policy communities that a problem existed for which his particular solution was required. One important community consisted of professional economists, and they had been extremely critical of the foreign investment content of Gordon's royal commission report, and continued their criticisms as he advocated his views within the Liberal Party (Azzi, 1999: 53, 79). Another important community resided inside government, especially officials in the Department of Finance and the Bank of Canada. Although he was the finance minister, Gordon did not have the support of senior officials within his department for his foreign investment policies. The situation was not helped by staffing decisions that would alienate senior officials from the outset. In the first of these, immediately upon taking office Gordon informed the long-serving finance deputy minister Kenneth Taylor that he would be replaced by Robert Bryce, who was then serving as clerk of the Privy Council (Smith, 1973: 137). Subsequently, however, Prime Minister Pearson delayed Bryce's release from his responsibilities as clerk, leaving Gordon to carry on with a disaffected Taylor in the preparation of the budget. Second, Gordon decided to bring his team of outside advisors into the minister's office, to the considerable consternation of Taylor and, especially, the department's assistant deputy ministers (Plumptre, 1977: 203; Azzi, 1999: 98), who disagreed profoundly with the advisors' proposals concerning foreign investment, first mounting a rearguard action to keep these measures out of the budget, and then, when their efforts failed, insisting that they were unworkable.[4] The Bank of Canada also had a jurisdictional interest in capital flows, and governor Louis Rasminsky expressed strong objections to the measures designed to promote the sale of shares to Canadians, especially the withholding tax provisions (Smith, 1973: 145–9; Azzi, 1999, 100).

The reservations of senior officials did not deter Gordon, who was determined to act quickly on his foreign investment program (Smith, 1973: 147). And because these measures were drafted for a budget, convention decreed that outside consultations had to be extremely limited, which meant that Gordon was unable to consult with cabinet colleagues or to gauge the reaction of organized groups to the proposals. This would be fatal for the budget measures, which 'aroused a storm of opposition both inside and outside the country' (Bliss, 1984: 5). Heads of the Montreal, Toronto, and Vancouver stock exchanges and the Investment Dealers' Association expressed concerns, and Gordon received delegations from the Toronto and Montreal exchanges (Smith, 1973: 162). The head of the Toronto exchange made clear his unhappiness with the takeover tax, although he did allow that the exchange could resolve the technical difficulties of administering it. However, Eric Kierans, the head of the Montreal exchange, made no such concession, instead launching a highly public attack on all the ownership measures (Azzi, 1999: 105). In this case then, organized interests were all pointing in the same direction, and their demand for the withdrawal of the budget measures was not offset by a strong defence by opposing interests that favoured them. As for the national mood, although public awareness and questioning of the role of foreign capital in the Canadian economy had been growing since the 1950s (Wolfe, 1978: 15), and was helped along by the Gordon

Commission hearings and the pipeline debate, as noted above, in 1963 Canadian attitudes were still generally positive towards foreign investment (Fayerweather, 1974: 14), so there was no strong climate of opinion that would offset the views of organized interests. Facing a barrage of criticism in the minority Parliament, Gordon withdrew the takeover tax and withholding tax increase.[5]

Shortly after the conclusion of the budget imbroglio, events in Canada's relationship with the United States demonstrated Canada's dependence on American capital, and its vulnerability to American action that threatened access to that capital. The episode served as a cautionary tale for both sides in the debate over the consequences of foreign ownership in Canada. In July 1963, the US introduced a special tax on purchases of foreign securities by Americans, designed to reduce the flow of American dollars abroad in order to overcome a persistent balance of payments deficit. The tax would hit Canada hard, forcing a rise in interest rates to prevent a serious loss of capital, and after initially refusing, senior US Treasury officials finally agreed to exempt Canada from the tax.[6] Although the US government drew no direct link between its tax and the Canadian foreign ownership measures, analysts concluded that Canada was not initially granted an exemption because of Gordon's budget,[7] and a senior US official made the point that the budget made it more difficult for the Canadians finally to secure an exemption (Azzi, 1999: 112–14). For those in the Gordon camp, this episode confirmed the costs to Canada of high levels of American investment, while for Gordon's opponents it confirmed the folly of interfering with capital flows, as his budget had done. In any case, the episode drove home the point that US interests had to be factored into Canadian agendas, policy ideas, and politics, a recurring theme in the investment story, as we show below.

Gordon's experience is instructive for our model of policy change. Advocates of particular agendas try to convince important people in and around government that they ought to give priority to certain problems, and ideas circulate in policy communities as proponents attempt to win adherents and attach solutions to problems. When a problem has been recognized and an appropriate solution has been accepted by a critical mass within key policy communities, then change can occur when the politics are right. For Gordon and his budget, critical changes in the politics stream provided an opportunity for policy change before he had achieved a widespread consensus on the need for action on the ownership problem, and on tax measures as the appropriate policy response. With substantial opposition in key policy communities, including among his own officials, with interest groups united in opposition to the measures, and without a supportive national mood, Gordon was a decision maker who had the power to bring about change, but a policy entrepreneur who had not yet created the necessary conditions to support change.

SCREENING FOREIGN INVESTMENT

The next stage in the evolution of investment policy unfolded very differently. Gordon had the tenacity required of policy entrepreneurs in his determination to keep the issue on the governmental agenda, and he succeeded when his return to the Liberal cabinet in 1967 led to the establishment of the Watkins task force. But the opposing forces were equally tenacious, ensuring that the evolutionary path would not be a smooth one. Finance minister Mitchell Sharp opposed the creation of the task force, and then successfully disputed Gordon's authority to choose its members (Smith, 1973: 309). Senior officials in Finance, Trade and Commerce, and the Bank of Canada also opposed the establishment of a task force, treated its work with derision, and then tried to suppress its report. Nevertheless, Watkins managed to generate a consensus among a diverse group of largely mainstream, albeit reformist, economists who agreed that, despite the substantial benefits of foreign investment, it could constitute a problem for Canada, and therefore should be monitored more systematically, while government encouraged more Canadian participation in the economy. The Watkins Report moved the foreign ownership issue back on to the governmental agenda, sharpening the definition of the problem facing Canada, and at the same time it moved away from the discriminatory tax-based measures for dealing with it that Gordon had advocated, in favour of a focus on scrutiny and maximizing the benefits from foreign investment while reducing the costs associated with it (Azzi, 1999: 158, 160, 161).

These changes in the problem and policy streams were important for the evolutionary development of investment policy, because they occurred at the same time as significant changes were underway in the politics stream. First, the national mood on the foreign investment issue was shifting more significantly in the late 1960s and early 1970s, as media coverage of the extent of American ownership and of American takeovers increased, and a strong trend developed toward less favourable views of foreign investment, because it was perceived to entail a loss of control over national affairs (Fayerweather, 1974: 13, 20; Molot, 1984: 169). In addition, the interest-group playing field that had been so dominated by business and finance in the 1960s added a new, highly visible player in 1970, when Walter Gordon joined with like-minded allies to form the Committee for an Independent Canada (CIC), which pressured the government to act on the recommendations of Watkins and then Gray. Finally, although the new Trudeau government initially showed little interest in the foreign ownership issue (Smith, 1973: 351, 352; Clarkson and McCall, 1990: 117), Trudeau's replacement of Mitchell Sharp in the critical finance ministry with Edgar Benson, a Gordon ally in the 1960s battles over foreign ownership, increased the probability of policy change.[8] As had not been the case in the 1960s, key elements in both the problem and politics streams had shifted in a way that increased the prospects for inclusion of the foreign investment issue on the government's decision agenda. What was needed was an alternative in the policy stream that would prove politically acceptable in the changed circumstances.

The successful policy that emerged from the Gray task force was, in the context of the times, 'an attempt to straddle the fence' (Bliss, 1984: 10), to find a middle ground between those who insisted that capital should be allowed to move unimpeded and those who insisted that there had to be some control over flows and purpose. The idea of passing legislation empowering the government to review, and set conditions for, takeovers, was defended for its flexibility and rationality, the bargaining power it conferred on Canada, and the fact that it was a measure that was familiar to international business (Government of Canada, 1972: 453–4). The cabinet debate that began over the recommendations of the Gray Report in the summer of 1971 intensified when, in August 1971, the US imposed a blanket import surcharge, plus measures to increase US exports at the expense of American investment abroad, as part of a more comprehensive strategy to deal with its balance of payments deficit. On this occasion, however, Canada's request for an exemption was refused. Recall that cabinet had agreed in July that a screening mechanism should be established to review significant foreign takeovers, but there was disagreement over the proper scope of review beyond takeovers. This episode influenced the debate, because ministers were concerned that the US measures would have a negative impact on the economy and depress planned business investment, and were therefore less inclined to be tough on foreign investment. As a result, the legislation that Gray introduced in May 1972 was narrow in scope, limited to takeovers, representing the lowest common denominator of agreement (Smythe, 1994: 194, 311, 312).

While problem, policy, and politics aligned in 1972, conditions in the political stream, including the Canada–US relationship, were right for only limited screening under the auspices of a government department. However, the election of 1972 changed that. Gray's original legislation, which had died with the election call, had been heavily criticized by the Committee for an Independent Canada (CIC) for restricting reviews to takeovers; the CIC had strong connections with the New Democratic Party, upon which the Liberal minority government now depended for parliamentary support. Under these circumstances, Roberto Gualtieri, the special advisor on foreign investment in Industry, Trade and Commerce, was able to deliver new legislation to his minister, Alastair Gillespie, that was much closer to the original Gray Report, which Gualtieri had a hand in writing along with the PMO's Joel Bell. Gillespie, an early proponent of screening, was able, with help from the PMO, to convince his reluctant cabinet colleagues, among them, as always, Mitchell Sharp, as well as finance minister John Turner, that the minority situation required the new, tougher legislation: a new agency would be created, and FIRA would screen not only takeovers, but also the expansion of existing, and the establishment of new, foreign-owned companies.[9]

With the establishment of FIRA in 1973, it had been twenty years since Walter Gordon first put pen to paper on the problem of foreign ownership, and it had taken the sustained efforts of Gordon, Watkins, Wahn, and Gray, among many others, to establish foreign ownership as a problem on the governmental agenda, finally defined in terms of its impact on Canada's development as an industrial economy. Since Gordon was a tax accountant by profession, it made sense for him to first think tax in 1956 when considering appropriate policy instruments to address the problem, but when the tax initiative crashed so spectacularly in 1963, it took almost ten years more for Conway's original idea of requiring government approval of equity sales to non-residents to be given expression in the requirement for government review of takeovers. That idea followed an evolutionary path through proposals from Watkins for a special agency to examine the behaviour of foreign-owned firms, from Wahn that the agency should assess performance against standards, and from Gray that it should negotiate benefit in exchange for access. When the industrial development problem was joined to the review solution in 1972, changes in political conditions were still required to bring the three streams together to produce the final FIRA legislation. Two critical components in Gordon's thinking had been lost along this evolutionary path to FIRA, however; namely, the assessment of the performance of existing foreign-owned firms, and the achievement of higher levels of Canadian ownership.

When political fortunes changed again in 1980, it seemed that the time might be right to remedy these deficiencies, since the newly elected Liberal government had campaigned for more Canadian ownership and greater benefit to Canada from foreign-owned firms. Herb Gray was returned to cabinet, and put in the driver's seat at Industry, Trade and Commerce to expand FIRA's mandate to review the performance of existing foreign-owned firms, and to assist Canadian companies to buy back foreign-owned firms or to counter foreign bids to take over Canadian firms. After a half-decade of experience with FIRA, developments in the problem and policy streams seemed to align again in such a way as to promote a further evolution in the policy of reviewing foreign investments, so that the agency would be given a greater role in achieving greater Canadian ownership and economic self-determination. Politics were not right for this change, however. There was substantial, unified opposition to the proposed changes from business lobby groups and the provinces (Smythe, 1994: 233–4; 1996: 195), and complaints about FIRA and its operations from American business and the US government increased significantly in this period (Beckman, 1984: 67). More ominously, in the summer of 1981 the US linked its unhappiness over FIRA to trade issues, and began to talk about trade retaliation. Gray's initiative was opposed in cabinet by Bud Olson, minister of economic and regional development and chair of the cabinet committee on economic development, and treasury board president Don Johnston, and in 1981 the proposals were rejected by cabinet. Instead, Olson's proposal for a resources-led industrial strategy was adopted (Tomlin and Molot, 1985: 6). In 1982, Gray was replaced as minister by Ed Lumley, who wanted to make FIRA more friendly to foreign investment, and the scope of FIRA's review authority was reduced (Smythe, 1994: 230, 237, 324).

While Canada retreated from its FIRA plans in the face of cabinet disagreement, and opposition within Canada and from the United States, it would not do so on the NEP. As already noted, energy minister Marc Lalonde was close to the prime minister, and could be assured of his support in cabinet, and he was further supported by a group of skilful policy entrepreneurs in Energy, Mines, and Resources (EMR), including Marshall Cohen, a very strong deputy minister who would take over the deputy's position in Finance in 1982, and Edmund Clark, an enterprising and creative assistant deputy minister with a Ph.D. in economics from Harvard (Foster, 1982: 74).[10] Clark had joined EMR in 1978, when Ian Stewart was deputy minister, and he was instrumental in developing the ideas behind the NEP, with Stewart's support. When Lalonde took the NEP proposals to cabinet, he did so in an alliance with finance minister Allan MacEachen (Doern, 1984: 41), an alliance that was facilitated by MacEachen's deputy minister, Ian Stewart, who had moved from Energy to Finance in 1980. Finally, although smaller Canadian firms that made up a majority of the industry opposed the NEP, the government was confident that Canada had a strong bargaining position vis-à-vis the energy sector (Smythe, 1996: 195) and confident that it was riding a wave of public support for its Canadianization policies. As a result, in 1980 the political conditions were right for an increased role for the federal government in the energy sector, a policy that would secure for Ottawa a larger share of the revenues that were being generated by rising oil prices, and the minister and his officials seized the opportunity presented by the coupling of the streams to secure adoption of their National Energy Program.

IN SEARCH OF FOREIGN INVESTMENT

What a coupling of the streams permitted, falling oil prices would undo.[11] By 1982, when the recession had hit Canada hard, with dropping oil prices and investment, and the problem became too little, rather than too much, investment, the Liberal government started to implement changes to its investment policy, modifying FIRA to make it more friendly to foreign investors. That incremental change was accelerated when the Conservative government was elected in 1984, and opted for the symbolic replacement of FIRA by Investment Canada. Although the new agency would continue to have the capacity to screen foreign investments, its principal purpose was to attract new investment and promote Canada as an investment destination. In addition, the NEP was modified to eliminate the provisions to which foreign investors had objected most strenuously. In this stage in the evolution of Canadian investment policy, dramatic changes in the economy led to the identification of a different investment problem, and political turnover produced more openness to foreign investment. This new approach was extended further when Canada entered into free trade negotiations with the United States, and, since Canadian investment policy would now be established through bilateral negotiations, we must turn to an examination of those negotiations to understand the next stage in the evolution of Canada's investment policy.

The US had indicated from the start of preliminary talks in July 1985 that they wanted any free trade agreement to include national treatment and right of establishment for investment; a central American aim in the negotiations would be to secure an agreement that would preclude any more FIRAS or NEPs.[12] For its part, Canada wanted to negotiate a new regime on American contingency protection, one that would remove the threat to Canadian exports from the application of US trade remedies—anti-dumping, countervail, and safeguard actions—to Canada. When the Americans first raised the investment issue at the negotiating table, however, Canada's chief negotiator, Simon Reisman, turned them back, asserting that Canada had never agreed to include investment in the trade negotiations. Reisman always intended to use investment as a trump card to secure Canada's goals on the trade remedies issue, and he finally put the issue on the table early in 1987, inviting an American proposal on investment. That proposal was presented by senior Treasury official Robert Cornell in April 1987, and it asked for the moon: in addition to national treatment, the Americans wanted to abolish Canada's capacity to review takeovers, and sought guarantees against the reintroduction of investment reviews or takeover legislation. Reisman refused to accept the proposal. Telling chief US negotiator Peter Murphy that it was so outrageous that it would be better to proceed as though no proposal had been made, Reisman handed it back. Undaunted, the Americans repeated the proposal in the working group that was established to negotiate investment, and for the next five months little progress was made. Essentially, Canada had already made its concessions on investment outside the negotiations, with the creation of Investment Canada and changes to the review procedures, and the Canadians wanted an agreement that would freeze the status quo (Hart, 1994: 236, 306).

This battle was finally joined in October 1987 when the two negotiating teams met in Washington, DC, for a last ditch effort to conclude a comprehensive free trade agreement. When the investment working group met, the Americans tabled a new proposal in writing, but it was an indigestible piece, composed by a 30-year Treasury veteran who tried to fit into one draft everything he had ever wanted to achieve on investment, incomprehensible even to his Treasury colleagues. The Canadians volunteered to redraft the US text, and then offered their complete rewrite back to the Americans as a single negotiating text from which both sides could work. Although the Americans were aiming at maximum access to Canada for American investors, they were forced to back off that position considerably as negotiations proceeded. The Canadian working group head, Andrei Sulzenko, adopted a very tough stance in the working group sessions with his counterpart, Robert Cornell, and was able to whittle away at American demands. This tough stand in the working group sessions helped finance minister Michael Wilson, who was handling the investment issue at the main negotiating table with his counterpart, US treasury secretary James Baker, since Baker was relying on advice from Cornell on how hard to push the Canadians. Reisman's April rejection of his original proposal had convinced Cornell that Canada could not be pushed too far on this sensitive issue, and he advised Baker that the US would have to be prepared to compromise. The Canadians incorporated the right to screen investment into the draft text, which the Americans accepted, but the US waived its reciprocal right to screen on the grounds that they did not wish to imitate a bad practice. The principle of grandfathering powers to review and restrict investment in specific sectors was also incorporated into the text. Most important here was agreement that any limits on Canada's power to review takeovers would not extend to the oil, natural gas, and uranium sectors. The US also agreed to a specific exemption for cultural industries from the investment provisions, as well as to a right of Canada to require divestiture to Canadians of cultural industries indirectly controlled by US firms.

However, the Canadians had to make some concessions to American demands for national treatment for US investors in order to achieve the tradeoff they wanted between investment and trade remedies. The crucial issue here became the threshold levels for review of foreign takeovers. It was agreed that Canada would continue to review major direct takeovers, but not smaller ones, and that the review of indirect takeovers would be phased out over three years, with the threshold for review increasing from $100 million to $500 million before ending reviews altogether. The question, then, was what threshold would be used to distinguish between major and smaller direct takeovers? Canada wanted the figure lower, and the Americans higher. Sulzenko told Cornell that the Canadians would not negotiate this issue in the working group, but instead would leave it to Baker and Wilson to settle on a figure, and they chose $150 million. Sulzenko then bought some additional room for review by insisting that the figure be phased in, with the review threshold moving in four annual stages from the then-current figure of $5 million to the agreed threshold of $150 million. They also persuaded the Americans to define the threshold in current dollars during the phase-in period, so that over the four stages the threshold would effectively be reduced, permitting the review of slightly smaller takeovers. Given the tough stance that Canada adopted in this bilateral exercise in making Canadian investment policy, it is worth noting that Treasury officials later came under heavy fire in Washington for conceding too much to the Canadians on investment. For their part, Treasury officials complained about being 'nickel-and-dimed' on the investment issue by the Canadians, and Baker himself was privately very unhappy over Canada's contentious behaviour on the issue.[13]

Canada's foreign investment policy moved further in the direction of openness in the bilateral negotiations with the US, granting national treatment, raising the threshold for the review of direct takeovers, and eliminating reviews of indirect takeovers. In addition, the agreement prohibited investment-related performance requirements that were trade-distorting. There the matter would have rested except, as noted in Chapter 2, for the emergence of the problem of investment diversion as a result of Mexico's decision to negotiate a free trade agreement with the United States. When Canada joined the others at the trilateral table, Canadian investment policy would once again be established through negotiations.[14] The investment issue posed particularly difficult problems for all three countries. The US wanted the provisions of the NAFTA investment chapter to conform to those contained in the maximalist bilateral investment treaties (BITs) that it normally negotiated to protect American investors. Canada, on the other hand, preferred the more limited obligations that were contained in the FTA. Each attempted to persuade Mexico to support the adoption of their approach.

In addition to the BITs versus FTA question, there were three basic issues at stake in the investment negotiations. The first concerned compensation in cases of expropriation. A typical American BIT stipulates that compensation must be 'prompt, adequate, and effective', but this was unacceptable to Mexico, because this was the language used by the US against Mexico when the Mexican government expropriated American oil companies operating in Mexico in 1938. Secondly, the US insisted that the chapter include provisions for arbitration proceedings between the investor and the state, and again the Mexicans objected. Finally, the Canadians wanted to preserve the right to screen investment that had been enshrined in the FTA. The US, however, having accepted the screening provisions of the FTA only reluctantly, now attempted to persuade the Mexicans that they should not be a part of the NAFTA.

Midway through the negotiations, the Mexicans accepted the idea of a provision in the chapter on investment that would allow arbitration to occur between investors and national states, and they agreed to language on expropriation that required the parties to pay compensation at fair market value without delay. These elements gave the Americans the BITs model they were seeking. The major issue left was investment screening, with the US seeking to reduce the scope for foreign investment review allowed by the FTA, and Canada resisting. Because US Treasury officials had come under heavy criticism in Washington for conceding too much to the Canadians on investment in 1987, the NAFTA Treasury negotiators were determined to reverse those concessions. The US initially persuaded Mexico to concede its ability to screen investments, but the Mexicans reneged on the deal under pressure from Canada. This episode strengthened the Americans' determination. Moreover, senior US officials expected Canadian movement on the screening issue as a quid pro quo for American acceptance, again, of the exemption of cultural industries from the agreement. The exemption for the cultural sector that Canada had secured in the FTA was a thorn in the side of the US entertainment industry, and they made certain that their pain was felt by NAFTA negotiators. The Americans had tried to keep culture on the table throughout these negotiations, but the Canadians insisted that the issue was non-negotiable. If that truly was the case, and the Americans were half convinced by Canadian intransigence that it was, then a price would have to be paid by Canada somewhere else on the agenda, and the Americans were looking for payment in the coin of investment screening. With the negotiations in their final phase, however, there was intense pressure on US negotiators to get an agreement, and the Canadians decided they could hang tough on the issue of investment. Reluctantly, the Americans agreed that Canada would retain its right to screen foreign investment, and Mexico would be granted the same right. However, with the strengthening of the prohibition on investment-related performance requirements in the agreement, the ability of Canada to bargain with firms to secure performance benefits in exchange for access, the original idea behind foreign investment review, was reduced.[15]

MAKING THE WORLD SAFE FOR CANADIAN INVESTMENT

Following the conclusion of the NAFTA negotiations, Canadian policy would focus on securing those same rights and protections for Canadian investors abroad through a series of bilateral negotiations to establish Foreign Investment

Protection Agreements (FIPAs). Although Canada made bilateral progress through the FIPAs during the 1990s, the going was slow, and a more comprehensive, multilateral approach would have been more efficient. However, multilateral progress was harder to come by. While the NAFTA negotiations were underway, Canada was also participating in the Uruguay Round of multilateral trade negotiations, where the US, with Canadian support, was pushing hard for a NAFTA-like agreement on investment. Instead, the negotiations produced an agreement on trade-related investment measures, or TRIMs, a very limited package of commitments, particularly in comparison to the NAFTA provisions (Smythe, 1996: 203). Unable to achieve much through multilateral negotiations in the World Trade Organization (WTO), in 1995 Canada reluctantly agreed to sidestep the WTO and follow the lead of the US and the European Union (EU) to negotiate a benchmark multilateral agreement on investment through the OECD, one that would set high standards on liberalization, protection, and dispute settlement, and would be open to non-OECD countries (Dymond, 1999: 28). However, after three years of work, the OECD negotiations were suspended without an agreement in 1998. Canada was still left with one more multilateral forum for the negotiation of investment provisions, namely the effort to create a Free Trade Area of the Americas (FTAA). Initiated in December 1994 at the Summit of the Americas in Miami, and formally started in April 1998, the FTAA negotiations engaged the 34 countries from North, Central, and South America (excluding Cuba) in an effort to fashion a comprehensive trade agreement by 2005, one that would include provisions on investment. In the negotiations, Canada and the United States pushed for the adoption of the NAFTA model on investment, but their efforts met significant opposition. In January 2005, the deadline for concluding an agreement expired, and in 2006 the prospects for an FTAA appeared to be slim. With progress on investment rules also blocked by a coalition of developing and industrializing countries in the Doha Round of multilateral trade negotiations, it seemed as though only bilateral channels were available for Canadian action on investment policy.

When the North American free trade agreement came into effect in 1994, Canada had come almost full circle from the open door that had prevailed in 1954, when Walter Gordon began his campaign against foreign ownership, to the right of establishment and national treatment that had been written into the NAFTA. Our analysis has tracked the protracted effort to get investment-related problems on the decision agenda, with ideas about how to deal with foreign investment evolving slowly and unevenly until a middle ground was found between those who argued for unimpeded capital flows and those who argued for controls, and a review process was put in place. That policy equilibrium lasted only six years, however, when the investment problem shifted and policy too began to shift in favour of more open access secured by international treaties. With this transformation, after more than fifty years at the centre of events in the stream of politics, the battle of agendas and ideas over investment policy may finally have come to an end.

C H A P T E R   4

Streams in the Trade Policy Process

As we did with foreign investment, in this chapter we first describe the changing agenda of trade problems that Canada has faced in the period since the end of the Second World War. Following this, we trace the evolution of ideas about trade policy alternatives, and finally, we examine the politics of trade policy during this period. Chapter 5 will bring the three streams together in an analysis of the evolution of Canadian trade policy.

THE TRADE POLICY AGENDA

Canada emerged from the Second World War as the third most important trade and industrial power in the world (Hart, 2002: 127). But the new Canadian industrial capacity, with its attendant prosperity, depended on international trade, and Canada had a trade problem. Actually, it was a balance of payments problem, and it stemmed from the structure of Canadian trade. The United Kingdom traditionally had been a strong export market for Canadian producers, but the war had left Britain depleted, with reduced demand for goods, and insufficient resources to pay for imports. Adding to the problem were Britain's decision in 1939 to suspend convertibility of the pound sterling, which continued after the end of the war, and Canada's decision to remain outside the sterling bloc, choosing instead to be part of an informal dollar group whose currency remained convertible (Muirhead, 1992: 12, 15). This choice resulted in British restrictions on imports from the dollar area. Thus, in the years immediately following World War II, Canada was selling fewer goods to the UK, and the pounds received for those sales could be used only to purchase goods from the UK (or other Commonwealth countries that were part of the sterling area). However, Canadian demand was primarily for goods imported from the United States, and that demand had surged with postwar prosperity. As a result, the US dollars paid by Canadians to purchase American imports far exceeded the US dollars earned by Canadians from the sale of products in US markets, and sterling from exports to the UK could not be used to pay for American goods. As a result, by 1947 Canada's growing balance of payments deficit provided an indicator of a serious problem.

When the American Marshall Plan was passed into law in April 1948, Canada's payments problem eased when Plan funds were used to finance British purchases from Canada (Muirhead, 1992: 27). However, the underlying problems affecting Canadian trade with Britain remained, forcing Canada to look elsewhere for export markets. The Liberal government saw the emerging multilateral trade system as a key element in achieving greater access for Canadian producers to foreign markets. However, after a very successful multilateral tariff negotiation was held in Geneva in 1947, subsequent rounds of negotiations, in 1948, 1950, and 1956, proved disappointing, as countries resisted efforts to open their markets and the use of non-tariff barriers grew in popularity. During this period, the US grew in importance as a market for competitive Canadian producers, taking 60 per cent of Canada's exports by 1957, up from 40 per cent in 1947. However, American commitment to liberal trade was under attack from domestic interests in the US, and Canadian exports were increasingly subject to restrictions or trade remedy actions (Hart, 2002: 148, 160).

While protectionist trends were growing internationally, and especially in Canada's most important export market, another trade problem was emerging closer to home. Although there had been progress since 1945 in reducing Canadian tariffs and other barriers to imports, by the mid-1950s Canadian industry still enjoyed relatively high levels of protection from foreign competition. This protection encouraged a continuation of import-substitution industrialization, whereby Canadian industry produced primarily for the domestic market, which was too small to allow firms to achieve the economies of specialization and scale necessary to compete successfully in export markets. When Walter Gordon's Royal Commission on Canada's Economic Prospects was established in the spring of 1955, John Young, a Yale University economist, was hired to conduct the commission study on the tariff. Young zeroed in on the tariff as the source of Canada's problem, identifying the negative effects of the tariff on secondary industry, and the very high cost of the tariff to the Canadian economy, as follows:

> In general and over the long run, increases in protection can be expected to lead to economic losses and decreases in protection to economic gains for the country as a whole. This follows not only from the direct effect the Canadian tariff has on the Canadian economy, but also from the effect Canadian commercial policy has on the treatment accorded this country's exports.[1]

The policy community was not yet ready to accept this neo-classical economic truth, however.

The problem with Canada's manufacturing sector as a whole that had been identified in Young's study for the Gordon royal commission characterized the automotive sector as well. High Canadian tariffs had led the big three

US-controlled manufacturers—Chrysler, Ford, and General Motors—to establish Canadian branch-plants to produce for the Canadian market, but production for a relatively small domestic market was not efficient, nor did it encourage the economies of scale that were necessary to develop export markets. In short, by the late 1950s, there was little prospect of growth in the Canadian auto industry, and in fact the industry was in decline, with rising unemployment and costs, and growing consumer dissatisfaction over high prices and limited choice (Hart, 2002: 241).

This structural problem made its way on to the governmental agenda in 1960, when the Diefenbaker government appointed a royal commission, chaired by University of Toronto economist Vincent Bladen, to undertake a study of the Canadian automotive industry. In his 1961 report, Bladen confirmed that the industry's problem was a lack of competitiveness, and demonstrated that industry inefficiencies were caused by the short, fragmented production runs designed to supply only the Canadian market (Hart, 2002: 241). Bladen's report produced the requisite indicators of an industry in trouble, and these secured a place for the issue on the government's decision agenda; however, the response to Bladen was simply an incremental adjustment of tariffs for the industry, whereby producers were allowed to recoup tariffs paid on imports of certain auto parts (known as duty remission).

A focusing event was necessary to sustain the government's attention on the problem, and this occurred in April 1964. The Modine Manufacturing Company, an automobile radiator manufacturer in Racine, Wisconsin, complained to US trade authorities that Canada's duty remission scheme represented what amounted to a subsidy to Canadian producers and asked that a countervailing duty of up to 25 per cent be imposed on imports of Canadian radiators into the United States. The Modine complaint would trigger an inquiry by the US Treasury Department, an inquiry that was likely to support the complaint (Hart, 2002: 242; Dawson, 2005: 160), thus putting at risk the entire duty remission scheme, and the industrial restructuring it was intended to produce.

Canada's automotive trade competitiveness problem was addressed through the 1965 Auto Pact, which provided a basis for the development of a large and productive Canadian secondary manufacturing sector. Even as that sector was rebounding throughout the remainder of the 1960s, however, another serious trade policy problem for Canada was surfacing, once again in the United States. By the end of the 1960s, the US faced a serious balance of payments problem and an erosion in its merchandise trade surplus because of an increase in American imports. As a result, the US government came under increased pressure to stimulate exports and restrain imports, and in August 1971 President Richard Nixon announced a series of measures intended to deal with the payments problem, including a 10 per cent surcharge on all imports.[2] There had been plenty of indicators of the growing American problem, with the media full of reports on the US payments and trade deficits, and the weakness of the American dollar. In addition, there were indicators pointing to Canada's role in the US problem— 1970 had produced a very large Canadian trade surplus in automotive products—and the Americans had provided feedback concerning the decline they noted in the US trade surplus with Canada. With almost 70 per cent of Canadian exports going to the American market in 1971, the serious implications of the surcharge for Canada were clear; between 40,000 and 100,000 jobs were estimated to be at risk from the expected decline in exports (Granatstein and Bothwell, 1990: 62, 64, 67). In this context, the Nixon measures provided a focusing event that secured a place for the trade problem on the government's decision agenda.

Another fundamental shift in the trade policy agenda originated in the unprecedented conditions of crisis and conflict that marked the early 1980s.[3] The Liberal government of Pierre Trudeau, elected in 1980, had adopted an ambitious national policy agenda designed to enhance the resources and visibility of the federal government.[4] The National Energy Program (NEP) was a central element in this overall strategy, one that had highly negative consequences for foreign investors in the Canadian oil and gas industry. When the government also announced its intention to tighten its regulation of foreign investment, the howls of outrage from the American business establishment led the US government to plan retaliatory trade measures, thus effectively targeting the Canadian Achilles' heel of trade dependence on the United States (Clarkson, 1982). Canadian producers faced a mounting tide of US protectionism: the number of American trade remedy actions against Canadian export practices increased significantly (Hart, 2002: 349), and specific legislation was introduced in Congress that would limit Canadian exports to the United States (Leyton-Brown, 1986: 185). This acute conflict, and the sense of vulnerability it created for Canadians and their government, represented a turning point for Canada in its relations with the United States. The Americans had overtly threatened security of access to a market on which Canada was overwhelmingly dependent, with profound implications for employment and investment. This stimulated a reassessment, on the part of both business and government, of the value to Canada of secure and enhanced access to the US market, an assessment that would take place within the context of an economic recession more severe than any experienced since the Great Depression of the 1930s.

The government's trade policy reassessment was undertaken through a task force organized under the Department of Industry, Trade and Commerce (ITC). As the trade task force conducted its review during 1982, the emerging economic crisis guaranteed that the threat to secure access to the American market for Canada's exports would be defined as the central problem for Canadian trade policy. In feedback from representatives of the Canadian business community and provincial governments, the task force was repeatedly told that the central goal of any trade policy should be to 'get the Canada–US relationship right'. The American market was fundamentally important to Canadian economic well-being, and preservation of that market required stability in the Canada–US relationship. In particular, the government had to find a means to protect Canadian exporters from the application of US trade remedies, primarily anti-dumping and countervailing duties, to Canadian exports. Thus, by the midpoint of the decade, a fundamental shift had occurred in Canada's trade policy agenda, and threats to Canadian access to the US market had become the number one problem on the governmental agenda.

The successful conclusion of the Canada–US free trade agreement in 1987 addressed the market access problem on Canada's trade policy agenda. However, the issue soon surfaced again, when, in 1990, Mexico indicated its desire to enter into bilateral free trade negotiations with the US. The Mexican initiative was problematic for Canada, since a Mexican–American free trade agreement would give Mexico the same privileged access to the US market that Canadian producers enjoyed, thus offsetting their advantage over Mexican exporters. In addition, Canadian exporters would be at a disadvantage compared to American exporters, since the latter would enjoy duty-free access to both Canada and Mexico. The consequences of the initiative were even more problematic for investment, however, since, as noted in Chapter 2, US involvement in two bilateral free trade agreements on the continent would attract investors to the United States, at Canada's expense. Thus, the Mexican initiative provided a focusing event, and recognition of the consequences of a hub-and-spoke arrangement for Canada was sufficient to bring the market access issue back on to the governmental agenda.[5]

The successful negotiation of NAFTA addressed the hub-and-spoke problem and reaffirmed the access to the American market that Canada had achieved originally in the bilateral free trade agreement with the US. However, market access issues did not disappear entirely, since the Americans continued to apply trade remedies to certain Canadian exports, prominent among them softwood lumber. Nevertheless, the 1990s marked a relatively tranquil period in bilateral trade relations (Hart, 2000: 94). That changed abruptly on September 11, 2001, when terrorist attacks on the US prompted American concerns about the security of their borders, and raised anew the problem of Canadian access (Hart and Tomlin, 2002).[6] The issue of security on US borders initially made its way on to the Canadian governmental agenda in 1996, when a proposal was introduced in the US Congress for changes to Section 110 of the *Illegal Immigration Reform and Immigrant Responsibility Act* (IIRIRA), changes that would require the documentation of every alien (including Canadians) entering and exiting the United States. Adoption of entry/exit controls at US ports of entry would seriously disrupt personal and business traffic between the United States and Canada, threatening Canada's access to the US market and causing severe cross-border traffic congestion. In the end, Canada was able to head off the implementation of controls, convincing key members of Congress, particularly from border states, that Canada was not the intended target of the legislation, and the unintended consequences for commercial traffic would be intolerable.

With this successful resolution, the issue dropped off the agenda until December 1999, when Ahmed Ressam was stopped while attempting to enter the United States from Canada with a car trunk full of powerful explosives. These were to be used, it was learned subsequently, in a terrorist attack on the Los

Angeles airport. Ressam had established himself in Canada over the previous three years under an assumed name, using a fraudulent Canadian passport. He was subsequently tried and convicted in a Los Angeles court. The incident was deeply embarrassing to Canada, and raised questions in US government circles about Canada's reliability as a security partner. In the aftermath of the Section 110 issue, the government was at pains to assert its reliability, but little was actually done to assuage American fears. However, the 110 and Ressam episodes did result in the development of information concerning the consequences of enhanced screening by US agencies at the border for the movement of Canadian goods and services across the border, and some alarming indicators were constructed of the dollar cost to manufacturers of delays.

It is important to note here that, while Canada acted to head off the application of 110 to Canadians, and to counter the fallout from the Ressam affair, the connection between US border initiatives and market access had not yet been identified as a problem deserving a priority place on the government's decision agenda. In fact, the government's response to Ressam was largely rhetorical, crafting and delivering messages intended to convince Americans that they had nothing to worry about on their northern frontier. That all changed, of course, with the occurrence of the focusing event provided by the terrorist attacks of September 11, 2001. The new measures that were immediately put in place by the Americans to screen entry into the United States from Canada had their predicted effects, with long delays severely impeding access to the American market for Canadian products. The border security–market access issue was suddenly thrust onto the decision agenda. In response, the government sought to assure US officials that Canada was playing its part in ensuring the security of North America, and to convince them that heightened security measures on the American side of the Canadian border were unnecessary. US officials, for their part, made it clear to Canadians that they required deeds, not words, and a variety of initiatives were taken, particularly on Canadian visa and refugee policies, to satisfy American concerns.

Finally, an issue is more likely to achieve a priority place on the governmental agenda when officials receive feedback about the inadequacy of existing policies and programs, and the government was in receipt of such feedback from a number of important Canadian advocacy groups in the aftermath of the September 11 attacks. A variety of business umbrella groups pressed the government to continue to deal with the security-access problem in order to protect Canadian commercial interests. The Canadian Council of Chief Executives, in particular, devoted considerable attention in its advocacy activities to Canada's relationship with the US, and in particular to the security-access problem. In summary, indicators of a problem at the border, feedback about the severity of the problem, and the crisis of the 9/11 attacks ensured that the security-access issue would have a place on the government's decision agenda, and policy entrepreneurs would soon attempt to couple this issue with proposals for deeper Canada–US integration, efforts that are described in Chapter 5.

TRADE POLICY ALTERNATIVES

Our focus in this section will be on the evolution of ideas about alternative trade policies and policy instruments that circulate in communities of specialists inside and outside of government. The severe balance of payments deficit experienced by Canada in the period immediately following the end of the Second World War, described previously, could not be ignored. In November 1947, in order to protect dwindling dollar reserves, the Canadian government announced its intention to impose restrictions on imports from, and travel to, the United States, and it requested a loan from the US Export-Import Bank to finance its deficit (Muirhead, 1992: 22). These could be only stopgap measures, however. For the longer term, what was first needed was better access to the US market in order to increase exports to offset the dollar drain, and second, a way to get US dollars to the UK, so the British could use them to purchase Canadian goods (Hart, 2002: 141).

To improve access to the American market, Canada approached the US, in October 1947, to explore the prospects for a comprehensive bilateral trade agreement that would provide greater access for Canadian products. The US responded with a proposal for a customs union, whereby the two countries would eliminate customs barriers to bilateral trade, and harmonize their external trade policies toward other countries. When this proved unacceptable to Canada, the Americans suggested a modified customs union, which they called a free trade area (Hart, 2002: 142), in which the two would eliminate customs barriers, but retain the right to their own external trade policy with respect to other countries. This would enable Canada to retain its system of tariff preferences with Britain and other Commonwealth countries.

In the end, a free trade agreement with the United States would have to wait for almost twenty years, and it would be restricted to the automotive sector. Instead, throughout the 1950s, Canadian trade policy followed a Janus-like path, attempting to improve access to international markets through multilateral trade negotiations, while continuing to protect domestic industries with high tariffs and tariff classifications, and trade remedies (Hart, 2002: 179–84). The idea that government should use trade policy to discourage imports and support industries producing for the domestic market had dominated policy thinking in Canada for 75 years, and was still in good currency in the mid-1950s. That idea was reinforced in the preliminary report of Walter Gordon's Royal Commission on Canada's Economic Prospects. Written by Gordon, the section on commercial policy recommended maintenance of the status quo on tariffs, keeping most rates at current levels, while eliminating preferential treatment for certain items. Professional economists were highly critical of those aspects of the preliminary report, calling them protectionist, and claiming that the proposed modifications would have the effect of substantially raising the tariff (Azzi, 1999: 52, 53). In fact, the study of trade policy undertaken for the commission by economist John Young argued for free trade, but his recommendation was rejected by Gordon, who repeated his initial recommendations in the commission's final report.

The trade policy debate that surfaced in Gordon's royal commission was playing out as well in Canada's automotive industry. In his own royal commission on the auto sector, Vincent Bladen had identified a competitiveness problem, and saw increased exports as the solution. He recommended that the Canadian tariff be used to encourage specialization in narrowed lines of production for increased exports. This would be achieved by allowing firms to count their export sales as part of their domestic production base, thus permitting them to import more parts on a duty-free basis. In addition, finished vehicles imported by Canadian producers would qualify for duty-free entry as long as minimum Canadian production levels were maintained. This proposed solution did not find favour among Bladen's fellow economists, who saw it as a scheme to manipulate the tariff to offer greater protection to the auto industry in order to subsidize exports. The Diefenbaker government also saw in Bladen's plan a way to protect the Canadian industry and subsidize exports, but these were viewed as positive features, and although the government did not adopt its specific recommendations, in October 1962 they did modify tariffs to allow manufacturers who increased exports of parts above base levels to recoup tariffs paid on imports of certain auto parts not already made in Canada. This duty remission program was designed to encourage increased Canadian production for export. The Liberal government subsequently broadened the program to provide for the full remission of duties on imports of vehicles and parts in exchange for increased production in Canada (Hart, 2002: 241, 242, 487, note 28).

When the duty remission program was threatened by the trade remedy complaint brought by Modine Manufacturing, some other way had to be found to protect the Canadian industry, while still promoting a sufficient degree of continental rationalization. This was achieved in the Automotive Products Trade Agreement, or Auto Pact, as it came to be known. Under the terms of that 1964 agreement (signed in January 1965), the US granted duty-free entry to original equipment parts and vehicles produced in Canada, provided they met a minimum level of Canadian and/or American value added. For its part, Canada agreed that qualified firms could import original equipment parts and vehicles from anywhere in the world provided they met certain performance criteria concerning the level and value of manufacturing activity in their Canadian facilities: they had to maintain at least a 75 per cent ratio of Canadian production of vehicles to their Canadian sales of vehicles, and ensure that vehicles produced in Canada maintained a specified level of Canadian content. In addition, the Canadian government received letters of commitment from the Big Three agreeing to increase the level of Canadian value added on a continuous basis and the value of Canadian production by at least 60 per cent of the value in growth in Canadian sales (Hart, 2002: 244).[7]

The free trade idea embodied in the Auto Pact did not spill over into other industrial sectors, at least not immediately. Instead, Canada would first try to resist economic integration with the United States, by searching out alternative markets that could serve as a counterweight to its growing dependence on the US. This idea originated in response to the 1971 US import surcharge, and was given expression in a paper published in 1972 under the name of external affairs minister Mitchell Sharp.[8] The paper described three options that were open to Canada in its relationship with the US, two of which were clearly included in order to be dismissed—maintenance of the status quo and closer integration. Knocking down these straw issues set the scene for the presentation of the preferred Third Option, as the policy came to be known, 'a comprehensive long-term strategy to develop and strengthen the Canadian economy and other aspects of its internal life and in the process to reduce the present Canadian vulnerability' (Sharp, 1972: 1). To achieve this goal, the paper called for greater diversification in Canada's external contacts and transactions in order to reduce vulnerability to the US, with the European Community and Japan identified as appropriate partners for this diversification (von Riekhoff, 1978: 89). For the next several years, Canada gave expression to this diversification strategy through efforts to enhance its trade and investment relationships with Europe and Japan.

Although the Third Option became the watchword for Canadian policy for several years, it was never credible among economists and practitioners in the trade policy community. Instead, their focus was on the market at hand, in the United States. Economists had long argued that Canada could not afford to isolate its economy behind high barriers to imports, and furthermore that Canadian producers required free and secure access to a larger market than their own domestic one to gain the efficiency benefits that came from long production runs. In 1975, the Economic Council of Canada issued a report reflecting this argument, and recommended that Canada pursue a strategy of free trade with the US.[9] The Economic Council report did not have a major impact on the evolution of trade policy ideas in the mid-1970s, coming as it did in the midst of the Third Option and FIRA, when the political focus was on vulnerability, diversification, and regulation. However, its themes were subsequently picked up in the early 1980s by economists on the staff of the Macdonald Royal Commission, who made Canada–US free trade the centrepiece of the trade policy debate. Coming to the same strategy from a different perspective, Canadian firms with an export interest were seeking increased access to the American market, and their views were reflected in a series of reports by the Senate Standing Committee on Foreign Affairs, in 1975, 1978, and 1982, which argued for bilateral negotiations to secure greater access (Hart, 2002: 363).

This evolution of trade policy alternatives in the 1980s continued in the task force that was struck by the Department of Industry, Trade and Commerce (ITC) in 1982 to examine Canadian trade policy.[10] The trade task force undertook its work in the context of the economic recession and increased levels of US trade remedy action, ensuring that its examination of Canada's trade policy would centre on securing access to the American market. And the Canadian business lobby saw to it that the negotiation of some form of trade liberalization arrangement was put forward as an option for consideration. In its report,[11] the task force played it absolutely safe, reaffirming the adequacy of the status quo and the centrality of the multilateral GATT system for Canada. Secondarily, however, it also raised the prospect of pursuing sectoral free trade arrangements with the United States as an additional option for the government to consider. The sectoral option was not without precedent, of course, since Canada already had the sectoral free trade agreement with the United States covering automobiles, described above, as well as two additional agreements on defence materials and agricultural machinery. In fact, in 1981, Canadian embassy officials in Washington, with Ottawa's knowledge, informally discussed broader sectoral free trade arrangements with officials in the Office of the US Trade Representative (USTR). This initiative was part of the Canadian effort to resolve the conflict with the United States over the NEP and FIRA. It did not proceed, however, because of opposition from within ITC in Ottawa.

In any case, the Liberal government subsequently decided to proceed with the effort to conclude sectoral arrangements, and the task of implementing the initiative from the Canadian side fell to Tony Halliday, an experienced trade official. In February 1984, he and his counterparts in USTR were ready to bring Canadian trade minister Gerald Regan and US trade representative William Brock together in Washington where they identified four sectors upon which officials from the two countries could focus. By June, however, little progress had been made in these preliminary discussions, principally because USTR was unable to bring American industries on board. Although Regan and Brock agreed to explore alternative sectors, nothing further was decided on the question of whether and when to begin formal negotiations. There the matter rested until a new Conservative government was elected in September 1984, headed by Prime Minister Brian Mulroney.

During their first few months in government, the Tories began to sketch the principal dimensions of what would become the Conservative policy agenda. In an economic and fiscal statement presented by finance minister Michael Wilson to the House of Commons in November 1984, the government identified its priorities of economic renewal and national reconciliation. Wilson also tabled a policy agenda, setting out a strategy for economic renewal. One element of the strategy was increased and secure access to markets for Canadian exports, especially in the United States. Referring to sectoral free trade, the Finance agenda noted: 'This initiative has generated public interest in exploring broadly-based bilateral arrangements with the US.' While the Tories were considering their options, think-tanks were enriching the policy debate with alternatives that went beyond sectoral arrangements. Research and consultations were underway in 1984 by the Royal Commission on the Economic Union and Development Prospects for Canada, chaired by Donald Macdonald,[12] and it was common knowledge in Ottawa circles that staff were pointing commissioners in the direction of comprehensive Canada–US free trade. In May 1985, the C.D. Howe Institute published a study of Canada's trade policy options (Lipsey and Smith, 1985), and recommended negotiation of a bilateral free trade agreement.

When that agreement was finally concluded by Canada and the United States in 1987, it was a big, broad deal, with 14 of its 21 chapters dealing with issues that cut across the entire economy, and 6 chapters dealing with vertical sectors of the economy, such as autos, energy, and agriculture.[13] Although many sections of the agreement simply consolidated or elaborated Canada's GATT obligations, others were path-breaking in relation to trade policy and law as it existed at the time, including provisions on investment, services, agriculture, and rules of origin. The agreement also institutionalized the bilateral relationship through the dispute-settlement provisions included in Chapters 18 and 19, the latter dealing with the anti-dumping and countervail trade remedies that had been at the heart of Canada's free trade aspirations.

With its free trade mission accomplished, the bilateral dimension of Canada's trade policy should have been set for the foreseeable future. However, Mexico's decision in 1990 to seek its own free trade agreement with the US brought the issue into play again. In response, Canada had three options: it could do nothing, allowing the Mexican–American negotiations to proceed with no Canadian involvement; it could negotiate its own bilateral free trade agreement with Mexico; or it could ask to be included in a trilateral Canada–Mexico–United States negotiation. The idea of a trilateral economic partnership had been raised in the United States in 1979, in the US Congress and in the National Governors Association, and Ronald Reagan made a 'North American Accord' a key plank in his 1980 presidential campaign (Wise, 1998: 7). Although the idea was taken up for discussion in US policy communities, it got little serious attention in Canada (Winham, 1994: 474). That changed with Mexico's bilateral free trade initiative, of course, and, as indicated previously, with the hub-and-spoke problem identified and acknowledged in relevant policy communities, the idea of a trilateral negotiation gained currency.

The North American free trade agreement (NAFTA) was modelled on the Canada–US agreement, elaborating on some chapters, such as investment and telecommunications, reorganizing others, such as national treatment and border measures, but adding only two new chapters, on intellectual property and competition policy (Winham, 1994: 503), as well as supplemental agreements on the environment and labour. While this was a very big deal for Mexico, because it applied broad new disciplines and obligations to the Mexican economy, for Canada (and the US) NAFTA largely represented an extension and modification of the disciplines and obligations that were already in place in the bilateral agreement with the US. Perhaps most important for Canada, the dispute-settlement provisions that had been achieved in its agreement with the US were included in NAFTA as well, ensuring their continuation. Also important to Canada was the inclusion of an article on accession, setting out the process by which additional members could be added to the agreement, that was intended to make future hub-and-spoke bilateral arrangements involving the US less likely.[14]

The conclusion of the Canada–US free trade agreement in 1987 and NAFTA in 1993, followed by the successful completion of the Uruguay Round of multilateral trade negotiations in 1994, represented a trade policy revolution for Canada (Winham, 1994: 507). In the decade since 1983, free trade had evolved from a concept promoted primarily by economists—and remaining controversial outside economics—to become conventional wisdom, and the dominant idea in the

Canadian trade policy community, inside and outside government. Moreover, free trade transformed Canada's trade relationship with the United States, leading to a prodigious growth in exports (Hart, 2002: 390), and increasing Canadian dependence on the American market.

With dependence comes vulnerability, and when Canadian access was threatened by US security concerns after the terrorist attacks on September 11, 2001, a variety of alternatives to the status quo circulated in policy communities. The US administration favoured establishing a security perimeter, which meant tightening security measures at points removed from the Canada–US border, on the North American perimeter, joint screening of goods and people entering North America, and greater harmonization of immigration and refugee policies (Haggart, 2005: 18). However, the Canadians preferred coordination to harmonization, and they prevailed, at least initially, when, in December 2001, Canadian foreign affairs minister John Manley and US director of homeland security Tom Ridge promised joint cooperation on security and migration at the border, and signed a 'Smart Border Declaration', which included a 30-point Action Plan for forward planning. The agreement rested on four declared pillars: 'the secure flow of people, the secure flow of goods, secure infrastructure, and information sharing, and coordination in the enforcement of these objectives.' The declaration and action plan consolidated the principal ideas that had emerged from two years of consultations between Canadian and American officials on ways to ease border problems, modified to address the post-September 11 security concerns of the US (Waddell, 2003: 61). In policy communities outside government, however, smart borders were not enough. Instead, policy advocates were promoting a fundamental shift in the Canadian–American relationship, one that involved deeper integration with the US, and these integration ideas are described in Chapter 5.

TRADE POLITICS

Our focus in this section will be on the political forces that drive trade policy agendas and ideas, identifying important shifts in the national mood, the direction of interest group pressures, and significant jurisdictional change and turnover in government. As Canada emerged from the Second World War, trade policy was in the hands of a small group of officials in the Departments of Finance, Trade and Commerce, and External Affairs who had handled trade negotiations for Canada since the mid-1930s (Hart, 2002: 120). Postwar economic planning for the Liberal government of Mackenzie King was led by deputy finance minister Clifford Clark, and the Canadians favoured the establishment of a multilateral, non-discriminatory trade system, under the auspices of a new international trade organization, that would ensure access to Canada's two traditional markets in the US and Britain. It would take another 20 years for that trade system to evolve, however, and almost 50 years to establish a World Trade Organization. In the meantime, in 1947 a multilateral tariff negotiation was held in Geneva, where Canada's principal negotiating partner was the US, and the two countries concluded an extensive agreement as part of the multilateral negotiations. As Canada's balance of payments deficit continued to worsen, Finance officials concluded that greater access to the American market was a necessary part of the solution. However, the trade relationship with the United States was a politically sensitive issue in Canada, and Canadian manufacturers were reluctant to give up the protection afforded them by Canadian tariffs, so politics demanded that bilateral trade liberalization be approached secretly, in the first instance, and finally not at all.

As it turned out, political forces in the 1950s favoured continued protection for domestic industries, with high tariffs and tariff classifications, and trade remedies, coupled with Canadian participation in a number of rounds of multilateral negotiations to reduce barriers to trade internationally. This had been the policy of Liberal governments since the war, the policy had been implemented by a relatively small group of officials who continued to dominate on trade issues, it was supported by organized business groups, and the public was supportive of any policy that promised a continuation of Canada's remarkable run of postwar prosperity. When Walter Gordon supported this status quo in his 1956 royal commission preliminary report, therefore, he was onside politically—but not analytically. His assistant director of research, Simon Reisman, challenged Gordon's position, claiming it did not reflect the results of research conducted on the tariff for the commission by Yale University economist John Young. In response, Gordon did not want to publish Young's trade study. However, Reisman had promised Young that the commission would publish his work, and when Gordon was advised that he had no choice but to publish, he prefaced the study with a disclaimer that attempted to discredit Young's analysis (Azzi, 1999: 57, 62). Despite opposition from economists and members of his own staff to Gordon's position in favour of restricting trade in order to protect local industries and jobs, his was a view that was generally shared in government circles. In addition, smaller, Canadian-owned manufacturers were deeply committed to continuing protection, and their interests were represented ably by the influential Canadian Manufacturers' Association.

Political conditions in 1960 were sufficient to secure a place for problems in the Canadian automotive industry on the Diefenbaker governmental agenda. The Canadian industry was dominated by the big three US-controlled manufacturers—Chrysler, Ford, and General Motors—and they had a stake in the success of their Canadian branch-plants. These multinationals worked closely with knowledgeable officials in the Department of Trade and Commerce to nurture the Canadian industry, and when its decline became apparent in the late 1950s, their mutual concern was sufficient to secure the appointment of Bladen and his royal commission. Although the Big Three indicated to Bladen their preference for industry rationalization in an integrated Canada–US market (Dawson, 2005: 180), political conditions were not ripe for that degree of change: the automotive file was secure under the jurisdiction of Trade and Commerce officials, who were inclined toward incremental change under a government nearing the end of its electoral mandate; and there was no strong pressure for change from organized interests, including the Big Three, nor was there anything in the national mood pushing in that direction.

Government turnover in 1963, when a Liberal minority government replaced Diefenbaker's Conservatives, did little to alter the status quo, at least initially. Trade and commerce minister Mitchell Sharp recognized the virtues of the duty remission program, as a means to stimulate secondary industry, increase exports, and decrease the current account deficit, as did finance minister Walter Gordon, and they agreed that it made sense to broaden the program, but did not consider going further. However, by 1964, when the Modine complaint threatened the program, and with it the Canadian industry, there had been further change in the political stream. The industry portfolio had been carved off the Department of Trade and Commerce in 1963 to create a new Department of Industry, with Bud Drury as the minister, and a substantial jurisdictional claim on the automotive sector that had, heretofore, been the responsibility of Trade and Commerce. In 1964, Simon Reisman became deputy minister of the department, and he would play a central role in the policy changes that occurred in the automotive sector.

By 1971, when the Nixon import surcharge seized Ottawa's attention, Reisman had moved to Finance, where he was now deputy minister, and the US measures would normally fall under the jurisdiction of his minister, Edgar Benson. However, on August 15, the day of Nixon's announcement, Benson was in Europe, as was Prime Minister Pierre Trudeau. As a result, Mitchell Sharp, deputy prime minister and minister of external affairs, had to deal with the problem, at least initially. Sharp was conversant with the issues at hand, having served in the trade and finance portfolios, and he managed the file until Benson returned, and then Benson, along with minister of trade Jean-Luc Pepin, travelled to Washington, DC, to deal with US officials, with Reisman as their principal advisor. Sharp, and others in official Ottawa, were shocked at the US actions (Gwyn, 1985: 121; Granatstein and Bothwell, 1990: 65), and Sharp's unease led him to take up the vulnerability problem in his own Department of External Affairs, at a time when the government was considering its options concerning US ownership of key sectors of the Canadian economy, and public concern was growing over the effects of American control.

Sharp's determination to formulate a policy to address Canadian vulnerability in the relationship with the United States, and the assignment of the task to his External Affairs officials, was critical to the development of the Third Option strategy to diversify Canada's international economic relationships. By the time the Third Option had died a silent death (Granatstein and Bothwell, 1990: 176) jurisdictional change was once again setting the stage for policy change in Ottawa. As indicated previously, the task force charged with reviewing Canadian trade policy in 1982–3 was organized initially in the Department of Industry, Trade and Commerce (ITC), reporting to the minister for international trade, Liberal Ed Lumley.[15] However, a major reorganization of ITC was undertaken in January 1982, in order to integrate federal industrial and regional development policies in a new Department of Regional Industrial Expansion (DRIE). As a result, the trade elements of ITC were split off and integrated into a reorganized Department of External Affairs as a new trade and economic wing reporting to its own minister for international trade, again Lumley. Consequently, in the spring of 1982 jurisdiction over the task force conducting the trade policy review was shifted to External Affairs, where it was supervised by Derek Burney, assistant undersecretary for trade and economic policy. Subsequently, Lumley was moved back to DRIE, and Gerald Regan became the trade minister who would receive the task force report.

These jurisdictional and ministerial changes were soon followed by even more significant turnover, when the Liberals under John Turner, who succeeded Trudeau as leader, were defeated by Brian Mulroney's Conservatives in September 1984. Mulroney was an activist prime minister on international policy files, especially those involving Canada's relations with the US, and his attention virtually guaranteed that the bilateral relationship would rank high on the governmental agenda. The trade policy review, as well as the consultations that were undertaken in the same period by the Macdonald royal commission, gave voice to organized groups who were virtually unanimous in their view that threats to secure access to the American market constituted a serious problem for Canada, and something had to be done to address it. Finally, the national mood, as represented in public opinion polls, was supportive of further bilateral trade liberalization (Hart, 1994: 71). In summary, elements in the stream of politics were aligned for change.

This was not the case for NAFTA, at least not initially. There had been neither governmental nor ministerial turnover: Brian Mulroney was still in power, and John Crosbie had been trade minister since the 1988 election that handed the Conservatives a renewed majority. There was no sustained pressure from organized groups for free trade with Mexico, and the 1990 recession had substantially eroded public support for the bilateral agreement with the US. Nevertheless, when a decision (or non-decision) was made necessary by Mexico's overture to the US, partisan considerations pointed in the direction of trilateral negotiations, and business groups and the public were supportive (Mayer, 1998: 48).

Negotiation of NAFTA was completed in August 1992, and the side agreements on labour and the environment were concluded in August 1993, both under the authority of Brian Mulroney's Conservative government. However, in October 1993, Jean Chrétien's Liberals won a majority government, after campaigning on a pledge to renegotiate NAFTA, a pledge that, in the end, was not fulfilled. Instead, Chrétien's new minister of international trade, Roy MacLaren, became an enthusiastic proponent of trade liberalization, with support from key ministerial colleagues Paul Martin in Finance and John Manley in Industry. While there was still opposition to free trade, opponents were outnumbered by the united front of organized groups that had been mobilized around the Canada–US agreement, and then NAFTA. In addition, public attitudes had evolved along with Canadian trade policy, so that trade was no longer the hot button issue it had been in the 1980s, and the national mood was much more receptive to liberalization.

However, US trade remedy action continued to be an issue that resonated in the politics stream, and in the first half of 2001 softwood lumber had Liberal trade minister Pierre Pettigrew's full attention. An agreement between Canada and the US to manage softwood lumber trade had expired in March 2001, and American lumber interests had immediately launched trade remedy actions against Canadian producers. At the start of the week of September 10, planning was underway for Pettigrew to convene a meeting in Vancouver, on September 14, at which he would meet with the men and women who serve as Canada's consuls general at diplomatic missions throughout the United States. The purpose of the meeting was to develop a coordinated strategy to blunt US trade remedy actions against Canadian softwood lumber exports to the US. A countervailing duty of almost 20 per cent on softwood imports from Canada had already been applied by the US government, and an additional anti-dumping duty was in the works; their combined effects could cost millions of dollars in exports and thousands of jobs in Canada.[16] It is fair to say that, as of September 10, softwood lumber was at the top of the policy agenda for the Canadian government in its relations with the United States.

That changed in an instant, when the shock of the September 11 attacks captured the attention of ministers and officials, and swept Canada's border with the US to the top of the policy agenda. John Manley, now foreign affairs minister, was named to head an ad hoc cabinet committee to deal with border security, but Foreign Affairs was not the lead department on the issue. Instead, a number of different government departments were involved in the border, including Citizenship and Immigration, Customs and Revenue, Justice, Solicitor General, and Transport, and their various approaches required coordination, and so in October a small task force of officials was established in the Privy Council Office, reporting to Manley, to coordinate discussions with the US. As these discussions moved forward, Manley was able to establish a positive working relationship with his US counterpart, director of homeland security Tom Ridge (Waddell, 2003: 59–60).

Initially, the national mood in Canada was strongly supportive of harmonizing Canadian and US policies along a North American perimeter, and of joint posts and US entry controls along the Canada–US border. However, the very high levels of support for a security perimeter soon declined, and by December 2001 a majority of Canadians believed that Canada had done enough to tighten border security. Business interests organized very quickly to press for action to enhance security and facilitate the movement of goods and people across the border. The Canadian Manufacturers and Exporters (CME) took the lead in establishing a Coalition for Secure and Trade Efficient Borders, made up of 40 Canadian business associations and individual companies, to press for Canadian action in three areas: offshore interceptions, at the North American perimeter, and at the Canada–US border. However, the coalition's specific proposals focused more on coordination than harmonization, and built on pre-2001 recommendations for border facilitation (Haggart, 2005: 33–4, 37). The Privy Council task force opted for the joint coordination approach, and led discussions between Canadian agencies and their US counterparts to formulate the Smart Border Declaration which was signed by Manley and Ridge in December 2001, and subsequently implemented under their supervision. However, even while implementation was underway, policy entrepreneurs were attempting to couple the security-access issue to changes that were underway in the political stream in order to advance their ideas for deeper integration in the Canada–US relationship, and these efforts are described in Chapter 5.

The Evolution of International Trade Policy

For much of the nineteenth, and well into the twentieth, century, Canadian trade policy reflected efforts to deal with the policies of the United Kingdom and the United States, and to find a special place for Canadian products in one or both markets through preferential access to the British market or reciprocal trade liberalization with the United States. In addition, starting in the late nineteenth century, the tariff was used as the principal instrument in an import-substitution policy that resulted in industries producing goods for the domestic market, often dependent on imported capital, technology, and even management (Hart, 2002: 45, 86).

THE SEARCH FOR MARKETS

The National Policy of high tariffs was instituted in 1879 by the Conservative government of Prime Minister John A. Macdonald after the failure to reinstitute the Reciprocity Treaty of 1854.[1] The 1854 treaty between Canada and the US was a limited free trade agreement, mainly involving natural resource products; most manufactured goods were excluded, in part because tariffs on them were an important source of government revenues. The Reciprocity Treaty contributed to a long period of prosperity in Canada, but in 1866 it was abrogated by the US, partly because of domestic economic pressure, and partly because of unhappiness over British–Canadian actions during the American Civil War. Canada's interest in reciprocity with the US originated in the ending of another special bilateral relationship with Britain. When Britain repealed the Corn Laws in 1846, it brought to an end imperial preference for its colonies' produce and forced the search in Canada for alternative markets. After Confederation in 1867, there were repeated attempts, in 1869, 1871, and 1874, to negotiate a new trade arrangement with the US, but these failed, primarily because of strong protectionist sentiments in the American Congress.

In this sense, Macdonald's National Policy of 1879 was a poor second choice, a reaction to US rejection of efforts to reinstitute reciprocity. The policy imposed high tariffs to protect Canadian manufacturing, but it was also intended as a device to persuade the Americans to agree to another free trade agreement. Throughout this period, free trade was politically popular in Canada, and became politically risky only after business interests had grown accustomed to the protection afforded by the National Policy. By the 1891 election, business support for protectionism was strong enough that Macdonald easily defeated the Liberals, who had campaigned on a free trade platform. However, 20 years later, the Liberal government of Wilfrid Laurier succeeded in negotiating a reciprocity agreement with the US, and the agreement was put to the electoral test in the election of 1911, when financial and manufacturing interests united behind Robert Borden and his Conservatives to defeat Laurier and the agreement. Although the 1911 election struck a serious blow against free trade, there were, nevertheless, several further behind-the-scenes efforts to revive it. Ministerial initiatives by Canada were made in 1922 and 1923, but died in the face of a protectionist drift in US policy. In 1935 and 1938, bilateral trade agreements were achieved under a new regime of US trade legislation designed to untangle the disastrous effects of the super-protectionist Smoot-Hawley Act, American trade legislation that had greatly worsened the Depression of the 1930s (Drummond and Hillmer, 1989).

When we pick up the trade story at the end of World War II, Canada's postwar industrial capacity and prosperity were fuelling a growing demand for imports and a search for expanded export markets. When dollar reserves dwindled to dangerously low levels in 1947, a trade policy response was deemed necessary, and Canada approached the US once again to explore the prospects for a comprehensive trade agreement. However, that approach was undertaken in strict secrecy (Muirhead, 1992: 22), reflecting the government's view of the sensitivity of the bilateral trade issue with the public and Canadian manufacturers. Nevertheless, when the Americans introduced the new idea of a bilateral free trade arrangement to Finance officials John Deutsch and Hector McKinnon, the two succeeded in convincing finance minister Douglas Abbott that it was worth considering. Trade and commerce minister C.D. Howe was supportive as well, and Prime Minister Mackenzie King authorized the negotiations (Hart, 2002: 142).

By April 1948, a preliminary agreement had been reached on the elimination of tariffs and quantitative restrictions on bilateral trade, immediately by the US and over a five-year period by Canada. However, when news of the negotiations leaked out, generating negative reaction in the Canadian press, Mackenzie King, close to retirement and concerned about his legacy, decided that the politics were not right for such an agreement, and brought negotiations to a halt (Hart, 2002: 143). King's change of mind also might have been caused by an easing of the payments problem when the US decided that Marshall Plan aid to Britain and Europe could be used to purchase goods outside the US, including from Canada (Muirhead, 1992: 22). Whether caused by change in the politics stream or by the abatement of the payments crisis in the problem stream, King's decision brought an end to the bilateral initiative.

That decision left Canada to rely on multilateral negotiations under the General Agreement on Tariffs and Trade (GATT) to advance its trade policy interests. However, successive rounds of multilateral negotiations in the 1950s failed to produce a significant opening of markets internationally, and Canadian exporters remained shut out of important markets in Britain and Europe (Hart, 2002: 156). Canada's dependence on the American market was growing, however, led by US demand for Canadian resources and industrial inputs, and financed by American capital, and with this dependence came increased Canadian vulnerability to US protectionism. Throughout the 1950s and early 1960s, successive governments sought alternative markets to offset the growing concentration of Canadian trade on the US, without success, and were increasingly preoccupied with managing the issues that arose out of the growing complexity in Canada's principal bilateral relationship. Finally, in 1964, the twin problems of American protectionism and industrial inefficiencies prompted Canada to once again consider bilateral solutions.

THE AUTO PACT

In January 1964, American President Lyndon Johnson proposed to Canadian Prime Minister Lester Pearson the establishment of an intergovernmental committee to explore continental rationalization of the automotive industry in Canada and the US. Canada rejected the proposal, and instead broadened the duty remission program designed to increase Canadian production and exports. US officials were unhappy with the program, as were some American firms. Although the big three US-controlled manufacturers—Chrysler, Ford, and General Motors—supported the duty remission program, US auto parts manufacturers did not, because they had the most to lose from Canadian protection and subsidization. The Liberal government's expanded program was having its intended effects, as Canadian auto exports to the US increased significantly in 1964 (Dawson, 2005: 159, 189), and American officials expressed alarm about Canada's approach (Hart, 2002: 242).

When Modine Manufacturing initiated its subsidy complaint in April 1964, it shifted the Canadian problem from a lack of competitiveness to a threat to market access for automotive products, a threat that was brought home to Canadian officials when they were told by the Americans that a Treasury inquiry into the Modine complaint would involve not only radiators, but all Canadian automotive exports to the US. The US government was pressing Canada to agree to participate in a bilateral effort to find an alternative program to solve the automotive problem, one that would make countervailing duties unnecessary. Canadian officials were largely convinced that the remission program was no longer viable, and most of the Liberal cabinet agreed that talks should be undertaken with the US to find an alternative solution. However, finance minister Walter Gordon argued that any mutually agreed solution would involve further market integration, to which he was opposed. In May, a report to cabinet by a committee of officials headed by Simon Reisman recommended that Canada enter into negotiations with the US to cut tariffs on automotive products and secure for Canada a specific share of the combined Canadian–American market (Dawson, 2005: 191–4).

In June 1964, cabinet, with Gordon's concurrence, agreed that an agreement with the Americans should be pursued. The threat of countervail had undermined the preferred duty remission approach to the industry's problems, and also eroded Big Three support for the remission program. Over the years, the Big Three had made significant investments in their wholly owned Canadian subsidiaries, and were open to any plan that would allow them to make better use of their Canadian facilities (Hart, 2002: 243). However, in 1961, they told Bladen they preferred an integrated Canada–US market, and in 1964 they certainly favoured a solution involving bilateral cooperation (Dawson, 2005: 179–80). Finally, a negotiated solution to the problem was an attractive means to avoid further conflict with the US. In 1963, Canada had engaged in two policy disputes with the United States, one involving Canadian budgetary measures on foreign investment, and the other over a special US tax on purchases of foreign securities by Americans, and the government preferred to avoid further conflict, this time over trade.

In summary, in 1964 the trade complaint provided a focusing event that secured a place for the automotive problem on the government's decision agenda, and the prospect of American trade remedy action undermined the viability of the existing duty remission program. Simon Reisman played the role of effective policy entrepreneur, bringing forward to cabinet a policy alternative that promised to secure market share for the Canadian industry through a negotiated agreement that would avoid further bilateral conflict with the US. This new policy alternative found favour in cabinet, with support from trade minister Mitchell Sharp and industry minister Bud Drury outweighing Gordon's opposition. With that decision made, Canadian automotive trade policy would now be established through bilateral negotiations, and so we turn to an examination of those negotiations to understand the next stage in the evolution of Canadian trade policy.

In June 1964, Philip Trezise, US deputy assistant secretary of state for economic affairs, and lead negotiator in the bilateral talks with Canada, suggested the creation of a limited customs union between Canada and the US covering the automotive sector (Donaghy, 1998: 453). However, when bilateral negotiations got underway in July, the lead Canadian negotiator, deputy minister of industry Simon Reisman, made it clear from the outset that Canada was looking, not for free trade in automotive products, but for a managed trade agreement, whereby Canada would secure certain minimum levels of production of automobiles and parts in Canada (Dawson, 2005: 211). To this end, negotiators reached early agreement on the following provisions: tariff reductions; expanded production and market share for Canada, and consultation to ensure measurable progress toward these objectives; and Canada's right to restrict imports if the Canadian industry did not grow at a satisfactory rate. However, the last provision was unacceptable to members of the US Congress, who would not agree to constraints on their right to retaliate against Canadian import restrictions, and was taken off the negotiating table. To substitute for that provision, the American negotiators proposed auto industry participation in the agreement:

> If industry were somehow formally obliged to meet the Canadian targets there would be no need for Canada to resort to unilateral trade restrictions that would be vulnerable to US retaliation because Canada would have some means to directly influence the actions of industry (Dawson, 2005: 226).

This effort to meet Canadian targets and satisfy Congress meant finding a satisfactory way of including industry in the agreement. To this end, Canadian officials developed a framework to persuade industry to expand production in Canada in exchange for reduced tariffs, and found industry supportive. Thus the idea of a dual agreement solution was conceived, whereby Canada would have an agreement with the US, as well as an agreement with the automotive manufacturers that would specify Canadian investment and production targets for each firm (Dawson, 2005: 243).[2] If targets were not met, then duty-free status would be rescinded.

Reisman and his team concluded the final terms of the bilateral agreement with the US in December 1964, and at the same time industry minister Bud Drury concluded agreements with the Big Three Canadian manufacturers, plus American Motors, on their investment and production targets under the agreement. The bilateral agreement contained asymmetrical obligations: 'Canada agreed to make its protection more efficient, and the United States agreed to exempt Canadian-origin parts and vehicles from its protection' (Hart, 2002: 244). In addition, in letters of commitment to the Canadian government, the Big Three agreed to meet the investment and production targets that had been established in their negotiations with Drury. With these safeguards in place, the agreement represented managed free trade, and marked an important shift for Canadian trade policy in this key industrial sector. With access to the American market threatened, the Canadian government chose to conclude a special bilateral trade liberalization agreement with the US, with substantial benefit to the Canadian industry. Nevertheless, it would be more than 15 years before a government would consider extending bilateral free trade to other sectors of the economy.[3]

THE THIRD OPTION

When US President Richard Nixon announced the imposition of a 10 per cent surcharge on all imports, deputy finance minister Simon Reisman advised that what was needed was an immediate visit to Washington to make it clear to the Americans that Canada was not part of their problem. A Canadian delegation subsequently made the trip in an effort to secure an exemption for Canada.[4] Their request was denied by treasury secretary John Connally, who considered Canadian imports, as well as US investments in Canada, to be very much a part of the US problem.[5] Although the import surcharge was removed in December, the effect on some Canadian government ministers and officials was profound.

Canada's high dependence on the US market made the country especially vulnerable to American policy initiatives, and the special treatment that Canada could count on in the past would apparently no longer be forthcoming. Mitchell Sharp, who had been the first to be notified of the US actions in August, was especially troubled by the episode, and he took the problem it raised back to his own Department of External Affairs. At a meeting of External Affairs officials in the week following Nixon's announcement, the idea of diversifying Canada's external economic relationships was first raised (Gwyn, 1985: 122), and subsequently a senior interdepartmental committee urged new economic ties with Europe (Granatstein and Bothwell, 1990: 66, 160). The task of fleshing out the idea was handed to Klaus Goldschlag, a senior European specialist in External Affairs, who developed a memorandum for submission to cabinet.

Sharp's initial involvement in the crisis provoked by the surcharge, as well as his previous experience as minister of both finance and trade, were important to his subsequent effort to develop an appropriate policy response, particularly because as minister of external affairs he had no jurisdiction over the key elements of what would become the Third Option, namely, trade and industrial policy. The jurisdictional issue was important in this case, because the international, and particularly the European, orientation of External Affairs made it much more likely that the department would produce a recommendation for the third, rather than the first (status quo) or second (integration), options. Sharp guided the paper through the cabinet process, where it encountered significant opposition from the Department of Finance and the Department of Industry, Trade and Commerce (ITC). Deputy finance minister Simon Reisman dismissed the Third Option as 'theatrical, mystical, idealistic', insisting that Canada was a North American country (Hart, 2002: 286), while ITC deputy Jake Warren was scornful of the initiative (Granatstein and Bothwell, 1990: 161, note 15). In the end, Sharp was unable to convince the cabinet to adopt the paper as government policy, and instead he was directed to publish it under his own name in a departmental magazine.

Primary expression of the Third Option was given in Canada's pursuit of the so-called contractual link with the European Community (EC), although Canadians had difficulty explaining to the Europeans exactly what they meant by this. Canada already enjoyed most-favoured-nation relations with EC members (offering one another their best tariff rates under the GATT), and they established early on that neither was interested in a preferential trade agreement. What Canada seemed to be proposing, at least in the EC view, was a symbolic instrument, devoid of content, while the EC was prepared to enter into an agreement that would provide a framework for economic and commercial cooperation (Granatstein and Bothwell, 1990: 165). In the end, Canada took what was on offer, a 1976 Framework Agreement on Commercial and Economic Cooperation that committed the parties to consult and establish working groups to examine the prospects for cooperative ventures. A similar framework agreement was concluded with Japan. Neither produced concrete results (Hart, 2002: 291, 292).[6]

FREE TRADE WITH THE UNITED STATES

In midsummer of 1985, Brian Mulroney was meeting with senior officials in his office on Parliament Hill.[7] The occasion was a discussion of an advance copy of the report of the Royal Commission on the Economic Union and Development Prospects for Canada, chaired by Donald Macdonald, who had been a minister in Pierre Trudeau's cabinet. The report contained a recommendation for the establishment of a free trade arrangement with the United States. According to those in attendance, Mulroney recognized the opportunity it presented for a bold policy initiative, and he relished the idea of using a former Liberal cabinet minister to give bipartisan legitimacy to the initiative. The volumes of the report arranged on his desk, Mulroney spread his hands over them and told the officials present in his office that summer day that he would use the report to beat Liberal party leader John Turner in the next election.

The decision to negotiate free trade was a fundamental policy shift on the part of the Canadian government, and it was certainly unanticipated at the beginning of the 1980s, even by those at the centre of the policy process. Few would have predicted that within three years Canada would propose sectoral free trade and that, two years later, it would offer to negotiate a comprehensive free trade agreement with the Americans. This decision involved a basic redefinition of Canada's relationship with the United States and represented a fundamental change in policy. We need to explain, first, how the issue of Canada's trade relations with the United States made its way to the top of the Mulroney government's decision agenda and, second, the policy process that led Canada to propose to the United States that the two countries negotiate a bilateral free trade agreement.

An explanation begins with the trade policy review that was undertaken in 1982. As noted in Chapter 4, severe recession and threats of American trade retaliation ensured that the attention of the task force undertaking the review would be focused on the problem of access to the US market, and Canadian business pressed for a bilateral liberalization solution to the access problem. Leading advocates included the Business Council on National Issues (BCNI), made up of major corporations operating in Canada, and the Canadian Manufacturers' Association (CMA). During 1982 and 1983, BCNI President Thomas d'Aquino was active in advocating negotiations for a comprehensive trade agreement as a means to guarantee access to the US market. Equally important, however, was the influential CMA's reversal of its long-standing opposition to free trade with the United States. The shift in jurisdiction over the review to External Affairs, under the direction of Derek Burney, was also important, since a free trade option, sectoral or otherwise, had less chance of emerging from ITC, with its mandate to protect and nurture Canadian industry. In addition, the jurisdictional change created an important role for Burney as manager of the task force. Nevertheless, the task force recommended a continuation of the status quo, firmly attached to the GATT system.

It was the task force's secondary prospect of sectoral free trade with the US, however, that caught the attention of trade minister Gerald Regan, a free trader from Nova Scotia. While stressing the report's reaffirmation of the GATT with his cautious cabinet colleagues, Regan persuaded them to go along with its sectoral option as well, despite the suspicions of the nationalist group in the Liberal cabinet. With cabinet endorsement in hand, Regan turned the report upside down at its presentation at a press conference in August 1983. Seizing on its most controversial element, he announced the demise of the Third Option and proclaimed the government's intention to pursue a limited free trade agreement with the United States. Regan's proclamation did not by any means reflect mainstream thinking in External Affairs. Alongside the trade policy review, a concurrent review of the Canada–US relationship was also initiated by External Affairs for submission to the deputy minister for foreign relations, and the review had reaffirmed the basic tenets of the Third Option. That report was overtaken by events, however. It was the trade policy review that provided the opening for fundamental change in Canadian–American relations as sectoral free trade negotiations became the preferred option of the Liberal government.

As noted in Chapter 4, those sectoral negotiations had made no progress by September 1984, when Mulroney and his Conservatives came to power. For the Conservatives, the problems with trade compounded the problem they faced in the Canadian economy. The minister of finance, Michael Wilson, was convinced by his officials that the economy was in a state of profound malaise, for which there could be no easy cure. In the fall of 1984, Wilson agreed with senior Finance officials that Canada could no longer tax or spend its way out of its economic troubles; instead, the country would have to grow its way out of the problems that beset the economy, and the key to this growth was a significant increase in Canadian trade. The Conservatives were still some distance from free trade at this early stage in their mandate, however. The Finance economic renewal statement, with its reference to increased and secure access to US markets, had not been prepared especially for the Conservatives, but was begun in May 1984 while the Liberals still held power. Nor was the concept of 'broadly-based bilateral arrangements' cleared through trade minister James Kelleher, who was not consulted on the Finance statement. Nevertheless, the autumn of 1984 saw pressures mount for the government to pick up the free trade idea, as Canadian business organizations and think-tanks engaged in a vigorous lobbying effort to shore up support for a comprehensive free trade arrangement (Doern and Tomlin, 1991: 103). Respected Canadian economist Richard Lipsey[8] and Wendy Dobson, then-head of the C.D. Howe Institute and later associate deputy minister of finance in Ottawa, launched what, for a think-tank, was an unprecedented personal lobby to promote the free trade option among key ministers, their staffers, and senior members of the bureaucracy. Their efforts, along with the trade policy studies prepared by the Macdonald Commission, helped to undermine many of the prevailing myths about free trade. In particular, they vigorously argued that, rather than representing a complete break with the Canadian past, the free trade option was quite consistent with Canada's commitment to trade liberalization throughout the postwar era and their position was given serious attention by a government committed to making Canada a better place to do business.

The fact that the new Conservative government was looking to establish a policy agenda made it particularly receptive to the arguments in favour of a comprehensive free trade agreement. In the event, the first, and very important, act of policy entrepreneurship came from an unlikely source: Donald Macdonald, chairman of the Royal Commission on the Economic Union and Development Prospects for Canada. Established by the Trudeau government in 1982, the commission was examining Canada–US free trade as part of its study of the Canadian economy. Although the commission had neither completed its studies nor framed its conclusions, Macdonald nevertheless announced in November 1984 that he favoured free trade between Canada and the United States as the principal long-term solution to Canada's economic problems.

Acknowledging that Canadians might be nervous about maintaining their sovereignty in a free trade arrangement with the United States, Macdonald nonetheless argued: 'If we do get down to a point where it's going to be a leap of faith, then I think at some point Canadians are going to have to be bold and say, yes, we will do that.'[9] Macdonald's call for a 'leap of faith' was a big news item in Canada. And because it was bipartisan and seemingly authoritative, his conversion provided important momentum to the free trade option at a critical juncture as the new government was considering its options. This endorsement was followed by a series of government reports and consultations that moved the Mulroney cabinet ever closer to a final commitment to negotiation.

The first of the reports was the product of a review of trade policy options initiated by Derek Burney in the Department of External Affairs. That review generated sharp conflicts, both in External Affairs and in the Department of Regional Industrial Expansion (DRIE), the successor to ITC. The conflict resulted from opposition to Burney's determination to put the comprehensive free trade option before the government. From a DRIE perspective, trade liberalization would threaten Canadian industries supported by an average tariff that was roughly double that of their American competition. In External Affairs, the opposition centred on traditional concerns over political autonomy. In the end, Burney was forced to override opposition from the most senior administrative levels of his own department, which wanted to suppress the free trade discussion. His task force presented comprehensive free trade as one of the options for Canada in the report prepared for Kelleher. Because the trade minister did not share the reluctance of his senior officials to consider all the options available to Canada in its relations with the United States, he released the report in January 1985 (Government of Canada, 1985).

This government discussion paper, while acknowledging the importance of multilateral trade liberalization, confirmed the need to seek enhanced and secure access to the US market. To this end, the paper suggested that some form of bilateral trade arrangement should be considered, and it set out the options available to Canada. These were the status quo, sectoral arrangements, a comprehensive trade agreement (the Conservative euphemism for free trade) to remove tariff and non-tariff barriers on substantially all bilateral trade, and a bilateral framework to discuss means to improve and enhance trade relations (a BCNI proposal). Although the paper was careful to avoid identifying a preferred option, it rejected the status quo as inadequate, sectoral arrangements as unattainable, and the BCNI framework as unnecessary (Leyton-Brown, 1985: 182). Clearly, the government was edging down the path to comprehensive free trade negotiations.

Another policy window was about to open in March 1985 in Quebec City at the so-called Shamrock Summit between Mulroney and Reagan, and policy entrepreneurs were ready to take advantage of it. The Shamrock Summit was orchestrated in exquisite detail by Prime Minister's Office (PMO) staffer and Mulroney confidant Fred Doucet. Working closely with Doucet was Derek Burney, who oversaw the drafting of the trade declaration to be issued by the prime minister and the president. Although the declaration contained no explicit statement of bilateral trade policy by either government, it did call for an examination of ways to reduce and eliminate existing barriers to trade. Mulroney and Reagan instructed Kelleher and Brock to report in six months on mechanisms to achieve this end. Following the summit declaration, Burney's External Affairs task force proceeded to flesh out the free trade option in preparation for the presentation of a recommendation to cabinet. They continued to encounter considerable opposition to a comprehensive agreement, both within External Affairs and from other departments. However, it was apparent that Canadian business was now solidly behind the initiative, and this could make all the difference in cabinet, especially with support from Wilson in Finance. With Canadian business onside, and with the backing of key ministers, Burney was determined to press ahead, despite continued opposition from senior officials.

The politics of the trade issue were right in other respects as well. Free trade was not only congruent with the government's agenda for economic renewal; it also served the Conservative priority of national reconciliation. The Western provinces had been deeply disaffected over the NEP, and Mulroney and his minister of energy Pat Carney wasted little time in undoing the NEP through the Western Accord, which reduced federal involvement in the oil and gas industry. There was also substantial support for free trade in the West, especially Alberta, long a stronghold of Conservative support. Alberta's Conservative premier Peter Lougheed, a strong supporter of the free trade option, was the principal exponent of Western grievances, and he held close counsel with Mulroney on the trade issue throughout this period. His support was important in shoring up Mulroney's resolve as the time for decision approached. Also important was the surprising degree of support for free trade in Quebec, home to a substantial number of inefficient Canadian industries that were the least likely to survive the elimination of protective barriers. The province's long-standing opposition to trade liberalization had been an essential element in shaping Canadian trade policy. All that changed, however, with the willingness of the Quebec business establishment to support free trade. This support would reinforce Mulroney's strategy to consolidate the Conservative landslide he had achieved in the province in 1984, and thus turn the political tables on the Liberals. Mulroney's path to the free trade decision was also smoothed by the presence of Tory governments in most of the remaining provinces, with the notable exception of Ontario. These premiers were ideologically sympathetic to the pro-market approach of the federal party, and they were deeply concerned about American protectionism. As a result, they were generally positive about negotiating a comprehensive trade agreement for enhanced and secure access to the US market, assuming, of course, that an agreement left untouched such 'non-trade' shibboleths as agricultural marketing boards and regional development grants.

Therefore, in the summer of 1985, the streams in the policy process had come together—a problem had been recognized, a solution had been developed and put forward, and a political change had made the time right for policy change. And policy entrepreneurs, both inside and outside government, were ready to take advantage of the policy window that was created by the merging of these streams. Shortly after the September 5 release of the royal commission report, to ensure that free trade would be tied to Macdonald, the prime minister indicated in reply to a question in the House of Commons on September 9 that the government had decided to pursue 'freer' trade with the United States. On September 26, Mulroney told the Commons that he had telephoned Reagan to ask him to explore with Congress Canada's interest in pursuing negotiations to reduce tariffs and non-tariff barriers between the two countries. This call, and the formal written proposal that followed on October 1, finally brought to an end four years of policy transformation in Canada.

This reconstruction of events between the decision to undertake a trade policy review in September 1981 and the September 1985 request for negotiations makes it clear that joining of the problem and policy streams alone would have been insufficient to drive this fundamental shift in policy. Change in the political stream was necessary as well. First, of course, was the timing of the failure of the sectoral initiative and the 1984 federal election, which produced Mulroney's majority government. In these circumstances, the significant partisan advantages that free trade offered the Conservatives made the option of comprehensive negotiations attractive. Mulroney was determined to offer a clear alternative to the centralizing, interventionist policies of the Trudeau Liberals and to build a lasting power base for his party. A policy that was market-oriented and had broad appeal in Western Canada and Quebec served both ends. The summer of 1985 also saw Mulroney and his ministers under fire for a lack of clear direction and purpose. Free trade offered the prospect of immediate partisan advantage to a government in search of a major policy upon which to fix. Finally, when the problem, policy, and politics streams were joined, key policy entrepreneurs took advantage of the policy window: d'Aquino and Lougheed aligned critical business and political interests, while Burney moved the policy process inexorably toward free trade.

As noted previously, the decision to negotiate a free trade agreement with the United States was a fundamental policy shift on the part of the government of

Canada. It is equally clear, however, that this shift in policy was not the product of a Conservative determination to fashion an agenda of major policy departures. There were significant changes underway in all three of Kingdon's policy streams: the problem was redefined to emphasize the need to ensure secure access to the US market; the range of policy alternatives was expanded incrementally to include comprehensive free trade; and, of course, the electoral, partisan, and interest group dimensions of the political stream had shifted. In hindsight, it is clear that there was nothing inevitable about the Conservative decision to seek free trade with the United States; rather, it was the product of the alignment of a complex array of conditions in three largely autonomous policy streams—conditions that evolved over a four-year period. Moreover, this alignment simply created windows of opportunity for key policy entrepreneurs who happened to be skilful, and lucky, enough to be able to exploit them before they closed. Free trade was not, therefore, a Conservative idea whose time had come; rather, it was a policy that had been thrust onto the agenda through a series of conjunctions of events and that was finally chosen as the result of cold political calculation.

With that decision taken, Canadian trade policy once again passed into the bilateral policy arena, requiring us to examine the Canada–US free trade negotiations in order to track the evolution of Canadian trade policy. As indicated in Chapter 3, the agreement concluded in 1987 was a very big deal, cutting across the entire economy and including obligations in new areas of trade, as well as path-breaking provisions concerning trade remedies. In order to render our task manageable, and because relief from trade remedies was at the core of Canada's decision to negotiate free trade, the bilateral negotiations over trade remedies will be the focus of our analysis here.[10] In Chapter 3, we indicated that a central American aim in the negotiations was an agreement on investment that would preclude any more FIRAs or NEPs. In turn, the Canadians wanted an agreement on contingency protection that would preclude the application of US trade remedies to Canada's exports. Canadian concerns centred on the use by the Americans of countervailing and anti-dumping duties against imports that were considered to be subsidized or sold at less than cost, respectively, and safeguards, used where there were sudden increases in exports.

Chief negotiator Simon Reisman first proposed the establishment of national treatment for the movement of virtually all goods and services between the two countries, a principle that would exempt Canada from key elements of US trade remedy law, since Canadian imports would be treated the same as goods produced in the US. When the Americans declined this proposition, Reisman next proposed the establishment of a regime to govern the use of trade remedy laws by defining new joint rules to discipline the practices, such as subsidizing and dumping, that triggered trade remedy actions in the first place. These rules would define exactly which practices were prohibited and which were permissible and would render trade remedies unnecessary. Again the Americans declined, arguing that negotiating limits on the application of US trade remedy laws was a non-starter because of almost certain Congressional opposition. There matters rested until September 1987, when the Canadian government suspended nego-tiations in an effort to force American movement on a number of critical issues, including trade remedies.

Congressman Sam Gibbons, chairman of the trade subcommittee of the US House of Representatives ways and means committee had an idea for resolving the impasse over trade remedies, and following suspension of the negotiations he presented it to Allan Gotlieb, Canada's ambassador to the US. Gibbons' pro-posal had two elements. First, he proposed that the contentious trade remedies issue be put aside for further negotiation, and that existing trade law continue to apply in the interim. Second, he suggested that some form of appellate proce-dure should be used to review applications of trade remedy law and resolve dis-putes, where necessary. The Gibbons proposal offered a different approach to the issue, focused not on changing the rules governing the use of trade remedies, but on disputes over the application of the rules already in place, and the use of a dispute-settlement tribunal to resolve differences. Initial reaction to the proposal was unpromising. Despite Gotlieb's advocacy of the idea, the new man in charge of the negotiations for Canada, Derek Burney, now the prime minister's chief of staff, was not convinced the concept addressed their security-of-access problem in any meaningful way; and US treasury secretary James Baker, the new man in charge for the US, was sceptical that the idea would find favour in Congress, based on initial opposition from a number of members of the Senate finance committee.

Gotlieb was convinced of the merit of Gibbons' proposal, however, and he convinced members of the Senate finance committee who were prepared to sup-port the proposal to express their views to Baker. Gotlieb then urged Burney to reconsider the tribunal idea, arguing that it was the only means to rescue the negotiations. When Baker called Burney to say that the US was prepared to take another look at the trade remedies issue, this time through the lens of the Gib-bons proposal, that was sufficient to restart the negotiations, on 2 October 1987. It did not take long, however, for the two sides to discover that they had pro-foundly different interpretations of the nature of the Gibbons proposal. The Canadians had taken the notion that existing trade remedy laws should con-tinue to apply, while the two continued to negotiate the trade remedies issue, to mean that there would be a freeze on existing trade remedy law. This was impor-tant because a freeze would prevent the US from introducing new measures designed to sidestep limits on the application of American trade remedies that resulted from tribunal decisions. Baker flatly rejected the proposal for a freeze, maintaining that he could not do a deal that would limit the constitutional authority of Congress to make or amend laws. There was disagreement as well over the structure and review powers of a binational tribunal, with Canada look-ing for a permanent court with broad powers of judicial review, and the Ameri-cans proposing a system of panels with rotating membership, and a very narrow concept of judicial review.

On the morning of October 3, the final day of negotiations,[11] the Canadians tried to craft a proposal that would address American objections to the concept of a freeze, while still protecting Canada from changes to US trade remedy law. This was achieved through a proposal that any changes in US trade law that named Canada would be subject to review by a binational panel, which would have watchdog powers to determine whether the changes were consistent with the bilateral agreement and the GATT, and whether their effect was to overturn a previous panel decision. This was intended to provide a facsimile of a freeze. They also proposed binational panels with broad review powers and the power to make judicially binding decisions. Although it would take all day, the Americans finally accepted the principle of binding decisions and the freeze facsimile, and as midnight approached, Baker offered a clarification on the review issue that the Canadian lawyers judged to be much closer to the Canadian proposal for broad review powers. This was sufficient to permit agreement between the two parties on this final element of bilateral free trade, embodied in Chapter 19 of the agreement, concerning binational dispute settlement in anti-dumping and countervail. In the end, Sam Gibbons' idea, so vigorously advocated by Allan Gotlieb, had provided the foundation for the policy solution the Canadians were seeking to address their security-of-access problem in the US market.

NORTH AMERICAN FREE TRADE

In March 1990, Prime Minister Brian Mulroney was en route to Mexico for a state visit when he received an in-flight telephone call from Derek Burney, now Canada's ambassador to Washington. James Baker, now American secretary of state, had just called Burney to say that the US had received a formal request from Mexican President Carlos Salinas for bilateral free trade negotiations with the United States. Salinas planned to inform Mulroney during his Mexican visit. Burney and Mulroney agreed that the prime minister would simply ask to be kept informed of developments while Canada examined the issue internally. Mulroney went further in Mexico City, emphasizing that Canada already had its free trade agreement with the US in place, implying that Mexican–American negotiations would not be of direct interest to Canada. Nevertheless, Mexico's action clearly was going to require a decision (or non-decision) by Canada.

To assess what Canada's position should be, a small task force was created within the Department of External Affairs and International Trade (DEAIT) to address the implications of a bilateral Mexico–US free trade agreement for Canada. The task force secured impact analyses from a variety of other government departments, and only the agriculture and textiles sectors were singled out as specific problem areas. In general, the impact analyses indicated that Mexican access to the Canadian market posed no threat, although in the longer term Mexico would provide moderately serious competition for Canada in the US market. While there was little cause for concern here, there was also little at stake for Canada in the Mexican market. However, Industry Canada identified a potentially serious problem for Canada in a Mexican–American deal, pointing out that the US presence in two bilateral free trade agreements on the continent—the hub-and-spoke arrangement—could lead to a diversion of investment dollars to the US as the only platform from which to serve all three North American markets.

As the task force continued its work during the summer of 1990, it became clear to Canadian officials that Mexico and the US were committed to negotiations, and pressure mounted for a Canadian decision. In August, trade minister John Crosbie presented a memorandum to cabinet in which four options were presented for consideration: continue to monitor developments; seek observer status at bilateral Mexican–American negotiations; negotiate a bilateral Canada–Mexico agreement; or, join Mexico and the United States in trilateral negotiations. The task force recommended the fourth option because it addressed all of Canada's interests in the issue: it offset the danger of investment diversion in a hub-and-spoke model; it prevented Mexico from getting preferential access to the American market through a better free trade agreement than Canada had with the US; and, it offered access to the growing Mexican market.

Although Crosbie and his DEAIT officials on the task force now favoured the trilateral option, the powerful Department of Finance had strong reservations, and the key ministers who sat on the priorities and planning committee of cabinet paid careful attention. Political considerations were also important for ministers. They realized that a trilateral agreement would likely emerge in time to provide a contentious issue for the next federal election. While the Mulroney government had won the so-called free trade election in 1988, defeating the opposition Liberals who campaigned on a platform opposing the Canada–US agreement, the economic times had begun to turn by 1990, as the approaching recession gathered momentum in Canada. As a result, few ministers relished another defence of free trade in the new circumstances.

On the other hand, the government was floundering in the aftermath of the failure of the Meech Lake Accord, a major initiative to satisfy Quebec's demands for constitutional reform. Blame for the failure, and the national malaise that resulted, was being pinned squarely on Brian Mulroney and his Conservative government. What was needed was a significant policy initiative around which government forces could rally. Crosbie argued that free trade was an issue on which they had won in 1988 and on which they could again join political battle with the opposition parties. In the end, ministerial combativeness, coupled with the reality that Canada could not prevent a bilateral Mexico–US deal, and could influence the terms of Mexico's access to the North American market most directly by being at the table, led to the decision to seek participation in the negotiations.

With Canadian trade policy back on the bargaining table, we need to turn again to an examination of the negotiation process to analyze policy change. As indicated in Chapter 4, NAFTA was a bigger deal for Mexico than for Canada, because it largely replicated the provisions of the bilateral agreement with the US. There were significant changes to the investment provisions, and these are described in our treatment of investment policy. In addition, the trade remedies issue that had been so contentious in bilateral negotiations between Canada and the US surfaced again in the trilateral negotiations, and this will once again be the focus of our analysis here.[12]

When trilateral negotiations opened on market access and trade rules in June 1991, Mexico began, as Canada had done during its bilateral negotiations with the US five years earlier, with a demand that the Americans agree to changes in US domestic trade laws, specifically rules governing the application of anti-dumping duties, on the grounds that the duties constituted non-tariff barriers (the Mexicans were less concerned with US countervailing duties, aimed at subsidies). Their opening position was to replace anti-dumping rules with competition law, which would govern the business practices, including pricing, of firms in all three countries. American chief negotiator Jules Katz insisted that the US administration was not going to assume the political risks associated with asking the Congress to pass changes to domestic trade law.

Although the Canadians had been down this dead-end path before, and had paid heavily for the trip, they nevertheless supported Mexican efforts to persuade the US to reform its anti-dumping rules. When the Canadians had recognized in the 1987 bilateral negotiations that the battle was lost on changing US trade laws, they had negotiated, as a substitute, the dispute-settlement provisions that were set out in Chapter 19 of the Canada–US agreement, whereby binational panels were empowered to decide whether the respective trade laws of each country had been applied properly. It would be a natural step to integrate the Chapter 19 provisions into NAFTA, and, in fact, the Canadians were eager to take this step, because there was emerging a difference of opinion between the US and Canada over the lifespan of the provisions. The bilateral agreement stated that they were to prevail for five to seven years, during which time the two countries would negotiate a new trade remedy regime. These continuing negotiations had not been successful, however, and were unlikely to be so within the prescribed timeframe (negotiation of the trade remedies issue had been shifted to the GATT Uruguay Round). Under those circumstances, the Americans were suggesting that the Chapter 19 provisions might expire, and the binational panel system would cease to operate.

Although the Canadians insisted that the panel system would continue, even in the face of a failure to negotiate a new regime within the five- to seven-year timeframe, they were eager to establish the provisions in a new agreement with no implication of a time limit, however tenuous. The Mexicans thought they could do better, of course. However, it was not clear at the outset of the negotiations whether they could achieve even the binational panel system, because the US Commerce Department indicated that Mexico would have to make very significant structural changes in the administration of its law and judicial review process before the US could consider the inclusion of a binational panel system to review countervail and anti-dumping cases. The Canadians, too, would press the Mexicans for these needed changes in order to ensure that the Chapter 19 provisions could be embedded in a trilateral agreement.

By the time negotiators from the three countries gathered at the Watergate apartment, hotel, and office complex in Washington, DC, for the final round of negotiation in August 1992, Mexico had abandoned its effort to persuade the US to eliminate anti-dumping, and instead was pursuing the inclusion of the dispute settlement provisions from the bilateral Canada–US agreement in the NAFTA. However, tensions were growing between Canada and the US over the issue. The subjection of American domestic trade remedy law to binational arbitration had been controversial in the US, especially among members of Congress, and subsequent Canadian challenges to American trade remedy actions that resulted in decisions against US practices produced further irritation. The danger for Canada in the negotiations over Chapter 19 lay, in the first instance, in the wording of Article 1906 of the bilateral agreement: 'The provisions of this chapter shall be in effect for five years pending the development of a substitute system of rules in both countries for anti-dumping and countervailing duties as applied to bilateral trade.'[13] Although they would not voice their apprehension, lest they give the Americans an opening to act, Canadian trade officials were concerned that the wording of 1906 could be taken to mean (and was by many) that failure to agree on a substitute system meant that all the provisions of Chapter 19—especially the highly valued dispute settlement system—would cease to exist as of 1993. As a result, Canada was, initially, determined to secure the inclusion of the Chapter 19 provisions in a trilateral agreement, and this had been conceded by the US at an earlier stage in the negotiations. Now, however, the Canadians were concerned about American proposals that, in the Canadian view, could have the effect of diluting the binding nature of the dispute settlement provisions. Although the American negotiators denied any such intent, Canadian suspicions remained, and tensions were growing between the two sides over the issue.

In the final stages of the negotiations, these tensions erupted in a serious conflict between Canada and the US over the Chapter 19 provisions. The conflict arose, initially, over Mexico's Law of Amparo, a provision of the Mexican Constitution that allows Mexicans to challenge the decisions of authorities. According to the US, Amparo opened the possibility that a Mexican firm could use the domestic courts to hold up, or block entirely, the implementation of a Chapter 19 panel decision concerning dumping or subsidies. This, said the Americans, raised the question of whether Mexico could guarantee that a panel decision would be enforced in Mexico. To deal with this problem, the Americans proposed the addition of a special review mechanism (SRM) to Chapter 19, along with criteria that would govern its application. In bilateral discussions with the US, the Mexicans indicated that they were prepared to see some amendments to the chapter, and this provided the Americans with an opening to try to secure changes in the application of Chapter 19.

Negotiations on dispute settlement were being handled by officials from Canada's Department of Finance, and they were opposed to any initiative to open up Chapter 19 for discussion, because of a concern that 'improvements' might, in reality, be used to erode the efficacy of the chapter. In particular, they were concerned that the SRM provisions might weaken Chapter 19 as it applied to Canadian challenges to US trade remedy actions. As American officials began to table specific language on criteria that would trigger the application of the SRM, Canadian fears grew. Essentially, their concerns centred on the possibility that the US proposals would change the standard for review of panel decisions, thus making them more easily subject to extraordinary challenge. Again, it is necessary to refer to the bilateral agreement in order to understand the significance of this aspect of Chapter 19.

Article 1904 of the bilateral agreement established an extraordinary challenge procedure that allowed either country to refer a binational panel decision to a special committee of judges for review, to determine whether a member of the panel had behaved improperly, or if the panel had violated procedural rules or exceeded its authority. In the event that the special committee determined any of these conditions existed, it had the power to refer the decision back to the panel for appropriate action, or to void the decision entirely, in which case a new panel would be established. This procedure was included in the bilateral agreement to guard against irregular action by a panel, or its members. The first extraordinary challenge of a panel decision was requested by the United States, in the spring of 1991 during Congressional consideration of the extension of fast track negotiating authority.[14] The case involved a finding by the US International Trade Commission (ITC) that subsidies to Canadian pork exports caused injury to US producers, and a subsequent binational panel review that overturned the ITC injury determination. It was reported in the press at the time that the American pork industry persuaded the administration to mount the extraordinary challenge in exchange for Congressional votes in support of the fast track extension (Davey, 1996: 276).

In any case, Canada maintained that the Americans were not making appropriate use of the extraordinary challenge procedure, arguing that it was never intended as simply another avenue of appeal for binational panel decisions. The special committee that was struck to hear the US extraordinary challenge agreed with the Canadians, noting that the procedure was 'not intended to function as a routine appeal', but instead was intended as a review mechanism 'for aberrant panel decisions' (Davey, 1996: 227). American officials, especially those in the Department of Commerce, were not pleased with the committee's finding, and the Canadians suspected that, in proposing a new special review mechanism for NAFTA's Chapter 19, the US was simply looking to create another avenue to appeal binational panel decisions that went against them. For their part, the Americans insisted that their intentions were benign, that they were only seeking to address a potential problem with Mexico's domestic law.

By the final stages of the negotiations, Chapter 19 had become a crunch issue for all three parties: Canada and the US were demanding specific changes in Mexico's domestic legal system in exchange for the extension of the Chapter 19 dispute settlement system to include Mexico; the US was pushing Canada and Mexico to accept the SRM as a condition for the inclusion of Chapter 19 in the NAFTA; and Canada was resisting the American SRM initiative, and trying to secure Mexican support for its resistance effort. Canada's problem was that Mexico was willing to accept the US conditions in exchange for the inclusion of the binational panel review system in the trilateral agreement. To correct this, the Canadians brought Len Legault, one of Canada's most seasoned trade policy officials, and one of the original authors of the Chapter 19 provisions in the bilateral agreement, directly into the negotiations.[15] In the words of a senior Canadian negotiator, 'Legault did a masterful job of educating the Mexicans with respect to their interests on this issue,' and in the process he threw a spanner in the works that the US was attempting to construct on Chapter 19.

The Americans were not amused. They believed that Legault understood very well the real nature of American objectives, but he said that, politically, the issue simply would not sell in Canada. Legault set out to define Canadian conditions for the operation of the SRM, which would be specified in Article 1905 of NAFTA's Chapter 19. He had to convince the Americans that the Canadian conditions would still allow Article 1905 to address US concerns about the Mexican system, while eliminating any threat that it might pose to the operation of the binational panel review system established under Article 1904. The result was bad feelings all around—the Canadians suspecting that the Americans were seeking to undermine Chapter 19, the Americans suspicious that the Canadians were planning some action that would have been curtailed by the SRM, and the Mexicans fearful that Canadian intransigence would lead the US to reject the application of Chapter 19 to Mexico.

Finally, Canada insisted that it was not prepared to pay the price the US was asking on Chapter 19 in order to get NAFTA, and trade minister Michael Wilson indicated that he had the prime minister's concurrence that the Canadians would break off negotiations over the issue, if they had to. In fact, negotiations were suspended, informally, but it was Mexico that brought about the suspension. Trade minister Jaime Serra said that the Mexicans would not participate further in the various working group negotiations until the Chapter 19 issue was resolved. They did so because they did not want the gains they were making on other issues to be undone by failure on the part of the US and Canada to reach agreement on Chapter 19. Mexico's action brought the negotiations to a standstill, freezing the process across the entire set of working groups. This was a major blow, so serious that, according to a senior negotiator, the impasse was never made public because the parties did not wish to further endanger the talks by revealing the significance of the problem that they faced. According to the Canadians, it took two days of this for the message finally to sink in with the Americans that Canada was in earnest about its objections. In the end, the Americans got their special review mechanism in NAFTA Article 1905, but its operations were circumscribed according to Canadian specifications, and Canada retained this key element in its trade policy, for which it had fought so hard in bilateral and trilateral negotiations with the US.

BEYOND NAFTA

As described in Chapter 3, while the NAFTA negotiations were underway, Canada was also participating in the Uruguay Round of multilateral trade negotiations. Those negotiations, which started in 1986 while Canada was negotiating its bilateral agreement with the US and carried on through the early 1990s, when

Canada was negotiating NAFTA, had finally concluded at the end of 1993. The result was a wide-ranging and ambitious agreement on a host of trade and related issues, as well as the creation of the World Trade Organization, an organizational framework within which countries could pursue rights and obligations (Hart, 2002: 418). A year later, in December 1994, Canada joined in the effort to create, by 2005, a Free Trade Area of the Americas (FTAA) among the 34 countries of the Americas (excluding Cuba). As mentioned previously, in January 2005, the deadline for concluding an agreement expired, and in 2006 the prospects for an FTAA appeared to be slim. In November 2001, Canada joined more than 140 other WTO member countries in Doha, Qatar, to launch a new round of multilateral trade negotiations. In addition to these multilateral initiatives, after the successful conclusion of NAFTA, Canada negotiated bilateral free trade agreements with Chile, Costa Rica, and Israel, and initiated free trade negotiations with a number of other countries and groups of countries.[16]

Although these initiatives were important, Canada's principal trading relationship continued to be overwhelmingly with the United States, and that relationship was tested anew when the events of September 11, 2001, severely impeded the access of Canadian products to the American market. Following the attacks, all the elements were in place for the establishment of the security-access issue as a problem on the government's decision agenda: there were a number of indicators that a problem existed on the border, and the measures of the dollar costs of delays that were developed by industry and government made the point rather dramatically; the crisis of September 11 provided a focusing event for officials, one that served as a compelling symbol not only of American vulnerability, but also of the way Canadian economic interests could be held hostage to US security concerns; and the government was in receipt of a steady stream of feedback about the need to keep the problem front and centre in Canadian concerns. The immediate policy response to the security-access problem was the Smart Border Declaration, and its 30-point action plan, which addressed US security concerns as well as Canadian concerns about the movement of people and goods across the border.

Policy entrepreneurs had grander ideas in mind, however. In the two years following the 9/11 attacks, a large number of papers, speeches, workshops, conferences, and opinion pieces dissected Canada–US trade, economic, and security issues from every conceivable angle and proposed a range of solutions, almost all of which called for deeper integration in the bilateral relationship.[17] Former Canadian ambassadors to the United States, Allan Gotlieb and Derek Burney, argued that only a major initiative would have the scope to attract US political interest and provide room for mutually beneficial tradeoffs. Gotlieb suggested the establishment of a joint community of law to foster joint rules, procedures, and institutions to govern common interests in creating a more open and more secure bilateral economic space, while Burney called for the two governments to work together on an initiative that addressed US concerns on the security front and Canadian priorities on trade and investment matters. Bank of Canada governor David Dodge challenged the two governments to pay serious attention to the benefits of deeper integration, including a more open and integrated labour market, allowing Canadians and Americans to work wherever opportunity beckons. The Canadian Council of Chief Executives advanced a strategy focused on reinventing borders, maximizing economic efficiencies, negotiating a comprehensive resource security pact, sharing in continental and global security, and developing institutions to manage the new partnership.

The C.D. Howe Institute commissioned a series of 'Border Papers' to create a better intellectual foundation for consideration of a joint Canada–US strategy that is big enough to attract US political attention and to address the full gamut of economic and security issues affecting bilateral relations. The series examined everything from the prospects for a customs union to the impact of enhanced security on bilateral trade flows. Hugh Segal, then-president of the Institute for Research on Public Policy (IRPP), made a series of speeches challenging Canadians to think big and creatively about Canada–US relations, with a view to developing new rules and institutions to govern joint interests, and IRPP economist Daniel Schwanen examined the pros and cons of further governance arrangements to foster deeper integration. Fraser Institute analysts built a case for more active efforts to link trade and economic and security interests, with a view to creating both more open and more secure cross-border ties. The Conference Board of Canada, after first arguing that Canada needs to approach the bilateral agenda incrementally, solving problems where it can and avoiding linkages to the extent possible, subsequently called for a Canadian debate on various options for securing access to the US market, up to and including a North American customs union. The Public Policy Forum held a number of consultations and sponsored research aimed at determining business attitudes toward the evolving Canada–US trade and economic agenda, much of which pointed to the need for a new round of bilateral discussions.

In the academic community, University of Alberta business economist Rolf Mirus circulated various papers arguing that Canada–US economic integration had reached the stage at which a customs union or common market arrangement is required to capture the full benefits of integration, and economists Tom Courchene and Richard Harris made the case for a common currency to advance Canadian macroeconomic and trade and investment interests. As well, McGill University legal scholar Armand deMestral advocated movement toward upgrading the legal commitments in the NAFTA, from intergovernmental treaty commitments to rights and obligations that have 'direct effect', allowing citizens to pursue rights under the agreement through the domestic courts, analogous to the direct effect that is central to the implementation of the treaties establishing the European Union. Finally, Carleton University analysts Bill Dymond and Michael Hart outlined the need to refine the trade and economic agenda in the light of the new security reality ushered in by the increased terrorist threat, calling for deepening integration.

There was a contra side to the debate as well. Nationalist critics, from Stephen Clarkson to Peter Newman, warned that any new initiative with the United States would threaten Canadian sovereignty and undermine Canada's ability to chart its own course. Economist Andrew Jackson argued that deeper integration would threaten the expression of distinctive Canadian values on defence, international affairs, and immigration and refugee issues, and would limit Canada's ability to shape industrial development, to control the energy sector, to move toward a more environmentally sustainable economy, to levy taxes at the level needed to maintain a distinctive Canadian social model, and to limit the effects of international trade and investment agreements. His colleague at the Centre for Policy Alternatives, Bruce Campbell, proposed as an alternative to the deeper integration approach, 'the deliberate pursuit of small steps', a strategy whose cumulative effect over time may lead the government to challenge NAFTA in key areas where national interests take precedence. Finally, Queen's political scientist Robert Wolfe argued that the need for action had been exaggerated, and that most issues were already well in hand, or could be addressed within the framework of existing rules and institutions.

However, these dissenting views were swamped by the flood of papers, speeches, workshops, conferences, and opinion pieces promoting change in the Canada–US relationship as a means to deal with the border security-market access problem. Certainly, in this period the policy community was being softened up by what amounted to a virtual drumbeat for deeper integration, and there is little doubt that policy entrepreneurs were trying to build acceptance for their policy preferences in the policy community and the general public, by presenting their ideas repeatedly and in many different forums. Although no tipping point was reached, where a single idea won general acceptance in the trade policy community, and members did not get on board a single policy bandwagon, the direction of the various ideas was clear, as they all pointed toward some form of deeper Canada–US integration. Therefore, by the end of 2003, a problem had been identified, and a consensus was building in the policy community around a particular solution. In this circumstance, policy entrepreneurs turned their attention to the politics stream, where conditions were somewhat more mixed.

As we indicated in Chapter 4, following the successful conclusion of the Canada–US and North American free trade agreements, the national mood in Canada was much more receptive to trade liberalization, including with the US. In a March 2003 survey, Liberal pollster Michael Marzolini found that 90 per cent of Canadians favoured closer economic ties with the US, and two out of three supported closer social and cultural ties as well. Canadians also demonstrated an awareness of the security-access problem, with 63 per cent indicating, in an October 2003 Ipsos-Reid poll, that enhanced border-security measures hinder bilateral trade. In sum, to the extent that politicians, and those who serve them, glean a sense of the national mood from public opinion polls, they would find support there for pursuing deeper integration with the US as a solution to the security-access problem. In addition, the organized political interests that matter most on trade policy were all calling for government action to ensure that the border would not stand as an impediment to the bilateral flow of goods and services, or to the ability to attract investment. In this regard, the major organized business interests—the Canadian Chamber of Commerce, Canadian

Manufacturers & Exporters, and the Canadian Council of Chief Executives—were all pushing in the same direction on the issue, toward some form of deeper integration.

However, the governmental elements of the politics stream were not as conducive to policy change. Paul Martin's installation as prime minister on 12 December 2003 touched off a substantial turnover of the key players in government, providing a major opportunity for change in policy agendas and alternatives. Typically, new ministers, and their senior officials, will bring new issues to the cabinet table, and the transition in power will provide an opportunity for policy entrepreneurs to pitch their problems and solutions to players who may be open to new ideas. Change, if it occurs, will not be sudden, however. The problem and policy advocacy activities that are currently in play, and that we have described in those respective streams, will be superseded by bargaining and coalition building among organized political interests and officials in the politics stream, as they seek sufficient adherents to tip the balance of support in a particular direction. That process was certainly underway during the first few months of the Martin government, when the prime minister made it clear that the Canada–US relationship was high on the government's policy agenda by creating a new cabinet committee on Canada–US relations, which he would chair, and appointing a parliamentary secretary to the prime minister with special responsibility for the bilateral relationship, supported by a secretariat on Canada–US relations in the Privy Council Office.

Thus, early in 2004, political circumstances seemed right for the elevation of the security-access problem on to the government's decision agenda, and for the identification of some form of deeper integration with the US as the appropriate policy response to the problem. The national mood was supportive, or at least permissive, organized political forces, at least those that had so far taken a stand, were pushing in that direction, a change of government produced new players who were actively looking for problems to solve, and solutions that might work, and, perhaps most important, the prime minister had taken personal charge of the Canada–US file. However, any decision regarding significant change in the bilateral relationship would have to wait until Martin had secured his own mandate to govern in an election that was widely expected in the spring. However, by midwinter, Martin's government was increasingly preoccupied with a growing scandal over dubious payments for promotional activities following the close 1995 Quebec referendum. The sponsorship scandal touched off a period of political instability in Ottawa, as the Liberal government first was reduced to minority status in June 2004, and then went down to defeat in a January 2006 election, which brought a minority Conservative government led by Stephen Harper to power. These political conditions were definitely not ripe for policy entrepreneurs to engineer a coupling of the security-access problem with their deeper integration solution, and what looked like a promising window of opportunity was closed, at least for the time being.[18]

The evolutionary path of Canadian trade policy in the 60 years following the end of the Second World War begins and ends with free trade with the United States. Following the abrupt abandonment of a bilateral free trade agreement in

1948, Canada sought to achieve its trade policy goals through a series of multi-lateral negotiations, each of which was significant in the degree to which it successfully reduced barriers to trade between the two North American partners. As a result, Canadian exports became steadily more concentrated on the American market, making security of access more important with each passing year, especially as protectionist forces gained strength in the US. When free trade was finally adopted in the mid-1980s, and reaffirmed in NAFTA, the stage was set for a huge increase in Canada–US commercial relations, producing what was, in most important respects, an integrated continental market. When the integrity of that market was threatened by international terrorism in the twenty-first century, Canadian action to prevent disruption was virtually guaranteed. It remains to be seen, if that threat continues, how agendas, ideas, and politics will combine to produce the next stage in the evolution of Canada's trade policy.

C H A P T E R   6

Streams in the Defence Policy Process

From the aftermath of the Second World War to the war on terrorism in the twenty-first century, Canada's national defence objectives have revolved around four constant pillars: the protection of the homeland and provision of emergency assistance in the event of natural disaster or threats to domestic peace; the defence of North America in cooperation with the United States; the support of like-minded allies through participation in the North Atlantic Treaty Organization (NATO); and contributions to collective security and international stability operations under the auspices of the United Nations Organization (UN).

The relative importance of these priorities on the policy agenda has shifted over the past six decades. Members of the Canadian defence policy community have championed alternative views about which of the four pillars should take precedence in shaping the Canadian military's force structure and deployments. Given, moreover, the challenges that arise from domestic and international politics, there have been numerous debates about how much funding the Canadian military and Department of National Defence (DND) needs to fulfill Canada's commitments, and about how DND and the Canadian Forces (CF) should be organized to best fulfill these obligations. Factors of continuity and change have at various times shaped national defence policy in Canada.

This chapter provides an account of the processes that led to the drafting of Canada's defence policy statements (usually called White Papers) of 1964, 1971, 1987, 1994, and 2005.¹ They are analyzed in terms of the three streams of public policy making: the problems they sought to address; the policy alternatives that were considered; and the bargaining that took place within the defence community, along with the international and domestic political circumstances that influenced defence policy making. Chapter 7 will bring the three streams together at critical junctures, which John Kingdon describes as policy windows, where opportunities for policy innovation and renewal are identified and exploited by leaders and policy entrepreneurs. Canadian defence policy entrepreneurs have succeeded in introducing policy alternatives at opportune moments when pressing problems have demanded solutions and the political environment was ripe for policy change. The defence policy statements, each the product of political turnover, are instances of such change.

THE DEFENCE POLICY AGENDA

This section will concentrate on the evolution of Canada's defence policy agenda from the 1950s to the early twenty-first century. Following the Kingdon framework, analysis of defence-related problems on governmental and decision agendas will include attention to objective indicators, focusing events, and feedback in shaping continuity and change on policy agendas.

During the early years of the Cold War, defence planners thought the preservation of Canadian sovereignty, within the new and evolving North American relationship, to be the primary problem in need of a solution (Milner, 1999: 158). The issue had arisen during the Second World War when the United States established a strong presence in the Canadian North; the Canadian government, after some hesitation, made it very clear that it was in charge of its own territory. For a few years after the war, the Liberal government attempted a balance: a very close cooperation with the US, including the exchange of personnel and observers, work toward common equipment and training standards and reciprocal access to military facilities, but 'no treaty, executive agreement or contractual obligation' (*Canada's Defence*, 1947, in Bland, 1997: 51–3). A treaty came, however, with NATO, signed by Canada, the US and other Western states in 1949 to counter the growing threat of the Soviet Union.

The Cold War led to ever more cooperation between Canada and the United States in the air defence of the continent: the building of three radar lines in Canada used substantial American resources and personnel and were designed to give early warning of incoming attacks. In 1957, with military officials in both countries arguing that the Canadian and American air defence systems should be coordinated and controlled by a joint command to ward off an attack on the continent, the North American Air Defence Command (NORAD) was established. James Eayrs, a leading authority on military questions, captured a common consensus when he wrote that a compelling international danger might force Canadians to forfeit their independence. If that moment should come, he believed, so be it—better that than capitulation to the Communists or nuclear annihilation (English and Hillmer, 1989: 37). Such was the fear of the Soviet Union, and such was the belief that the United States was a good friend and a necessary ally. For many Canadians, as well as for their political leaders, the problem now seemed less a matter of sovereignty than security.

The government that introduced NORAD was not the one to which Canadians were accustomed. John Diefenbaker's Conservatives had won the election of 1957, bringing 22 years of Liberal rule to an end. A sympathetic Republican administration was in power in the United States, and Diefenbaker got on extremely well with his counterpart, President Dwight Eisenhower. In addition to the signature of NORAD, Diefenbaker agreed to acquire air defence systems that required nuclear warheads. The prime minister's early policy preference for close cooperation for North American defence responded to the prevalent geopolitical conditions of Cold War, namely, the threat posed to North America by Soviet bombers and ballistic missiles. Indicators showed that, by the 1950s, the Soviet Union possessed nuclear arms and increasingly sophisticated long-range bombers that could reach North America. The October 1957 launch of the Soviet 'Sputnik', the world's first artificial satellite (Collard-Wexler et al., 2006: 64), demonstrated to the West the extent of the USSR's technological advancement and raised the stakes in the competition for mastery of outer space.

The acquisition of nuclear weapons for Canada's defences was apparently the next logical step in the integration of North American strategic systems. Indeed, the Diefenbaker government announced this as its intention in 1959. However, contradictory feedback from within the Conservative cabinet prevented the government from making an official decision. The defence minister, Douglas Harkness, wanted Canada to follow through on the commitment to take the warheads. Meanwhile, Howard Green, the minister at External Affairs, was an all-out opponent of nuclear arms. So too were a group of Canadian and other scientists who had come together in 1957 at the inaugural meeting of the Pugwash Group, an organization that would become a powerful voice for nuclear disarmament in Canadian civil society. Agenda instability ensued. Yet nuclear disarmament was never really a viable option. If adopted, a disarmament policy would have completely destabilized the highly integrated Canadian–American defence relationship: in the tense Cold War atmosphere of the times, that was simply not going to occur.

What seemed more possible, however, was to put a stop to the introduction of nuclear weapons into Canada. Feedback from Canadians and organized interest groups in civil society indicated support for this course of action. This trend was reinforced by the prime minister's personal dislike of US President John F. Kennedy, who won the election of 1960. The new American administration was as anxious as the last for Canada to accept its responsibilities to North American defence by acquiring nuclear warheads. But the charismatic Kennedy rubbed Diefenbaker the wrong way, reinforcing the prime minister's nationalist inclinations and colouring the way he saw the issue of Canadian–American relations. Diefenbaker made it clear that neither he, nor Canada, would be pushed, but he never fundamentally challenged the idea of nuclear weapons for Canada. Instead he did nothing, or next to nothing, month after month, year after year. The result was policy stagnation on the government's decision agenda. This was continuity, but continuity of a particularly damaging kind.

It took an international crisis of global proportions to propel the Canadian defence policy agenda toward action. In May 1961 the brash Kennedy, far more popular in Canada than Diefenbaker, came to Ottawa to visit the prime minister. Publicly he prodded the Canadians to be better allies in his anti-Communist crusade, while privately he urged Diefenbaker to fulfill his commitments on nuclear weapons. Diefenbaker resisted, and the atmosphere was poisonous. The relationship, already off to a bad start, got worse in October 1962 when Kennedy revealed that the Soviets had deployed missiles in Cuba, friendly to the USSR and only 150 kilometres away from the Florida coast. As the US faced the Soviets in a confrontation that seemed likely to lead to an all-out war, with the life of the world on the line, Diefenbaker refused to order the Canadian forces in NORAD to go onto an immediate alert, matching the higher US alert status. So defence minister Harkness and the military chiefs went on alert behind the prime minister's back. After a tense 13 days, Kennedy came to an accommodation with the Soviet Union. Diefenbaker had eventually supported the tough American line, but too late, in the view of the US administration and of many Canadians, who judged that the reaction of their government had been 'hesitant, uncertain, and inglorious' (Granatstein, 1981: 352–3).

The Cuban missile crisis focused the attention of many Canadians on the very serious threat posed by a nuclear-armed Soviet Union. Diefenbaker was slow to respond to these public priorities. Negative feedback from domestic constituencies, combined with a public rebuke from the Americans about the prime minister's delays over the nuclear warhead issue, precipitated a crisis of confidence in the Conservative government soon after the Cuban scare. The government fell in March 1963 and the country was soon in the midst of a divisive, and hard-fought, election campaign. Diefenbaker whipped up nationalist sentiment and sovereignty concerns with the argument that the Americans were out to use Canada as a storage dump for their nuclear weapons. He campaigned hard and well but, in the end, the Liberals led by Lester B. Pearson won a minority government with a promise to accept the nuclear weapons in the name of Canadian security and alliance solidarity with the Americans. The strong showing by the Conservatives, however, indicated that anti-Americanism remained a potent rallying force for many Canadians, not least in Quebec—and anti-Americanism, then on the rise in Canada, suggested a defence policy that concentrated on Canadian interests.

Problems and priorities shifted again with the election of the Liberals, precipitating changes on the governmental and decision agendas. The Pearson governments (1963–8) were committed as a first priority to 'restoring sound and steady management of the nation's business' (Carrington, 1968: 295) after the policy chaos of the Diefenbaker years. It was a minority government, but one pledged to action, and to clean, progressive, and modern policies. In defence, the goal was to establish firm control of the military and of military expenditure (Bland, 1997: 58). Feedback resulting from an internal review of the defence department indicated that there was little cooperation or coordination between the three military branches, resulting in inefficiencies, duplication, and suboptimal outcomes. This conclusion was strongly buttressed by the findings of the Royal Commission on Government Organization, which reported in 1962–3 that National Defence contained too much bureaucracy and too much administration relative to military effectiveness, not to mention a duplication and triplication of services (Granatstein, 1986: 225; Hellyer, 1990: 36). Unification of the three armed services rose onto the Liberal government's decision agenda as the best solution to overblown defence costs and the problem of military inefficiencies. It was also expected that unification would free up defence dollars for investment in military equipment and more commitments to NATO and peacekeeping operations abroad, all without increases to the defence budget. The defence White Paper, issued in late March 1964, sought to reduce service rivalries, promote efficiency, and give the government greater control over the military; all three services were to come under a unified defence staff headed by a single officer, the Chief of Defence Staff (CDS).

The budget consideration can make or break policy proposals on governmental agendas (Kingdon, 2003: 105–9), but the problem was not only one of cost cutting. Developments in the confrontation between the superpowers shaped defence minister Paul Hellyer's policies as well. According to American and Canadian defence experts, an all-out nuclear exchange was now the least likely war scenario (Saywell, *CAR*, 1963: 338). Instead, many Western officials feared that the USSR would test NATO's resolve by mounting a much smaller non-nuclear challenge in Western Europe. A nuclear response to a non-nuclear challenge would not be credible. The American doctrine of 'flexible response' thus called for NATO to tailor its military response to fit with the severity of a Soviet attack (Bland, 1995: 69). This redefined the Cold War problem for Canadians: the need now was to develop more conventional forces. Hellyer, for instance, recognized that 'for our air division [in Europe] that meant acquiring hardware for a dual role—conventional, in addition to nuclear' (Hellyer, 1990: 34). What was more, a greater number of conventional forces might be needed to address 'brushfire' wars in the developing world. Canada, just having acquired nuclear weapons for its forces, was already moving away from them, and the Pearson government was acknowledging the continuing importance of conventional forces.

The diminishing attention afforded to nuclear weapons on the Canadian defence policy agenda represented one area of continuity between Pearson and his Liberal successor, Pierre Elliott Trudeau (1968–79, 1980–4). Another was Trudeau's decision to act on the previous Liberal government's pledge to freeze the military budget and cut personnel levels to 83,000. In most other respects, however, Canadian defence policy during the early Trudeau era was shaped by significant changes in priorities and perspectives. Above all, the new prime minister placed the problems of Canadian sovereignty and national unity at the heart of defence policy making. Focusing events at home caught the attention of the government, making the ongoing, but apparently improving, Cold War predicament seem less immediately important by comparison. The first great problem facing the Trudeau government was the October 1970 FLQ crisis, when terrorists demanding the separation of Quebec from Canada murdered a prominent provincial politician and kidnapped a British diplomat, which in turn brought the armed forces into the streets in large numbers. Coupled with the sailing of a US oil tanker, the *Manhattan*, through Canada's Arctic waters in 1969 in apparent defiance of Canadian sovereignty in the North, the FLQ crisis reinforced nationalist arguments that defence began at home and reminded

Canadians that the military played a critical, if rarely seen, part in preserving their personal safety and domestic security. An emphasis on sovereignty was a natural response to the sense of a vulnerable homeland.

Meanwhile, the Cold War problem was also perceived differently, bringing the focus back to continental defence. While Pearson's Cold War had led him to acquire more military equipment to support a flexible force structure and peace-keeping operations abroad, Trudeau's Cold War would be fought at and near home. Canadian national security was inexorably linked to NORAD and the pro-tection of the United States' retaliatory nuclear capabilities. For the prime minis-ter, however, this did not necessarily require complete integration into American schemes for security. The Trudeau government's abandonment of nuclear weapons in Europe by 1971 was an important departure in this respect.

The 1971 defence White Paper, *Defence in the 70s*, reversed the priorities stated in 1964, from the collective good of Canada and its allies to Trudeau's preoccu-pation with the future of the country itself. The 'first concern' of the White Paper was to ensure that Canada continued to be 'secure as an independent political entity' (Saywell, *CAR*, 1971: 293). In policy terms, this translated into prioritizing the protection of Canadian sovereignty, assistance to civilian author-ities (a role known as aid of the civil power) and continental defence commit-ments through NORAD over expeditionary commitments to Western allies abroad. Contributions to UN peacekeeping operations would, moreover, be select and conditional upon the likelihood of success. The idea got about that defence was just another 'government program'. Spending on it would be partially deter-mined by the goals of other departments, and defence would be expected to con-tribute to those goals. A further indication of control and discipline was suggested by the announcement of a Management Review Group (MRG) to eval-uate military organization.

An iconoclastic and activist prime minister did not, ultimately, overcome fac-tors of continuity in shaping the Canadian defence policy agenda. Over the remaining 13 years of the Trudeau government, defence returned to its low rank on the governmental agenda, although there were incremental increases to the military budget over time. The NATO alliance and peacekeeping also regained some lost ground on the governmental agenda, and pressures from south of the border in the early 1980s led Ottawa to allow the United States to test cruise mis-siles in Canada.

With the election of a Conservative government (1984–93), a stark Cold War vision returned as the primary determinant of Canadian defence policy. Prime Minister Brian Mulroney called for a robust defence in keeping with Canada's traditional international roles and commitments. Part of this entailed a high pri-ority for closer defence ties with the US: the Mulroney government was out to please and support the United States (Ripsman, 2001: 101, 105). The defence problems of the mid-1980s also conspired in the direction of bold change. Fore-most amongst Canada's defence policy problems, and seen as such by govern-ment (Bland, 1993: 219) was the commitment-capability gap. Despite years of growing defence budgets and several major equipment procurements, the CF appeared to lack the resources necessary to fulfill its international commitments and domestic duties. The military was uncomfortable with the direction of policy under the Liberals, and deeply unhappy about both a lack of resources and of respect given them by the Trudeau-ites. NATO allies regularly complained that Canada was not contributing enough for collective defence. Meanwhile, the conditions of détente (diminished tensions between the superpowers) had dissipated, making the commitment-credibility gap seem even more serious. Battles raged between American and Soviet proxies in the developing world, and the United States and Soviet Union were locked in an intense arms race.

New indicators of an escalation in the Cold War arms race had clear implications for the North American strategic environment, posing further problems. Under the Trudeau Liberals, Canada and the United States had begun negotiating modernizations of the continent's air defences. Given Soviet investments in new bomber and missile technologies, the improvement of North America's aerospace defences appeared prudent. In 1983 President Reagan announced that the United States would begin developing a space-based ballistic missile defence system. Known as the strategic defense initiative (SDI), the system aimed to destroy ballistic missiles launched against the United States; its allies and the US invested several billion dollars in research and development of space-based interceptors (Collard-Wexler et al., 2006: 147). As an aerospace defence mechanism, moreover, SDI would rely on ballistic missile warning and assessment data transmitted from NORAD. Hence, discussions about the future of NORAD and North American air defence necessarily involved a determination of Canada's involvement with SDI. Relations with the United States were further complicated by the recurring dispute over the Northwest Passage. In 1985 an American ice-breaker, *Polar Sea*, sailed through the Northwest Passage, reviving Canadian concerns about their Arctic sovereignty and surveillance capabilities. Adding to these worries was the presence of Soviet and American nuclear submarines in Canadian Arctic waters. Lacking nuclear-powered submarines of its own, Canada was unable to track these vessels. The *Polar Sea* incident became symbolic of the fragility of Canada's sovereign claim over the Arctic and focused the attention of Canadian policy makers on the need to address this problem.

Defence policy under the Mulroney Conservatives was ambitious. The overarching objective was to perform both continental defence and collective security roles better than the previous Liberal governments, all the while giving Canada's sovereignty interests in the North their due. A concern for resource overstretch motivated a 1985 proposal from Mulroney's defence minister, Erik Nielsen, to examine the feasibility of withdrawing all Canadian forces from Europe, but this alternative was quickly rejected by high-ranking DND officials, demonstrating the difficulties of overcoming factors of continuity in the bureaucratic culture and ideas of the defence community. Canada's commitment to NORAD was also renewed, with the important provision that the binational Canada–US command structure would retain its aerospace warning and assessment functions, despite the government decision that there would be no formal Canadian involvement with SDI research. Significantly, in the interests of achieving favourable terms for

Canada in the NORAD renewal negotiations, future participation in an American Ballistic Missile Defence (BMD) was not ruled out (Lagassé, 2006).

In June 1987, the Mulroney Conservative government released Canada's most far-reaching and controversial defence White Paper. The paper outlined recommendations for higher defence expenditures and investments in military equipment including new tanks for use by the Canadian Forces (CF) serving with NATO in Europe, new destroyers for the Canadian navy, maritime patrol aircraft, and nuclear-powered attack submarines to patrol Canada's Arctic waters. The last of these responded to two problems on the governmental agenda simultaneously: the promotion of Canadian sovereignty in the North and Cold War deterrence against Soviet intrusions into Canadian waters. The Conservatives acted as if budgets did not matter in their efforts to expand Canadian influence on the world stage and reassure traditional allies of Canada's usefulness as a defence partner.

Budgets, however, did matter to opposition parties in Parliament and influential figures within the Conservative Party, led by the minister of finance. Feedback from the Canadian public registered opposition to the recommendations of the White Paper, as voices from the peace movement combined with broader constituencies wary of the Mulroney government's perceived harmonization with hawkish American policies. Finally, geopolitical indicators heralding the end of the Cold War were increasingly persuasive. A Canadian policy agenda that prioritized a defence stance designed for a bipolar world was quickly becoming obsolete. Change was both necessary and inevitable; by 1989, the White Paper, *Challenge and Commitment*, was in the dustbin.

The Chrétien Liberals were the first government to be elected in the post–Cold War era. Their defence policy agenda would clearly look very different from that of their predecessors, and most especially from the Mulroney Conservatives. Thirteen months after their election, the Chrétien government (1993–2003) released the 1994 Defence White Paper. It stood out for its grasp of the post–Cold War security environment, and promotion of affordable defence policies designed to secure the Canadian national interest in a time of great fiscal imbalance.

The problem window was open, with a vengeance. The most urgent problems on the governmental agenda were the budget deficits and national debt that played an important part in undoing the 1987 White Paper. Quantitative indicators showed that Canada was on the brink of insolvency: the national debt had doubled over the previous decade and the federal deficit had never been higher (Goldenberg, 2006: 114). International lenders were about to lower the country's credit rating. Chrétien and his finance minister Paul Martin understood that a massive reduction in federal expenditures was necessary to save Canada from international ruin. To be meaningful, these reductions would have to be imposed on every federal program and department, including healthcare and postsecondary education, but as the only significant pool of discretionary spending the defence budget was especially vulnerable to cuts. With the end of the Cold War and absence of a direct military threat to Canada, it was thought that the country's military capabilities could be curtailed without endangering Canadian national security in the short-term. Martin's first budget, early in 1994, contained a number of military cuts, including some base closures.

The Liberals decided to focus on the problem of military expenditure as the primary target of their remaking of defence policy. The economic crisis was a focusing event that threatened the maintenance of the status quo. Feedback from the top also seemed to support changing priorities on the defence policy agenda. Conventional war-fighting with NATO allies had given way to peace-keeping, humanitarian tasks, the protection of Canadian sovereignty and aid of the civil power, alternatives that were both less costly and suited to the changing security climate. Although global 'common security' was not a new idea, the end of the Cold War elevated it as a viable alternative on the governmental agenda.

Change, apparently, was in the air. But the military establishment and CDS were fervently opposed to any changes that would undermine the ability of the CF to carry out missions across the full spectrum of military options, from sovereignty protection and civil tasks at home to traditional combat roles and collective security obligations abroad. Canada's military-bureaucratic culture favoured the status quo over innovation. There were other countervailing pressures from the military in the direction of forging closer ties with the world's sole remaining superpower through cooperation in the defence of North America and contributions to UN and NATO endeavours alongside the American armed forces. Prime Minister Chrétien was also wary about making drastic changes to policy, despite the importance of the budget consideration in a climate of fiscal limitation and restraint.

The 1994 White Paper represented a response to factors of both continuity and change in the early years of the post–Cold War era. The CF would be smaller and leaner, funded by less than 60 per cent of the expenditures allocated by the 1987 White Paper. Expectations of performance and capabilities would be adjusted accordingly. However, the CF would remain a multipurpose, combat-capable force, with the ability to serve in a full spectrum of potential operations at home, on the continent and overseas. The Liberals' White Paper was a compromise package that stopped short of fully satisfying any one camp in the setting of the defence policy agenda.

The 1994 defence policy statement identified a range of issues for the post–Cold War era. These included ethnic hatreds, failed states, rogue regimes, and the proliferation of weapons of mass destruction. The emergence of such threats in the problem stream made the limitation of Canada's overseas commitments more difficult. Despite the White Paper's recommendation that the military should be deployed selectively, the government committed CF units to a wide variety of UN and NATO operations, including tougher and broader peacekeeping roles and the 1999 war in Kosovo. The Canadian Navy also cooperated closely with its US counterpart in enforcing sanctions against Saddam Hussein's Iraq. By 1999, defence expenditures had begun to go up. Then came the terrorist attack on New York and Washington on September 11, 2001. National security and defence policy shot towards the top of the government's decision agenda.

September 11 focused the attention of the business lobby, trade specialists, and government in Canada on the economic and political costs of being perceived by the United States to be a security liability or defence free-rider. Feedback from these influential groups in the aftermath of the terror attacks, and indicators of a problem at the border, questioning existing defence policies and approaches, pushed the so-called security-access problem high on the governmental agenda. 'Security-access' was the business lobby's appeal for a strategic arrangement for protecting Canada's share of the American market and meeting US-defined continental defence and homeland security objectives, including policies for immigration, border infrastructure, and civil policing. The Canada–US Smart Border Accord of 2001 signalled the Chrétien government's serious attention to the security-access problem. However, some members of the business community advocated deeper integration—a 'grand bargain' that would include a North American Security Perimeter, a repackaged version of the traditional Canadian national defence objective to protect North America through closer defence ties with the United States. Canada moved with speed to bolster its border defences but, to the chagrin of some trade advocates and the American administration alike, chose not to support the 2003 intervention in Iraq.

When Paul Martin became prime minister in December 2003, defence policy became an integral part of his initiative to restore Canada's clout in the world and rebuild the Canada–US relationship. The Martin government (2003–6) was faced with four concrete problems that had accumulated on the governmental agenda and helped to account for the attention defence was receiving and the tough-minded policy alternative that was emerging. Shortfalls in the CF's core capabilities and operational readiness were the first problem that the Martin government confronted. While the cause of the military's difficulties was debatable, few doubted that the CF was in a troubled state. By 2003 the army and navy were asking for a deployment pause to give their soldiers and sailors a much needed rest, while two-thirds of the air force's tactical airlift planes were proving to be unserviceable. Media outlets and the defence lobby lamented the state of the CF's aging platforms, Canada's relatively low defence expenditures, and the services' small number of combat-capable personnel. Although the CF's performance in the war on terror between the fall of 2001 and December 2003 was commendable, the Liberals and the defence department were aware that the armed forces were saddled with an untenable commitment-capability gap. The Martin Liberals made clear their determination to find ways to bridge the gap.

The role of the CF in countering terrorism was a second problem. As indicated by the Chrétien government's post-9/11 investment in intelligence assets and border security, domestic counterterrorism was largely the purview of civilian agencies. Yet the military was not peripheral to Canada's counterterrorism efforts. Military contributions to consequence management measures, emergency preparedness, and coastal surveillance were taken for granted. What had yet to be decided was how many CF resources, units, and personnel should be dedicated to domestic counterterrorism and consequence management. Complicating this calculus was the generally accepted notion that the military's role in protecting Canadians from terrorism was an expeditionary one; that is, it would take place abroad. Specifically, most strategic analysts held that the military's most effective contribution to counterterrorism was dismantling terrorist safe havens abroad, and killing and capturing terrorist operatives before they reached North America. Hence, it appeared that the ideal solution was to increase both the CF's role in domestic consequence management and the military's expeditionary deployments, an impossible feat under the existing defence budget. Addressing the issue of how, or whether, the CF could be asked to do more to protect Canadians at home, while simultaneously defeating terrorist groups overseas, was a question both the Liberals and DND felt compelled to address.

A third problem with which the Liberals grappled was the belief that Canada's international stature was in decline. With defence expenditures totalling only 1.1 per cent of GDP and the CF's shortfalls receiving wide media coverage, policy makers inside the government and commentators outside expressed concern that the country was turning its back on the world, and on its lengthy and distinguished record of international influence. Raised on tales of Canada's past greatness in international affairs and viewing their country as a paragon of peace and prosperity, Canadians believed, as a book chain's sloganeering had it, that 'the world needs more Canada'. Yet, foreign observers agreed that Canada had become less important in global politics. Canada's inabilities to mount independent military operations or rapidly deploy forces overseas were cited as factors that contributed to the country's diminishing influence. The Martin government's integrated international policy review was meant to highlight policies that would reverse this perceived Canadian decline.

Defence relations with the United States were a last problem set. Martin inherited three Canada–United States defence issues from his predecessor. First, a decision would have to be made regarding the binational planning group (BPG) for continental defence and the possible expansion of NORAD. Second, Canada's role in the American BMD system would have to be clarified. Third and most important, Ottawa's outlook on the war on terrorism and the CF's role in American-led operations would have to be clarified. The war in Afghanistan showed that Canada was willing to fight alongside the United States military, but Ottawa's stand on the Iraq war suggested that Ottawa preferred the cloak of internationally sanctioned, multinational operations. A balance would have to be struck between Canada's interest in fighting the war on terror next to the United States and the preference of many Liberals and many Canadians for multilateral optics and peacekeeping guises.

An early draft of the Martin defence policy statement argued that the CF should take on fewer international commitments, and use the money and resources saved closer to home for continental defence and domestic consequence management. This all sounded very close to the approaches under the Trudeau government, notwithstanding a different kind of twenty-first-century terrorism that was simultaneously 'homegrown' and transnational. Continuity was also present in the Martin government's decision to opt out of BMD in early

2005, echoing the Mulroney government's decision not to participate in the Reagan government's SDI program. Like the Conservatives, the Liberals had made their decision only after signing a separate agreement ensuring that NORAD would retain its warning and assessment function whether or not Canada was officially part of BMD (Lagassé, 2006).

The choice of army general Rick Hillier as chief of the defence staff consolidated a shift in the defence policy agenda away from cost cutting and niche continental security roles and toward an expansive vision for the CF to address the complex realities of a post-9/11 world. The defence policy statement, released in the early months of 2005, reflected Hillier's concept of a renewed and transformed CF, in keeping with the broader objectives of the prime minister to restore Canada's 'role of pride and influence in the world', the title of the government's *International Policy Statement* (Government of Canada, 2005a). The cabinet promised to inject $13 billion in new defence expenditures over a five-year period, a significant departure from long-term trends. Many of the items on the Martin Liberals' defence policy agenda, like the defence of North America in cooperation with the US and the maintenance of international peace and security through the UN and NATO, reflected the concerns of their predecessors. However, the emphasis on the intensity of new threats in a post-9/11 security climate added weight and urgency to existing alternatives on the policy agenda to restructure and reform the Canadian military.

When the Conservative government of Stephen Harper came to power in January 2006, much of the groundwork for change in Canadian defence policy had already been laid by the outgoing Liberals. The agenda for change had been set and it was now up to the Conservatives to act upon their promises to rebuild the military and restore its prestige as a proud Canadian institution.

DEFENCE POLICY ALTERNATIVES

This section will focus on the evolution of ideas about defence policy alternatives circulated among members of specialist communities in and around government.

When Prime Minister Diefenbaker agreed in 1959 to acquire weapons systems that required nuclear warheads, he was responding to dominant ideas in domestic and international policy communities that supported nuclear deterrence as the solution to the Soviet threat. The nuclear warheads, moreover, were seen by defence minister Douglas Harkness and the military establishment as a necessary part of the joint Canada–US air defence system, or North American Air Defence Command (NORAD) established in 1957. Nevertheless, not all Canadians or Canadian politicians, including minister of external affairs Howard Green, believed that the acquisition of nuclear arms served the best interests of continental or international security.

The prime minister took the weapons but not the warheads. A divided domestic policy community contributed to policy fragmentation and Diefenbaker's indecision. With the Department of National Defence and the Department of External

Affairs at loggerheads, the prime minister could not make up his mind whose advice to follow. Seizing upon the window of opportunity born of bureaucratic in-fighting and Diefenbaker's antipathy to US President Kennedy, Green advocated nuclear disarmament. The stance had the backing of other important people in the government, deputy minister of external affairs Norman Robertson not the least. The feasibility of this alternative, however, was called into question by the prevailing conditions of the Cold War, especially as they related to the integrated Canadian–American defence relationship.

A less radical policy alternative was to put a stop to the introduction of nuclear weapons into Canada. This was an idea that proved to be popular both in and outside of government. Leading public interest groups, including women's organizations such as the Voice of Women, favoured this alternative, as did the opposition Liberals up until the end of 1962. But a policy alternative, a core of supporters within the policy community, and policy entrepreneurs were not enough to foster change. The prime minister was not onside, neither were military leaders. Diefenbaker was not about to change Canadian government thinking on an issue that went to the heart of the country's alliance politics and the relationship with the United States.

Diefenbaker's refusal to play the Cold Warrior, and come out in favour of nuclear warheads, or to definitively reject the weapons in favour of an anti-nuclear stance, led to his defeat in 1963. The Liberal government of Lester Pearson that succeeded him would not make the same mistake. One of the first acts of the new government was to acquire the nuclear warheads that John Diefenbaker had avoided so clumsily. The Liberals made a further promise to establish a parliamentary committee on defence, which also was quickly done.

The Liberals also moved, under the very forceful defence minister Paul Hellyer, to assert greater control over the military and military expenditures. The parliamentary committee set to work on Canadian defence, but Hellyer saw their studies as purely advisory. He would undertake an internal review, and he would carry a White Paper to the cabinet. As the minister surveyed his fiefdom, he immediately found it suffering from 'a deeply-rooted disease—the existence of three independent and competing legal entities in an era when technology and common sense demanded one' (Hellyer, 1990: 32, 36). Each of the services had drafted individual war plans and acquired equipment without consulting one another. To the defence minister, the solution to these redundancies was the unification of the services: placing the army, navy, and air force in a single organization under a single chief, ridding the Canadian military of duplicate functions and imposing closer cooperation among the branches. This would allow the government to better monitor the services and their activities, ease some of the resistance ministers had faced when trying to implement novel policies and directives, and streamline the administration of a cumbersome defence department. The idea of unification had the important support of Prime Minister Pearson, who had suggested something along these lines in the House of Commons in 1960 and General Charles Foulkes, the retired chairman of the Chiefs of Staff Committee and the most respected soldier in the country, as well as some other former senior military officers (Hellyer, 1990: 38–40). More problematic, however, were the current members of the Canadian military, whose opposition to Hellyer's plans stemmed from their eagerness to protect existing roles, funding pools, and traditions.

Efficiency alone justified Hellyer in his drive to unify the Canadian forces, but the measure offered other benefits. Specifically, Hellyer hoped that unifying the services would secure enough savings to acquire more equipment and commit more resources to NATO and the peacekeeping operations of the Canadian Forces, without increasing the defence budget. Ten years before, 42.9 per cent of the military budget had gone for equipment; by the early 1960s, the figure was 13.6 per cent (Granatstein, 1986: 225). Hellyer wanted the equipment budget to find its way to 25 per cent. He told the defence committee that Canada had 'the best housed, best dressed and best fed but most poorly equipped force in the western world' (Saywell, *CAR*, 1963: 339).

The idea for unification of the armed services was also a solution, the defence minister asserted, to the changing conditions of the Cold War. Hellyer told the parliamentary committee that the world had moved on from the darkest days of the Cold War. An all-out nuclear exchange was in his view now the least likely war scenario (Saywell, *CAR*, 1963: 338). Because the superpowers possessed enough nuclear weapons to destroy each other many times over, a Soviet or American nuclear attack on its adversary would be suicidal. The idea circulated among Western defence planners that the USSR would test NATO's resolve by mounting smaller challenges in Western Europe. In such a case, the costs to human life made the nuclear alternative untenable. Instead, the US secretary of defense, Robert McNamara, proposed the adoption of a doctrine known as 'flexible response', meaning that NATO should tailor its military retaliations to fit with the severity of a Soviet attack. Hellyer agreed that the most probable Soviet aggression would not be with nuclear arms, 'and the problem would be to meet fire with appropriate fire in an effort to prevent escalation' (Hellyer, 1990: 34). The money saved through unification would enable the Canadian Forces to adapt to these changing realties (Bland, 1995: 88), and to become a more flexible fighting force with the ability to fill various collective security and defence roles at home and abroad.

The 1971 defence White Paper, issued by the government of Pierre Trudeau, was a sharp turn away from the Hellyer exercise. *Defence in the 1970s* was formulated as a response to seven interrelated ideas circulating in domestic policy circles. First of all, in an era of détente, when relations between the Soviet Union and the US had cooled down, the Cold War problem was receding from its privileged position at the top of the government's decision agenda. This suggested and justified a less robust Canadian stance towards the Soviet Union. Second, against the background of the Vietnam War and a troubled US domestic scene, the Canada–United States partnership was unsettled. A tougher attitude toward Canada was also apparent in the administration of Richard Nixon, which was unwilling to treat Canada as in any way 'special'. Third, the safeguarding of the homeland was much on the minds of politicians and their voters. There had been a police strike in Montreal in 1969 and riots at the Kingston Penitentiary in 1971, while, jammed in between those incidents, a major internal security crisis hinted at wider eruptions to come when the Front de libération du Québec (FLQ) mounted a terrorist threat in 1970. In addition, the protection of Canadian sovereignty had become a live issue after the sailing of the US ship *Manhattan* through Canada's Arctic waters in 1969 (Head and Trudeau, 1995: 30).

As costs rose and with the 1967 expulsion of Canadian soldiers serving with UNEF, peacekeeping had fallen out of fashion, a fourth consideration. Fifth, inflation was on the rise: the term of the time was the wage-price spiral, and it left little room for defence expenditure. Sixth, there was the political perception that the Department of National Defence's administration needed to be brought under control: it was asking for too much and was apt to think it ought to set defence policy rather than the government (Bland, 1993: 216). The new government complained of the lack of civilian input into defence policy, lingering inefficiencies with the department's fiscal and procurement processes, and the military's perceived tendency to resist cabinet directives. Lastly, the morale of the CF was dragging, with unsympathetic politicians, reduced force levels (102,000 in 1968; 90,000 in 1971), base closures, static budgets, and little money for new equipment (Dobell, 1985: 267).

With all these concerns in mind, the prime minister's solution was to make defence policy follow from foreign policy, not the other way around. And as to foreign policy, that had to be brought home, freed from the Pearsonian internationalists who put the world first, rather than their country. Trudeau's *Foreign Policy for Canadians* statement in 1970, which received favourable notices from the media, placed the emphasis on things national, domestic unity and economic growth in particular, the latter preoccupation prompting analyst James Eayrs to quip that foreign policy would now be 'for beavers' (Saywell, *CAR*, 1971: 293, 306). Nevertheless, by the end of Trudeau's term as prime minister, internationalist ideas had returned to vogue, motivating the government to assume more active foreign and defence policies. Military spending accordingly inched back up.

But the window for a true renaissance for the military and defence priorities would not be opened until the election of another government. Under the Mulroney Conservatives, a defence policy White Paper was released in 1987, entitled *Challenge and Commitment—A Defence Policy for Canada*. Written before the collapse of the Soviet Union and end of the Cold War, it put forward a distinct policy alternative—a strong Cold War defence vision—that was framed as an explicit rejection of 15 years of Trudeau government practice.

Mulroney's first defence minister, Robert Coates, arrived at DND with a number of ideas for refurbishing the military. To improve morale, Coates announced that the services were to be issued distinct uniforms, and unique ranks were reinstituted in the navy as well—this was a small step away from the Hellyer revolution, but it was not accompanied by any reorganization of the CF's unified force structure. Coates doubled the procurement of new naval frigates from 6 to 12 and suggested an extra $10 billion in defence spending. Finance minister

Michael Wilson, however, stood in the way of any increases. Coates, at any rate, was soon gone, the victim of a sordid little scandal.

Unlike Coates, his successor as minister[2] was a powerful figure in the government. Erik Nielsen completed the Canada–United States air defence modernization negotiations begun by the Trudeau Liberals, confirming that continental defence remained a central facet of Canadian defence policy. He then turned to the policy review. While Coates had intended to encourage a public debate about defence matters, Nielsen decided that the review should be internal to DND. That way it would be faster and better informed. Perhaps reacting to the Finance department's reluctance to increase defence spending or echoing a sentiment that the CF should focus more on Canada's specific national interests, Nielsen began by asking the policy group at DND to examine the feasibility of withdrawing all the CF from Europe. A memo outlining a CF withdrawal from Europe was drafted and circulated among high-ranking DND officials. Many were shocked, among them the assistant deputy minister in the policy group, John Anderson. He encouraged his minister to travel to Washington and other NATO capitals to discuss the idea with Canada's allies. American and Western European defence ministers were predictably unhappy that Ottawa was considering a further retreat from its NATO commitments. Nielsen quietly dropped the proposal. Anderson had succeeded in undermining his political superior's policy alternative without challenging ministerial authority. Reputational hazards, and alliance politics, in the international sphere were persuasive. Nielsen had to concede.[3]

While Nielsen and senior DND officials were negotiating the NORAD renewal, the Mulroney government released the preliminary findings of its foreign policy review. Internationalist in outlook, the review declared that Canada should expand its global efforts in a number of areas, from arms control to development. The review also touched on the commitment-capability gap, the maintenance of a strategic balance between the superpowers, and the importance of protecting Canadian sovereignty in the Arctic. The emphasis on the Arctic was a clear reflection of concerns about both the *Polar Sea*, a US coastguard ice-breaker that had in 1985 challenged Canada's sovereignty claims over a 200-mile zone off the Arctic Archipelago, and foreign submarine activities in Northern waters. Canada had a unique security interest that could be undermined by friends and foes alike. What military capabilities might it need to guard that interest, as well as the numerous other capabilities implicit in the performance of traditional collective security and continental defence obligations?

Perrin Beatty, at 36 already seasoned as a cabinet member in the Clark and Mulroney governments, replaced Nielsen as minister of national defence in June 1986. He was a surprise appointment, having no background, aptitude, or experience in the area. Certainly Beatty was surprised. 'You're kidding,' he said to Mulroney when asked to assume the defence portfolio. The prime minister told him that it was no joke, and Beatty was off to National Defence headquarters. By his own recollection, he arrived there with the biases against the military shared by so many young men of the Vietnam War era. These did not last. The minister was won over by the senior civilians and CF personnel that now surrounded him, led by chief of defence staff Paul Manson, deputy minister Bev Dewar, and the new assistant deputy minister for policy, Robert Fowler. Beatty's judgement, quickly formed, was that they were dedicated, knowledgeable, and thoroughly professional servants of Canada, not at all the clichés thrown up by the anti-military rhetoric of the 1960s and 1970s. His mandate from the prime minister was to reconstitute the CF as an influential, effective fighting force, and to construct a White Paper around that concept. Beatty facilitated change at a time of policy renewal, in accordance with predictable cycles of investment and disinvestment in Canadian national defence (Kingdon, 2003: 186–7). He conceived of his role as one of team leadership, actively encouraging entrepreneurial activity from the experts within the department, and acting as the department's external entrepreneur—inside the cabinet room and with the public.

Beatty reignited the defence review with the dynamism and energy he had displayed in earlier cabinet portfolios. At the core of the vision the minister and DND officials developed for the new defence program was the notion that a state could not be sovereign if it depended on others for its protection or had to be overly deferential toward a powerful neighbour. The linchpin of defence policy, as DND policy experts advised and as Beatty expressed it, was the protection and enhancement of 'our rights and responsibilities as a sovereign nation' (Eayrs, 1987: 11). Beatty had no intention of releasing a purely rhetorical document, instead wanting his White Paper to be well informed and honest about the military's shortfalls and the investments needed to correct those deficiencies. More than policy renewal, what was needed was sweeping changes to how government, and Canadians, perceived the military and its contributions to national life. The Canadian military Beatty so quickly came to respect deserved no less, given the sacrifices Canada asked them to make and the burdens they had been forced to shoulder for years of overstretch.

The White Paper, *Challenge and Commitment*, included an increase in real defence expenditures, the acquisition of modern equipment and refurbishment of older platforms, the full implementation of the 1985 NORAD modernization program, and steps to further Canadian aerospace defence capabilities. Canadian commitments to NATO, moreover, would continue with a renewed emphasis on the defence of southern Germany. Maritime surveillance in the Arctic would also be stepped up with the acquisition of nuclear-powered submarines. But with the end of the Cold War, the popularity of ideas for renewal and reinvestment outlined by the 1987 White Paper was short-lived. In 1989, the federal budget for defence was cut by $2.7 billion over five years and plans for military procurement were scrapped.

When the Liberal government of Jean Chrétien came to power in 1993, budget deficits were everything: cost cutting and efficiency were the dominant ideas circulating among policy experts in and around government. The problem of money fed into the problem of what kind of military was needed for a post–Cold War world; one alternative would be uniquely suited to domestic and peace support operations, while another option would be a force designed to operate across the spectrum of conflict. Defence objectives and force-structuring choices were thus on the governmental agenda. In the 1990s the Canadian military were deployed on a variety of operations, ranging from a conventional war-fighting operation in the Persian Gulf, to peace enforcement in the Balkans and Africa, to aid of the civil power at Oka, Quebec, during a confrontation between government authorities and a group of Aboriginals in the summer of 1990. On the one hand, Ottawa's penchant for deploying the military on UN and domestic operations suggested that the CF might forgo war-fighting capabilities in favour of a constabulary role, as more an armed police than a traditional military. While this type of force structure would limit the CF's ability to take part in future conventional wars, it would cost less to maintain and would fit with Canadians' perception of themselves as the globe's pre-eminent peacekeepers. On the other hand, the Persian Gulf War had demonstrated that conventional wars were not impossible in a post–Cold War world. Indeed the Gulf War had become a symbol, for some, of a new dawn for international cooperation and collective security in the aftermath of the Cold War. Were the CF to lack units equipped to participate in another such war, Canada's reputation as a reliable military ally and collective security contributor would vanish.

These questions about the future shape of the CF were clearly linked to the problem of Canada's defence relations with the United States. With the Soviet Union gone, the United States was the sole remaining superpower; the immediate post–Cold War era was a time of unrivalled American hegemony. The defence of North America and contributions to UN and NATO endeavours alongside the American armed forces could serve the Canadian national interest in two ways. First, defending the continent in cooperation with the United States reassured Washington that Ottawa took American national security seriously and that Canada was not a defence liability. Second, since the United States fielded the largest and best-equipped military in the world, UN and coalition operations in cooperation with the US would allow Canada to help maintain international security while cutting defence expenditures. Hence, the Canadian military embraced the policy alternative of closer ties with their US counterparts and sought means to enhance the capacity of the CF to operate in the same environment as US forces.

Chrétien's first minister of defence, David Collenette, was charged with the preparation of a new defence White Paper. Paul Martin, the Liberal finance minister, was pushing for deep cuts while Lloyd Axworthy, the minister of human resources and the Liberals' foreign policy expert, made peacekeeping his priority on the defence policy agenda. Outside government, these ideas were shaped into a comprehensive policy package by the Canada 21 Council, chaired by Ivan Head and directed by Janice Stein of the University of Toronto. The council advocated a move away from high-intensity combat responsibilities to an emphasis on peacekeeping, the delivery of humanitarian aid, the protection of Canadian sovereignty and aid of the civil power. This, the council argued, would be cheaper and well suited to deployments on most UN operations. In addition, they urged Ottawa to use preventive diplomacy to halt the spread of weapons of mass destruction, help resolve disputes between and within states, and address the emerging threat of environmental degradation (Stein, 1994). The council had the support of several Bloc Québécois and NDP MPs, who played a critical role in 'softening up' the policy community and encouraging receptivity in parliament to Canada 21's ideas during the policy review process.

At the other end of the policy spectrum, civilian and military officials at DND, including the respected CDS General John de Chastelain, were unified in their staunch opposition to Canada 21's defence policy alternative. This camp in the domestic policy community argued that abandoning the CF's combat-capabilities would handicap the country, hollow out Canada's international reputation, and hamper a safeguarding of the Canadian national interest. The maintenance of a multipurpose, combat-capable force with the flexibility to participate in many kinds of missions at home and abroad was the alternative favoured by the defence establishment. DND sought to dissuade the government from implementing the recommendations of the Canada 21 Council.

A report from the Special Joint Committee on Canada's Defence Policy, established to gather expert advice and parliamentary input, supported the status quo as defended by DND over the innovative alternative advocated by Canada 21. Budgets, however, remained an abiding consideration and the more ambitious elements of the draft (emerging out of consultations with senior military officers) were subsequently amended to account for the government's planned budget cuts. The 1994 White Paper was in tune with the economic conditions of the day, scaling down the CF both in terms of civilian and military personnel. Nevertheless, rather than the niche alternative advocated by the Canada 21 Council, Canada would retain a fighting force with the ability to operate across the full spectrum of potential operations. Continuity prevailed over change in the Canadian defence policy community, as the voices of the defence establishment and senior bureaucrats proved more persuasive than Canada 21's contribution to the defence policy debate.

In December 2003, Paul Martin became prime minister of Canada, succeeding Jean Chrétien. They were both Liberals, but Martin promised more dynamic governance, and nowhere more than in international affairs. He initiated a foreign and defence policy review shortly after he became Canada's head of government. In April 2005, his government released a defence policy document as part of an *International Policy Statement* that aimed to integrate foreign, defence, development, and trade policies. At the heart of the new government's initiatives was the acknowledgement that policy renewal would require more resources and dedicated funding. With Canada's economic house now in good order, defence spending was becoming a more attractive and viable policy option.

There was, moreover, an unusually unified constituency of support for increased defence spending in the domestic policy community and among Canada's political elites. The opposition Conservatives had also promised to increase the defence budget, as did the NDP, albeit with the caveat that new defence dollars should fund peacekeeping operations and improve soldiers' welfare, rather than enhancing war-fighting capabilities and equipment and rendering the CF more interoperable with the American armed forces. Influential individuals and groups within the policy community, including Wendy Dobson of the C.D. Howe Institute, former Canadian trade negotiators Bill Dymond and Michael Hart, and Thomas d'Aquino of the Canadian Council of Chief Executives, also supported increased spending on security as part of a 'deeper integration' of North America. The 'Big Idea' was that the Canadian interest in a seamless border and a shield from US protectionism could realistically be achieved by meeting US security objectives (Jackson, 2003: 32–3).

Change took the immediate form of the Martin government's first defence minister, David Pratt. Closely tied to and admired by the defence community, Pratt had endorsed a Canadian contribution to the Iraq war, loudly advocated higher defence spending, and was a strong supporter of a Canadian commitment to US Ballistic Missile Defence planning. Early on indeed, in a January 2004 letter to American secretary of defense Donald Rumsfeld, Pratt all but declared that Canada would take part in missile defence. That letter had the approval of the Prime Minister's Office. Martin's selection of Pratt, it seemed, heralded an era of increased military spending and closer Canada–United States defence relations.

DND headquarters greeted Pratt's arrival with cautious optimism. Within Kenneth Calder's policy group, there was the sense that the new defence minister would be able to push a Canadian role in missile defence through Cabinet. Pratt's ability to secure substantial defence dollars, however, was doubted. While there was hope that the defence budget might rise, the policy group assumed that the amount would not be enough to bridge the commitment-capability gap, especially if the CF was expected to contribute additional resources to continental defence. Given these budgetary limitations, defence officials sought to devise a policy alternative that would protect existing capabilities and contribute to bolstering homeland security as well as meet the test of fiscal feasibility. A draft defence policy statement during the first months of the defence policy review argued that the CF should take on fewer international commitments. The money saved could be used to bolster the CF's homeland and North American defence capabilities. Likewise, if the military deployed on fewer expeditionary operations, the CF could dedicate more resources to domestic consequence management capabilities. This assessment of Canada's military options was echoed in the government's *National Security Policy*, published by the Privy Council Office in April 2004. It declared that the CF would be deployed more selectively and strategically, a subtle acknowledgement that the military's past operational tempo was excessive and detrimental to the armed forces's long-term viability. In addition, the *National Security Policy* hinted that the CF would be asked to devote more time, personnel, and resources to domestic and continental security measures.

The arrival of another defence minister in the person of Bill Graham after the June 2004 federal election changed the direction of the defence policy review. Graham came to the post directly after serving as minister of foreign affairs and was, therefore, more apt to see defence policy as part of a broader foreign policy agenda. Consequently, he favoured a policy alternative that would see Canada play an activist role overseas rather than recede into the shadows of Fortress

North America. Yet Graham also understood the importance of placing the frayed Canada–US relationship on a better footing in the aftermath of Canada's decision not to support the 2003 US intervention in Iraq. Pratt's efforts to increase the defence budget and bring Canada into the US missile defence system continued to be high priorities on the defence policy agenda. Clearly, a policy that would both expand Canada's presence abroad and ratchet up the country's continental capabilities could not be achieved without a considerable increase in defence spending. Graham persuaded the cabinet to accept a considerable jump in expenditure.

Softening up the policy community was made easier by the entry into the equation of a new chief of the defence staff, General Rick Hillier, who had entrepreneurial ambitions right from the start to transform the Canadian military into a force that could address the realities of a post-9/11 world. Hillier had considerable experience with and knowledge of the US army, and he was much impressed by the American concept of the three-block war, a strategic formula for fighting asymmetrical wars that involved the carrying out of humanitarian, policing, and traditional combat roles simultaneously. He believed that failed and failing states were crucibles for extremism and terrorism and, therefore, the most pressing contemporary threat to international peace and security. His ideas quickly gained a wide following, not least with the prime minister and minister of defence. Hillier assumed control of the government's defence policy review, and was effectively given the freedom to shape it as he wished. When the defence policy statement was published in early 2005, it was very much a reflection of Hillier's ideas for a reinvigorated Canadian military, prepared to take on three-block stabilization operations in failed and failing states. This came with a pricetag of an additional $13 billion over the next five years, but it was an amount that the prime minister was willing to pay. So too, apparently, were many Canadians.

The three-block-war alternative survived the defeat of the Martin government by the Conservative opposition led by Stephen Harper in the January 2006 federal election. Harper was already a convert to Hillier's vision and, like Prime Minister Martin before him, sought to do his part to reassert Canada's international influence. The announcement of a $15 billion funding package for the military in the summer of 2006 signalled that security and defence would remain major priorities on the Conservatives' decision agenda. The extension of the CF mission in Afghanistan to 2009 implemented the Liberal government's policy recommendations for a three-block war, although critics argued that the subordination of diplomatic and development initiatives to military operations did not represent a 'whole-of-government' commitment to that part of the world.

DEFENCE POLITICS

This section will focus on the politics of defence policy making, particularly the shifts in national mood, direction of interest group pressures, and significant

jurisdictional change and turnover in government that influence policy entrepreneurs and the relative success or failure of competing policy alternatives on
the governmental agenda.

The Diefenbaker government's (1957–63) indecision over the issue of acquiring nuclear warheads was shaped by competing bureaucratic cultures and perspectives in the making of Canadian defence policy. The Department of External
Affairs and Department of National Defence assumed opposite sides of the
nuclear weapons debate, with the former pushing for nuclear disarmament and
the latter calling for Canada to take the warheads as part of the country's obligations under the NORAD alliance. In this case, jurisdictional competition made
decision making more difficult—indeed preventing any decision from being
made at all. The stalemate was only made worse by the election in 1960 of US
President John F. Kennedy, a leader the prime minister did not trust or like. The
feeling was mutual, and the continuity of cooperation that had characterized
Canadian defence policy toward the United States was shaken for the first time
in almost 20 years. The national mood was also split between those advocating
for a strong Cold War stance with the Americans and organized interest groups
pushing for nuclear disarmament.

In the context of prevailing geopolitics, putting a stop to the introduction of
nuclear weapons into Canada was a less radical, and more possible, policy
option. It was an attractive idea that had a good deal of public support (Granatstein, 1981: 342). A growing and vocal component of Canadian civil society,
including prominent church and women's groups, agreed with the views of the
two leading advocates, foreign minister Howard Green and his deputy Norman
Robertson; it was also the policy of the Liberal Party, headed by Nobel Peace Prize
winner Lester B. Pearson. National unity considerations were another factor, as
Ottawa's defence policy, and the spectre of nuclear warheads, faced growing
opposition in Quebec throughout the 1950s (Rioux, 2005: 18).

The prime minister, however, remained constrained by broader political concerns, namely, Canada's alliance politics and the relationship with the United
States. As much as the national mood and advocates within government made
an anti-nuclear stance politically attractive, the hard realities of the Cold War
dictated that change could only go so far. Division within the government and
bureaucracy led to an incoherent and fragmented Canadian defence policy that
worried and puzzled the US administration.

The next crisis for the weakened Diefenbaker came soon, toppling him from
power. The Americans, tired of the prime minister's delays over the nuclear warhead issue, made their concerns public early in 1963. Diefenbaker was reneging
on commitments clearly undertaken, they said. At the same time the opposition
Liberals switched sides in the debate, coming out in favour of taking the
weapons. Public backlash over perceived mishandling of the Cuban missile crisis,
a divided and weakened Conservative government, and an openly critical American administration led by a charismatic president, had handed the Liberals an
opportunity to regain the reins of power that was simply too good to pass up.
Pearson couched his about-face in the language of a responsible friend and

neighbour: 'I am ashamed if we accept commitments and then refuse to discharge them' (Hillmer and Granatstein, 1994: 205). Pressure mounted on Diefenbaker to clarify the situation, but he would not—or could not. Harkness resigned from the cabinet, as did others. The government fell on a vote of non-confidence in Parliament on March 8.

In the ensuing election, Pearson at first had public opinion firmly on his side, but Diefenbaker fought back. There was always a segment of the population for whom other policy considerations invariably took a back-seat to the problem of Canadian sovereignty—especially vis-à-vis the United States. Québécois opposition to nuclear weapons, moreover, had clearly reached a tipping point by 1963 (Gow, 1970: 114). When Diefenbaker angrily insisted that Canada would not be pressured into taking US nuclear weapons, his words were much more an appeal to nationalists of all stripes than they were to the many organized interest groups mobilizing against nuclear weapons. Pearson won the election, one of the very few in Canadian history when national defence was an issue, but was deprived of a majority government by Diefenbaker's vigorous campaigning.

Despite the Liberals' minority government status, it was dedicated to action and, in particular, to taking control of the military and military expenditures (Bland, 1997: 58). The time was suddenly ripe for change. The public, shaken by near-nuclear war over Cuba and the near-disintegration of the Canadian–American defence alliance in 1962–3, was receptive to movement and ideas. Within the cabinet, the minister of finance, Walter Gordon, was intent on bringing the government's expenditures under control (Gordon, 1977: 138–9). Politics in the international sphere were also in a state of flux. After the Cuban crisis, the Cold War seemed to be thawing: a partial international nuclear Test Ban Treaty was signed by Canada on 8 August 1963. Suggestions for the restructuring and reordering of the armed forces were in the politico-bureaucratic air.

Meanwhile, political turnover within the defence ministry came in the shape of an ambitious, deeply moral, and aggressive young minister who was ready to seize control of the defence agenda—with the active support of the prime minister. When Hellyer became minister, he moved decisively, cutting programs and cancelling others, like plans for naval frigates. Although he may have preferred the finance minister's seat, Hellyer made the most of the defence portfolio, seeing it as a 'tidy ship' for his political fortunes (Bland, 1995: 69). His dynamism, in the words of the *Canadian Annual Review*, won him 'wide acclaim' and created 'an appropriate atmosphere' for a new defence policy (Saywell, *CAR*, 1964: 214), to take the form of a White Paper, a formal declaration of government intentions.

Hellyer's proposal to unify the armed services had the support of the prime minister as well as of several former senior military officers (Hellyer, 1999: 38–40), but the defence community was split with many current members of the Canadian military opposed to the minister's initiative. The existing force structure was advantageous to members of the military elite and each sought to protect their own policy turf from intrusions by government or some other centralized authority. This was a form of clientelism that could very easily have resulted in governmental inertia (Kingdon, 2003: 152). The Department of External Affairs, complaining that they had been excluded from the decision making, joined forces with the air force and navy chiefs to oppose the defence minister's policy agenda. Nevertheless, few concessions were made to Hellyer's critics in the bargaining process. Prime Minister Pearson continued to support Hellyer, signing off on his draft White Paper without significant revision. Geopolitical constellations also seemed favourably aligned. Unification appeared to be the right alternative for Canada in adapting to the American flexible response doctrine for NATO; the money saved from avoiding the duplication of functions could buy more equipment and resources for use by the CF, across a range of options, serving with the country's allies. Most importantly, from the point of view of the prime minister and minister of finance, costs would be kept in check.

Political turnover was again a significant factor in Canadian defence policy when a Liberal government, led by Pierre Trudeau, was elected in 1968. This was a prime minister who refused to tow the traditional line. Though far from an expert, Trudeau was an intellectual with strong convictions about world affairs. He believed that good-versus-evil views of the Cold War were simplistic, aggravated an unnecessary superpower conflict, and prevented Canada from pursuing policies that served its national interests rather than those of the NATO allies. Trudeau, indeed, had been prominently quoted as saying that NATO ran Canadian foreign policy (Granatstein and Bothwell, 1990: 8). Moreover, it was an era of détente, a word coined to describe a relaxation in superpower tension that was characterized by a willingness to find areas of agreement. The prime minister believed that the time was right to bring foreign and defence policies home and for national interests to come before ambiguous international obligations to collective defence. Trudeau would wield considerable control over the drafting of the defence White Paper.

Prime Minister Trudeau was also, in many respects, in tune with changes taking place in the national mood. The politics of the time were nationalist. There had been some of that in Hellyer's desire to build unified armed forces but by late in the 1960s the political discourse was dominated by the view that Canada had to find its own way in the world. Washington's increasingly forceful prosecution of the Vietnam War had disillusioned Canadians and made them question the intimate relationship with the United States. A distinction had to be drawn between Canada's positions and American foreign and domestic policies that might, Canadians feared, overwhelm their own. Book after angry book, with titles like *The Star-Spangled Beaver*, excoriated Canada's silent surrender to the Yankee dollar and the US war machine. Defence analyst James Eayrs, so certain in the early 1960s that Canada's sovereignty mattered less than its security, was advocating neutrality late in the decade. There was nationalism of another sort too, as Quebec's Quiet Revolution propelled it toward separate status and away from Canada. Trudeau thought that it was Canada that needed saving, not the world. Many Canadians, wondering about the country's future, could not help but agree.

The popularity of United Nations peacekeeping had also diminished since the heady days of Pearson and his Nobel Peace Prize. The operation in the Congo (1960–4), to which Canada had contributed mightily, had divided UN members and almost bankrupt the world body, while Canada's contingent in UNEF in the Middle East had been unceremoniously shown the door by Egypt's President Nasser in 1967, souring Canadians on peacekeeping and causing many to question why so much money had been spent, for so little result.

The calculus of putting unity and national development to the fore, and the world in the background, arose from Quebec nationalism, concerns about the economy, fears of American power and influence, and from the anxious national moods that accompanied them. On the other side of the equation, Pearsonian internationalists, pro-defence advocacy groups, and those with ties to the demoralized CF were the natural critics of the new direction in Canadian strategy. Although the prime minister continued to prioritize Canadian sovereignty and continental security over overseas commitments, Trudeau accepted that the political climate was such that the internationalists were still powerful. Organized political forces in and around government would be effective in limiting the scope of cuts to defence spending, the size of the military and Canada's NATO contributions. A 1969 DND review, which considered pulling the Canadian Forces out of Europe, never came to light. Nevertheless, Canada's NATO-Europe contribution would be cut by half and the nuclear weapons role in Europe would be discontinued.

There was no input (and no request for input) into the unilateral NATO decision from the United States, but there was understanding. The American secretary of defense, Melvin Laird, respected Ottawa's decision to reduce Canada's contribution to NATO, especially in light of the Nixon administration's own desire to scale-back global commitments. Indeed, the Canadian force reduction in Europe set an interesting precedent. Should détente last and the superpower conflict stabilize, the United States might decide to cut its own force levels in Europe. Some of Trudeau's reasoning could then be repackaged to justify American retrenchment. The US national security advisor Henry Kissinger did not demur, while the influential senator William Fulbright cited the Trudeau initiative to promote the reduction of American forces in Europe. Politics south of the border would not impede the momentum for change.

When the Mulroney Conservatives came to power in the 1984 federal election, American opinion would not be so easily taken for granted. As is so often the case when political turnover occurs at the executive level, policy change was driven by the new government's desire to distinguish itself from its predecessor. The new prime minister pursued a defence policy agenda that was much more in keeping with traditional Cold War ideas about collective defence.

The national mood, however, was contradictory. It called for more attention both to home defence *and* overseas defence. There was a widespread sense that Trudeau had presided over a rust-out of the Canadian military, and that Canada had acquired a reputation as a bad ally in NATO, living off the efforts of others

(Bland, 1993: 220). A peace movement also thrived, a loose collection of labour, feminist, student, and anti-nuclear groups galvanized by the stridently anti-Soviet US President Ronald Reagan. They were not part of the Conservatives' electoral base, however, and the government was clear from the first instance about what they thought the public wanted and the country needed. They were determined to nourish the military they believed the Liberals had starved and reclaim the international stature they were sure Trudeau had squandered.

Because better relations with the United States was one of the prime minister's major personal objectives, Washington's views about Canadian defence policy were important. The conditions of détente had dissipated and President Reagan's secretary of defense, Caspar Weinberger, pushed Canada to strengthen its con-tributions to NATO. Weinberger also invited Canada to take part in the Strategic Defense Initiative (SDI) and was eager to complete the continental aerospace modernization negotiations. The Reagan administration's 'call to arms' (Hampson, 1988: 68) in the fight against what he dubbed the 'evil' Soviet 'empire' set an example for many Conservatives. The Mulroney government gave a high pri-ority to closer defence ties with the United States: they were determined to build political capital in Washington (Ripsman, 2001: 101, 105).

The renewal of the NORAD agreement and the question of Canadian participa-tion in SDI represented the delicate bargain struck by the Conservatives in bridg-ing the gulf between the national mood in Canada and the expectations of American defence partners. After a year of contentious public and political delib-erations, the Mulroney cabinet declared that Canada would not be directly involved in SDI research. Yet Ottawa also stated that the Canadian government did not consider SDI research to be a violation of international treaties, such as the 1967 Outer Space Treaty (Collard Wexler et al., 2006: 45–6), as critics of the system claimed. Nor did SDI research contravene the popular Anti-Ballistic Mis-sile (ABM) Treaty, the Mulroney government noted, since this agreement only banned the *deployment* of a missile defence system. This carefully crafted position left open the possibility of a future Canadian role in ballistic missile defence. Leaving this possibility open was vital for Canada leading up to the NORAD renewal negotiations. Had Ottawa explicitly rejected a Canadian role in missile defence, NORAD might have lost its aerospace warning and assessment functions, which would have called the binational command's usefulness into question. In 1986 the Mulroney government's strategy paid dividends. The NORAD agreement was renewed, the binational command kept its aerospace warning and assess-ment functions, and Canada avoided a formal role in SDI research without ruling out future participation in an American BMD (Lagassé, 2006).

As for the Mulroney government's broader defence policy agenda, domestic and international politics were to conspire against its implementation. Orga-nized peace interest groups came together to oppose the defence review's ambi-tious program of increased spending and military procurement. Within Parliament, both the Liberals and NDP challenged key components of the Con-servative agenda, including the acquisition of nuclear-powered submarines. Important members of the Conservative cabinet, such as minister of external affairs Joe Clark and finance minister Michael Wilson, expressed opposition to the defence White Paper. The latter was particularly concerned with the projected increases to the defence budget, in light of the country's emerging debt crisis. The prime minister's power to shepherd his defence agenda through to implementation was dealt a blow when the 1988 election resulted in a reduced majority of seats. The free trade controversies had probably also made Mulroney more cautious about pursuing policies that Canadians might associate with hawkish American approaches, although the Americans themselves (as we saw) opposed aspects of the White Paper. By the time of the Soviet collapse, *Challenge and Commitment* had already become a dead letter. The transformation of the geopolitical landscape confirmed and reinforced the government's changing direction.

The Chrétien government was faced with a domestic political climate that, for the most part, saw defence spending as an unnecessary drain on already limited public resources. Canadians' first priorities were domestic ones. The new Liberal government understood that it could not justify cutting any other department or social services until a significant amount of money was extracted from the defence budget. Canadians could not be asked to weaken their healthcare and education programs while a large military structure facing no plausible threat was kept in place. In a similar vein, Chrétien knew that if the Liberals blinked on defence cuts, bureaucrats in other departments would be emboldened to mount their own opposition against the deficit measures.

Nevertheless, the Canada–United States relationship continued to be a political determinant of Canadian defence policy, counterbalancing calls for massive defence spending cuts. Although the United States government was never directly consulted over the course of the defence policy review, it was understood that Washington would express displeasure with the Canadian government if Canada's military expenditures fell too dramatically. Despite the apparent absence of a direct threat to North America, the United States expected that the CF should be able to contribute effective continental aerospace defence forces and to deploy adequately equipped units on stabilization operations overseas. Ottawa would not allow Washington to dictate Canadian policy, but part of that policy had always been to do 'just enough' so that defence did not become a major irritant in the bilateral relationship (Sokolsky, 2004: 10–11). The Liberal minister of national defence, David Collenette, rapidly established a close relationship with American defense secretary William J. Perry, appointed in February 1994. Perry was always polite about US imperatives, unlike NATO defence ministers from Britain and Germany, who let Collenette know just how disappointed they were in the aftermath of Canada's withdrawal of its NATO troops from Europe in 1992.

The Canadian military, under the rubric of interoperability, advocated closer ties with their US counterparts, both to reassure the Americans and as the most efficient way for Canada to contribute to building international security. But public opinion and national unity concerns represented a constraint. Quebecers were consistently the least supportive of increased defence spending, an attitude that represented a general feeling that Canadian defence policy too often responded to foreign interests rather than the values and interests of Canadians (Rioux, 2005: 20–1). A policy alternative with too much emphasis on the bilateral Canada–United States military relationship might make Ottawa seem subservient to Washington and indifferent toward other defence obligations. A balance had to be struck and explanations found for a public admiring of the US but chronically wary as well.

Against this background, the Liberals were anxious to play the politics of differentiation that the turnover of government offered. The Mulroney era had come in the public mind to stand for excess, scandal, and grandiosity. Chrétien promised to be the un-Mulroney, delivering clean, efficient, no-nonsense government. Mulroney had brought recession and deficits. Chrétien pledged that he would deal effectively with the economy. Mulroney had been associated with very close relations with the US—too close for the public, opinion polls revealed. The 1987 defence White Paper had overreached, right down to its glitzy cover and glossy photographs. The Liberals' White Paper would be a realist's statement, aligning the defence problems of the country with the world and the economy as it was, not as some Conservative politicians of the 1980s had wished it might be. Chrétien's reading of the national mood contributed to the Liberals' decision to aim at the problem of military expenditure as the primary target of their remaking of defence policy. Canadians' traditional preference for 'butter' over 'guns' had been amplified by the end of the Cold War. There was apt to be little opposition to the idea of a smaller military establishment, particularly in the wake of a very public scandal after Canadian soldiers brutalized and then murdered a teenage boy in Somalia. The spotlight shone on the crack Airborne Regiment, and not favourably. It was disbanded in early 1995.

The recommendations of a new, and influential, public interest group, the Canada 21 Council, gained a wide hearing but did not ultimately make its way into government policy. Organized political forces and elites within DND were able to overcome Canada 21's innovative policy alternative to refashion the CF into a 'common security' force. The department of defence's successful bargaining over the direction of policy was built, in part, on improvements to communication strategies and policy coherence resulting from efforts to transform DND's policy staff into a true 'policy shop'. The defence department was able to parlay the government's concerns with cost-cutting into a credible defence of the, albeit leaner, status quo.

Chrétien's successor, Paul Martin, wanted to do something newer and braver with foreign and defence policies: the integration of diplomatic, defence, and development policies in a 'whole-of-government' approach. Turnover played an important part in this thinking. Martin had brought Chrétien down, winning the Liberal Party over to the idea that the old man had had his day and forcing the prime minister's resignation. Martin had been for nine years Chrétien's finance minister, responsible for the mid-1990s cuts in the defence and foreign affairs budgets, but he associated himself with the school of thought arguing that Canada's international power and reputation had declined unacceptably in recent years (Molot and Hillmer, 2002). As prime minister, Martin would restore Canada's place of pride in the world. Part of the solution was to spend more on defence since this was also a prerequisite for building a close Canada–United States relationship. What is more, he would be the anti-Chrétien, vibrant and expansive after a decade of pale, frugal, prudent government. Martin gave interviews when he became prime minister in which he predicted his own very different decade in power. One indication of changing government preferences was an ostentatious prime ministerial visit to the defence department shortly after Martin took power.

Pressure from Washington was another political factor influencing Martin's decision to adopt a more forceful defence posture. When he was named United States ambassador to Canada in 2001, Paul Cellucci was given a single directive from American secretary of state Colin Powell: encourage Ottawa to reinvest in the Canadian military. The American envoy did so, repeatedly, forcefully, and publicly (Cellucci, 2005). Washington's message likely hit a nerve, even at a time when the US administration was unpopular in Canada.

The September 11, 2001, terror attacks contributed to political pressures from south of the border for increased Canadian defence spending. It also created a new domestic constituency in the business and trade communities to push for defence hikes and investment in national security infrastructure. Support for higher military expenditures crossed party lines as well. During the 2004 election campaign, the Conservative Party promised to increase the defence budget by $18 billion. Leader Stephen Harper's only displeasure with Liberals' own plan, $13 billion extra over five years, was that it was insufficient. Typically sceptical of defence expenditures, the New Democrats also admitted that more money for the CF was necessary.

The unusually unified support for increased defence spending among Canada's political elite reflected trends in the national mood that also favoured a substantial reinvestment in the Canadian military. The defence movement's relentless lobbying was without doubt partly responsible for the public's newfound interest in the CF. Nearly every journalistic report about the Canadian military included a reference to the CF's low level of funding. Most media outlets turned to members of the defence lobby for expert opinions about the military. If an accident or tragedy befell the CF, underfunding was often cited as the probable cause. Publications such as the reports of the Senate Standing Committee on National Security and Defence and the Conference of Defence Associations received a level of media attention usually reserved for healthcare debates. Pro-defence academics were among Canada's premier public intellectuals. J.L. Granatstein's book *Who Killed the Canadian Military?* was a national bestseller. Douglas Bland's edited volume *Canada Without Armed Forces?* was read by the prime minister; Bland was among Martin's most trusted advisors on the military. A few contrarian academics and left-wing think-tanks questioned the defence movement's statistics and premises, arguing that in relative terms defence expenditures were high, but they had little influence with decision makers or members of the general public and, consequently, little impact on what had become received wisdom.

Despite agreement on the necessity for increased defence expenditures, the public and the defence movement disagreed over the future of Canada–United States relations. While the pro-defence movement urged the Martin government to endorse a Canadian role in the US Ballistic Missile Defence (BMD) system and expand NORAD, public opinion by a small margin rejected missile defence and was lukewarm about cooperating more closely with the Americans in North America. Most members of the defence lobby argued that Canada had a vital interest in deploying the military to combat hostile groups and regimes as part of the United States' global war on terror. Prominent members of the movement had also encouraged Canada to take part in the Iraq war.

Canadians' disaffection with American President Bush and his administration's unilateral foreign policies, on the other hand, steered the public toward a preference for multilateral, UN-sanctioned operations. A majority of Canadians, therefore, preferred deployments of the CF on multinational peace support operations instead of American-led counterterrorism missions in places like Afghanistan. Public sentiments were reflected in an April 2004 poll finding that fighting terrorism abroad (that is, military interventions) ranked the lowest among Canadian's foreign policy priorities (POLLARA, 2004). Martin was well aware of this current running through the national mood: wariness toward the US seemed everywhere. Shortly before its defence policy statement was released, the Martin government announced that Canada would not take part in BMD. Despite the contradictions, the upward trajectory of defence in the Canadian national mood was unmistakable. People cared about their military, and that made the government more apt to care.

With elements in the political stream conducive to significant policy change, Martin moved to take advantage of the opportunity to pursue a more vigorous defence stance. This was to take the initial form of the government's 2004 *National Security Policy*, which prioritized North American defence and domestic consequence management over expeditionary operations abroad. This assessment was based upon existing budget allocations but public opinion also seemed to support this alternative over military engagements abroad; the same 2004 poll that attributed the least public support for military interventions abroad also ranked fighting terrorism at home as highest on the list of Canadians' spending priorities (POLLARA, 2004).

A turnover at the ministerial level when Bill Graham replaced David Pratt as minister of defence brought a new policy option to the fore. Graham would push for more spending and a larger overseas presence as well as improvements to border and homeland security. But first on Graham's agenda was BMD. In August 2004, Canadian and American defence officials signed an agreement permitting the binational NORAD command to transmit its ballistic missile warning and assessment data to BMD command and control. This achieved two objectives. First, the sharing of data ensured that NORAD could retain its warning and assessment function whether Canada was officially part of BMD or not. Second, the agreement laid the foundation either for an official Canadian role in BMD, or for a decision to stay aloof from BMD. Should Canada accept a role in BMD, the agreement could be used to argue that the choice followed naturally from the August document. If the Canadian government declined a role in BMD, the argument would be that Ottawa had already given the United States everything it needed, since the Pentagon was not planning to build any missile interceptors on Canadian soil. Whatever decision the Martin Cabinet made, the August 2004 agreement signalled that Canada was a reliable ally, and would not complicate the United States' BMD plans even if official participation in missile defence was declined—as it was in early 2005 (Lagassé, 2006).

Turnover in the office of the CDS amplified the trends emerging in government and the national mood. General Hillier became a vocal, and effective, advocate for increased military expenditures and equipment procurement, as well as for an internationally active CF, doing its part to stabilize failed and failing states in a post-9/11 world. Hillier was a charismatic and effective communicator of ideas, building political capital at the top with the prime minister and minister of defence, as well as among his policy staff and members of the armed forces. Bargaining, in the traditional sense, was minimal and ideas proved more potent than poker politics or strategic tradeoffs. The three-block war and the associated concept of 'whole-of-government' stabilization and reconstruction became the focus of the Martin Liberals' 2005 defence policy paper.

Following the 2006 election of a Conservative government led by Prime Minister Stephen Harper, the political climate underwent a period of flux. National defence and security increasingly competed with other foreign and domestic policy concerns, such as environmental degradation and climate change. Development perspectives returned to greater prominence, perhaps in response to criticism over the operation of the Afghanistan mission. Critics south of the border, bolstered by the return of the Democrats to majority status in the US Congress, challenged exclusively military approaches to stabilization as a solution to the ongoing crisis in Iraq. Nevertheless, defence policy remained a high priority on the Conservative's governmental agenda as political elites and influential lobby groups continued to promote investments in the Canadian military in the interests of continental security and international obligations abroad.

CHAPTER 7

The Evolution of National Defence Policy

This chapter concentrates on Canada's defence statements of 1964, 1971, 1987, 1994, and 2005, as instances of policy change, renewal, or innovation. In each case, policy entrepreneurs identified opportunities to advocate their favoured policy alternatives, either as solutions to pressing problems or in response to political conditions thought to be susceptible to successful advocacy. The opening of problem windows, where new problems or new problem-definitions made for changes on governmental agendas, frequently played a part. However, the process that led to the policy statement always began with political turnover. A new minister assumed office with a mandate for change and was at or near the centre of the entrepreneurial activity that generated the policy paper. Only in the 1964 case, however, did the minister himself drive that change; usually ministers were driven by change and they sometimes found themselves trying to manage it. Defence ministers, often short-lived and in a role not thought to carry great political weight, are seldom entrepreneurs, although they play an important role in identifying key actors, problems, and constraints as well as politically expedient ideas. Fortuitous political conditions are the most important factors in elevating policy alternatives onto decision agendas, transforming ideas into formal statements of government intent.

THE 1964 WHITE PAPER

The political window for the 1964 White Paper opened with a change in administration and the election of a Liberal minority government pledged to action. The goal of the Pearson government was from the beginning to establish firm control of the military and of military expenditure (Bland, 1997: 58). Paul Hellyer was the choice for defence minister. He had been a key figure in convincing Pearson and the Liberal Party to accept the notion of nuclear weapons for Canada just before the 1963 campaign. At age 40, he already had 15 years of experience as a Member of Parliament, including a stint as associate defence minister in the middle 1950s, in the last days of the Louis St Laurent government. Before that he had briefly been a soldier and an airman at the end of the Second World War, where he had acquired strong views on what he thought was the predilection of the armed forces for waste and mismanagement. An admirer of American secretary of defense Robert McNamara's campaign to impose greater civilian control over the military, Hellyer was determined to do the same in Canada (Bland, 1995: 71). Like McNamara, he had a business sense and had used it to make a good deal of money, so that he had the freedom independent wealth can give a politician.

Hellyer became the primary policy entrepreneur, attaching his policy alternative of centralized control over, and unification of, the armed services to perceived problems. The minister kept the White Paper as much to himself as he could. He himself wrote the first draft out in longhand, sometimes relying on departmental documents to cover routine matters. For the sections involving 'major change,' he recalled, 'I was on my own.' Once the document was roughed out, the political and bureaucratic bargaining began, with the impatient minister driving the process forward. The paper went first to the deputy minister, senior military men, and departmental officials; this yielded a few small suggestions but nothing major. Hellyer's aim to have a more adaptable Canadian Forces (CF) was in line with studies produced by the army and navy in the early 1960s, which in turn were reinforced by Canada's expanding peacekeeping experience and American discussions of a flexible response doctrine for the North Atlantic Treaty Organization (NATO). Pre-existing ideas in domestic and international circles, as well as emerging practices on the ground, had thus prepared the policy community for innovation.

Hellyer, however, had held back the sections on his central idea of the reorganization of the military structure into a unified command, in order to make sure that he had the prime minister's approval. Once that was secured, those parts were shown to the department, with mixed reactions from the military. The army was favourable, but the air force and especially the navy expressed reservations. The chairman of the Chiefs of Staff Committee, air chief marshal Frank Miller, wanted to remove Hellyer's wording about integration of the DND headquarters structure as simply a phase on the way to unification of the armed forces. Miller also opposed the adoption of dual nuclear and conventional roles for the air force in Europe; he and the air force, Hellyer believed, were 'on the wrong track in [their] preoccupation with nuclear war'. The defence minister, bolstered by the prime minister's support, held firm. The prime minister and the government would not agree to an exclusively nuclear role for the air division in Europe. Nor was Hellyer about to hide the fact that unification was the ultimate object of his reorganization. The minister was prepared to consider, and to make, drafting alterations, but nothing that affected the thrust of his recommendations. 'It is the issue,' he wrote in his diary at the time, 'of who is going to set policy—the military or the government.' The paper, changed very little, went off to Pearson (Hellyer, 1990: 34, 43–5).

For a while, a fragmented policy community produced agenda instability, making the success of Hellyer's ambitious new policy agenda far from certain. The air force and navy continued to fight, now with the assistance of the Department of External Affairs, which complained that consultation had not taken place and that the foreign ministry must have a part in decision making. The prime minister wavered just enough to agree to a delay while a committee of officials reviewed the text. Hellyer's memoirs record his 'acute apprehension' at this point. When the Defence Committee of the cabinet met informally on 21 February 1964, the minister's concerns increased, but in a way he found perplexing. No one raised problems about integration and unification, which Hellyer thought the controversial item on the agenda. Instead there were questions about Canada's NATO contribution, and desires to cut it back. Foreign minister Paul Martin wanted to bring the sizeable Canadian contingent in Europe home, while finance minister Walter Gordon wished to slash defence expenditures by another $500 million (Hellyer, 1990: 45–7).

The prime minister said that he would revise the paper and return it to Hellyer. Much to the defence minister's surprise, the prime minister hardly touched the document. It was left in tact, and Hellyer could now boast of Pearson's full support. The boss had signed off on the White Paper. With the prime minister's support confirmed, Hellyer's bargaining position was greatly enhanced, enabling the defence minister to present his paper to cabinet as a *fait accompli*. When the cabinet Defence Committee met again a month later in March, committee members approved the document as it had come to them, despite the presence of the sceptical defence chiefs, many of whom had come to voice their opposition at Hellyer's urging. The White Paper had survived parliamentary and bureaucratic haggling substantially in the form it had originally been written. Hellyer rushed his paper into print even before the full cabinet gave its blessing, which it duly did (Hellyer, 1990: 47).

The White Paper, issued in late March 1964, faithfully reflected the minister's views. To reduce service rivalries, promote efficiency, and give the government greater control over the military, all three services were to come under an integrated defence staff headed by a single officer, the chief of defence staff (CDS). This would streamline operations and planning, free up funds that could go to the military's depleted capital equipment budget, and serve as the first step toward complete unification of the three services. The objectives of defence policy were the traditional ones, listed by Hellyer as contributions to United Nations collective security; Canada's commitments to NATO and the collective defence of the West; the cooperative defence of North America alongside the United States; and the defence and protection of Canada itself. The CF, however, would change radically 'to produce a mobile capability ready to respond quickly to new commitments' (Bland, 1997: 60). It would be structured as a distinctive, independent force, capable of operating anywhere, with anyone, across the range of conflict, from peacekeeping in the developing world to participation in a major war in Europe. As demanded by the prime minister and minister of finance, the new CF would have a smaller budget. Defence expenditures for fiscal year 1964–5 were cut to 3 per cent of gross domestic product (GDP), the lowest percentage since the beginning of the Korean War. The age of big Canadian defence spending was over.

Hellyer's unification of the armed forces, completed in 1967, ultimately failed to solve many of his department's administrative and fiscal woes. Although merging service functions did save some money, the purchasing power of these additional dollars was swallowed by inflation. Nor did unification fuse the services as tightly as had been hoped. When working alongside Canada's allies in North America and Europe, the services continued to operate as independent military elements. By the late 1960s, therefore, it seemed that the only notable effects of unification were a growing malaise among military personnel clad in the drab olive green uniform of the unified CF, and a concentration of power in the office of the CDS. Indeed, as the principal source of military counsel to the government, the CDS and his staff appeared to hold greater sway over Canadian defence policy than any of the three competing service chiefs could have exercised before unification.

DEFENCE IN THE 1970S

In 1968, problem and political windows opened simultaneously, providing an unprecedented opportunity for policy innovation. Change, however, would not be in the direction of program renewal and reinvestment as advocated by the military establishment. The new prime minister, Pierre Elliott Trudeau, was an iconoclastic leader attuned to the broader societal upheavals of the 1960s and 1970s. *Defence in the 70s*, the new government's White Paper, reversed the priorities stated in 1964, from Hellyer's brief for the collective good of Canada and its allies to Trudeau's preoccupation with the future of the country itself. The 'first concern' of defence policy, *Defence in the 70s* stated, was to ensure that Canada remained 'secure as an independent political entity' (Saywell, *CAR*, 1971: 293).

The prime minister was the White Paper's opportunist-entrepreneur, taking advantage of the confluence of problems, politics, and a viable policy option, and driving change (not without resistance) from the centre of government. The White Paper was released in August 1971, but the process of which it was a culmination began soon after Trudeau took power. His first defence minister, Léo Cadieux, and the CDS, General Jean Allard, were quick off the mark to counter the prime minister's view that Canada's alliances did not serve its interests. Two Cadieux-Allard studies, *Rationale for Canadian Defence Forces* and *Defence Policy Review 69*, presented to cabinet in July 1968 and February 1969 respectively, argued that Canada should remain fully committed to NATO and the North American Air Defence Command (NORAD). Canada's contributions to NATO, the studies argued, were vital for the maintenance of a stable deterrent against the Soviets, and NORAD discouraged Moscow from building a larger bomber fleet. *Defence Policy Review 69* warned that Ottawa would have to invest massively in defence to build an independent deterrent if Canada abandoned NATO and NORAD and declared itself a neutral state. Cadieux and Allard's positions were supported by high-ranking External Affairs and DND officials, cabinet ministers Paul Hellyer, John Turner, and Paul Martin, and the minister of external affairs, Mitchell Sharp. At this stage in the policy-making process, the prevailing continuity of attitudes and bureaucratic culture among key personnel created a dissonance between the policy direction advocated by the prime minister and what was perceived to meet criteria of 'feasibility' and 'value-acceptabilty'. An influential group of internationalists, with a retired Pearson among them, successfully prevented the prime minister from recasting defence policy during his first months in office. The time had not yet come for Trudeau's Canada-First defence policy.

Undaunted, Trudeau asked his principal foreign policy advisor, Ivan Head, to conduct a policy review that would exclude input from the Department of National Defence (DND) and the Department of External Affairs (DEA). Assembled by a small team of Privy Council Office (PCO) and Treasury Board officials, Head's review, titled *A Study of Defence Policy*, was presented to Cabinet on 29 March 1969. It proposed that the military be reduced from 100,000 to 50,000 personnel within 10 years and that it concentrate on the protection of Canadian sovereignty and assistance to civilian authorities (aid of the civil power). Only 1,800 CF personnel were to stay in Europe as part of NATO. Head's study further advocated that these shrunken Canadian NATO forces relinquish their nuclear weapons.

Cabinet was deeply divided over *A Study of Defence Policy*. The president of the Privy Council and a Trudeau favourite, Donald Macdonald, complained that Head's group was too timid; Macdonald and his supporters pushed for a complete withdrawal from NATO. Sharp, Cadieux, and other internationalist ministers replied that Canada's NATO allies would be horrified by deep cuts. Although Sharp and Cadieux were willing to entertain some scaling-down of Canada's NATO commitments, they thought Head's reductions unacceptable. The prime minister supported Head's scheme. Trudeau recognized that Canada could not abandon NATO altogether, yet he was equally determined to secure a sharp reduction in the number of CF personnel stationed in Europe. He stated that Canada's true interests lay in protecting its sovereignty and in helping defend the United States' retaliatory nuclear forces under the auspices of NORAD. Any other defence commitments were optional, not obligatory. The political climate was such that the reductions in defence spending, the size of the military, and Canada's NATO contributions could not be as drastic as those envisaged by Head. Still, as events continued to unfold, it would become increasingly clear that the prime minister was less interested in the consensus politics of his predecessors than in shaping Canadian policies in a direction consistent with his own personal vision.

Trudeau unveiled an outline of his government's defence policy in April 1969. Canada's top defence objective was the protection of Canadian sovereignty, and the second priority was the defence of North America alongside the United States. Next in the hierarchy was a 'fulfillment of NATO commitments', although the government would 'take early steps to bring about a planned and phased reduction of the size of the Canadian forces in Europe'. Last on the list, and receiving no ringing endorsement, was 'the performance of international peacekeeping roles as we may from time to time assume'. Cuts ensued. CF personnel were reduced from approximately 100,000 to between 80,000 and 85,000, and the defence budget was capped at $1.8 billion, a sum that amounted to 2 per cent of GDP, the lowest level of Canadian military spending since the 1950s. On 19 September 1969, after a debate that nearly tore the cabinet apart, Cadieux announced the government's plan to reduce Canada's NATO–Europe contribution by half, down to 5,000 army and air force personnel, and to abandon the country's nuclear weapons.

The stage was set for a defence White Paper that would provide context and confirmation for these changes, setting policy into stone. The man charged with drafting it was Donald Macdonald, who was appointed minister of national defence in September 1970. The minister, who had pushed for his first major assignment with real resources to deploy, was suspect in DND. 'We've had one ambitious young minister,' an unnamed officer said publicly just before Macdonald's appointment, referring to Hellyer. 'I'm not sure we can stand another.' Instead of worrying exclusively about what he thought a remote threat of nuclear holocaust, Macdonald agreed with the prime minister that the most pressing problems on the government's decision agenda were Canadian sovereignty and domestic terrorism. Immediately upon entering cabinet, Macdonald told the *Montreal Star* that he was in some respects an 'anti-militarist', although he supported 'a substantial military establishment' and could not 'conceive' of more cuts in force levels or at NATO 'at least for the foreseeable future'. In the same interview, Macdonald said he was afraid that US domestic violence and unrest would seep into Canada. A trained and disciplined CF must be present to deal with any problem that might arise on domestic soil in that respect (Saywell, *CAR*, 1970: 361–2).

Focusing events at home caught the attention of Trudeau and Macdonald, downgrading the ongoing but apparently improving Cold War predicament on the governmental agenda. The first great problem Macdonald faced as defence minister was the October 1970 FLQ crisis, when terrorists bent on Quebec independence held a British diplomat captive for months and murdered a provincial cabinet minister. Coupled with the impact of the voyage of the American oil tanker *Manhattan* across the Northwest Passage in 1969, in apparent defiance of Canadian sovereignty, the FLQ crisis reinforced nationalist arguments that defence began at home and reminded Canadians that the military played a critical, if rarely seen, part in preserving their personal safety and domestic security. The government's emphasis on sovereignty was a natural response to a sense in the national mood of a vulnerable homeland.

Macdonald's mandate came directly from Trudeau. The prime minister told Macdonald that his White Paper would have to respect the defence spending freeze and NATO reductions announced the year before. He could not ask for more money, but neither should he attempt further to reduce Canada's NATO commitments. In addition, the prime minister wanted the White Paper to address DND's administration. Having seen how successfully the defence bureaucracy could resist policy change, Trudeau sought to make DND and the CF more responsive to political authority. Like Hellyer before him, Macdonald chose to marginalize DND and the CF and concentrate his attention on the prime minister. The department and military might be consulted, but policy would be set at the top.

As the paper's principal author, Macdonald commandeered Gordon Smith, a young DEA official who could speak authoritatively about defence, but was unattached to DND and its institutional interests. Smith, who had a doctorate in political science, began work in the fall of 1970. To ensure that his final draft met the prime minister's expectations, Smith worked with Ivan Head, who could be trusted to provide Smith with an accurate reading of the prime minister's opinions and predilections. Smith's closest collaborator was Macdonald, who made revisions to nearly every version of the paper. Smith was also in regular contact with DEA and the military: he understood that External Affairs and National Defence were jealous of their jurisdictions, but allowed them little say in what he was writing. DND officials were unhappy with a device that they thought would be used to mask further reductions of money and personnel. Yet the military afterwards claimed that they found their way into the process by making the case that their views on equipment and strategy had to be included if the armed forces were to protect the country (Granatstein and Bothwell, 1990: 236–40).

Drawing directly and deliberately on the prime minister's April 1969 defence policy statement, *Defence in the 70s* listed Canada's objectives as beginning with Canadian sovereignty and ending with contributions to select UN peacekeeping operations. The government promised to enhance the CF's surveillance and reconnaissance capabilities, with particular emphasis on Canada's northern regions, and highlighted aid of the civil power and the enforcement of peace and order within Canada. The *Manhattan* and the FLQ crisis were the clear subtext.

The Cold War problem was redefined, this time with a focus on continental defence. The White Paper noted that the continuation of the superpower confrontation made an effective defence of the continent another inescapable obligation. While Hellyer's Cold War had led him to acquire more military equipment to support a flexible force structure and peacekeeping missions abroad, Trudeau's Cold War would be fought at and near home. Canadian national security was inexorably linked to NORAD and the protection of the United States' retaliatory nuclear capabilities; however, there were to be important alterations to Canada's continental defence force posture, including the abandonment of nuclear-tipped surface-to-air missiles.

With respect to Canada and NATO, *Defence in the 70s* aimed to explain and justify the force-level reductions announced in September 1969, but the views of the government's NATO supporters were also implicit in the White Paper. Canada's obligation to help defend Europe in times of emergency was acknowledged and the neutrality option disavowed. As to peacekeeping operations, the White Paper stipulated that such missions had fostered feelings of frustration and disillusionment. Citing a lack of clear mandates, the absence of cooperation among belligerents, and insufficient resources, the document stated that Canada would avoid future peacekeeping activities that appeared unlikely to succeed. Unhappy peacekeeping experiences in the Congo and Middle East were clearly on the government's mind. In the Congo during the early 1960s, Canadian peacekeepers had often found themselves in combat conditions during an operation that demonstrated the danger and expense of keeping the peace within a state that was disintegrating. Then, in 1967, Canadian soldiers serving with the United Nations Emergency Force (UNEF) had been expelled from Egypt.

Apart from nine months in 1979–80, Trudeau was in power for the next 13 years. Defence was never again high on the governmental agenda. Macdonald was succeeded by a series of short-term defence ministers and the work of the Management Review Group, announced in the White Paper, tended to shift the balance in the department toward civilian bureaucrats and away from the military (Bland, 1993: 218–19). There were no more Trudeau White Papers, and the government drifted back to the centre in its defence and foreign policy. NATO and peacekeeping came back into some favour, and in the early 1980s Ottawa allowed the United States to test cruise missiles in Canada. Military spending inched back up, but despite better defence budgets and several major equipment procurements, there was a long list of equipment in need of modernization or replacement. Other NATO governments made plain their feeling that Canada was 'free-riding' on the efforts of its allies.

Defence was only a minor theme during the 1984 election, but the platform of the opposition Conservatives did promise to bridge the gaps between the military's commitments and its capability, increase defence expenditures by 6 per cent per year, and recruit additional CF personnel. Opposition leader Brian Mulroney also promised to improve relations with the United States and to refurbish Canada's international image. The Conservatives breezed to a big victory, and a review of Canada's foreign and defence policies was launched soon after.

CHALLENGE AND COMMITMENT: A DEFENCE POLICY FOR CANADA, 1987

The new administration was inherently sympathetic to the views of the defence establishment. The political window, in other words, was open to policy alternatives that matched the Mulroney government's unambiguous Cold War defence vision. The solution would also, and almost obligatorily so, be framed as an explicit rejection of 15 years of Trudeau government practice.

Perrin Beatty, Mulroney's third minister of national defence in only two years, was appointed in June 1986. He took particular aim at the writing of a defence White Paper, turning to a cadre of upper-level officials and military at the Department of National Defence to guide the evolution of policy in accordance with overall government directives. Among the senior civilian and CF personnel at DND, the new assistant deputy minister for policy, Robert Fowler, stood out as the primary policy entrepreneur for his knowledge, energy, and determination to rebuild the forces. He recommended, to take a prominent instance, the acquisition of nuclear-powered (but conventionally armed) submarines for the Canadian military. The submarines would allow Canada to patrol the Arctic clandestinely, project power across the world's oceans, and establish a near-perfect deterrent against unwanted incursions, either in Canadian waters or overseas. These were to be attack submarines, providing the navy with the ability to flex Cold War muscle against the Soviets, although they were justified by the minister primarily in terms of their role in the promotion of Canadian sovereignty (Eayrs, 1987: 10–11).

Together with CDS General Paul Manson and the deputy minister, Bev Dewar, Fowler and the minister of defence met regularly during the summer of 1986. Dewar held only a watching brief over the meetings, leaving the strong-minded Fowler to speak for the senior civilian cohort of the department. Fowler played the key role in crafting the White Paper's fundamental policies, principles, and prescriptions, and ensuring with Beatty and Manson that the services would have a critical part in setting the document's force-structuring proposals. They agreed that the White Paper should address the issue of Canadian sovereignty, the Cold War struggle against the Soviet Union, the commitment to NATO, and the importance of continental defence; outline equipment recapitalization and modernization programs, funded on a steady and predictable basis; and push for better ties between the military, industry, and civil society. These policies would be grounded in a strongly worded declaration about the existential threat posed by the Soviet Union and of Canada's unabashed alignment with the West, a course independently chosen in the Canadian national interest. An explicit aim was to combat the questioning of defence policy by a sizeable contingent of organized civil society groups, which by the mid-1980s had gained sufficient internal cohesion and organizational capacity to qualify as a peace movement (Coulon, 1987).

The drafting of the White Paper began in earnest in late 1986. Fowler tasked Kenneth Calder, his director of strategic analysis, to write the document. Calder's instructions were to minimize conflicts and build consensus within DND. However, this did not imply that the services were given a free hand. Even in a time of plenty, Fowler knew that not all service desires could be fulfilled; the White Paper would not be all things to all service people. In spite of this constraint, the services were actively consulted. Rather than excluding the CF from the planning process, as had been done in 1964 and 1971, this process made them a partner. The military was asked to inform Calder of the capabilities required to bridge the commitment-capability gap, strengthen Canada's position in the Canadian–American defence relationship and NATO, and protect Arctic sovereignty. Those recommendations that survived civilian scrutiny were then included in drafts of the White Paper.

A key bargaining role was assumed by Manson, a deft operator who attempted to bring the army, navy, and air force perspectives together into a single coherent program (Bland, 1993: 221). While not entirely successful, he was assisted in his goal by the fact that the government was convinced of a crisis in the military and was anxious to staunch what the White Paper would call 'the unplanned and pervasive deterioration in the military capabilities of the Canadian Forces'. With government opinion favourably aligned with their own, Fowler and Manson perceived that the political window had opened; military renewal was solidly at the front of the governmental agenda.

Manson had strong ideas about renewal, deriving mainly from his experience as a fighter pilot with NATO in Europe, where he had flown aging Starfighters on the front line of the Cold War. He knew the Soviet threat firsthand, and he believed that Canada's ancient equipment did not serve Canada and its alliance well. He also had broad experience in the Ottawa bureaucracy and had successfully engineered the acquisition of new fighter aircraft for the CF. He was well equipped for the series of meetings with individual cabinet ministers that was part of the education campaign he and other senior staff undertook as an exercise in softening up political opinion, and for doing battle at meetings of the cabinet foreign affairs and defence committee. There, a far-reaching White Paper was tested and successfully justified before a sometimes hostile membership, led by Joe Clark, the foreign minister.

Manson disagreed with his minister only in one respect. Rather than putting the emphasis on sovereignty, as Beatty insisted, Manson thought the real point of the exercise was to contribute responsibly and well to collective deterrence of the Soviet Union at a time of high tension in the Cold War. As it happened, and as the prime minister's introduction to the document demonstrated, the White Paper gave equal weight to both purposes when it set out its rationale for major change in Canadian defence policy.

Draftsman Calder's task was to link the military's recommendations with the overarching defence policy objectives set out the previous summer. Fowler meanwhile had the proposed force structure costed. Cabinet would be given both a set of policies and the price of implementing them. With Calder's writing completed, and both the details and the wording finalized around Beatty's dining-room table, the new policy was carefully conceived and demonstrably feasible, paving the way for elevation to the government's decision agenda.

The draft White Paper argued that the Soviet military threat was real and increasing, and made the case for a funding program that would match the challenge ahead. The problem and the solution were mutually reinforcing; as military investment and renewal ascended to prominence on the Mulroney governmental agenda, this became justified as a solution to a real Cold War problem (Kingdon, 2003: 178). The funding timetable envisaged was a 15-year increase in real defence expenditures beginning with 2 per cent a year after inflation and ending with 5 per cent annually in the outer years, along with additional appropriations for the acquisition of modern equipment and refurbishment of older platforms. Canada's NORAD forces would continue to protect the United States' retaliatory nuclear capabilities, the 1985 NORAD modernization program would be fully implemented, and steps would be taken to strengthen Canadian aerospace defence capabilities. Canada's commitment to conventional deterrence would necessitate a renewed emphasis on the defence of southern Germany, along with the elimination of the impractical promise to send forces to Norway in time of crisis, and the acquisition of new tanks for the CF's mechanized brigade stationed in Europe. At the same time, the Canadian navy would increase its presence on the Pacific Ocean, modernize its destroyers, buy more maritime patrol aircraft and new helicopters, and press forward with plans to acquire twelve frigates. To enhance the CF's presence in the Arctic and deter intrusions into Canadian waters, Fowler's nuclear-powered submarines (SSNs) were prominently in view.

Beatty, Fowler, Manson, Dewar, and DND policy staff frequently saw their counterparts from other countries during the period, often as part of the regular meetings that populated the NATO and Canadian–American military relationships. But Canada's allies were not explicitly consulted about the White Paper. They were, indeed, ambivalent about the ambitious Canadian plans. US defense secretary Caspar Weinberger liked the Cold War rhetoric (Gotlieb, 2006: 466), but the submarine fleet and the abandonment of the Norway commitment were particular targets of unhappiness in Washington and other alliance capitals. The two criticisms were brought together by those who contrasted Canada's desire to spend copiously on expensive nuclear submarines with the willingness to leave NATO's northern flank begging. Charles Doran, an American academic commentator, thought that the Canadians were too intent on questions relating to what he termed the 'political imagery of sovereignty', and not enough on the imperatives of alliance security. He wondered if US officials regretted their insistence on the 1985 *Polar Sea*'s trek through Arctic waters, which had given such a boost to the sovereignty debate in Canada. Certainly officials in the United States, and particularly the US Navy, made it clear—and public—that they were concerned by the nuclear sub program. Where would Canada get them, and how would the navy learn to run them? Would they operate in concert with the US, or would they be used to challenge American submarines in northern waters (Eayrs, 1987: 11)? Nevertheless, Canada was announcing substantial increases in defence spending, and that was bound to be welcomed throughout NATO, where the country's 'free rider' status was often noted and widely deprecated (Doran, 1987: 8–9). This mixed picture demonstrated that the prime drivers for the 1987 change in defence policy were coming from inside the country, not from outside. They were, in fact, coming from the defence department and its entrepreneurial assistant deputy minister for policy.

Beatty met strong resistance when he submitted his draft to the full cabinet. As he had done at the cabinet committee level, foreign minister Clark questioned the acquisition of nuclear submarines and expressed discomfort with the document's Cold Warrior tone. A sharp rebuke was also issued by finance minister Michael Wilson, who said that the defence spending increases outlined in the document were unaffordable in light of the alarming growth of the country's debt-to-GDP ratio, the result of accumulating annual deficits. He sought to prevent the White Paper from ever being released. Budgeting, again, had reared its uncompromising head, this time to the detriment of the circulating policy alternative. Nevertheless, prime ministerial leadership rescued Beatty's defence document. Mulroney was ready to commit his government and his personal prestige to it. With the prime minister's support, Beatty won the day. Cabinet instructed DND to go forward with a final draft of the paper, although Beatty had to compromise on the funding timetable—the CF would get their increases in real expenditure but not a guarantee for the long haul, and not a 15-year funding formula.

Challenge and Commitment, its title reflecting its bold contents, was released in June 1987. Yet it all quickly came to naught as domestic events and broad public opposition made the defence review's ambitious program of action politically untenable. The peace movement assailed the White Paper's muscular rhetoric—the promotion of an accelerated Canadian military space program and the proposed acquisition of submarines that were incorrectly said to carry nuclear weapons. Both the Liberals and the NDP added questions about the cost and logic of the submarines. Within the government, Wilson put up obstacles to the White Paper's funding program and gained adherents in the Conservative caucus.

Beatty's influence began a steady decline, while the prime minister's own political capital was depleted after his re-election in 1988 resulted in a reduced majority of seats. The election fight over free trade with the US had reinforced the impression that Mulroney was in the Americans' hip pocket, a factor that may have made him more wary about a defence program fuelling the image of a government too anxious to mimic Washington's Cold War policies. With domestic opposition and budget deficits, the policy window for military renewal closed. Mulroney abandoned his support for higher defence expenditures. There would be no additional tanks, no new aircraft, no nuclear-powered submarines, no space-based surveillance satellites. In 1991 the decision not to increase defence expenditures was transformed into another round of defence budget cuts. By then it was clear, even to a government that was late to concede the fact, that the Cold War was over. The Soviet Union had collapsed. Events in the international political stream thus confirmed and reinforced the government's changing direction.

In the early 1990s the military was busily engaged in operations thrown up by the opportunities and dislocations caused by the end of the Cold War. Mulroney believed, with US President George H.W. Bush, that a 'new world order' was unfolding. Canada took part in the first war of the post–Cold War era, the UN-authorized and American-led Persian Gulf War of 1991, and CF deployments on peacekeeping operations boomed. Following the 1987 White Paper's recommendation, the prime minister finally let a contract for the purchase of EH-101 replacements for Canada's aged Sea King maritime helicopters, only to have it become a major issue in the 1993 federal election campaign. After he was elected prime minister, trouncing Mulroney successor Kim Campbell, one of Jean Chrétien's first acts was to cancel the helicopter acquisition program, a portent of things to come. A review of defence and foreign policy, promised in the campaign, was also set in train.

THE 1994 DEFENCE WHITE PAPER

The post–Cold War security environment opened a problem window in Canada. The end of superpower bipolarity in the international system made way for potential changes that could be far more unpredictable than ordinary shifts associated with cycles of policy renewal. More was at stake, in short, than investment and disinvestment in national defence. Voices in academia, civil society, and some of the well-connected members of government circles spoke out for alternatives to traditional war-fighting in a globalizing and postmodern world. More importantly, in the early 1990s the budget crisis loomed large, a structural imperative personified in the minister of finance, Paul Martin.

The economic crisis focused the attention of the country's leadership and policy makers on the costs of maintaining the military status quo, with a multipurpose, combat-capable CF. Feedback from the top indicated to an influential group within the policy community that the time was right to place a policy alternative on the government agenda. Inside the cabinet the powerful Martin advocated deep cuts that could change the shape and direction of the military, while Lloyd Axworthy, the minister of human resources and the Liberals' foreign policy critic when they were the opposition party, had long advocated a peace-keeping-centric defence policy. Nor were the prime minister and his principal policy advisor, Eddie Goldenberg, friends of the military. As leader of the opposition, Chrétien opposed a Canadian commitment to the Persian Gulf expedition and he had campaigned in the election of 1993 with the promise that he would kill the helicopter contract and get the economy back on track. He backed Martin's cost cutting to the hilt.

Outside government, these ideas were given coherence by the Canada 21 Council, chaired by Ivan Head from the Trudeau days, directed by Janice Stein, a political science professor at the University of Toronto, and including the former defence minister, Donald Macdonald. The council sought to steer the armed forces away from combat-capabilities. Rather than equipping the military to fight conventional wars, the CF should field forces suited to peacekeeping, the delivery of humanitarian aid, the protection of Canadian sovereignty, and aid of the civil power. The council noted that such a force structure would be affordable and suited for deployments on most UN operations. Underlying the council's position was the notion that Canadian defence policy should serve a global 'common security'. This was not a new idea, but the end of the Cold War created a window of opportunity to push for wider acceptance and elevation onto decision agendas. The council was backed by several Bloc Québécois and NDP MPs, who kept Canada 21's ideas floating around Parliament Hill during the policy review process.

Even if they diverged on other issues, civilian and military officials at DND agreed in private that the council's proposals had to be defeated and discredited. Their alternative to Canada 21's alternative was a multipurpose, combat-capable military force, flexible enough to take on a wide spectrum of missions at home and abroad. DND hoped that the government would agree that Canada 21's was the wrong solution to the challenges of the post–Cold War world. In fact, defence officials decided to proceed on the assumption that they knew best what the government really wanted and needed.

Robert Fowler, now deputy minister of defence, was a realist who was concerned above all to ensure the survival of DND at a level that would keep a working department and its core competencies intact. Fowler's senior position in the public service, previous entrepreneurship for the Mulroney defence review, and political acumen made him a formidable policy entrepreneur. Entrepreneurship, in this case, did not involve a new idea (Kingdon, 2003: 124). Fowler sought to demonstrate the importance of preserving traditional force structures and military roles to meet post–Cold War problems. Using his wide bureaucratic experience and his sure knowledge that the rest of government had little interest in defence, or knowledge of it, he was able to protect DND's core assets, and along with them the department's decision-making turf.

With the clear intent to weather the storm of forthcoming cuts to defence spending, Fowler moved to use the budget constraint to the department's advantage. If DND stayed within the budget constraint imposed on it, the deputy minister realized that the defence department would be given a wide degree of discretion in setting policy. His reasoning was cunning: if cabinet insisted on certain defence policies or capabilities, such as those proposed by Canada 21, the defence department could argue that additional funds or fewer cuts were needed to provide those capabilities. Simply put, once the government waded into the policy questions, DND could use the government's policy preferences to demand more dollars for defence. Accordingly, Fowler recognized that there was no true threat to DND's policy-making prerogative, since the government would not risk the cost associated with an insistence that the defence department follow a set of prescribed policies. Finance minister Martin's mandate was to put the country's economic house in order. It did not ultimately matter to him what shape the CF would take, so long as it was an affordable one. If DND could better Canada 21's niche alternative in terms of capability, and if the CF could absorb the cuts imposed on it without a fundamental rethinking of force structures and operational roles, then defence officials would be free to set the policy they wanted.

The chief of the defence staff (CDS) was army General John de Chastelain. He had been the CDS from 1989 to 1993, a period during which he had dealt coolly with the Aboriginal crisis at Oka and the expedition to the Persian Gulf, winning accolades from politicians and the public. Early in 1993 he was named ambassador to the United States, but at year's end he received word from the clerk of the Privy Council that the Chrétien government was replacing him with a career diplomat who had the considerable advantage of being the prime minister's nephew. De Chastelain was asked to come back as CDS, despite his having already served a full term in the office. He refused the offer. The prime minister requested that de Chastelain visit him, and was able to prevail upon the general to resume his former duties. Tough times for the military were coming, said Chrétien, and a return to National Defence headquarters was the only way that de Chastelain could be sure that his vision for the future of the CF would be on the governmental agenda. To Chrétien, de Chastelain was undoubtedly a known quantity and his solid reputation in Quebec was bound to be an asset in the soon-to-come independence referendum. For his part, de Chastelain only (and very reluctantly) accepted a return to his old post so that he could fight for a CF that would continue to be able to carry out missions across the full spectrum of military options. De Chastelain was familiar with DND headquarters and personalities, and had a particularly good relationship with Fowler. No learning curve was necessary and the CDS would be a useful ally for the entrepreneurial deputy minister in his bid to protect the status quo.

DND interests had another weapon in the bargaining over the direction of policy that was to ensue. The experience gained by Fowler and Kenneth Calder in drafting 1987's *Challenge and Commitment* had taught them a valuable lesson: defence White Papers should not be written at the last minute or without organized expertise. They agreed that DND's policy staff should be transformed into a true 'policy shop'. Rather than merely offering advice, the policy group would produce regular policy updates, improve their studies of developments in the international security environment, and work to better match the CF force structure with the constraints imposed by the defence budget. In other words, DND sought to become an indispensable part of the feedback loop to which governments, and the government's economic departments, responded.

Between 1989 and 1993, four updates were written by the policy staff, and their influence over the direction of Canadian defence policy grew. The 1991 *Statement of Defence Policy* and the 1992 *Canadian Defence Policy* documents reflected the policy group's leading role in reconciling lower defence expenditures with Canada's continued interest in promoting international and domestic stability, at the same time as dedicating forces to sovereignty protection operations. The empowerment of the policy group coincided with the rise of Fowler and Calder within the defence department hierarchy. Fowler was appointed deputy minister in 1989 and Calder assistant deputy minister (policy) in 1991. When the Chrétien Liberals initiated their foreign and defence review in late 1993, the policy mavens were well positioned for advocacy. The policy group, led from the top by Fowler and on the ground by Calder, was determined to prevent Canada 21's policy alternative from finding its way onto the decision agenda, and to influence the government in the direction of a readily adaptable and realistic policy solution that would meet the problems posed by economic difficulties and international uncertainties.

Defence minister David Collenette was not an advocate for change, rather a manager of it. On the one hand, he was being driven by demands for cost cutting emanating from the Prime Minister's Office and the Department of Finance. On the other hand, placing a high premium on defence and having jurisdictional responsibility for DND, he was concerned that cuts, if they went too deep, could make a mockery of the CF. Furthermore, Collenette wanted his review to be more than a mere justification of lower expenditures. He believed that the end of the Cold War offered Canadians an opportunity to debate publicly Canada's defence objectives and the role of the CF, and he valued parliamentary inputs into the process. To this end, he welcomed the establishment of a Special Joint Committee on Canada's Defence Policy in February 1994. The Joint Committee was mandated to gather expert advice about alternative directions for Canadian defence policy and the CF force structure. The minister wanted its findings to be reflected in the White Paper. At first Collenette viewed DND headquarters with some scepticism. He was well aware that the department was full of entrenched interests and that its bureaucrats were practised at getting their way. Quickly, however, he came to respect the policy group, Fowler and Calder in particular, and found an ally in the CDS.

In early 1994, Daniel Bon, the director general of policy planning at DND, was asked to draft a guidance document for the minister to give to the Special Joint Committee. As a tough former parliamentary defence committee staffer, and a gifted and precise writer, Bon was well equipped for the work, which was quickly completed. His next step was to begin a 'working paper', meant to provide ready-made material when the time came to formulate a new White Paper. The working paper detailed the state of the international security environment, Canada's domestic security and sovereignty protection requirements, and the logic of maintaining a healthy Canada–United States defence relationship and of fielding multipurpose, combat-capable military forces that would help meet NATO commitments. The North Atlantic Alliance had emerged at the end of the Cold War with a changing focus. It was in the beginning stages of evolution toward a new 'strategic concept', a humanitarian thrust somewhere between peacekeeping and war-fighting that provided new mandates and legitimacy for the military alliance. Significantly, the roles envisioned by NATO supported the status quo in terms of equipment and expenditures. Canada's membership in the new NATO, and the country's voice in alliance decision making, required many of the same capabilities as were required during the Cold War. However, the working paper did not include any mention of CF force structure changes. The policy group knew that these decisions must be delayed until the findings of the Special Joint Committee were made public.

Collenette's activities took place on a different level from his civilian and military advisors. The defence minister discussed alternatives with members of the academic community, including Canada 21's Janice Stein, military historians J. L. Granatstein and David Bercuson, and the editor of *Canadian Defence Quarterly*, John Marteinson. These consultations exposed Collenette to a variety of views, but only reinforced his belief that the integrity of the military as a fighting force had to be maintained. He had a cooperative colleague in the foreign minister, André Ouellet, who had been chosen over Axworthy for the position. Ouellet was easy to get along with and preoccupied with other issues, the coming referendum in Quebec not the least. When Bon's working paper was circulated to interested government agencies in the late summer of 1994, the Department of Foreign Affairs expressed its approval.

In the fall of 1994, the Special Joint Committee released its report on the future of the CF and Canadian defence policy. Titled *Security in a Changing World*, the document favoured the maintenance of multiple combat-capabilities for the

Canadian military; a continuance of the country's NATO membership and role in NORAD; and continued expeditionary CF deployments on UN operations to maintain international peace and security. In addition, the Committee acknowledged that budget cuts would force DND to rethink the CF force structure, proposing that headquarters staff at DND be reduced by 50 per cent and that a quarter of Canada's CF-18 fighter/bombers be put to rest. Yet the Canadian navy ought to retain a fleet of 12 frigates and 4 destroyers, combat forces should be increased by 3,000 personnel, and reserves could be used to reinforce regular units on combat operations. The report is best explained as a strong endorsement of the status quo, and a rejection of the Canada 21 Council's 'common security' force in keeping with a peacekeeping-oriented defence policy. This conclusion was not surprising. Fowler's skilful entrepreneurship had clearly, and successfully, made the link between a traditional CF and affordability. De Chastelain had also made a forceful case to the committee, a good number of whom had links to the defence community (Lawson, 1995: 102–3). DND officials worked closely with committee staffers throughout.

DND rushed headlong toward a draft of the White Paper. Through Calder, Fowler gave Bon simple and limited instructions: to hold to the line taken by the Joint Committee, except in those few areas where the minister was not prepared to follow, and to give the military as much of what it hoped for as seemed possible within the constraints imposed by budgetary realities. Bon added to his drafting team an experienced policy hand, well known and respected throughout the department for his knowledge of force structuring, procurement, and organizational matters. The policy group knew how deeply the government wanted to slash. So too did their partners in the exercise, the staff of the vice chief of the defence staff (VCDS), who were at the time also spearheading DND's work on Program Review, the government-wide exercise intended to drastically cut back federal expenditures, and who knew only too well where future funding lines would be drawn. Given its responsibility for force structuring and procurement planning, the VCDS Group also coordinated overall military responses to options the policy drafters were putting forward. Emerging from these negotiations, the policy group's draft outlined more cuts than the parliamentarians had suggested.

Senior military officers not directly involved in the process were shocked by what they saw. The dissatisfactions of the individual service environments—land, sea, and air—gathered steam as the three-star generals and assistant deputy ministers heading the various DND and CF units came together at meetings called by Fowler and the CDS for the purpose of finalizing a draft to be sent to the minister. Everyone knew that cuts were coming, but the military rejected the policy group's assessment that the cabinet would demand real and major reductions. The services' priority was to salvage as much of possible of existing and planned capabilities. They insisted that a new draft be written that reflected their demands. Once completed, that was what went to the minister. The defence community had divided over the extent to which the budgetary constraint would limit future military roles and the acquisition of new capabilities. For now, the realist policy shop would defer to the traditionalist practitioners.

The new draft would not survive for very long on the governmental agenda. Collenette promptly rejected the document's directions for the future of the CF. He had little difficulty with the general policy chapters, and indeed he had commented on a number of earlier versions of them, but he was unimpressed by the final chapter, entitled 'Implementing Defence Policy'. That section, he insisted, would follow the 'intent' of the Joint Committee, but it would also have to match the CF's force structure to the government's planned budget cuts. The committee report's recommendations about the future size of the CF had been too generous. Revisions were ordered to mandate much deeper cuts than that body had envisaged. Collenette worked closely with a small group of senior civilians and military advisors led by Fowler, and including de Chastelain, the VCDS, and Calder. The drafting team shifted the thrust of the offending chapter back to where it had pointed before the bargaining among senior staff.

Cabinet gave its approval to the White Paper in late autumn 1994. Collenette's colleagues on the left fought back, leaking the document to the *Globe and Mail* and mounting a campaign to make the case to Canadians that the military and the status quo had emerged from the fray with scarcely a scratch. The minister, intent on containing the storm, telephoned Chrétien, who was in Europe, and received permission to present the opposition with a *fait accompli* by rushing the White Paper into print. It was produced in-house overnight, the final product looking like it had been hand-stapled and reproduced straight from a lowly assistant's personal computer.

Released on December 7, the Liberal Defence White Paper announced a smaller, leaner CF able to do less, but still within the traditional framework of a multipurpose force. Working against the wishes of some of the senior military but also rebuffing Canada 21's prescription for the future, Collenette projected a CF of 60,000 by century's end, down from 74,000, along with deep reductions in DND's civilian personnel. The White Paper had emerged from the policy window as a compromise package, reflecting competing alternatives in the policy community, a changing international landscape, as well as the Chrétien government's general reticence to alter the status quo fundamentally. Instead, the government would be selective in taking on commitments, and the military would have to make do with less than 60 per cent of the expenditures assumed by the 1987 White Paper. Canada would still retain a fighting force, however, adaptable to the full spectrum of potential operations at home, on the continent and abroad.

The Chrétien Liberals had no qualms about implementing force structure changes. Until Ottawa was confident that its budget deficit was under control, there would be no new money for the CF. Spending was cut to $9.5 billion in 1995, reducing defence expenditures to 1.4 per cent of GDP, the lowest percentage since 1947. There was harsh feedback from critics in the defence community, who complained bitterly about the cuts, while the backers of the Canada 21 concept regretted a document they thought out of touch with the realities of the post–Cold War world. Fowler and CDS de Chastelain, however, were content with the package the White Paper presented, believing it was the best that could be obtained. Meanwhile, the national mood was elsewhere, preoccupied by the national debt and the referendum on Quebec independence.

The White Paper underlined the importance of the preservation of global stability as a vital national interest. Despite an easing of great power tensions, the document pointed to the serious threats caused by ethnic hatreds, failed states, rogue regimes, and the proliferation of nuclear, chemical, and biological weapons. This was also in keeping with developments in the international sphere, as NATO staked out a broader mandate beyond the purview of collective self-defence. The emergence of new threats in the problem stream, indeed, made limitations on Canada's overseas commitments difficult. Ignoring their White Paper's recommendation that the military should be deployed selectively, the government committed CF units to a wide variety of UN and NATO operations in the 1990s, including those fitting under a widening peacekeeping rubric and the 1999 war in Kosovo. The Canadian navy also cooperated closely with its US counterpart in enforcing sanctions against the brutal regime of Saddam Hussein in Iraq. Beginning in 1999, defence expenditures began to creep back up.

After the terrorist attacks on New York and Washington on September 11, 2001, Canada took a major role with the US in the Afghanistan war. In 2003, the Chrétien government decided against participation in President George W. Bush's war in Iraq, but that was the exception proving the rule: the United States remained Canada's closest defence partner. Nevertheless, the disagreement over Iraq caused deep fissures in the relationship of Canada and the US and the two leaders. Added to that was a powerful distaste for the US president in Canada's public mood, tempting politicians (and prime ministers) to indulge in anti-American rhetoric that itself created problems between Canada and the United States.

2005 DEFENCE POLICY STATEMENT

When Paul Martin succeeded Jean Chrétien as prime minister of Canada in December 2003, both problem and political streams were favourably aligned for policy innovation. This took the form of a foreign and defence policy review, initiated shortly after the election, in which the stated aim was the integration of foreign, defence, development, and trade policies into a 'whole-of-government' approach. Martin also promised to take advantage of the opportunity to pursue a more vigorous defence stance, taken in cooperation with the United States.

The direction of changes to policy, as eventually reflected in the 2005 *International Policy Statement* (Government of Canada, 2005a), only became clear after a turnover of personnel at the senior levels of the defence hierarchy. Shortly after the Liberal government released Canada's first ever national security policy in April 2004, the Martin Liberals lost their parliamentary majority in the June 2004 federal election. As part of his post-election cabinet shuffle, Martin named Bill Graham as defence minister and gave him wide leeway to run the department as he wished. A new military star was meanwhile rising fast: Major-General Rick Hillier, the chief of the land staff, recently returned from duty as a deputy corps commander with the United States' Central Command. Having commanded forces on domestic missions, in the Balkans, and in Afghanistan, Hillier was a Canadian general who knew how to 'get things done' and who respected those who did the same.

Hillier was touted as a man with a vision of how the Canadian military should be transformed to address the realities of a post-9/11 world. Drawing on his and his colleagues' operational experience since the early 1990s, Hillier wanted the CF to embrace the United States Marine Corps' concept of three-block warfare, so that the Canadian military would be equipped and trained to provide humanitarian assistance, carry out policing duties, and fight enemies concurrently. Hillier admitted, however, that transforming the CF to meet the demands of the three-block war would take time, money, and above all, unwavering political and public support.

Political support was forthcoming. Fortuitous events and Hillier's considerable acumen as a policy entrepreneur combined to build support for his innovative alternative for the CF. After meeting privately with the general, Martin and Graham were taken by Hillier and his vision. Martin concluded that the three-block war concept fit perfectly with his own nascent policy proposal to integrate Canada's foreign, development, and defence policies. The prime minister was drawn to the idea of allowing the military to get into action more rapidly and efficiently.

Graham found a kindred spirit in Hillier. Both thought the CF should be more active overseas, be able to deploy independently, and be better trained, equipped, and funded. Previously the minister of foreign affairs, Graham's personal experience motivated a shift in problem definition from continental security to international security. For the new minister, there was a direct relationship between expeditionary military deployments and influence in international affairs. Graham also appreciated the importance of rebuilding a solid Canada–United States relationship after the Iraq war schism. Accordingly, he continued efforts to increase the defence budget and involve Canada in the United States' missile defence system. However, the new problem window would require new solutions and involve new costs. Graham was disappointed when he read the government's previous draft defence policy statement with its tilt toward domestic/continental capabilities and call for a lower operational tempo. The new minister reshaped the government's policy agenda, moving it in the direction of a vigorous overseas presence. When deputy minister Ward Elcock and the policy group informed Graham that the CF could not do more both at home and abroad under the existing defence budget, the minister replied that he would press cabinet to accept a considerable increase in defence spending. He asked that a second version of the defence policy statement be written, one predicated on a substantially larger defence budget.

The meeting of minds occurred at an opportune moment. Similar ideas on the defence policy agenda benefited from the spillover of political capital already secured for the whole-of-government initiative. In the autumn of 2004 the position of CDS came open, and the announcement came quickly that Hillier would take over the leadership of the CF. Though he officially assumed the post in February 2005, news of Hillier's appointment and prime ministerial backing gave him considerable influence within the defence department before that date. Hillier wasted no time. By late 2004, the CDS-in-waiting was taking control of the government's defence policy review.

Hillier refined his defence policy vision and transformational ideas by enlisting the assistance of a group of 'tiger teams'—a collection of senior military officers sympathetic to Hillier's views, who were charged with converting sceptics and sidelining dissenters. As Kingdon's model asserts, ideas can be more potent tools than traditional notions of power or pressure in 'softening-up' policy communities. Bargaining, therefore, was minimal. The DND's policy group was tasked with writing a version of the defence policy statement that favoured the CDS's policies, force structuring objectives, and procurement goals. The policy group's first drafts were circulated around Foreign Affairs Canada, the Canadian International Development Agency, the trade department, and the Privy Council Office. Minor edits and additions were suggested by various officials within these departments, but the thrust of the document stayed true to Hillier's tenets.

Believing that a true transformation of the CF could only come from within the armed forces, deputy minister Elcock saw Hillier's appointment as an opportunity to bring real change to Canadian defence policy. He was an unequivocal Hillier backer. It was the navy and air force that mounted the strongest opposition to Hillier. Hillier's procurement plans and force structuring proposals tended to be focused on land forces overstretched by commitments in Afghanistan. Unless they intervened in the policy process, naval and air force officers feared that their environments might be reduced to support roles, such as transport. Accordingly, the navy and air force pressured Hillier and his staff to be mindful of their services' particular requirements and contributions to a well-rounded CF. In the end, the CDS proved more open to the navy's appeals.

The final draft of Canada's new defence document was ready in the early months of 2005. Though it was published as part of the integrated *International Policy Statement*, the defence policy statement was essentially a stand-alone document that reflected the concerns, hopes, and precepts of an entrepreneurial CDS filtered through a like-minded prime minister and minister. Prime Minister Martin, indeed, carefully read every draft. His contributions included the addition of more references to Canada's interests in the North. Nor would the budget constraint be allowed to be insurmountable in this case. The government simultaneously announced the increase of Canadian defence spending by $13 billion over a five-year period, an amount that pleasurably stunned the defence community and confirmed the prime minister's commitment to rebuild the CF. Personalities, namely, the prime minister, the minister of defence, and especially the persuasive chief of the defence staff, had overcome the predictable structural constraints of budgets and existing resource allocations. Martin's support of the new CDS was also beyond question, and it was widely known, helping Hillier ensure that DND fell into line with his plans.

With the exception of small alterations made to render the document less controversial, and more amenable to public consumption, the defence policy statement reflected Hillier's swashbuckling notion of a renewed and transformed CF. In contrast with previous policy drafts that stressed the necessity of reducing the CF's operational tempo and concentrating on domestic functions, the crux of the document was the CDS's belief that spending increases would, and should, allow the military to do more overseas. Similarly, the statement's force and command structure reforms, procurement plans, and focus on three-block stabilization operations in failed and failing states all came directly from Hillier. While the backing of the prime minister and the defence minister provided the document's crucial context, placing defence high on the governmental agenda, it was Hillier who was the principal policy entrepreneur driving the policy process forward towards decision making and implementation.

Like the 1994 White Paper and the 2004 *National Security Policy*, the defence policy statement listed Canada's defence objectives as the protection of Canada and Canadians, the defence of North America in cooperation with the United States, and the maintenance of international peace and security via the UN and NATO. Where the statement differed from its predecessor White Paper was in its emphasis on the intensity of the threats Canada faced in a post-9/11 world. According to the statement, the gravest problems for Canada and for global stability at the dawn of the twenty-first century were failed and failing states, terrorism, weapons of mass destruction and their proliferation, and the continuance of intra- and interstate wars. The aim of the document was to outline a restructuring and transformation of the Canadian military that would assist the CF in addressing these dangers. With the Liberal promise to increase the defence budget by $13 billion over five years, the defence policy statement was confident that the CF could be rebuilt and restructured, while also promoting Canada's interests and values, protecting Canadians, and reclaiming the country's international prestige.

While it had from the beginning favoured closer Canadian–American defence ties, the government was only too aware of the low esteem Canadians had for the US administration of George W. Bush. Noting that the security of Canada and the United States was intertwined, the defence policy statement argued for closer continental defence ties, including the improvement of North American maritime security, as would later be reflected in the May 2006 NORAD renewal agreement. Yet, with an eye to electoral, partisan, and pressure group factors, the document made no mention of CF operations overseas with the American armed forces and was evasive about interoperability with the United States military and the CF's links with the American armed forces in Afghanistan. Instead of advocating future CF deployments alongside the United States military, the defence policy statement used euphemisms such as 'participating in less formal coalitions of like-minded states' and retaining 'a spectrum of capabilities to operate

with our allies on international missions'. Cooperation with the US on continental security issues was easier to sell than overseas expeditionary roles under
the rubric of the US-led war on terror. Policy entrepreneurs were mindful of the
national mood and careful to craft a policy alternative that would be a politically
palatable solution to perceived problems. Hillier and the Martin Liberals could
not have achieved such profound, and fiscally ambitious, changes to the policy
agenda without the support of the Canadian population.

Despite many Canadians' opposition to automatic harmonization with American military methods and strategic goals, the national mood was more
favourable to defence spending than it had been since the 1950s. Organizations
such as the Conference of Defence Associations, the Council for Canadian Security in the Twenty-First Century, and the Canadian Defence and Foreign Affairs
Institute, unhappy with the pace of changes, had combined to make a powerful
case that the Liberals were not doing enough, notwithstanding the elevation of
defence high onto the Martin agenda from the beginning of his tenure as prime
minister. Added to these traditional advocates for national defence priorities was
a new pro-defence constituency of prominent voices in the trade and business
lobbies. The C.D. Howe Institute and the Canadian Council of Chief Executives
were among the public interest groups that crossed over from the commercial
domain to push for border infrastructure projects, the rebuilding of Canada's
military and closer security coordination at home and abroad (Welsh, 2004:
77–8). In the view of the public too, it seemed, more still had to be done.

When an election was called in 2006, the Conservative opposition under
Stephen Harper seized the opportunity to make defence an issue in the campaign. When they won power, the Conservatives championed the military,
increased defence spending, and extended the mission to Afghanistan by
another two years, to 2009. They were intent on demonstrating that they were a
new government determined to make the CF once again an institution capable of
meeting serious threats around the world as well as at home. Political turnover
was generating the same dynamic in defence policy that it had so many times
before.

C H A P T E R   8

Streams in the Development Policy Process

This chapter traces the evolution of Canada's international development policy agenda from the origins of the Cold War to the present. The discussion is divided into three sections. The first section, the problem stream, explores how the international development policy agenda evolved over more than five decades, identifying both the major problems that surfaced on the government's agenda and ideas about how those problems should be addressed. Intellectual turbulence in international development circles about how best to promote economic and social development has reverberated within Canada, posing its own, unique challenge in the formulation of policy. The second section describes the main actors and institutions in development policy. It explores the role of pressure groups, non-governmental organizations, and international institutions in shaping Canada's development policy agenda, along with the policy networks that influenced critical policy choices. The final section discusses the political forces that have driven policy agendas and ideas forward, highlighting those elements that relate to electoral, partisan, and pressure group politics. Chapter 9 will bring the three streams together at critical junctures, where opportunities for innovation and renewal are grasped by policy leaders or entrepreneurs.

THE DEVELOPMENT POLICY AGENDA

The evolution of Canada's aid policies since the end of the Second World War must be viewed within the context of a changing international development policy agenda, one that has been shaped by a combination of geostrategic and international institutional interests, changing ideas about the purpose and function of overseas development assistance, and the ebb and flow of political pressures in Canada's special bilateral relationship with the United States. International dynamics and events spilled over into the domestic Canadian arena in the form of objective indicators, focusing events, and feedback on

Canada's foreign and development policies. In this section, we trace the evolution of that international policy agenda and how it has influenced Canadian policy over the course of more than a half-century.

In the early years, Canada's aid policies were dictated by the Cold War problem of geostrategic rivalry between the United States and the Soviet Union. As the superpower contest for regional spheres of influence spread from the European theatre to Asia and the Cold War turned hot in the Korean peninsula, international development assistance came to be seen as a vital instrument of foreign policy and as a tool to promote democracy and stave off the threat of Communism in the newly decolonized states of the developing world. The Marshall Plan (1947), which had done so much to resuscitate the economies and polities of Britain and Western Europe, was seen as a model for global assistance, especially for the countries of South Asia, which were struggling with a host of social and economic ills that threatened their newfound freedom. But when it became apparent that the resources and political will were simply not available to recreate the Marshall Plan, policy makers were forced to look to other instruments.

One such instrument was the Colombo Plan, which laid the foundations for 'Co-operative Economic Development' in South and Southeast Asia. The main recipients were India, Pakistan, and Ceylon (now called Sri Lanka). Canada's decision in 1950 to participate in the Plan alongside Britain, Australia, and New Zealand was a controversial one. Some senior Canadian officials felt the Plan was a temporary expedient to thwart the Communist menace and others were downright sceptical that it would work. These sceptics preferred to use the United Nations as the main instrument for Canadian technical assistance abroad, rather than ad hoc arrangements like the Plan. This changed with the North Korean incursion into South Korea in June 1950. The Korean War was the crisis or focusing event that caused Canadian decision makers to rethink their position on the nascent Colombo aid initiative in the context of the Communist threat in Asia. Building upon this problem window, Lester B. Pearson, secretary of state for external affairs and the main Canadian champion of the Colombo Plan, was eventually able to persuade prime minister Louis St Laurent to commit funds to it. Canada's participation in Colombo was soon followed by technical assistance programs in Africa and the Caribbean and Canadian contributions to various multilateral relief efforts, including those of the United Nations.

The Cold War problem was supplemented by concerns closer to home. Food aid became one of the cornerstones of Canadian Official Development Assistance (ODA) under Prime Minister John Diefenbaker's government, which came to power in 1957. Diefenbaker, a native of Saskatchewan, had the strong support of Prairie wheat farmers who were keen to find ways of getting rid of their massive wheat surpluses. In 1956–7 food aid accounted for just 3 per cent of Canadian ODA, but two years later it had risen to almost 50 per cent of total ODA (Lloyd, 1960: 198). In the years that followed, food aid continued to be a way to dispose of Canada's substantial agricultural surpluses and reduce the costs of carrying excess inventory. The Canadian Federation of Agriculture (CFA) and the

National Farmers Union (NFU) were chief lobbyists for Canada's food aid programs (Charlton, 1992: 94–119).

Although Canada was an active supporter of the Colombo Plan, its ODA contributions during the 1950s and early 1960s were extremely modest. Canada's contribution stood at the bottom of the list of donors—a paltry 0.14 per cent of GNP in 1963–4 (Cohen, 2003: 78). Soon Canada came under pressure from its allies, particularly the United States, to increase its aid commitments. Negative feedback from south of the border notwithstanding, neither St Laurent nor Diefenbaker was prepared to give a major boost to aid spending.

With the election in 1963 of a new Liberal government led by Lester B. Pearson, Canada's ODA transfers witnessed a major increase as Canada's aid budget doubled in size. Pearson endorsed the UN target of one per cent of donor country GNP in transfers to developing countries. As Cranford Pratt argues, it was not simply Cold War politics and pressure from the United States, the world's largest ODA provider, which drove Canadian aid policies. Nor was this increase in development assistance motivated simply by a desire to find outlets for Canadian exports of goods and services in the developing world. Rather, it was Pearson's personal commitment to a more 'humane internationalism' directed at helping the world's poorest countries (Pratt, 1996: 341).

Canada's engagement in development assistance and cooperation in the late 1960s and early 1970s paralleled the experience of many of the industrialized developed countries, which established their own aid organizations. Feedback from development thinking in international circles in these early years subscribed to the 'take off' thesis of economic growth—namely, that all societies have to pass through a critical interval in their economic development where the traditional obstacles to achieving steady economic growth are finally overcome (Rostow, 1971). It was generally believed that development assistance could help lay the foundations for steady economic growth by promoting the commercialization of agriculture, boosting domestic consumption, and raising the level of savings and capital investment.

However, it was not long before ideas about the right path to development changed as the traditional development model, which stressed the importance of capital intensive projects such as dams, roads, and major infrastructure projects, was challenged by those who believed that social and not just physical capital should also be the focus of international assistance efforts (Browne, 1999: 20). These critics believed that education, health, and the provision of basic social services were necessary accompaniments to the development process. Evolving perspectives on the problems of human development were reflected in the *Report of the Commission on International Development* (Pearson, 1969), chaired by Pearson after he stepped down as Canada's prime minister. The report is perhaps best known for calling on developed nations to target 0.7 per cent of their GNP to international development assistance. The 0.7 per cent of GNP target became a recurring symbol of commitment to the international development agenda, but it is a target that only a handful of countries, Canada not among them, has attained. Other recommendations from the report were the creation of a framework for free and equitable international trade; mutually beneficial flows of foreign private investment; better partnerships, clearer purpose, and greater coherence in development aid; revitalized aid to education and research; and a strengthened multilateral aid system.

During the early years of the new Liberal government, led by Pierre Elliott Trudeau who succeeded Pearson in 1968, Canada's aid policies became even more focused on the needs and development challenges of the world's poorest countries. At the same time, the Canadian International Development Agency (CIDA) came under pressure from other corners of the bureaucracy to channel aid to richer developing countries that would be more receptive to buying Canadian goods and services (Pratt, 1996: 342). The government's five-year *Strategy for International Development Cooperation* (1975) declared that Canada 'would harmonize various external and domestic policies which have an impact on developing countries, and . . . use a variety of policy instruments in the trade, international monetary and other fields in order to achieve its international development objectives' (ibid.: 18). The government also pledged that 'the development assistance program will direct the bulk of its resources and expertise to the poorest countries of the world' and that 'particular attention [will] continue to be given to the hardcore least developed countries identified by the United Nations' (ibid.: 26). Among the other priorities outlined in the *Strategy* were official debt forgiveness for the poorest countries, a policy of 'untying' aid (that is, not making it conditional on purchases of Canadian goods and services) and greater investment in agricultural production, especially for those countries that were the recipients of food assistance.

The humanitarian and needs-based orientation of Canadian ODA policy proved to be short-lived as Canada's assistance policies and even the fundamental premise of ODA came under attack from a variety of different quarters. During the 1970s, although some developing countries, especially those in East Asia, were experiencing the benefits of trade liberalization and underwent rapid economic growth, others, especially in Latin America, Africa, and South Asia, did not. Economic instability and crises focused attention on trade as a better alternative to aid and bolstered the argument that developing countries should abandon their import substitution polices as quickly as possible (Browne, 1999: 73–94). Within international institutions like the IMF, World Bank, and the OECD/DAC (Organization for Economic Cooperation and Development/Development Assistance Committee), a new belief in the importance of markets as the path to development and economic prosperity also took hold.

However, in many developing countries a new generation of scholars and policy analysts associated with the *dependencia* school of thought argued that trade between the developing and the developed world was a one-way street and that the only way developing countries could move forward was to raise tariffs, reduce their exposure to the crippling forces of international competition, and curb their overall dependence on the global economy by restricting and controlling foreign investment (Frank, 1969; Cardoso and Enzo, 1979; Kapoor, 2002). The creation of the OPEC (Organization of Petroleum Exporting Countries) cartel and its successful efforts to raise oil prices in the 1970s, leading to an oil crisis in the West, gave further comfort to those who saw self-sufficiency and protectionism as the path to economic advancement.

Developing countries continued to beat the drum for a redistribution of global wealth and income, debt forgiveness, and a more level economic playing field in successive rounds of UNCTAD (United Nations Conference on Trade and Development), but without gaining much in the way of concessions. Even countries like Canada, which were willing to lend a sympathetic ear to their demands, grew increasingly impatient, especially after the acrimonious exchange at the Cancun Summit in October 1981, co-chaired by Trudeau and Mexican President José López-Portillo, buried any lingering hopes that a new dialogue in North–South relations could be launched.

On the domestic front, a series of highly publicized scandals in some of CIDA's assistance programs, coupled with Canada's own economic problems, marked by a rapid rise in inflation and a growing federal deficit, eroded public support for ODA. Canada's development priorities began to shift in the direction of supporting Canadian trade and investment abroad by channelling development assistance to those middle-income, developing countries where economic fortunes were rising. As CIDA began to show greater favour to Canadian exporters and investors, especially those who were internationally competitive, the goals of poverty alleviation and helping the world's poorest countries began to receive less attention.

Was there an inevitable shift in CIDA's policies in the late 1970s and early 1980s toward a more commercial orientation, stressing the integration of aid policy with foreign policy and its linkage to Canada's international economic and commercial interests? Feedback came with equal fervour from opposite ends of a fragmented development policy community. On the one hand, neo-liberal economists in the IMF and World Bank, espousing the value of free markets and the removal of barriers to trade and investment, criticized the traditional paradigm, with its emphasis on donor-led development. On the other hand, a new generation of scholars in developing countries argued that ODA, much of which was tied to concessions from those developing countries in trade and investment, was just another manifestation of neo-colonial imperialism (see Escobar, 1994: 53–101; Leys, 1996: 45–106). Indicators of rapid population growth in developing countries, mounting poverty, and the apparent failure of the Western modernization model to take hold, persuaded many in the non-governmental organization (NGO) community that a more targeted and focused 'basic needs' approach was required to help people in the developing world escape the poverty trap.

With the debt crisis in full swing in the 1980s and the imposed World Bank/IMF structural adjustment programs that many countries in the developing world soon found themselves labouring under, the debate only intensified. The publication of the *Report of Independent Commission on International Development Issues* (1980), chaired by the former West German chancellor, Willy Brandt, underscored the growing divide between redistributive, assistance-based versus market-driven approaches to the development challenge. The commission argued for a new political compact between North and South and a Marshall Plan-style program of aid and development assistance that would kick-start development in the South, especially in the poorest countries. Mounting concerns about the worsening health of the global commons also entered development discourse later in the decade with the publication of the report of the World Commission on Environment and Development, chaired by former Norwegian Prime Minister Gro Harlem Brundtland (1987). That document moved 'sustainability', which it defined in social and environmental terms, to the centre of the economic development agenda, recombining old agendas and ideas into the new motif of sustainable development.

In the 1970s and 1980s, greater attention also began to be paid to marginalized and/or disempowered groups, such as women and rural workers, in the development process. This shift was part of the movement toward a 'basic needs' approach in development, which was initially championed by the International Labor Organization (ILO) and subsequently endorsed by the UN General Assembly (International Labor Organization [ILO], 1976; Emmerij, Jolly, and Weiss, 2005: 215–16). The ILO explicitly recognized the importance of including gender in this new approach, arguing that the basic needs strategy had two facets—to enable women 'to contribute more effectively to the satisfaction of their families' basic needs' and 'to ease their work burden while furthering their economic independence and their more equitable integration into the community' (ILO, 1976: 61). Gender issues received great prominence at the first UN Conference on Women, held in Mexico City in 1975, an event timed to coincide with International Women's Year. The United Nations General Assembly passed several resolutions on Women in Development, among them a resolution declaring a 'Decade for Women' that urged governments to implement and assess gender issues and outlaw gender discrimination in all sectors of society. Further UN conferences on women were held in the decades that followed—Copenhagen (1980), Nairobi (1985), and Beijing (1995). The OECD/DAC also promoted the integration of women in the development process through its 'Guiding Principles to Aid Agencies for Supporting the Role of Women in Development' (Morrison, 1998: 239). The mainstreaming of gender equality into development discourses had followed from a series of initiatives at the international level including focusing events and the creation of indicators to gauge the successful implementation of Women in Development principles.

The growing disquiet at the international level about the purpose and role of ODA in development was mirrored in Canada's own public debate about CIDA's future direction. Many NGOs became increasingly vocal about CIDA's failure to make poverty alleviation and 'humane internationalism' the cornerstone of Canada's development assistance abroad. The publication in 1987 of the House of Commons Standing Committee on External Affairs and International Trade (SCEAT) report, *For Whose Benefit,* which was chaired by William Winegard, lent powerful political expression to these concerns, forcefully arguing that Canada had an ethical responsibility to help the world's poorest countries. The report contained a total of 115 recommendations, many of which urged that human needs and human resource development should take priority over geopolitical or commercial interests in Canada's development assistance programs. The report also introduced the problem of human rights into the development equation by recommending that CIDA should use aid to promote and protect human rights. It called for far-reaching administrative reforms that would place many more CIDA officers in the field, where they could see and understand development challenges firsthand. In addition, it advocated the creation of a special advisory council composed of outside experts who could provide long-range, strategic advice to CIDA. Finally, it called on the government to make a formal commitment not to lower Canada's ODA below 0.5 per cent of GNP.

It was a broadside assault on Canada's ODA policies. However, Brian Mulroney's Conservative government of the time and its foreign minister, Joe Clark, who was supportive of the recommendations contained in the Winegard Report, did not introduce far-reaching reforms in the programming orientation and delivery of Canada's ODA. Instead, in its response to Winegard, which was contained in two documents, *To Benefit a Greater World* (1987) and CIDA's own report, *Sharing Our Future* (1987), the government backtracked on many of Winegard's recommendations. There was rhetorical support for advancing human rights via ODA; bilateral assistance programming would increase and not diminish to the richer developing countries; donor recipients would have to conform to World Bank/IMF oversight; and broader, Canadian foreign policy and trade objectives would continue to inform Canada's ODA. The government did yield to some of the humanitarian and development recommendations of Winegard by endorsing the general proposition that 'Canada's development assistance efforts would be "guided first by humanitarian concerns"' (Morrison, 1998: 291) and acknowledging the need to alleviate poverty and address the social and economic downside effects of structural adjustment (ibid.: 294–5).

Other factors came into play as well. As a direct consequence of Canada's growing fiscal deficit and burgeoning debt load, the Conservative government was forced to cut federal spending. The year 1989 witnessed the beginning of several major cutbacks to the ODA budget and the abandonment of the ODA goal of 0.7 per cent of GNP. This year has been called 'the beginning of the period of a long decline' in Canadian foreign policy that was to last more than a decade as the federal government struggled to bring the deficit under control (Greenhill, 2005: 5). This 'decline' began in the years of the Mulroney government and was to continue under the Liberals, led by prime minister Jean Chrétien, who took office in 1993. It lasted into the early years of the twenty-first century, when the federal deficit was finally brought under control and Canada's economic prospects brightened.

During the 1990s, there was a further shift in the way the development assistance problem was defined in international and domestic policy circles (see, for example, Rodrik, 1999: 23–102). In global terms, ODA allocations for developing countries by OECD countries began to decline in both absolute and relative terms. However, private capital flows to developing countries began to increase markedly, especially as those developing countries began to experience economic recovery (North-South Institute, 2004: 7).

International development assistance efforts in the 1990s were also buffeted by new geostrategic and global developments that would solve old problems while simultaneously creating a roster of new ones. The end of the Cold War in the late 1980s eliminated one of the strategic imperatives for ODA, which was to reduce the risk that developing nations would turn to Communism and fall into the Soviet/Chinese orbit. However, with the collapse of the Soviet empire in Eastern and Central Europe, new claimants on development assistance budgets emerged. Many of the former members of that bloc needed help with their efforts to make the transition from centrally planned to market-based economies. The large size of their expatriate populations in many Western countries, including Canada, meant that there was also strong, domestic, political pressure to help these countries succeed with their political and economic transitions.

The end of the Cold War also marked the high watermark in international conflict (see *Human Security Report*, 2005). Many of these conflicts were products of the Cold War and superpower rivalry in different regions of the globe. With the end of the Cold War, many of the world's civil and regional conflicts began to draw to a close as the combatants, wearied by prolonged years of fighting and confronted with the prospect of losing their superpower sponsors and external bases of support, looked to negotiated political solutions as a way out of their impasse. Because of the high level of UN involvement in the negotiation and implementation of the peace settlements that ended these conflicts, members of the international community, including Canada, came under pressure to channel humanitarian and development assistance into the tasks of social, economic, and political reconstruction in war-torn states to speed their recovery and reduce the chances that conflict would recur. Nowhere was the need more apparent than in the sub-Saharan region of Africa, which experienced the lion's share of civil and interstate wars in the 1980s and 1990s. The rapid growth in the numbers of people infected by crippling diseases like HIV/AIDS, especially in sub-Saharan Africa, further complicated the development equation by creating a new set of pressures on development assistance, particularly in the areas of public health, education, and disease prevention.

As Mark Duffield (2001) and others (see Craig and Porter, 2006: 31–94) have argued, two big structural dynamics were at play in the 1990s. Neo-liberal orthodoxy, which celebrated the virtues of economic growth, the removal of trade barriers, and structural adjustment, was increasingly delegitimized, giving way to a new orthodoxy that stressed the virtues of 'good governance', the strengthening of civil society, and the development of democracy (Halperin, Siegle, and Weinstein, 2005: 203–30). Donor governments and aid agencies in OECD countries, whose commitment to conflict resolution and social reconstruction in war-torn societies and conflict zones grew during this same period, increasingly viewed the development challenge in terms of preventing the recurrence of conflict and ensuring, at a minimum, that development processes would not contribute to political instability by enriching and empowering some groups at the expense of others. The marriage of development orthodoxy with the 'new' liberal peace—the idea that the democracy promotes prosperity and peace—led to a new discourse of 'failed states' and the notion that developing countries would have to be directly transformed if they were to escape the poverty–underdevelopment–conflict trap. The engines of such a transformation were to be not just states, but NGOs, UN agencies, international financial institutions, and the private sector. This enlarged and disparate international community of development experts, stakeholders, financiers, practitioners and advocates would have to work together to secure the wholesale social transformation of developing countries.

The discourse of 'failed states', however, sat somewhat uncomfortably with the traditional orientation of the development community toward poverty alleviation, which, by the mid-late 1990s, had converged on the objective of reducing *extreme* poverty. This is because many members of the development community worried openly about the consequences of falling aid shares in the world's least developed countries, many of them in sub-Saharan Africa, where real per capita incomes were declining or stagnant (Canadian Council for International Cooperation [CCIC], 1994a, 1994b, 1994c, 1994d).

In order to make aid programming more effective, many also wanted to see the establishment of concrete benchmarks or targets to counteract donor 'fatigue' and mobilize political support. Following several major international conferences, a series of international development indicators or targets were eventually identified. In 1996, the OECD called for a reduction by one-half in the proportion number of people living in extreme poverty by 2015 as well as universal primary education in all countries by 2015, along with gender equality, access to universal primary health care and reduction in infant mortality (OECD/DAC, 1996). These targets were subsequently endorsed by OECD/DAC members, G8 countries, and the IMF and World Bank. The Millennium Development Goals (MDGs), which were approved by the United Nations General Assembly in 2000, also established general poverty reduction targets, suggesting that there was an emerging international consensus, if not about means then at least about general development goals and the importance of paying greater attention to human rights and human development. The Millennium Summit was clearly a major focusing event and turning-point in addressing the interdependent challenges of post–Cold War development. Summing up these new trends and approaches to development thinking, Emmerij, Jolly, and Weiss (2003: 230) argue that although 'neo-liberal orthodoxy and Western influence remain internationally dominant . . . the Millennium Summit of September 2000 outlined a new development agenda for the UN and opened up the possibility for a new and more balanced partnership with the Bretton Woods institutions and with the World Trade Organization. It is worth noting that this is the first time the World Bank and IMF have accepted outcome goals, as opposed to the process goals of structural adjustment in the 1980s.'

The notion that donors should work together and coordinate their efforts to reduce duplication and achieve maximum efficiency became part of the new mantra (Stiglitz, 1998 and 1999; World Bank, 2006). The proliferation of donor relationships, projects, and requirements in partner countries was widely perceived as a long-standing problem in many bilateral aid programs. There was an emerging consensus about the need for a tighter focus to ODA, stronger partnerships, and improved coordination among donors to avoid duplication of effort and waste. There was growing acceptance of the principle that aid programs should be evaluated on the basis of their 'results', with better monitoring and evaluation of those programs (World Bank, 2000). Many countries, including Canada, saw the need to concentrate development programming by moving away from funding individual projects to a more comprehensive, programmatic approach that would target aid to clear, defined, strategic priorities where the results could be measured. Development trends in aid effectiveness also corresponded to an emerging consensus among Canadian foreign policy circles around a 'niche' approach to international engagement in an increasingly complex world.

The philosophy of development assistance that emerged in the 1990s stressed the importance of 'local ownership'. This meant that donors would develop programming priorities in close consultation with host country governments and in a way that would allow recipient countries to feel that assistance programs were tied to their own national (and local) priorities and requirements rather than those of donors. This approach required much higher levels of consultation and coordination among donors than had been the case. It also meant that donors would have to be extremely knowledgeable about social, economic, and political conditions in recipient countries. However, there was obviously a continuing tension between donor objectives and those of recipient countries—one that was not easily resolved by the new rhetoric of 'local ownership' and responsiveness to local needs and aspirations. This is because development agencies in donor countries had to be accountable to their own public and political masters in deciding where ODA monies should go.

Canadian aid officials subsequently embraced many of these ideas and approaches to ODA, which reflected an emerging consensus in international development circles about the principles and the goals of effective development assistance. The idea that donors should work together through multilateral channels to allocate aid, identify and select countries where it was needed most, and develop programming priorities also seemed a good way to depoliticize ODA and ensure that development assistance programs were locked into long-term partnerships and commitments. CIDA's policy statement in 2002 argued for a 'comprehensive development model' growing out of 'a set of broadly endorsed objectives'. This new model was to be based on a 'balanced approach, which addresses the political, economic, social, and institutional dimensions of development'. The statement also stressed 'the importance of getting governance right', ensuring 'the proper sequencing of reforms', and the need to build 'capacity to ensure sustainability'. But, above all, the central principles for effective development were to be 'local ownership; improved donor coordination; stronger partnerships; a results-based approach with improved monitoring and evaluation of development programs; and greater coherence in those "non-aid" policies of industrialized countries than can have a profound effect on the developing world' (Canadian International Development Agency [CIDA], 2002a).

DEVELOPMENT POLICY ALTERNATIVES

Crucial ideas about the direction of Canada's international development assistance policies have been influenced by a changing constellation of actors, institutions, and interests that together constitute specialist communities at the domestic and the international level. Some ideas have clearly had greater traction than others in the evolution, development, and implementation of Canadian assistance policies. And the power of these ideas has tended to ebb and flow in direct proportion to the energy, political skill, and effectiveness of their advocates and the presence—or absence—of bureaucratic and political entrepreneurs who carry these ideas forward and secure their acceptance.

Until 1968, Canada's development policy community was small and self-contained. Those involved in policy advocacy were politicians and senior bureaucrats who generally tended to enjoy close, direct, working relationships. Neither the public nor Parliament were actively engaged in the policy process and there were no NGOs or civic associations that mobilized around development issues or lobbied government policy. To the extent that the public was 'engaged' in the formulation of aid policy, it was largely through traditional political channels and politicians who wished to curry favour with particular regional economic interests standing to benefit directly from government policy.

Canada's aid policies were obviously not developed in a vacuum. International pressures impinged on policy at every turn. They came from the Cold War and Canada's most important allies—the United States, which was the leader of the free world against Communism, and Britain, which had strong historical ties with its former colonies, including countries like Canada, Australia, and New Zealand. During these early years, international institutions, like the United Nations and its affiliated agencies or the fledgling DAC Group of the OECD, were not critical influences on Canadian aid policy.

Canada's own internal bureaucratic capacities in the development field were quite limited. Prior to Canada's decision to join the Colombo Plan in 1950, all of Canada's international assistance went to the UN, specifically to the UN's Expanded Program of Technical Assistance. After Canada joined the Colombo Plan, ODA was managed through the Technical Cooperation Service (TCS) in the Department of Trade and Commerce. As Canada's commitment to Colombo quickly grew from the initial contribution of $400,000 in 1950 to $25 million in 1951–2, TCS was replaced by the International Economic and Technical Cooperation Division (IETCD). In 1958, IETCD was upgraded to the Economic and Technical Assistance Branch (ETAB) in Trade and Commerce. In 1960, ETAB was replaced by the External Aid Office (EAO), under a director general with the rank of deputy minister who reported directly to the secretary of state for external affairs. Throughout this bureaucratic evolution, however, those officials responsible for managing Canada's aid disbursements construed their role narrowly as one of offering technical and administrative—not broader—policy advice. Policy entrepreneurship was further hampered by the fact that they were not 'career' professionals.

The absence of a mobilized, policy advocacy constituency either within the Canadian government or outside of it—certainly in the sense that we would understand such a community today—meant that Canada's ODA policy was made by the politicians and those who stood at the very senior ranks of the public service. This lent greater coherence to Canadian policy, but it also meant that policy was driven by the dictates of personality, ideas, the presence (or absence) of cabinet solidarity, and the overall priorities of the government of the day.

It is also quite clear that Lester Pearson, who served as Canada's secretary of state for external affairs from 1948–57, was the 'policy entrepreneur' par excellence in the shaping of Canada's ODA policies and commitments during these early years. Through the sheer force of his personality and his powers of persuasion, Pearson was able to cajole his cabinet colleagues and pressure his cautious and somewhat reluctant prime minister, Louis St Laurent, to commit Canada to the Colombo Plan and then secure a sizeable increase in Canada's foreign aid disbursements. As we see in Chapter 9, Pearson's ideas about the purpose and function of development assistance—and his support for the Colombo Plan, in particular—were motivated by a combination of realism and idealism. As a realist, Pearson believed that it was vital that Canada support 'democracy's answer to the spread of Communism in Asia' (quoted in Pearson, 1993: 52). As an idealist, Pearson believed that Canada had an obligation 'to assist in raising the standard of living of friendly peoples on the other side of the globe whose well-being and stability are of importance to the whole of the free world—ourselves included' (ibid.: 61).

When the government changed in 1957, Canada's aid policies came under the direct influence and control of Conservative Prime Minister John Diefenbaker, who, having won his election with the support of Prairie farmers, became the policy entrepreneur who elevated food aid as a cornerstone of Canada's policies. Diefenbaker's motivations were simple—to ensure that Canada's enormous wheat surplus had a market abroad. Under Diefenbaker, Canada's food aid quickly rose from 3 per cent of total ODA disbursements in 1956–7 to almost 50 per cent in 1958–9. Ideas clearly played less of a role in Canada's ODA in this period than electoral politics.

After winning the federal election of 1963, Prime Minister Pearson was once again able to place his personal stamp on Canada's development policies. Canada's ODA contributions increased dramatically. Pearson more than doubled the size of Canada's aid budget between 1963 and 1965. The government also began to support Canadian NGOs, with the Canadian University Services Overseas (CUSO) becoming the first development NGO to receive financial support from the government. Pearson also appointed Maurice Strong, a Canadian businessman, to head the External Aid Office (EAO) in the Department of External

Affairs. Strong became the next entrepreneur par excellence in the evolution of Canada's development policies.

Pierre Trudeau's election as leader of a new Liberal government in 1968 was important in a number of respects. As a result of Strong's lobbying, the EAO was changed to the Canadian International Development Agency (CIDA), with Strong as its first president. The creation of an independent development agency meant that there was now a proper administrative and implementing agency to oversee Canada's development partnerships. Under Trudeau, who wished to put a French face on Canadian foreign policy, Canada also began to pay greater attention to the needs of francophone Africa in its development assistance programs, balancing Canada's longstanding commitments to Commonwealth countries in the developing world, which had begun under the Colombo Plan (CIDA, 1971; Gérin-Lajoie, 1976; Sabourin, 1976).

Paralleling the creation of CIDA was a rapidly expanding local NGO sector, which also became involved in policy advocacy. Until the late 1960s and early 1970s, most of the NGOs involved in humanitarian and overseas development assistance were branches of international—that is, British or American-based—NGOs. This included NGOs like CARE, OXFAM, and Save the Children. This was also true of Quebec-based NGOs, which were also largely of foreign origin. However, with the growth of funding opportunities through CIDA and/or funds raised from private sources, the Canadian NGO community grew by leaps and bounds. The work of these NGOs included direct participation and responsibility for managing overseas projects and programs, development education, and public policy advocacy. Recognizing the need to coordinate their efforts at the national level, the Canadian Council for International Cooperation (CCIC) was created, which by the mid-1980s had well over a hundred institutional members and a mandate that included policy advocacy, representation and defence of NGO interests, information sharing, and government relations. CCIC also formed regional committees in the different provinces, including Quebec. Over its many years of operations, CCIC has been a firm and unwavering advocate of the need for Canada to raise its ODA levels and to target its programs to the world's poorest countries.

Other players in the advocacy community include the North-South Institute, which has focused much of its work on public policy research, including the areas of financial assistance and debt relief, and regionally focused groups like the South-Asia Partnership, Solidarité Canada Sahel, Partnership Africa Canada, various church groups, and the International Development Research Centre (IDRC), a government-funded and -operated Crown corporation committed to promoting and strengthening research capacities in the developing world.

The degree of policy influence exercised by these groups has tended to fluctuate over the years. Although they have been unable to change the general direction of aid funding, including the severe cutbacks (in real terms) to its budget that CIDA experienced during the 1990s, they have been effective champions of ODA in the media and on Parliament Hill, especially when parliamentary committees have conducted hearings on Canada's foreign and development policies and issued reports.

During the prime ministerships of Brian Mulroney and Jean Chrétien, Canada's ODA policies continued to be shaped, at the macrolevel, by prime ministerial and cabinet priorities. However, this period also witnessed growing levels of parliamentary engagement and debate about the content and future of ODA. The *Report of the Special Joint Committee of the Senate and the House of Commons on Canada's International Relations* (1986), which was chaired by Tom Hockin and Maurice Simard, and the subsequent *Report of the House of Commons Standing Committee on External Affairs and International Trade* (1987), which was chaired by William Winegard, were attempts to define new priorities for ODA. In both exercises, there were substantial levels of public consultation and engagement.

The Liberals issued their own policy statement, *Canada in the World* (DFAIT, 1995b), after they assumed power under Jean Chrétien. Again, the release of this report came after extensive public consultation and discussion and a parliamentary study by the Special Joint Committee Reviewing Canadian Foreign Policy (SJC-CFP) (1994), which was chaired by Liberal senator Allan MacEachen.

The presidents of CIDA have played an entrepreneurial role in shaping ODA priorities. Some presidents were clearly more effective than others in bringing their own ideas and agendas to the policy table. In the early years, Maurice Strong, Paul Gérin-Lajoie, and Marcel Massé were clearly important architects of Canada's aid policies. In later years, Margaret Catley-Carlson, Marcel Massé (who occupied the presidency twice), and Leonard Good were influential in softening-up domestic constituents and placing their own special imprint on Canada's development agenda—gender and human rights (Catley-Carlson), structural adjustment (Massé), and donor coordination and local ownership (Good). Personality, bureaucratic skill, and talent explain some of the variations in presidential effectiveness as entrepreneurs in the making of Canada's development policies.

During the years of fiscal austerity in the 1990s, when Canada's ODA budget fell by more than 30 per cent in real terms to just 0.25 per cent of GNP in 2000, there were few inside or outside of government, other than the NGO community and the occasional editorial in Canada's newspapers, who rallied to CIDA's defence. But the effect of these cuts and a comprehensive review of programming across all federal departments sharpened policy priorities and initiated a process of 'management renewal' and a shift toward 'results-based programming' (Morrison, 1998: 412). In an effort to rekindle its partnerships and build public support, CIDA tried to situate Canada's development assistance programs within a broader global strategy and the emerging 'consensus' within the wider, international development community about how development assistance should be carried out. This strategy, which focused on pursuing real targets in poverty reduction, improving coordination among donors, and moving ODA programming closer to the local needs and priorities of developing countries—all in the ultimate pursuit of 'sustainable development'—had initially been developed within the DAC of the OECD and later given strong endorsement and programmatic focus by the World Bank. CIDA's adoption of the OECD/DAC and World Bank's approach to development assistance also had other attractions. By working much more closely with other donors, CIDA would be able to insulate, at least partially, Canada's aid programs from unwanted political interference.

International organizations, particularly in recent decades, have played an important part in introducing ideas into Canada's development policy stream. The OECD's DAC, the Bretton Woods institutions (notably the IMF and the World Bank), and the United Nations Development Programme (UNDP) have been the most influential. However, it would be a mistake to simply view CIDA as a mere 'cue taker' of the policy ideas and proposals generated by international institutions. To some extent, the agency itself has been a policy entrepreneur in helping to shape the international development agenda through its ongoing dialogue with other donors in intergovernmental bodies and forums. These dynamics underscore the integration of development as a pillar of Canadian foreign policy.

The OECD's DAC is a consultative body that was created in 1960. Its mandate is 'to consult on the methods for making national resources available for assisting countries and areas in the process of economic development and for expanding and improving the flow of long-term funds and other development assistance to them' (Führer, quoted in Hampson et al., 2002: 163). The DAC is directed by the development cooperation ministers and heads of aid agencies of OECD members. It has a secretariat and a research unit that issues an annual report on development cooperation as well as specialized studies on different development issues. During its almost 50 years of operations, the DAC has issued numerous reports and recommendations to member countries on both policy and operational matters, including recommendations on 'best practices'. Although the OECD's thinking on development has generally tended to lean toward free market principles, including support for the liberalization of trade and unrestricted flows of capital, it has also stressed the importance of sustainability, human development, and, in recent years, the complex linkages between development and conflict (ibid.: 164–8).

The DAC's 1996 Report, *Shaping the 21st Century: The Contribution of Development Cooperation*, has arguably been one of the most influential contributions to the evolution of international development policy. The report argued that 'ways must be found to finance multilateral development cooperation that are adequate, efficient, predictable, and sustainable' (OECD/DAC, 1996: 2). It proposed a 'global development partnership effort' that would centre on the following goals: 'a reduction by one-half in the proportion of people living in extreme poverty by 2015'; 'universal primary education in all countries' by the same date; 'demonstrated progress toward gender equality'; 'a reduction by two-thirds in the mortality rates for infants and children under age 5'; 'access through the primary health-care system to reproductive health services for all individuals'; and 'the current implementation of national strategies for sustainable development in all countries by 2005, so as to ensure that current trends in the loss of environmental resources are effectively reversed at both global and national levels by 2015'. In order to achieve these goals, DAC members committed themselves to a 'willingness to make mutual commitments with our development partners', 'improved coordination of assistance in support of locally-owned development strategies', and better 'coherence between aid policies and other policies which impact on developing countries' (ibid.). In stressing the importance of coordination, the DAC has reached out to donors, multilateral development institutions, the UN system, and the private sector. Its agenda now includes such issues as the international financial architecture, corporate governance, and partnership and the governance of aid (OECD/DAC, 2000).

The Bretton Woods institutions, notably the IMF and the World Bank, have been valuable players in development and reconstruction processes. During the 1980s and 1990s, the International Monetary Fund was especially influential. This is because it was instrumental in setting the terms of conditionality for the world's most indebted countries as they struggled with their mounting debt burden and were forced to renegotiate (or cancel) their loans. In the process of helping developing countries address their balance of payments difficulties, the IMF required them to submit to wide-ranging reforms that included raising taxes, cancelling state subsidies, and trade and investment liberalization. Along with World Bank and the United States Treasury Department, the IMF was a proponent of the so-called Washington consensus in the late 1980s, a set of policies focusing on fiscal discipline, tax reform, competitive exchange rates, redirection of public expenditures towards health, education, and infrastructure investment, and market deregulation.

The World Bank, originally known as the International Bank for Reconstruction and Development, was meant to provide aid to Europe in the aftermath of the Second World War. The Bank soon shifted its focus to helping Europe's former colonies as they struggled to gain their economic footing after receiving their independence. The Bank's influence comes from its substantial lending programs, which run into the tens of billions annually, and its sheer size, which makes for its sway over private, bilateral, and multilateral institutions. Through its 'conditional' financing programs, the Bank exerts enormous leverage over the policies of developing countries.

The Bank's approach to development in the South has passed through four distinct phases or stages (Hampson et al., 2002: 154): industrialization and investment in large-scale capital projects in the 1950s and 1960s; poverty reduction, basic needs, and income redistribution in the early 1970s; fiscal policy reform, public sector efficiency, and structural adjustment in the late 1970s and 1980s; and a greater focus on sustainable human development, infrastructure development, and sectoral development and adjustment (especially in agriculture and integrated rural development) in the 1990s and early twenty-first century. The return to a more people-centred approach to development in the fourth phase was very much driven by the entrepreneurship of the Bank's president at the time, Paul Wolfensohn.

Much of the Bank's newest principles and thinking about development, especially its *Comprehensive Development Framework* (CDF) (Stiglitz, 1999; World Bank, 2006), contain more than a residual echo of the DAC's *Shaping the 21st Century.*

This is no accident because many of the same countries and donors are important players in both of these institutions, forming a closely knit policy community that generates common outlooks, orientations, and ways of thinking (Kingdon, 2003: 119). Like the DAC, the CDF stresses local country ownership of development efforts, extensive partnerships across government and other sectors of society, a longer-term vision of the development agenda that is based on extensive consultations within recipient countries, and greater attention to structural and social concerns (that have equal relevance to macroeconomic and financial concerns). The Bank has taken the lead in developing requirements for highly indebted poor countries to produce Poverty Reduction Strategy Papers (PRSPs), which are intended to establish clear guidelines for how international aid relief is to be used, and other policy instruments such as medium-term expenditure frameworks, sectorwide approaches, and poverty reduction strategy credits that can be adapted to meet these new principles and the commitment to results-based management.

The United Nations Development Program, which was established in 1967, is the fourth column in this international institutional edifice. The United Nations Economic and Social Council (ECOSOC) exercises oversight over the program, as it does for the UN's other social and economic programs and agencies like the UN Children's Fund (UNICEF), the Food and Agricultural Organization (FAO), the World Food Program (WFP), and the World Health Organization (WHO). UNDP is the chief coordinating instrument for the UN's work in the development field. It has a sizeable presence on the ground in developing countries through its field offices and resident coordinator. In 1990, UNDP launched its 'human development index', which ranks countries on the basis of their performance in such areas as education, life expectancy, and infant mortality, an annual exercise that regularly captures international headlines. UNDP is also involved in helping to co-manage the UN's Global Environment Facility and the UN Environment Program.

In the late 1990s, UNDP initiated a series of studies that attempted to redirect the development discourse in the direction of global public goods (GPGs), which are underprovided at the global level and have disproportionate, adverse impacts on developing countries (see Kaul, Grunberg, and Stern, 1999; Kaul et al., 2003). In addressing how various global public goods, such as peace and security, equity and justice, environment and cultural heritage, health, knowledge and information, international trade and financial stability, might be more effectively provided through global systems of governance, UNDP proposed a radical rethinking of the traditional principles of international development cooperation and financing mechanisms, which some considered to be too constraining to address the problems of global public goods provision. The UNDP's human development reports and indexes can be seen as part of an ongoing effort to refine concepts and focus public awareness and political decisions on those human security problems requiring collective action by the international community, such as the HIV/AIDS or global funding for efforts to combat major infectious diseases. However, this ambitious, if unwieldy, agenda created its own confusion and ambiguities. Policy fragmentation among disparate interest groups, states, and stakeholders advocating different aspects of the human security agenda, and especially relative to the unified policy networks and outlooks of the Bretton Woods institutions, created agenda instability.

Although some major donor countries, like Sweden and the United Kingdom, have gone so far as to embrace the notion of global public goods and to incorporate GPGs into certain aspects of their foreign and development policies, Canada has been far more cautious, in part because of the implications for the machinery of government of creating a separate funding mechanism that would be entirely devoted to global problems and that would fall outside of the traditional development assistance envelope. Human security in the form of landmines initiatives, efforts to establish an International Criminal Court and civilian protection in situations of armed conflict found a home at the Department of Foreign Affairs and International Trade. However, the broader public goods agenda did not fare as well in Canadian development circles. Although IDRC helped fund the UNDP studies, there have been no obvious champions within the Canadian bureaucracy to reorient development assistance in the direction of global public goods.

DEVELOPMENT POLITICS

The political stream, paralleling the problem and policy streams, contains elements such as public mood, pressure group campaigns, and elections, which produce changes in leadership and the party composition of Parliament. A new government may be more receptive to certain ideas than others, depending on its ideological orientation. And pressure group campaigns that are mounted by interest groups may be more effective in changing the policy agenda because a new government is more responsive to their ideas and policy proposals. Significant jurisdictional changes also shape policy outcomes as new actors and additional resources come into play.

The national mood has generally supported development assistance in Canadian foreign policy, and the mood has not changed appreciably even with changes in government. However, public support for ODA, which is reflected in opinion polls, masks deeper ambivalences about its purpose and importance. While some Canadians prefer to see aid tied closely to Canada's national economic and political interests, others believe that aid should be an instrument to combat poverty in developing countries. The number of Canadians who view development assistance as a high priority in Canada's international policies has fallen in recent decades.

During the 1950s and 1960s, ODA was viewed as a tool in the global struggle against Communism. But this ideological rationale was also infused with strong humanitarian overtones and a commitment to promoting a more humane and just international order. After the 1956 Suez Crisis, which won a Nobel prize for Lester Pearson, Canadians' expectations about the country's role in the world increased (Lyon, 1964: 3). Development assistance—along with peacekeeping—was viewed as the cornerstone of Canada's middle power, internationalist vocation (Doxey, 1989; Cohen, 2003). During the vaunted 'golden age' of Canadian foreign policy, the government moved on a number of fronts to strengthen its aid programming overseas. For the first time, the government began to provide funds to Canadian development NGOs by establishing a special NGO program. At the same time, bureaucratic responsibility for Canada's bilateral and multilateral development assistance polices came to be concentrated in the External Aid Office of the Department of External Affairs. A concerted effort was made to recruit for and develop a 'career service' of development assistance professionals (Spicer, 1966: 115–17). Maurice Strong, an individual with extensive private-sector experience, was appointed to head Canada's aid office in 1966. Two years later, the EAO became a separate entity from the Department of External Affairs and was renamed the Canadian International Development Agency (CIDA) with Strong as president, a rank equivalent to that of deputy minister in other government departments. The establishment of a separate agency with jurisdiction over Canada's development agenda set the stage for greater autonomy in policy perspectives, a shift that would sometimes lead to friction between CIDA and the foreign affairs establishment.

As Canada's ODA contributions grew steadily during the 1960s and early 1970s, reaching their peak in 1975 when ODA accounted for 0.53 per cent of GNP, there was little public discussion (or criticism) of ODA. That was to change in the 1970s, when a series of highly publicized scandals about some of CIDA's projects in Africa severely damaged the agency's image and prompted demands for a parliamentary inquiry into CIDA's management practices and aid allocations. It took a long time for CIDA to recover from the battering it suffered in the media. Opinion polls taken in the late 1970s suggested that Canadians continued to support ODA, but the level of support was not as robust as it had been in earlier years (Morrison, 1998: 140).

Attitudes did not change significantly in subsequent decades. A national opinion poll commissioned by CIDA in 1987 'confirmed widespread support among Canadians for Canada's ODA program and policy. Only 18 percent of those queried thought that the Canadian government was spending too much money on ODA while a majority (66 percent) thought that Canada should be among the more generous donor countries in the world' (Clarke, 1990: 196). A similar observation was offered in the late 1990s: 'the long-term trend has shown little significant change upward or downward, and it remains at the relatively high levels that have prevailed for the better part of two decades'. However, in more recent years 'the Canadian consensus over foreign aid is weaker and more fragile than what is often suggested'. As aid budgets were slashed in the 1990s, only a small majority of Canadians favoured an increase in them, although a strong majority continued to express their support for the general principle of development assistance. Surveys also show that Canadians harbour doubts about the effectiveness of aid programming, with some believing that it does not make much of a difference to poor countries and others that it is 'used for self-serving purposes, and is being wasted by bureaucrats and dictators alike' (Ian Smillie, quoted in Noel, Thérien, and Dallaire, 2004: 16, 27).

Canadian levels of public support for development assistance put it in the middle of the pack among OECD countries. Comparative polling data show that northern Europeans are the most strongly committed to development assistance, while fewer than half the American population support foreign aid (ibid.: 17–19). Canadians are ideologically divided in their views about development assistance; those who identify themselves as liberals and as socially progressive strongly support development assistance, but conservatives are more skeptical (ibid.: 41). Development assistance tends to fall at the lower end of the list of Canadian priorities for government spending. Domestic economic and social concerns have consistently been at the top of the list. Among international concerns, the environment and global political stability ranked higher in the 1990s than poverty alleviation and support for developing countries, especially during the past decade (Kirton, 1994). Perhaps most telling, there was a steady erosion in the importance assigned to development assistance as an international priority from the 1970s to the 1990s. The level of support dropped 'by almost two-thirds, from 58 percent in 1979 to 39 percent in 1984 and to 23 percent in 1990' (Munton, 2002–3: 162).

If public opinion polls are one measure of the national mood, media reportage is another. Most studies of media coverage of Canada's development assistance policies find that coverage is limited if not 'inadequate'. As Erica Martin observes, 'During the massive spending cuts of the ODA envelope throughout the 1990s, the media generally remained silent and this silence has been identified as minimizing policy discussion. . . . Due to the media's omission, few Canadians were aware of the spending cuts that occurred and this may have contributed to the public's current tendency to overestimate levels of spending' (Martin, 2005: 31). To the extent there has been coverage, it has generally tended to be unsystematic, sporadic, and focused on 'crisis situations rather than long-term development' (ibid.: 37). All this suggests that, as a barometer of national mood, the Canadian media's view of ODA has generally been one of indifference except when crises or scandals have erupted to make headlines.

Pressure group campaigns to boost ODA spending have typically been led by the NGO community and groups like CCIC (Canadian Council for International Cooperation), which have consistently lobbied for increases in ODA. However, these groups were unable to arrest the steep decline in Canadian aid spending in the 1990s, when Canadian ODA performance, measured by ODA to GNP ratio, sank from 0.45 per cent in 1991 to 0.27 per cent in 1998. Calls for a more coherent approach in Canada's relations with the developing world that would be centred on devoting the lion's share of CIDA programming to promoting sustainable human development and reducing the use of ODA for commercial purposes had little traction.

Draimin and Tomlinson (1998: 143) attribute this decline to fiscal pressures and 'the implementation in the 1990s of neo-liberal economic policies in Canada and abroad' that fractured the 'strong postwar consensus on social values and the response of the state to its citizens'. As a consequence, they argue, government, think-tanks, and even NGOs increasingly 'questioned the rationale and goals for donor programs' and their relevance 'in the face of increasing globalization' (ibid.). Such a change in national, and even international, mood is notoriously hard to measure. However, Draimin and Tomlinson find evidence for this breakdown in the dearth of ideas and proposals for reform in the Liberal government's 1994 foreign policy review and the government's response in 1995, *Canada in the World.* They argue that the absence of a clear reform agenda, fiscal restraint, and 'an absence of government leadership on the "big picture"/frame-setting aid issues' meant that any policy innovation in CIDA was only at the margins and confined to modernizing CIDA's bureaucratic procedures and management systems (ibid.: 144). To the extent that a new paradigm of development assistance emerged during this period, Draimin and Tomlinson believe it was driven by a preference to expand private-sector involvement in developing countries, promote government deregulation, and support a global trade and investment regime centred on the rights of private capital and expanding market opportunities.

Sometimes elections and/or leadership changes have accompanied major changes in policy—for example, Pearson's election as prime minister in 1963, which saw a boost in aid spending, the establishment of CIDA under Trudeau, coupled with new aid programs in francophone Africa. At other times, they have not. The steady decline in ODA, which began under Mulroney and continued under Chrétien, was driven by budget deficit fears and the desire of both leaders to rein in runaway public expenditures. Too much political turnover also creates its own special problems. In a period of just four years (1996 to 2000), CIDA had four ministers of international cooperation. This contributed to a widely criticized lack of focus and clear strategic direction in Canada's aid policies in the late 1990s.

By the turn of the twenty-first century, the picture changed in a more positive direction. Having wrestled Canada's deficit to the ground, the federal government announced a series of important funding and policy decisions in 2002, including a commitment to increase Canada's international assistance programming by 8 per cent per annum until 2010, with the aim of reaching the ODA UN target of 0.7 per cent of GNP. The government announced a series of wide-ranging measures to support development on the African subcontinent, including a $100 million investment fund to support the private sector in Africa. The government also committed itself to allocate half of its ODA increases to Africa and to adopt the DAC recommendation of untying Canadian ODA to developing countries, particularly in the areas of financial and project assistance (OECD/DAC, 2003: 11).

Prime Minister Jean Chrétien's own leadership in his legacy-building last years in office drove much of this turnaround, as did bureaucratic players within CIDA.

As host of the G8 Kananaskis Summit in Alberta in 2002, Canada spearheaded the G8 Action Plan for Africa and was directly responsible for inviting the heads of five African countries, representing the New Partnership for Africa's Development (NEPAD) to the summit meeting itself (Fowler, 2003; CCIC, 2004a). These had been preceded by the prime minister's own visits to Africa and a series of nationwide, public consultations that had taken place on Canada's foreign policy priorities. Describing what it viewed as 'major policy breakthroughs in aid volume and on the wider policy coherence front', the OECD's DAC commended CIDA for 'broadening and deepening the organizational change process' and moving CIDA to 'a programme and country focused organization operating within the framework of developing country driven strategies, aimed notably at poverty reduction and the achievement of the Millennium Development Goals' (ibid.: 12). CIDA's own strategic statement on aid policy, *Canada Making a Difference in the World—A Policy Statement on Strengthening Aid Effectiveness* (2002) reflected this increased focus on Africa as well as Canada's commitment to the UN's MDGs.

In September 2002, CIDA joined other donors in formally committing Canada to structure development assistance around program-based approaches (PBAs) to implement PRSPS in developing countries. By the end of 2004, 45 PBAs 'were operational or under development' accounting for 'roughly 15 percent of CIDA's share of the ODA budget by 2005/06'. The fact that the *International Policy Statement* (IPS) (Government of Canada, 2005a), which was issued later by Prime Minister Paul Martin's Liberal government, was based primarily on CIDA's 2002 report, with few substantial changes, indicated that Canada's development policy was not a priority for reform. However, some members of the NGO community warned that these new approaches to donor disbursements were 'continuing to impose their own far-reaching conditions in the aid relationship' and in a way that 'removed the political locus for national decision-making away from the political checks and balances where citizens should have a significant role in influencing public policy' (CCIC, 2004b: 3, 21).

Prime Minister Harper's new Conservative government pumped fresh infusions of cash into ODA in its 2007 spring budget—much of it to be directed toward development and reconstruction efforts in Afghanistan and Iraq. However, rumblings about the need to undertake a major overhaul of Canada's ODA policies had yet (at the time of writing) to be translated into a concrete package of new policy initiatives by the Harper government.

In the next chapter, we explore how these three streams—problems, policies, and politics—merged in the concrete formation of Canada's development policies. It analyses those episodes where policy changed, as well as those episodes where, although some of the conditions conducive to change were present, there was not a convergence of the three streams because the critical ingredient of leadership was missing. That leadership in the development arena has come from individuals who display remarkable qualities of imagination, insight, personal drive, and ambition, even when the odds are stacked against them. Above all, they are individuals who have a keen sense of opportunity. Our story correspondingly shifts from a description of the role of ideas, institutions, and political forces mobilizing around a particular policy agenda, to a discussion of how policy entrepreneurs instigate and direct policy change.

The Evolution of
International Development Policy

From the early days of Canada's involvement in the Colombo Plan to the twenty-first century, Canada's development assistance policies have moved through several phases or turning points. These stages are marked by a change—sometimes major, occasionally more modest—in the general orientation of Canadian development assistance policies. In this chapter, we explore the motivations and forces behind those episodes of change, when a new policy window opened and there was an opportunity to explore alternatives to existing policies. In each instance, policy change was driven by a major international crisis or new international developments, the convergence of changing agendas, the presence (or absence) of available policy alternatives, and/or by politics of the electoral or partisan variety. Our story also concentrates on the role played by policy entrepreneurs who were the engineers of change and exploited these moments of opportunity. Many of these individuals clearly had the right mix of personality, authority, political connections, and negotiating skills to advance policy in new directions. It was simply not the case that they happened to find themselves in the right place at the right time.

The history of Canadian ODA, however, is not simply one of innovation and change. It is also one of stagnation, confusion, and frequently a lack of strategic focus and direction. The inability of the Canadian International Development Agency (CIDA) to bring new thinking and solutions to development problems was often due to a lack of leadership at critical moments in the organization's history when pressure and circumstance would argue for change in policy direction. This was especially true during the mid-1970s and later on in the 1980s and 1990s when CIDA's budget was cut, and Canada's Official Development Assistance (ODA) spending and programming went into serious decline.

The problem during these hard times was not simply a lack of leadership. Leadership alone cannot open policy windows, especially when elements in the problem and politics streams are not in alignment. The 1990s were a period when the development paradigm was once again being challenged and redefined as new problems emerged on the world stage in the Cold War's aftermath. Beginning in the mid-1990s, policy convergence among development, security, and prosperity agendas led to bureaucratic competition with the Department of Foreign Affairs and International Trade (DFAIT), depleting already limited resources at CIDA. The public mood was also changing. Although Canadians continued to express their support for ODA, it was not high on their list of international priorities and there was no rallying cry to reverse years of decline. Canada's non-governmental organization (NGO) community was also not terribly effective in pressuring the government to change the direction of its development assistance policies. A general lack of media attention to development issues meant that the public was not well informed about development questions. In this respect, there was no alignment of policy agendas, ideas, and politics during this period, with the result that ODA fell hostage to narrow entrenched political and economic interests.

LESTER PEARSON AND THE COLOMBO PLAN

Canada's support for the Colombo Plan is a story of enlightened leadership that exploited a window of opportunity, brought on by the Korean War, to initiate change. As Keith Spicer observes, 'for five years following the Second World War, Canadian development aid flowed only through the multilateral channels of United Nations Specialized Agencies. During this time, there was no central Canadian office to receive and process requests for aid. Grants to UN agency funds were studied by the Department of Finance, in consultation with Bank of Canada and the Department of External Affairs; while administration of UN training programmes in Canada and the recruitment of Canadian experts for UN service grew empirically, on lines of ministerial specialization' (Spicer, 1966: 93–4). However, the exclusive UN focus to Canada's development assistance programming was to shift with Canada's decision to participate in the Colombo Plan. So too did the practice of Canada's assistance and the expansion that took place in the decade that followed the 1950 Colombo Conference (Spicer, 1966: 95–100).

The stage for Canada's entry into development assistance was set at the April 1949 Commonwealth meeting in London, England. It dealt with the admission of the newly independent states of India and Pakistan into the Commonwealth, an international organization made up of Britain and its former colonies. Lester B. Pearson, Canada's secretary of state for external affairs, was keenly supportive of India's and Pakistan's membership (see Cavell, 1954–5). Yet other Commonwealth leaders were deeply concerned about India's decision to adopt a republican-style constitution, which contradicted the Commonwealth's allegiance to the British crown. Pearson was nonetheless passionate about retaining an association with India, so that the Commonwealth would become 'multilateral' and 'multiracial'. Pearson also took seriously Indian Prime Minister Jawaharlal Nehru's warnings that India's fledgling democracy was already being threatened by Communism and the dire poverty of its citizens. Upon visiting Colombo and other parts of Asia later in that same year, Pearson became convinced that the only way to curtail the threat of Communism and totalitarianism in the region was through a combined policy of 'self help and mutual aid'. A program of assistance to lift peoples out of poverty in these strategically important newly independent states was perceived to be the best solution to the seductive powers of political socialism. Pearson saw 'little value in preaching the virtues of the democratic way of life to starving people' and viewed economic and technical assistance as a practical way to promote democracy (Pearson, 1973: 49–51, 107–8).

The problem window had been identified and Pearson was an able entrepreneur, but there was little appetite in the Canadian government for a Commonwealth aid program for Asia. Pearson and the minister for fisheries, Robert Mayhew (who had accompanied Pearson on his travels), recommended that Canada contribute $500,000 per year to the proposed Commonwealth technical assistance program. But finance minister Douglas Abbott did not like the idea, and, instead, took one-fifth of this amount and put it toward the UN technical assistance program. At the same time, Canadian officials were ordered to merge both the Commonwealth and UN programs in order to avoid a duplication of effort in the two different multilateral institutions. As Geoffrey Pearson writes, 'this housekeeping approach to international programs was no doubt worthy of the auditor mentality of the Department of Finance, already troubled by the prospects of new commitments to NATO (North Atlantic Treaty Organization), but it boded ill for any large-scale Canadian effort to extend capital assistance to the Asian members of the Commonwealth' (Pearson, 1973: 54).

The invasion of South Korea by North Korean forces on 25 June 1950 escalated concerns about Communism in Asia and underscored Pearson's urgent appeals for increased and rapid support to the new Asian members of the Commonwealth. A window of opportunity opened. At the London Consultative Meetings of Commonwealth officials, which took place in September, the Canadian delegation was given more flexible instructions. Canada lent its agreement to a six-year assistance plan for the Commonwealth's new Asian members. But the precise size of the Canadian contribution was still contentious in cabinet, with the minister of finance opposing Pearson and Mayhew. Eventually, Pearson's arguments won the day. On 7 February 1951 the Canadian government approved a grant of $25 million to be made available to the Colombo Plan, a grant that was renewed the next year and then increased subsequently.

The Plan had bipartisan support and had the advantage of being an initiative taken independently of the United States. Yet, as Geoffrey Pearson argues in a fine study of his father's diplomacy, 'it is not certain these arguments would have prevailed, had not St. Laurent and Pearson come to believe through their first-hand contacts with Asian Commonwealth leaders, especially Nehru, that Canada had a key role to play in building ties with India and Pakistan, all the more so as the prospect of an American-led war with China [over Korea] loomed large' (Pearson, 1993: 60). Canadian leadership in the consolidation of the new

Commonwealth was possible because the opportunity was seized at a propitious moment, when problem and politics converged.

MAURICE STRONG AND THE ESTABLISHMENT OF CIDA

The establishment of the Canadian International Development Agency (CIDA) in 1968 marked another turning point in the evolution of Canada's development assistance policies and a shift away from ODA as a form of charity to development and partnership. This change was the result of a clear merging of the three streams of problems, policies, and politics. The international development policy agenda was changing as donors realized that a much more comprehensive and sophisticated approach to development was required than simply providing aid to developing countries. Many of these new ideas were reflected in the *Report of the Commission on International Development* (Pearson, 1969), which was sponsored by the World Bank and chaired by Lester B. Pearson.

Conditions at home were favourable to new ideas and policy alternatives. As Canada's administrative capacities grew with the substantial increase in ODA spending under Pearson, these new ideas entered the policy stream. The 1968 transition in the government's leadership from Pearson to Pierre Trudeau, moreover, created a window of opportunity in the politics stream for policy innovation and a different approach to the way the government administered its development assistance programs. Finally, the arrival of a new set of policy entrepreneurs, most notably in the person of Maurice Strong, who became the first president of CIDA, allowed for the coupling that linked problems and solutions to the new government's decision-making agenda.

In a bold move, Pearson had appointed Strong, a businessman with no prior government experience, to succeed Herb Moran as director of the government's External Aid Office (EAO) in 1966. This came as the Pearson government was doubling Canada's aid budget. Under Pearson, the government also began to fund Canadian NGOs, with the Canadian University Service Overseas (CUSO) as the first to receive direct government support. Canada supported the founding of the African Development Bank and also became a charter member of the Asian Development Bank.

Strong was a self-made millionaire. At the age of 33, he had become president of the Power Corporation, one of Canada's largest and most important corporate entities. He had a strong philanthropic bent, having been active with the Overseas Institute of Canada, CARE, and the Red Cross. Strong also served as international president of the YMCA and, in that capacity, spoke about the importance of strengthening Canada's international role. The initial suggestion to Pearson to appoint Strong as head of the EAO came from J. Roby Kidd, head of the Overseas Institute. When Pearson offered him the post, Strong agreed on the condition that EAO be reformed to become the focal point for Canada's bilateral and multilateral assistance programs (Morrison, 1998: 58).

With his appointment to the EAO, Strong subjected the entire organization to a full-scale review. He recruited Denis Hudon, Canada's executive director of the

World Bank, to help him. The bureaucracy of the Department of External Affairs, the EAO's home, resisted Strong's reformist agenda and assertions of bureaucratic independence. There were challenges from the outside too, especially a growing disquiet in international circles about the utility of aid. Some argued that the promotion of international trade through the removal of tariffs and other non-tariff barriers was the way to achieve economic growth and development. Many developing countries favoured protectionist policies that would help their infant industries and resorted to rent-seeking policies in the form of various kinds of taxation that enriched state coffers (and private pockets). Within Canada, there was an increasingly powerful, mobilized constituency that wanted the government to use ODA to promote Canadian business by tying project funding to the purchase of Canadian goods and services.

Strong fought off these pressures. He was able to help secure the passage of legislation that eased some of the restrictions on tied aid and allowed for up to 25 per cent of project funds in developing countries to be spent on local, as opposed to Canadian, goods and services. Under Strong, Canada also supported the establishment of the Commonwealth Technical Assistance Program (1967), the forerunner to the Commonwealth Technical Cooperation Program, which was established in 1971. Notwithstanding his entrepreneurial abilities, Strong was unable to fully realize his bureaucratic ambitions until the election of a new Liberal government headed by Pierre Trudeau in 1968. In Trudeau, Strong found a leader who was receptive to his ideas about change and the need for reform. On Strong's recommendation, Trudeau moved quickly to change the EAO into CIDA, a reform that was carried out in the new Liberal government's first year in office and was aimed at underscoring the principle of partnership in development. Although there was no formal legislation that was introduced in Parliament to bring about this change in CIDA's status, the consequences were profound and far-reaching. With CIDA's creation, the Canadian ODA budget grew dramatically. In fact, so rapid were the increases that CIDA was not able to disburse all the funds it received.

Strong moved quickly to recruit talent to help lead the agency. Among the individuals he brought into the agency were Donald Tansley, the former deputy minister of health in Saskatchewan, who became CIDA's first vice president; Joseph Hulse, a food scientist; and Clyde Sanger, a journalist who oversaw communications (Morrison, 1998: 65). Tansley initiated a major review of CIDA programming in an effort to make planning and operations in recipient countries the central focus of development assistance. CIDA began aid programming for francophone Africa in order to give better recognition to Canada's bicultural status at a time when separatism was growing in the province of Quebec and its government was openly challenging the federal role in foreign policy. Strong's other achievements included the funding of a NGO program, cementing CIDA's ties with Canada's NGO community; the harnessing of the talents and energies of Canadian business and industrial firms in development (ibid.: 71); and the founding of a new think-tank, IDRC (International Development Research Centre), to carry out research and projects 'where assistance is likely to have the greatest impact on development' (Peters, 1969: 15). Strong also downgraded the importance of food aid, which had come under increasing criticism, in Canadian ODA. It dropped from 50 per cent to roughly 30 per cent of ODA.

Although Strong's forcefulness and unorthodox tactics made him unpopular with the bureaucracy, especially with officials in the Department of External Affairs, his close relations with Pearson and Trudeau meant that his ideas usually carried the day. Canada's foreign aid reached almost 0.28 per cent of GNP in 1968–9, rising again to almost 0.4 per cent in 1970–1 (Cohen, 2003: 85). The Trudeau government also formally endorsed the recommendations of the Pearson Commission that ODA should reach 0.7 per cent of GNP. By the time Strong left CIDA in 1970, development assistance had become a central pillar of Canadian foreign policy. The government's *Foreign Policy for Canadians* document of that year acknowledged as much in making it clear that ODA was 'an integral part of Canada's foreign policy', a way for Canada to establish its international significance and make a 'distinctive Canadian contribution' (quoted in Morrison, 1998: 211).

The momentum that CIDA harnessed under Strong's leadership continued with his successor in the presidency, Paul Gérin-Lajoie. In the 1975–6 fiscal year, Canada's ODA to GNP ratio reached 0.53 per cent, the highest level it has ever attained (see Gérin-Lajoie, 1976). But CIDA's capacity to manage those resources effectively came under public criticism and parliamentary scrutiny after a series of highly publicized scandals broke in the press in the mid-1970s. These scandals tarnished Gérin-Lajoie's legacy. His immediate successor, Michel Dupuy, who led the organization from 1977 to 1980, had to devote much of his presidency to restructuring and overhauling CIDA's financial planning, accounting, and monitoring systems (Morrison, 1998: 146). Over this period, the challenges of implementation and controversies in the politics stream closed the window for initiating substantive policy changes or renewal.

MARGARET CATLEY-CARLSON AND THE POLITICS OF GENDER EQUALITY AND DEVELOPMENT

As Razavi and Miller (1995: ii) point out, 'the international women's movement, punctuated by the United Nations World Conferences on Women, has since the 1970s called on international development agencies and governments to "integrate" women into the development process'. The first institutional response was the establishment of Women In Development (WID) bureaus in development agencies in donor countries, which funded and/or executed a variety of women's projects. However, by the mid-1980s, 'due to the slow pace of progress in women's status and well-being, and the continued marginalization of women-specific projects, the need for new strategies became apparent. In this context, "mainstreaming" gained currency among international agencies and governments as a new strategy aimed at bringing women's concerns into the center stage of development' (ibid.).

Where did Canada and CIDA stand on this global movement to 'mainstream' gender into the development process? In some areas, Canada was at the forefront of the movement to promote gender in development. However, it was not until Margaret Catley-Carlson, the first woman to be appointed to the presidency of CIDA (1983–9), assumed her post that gender was pushed to the top of CIDA's agenda. Her appointment, which itself created a window of opportunity for policy change on this important issue, accompanied rising domestic and international pressure to place a more human face on development, with greater attention to human rights, women, and the environment (Morrison, 1998: 221). When problem and politics converged around the promotion of women's role in development, a Canadian entrepreneur was ready to mobilize for the cause.

The women in development, or WID, agenda benefited from a spillover of concerns in other domains of domestic politics (Kingdon, 2003: 190–4). Women's issues were prominent in Canadian politics well before they surfaced on the government's development agenda. In the 1960s and 1970s, the women's movement gathered momentum and women's groups in anglophone and francophone Canada successfully lobbied for a Royal Commission on the Status of Women (Rankin and Vickers, 2001). Trudeau's Liberal government supported the initiative because it integrated the concerns of francophone and anglophone Canadians at a time when national unity was a major government priority. Among the recommendations of the Royal Commission was an 'implementation committee' for women. In 1971, the government created the post of minister responsible for the status of women. This was followed in 1973 by the creation of the Advisory Council on the Status of Women, which was subsequently replaced by the National Action Committee on the Status of Women.

The first World Conference on Women, sponsored by the United Nations and held in Mexico City in 1975, placed gender at the forefront of international attention. Member of Parliament Coline Campbell, who headed the Canadian delegation to the conference, was an effective promoter of WID and a Canadian commitment to the integration and equality of women in aid programming. The conference was timed to coincide with International Women's Year and the start of the UN's Decade for Women. That same year the UN General Assembly passed several resolutions on women in development (UNGA Resolutions 3490, 3503, 3519, 3520, and 3523), including the recommendation 'that all international technical and financial assistance programs and agencies should give sustained attention to the integration of women in the formulation, design, and implementation of development projects and programmes' (UNGA Resolution 3524). The ILO (International Labor Organization) (1976) stressed the importance of gender equality in its 'basic needs' strategy for development, and other UN agencies integrated the principles of gender equality into their programming. So too did the OECD (Organization for Economic Cooperation and Development), which emphasized the importance of integrating women into development programs (Morrison, 1998: 239).

With the Liberal government's announcement in 1976 that it was creating a new agency, Status of Women Canada, Canada became the first country in the world to formally announce that it was incorporating the UN's women in development guidelines into its policies and programs. CIDA's policy branch created a 'one person responsibility centre' to oversee WID. However, other than issuing general WID guidelines for integrating women into existing development strategies, there was no real strategy to achieve gender equality in actual program implementation.

Catley-Carlson's appointment as president of CIDA proved critical to making WID a concrete reality. After a distinguished career in Canada's foreign service, and postings in CIDA as a vice president and then senior vice president, Catley-Carlson was exceptionally well qualified to take the helm. At a time when donor fatigue was setting in, and many of the economies of Western countries, including Canada, were in deep recession, Catley-Carlson made it her mission to improve CIDA's image by deepening the agency's relationships with the media, NGOs, and the Canadian public (Morrison, 1998: 221). Her entrepreneurial efforts in this regard benefited from excellent communications skills that enabled her to reach out to different constituencies and build a national mood supportive of the WID agenda. In addition to integrating women in development, her priorities included strengthening the role of the private sector in the development process and advancing environmental sustainability in development programming (ibid.: 227).

One of Catley-Carlson's first initiatives was to establish the WID Directorate in CIDA's policy branch and appoint Elizabeth McAllister, who was the WID coordinator in CIDA, as the unit's first director. McAllister had extensive experience in implementing affirmative action plans elsewhere in the bureaucracy. She recognized that her role had shifted 'from being an advisor to being a person who would create palatable policy that others could apply'. She also understood that she still did not have the power 'to implement their application: I could only persuade' (quoted in Faveri, 1992: 72).

In 1984 McAllister proposed a new approach to WID in CIDA in a document entitled 'Managing the Process of Change: Women in Development' (CIDA, 1983). It called for a change in CIDA attitudes and the institutionalization of a 'systemic/accountability response' that would mobilize resources and bring about organizational change in CIDA. McAllister's proposals were instrumental in shaping Catley-Carlson's own new directives for WID, which appeared in the form of a comprehensive WID goal statement and policy framework in November 1984 (CIDA, 1986: 3). The operational objectives outlined in the statement became the basis for a five-year action plan for the agency to promote WID both internally in CIDA operations and through Canada's international partnerships.

Among the various measures adopted by CIDA 'to foster the active participation of women in the development process' were the creation of a senior-level steering committee to oversee the integration of WID in all aspects of CIDA programming; the development of specific plans and sector guidelines to ensure that women were both 'agents' and 'beneficiaries' of development; and special new staff training programs, developed in cooperation with Harvard University, designed to provide CIDA managers 'with a method of analysis that will assist them to better incorporate women in the development activities financed by CIDA abroad'. CIDA also formally committed itself to promoting the integration of WID in multilateral agencies and forums in which Canada was a member (CIDA, 1986: 4–6), which it did vigorously and successfully. CIDA was a major supporter of the new UN Fund for the Development of Women and Women's World Banking, an international NGO that was established to help women in the developing world in their business endeavours.

Catley-Carlson viewed WID as one of her most substantial achievements at CIDA (for a critical perspective, see Pfister, 1989). Her success in institutionalizing WID in the agency was reflected in the valuable role that CIDA and Canada would play in subsequent decades in promoting gender equality in poverty reduction, health, basic human needs, children, population, human settlements, and social and sustainable development (Status of Women Canada, 1996). By the mid-1970s, the essential role of women in development had been recognized by both international and domestic policy communities. Catley-Carlson's leadership, and that of key individuals such as Elizabeth McAllister, was essential to this transformation, whereby WID and gender equality became a defining priority in Canada's development assistance policies (see, for example, CIDA, 1996a, 1999; Tiessen, 2003).

MARCEL MASSÉ, STRUCTURAL ADJUSTMENT, AND THE NEW AUSTERITY

The year 1989 was an extraordinary one in international affairs. Changes occurred at such a pace in Eastern Europe and the Soviet Union that observers in the West were caught by surprise. The destruction of the Berlin Wall in that year symbolized the revolution underway in Eastern Europe, as the Communist regimes of Poland, Hungary, East Germany, Czechoslovakia, Bulgaria, and Romania fell because of popular pressures for reform. It was also an important year domestically as the federal government, confronted by Canada's ballooning fiscal deficit and crippling debt, was finally forced to confront the consequences in the budget of April 1989. Minister of finance Michael Wilson's budget committed the government to reduce federal spending while raising new taxes through a variety of new measures that included a goods and services tax (GST). The government announced that it would accelerate the sale of publicly owned corporations in the transportation and energy sectors and cut transfer payments to the provinces for healthcare and education. Canada's ODA budget came in for some of the biggest cuts of all. Under the budget plan, ODA expenditures would be reduced by about $1.8 billion over the next five years. Although foreign aid only accounted for 3 per cent of total federal expenditures, it would be cut by almost 23 per cent. The government also abandoned its earlier commitment to accept a target for ODA growth to 0.7 per cent of GNP by 1990 (Clarke, 1990: 198).

Development thinking was in turmoil. The ending of the Cold War meant that the traditional rationale for development assistance, as a tool to fight Communism, had completely evaporated. In its place stood two very different ideas about ODA—the humanitarian (or traditional liberal) vision versus a new (conservative) economic orthodoxy. The humanitarian vision, which viewed ODA as an instrument to help the poorest of the poor, had been emphasized in two reports that were issued during the Mulroney government's first term. The Simard-Hockin Report on foreign policy, *Independence and Internationalism* (1986), argued that development policy should not be used exclusively for trade promotion purposes, but instead to counteract 'the tendency towards have and have-nots and for promoting the development of the poorest regions' (quoted in Morrison, 1998: 274). The special report of the House of Commons Standing Committee on External Affairs and International Trade, entitled *For Whose Benefit?*, chaired by William Winegard, delved deeply into the purposes of development assistance. After extensive consultations at home and abroad, it identified three priorities for ODA: humanitarian ('to alleviate human suffering and promote social justice'); political ('to increase stability and peace'); and economic ('to support the economic growth of developing countries') (quoted in ibid.: 191). It stressed the importance of strengthening human and institutional capacities in developing countries and in a manner that was consistent with the principles of sustainable development.

In international circles, development thinking was moving in the opposite direction, embracing a neo-liberal ideology that stressed the principles of sound economic management, the importance of free and open markets for trade and investment, divestment of state-owned enterprise, shrinkage of the public sector, fiscal austerity, and reductions in social subsidies provided by the state. As indicated in Chapter 8, the IMF (International Monetary Fund) and the World Bank were the major, international institutional advocates of this new orthodoxy.

Crippled by rising levels of debt, high unemployment, and declining terms of trade, many developing countries in the 1980s had found themselves falling under 'structural adjustment' programs that were mandated by international financial institutions. In order to be eligible for new loan, and/or a rescheduling of their existing debt obligations, developing countries had to submit themselves to a rigorous program of reforms that reduced public expenditures and the role of the state in the economy, eliminated trade barriers, and created a more welcoming environment for international investors. In practice, this meant the elimination of food subsidies, drastic cuts to healthcare and education, and a major reduction in public services, with the burden of these adjustments falling disproportionately on the poor.

Given domestic and international cross-currents, and a fragmented development policy community, it was not entirely clear where Canada's development assistance policies would land during this time of transition. Political conditions were ambiguous. The members of Prime Minister Mulroney's Progressive Conservative government were split between those who subscribed to neo-liberal (that is, conservative) orthodoxy in the management of Canada's international relations (like minister of finance Michael Wilson) and those 'red Tories', like Joe Clark, Douglas Roche, and Flora MacDonald, who favoured a foreign policy that was attentive to the welfare needs of world's poorest citizens and promoted human rights. The prime minister's own thinking seemed to fall somewhere in the middle.

With Marcel Massé's appointment to CIDA's presidency in 1989, Canada's ODA policies landed on the conservative side of the equation. Massé was not new to the file, having served briefly as CIDA's president in early 1980s. His first presidency was generally unremarkable. He espoused the new rhetoric of 'basic human needs' in aid programming, oversaw a further expansion of CIDA's budget, initiated a variety of image-building outreach programs, and advanced a series of modest internal management reforms.

In the intervening years between his two presidencies, Massé had served as Canada's representative at the International Monetary Fund (IMF). His years at the IMF had clearly influenced his own thinking about the nature of the development challenge. Massé became a champion of structural adjustment and was instrumental in the IMF's efforts to organize a structural adjustment program among major donors for Guyana.

In one of the first speeches he gave on his reappointment to CIDA, Massé stated that 'structural adjustment looks more relevant with every day that passes'. He went on to say that 'CIDA has taken the leap of faith and plunged into the uncharted seas of structural adjustment. . . . Structural adjustment figures among the priorities for Canadian development assistance' (quoted in ibid.: 203). Over the next several years, CIDA began to work closely with the Department of Finance in the formulation of structural adjustment programs by providing inputs into the Policy Framework Papers, the blueprints for economic reform that were prepared by the IMF in close consultation with the World Bank and at the field level in Washington and through the Canadian Executive Director's offices (O'Neil and Clark, 1992: 224).

With each new federal budget came further cuts to ODA. Depleted resources increased the competition among disparate Canadian stakeholders for control over the development agenda. Massé's enthusiasm for structural adjustment put him on a collision course with Canada's NGO community that continued to beat the drum of poverty reduction and ODA increases. Officials in the Department of External Affairs, including the ministers (Joe Clark and then Barbara McDougall, who succeeded him in 1991), were wary of Massé, if for somewhat different reasons than the NGOs. They were suspicious of his bureaucratic intentions and obvious desire to assert CIDA's independence from its foreign affairs' political masters. External Affairs did not like Massé's overt expressions of independence because it challenged the department's long-held view that aid policy should be subordinate to foreign policy. External Affairs was keen to see aid monies flow toward the newly independent states of the former Soviet Union, in order to help them consolidate their independence and democratic reforms. It also wanted more flexible aid programming to meet the growing number of humanitarian crises that were engulfing sub-Saharan Africa, especially in the Horn of Africa.

The Interchurch Fund for International Development, the Churches' Committee on International Affairs, and the Canadian Council of Churches (Interchurch Fund for International Development, 1991: 6) issued a scathing attack on Canada's ODA under the provocative title, *Diminishing Our Future: CIDA: Four*

Years After Winegard. The report charged that 'CIDA's practice has been reshaped since the Winegard Report . . . [and that] structural adjustment programs in developing countries has become its chief focus.' It alleged that 'Massé clearly believes that the economic practices and policies of Third World governments bear primary responsibility for Third World poverty' (ibid.). It recommended that CIDA should 'no longer link Canadian bilateral assistance to the acceptance of IMF conditions by recipient countries', but should 'formally endorse the priorities which underlie the Winegard Report' by affirming that 'CIDA's central objective should be to aid the poorest countries and peoples rather than promote IMF Structural Adjustment Programs and the advancement of Canadian commercial interests' (ibid.: 10). Echoing long-standing demands of the Canadian development community to deny bilateral development assistance to countries where there were gross and persistent violations of human rights, the report called for 'staffing and organizational changes' in CIDA to ensure that human rights' considerations were properly integrated into CIDA's decision-making processes (ibid.).

Despite his efforts to lead CIDA in new directions, Massé was not unresponsive to these concerns. Nor, as his earlier advocacy for the basic needs agenda indicated, did he consider macroeconomics to be the sole solution for the world's development problems. Confronted with these criticisms and mounting pressures, Massé issued a new mission statement, which was contained in a memorandum dated 28 March 1991. This statement was released only after extensive consultations between Massé and the members of his staff. The memorandum suggested that the concept of 'sustainable development', which was first articulated by the Brundtland Report in 1987 and had become fashionable in development policy circles, should be the cornerstone of Canada's aid policies. But it should also be based on five pillars: economic sustainability (which would promote the efficient allocation of resources in developing countries); social sustainability (for example, support for healthcare and basic education programs targeted at specific social groups, especially women); environmental sustainability (through the continued implementation of environmental assessment procedures, which had been strengthened by staff training and the creation of CIDA's environmental division); political sustainability (stressing a respect for human rights in aid programming); and cultural sustainability (taking greater account of local values and cultures in aid policy) (O'Neil and Clarke, 1992: 222–9).

Massé's tenure was marked by several other developments. The government's February 1991 budget created an international assistance envelope to provide ODA funding to Eastern Europe and the new states of the former Soviet Union in order to assist them with their economic and political transition to market-based democracies. Because there was little 'new' money in the federal budget for CIDA, however, these programs came at the expense of its long-standing programs in Africa and elsewhere in the developing world.

Human rights conditionality loomed larger in bilateral assistance. Thus, aid allocations to Kenya, Sri Lanka, Haiti, China, and Indonesia were either suspended or reduced because of human rights abuses in those countries (CCIC,

1994c). The growing importance of human rights in Canadian foreign and development policy during this period were driven by the prime minister himself. Prior to the Harare Commonwealth Heads of Government Meeting in October 1991, and in subsequent statements at the Francophone summit in Paris in November 1991, Mulroney announced that Canadian aid would henceforth be conditional on human rights performance. With the upsurge of democracy in the newly independent states of Eastern Europe and the former Soviet Union, and growing public protest in Africa against authoritarian regimes, along with the establishment of new, multiparty democracies in countries like Benin, Gabon, Kenya, Mali, Togo, and Zambia, Mulroney's activism on behalf of human rights and democracy was welcomed by many and was a critical ingredient in Massé's successful entrepreneurship in this domain.

Massé also launched a strategic management review of the agency, which began with an external consultant's report prepared by the Quebec management consulting firm, SECOR. The firm's unwieldy 403-page report focused on the escalating costs of CIDA's aid dispersion and identified a myriad of problems with the agency—among them, the dispersion of aid across too many countries, programs, and institutions; CIDA's cumbersome, complex, and rigid contracting processes; and its liberal use of consultants. Massé asked his deputy, Douglas Lindores, CIDA's senior vice president, to review the report and draft a detailed set of recommendations. After many more consultations and discussion, Lindores produced his report. However, when the recommendations were subsequently presented to minister for external relations Monique Landry and then to cabinet for approval, the government balked. The politicians were completely taken aback by the wide scope of the proposed reforms, especially with an election call in the offing. Massé's own departure from CIDA in January 1993 meant that the implementation of these reforms was left to his successors (see Morrison, 1998: 335–46). Thus, partisan interests and the turnover of personnel put up barriers to the reform of policy practices and changes to development agendas.

Under Massé's leadership, the window of opportunity, in this case the opportunities presented by the more or less steady growth of CIDA's budget during the 1970s and 1980s, began to close. Canada's ODA to GNP ratios began to fall, from a high of 0.5 per cent in 1988–9 to 0.43 per cent in 1993–4. Aid programs in sub-Saharan Africa were especially hard hit. Canada cancelled its aid programs in Tanzania (until then, CIDA's largest program in Africa) and Ethiopia, decisions that were extremely controversial (Morrison, 1998: 372). Canada's ambassadors in those countries were given no prior warning when projects were abandoned and were not able to discuss why the decision had been made.

Massé alone was not responsible for this state of affairs. The chief responsibility lay with his political masters and the minister of finance. However, Massé's own political philosophy about ODA's role in economic development, stressing the principles of efficiency and the policies of structural adjustment in the development process, was very much in keeping with the spirit of the times. He was not someone to rush to the barricades, as many in the NGO community wanted.

And the national mood, which had become increasingly sceptical about ODA, meant that it was difficult to rally public support in CIDA's defence.

It would be unfair to paint Massé's legacy in stark terms. He gave substance to the rhetoric of sustainable development in CIDA's policies, and following the cues that came from the prime minister himself, Massé made human rights a priority in ODA. Although he was not successful in bringing about much-needed internal reforms, he understood the depth of CIDA's managerial malaise and the need to streamline the bureaucracy and narrow Canada's aid priorities. He was also prepared to respond to his critics inside and outside of government.

STAGNATION AND DECLINE IN THE 1990S: AN ABSENCE OF LEADERSHIP?

Although the end of the Mulroney era, and of Massé's own tenure at CIDA, marked the beginning of ODA's demise, at least in budgetary terms, the most savage cuts were to come with the election of a new Liberal government in 1993 led by Prime Minister Jean Chrétien. The changes to ODA policy that began under the Conservatives accelerated sharply under the new Liberal government as it wrestled with the country's massive public debt and fiscal expenditures that had clearly run out of control.

At the outset of the Chrétien era, it looked as if things might be different. In the Liberal government's 1995 foreign policy review, *Canada in the World* (DFAIT, 1995b), three foreign policy objectives were identified: promotion of prosperity and employment, protection of security, and the projection of Canadian values and culture. CIDA's own mandate in this context would be 'sustainable development in developing countries, in order to reduce poverty and contribute to a more secure, equitable and prosperous world' (quoted in Draimin and Tomlinson, 1998: 150). Priorities for development assistance would focus on basic human needs, women in development, infrastructural services, human rights, democracy and good governance, private-sector development, and the environment. The statement contained no major blueprint for ODA reform or a renewed focus on poverty alleviation, which many in the development community had urged in their appearances before the Special Parliamentary Committee Reviewing Foreign Policy the previous year (ibid.).

In the years that followed, there would be little program innovation as Canada's total aid disbursements fell from 0.38 per cent of GNP in 1995 to 0.27 per cent in 1998 and 0.26 per cent in 1999. The lack of innovation is hardly surprising because so much of CIDA's bureaucratic energies were diverted internally into managing budget cuts. Although Canada's falling aid contributions paralleled the decline in the OECD as a whole, 'Canadian trends [were] even more sharply defined relative to other donors' (ibid.: 144). The impact of this decline was especially felt on Canada's aid programming in the poorest region of the world: 'aid to sub-Saharan Africa . . . declined in nominal dollars by 30.4 per cent between 1992–3 and 1996–7, a rate greater than that for either ODA as a whole (21.2 percent) or bilateral aid (16.8 percent)' (ibid.: 153–4).

There was periodic, and negative, feedback from the international community. Reviewing Canada's aid performance toward the end of the decade, the OECD's DAC (Development Assistance Committee) was highly critical of Canada's aid volume and performance. It noted that reductions in ODA raised real concerns about Canada's ability to meet expectations about its role in the world and that Canada's reputation was suffering as a consequence. The review questioned the wide geographical dispersion of Canada's aid programming, recommending greater concentration on a limited number of countries. It expressed strong concerns about the overwhelming number of programming priorities and the absence of clearly defined and measurable objectives consistent with available financial and human resources. It suggested that there was a real need to re-examine the efficiency of 'tied aid as a means of promoting Canadian exports and employment alongside the costs and benefits of tied aid to developing countries' (OECD/DAC, 2003: 73). It also called for 'initiatives, partnerships and accountability systems' that 'reinforce rather than weaken the all-important partnerships with developing countries' (quoted in CCIC, 1998: 2).

The efforts of Prime Minister Jean Chrétien and his finance minister, Paul Martin, to slay Canada's fiscal deficit lay behind much of CIDA's troubles and budgetary difficulties. ODA was obviously not the only government program to suffer during these years of fiscal austerity. Social programs, especially in education and healthcare, were also cut to bring the deficit under control. And there were lean pickings for Canada's military, which had to make do with smaller forces and deteriorating equipment.

The problem was not simply one of resources. It was also one of leadership. Huguette Labelle, CIDA's president from 1993–9, served under a revolving door of political masters. From 1993 to 1996, André Ouellet, the minister of foreign affairs, was responsible for Canada's development assistance. As the prime minister's Quebec lieutenant, he used his position to steer government contracts toward his home province. In 1996, however, Chrétien created a separate portfolio, the minister for international cooperation, with direct responsibility for CIDA. In fairly rapid succession, three different individuals occupied the post from 1996 until 1999—Pierre Pettigrew (25 January 1996 to 3 October 1996), Don Boudria (3 October 1996 to 10 June 1997), and Diane Marleau (11 June 1997 to 2 August 1999). As Draimin and Tomlinson astutely observed at the time, 'The lack of consistent political leadership undermines the capacity of the aid program to be an advocate for sustainable human development within Canadian foreign policy' (1998: 161).

When Lloyd Axworthy assumed the post of foreign minister in 1996, a post he held for the next four-and-a-half years, he tried to promote greater levels of policy integration with other parts of government in the domain of international policies (International Trade, International Cooperation, and the secretaries of state for Latin America/Africa and Asia) by hosting regular meetings. However, recurring tensions between CIDA and Foreign Affairs over policy and resource allocation issues, heightened by the difficult (though modestly improving) fiscal climate, were such that they undermined Axworthy's desire 'to build common cause with Cabinet colleagues' (ibid.: 162). Notwithstanding its human development underpinnings, Axworthy's human security agenda proved difficult to sell, at least initially, to CIDA. Over time, however, there was a greater melding of these two agendas, especially in efforts to direct humanitarian and development assistance toward the victims of armed conflict, especially women and children (see Axworthy, 1997; CIDA, 2001c; Donaghy, 2003).

REVERSING THE 'LONG DECLINE': ODA IN THE TWENTY-FIRST CENTURY

At the turn of the new century, Canada's development policies began to experience something of a revival. There were a number of factors that explain this turnaround. First, the special problem of budgets in the agenda-setting stream seemed no longer pertinent. The improving health of the Canadian economy and federal coffers meant that government spending was on the rise. This factor alone created new windows of opportunity. Second, the appointment of Leonard Good as CIDA's president in 1999 breathed new life into the agency, giving it the leadership, focus, and sense of direction it had lacked. Third, in the aftermath of the September 11, 2001, terrorist attacks in the United States, international affairs was suddenly on everybody's agenda. In the context of the new transnational terrorism crisis, international development policy concerns shifted toward defence and security and in the direction of alleviating what some considered the 'root causes' of terrorism and global insecurity—poverty and chronic 'underdevelopment' in the face of globalization.

Good had strong academic credentials, with a Ph.D. in economics from the University of Western Ontario. He had just left his post as Canada's executive director on the board of the World Bank, a position he held from 1994 to 1998. Before that he had been Canada's deputy minister of the environment (1989–93) and earlier served in a variety of senior positions in the Department of Energy (1979–87). Good appointed Brian Emmett as his vice president for policy. Like Good, Emmett had an economics background, having also trained at the University of Western Ontario and the University of Essex in the United Kingdom. Emmett had followed Good from the Department of Energy to Environment Canada where he had served as assistant deputy minister for corporate policy. Along with Good, he had played a central role in the development of Canada's Green Plan (a package of environment-friendly policy initiatives). Emmett's mandate was to improve the efficiency of Canada's development assistance policies to poor countries.

It did not take Good long to state his priorities. He openly declared his strong support for the recommendations of the OECD/DAC report, *Shaping the 21st Century* (1996), and the lessons that were contained in World Bank's own *Comprehensive Development Framework* (2006; see also Stiglitz, 1998 and 1999). These included the principles of country ownership for development, closer relations with civil society, donor cooperation, realistic timeframes, the notion of a more balanced approach between structural macro policies and social policies (CCIC,

2001: 3–5). Good's emphasis coincided with mounting government and public concerns about 'aid effectiveness'. This alignment of problem and politics paved the way for Good's proposal to develop a new business model for CIDA that was less project-oriented and more focused on overall program delivery and results. As Emmett pointed out, there was now much greater emphasis in the Canadian public sector in 'getting results, transparency, and accountability' (ibid.: 8).

CIDA's new development policy was outlined in its September 2002 policy statement, *Canada Making a Difference in the World: Strengthening Aid Effectiveness* (CIDA, 2002a). The statement laid out priorities and principles, and announced two changes in strategy: a shift from individual, project-based approaches to more comprehensive and policy directed so-called program-based approaches. The latter would also focus future CIDA spending on a much smaller number of recipient countries.

To see the significance of these two strategic changes—and gauge their coherence and durability—it is first worth recalling the rich abundance of development policy priorities that CIDA had compiled over the preceding decade (the following discussion draws from Hampson and Hay, 2004). The 1995 foreign policy review, *Canada in the World*, asserted 'six program priorities' for ODA: basic human needs; women in development; infrastructure services; human rights, democracy and good governance; private sector development; and the environment. CIDA's 2002 policy statement observed that 'these priorities cannot be seen as providing a focused agenda for CIDA. Rather, there is a broad menu of thematic options.' Whether as priorities or options, the six remained embedded in CIDA's policy scheme.

In September 2000 CIDA formally adopted for itself four 'social development priorities': health and nutrition; HIV/AIDS; basic education; and child protection. At the same time, 'gender equality' and 'mainstreaming' were declared integral to all four of these priority areas (CIDA, 2000a; see also CIDA, 2001b and 2001c; CIDA, 2002b). These social development priorities were reaffirmed in CIDA's 2002 policy statement (CIDA, 2002a), along with a commitment 'to double CIDA's investment in social development over a five-year period with specific targets in each of the four areas for each year through to 2005'.

Two further priorities materialized in 2002, shortly after Susan Whelan joined the cabinet and became minister responsible for CIDA. Henceforth, explained the minister in her foreword to the 2002 statement, 'CIDA will give added emphasis to rural development and agriculture.' This emphasis was described as a contribution to economic growth and poverty reduction, and to reversing the decline in agricultural investments recorded in developing countries through the 1990s. The formal policy was outlined in CIDA's 2003 paper on *Promoting Sustainable Rural Development Through Agriculture* (CIDA, 2003a). Finally, CIDA's new policy for revising its framework for private-sector development was enunciated in another paper, *Expanding Opportunities for Private Sector Development* (CIDA, 2003a and 2003b).

Many CIDA priorities were being added but none subtracted. In the Canadian policy process, it had long proven easier to declare a new priority or focus than to abandon an old one. The operational salience of any development priority was diluted by the appearance of competing priorities. However, the move from project-based to program-based approaches, which had been directed by Good and Emmett, did constitute a major new policy initiative. Announced in the 2002 policy statement, CIDA explained the transition in part as an outgrowth of principles articulated in *Shaping the 21st Century*, the influential 1996 report by the DAC, the OECD's Development Assistance Committee. The five principles recited by CIDA included local ownership; improved donor coordination; stronger partnerships between donors and recipients; a results-based approach, with better monitoring and evaluation; and greater coherence between aid and non-aid policies in trade, investment and technology transfer. As well, CIDA added 'three other factors . . . of central importance to the effective use of aid investments': good governance; building capacity in poor countries to support sustained development; and engaging civil society in recipient countries. Eight more principles and 'factors' had thus been injected into CIDA's pre-existing priorities, thus diluting earlier efforts to bring some discipline and a narrower, more targeted focus to ODA.

The arguments for program-based approaches were strong, meeting many of the criteria for survival in the policy stream. These approaches would help to reduce costs otherwise attached to multiple and separately administered projects. They would also minimize burdens on developing-country capacity, while expanding that capacity. And they would encourage more efficient coordination among donors, while promoting local ownership. CIDA's adoption of program-based approaches was consistent with the Poverty Reduction Strategy Papers (PRSPs), first conceived at the World Bank and the International Monetary Fund. Further still, they meshed with the Sector-Wide Approaches (SWAps), which were gaining ground in the ODA community. CIDA's objective, put simply, was to align its program-based approach for any developing country with that country's PRSP and SWAps—all for a comprehensive, coordinated, and locally owned development strategy. Values and interests were both served by the new approach to selecting aid partners and programs.

The second significant change confirmed in the 2002 policy statement was the determination to focus aid on fewer countries. Despite an earlier notional focus on 30 countries and regions, the statement said, bilateral Canadian aid was really being dispersed across about one hundred countries. Of all the donor countries, Canada was among the least concentrated in its aid allocations, a point that had been made a decade earlier in the SECOR report on CIDA and repeatedly since. As a corrective, the statement committed CIDA to focus on a particular category of developing country: those that are poor, but have 'functioning governments, albeit with weak capacity'. The needs in these countries for external resources may be substantial, 'but they are also committed to taking ownership of their development challenges'. CIDA would concentrate on countries with 'a high level of poverty as measured by income per capita and a commitment to development effectiveness, as demonstrated through efforts to improve governance, ensure local ownership of poverty reduction strategies, end corruption and make effective use of aid monies'. In addition, 'special consideration may also be given to countries with the potential to exercise regional leadership'.

The logic of concentrating ODA on a smaller number of promising recipient countries was undeniable, especially if CIDA's program-based approaches were to reach the necessary critical mass to make any genuine or lasting difference. Aid increments would have no noticeable sector-wide or economy-wide impact if they were dispersed too thinly to have effect anywhere. The discourse of 'niche diplomacy' making the rounds in Canadian foreign policy circles added to the acceptability of aid concentration around a selective group of development partners.

The 2002 policy statement did not spell out which countries would qualify under CIDA's new standards. The nine chosen recipients were publicly named in CIDA's spending plan, issued with all other departmental and agency estimates by the Treasury Board Secretariat in February 2003. Senior CIDA executives professed confidence that the list of nine—Bangladesh, Bolivia, Ethiopia, Ghana, Honduras, Mali, Mozambique, Senegal, and Tanzania—would remain intact for the foreseeable future (Treasury Board Secretariat, 2003). Elaborate multiparty agreements were to be put in place, binding donor and recipient governments and international institutions. Notably, six of the nine were countries in Africa, a region to which Canada was committed by prime ministerial declaration and G8 undertakings at the Kananaskis Summit, hosted by Canada in 2002, and again, in 2003, at the G8 Summit in Evian, France.

The durability and coherence of the policy were to prove tenuous, however. CIDA's nine chosen focus countries did not correspond unambiguously to the developing countries of deepest interest to Foreign Affairs (or National Defence). There was subsequent pressure to enlarge the list, even if not to remove any countries from it. Moreover, other problems and political interests and developments in adjacent areas of Canadian foreign policy spilled over into the development domain. As a result of Canada's military commitments in Afghanistan, that country soon came to represent Canada's largest aid commitment, even though it had not presented itself as credibly qualified under CIDA's earlier declared priorities.

CIDA's program-based approaches were firmly rooted in development principles articulated by the OECD's Development Assistance Committee and the World Bank, and were intended in part to stem the capacity drain on recipient countries associated with managing multiple projects. However, program-based approaches typically involve bigger sums of money than project-based approaches, and they rely heavily on reasonably smooth and coordinated implementation over several years. As a result, program-based approaches carry their own risks. Because they demand more time, more money, and more complexity, they are vulnerable to setback, blunder, and political retreat, either in donor or recipient governments. Sooner or later, events would test the true commitment of CIDA, and of Canadian ministers, to these approaches.

Some critics argued that the durability of CIDA's program-based approaches would be further challenged by a tension inherent in the approaches themselves—the tension between local ownership (by the developing country) and the accountability that donor governments owe to their own taxpayers. These tensions are even more acute in the case of PRSPs, which can give the appearance of imposing 'local ownership' on roughly the terms dictated by donors (CCIC, 2004b).

CIDA's engagement in more comprehensive development approaches, locking its programming into extensive arrangements with other donors and recipient governments, meant that any disengagement from such agreements would inevitably attract political and financial exit costs for Canada. This would tend to discourage alteration of CIDA commitments once made, reducing flexibility, although increasing durability. As noted above, CIDA's program-based approaches also placed a premium on good governance of every kind, from specific program management to the overall government of a developing country.

These changes in policy were accompanied by formal commitments of new money, reversing years of decline in Canada's ODA budget. In 2002, the government announced that the international assistance envelope, of which ODA comprised roughly 80 per cent, would be increased by 8 per cent per annum until 2010, effectively doubling Canada's ODA at the decade's end. In its February 2003 budget the government reaffirmed this promise. This commitment, said finance minister John Manley, 'reflects the understanding that you cannot have a world of peace unless you address the world of need' (Hampson and Hay, 2004). At least half these budget increases were allocated to Africa, as part of Canadian support for the New Partnership for Africa's Development (NEPAD) and the G8 Africa Action Plan. The 2003–4 international assistance envelope was set at $2.9 billion, of which $2.3 billion was ODA to be spent through CIDA. Among non-ODA commitments: up to $1 billion over 10 years—$100 million yearly—were allocated to the G8 Global Partnership Against the Spread of Weapons and Materials of Mass Destruction, mostly in Russia, under the management of the Department of Foreign Affairs.

Increased aid to Africa was an important policy priority during this period. During the 1990s, bilateral aid to Africa had been particularly hard hit by the cuts to CIDA's budget. This was to change with Canada's hosting of the G8 Kananaskis Summit in 2002 and the announcement of the Africa Action Plan. The new focus on Africa in Canadian foreign policy and aid priorities was led by the prime minister himself. Although Chrétien's newfound advocacy took some by surprise, his interest dated back to the mid-1990s when the Canadian government sought to establish a multinational force to assist refugee repatriation in Zaire's eastern provinces following the Rwandan genocide, which had prompted the flight of vast numbers of refugees to neighbouring countries (Smith and Hay, 1999). The prime minister's growing interest in and knowledge about the region, and his direction of Canada's African policies, was likely assisted by Raymond Chrétien, the UN secretary-general's special envoy to the Great Lakes region during the Zaire crisis. Chrétien was also the prime minister's nephew, a familial connection that gave him privileged access to the Canadian leader.

Immediately after the Genoa Summit of 2001, Chrétien appointed Robert Fowler, Canada's ambassador to Italy, to become his personal representative for the 2002 G8 meeting. Chrétien made it clear from the beginning that he wanted to put Africa firmly on the international agenda. As Fowler recalls, 'From Genoa, in July 2001, it was crystal clear Prime Minister Chrétien would insist that the Canadian Summit he would host in 2002 would be an all-encompassing effort to end Africa's exclusion from the rest of the world and reverse the downward-spiraling trend in the quality of life of the vast majority of Africans' (Fowler, 2003: 223). To that end, he invited those African leaders who were the creators of the New Partnership for Africa's Development to join the discussions at the summit.

One of the major achievements of the summit was the announcement of a new Africa Action Plan, providing 'a long-term framework for a productive partnership between G8 countries and the 53 nations of Africa' (ibid.: 229). To underscore Canada's own commitment to the Plan, Chrétien announced that Canada was setting aside $500 million in new monies for a Canada Fund for Africa. The allocations of the fund would focus on three areas: fostering economic growth, including increased market access and encouraging public sector investment; strengthening institutions and governance; and investing in people and the future of Africa, including health and nutrition, water and agriculture, and basic education.

Just prior to its defeat in the January 2006 federal election, the Liberal government of Paul Martin released its *International Policy Statement on Diplomacy, Defence, Development, and Commerce* (Government of Canada, 2005a). The IPS had been a work-in-progress for almost two years before it was finally released, its delay affected by the Liberal leadership transition from Chrétien to Martin and the federal election of 2005.

Paul Martin and Bill Graham, who occupied the post of foreign minister and then defence minister in the Martin government, were the central players in the initiation of the overall foreign policy review. Much of the drafting of the IPS was carried out by officials in Foreign Affairs and an interdepartmental committee. Officials in the Prime Minister's Office (PMO) were careful to scrutinize the final document and make changes that reflected the prime minster's concerns. Paul Thibault, CIDA's president from May 2003 until May 2005, seems to have played only a marginal role in the IPS. His successor, Robert Greenhill, who was appointed while he was still working on the 'External Voice Project' at the Canadian Institute of International Affairs (CIIA) had somewhat greater influence (Greenhill, 2005). His work with the International Development Research Centre and the CIIA was instrumental in shaping some of the general ideas in the policy statement.

The development section of the IPS statement did not depart substantially from CIDA's 2002 *Report on Aid Effectiveness*. The most influential change in indicators was the growing attention to the issue of failed and failing states and the related focus of terrorism. This, and the increased focus on Africa, where many states were struggling to avert real decline in per capita incomes, were mutually reinforcing issues. Many of the commitments outlined in the development section drew heavily on earlier announcements, such as the Canada Fund for Africa and the G8 Africa Action Plan. Security and human rights were also highlighted to some degree. As critics noted, however, the development section of the IPS seemed almost an afterthought, lagging behind diplomacy, defence, and trade. That section of the IPS, moreover, was not tightly focused and contained major gaps in its discussion of development challenges and the list of priorities it outlined for ODA (Government of Canada, 2005b).

The 2005 IPS made a point of stressing that aid should be focused on a narrower range of countries. Advocating greater concentration was by now an old idea, but the fact was that the IPS actually increased the number of countries from the 9 that had been identified by Treasury Board in 2003 to 25. The numbers rose because more African countries were added to the list. The government committed itself to shift two-thirds of all bilateral development aid to the 'new' list of 25 development partner countries by 2010. The war in Iraq and the U.S.-led coalition in Afghanistan also strongly influenced the focus of Canadian development assistance at the time of the IPS release, as Afghanistan moved to the front of the queue of recipients of Canadian bilateral assistance and Canada began to plough aid dollars into Iraq's reconstruction. So too did Canadian involvement in Haiti, which was also drawing heavily on Canadian development assistance. But these three countries were not even mentioned in the list of 25 development partners.

How much traction would the Liberal approach to development have with Stephen Harper's Conservative government, elected in January 2006? The Conservatives' perspective on foreign policy seemed very different, and certainly more muscular, with an emphasis on alignment with the US and a strengthened military. Yet many of the IPS's recommendations about breaking down bureaucratic 'silos', improving policy coordination, and integrating the so-called 3Ds—defence, diplomacy, and development—were as uncontroversial as they were unobjectionable. The Harper government's commitment to a 'whole of government' approach to international affairs, 3D in all but name, suggested that some things were not about to change.

ENTREPRENEURSHIP IN DEVELOPMENT

This chapter has reviewed some of the most important episodes of agenda and policy change in Canada's development assistance policies since the end of the Second World War. As this account of those policies has stressed, policy entrepreneurs exploited windows of opportunity to bring about policy change and innovation. These windows emerged during times of crisis (the Korean War and the Colombo Plan), as a result of political turnover, produced by either a change in leadership and/or a change in government (for example the creation of CIDA under Trudeau), and even as a consequence of international systemic change (the fall of the Berlin Wall in 1989 and the end of the Cold War). Entrepreneurs identify problems, and shape how problems are perceived and interpreted by decision makers and publics, creating opportunities for new ideas and policy alternatives to rise onto governmental and decision agendas.

Entrepreneurship has many qualities—the ability to reason with others, to forcefully express new concepts, to convey ideas through the media and other public forums, and to mobilize constituencies inside and outside of the bureaucracy in support of new policies. One of the most important entrepreneurial assets is sheer tenacity, advancing a cause even when others are strongly opposed to it. Pearson displayed such qualities in promoting Canada's involvement in the Colombo Plan. Strong was equally dogged in promoting the creation of a free-standing aid agency. Similar levels of determination were evident in the ways Catley-Carlson, Massé, and Good advanced their own policy agendas during their respective presidencies.

Leadership is also about advancing ideas that can solve real problems, but where do policy entrepreneurs get their ideas? They can be acquired through professional experience, on-the-job learning, or places of work, where individuals are exposed to new ways of thinking. Pearson's internationalist vision and his ideas about the importance of development assistance were influenced by his international travels as Canada's secretary of state for external affairs and his personal contact with Asian leaders. As a businessman, Strong saw the importance of marketing Canadian ODA through an independent administrative mechanism, CIDA, which would give Canadian aid programming much-needed, international visibility and profile. As a woman who had risen through the ranks of a male-dominated foreign service, Catley-Carlson understood the challenges of ensuring that more than lip-service was paid to gender equality in CIDA and that extensive levels of training and professional development were required to make women in development a reality. Massé's and Good's experience in international institutions that were the sources of much development thinking and policy research in the 1980s and 1990s had an undoubted impact on their respective agendas and priorities at CIDA.

Entrepreneurship is about timing and seizing opportunity to advance policy agendas at ripe moments by joining policy with politics. In urging Canada's involvement in the Colombo Plan, Pearson recognized that, unless Canada and other Commonwealth countries supported the newly independent states of Asia, their democratic future and independence would not be secure. He successfully exploited Canada's participation in successive meetings of Commonwealth ministers to persuade Canada's prime minister, Louis St Laurent, that the conflict in the Korean peninsula could spill over to other countries in Asia unless Canada and other countries made a serious commitment to their economic development. Maurice Strong saw opportunity in the leadership transition from Pearson to Trudeau to press his case for an independent development agency. He capitalized on the national mood, which supported a strong Canadian role in international affairs, to secure major increases in ODA. Although gender equality had long been on the domestic and international policy agenda, Catley-Carlson saw an opportunity with her appointment at CIDA to advance the rights of women in development. Massé's commitment to structural adjustment during his second term as president was compatible with the ideological orientation of the Mulroney government, eroding public support for

ODA, and the emerging climate of fiscal austerity. Massé believed that ODA would not only have to be strategically deployed but also that there would be less of it in the post–Cold War environment.

When a window of opportunity for ODA policy opened at the turn of the twenty-first century with improving fiscal and economic fortunes, CIDA's new leadership understood that it could not carry on as before at the agency. Here was an opportunity to promote some of the ideas about donor coordination, partnership, and allocative efficiency that had been discussed in international circles since the mid-1990s. At the same time, mounting public concern about transparency and accountability in the public sector demanded a fresh approach to aid and development. After many years of stagnation and decline, development policy began to move in new directions.

CHAPTER 10

Streams in the Human Security Policy Process

In this chapter, we trace the development of agendas and ideas about human security, particularly those that followed the end of the Cold War. Since much of the activity on human security issues occurred in international institutions and policy communities beyond Canadian borders, our analysis of developments in the problem and policy streams will reflect that international focus. In the politics stream, however, domestic developments played an important role in the successful integration of human security ideas and problems into Canada's international policies, and our analysis will trace the political forces that produced distinctly Canadian agendas and alternatives.

THE HUMAN SECURITY POLICY AGENDA

Understandings about the emerging problem of human security at the turn of the last century advanced along two distinctive, if interrelated, tracks. At one level, the concept of human security was presented as an alternative to the state-centred paradigm of 'national security' that had so dominated international relations during the Cold War. When the Cold War ended and the risk of a nuclear confrontation between the two superpowers receded, there were calls in some quarters to widen the security agenda to include new components such as economic security, food security, health security, environmental security, and personal and community security. This concept emerged most forcefully in the United Nations Development Programme's (UNDP's) *1994 Human Development Report*, which bluntly stated that security should be viewed at the human level and was framed in terms of the security concerns of people in their daily lives. The report stated: 'For most people, a feeling of insecurity arises more from worries about their daily life than from the dread of a cataclysmic world event. . . . In the final analysis, human security is a child who did not die, a disease that did not spread, a job that was not cut, an ethnic tension that did not explode into violence, a dissident who was not silenced. Human security is not a concern with weapons—it is a concern with human life and dignity.' In proposing a new concept of security based on an expansive understanding of the different threats to human security, UNDP argued for a transition in the security agenda that would involve two basic changes: a shift away from territorial security to a much greater emphasis on peoples' security; and 'from security through armaments to security through sustainable development' (UNDP, 1994: 22, 23).

The UNDP identified six principal challenges while suggesting that the 'real threats to human security in the next century will arise more from the actions of millions of people than from aggression by a few nations.' Unchecked population growth (along with diminished prospects for development) was cited as one of the main threats to human security in the twenty-first century. Demographic pressure was presented as a source of human poverty, migration, and environmental degradation, problems that feed upon each other and result in a vicious cycle of underdevelopment. Second on the list were disparities in economic opportunities as a result of growing inequality between the richest 20 per cent of the world's population and remaining 80 per cent whose incomes had fallen steadily over the past three decades. Third were migration pressures resulting from growing population and limited economic opportunities in many developing countries. Fourth was environmental degradation, including harmful gas emissions, greenhouse gases, deforestation and destruction of wetlands, and accelerated destruction of coastal marine habitats. Drug trafficking, particularly in narcotic drugs, was fifth on the list of threats. The report noted that drug trafficking posed one of 'the most corrosive threats to human security' because over the past 20 years the 'narcotics industry had progressed from a small cottage enterprise to a highly organized multinational business' (ibid.: 36). Finally, the sixth global threat was international terrorism. Although the report observed that absolute numbers of incidents of terrorism were dropping, casualty rates remained high (well over a thousand people per year) and focus of terrorist activity was now global, rather than limited to one or two regions in the world.

In the eyes of some, however, this very broad interpretation of human security failed to address the growing threat to civilians and non-combatants from, what some perceived as, a worldwide explosion in the outbreak of interethnic warfare and civil violence in many developing countries, Africa, and the territories of the former Yugoslavia and Soviet Union. As Neil MacFarlane and Foong Khong write: 'In the mid-1990s, and in view of the egregious violations of human rights characteristic of much post–Cold War internal armed conflict, some concluded that the focus on development of the UNDP's approach to security distracted attention from increasingly serious problems of basic protection of human beings involved in war' (2006: 164).

A report published by Canada's own Department of Foreign Affairs and International Trade (DFAIT) also reflected this concern: 'A growing number of armed conflicts are being fought within, rather than between states. The warring factions in these civil wars are often irregular forces with loose chains of command, frequently divided along ethnic or religious lines. Small arms are the weapon of choice and non-combatants account for eight out of ten casualties. Once considered merely "collateral damage," civilians are being thrust into the epicenter of contemporary war' (DFAIT, 1999b: 1).

In suggesting that the most pressing human security problem was safety from violence and the protection of basic human rights, this narrower conception of human security drew on a long-standing, moral distinction between combatants and non-combatants in warfare. It also reflected a belief that innocent civilians should be protected from violent threats and, when they are harmed or injured, the international community has an obligation to intervene and assist. This view dates back to The Hague Conventions with Respect to the Laws and Customs of War on Land of 1899 and 1907, and the Geneva Conventions of 1949, which gave universal expression and legal sanction to these principles. Other norms of warfare, which were eventually given expression in international treaties, included the principle that individuals who were sick, wounded, or made prisoners of war should not be harmed. The Geneva Conventions of 1864, 1906, 1929, and 1949 codified this principle as well as the legal obligations that fell on the parties to these conventions regarding the wounded and the sick. Along with the Hague Conventions of 1899 and 1907, the Geneva Conventions also laid down detailed standards safeguarding the humane treatment of prisoners.

Humanitarian concerns for the life and welfare of human beings exposed to ravages of war in earlier times, had led to various prohibitions on the production, use, and stockpiling of certain kinds of weapons that are indiscriminate, or particularly injurious, in terms of their ability to prolong the suffering of victims. The Declaration of St Petersburg of 1868, for example, prohibited the use of lightweight projectiles charged with explosives or inflammable substances. The Hague Declaration of 1899 prohibited the use of expanding or dum-dum bullets. Over the years international conventions prohibiting the production, use, and stockpiling of chemical, gas, and bacteriological instruments of warfare have also been negotiated, as have a large number of treaties regulating the production and development of nuclear weapons. In addition to controlling the production and prohibiting the use of weapons of mass destruction, by the middle to late twentieth century there was also growing interest in controlling the production, sale, and use of conventional weapons that have the capacity to harm or maim civilians. The anti-personnel landmines treaty that was signed in Ottawa in 1997 was a leading example of these efforts.

In the 1980s and early 1990s, long-standing humanitarian concerns had evolved into a growing awareness, in both government and non-governmental circles, that new approaches were necessary—particularly to address the needs and interests of victims of, and perceived growth in, the outbreak of intercommunal violence around the globe. Many came to believe that the challenge was not simply to provide emergency and humanitarian relief to victims of armed conflict, but also to address the underlying causes of this conflict and violence. Within the UN itself, consensus was building around more systematic and strategic approaches to prevent those conflicts that had just ended (usually as the result of a negotiated peace settlement) from re-escalating after the international community withdrew its peacekeeping forces and stopped providing humanitarian relief and assistance. Many senior officials and academics, including the secretary-general of the United Nations, argued for a broader conceptual approach as well as the creation of new strategies and tools to promote human security in war-torn societies (Boutros-Ghali, 1992). In the 1990s, peacebuilding and conflict prevention came to be viewed as instruments of human security, particularly in those settings where a fragile peace accord had been negotiated but where the dividends from the peace process had not yet been consolidated. In his *Agenda for Peace,* former UN secretary-general Boutros Boutros-Ghali defined peacebuilding as a broad set of activities that 'tend to consolidate peace and advance a sense of confidence and well-being among people' (1992: 55).

The much-publicized 1997 report of the Carnegie Commission on Preventing Deadly Conflict also spelled out the multiple challenges of promoting human security in civil conflict situations: 'the need to prevent deadly conflict is increasingly urgent. The rapid compression of the world through breathtaking population growth, technological advancement, and economic interdependence, combined with the readily available supply of deadly weapons and easily transmitted contagion of hatred and incitement to violence, make it essential and urgent to find ways to prevent disputes from turning massively violent. . . . [P]reventing deadly conflict is possible. The problem is not that we do not know about incipient large-scale violence; it is that we often do not act' (Carnegie Commission, 1997: xvii).

Among the pivotal focusing events that compressed the human security agenda into its narrower 'safety' and 'protection-of-civilians' form and elevated it onto the policy agenda were the wars in the Balkans and the genocide in Rwanda. Some argue that UN mandates began to change earlier with the humanitarian crisis that occurred in Iraq in the spring of 1991; when Saddam Hussein's military forces attacked Kurdish populations in northern Iraq, three of the permanent members of the Security Council—the United States, Britain, and France—worked to secure a resolution (UNSC Resolution 688) establishing an air exclusion zone over Iraqi territory in order to prevent further attacks on civilians (MacFarlane and Foong Khong, 2006: 167). In response to a humanitarian crisis in Somalia that broke shortly after, resulting from the civil war in that country, the Security Council invoked Chapter VII of the UN *Charter*—determining that the situation presented a threat to international peace and security and authorizing the delivery of humanitarian assistance to those affected populations that were in dire need.

But it was the civil war in Bosnia, occurring as it did on Europe's doorstep, that dramatized the costs of human suffering and the egregious violations of human rights that occur in such conflicts. A series of UN Security Council resolutions based on Chapter VII of the UN *Charter* called on the international community to address the deteriorating humanitarian situation in that country. When the situation in Bosnia worsened, the council called for the establishment of an International Criminal Tribunal for the Former Yugoslavia to investigate and prosecute those guilty of war crimes and, eventually, the council took steps that included the authorization of a direct use of force to halt the conflict. In the case of Rwanda, the notable lack of action by the council, even when confronted with compelling evidence that the most appalling genocide was taking place, is a blight on its record, even now. Even so, the council did eventually pass a series of resolutions that acknowledged the gravity of the situation as posing a direct threat to international peace and security.

These and other major humanitarian crises, including the crackdown in East Timor following elections held in the secessionist province, were focusing events that helped to generate support for a series of major, new, human security initiatives, including the anti-personnel landmines treaty, the establishment of an International Criminal Court, and the responsibility to protect (R2P) doctrine. However, the realities of ethnic and armed conflict in the world were, somewhat, at variance with public and political perceptions. As the *Human Security Report* (Human Security Centre, 2005: 3) published by the Liu Institute for Global Issues at the University of British Columbia noted: 'in the early 1990s, at precisely the point that media commentators in the West began to fret about a worldwide explosion in ethnic violence, the number of armed conflicts began to drop'. The report states that between 1946 and 1991 'the number of state-based armed conflicts being fought worldwide trebled, with most of the killing taking place in poor countries' (ibid.). However, the end of the Cold War 'brought remarkable changes to the global security climate. Security pessimists saw the upsurge of secessionist violence in the former Soviet Union, the dissolution of the Yugoslavian federation, genocide in Rwanda, and other ethnic confrontations as portents of an increasingly violent future' (ibid.). According to the Liu Institute report, this pessimism was quite unfounded: 'Between 1992 and 2003, . . . the number of armed conflicts . . . dropped by 40 per cent. The number of wars—the most deadly category of armed conflict—declined even more sharply' (ibid.).

What is also quite striking is that the wars of the 1990s witnessed fewer battle-related deaths than earlier times. This trend is partially explained by the fact that most wars in recent years have been fought in developing countries 'with armies that lack heavy conventional weapons—or superpower patrons. In a typical low-intensity conflict weak government forces control small, ill-trained rebel forces equipped with small arms and light weapons' (ibid.: 5). But, tellingly, these are also conflicts where assaults on non-combatants became commonplace: 'skirmishes and attacks on civilians are preferred to major engagements. Although these conflicts often involve gross human rights abuses, they kill relatively few people compared with the major wars of 20 or more years ago' (ibid.: 5).

The data on genocide and other deliberate killings of civilians also point to a similar trend. There was an 80 per cent decline in deaths resulting from genocide in the 1990s 'despite Rwanda, Srebrenica and a host of lesser massacres' (ibid.: 40).

Nevertheless, the symbolism of the wars of the post–Cold War era was far more important than any statistical indicators of declining trends in the level and frequency of violence and armed conflict. On the one hand, the end of the Cold War heightened expectations that the world would soon become a more peaceful, less dangerous place. On the other hand, the brutal murder of eight hundred thousand Tutsis in Rwanda over one hundred days in 1994, occurring as it did under the watch of Canadian-led UN peacekeeping forces, flew in the face of such expectations. The failures of the United Nations Assistance Mission in Rwanda (UNAMIR) served as a powerful demonstration of the international community's indifference to such atrocities. So, too, was the much-publicized round-up and massacre by Serb forces in July 1995 of more than seven thousand Muslim men and boys in the Bosnian town of Srebrenica—a town that the UN had designated a 'safe-haven' (ibid.: 40).

The brutal symbolism of these atrocities against civilians was reinforced by the so-called CNN effect. Television had—in an earlier time—brought the Vietnam War viscerally into living rooms around the globe. With the advent of 24-hour news networks, there was simply no way that the public could avoid the brutality of these conflicts and their appalling costs in terms of human suffering. If television was responsible for a new moral affinity between victims and viewers, it was the advent of the Internet that provided the immediate impetus to action. The global public responded to cries for help, issued in real time, creating a more potent sense of urgency than any journalist could by writing about events, hours, days, or weeks after the fact.

The ethical imperatives and practical challenges of the expanded human security agenda landed on Canada's doorstep with the appointment of Lloyd Axworthy as Canada's foreign minister in January 1996. The three major human security initiatives that were pursued by Lloyd Axworthy during his four and a half years in office were the 1997 treaty banning anti-personnel landmines; the 1998 Rome Statute that provided for the establishment of an International Criminal Court (ICC); and the responsibility to protect doctrine, which emerged from the report of the International Commission on Intervention and State Sovereignty (ICISS). The ICISS commission and report both enjoyed the strong backing of the Canadian government during, and after, Axworthy's tenure.

HUMAN SECURITY POLICY ALTERNATIVES

These three issues were also ones that engaged and mobilized civil society and provided Axworthy with an opportunity to work directly with non-governmental organizations to advance Canada's national foreign policy goals—goals that included not just the advancement of a human rights agenda and Canadian values, but also the democratization of Canadian foreign policy itself.

Axworthy's engagement with civil society dated back to his student activism in the civil rights movement and his involvement with local NGOs in municipal politics in his hometown of Winnipeg. Notes John English, himself close to the process, 'Axworthy applied this same approach when he served as foreign policy critic in the early 1990s.' He worked closely with academic specialists, human rights organizations, cultural groups, and NGOs to develop Liberal foreign policy.

In his 1992 summary of Liberal foreign policy, he recognized 'the need for promoting within Canada much stronger involvement of our non-governmental organizations, churches, universities, business organizations and aboriginal groups' (English, 2001: 104). Axworthy's commitment to opening up the policy process transformed the relationship between the DFAIT and the NGO community. This new populist approach, which paralleled a groundswell of public interest in Canada's role in the world, shifted the centre of gravity in Canadian foreign policy toward new interests and a more value-based orientation. NGO activists, who were champions of human rights, the environment, peacebuilding, democratic development, and good governance, suddenly found that the doors were open, at DFAIT, to public engagement and discussion.

One of Axworthy's instruments for engaging the public in policy development was the Canadian Centre for Foreign Policy Development (CCFPD), which was established in early 1996 and headed by a former NDP staffer, Steven Lee. The centre was created to make good on the government's 1995 foreign policy statement that promised 'the voice of Canadians would be heard in the foreign policy process' (Lee, 1998: 57). The centre also provided 'regular input and feedback with various branches of DFAIT to raise awareness of policy development needs, contribute public views to policy-making, and inform citizens about the results of their work and continuing policy development.' The centre also developed a 'consultation, comment and feedback' system within the department, working closely with DFAIT's policy-planning staff (ibid.: 58). One of the responsibilities of the centre was to organize the minister's National Forum on Canada's International Relations. The purpose of these meetings was to engage the public and generate policy ideas that could contribute to public policy. Participants in these annual gatherings included local community leaders, journalists, business, labour, and professional groups such as academics, experts, and foreign affairs NGOs. The centre also organized short, one-off briefings for the minister and his senior officials on issues such as Canada's policy options in Bosnia, NATO enlargement, and the human rights situations in Nigeria and Burma.

Axworthy's 'consultative imperative' was not entirely unprecedented. Previous foreign ministers, such as Joe Clark who served as secretary of state for external affairs under Prime Minister Brian Mulroney, had consulted widely with public interest groups on a variety of foreign policy issues. But Axworthy appeared more committed than his predecessors to 'democratizing' foreign policy and his human security agenda was instrumental in opening 'the door to civil society engagement' in the policy process (Van Rooy, 2001: 262).

Although Canadian-based NGOs developed close relationships with the foreign minister and lobbied him on major issues, such as the appalling human rights situation in Burma (now Myanmar) and the plight of children in war-torn societies, they were not the primary actors responsible for setting Axworthy's human security agenda. Instead, international NGOs were the policy entrepreneurs, par excellence, and it was their efforts that drove the international campaign and agenda on such issues as landmines, the ICC, and small arms. International campaigns around the first two of these issues had gathered sufficient momentum that Axworthy, upon becoming foreign minister, was presented with a golden opportunity to seize the initiative and exercise leadership.

The first call for a landmines ban came from a quasi-intergovernmental body, the International Committee of the Red Cross (ICRC). As John English notes, the 'origins of the ban movement lay in the attempt by the ICRC in the 1970s to reinvigorate the century-old tradition of international humanitarian law'. These efforts led to the UN Convention on Certain Conventional Weapons (CCW), which was negotiated within the forum of the UN's Conference on Disarmament (CD). The second protocol of the CCW dealt with the 'Prohibitions or Restrictions on the Use of Mines, Booby-traps, and Other Devices' (English, 1998: 122). ICRC officials, who were pushing vigorously for the convention, were responding to the use of landmines in a wide variety of different conflict settings in Africa, Asia, and elsewhere, where ICRC officials observed first-hand the devastating humanitarian consequences of landmines.

Along with the ICRC, other early champions for a landmines ban were a variety of largely American civil society actors. The head of the Vietnam Veterans of America Foundation, Robert (Bobby) Muller was so moved by his own encounters with landmine victims that he began to work closely with US Senator Patrick Leahy of Vermont to establish a fund to aid mine victims and to introduce legislation in the US Congress to ban landmines exports. The resulting legislation, which was signed by President George H.W. Bush in 1992, called for a moratorium on American landmine exports that was extended several times, and subsequently signed into law by President Bill Clinton.

Realizing that he would need coalition partners, Bobby Muller forged links with Medico International and other humanitarian NGOs who were keen on banning landmines. In 1992, the International Campaign to Ban Landmines (ICBL) was formed, headed by the well-known activist Jody Williams. Williams, Muller, and ICRC President Cornelio Sommaruga came together to lobby governments around the world to support the idea of a ban.

Initially, the focus of the advocacy campaign was the United Nations General Assembly (UNGA) and the CD. UN General Assembly Resolution 48/7 of 19 October 1993 requested the secretary-general to submit a comprehensive report on the problems caused by mines and other unexploded devices. This resolution was followed by a second one on 16 December 1993 calling for a moratorium on the export of anti-personnel landmines. The resolution noted 'with satisfaction that several States have already declared moratoriums on the export, transfer or purchase of anti-personnel land mines' and called upon all '[s]tates to agree to a moratorium on the export of anti-personnel land mines that pose grave dangers to civilian populations' (United Nations General Assembly, 1993).

When international support for a landmines ban grew, the government of the United States endorsed the proposal. In his 1994 address to the UN General Assembly, President Clinton called for a global ban on landmines. Backing up the president's call to eliminate the scourge of landmines was a US State Department report *Hidden Killers: The Global Problem with Uncleared Landmines* (United States Department of State, 1994) that painted a picture of an endless, perhaps insurmountable, challenge. The report estimated that there were anywhere between 80 to 110 million landmines littered around the world and that, although perhaps up to 80,000 of these were being removed on an annual basis, another 2.5 million were still being planted.

The first CCW Review Conference was held in Vienna from 15 September to 13 October 1995, with the objective of strengthening the anti-personnel land-mines (APL) protocols in the CCW. At the time, the UN's own estimate was that there were 110 million APLs to be located and cleared in 64 countries, and that the pace of mine deployment was increasing rather than diminishing (Freden-burg, 1997: 5). Forty-four countries attended the review conference, and the ICBL and a number of NGOs attended as observers. In both their briefings to the dele-gates and in their public statements to the media, the NGOs reiterated their call for a complete and immediate ban on landmines—a call that was supported by a number of countries including Austria, Denmark, Germany, Ireland, Mexico, Norway, and Sweden. The conference did not make much progress in reaching a consensus on a ban or even more stringent controls on the production, export, and use of landmines, although it did reach an agreement on banning the use of Laser Blinding Weapons. Part of the reason for the impasse was that Western defence establishments shared the view that the humanitarian problems were, in reality, caused by the indiscriminate use of landmines by guerrilla and non-professional armies who target civilians. Such groups would not be easily cov-ered, or regulated, by any kind of international convention. Many in the military were also of the view that as older APL systems were replaced by self-neutralizing (SN) or self-destructing (SD) APLs, otherwise known as 'smart mines', the risk to civilians and non-combatants would diminish. Further, there was a lack of consensus at the conference on how to verify a possible ban, or to police more stringent restrictions on the production and use of landmines. Signifi-cantly, Russia, China, and India were opposed outright to any kind of ban on landmines.

In spite of the miniscule progress, advocates of the ban drew inspiration from the conference, as well as from a surprising call for a landmine ban from Presi-dent Ramos of the Philippines in December 1995. Coming from a government that was engaged in a major counterinsurgency operation against local guerrillas who were using landmines, Ramos's statement attracted considerable interna-tional attention. It should also be noted that at the G7 Summit, held in Naples earlier in the year, Canada's prime minister Jean Chrétien had discussed the issue of a landmines ban with his fellow leaders. The discussion occurred despite the fact that his government had not formally expressed support for a ban. That sup-port would come later, when political change in Canada elevated the landmines problem, and the ban solution, onto the government's decision agenda for action, a policy process that is described in Chapter 11.

The subsequent success of the landmines treaty proved to be instrumental in Axworthy's willingness to support those officials within DFAIT who were keen to use Canada's newfound profile to champion another dimension of human secu-rity, namely, the establishment of an international criminal court.

The origins of the ICC date back to the creation of the United Nations, which affirmed the 'principles of international law recognized by the Charter of Nuremberg'. Using this as a starting point, the UN General Assembly, as well as the International Law Commission (ILC),[1] took numerous actions that served to further the development of international criminal law. For example, the 1948 Genocide Convention explicitly recognized the jurisdiction of a future international criminal court. Grave breaches of the 1949 Geneva Conventions were characterized as international crimes.

Members of civil society were integral to the progress of the UN system. The UN *Charter* explicitly institutionalized the notion of social representation by allowing for 'consultative status' for certain NGOs within the Economic and Social Council (ECOSOC). Groups also operated within the Human Rights Commission, its working groups, and the Human Rights Committee. NGOs facilitated norm building by focusing attention on issues, setting standards, and monitoring compliance. Similarly, the creation of the ILC gave international jurists a forum within which to formulate ideas and codification programs. In sum, the postwar world witnessed a 'global associational explosion' (Fisher, 1997: 440). Civil society actors used the Cold War period to improve their organizational capacities and to adapt to the new institutional procedures created by the UN system (Korey, 1998).

In 1947, UNGA gave the ILC a mandate for the codification of international criminal offences. The ILC was also to determine whether the creation of a court was desirable. There was little consensus within the ILC with which to proceed with the project: one report, written by Ricardo Alfaro, found the creation of a court to be both desirable and feasible; another report, written by Emil Sandstrom, concluded that a court was not desirable, given the lack of existing mechanisms for state cooperation. Although the ILC completed the *Draft Code of Crimes Against Peace and Security* in 1954, the body did not possess the consensus needed to develop a draft statute for the creation of an international criminal court.

This lack of consensus, however, was largely irrelevant, given that the UNGA would effectively remove the issue from the ILC's perusal. Progress was thwarted by state parties through the creation of an institutional 'catch-22': an international criminal court could not be created without the establishment of a draft code of offences, and a draft code could not be completed without agreement on the definition of aggression (Ferencz, 1992). State parties would only conclude their work on aggression in 1974, long after the project had been effectively shelved.

There was a limited attempt to revive the project in the late 1970s, in large part because of the international community's united front against the apartheid regime in South Africa. During the creation of the Apartheid Convention, the eminent legal scholar Cherif Bassiouni prepared a report concerning an 'enforcement mechanism' for the UN Human Rights Commission. The resulting draft statute was considered at the UN's Sixth Congress on Crime Prevention and the Treatment of Offenders. Favourable feedback from UN member states was subsequently thought of as giving the ILC a renewed mandate to study the creation of an international criminal court. Thus, the ILC appointed a special rapporteur to revisit the *Draft Code of Crimes* in 1982, and reports were issued from 1982 to 1988.

Despite these efforts, it was clear that progress on the code was practically nil. The lack of substantive momentum must be viewed in light of the rivalries of the Cold War. The USSR and the US were not in favour of the creation of an international criminal court, given the scope of actions taken in their own spheres of influence. In addition, the USSR had a unique view of human rights based on Communist ideology that would have made agreement over jurisdiction and subject-matter impossible. Preoccupation with Cold War imperatives thereby ensured that peace and justice remained distinct and separate.

Several events in the late 1980s signalled a change in state attitudes. The first was the decline of US–Soviet hostilities that removed many of the political impediments to the creation of an international criminal court. In 1987, USSR General Secretary Gorbachev expressed the desire for the creation of a global security plan in a letter addressed to the UN. One hallmark of this proposal was the importance placed on the strengthening of an internationally enforceable rule of law. It was clear that Soviet opposition to the creation of an international court was diminishing.

Further, the end of the Cold War allowed states to explicitly recognize the need for legal mechanisms to control problematic transnational behaviours. States were increasingly concerned about 'new' security threats, such as drug trafficking, terrorism, and hijacking (Gilmore, 1995). A coalition of Caribbean states, led by Trinidad and Tobago, was adamant in its calls for the creation of a court to deal with such issues. The voices of these small and vulnerable states led the UNGA to request the ILC to prepare a report on international jurisdiction with respect to drug trafficking. Also at this time, an NGO Committee of Experts, chaired by Cherif Bassiouni, submitted a *Draft Statute for the Establishment of an International Criminal Court* to the Eighth Congress on Crime Prevention and the Treatment of Offenders. The congress responded affirmatively and urged the ILC to step up its work.

The United States also recognized the need to deal with issues such as drugs and terrorism. The 1988 American *Anti-Drug Abuse Act* gave an explicit mandate to the president to begin negotiations for the establishment of an international criminal court tasked with prosecuting international drug traffickers. In 1989, the US House of Representatives passed a resolution encouraging the president to act in this respect. The president's mandate was encouraged and broadened beyond drug trade offences by the 1991 *Foreign Appropriations Bill*. Congressional support was ensured by the active leadership of Republican Senator Arlen Specter and Republican Congressman Jim Leach, both members of the Parliamentarians for Global Action organization (Anderson, 1991; Bassiouni and Blakesly, 1992).

Positive American attitudes were also secured by the Gulf War, which illustrated the ability of the international community to act collectively, albeit for a brief moment. An international criminal court seemed both desirable and feasible. Such a court would punish the 'Saddam Husseins' of the world and avoid extradition conflicts like the one the US was experiencing with Libya over the destruction of Pan Am Flight 103 (MacPherson, 1998). By 1994, the court had become a centrepiece of President Clinton's foreign policy agenda (Wedgwood, 1998).

Powerful states had, belatedly, come onside, but civil society actors were instrumental in creating, and maintaining, the momentum behind the creation of a court. The end of the Cold War had led to a proliferation of international human rights groups. These groups had transnational linkages and many reported increased contact with governments (Smith, Pagnuco, and Lopez, 1998). The 1993 World Conference on Human Rights in Vienna demonstrated that NGOs had expanded their influence and procedural repertoire; of the 1,400 to 1,500 NGOs in attendance in Vienna, 248 had consultative status and NGO participants numbered 593 (Nowak, 1994). Working with these groups, international jurists continued to agitate for the creation of the court. Development-oriented groups were also becoming interested in the creation of a court, as they experimented with truth commissions in nations torn apart by violent conflict (Edwards, Hulme, and Wallace, 1999).

The international community (and its institutional machinery) responded rapidly to the softening of American attitudes. The ILC came under increasing pressure to consolidate its work; the ILC created an ICC working group in 1992, so as to identify how the ILC could proceed with the creation of a court. The first comprehensive draft statute was completed and submitted to the UNGA in 1993. The fact that the draft was submitted to the UNGA before it was officially adopted by the ILC illustrates that its completion was viewed as a political priority. The UNGA passed a resolution urging the ILC to continue its work, and encouraging states to submit their concerns regarding the draft statute to the Working Group of the ILC, now chaired by Australian James Crawford. The revised draft statute of 1994 attempted to both identify, and solve, the political problems inherent in the creation of the international criminal court (Crawford, 1994).

Support for the creation of a court was further buttressed by the Yugoslavian and Rwandan conflicts, where abuses were committed that clearly invited an international response. International human rights groups worked with the media to sustain public pressure on national governments and international institutions to address this issue (MacPherson, 1998). The Security Council's creation of the International Tribunal for the Former Yugoslavia (ICTFY) in 1993 and the International Tribunal for Rwanda (ICTR) in 1994 affirmed the need for judicial structures to address atrocities committed in times of conflict. Yet the failed attempts of the Security Council to 'micro-manage' judicial processes in an ad hoc fashion contributed to 'tribunal fatigue'. This fatigue manifested itself in continued calls for the creation of a permanent international criminal court.

There was also growing momentum behind the project within UN machinery. The Ad Hoc Committee for the Establishment of the International Criminal Court, composed of state representatives, was formed in 1994 and tasked with facilitating consultation between state parties regarding the ILC draft statute.

Further, a Preparatory Committee (PrepCom) was created in 1995 to streamline the organization of formal negotiations. The PrepCom met six times, and was chaired by Adriaan Bos of the Netherlands. Each session organized discussions around specific issue-areas, and permanent working groups were established and tasked with the definition of war crimes, general principles of international law, penalties, procedural matters, and state cooperation. The working groups were assisted by drafting committees, which worked on compiling the bracketed negotiating text (Hall, 1997; 1998a, b, and c).

Civil society actors were active during the PrepCom sessions, their ability to influence state behaviour and agitate for change proven by the conclusion of the landmines treaty. This time around, non-governmental groups coordinated, and maximized, their influence through the creation of the Coalition for the International Criminal Court (CICC),[2] led by the World Federalist Movement's William Pace. National and regional coalitions were also formed to lobby domestic governments. The CICC particularly sought to ensure that developing states, which feared that the court would become a tool of Western domination, would support a court. Civil society actors worked tirelessly to keep the creation of the ICC on international and domestic agendas, and, with the assistance of the information superhighway, publicized progress as it was made. Although NGO participation within the PrepCom sessions was curtailed as states focused on the more politicized issues, their efforts would be rewarded. In December 1997, a PrepCom resolution authorized the UN Diplomatic Conference of Plenipotentiaries on the Establishment of an International Criminal Court, to begin in June 1998.

Unlike the landmines and ICC campaigns, governments, rather than civil society, set in place the processes leading to the promotion of the responsibility to protect doctrine as an emerging norm of international relations. Canada, in particular, was instrumental in spearheading an international debate surrounding the limits of absolute sovereignty in an age of interdependence and universal human rights. Through the forming of like-minded coalitions, engineering of agreements and facilitating the negotiation of compromise solutions, Canada assumed the role of an entrepreneurial leader (Riddell-Dixon, 2005).

At the heart of the notion of a responsibility to protect is the evolution of state sovereignty as a guiding principle of international relations. Arguably, legal norms and state practices in areas of human rights, the environment and trade had already provided precedents for R2P. The founding document of the United Nations balances the principle of non-interference in the internal affairs of sovereign states under Article 2 against Article 55 that calls upon all member states to promote the 'universal respect for, and observance of, human rights and fundamental freedoms for all'. When the UN Human Rights Commission was established in 1946, it provided for states to investigate the internal human rights abuses of other states in extreme cases. In the environmental domain, the idea of sustainable development that came out of the 1987 Brundtland Commission embodied a consensus behind the development of global standards against which to evaluate the policies of individual states, even in the absence of transboundary effects (Brunnee and Toope, 2006: 7–8). Finally, the international legal regime governing trade and commerce between nations is the most complete and binding system under contemporary international law, limiting states' domestic regulatory freedoms at the same time as opening markets and protecting the rights of exporters and investors.

Notwithstanding these examples in law and politics of incursions into state sovereignty, the responsibility to protect went much further along the continuum toward a fundamental transformation of the sovereign states system. In what Anne-Marie Slaughter (2005) has deemed a 'tectonic shift' in the definition of sovereignty, the responsibility to protect creates a 'generalized set of interlocking obligations owed to states and to persons' (Brunnee and Toope, 2006: 8). Sovereignty became a 'dual responsibility'. In the international sphere, sovereignty implied a duty to respect the sovereignty of other states in accordance with traditional principles of non-interference. Where sovereignty as the 'responsibility to protect' differed was in its domestic function to 'respect the dignity and basic rights of all people within the state'. Making peoples and individuals equal subjects of responsibility, to which state behaviour was accountable, changed the rules of the game. In situations of extreme human rights abuse and humanitarian crises resulting in actual or apprehended large-scale losses of life or large-scale ethnic cleansing 'the principle of non-intervention yields to the international responsibility to protect' (ICISS, 2001: xi, 8). Intervention by third parties based upon R2P could consist of all actions up to, and including, the use of force as a last resort.

The responsibility to protect has been characterized by some as a re-packaging of humanitarian intervention. This latter idea had emerged out of the evolution in foreign policies and practices following the end of the Cold War. In the early 1990s, the United Nations deployed wider peacekeeping missions to Somalia, the former Yugoslavia, and Rwanda in response to incidences of intrastate conflict, genocide, and ethnic cleansing. Wider, or second-generation, peacekeeping came to challenge the traditional principles of consent, minimal force, and impartiality governing peacekeeping operations by the UN (Bellamy, Williams, and Griffin, 2004: 143–5). For Canada, the 1999 Kosovo intervention led by the North Atlantic Alliance (NATO) represented a turning point for the human security policy paradigm from a soft power agenda of networking and norms development to a harder-edged application of proportional force to protect civilians from violence and egregious harm. The foreign minister was himself an entrepreneur for the re-orientation of human security away from broader human development issues in favour of a narrower 'freedom from fear' approach. Events in the Balkans, and at Dayton in the aftermath of the Bosnian war, were significant. The combination of resurgent nationalism, religion, political ambition, and complete disregard for human life was, so it seemed to Lloyd Axworthy, a new type of problem requiring fresh solutions. His personal dealings with Milosevic and other Balkan leaders had been a lesson in cunning and cruelty. Axworthy recalls his encounter with the Serbian president in April 1996 with the following description: 'He was a smart man, but also a dangerous one who rode the winds of extreme nationalism and religious holy war for political gain. He would not be won over by blandishments from the West.' As Axworthy wrote in his memoirs after the end of his term as foreign minister, the Balkans was 'an eye-opener into the saga of Kosovo . . . two years later' (Axworthy, 2003: 170, 176).

The Kosovo intervention was framed by the Canadian government as the first war carried out in the name of human security (Heinbecker, 2000: 15). The international community had acted to protect the right to freedom from fear of the majority Kosovar Albanian population in the southern province of the disintegrating former Yugoslav Republic against the threat posed by Milosevic's Serbian Forces. However, problematic from the point of view of international law, and for the Canadian government, was the fact that the intervention had been carried out by NATO without prior authorization from the United Nations Security Council. Indeed, according to Paul Heinbecker (1999), the assistant deputy minister of global and security policy, 'Canada had tried several times in several ways to see whether the Council could be brought to act responsibly' but to no avail. Russian and Chinese vetoes would inevitably block any Security Council resolution authorizing collective action. Axworthy was clearly frustrated with Security Council intransigence despite a dire humanitarian crisis, noting in a speech before the UN General Assembly in September 1998, 'to remain credible, the Council must re-examine the traditional interpretation of its mandate . . . [and] broaden its horizons in addressing emerging threats which impact on our security' (DFAIT, 1998).

Following the 1999 Kosovo war, domestic consensus crystallized in Canadian communities of academics and foreign policy experts around an expanded human security mandate; a commitment to the protection of peoples 'also requires a commitment to back diplomacy with the threat of military force and, when necessary, the use of force' (Heinbecker, 2000: 16). Moreover, NATO had presented Canadian policy makers with an effective vehicle to lead robust responses to humanitarian crises in the absence of a viable alternative from the United Nations. This was all music to the ears of the defence establishment and defenders of military budgets and capabilities. Humanitarian interventions, particularly in robust forms like the Kosovo and Bosnia missions, bolstered the role of the Canadian Forces (CF) as an instrument of foreign policy and, therefore, its claim to a share of government spending. Axworthy was so persuaded by the importance of the CF in carrying out humanitarian and reconstruction tasks like mine clearance that he, in turn, persuaded CIDA to channel a portion of Canadian assistance funds to Bosnia through Canadian soldiers (Axworthy, 2003: 175). After Kosovo, the ideological and operational divide between hard and soft power narrowed and converged around a newly robust version of human security (Smith-Windsor, 2000; Rigby, 2001).

Nevertheless, the right to humanitarian intervention was not universally accepted among members of the international community. Most countries, with the exception of Belgium, abstained from asserting a general norm of humanitarian intervention and instead invoked a 'moral duty' or a 'necessity to act' when characterizing the Kosovo intervention (Brunnee and Toope, 2006: 3). Concerns among developing countries about the potential for neo-imperialist incursions by the West into sovereign states, especially in the absence of UN Security Council authorization, impeded the momentum for a customary right to humanitarian intervention. In Canada, as well as in other Western countries, similar concerns arose that an expanded mandate for collective action and forceful interventions based upon humanitarian premises might result in unchecked expressions of unilateral power serving the interests of influential states (CCFPD, 2000). The United Nations had been sidelined by the Atlantic alliance, and its *post facto* decision not to condemn the regional organization was not a persuasive indication of the world body's credibility or, indeed, that of NATO. Both legality and legitimacy were at stake in drawing general conclusions for international law and international relations from NATO's actions in Kosovo.

National forums and conferences hosted by the CCFPD brought together Canadian interest groups, academics, lawyers, foreign policy experts, and government officials to debate the problem of humanitarian intervention and develop policy ideas for elevation as alternatives on the governmental agenda. The most important message coming out of these foreign policy dialogues was the need to develop clear criteria for collective actions taken by the international community on behalf of human rights. This was necessary to prevent potential abuses of armed humanitarianism as well as to avoid charges of Western neo-colonialism by developing countries (Geislerova, 1999: 16). United Nations reform to support changing norms surrounding humanitarian interventions also emerged as a pressing theme of these consultations (CCFPD, 2000: 4). Bringing ideas and policy recommendations together as a coherent policy alternative was the next logical step. Canadian foreign policy experts were charged with developing a framework for human security–style interventions within a broader mandate for UN reform.

Movement toward reform and renewal at the United Nations was already underway. Axworthy and Canada's ambassador to the UN, Robert Fowler, had only to take advantage of emerging trends in order to build support for Canadian proposals and initiatives. In September 1999, the secretary-general released a landmark report entitled *The Protection of Civilians in Armed Conflict* that had been developed in close collaboration with Canadian diplomats during Canada's term as a non-permanent member of the Security Council beginning in February 1999 (DFAIT, 2000b). Canada used the secretary-general's report as a launching pad for a process of intergovernmental bargaining at the UN, at international conferences, and through bilateral meetings with UN member states. Engaging intergovernmental bodies, such as the International Committee of the Red Cross and Human Security Network, as well as NGOs and research think-tanks, such as the World Federalist Movement, the Carnegie Foundation, and the International Peace Academy, was part of the process of persuasion. Canadian diplomats pushed for a new international consensus on balancing sovereignty rights and human rights in an age of interdependence. When secretary-general Kofi Annan called upon the international community to 'address the prospects of human security and intervention in the next century' (ICISS, 2001: 15) in his opening address to the General Assembly in September 1999, specialized publics and the international policy community had already been 'softened' to the idea of change. Canadian entrepreneurs, too, were ready to assume international leadership with a proposal for an innovative forum for debate.

Two senior officials at Canada's Department of Foreign Affairs and International Trade, Don Hubert and Jill Sinclair, proposed an international commission of experts and politicians to take on the problem of reconciling human rights with state sovereignty (Axworthy, 2003: 191). The International Commission on Intervention and State Sovereignty (ICISS), as it came to be called, was designed to be a catalyst for debate and political engagement as well as a statement of principle. As Axworthy explained at the launch of the commission, in sponsoring ICISS Canada hoped to 'foster global political consensus on how to move from . . . paralysis, towards action in the international system, particularly through the United Nations' (DFAIT, 2000a).

The ICISS report set out a 'responsibility continuum' (Brunnee and Toope, 2006: 8) that moved from preventive actions to reactive interventions—including the use of political, economic, and military sanctions—and postconflict rebuilding. The second pillar after preventive actions, the responsibility to react, was both the most contentious and most complete package of ideas and prescriptions. Earlier debates surrounding humanitarian intervention had revolved around issues such as the appropriate benchmark warranting intervention and the critical decision to use force, as well as whether countries had unilateral or collective rights to intervene on behalf of human rights. Policy alternatives for humanitarian intervention had included wider peacekeeping operations by the United Nations in Bosnia and Somalia, non-defensive NATO campaigns outside of the traditional North Atlantic theatre of operations in Kosovo, interventions of coalitions of the willing—such as that led by Australia in East Timor, or alternatives that fell in the grey area between UN authorization (*ex post facto*) and unilateralism, as in Liberia and Sierra Leone.

The ICISS report's solution was to establish a set of six criteria regulating military interventions for human protection purposes, namely: right authority; just cause; right intention; last resort; proportional means; and reasonable prospects (ICISS, 2001: 32). Of these, the first two precautionary principles were critical. On the question of right authority, the report notes that 'there is no better or more appropriate body than the Security Council to deal with military intervention issues for human protection purposes' (ICISS, 2001: 49). Moreover, the commission recommended that Security Council authorization 'must in all cases be sought prior to any military intervention being carried out' (ICISS, 2001: 50). The primary authority of the UN to govern the use of military force in response to humanitarian crises was explained in legal terms (with reference to the UN *Charter* and customary norms) as well as with reference to the world body's universal membership, political legitimacy, and value acceptability among members of the international community (ICISS, 2001: 52). However, the commission did acknowledge that limitations in capabilities, failures of political will, as well as the democratic deficit and the Permanent Five veto-power system of the Security Council might require the UN to work more closely with regional and subregional organizations in 'partnerships of the able, the willing and the well-intended—and the duly authorized' (ICISS, 2001: 52–3). These partnerships did not preclude the necessity for prior authorization, whether through the Security Council, or, if this is impossible, through the General Assembly's 'Uniting for Peace' procedures (ICISS, 2001: 54). According to Thomas Franck, speaking in 2006 at the Foreign Affairs building in Ottawa, the difference between humanitarian intervention and the responsibility to protect was that the first represented a unilateral right of intervention based on *erga omnes* obligations to the international community while the latter reinforces the role of the United Nations as the leading institutional guarantor of human rights and international peace and security (Franck, 2006).

The 'just cause' clause of the ICISS report sought to resolve the ambiguity over the threshold for military action by limiting R2P interventions to incidences of 'large scale loss of life, actual or apprehended', with or without intent, or 'large scale "ethnic cleansing", actual or apprehended' (ICISS, 2001: 32). Significantly, the report does not justify the use of force to overthrow non-democratic governments (Ignatieff, 2005). Nor, however, does the report limit interventions to responses to international crimes like genocide, presumably opening the door to collective action in cases where massive human rights violations have not reached the threshold of international crime (Brunnee and Toope, 2006: 10). The scope for action is also widened by the provision that both actual and 'apprehended' threats are sufficient causes for robust international action.

Following the publication of the ICISS report, Canada exercised entrepreneurial leadership to promote the responsibility to protect. These efforts were largely regarded as diplomatic successes, in particular the inclusion of R2P principles in the 2005 UN World Summit Outcome documents. Critics maintain, however, that Canadian leadership can only go so far when the political will in the wider international community is absent. According to one view, the Summit Outcome impeded the momentum that had been building for the Security Council to adopt a resolution establishing commonly agreed upon criteria governing the use of force for human protection purposes. The threshold criteria for collective responses were also further limited at the Summit to incidences of international crime (Brunnee and Toope, 2006: 10–11). Moreover, the ICISS report's reference to the threat of harm as a triggering event, as well as actual incidents of violence, was notably missing. Similarly absent was the commission's recommendation that Permanent Five states abstain from exercising veto rights with respect to actions required to 'stop or avert a significant humanitarian crisis' where vital national interests are not involved (ICISS, 2001: 51). Finally, omitted from the Summit Outcome was significant attention to the conflict prevention agenda (Brunnee and Toope, 2006: 9).

Clearly, the responsibility to protect, at least in the form embodied by the 2001 ICISS report, had not achieved the broad consensus necessary to reach the tipping point where a persuasive and innovative idea becomes a viable alternative on governmental and decision agendas. Canadian entrepreneurship to promote human security had profound limits.

HUMAN SECURITY POLITICS

One factor in the successful mobilization of human security onto the official governmental agenda was a confluence of elements in the political stream that made the time right for policy change. Shifts in the national mood, the direction of interest group pressures, and the impact of jurisdiction and turnover in government each contributed to creating an opportune moment for human security:[3] a compelling idea suited to changes in the global security climate as well as national politics.[4]

Human security emerged onto the Canadian governmental agenda in the years following the end of the Cold War. The Conservative government of Brian Mulroney (1984–93) had initiated a change in Canadian foreign-policy principles and practices away from cautious middle-power engagement and toward active promotion of the 'new world order'. Notably, this resulted in wider peacekeeping and peace enforcement in the former Yugoslavia, Somalia, and Haiti, missions with more robust mandates in situations of intrastate and ongoing conflict involving multiple belligerents. The nature of these conflicts made civil and peacebuilding efforts focused on the needs of civilian populations a constituent part of the new peacekeeping in addition to promoting the security of states.

Underlying the transformation of peacekeeping were changing discourses surrounding security. Under the Conservatives, Canada participated in development projects and peacekeeping missions in Central America, commissioned studies through the International Development Research Centre (IDRC), and began to integrate the development and security agendas into a more holistic 'human security' package (Ross, 2001: 75–93). Development NGOs and the Central American lobby—including the Canadian–Caribbean–Central-American Policy Alternatives (CAPA) group which hosted a series of international roundtable discussions attended by NGOs, bureaucrats, parliamentarians, and academics in the mid-to-late 1980s—became active participants in defining the government's new security agenda, greatly influencing future decision makers including Liberal foreign affairs critic Lloyd Axworthy (ibid.: 90).

New approaches to foreign policy were delayed responses to long-term trends toward non-traditional and non-territorial interpretations of security (Cheung-Gertler, 2006b). From the 1960s 'counterconsensus' mobilizations against Cold War militarism had emerged a broad-based movement that included diverse civil society groups like Project Ploughshares, the Canadian Council for International Cooperation (CCIC), Oxfam, and the National Action Committee on the Status of Women (Neufeld, 2004: 107–23). In the early 1990s, two reports based upon civil society consultations and submissions planted the seeds of the human security idea: *Transformation Moment*, cosponsored by a number of NGOs including CCIC (1992); *Towards a Common Future*, based on submissions to the CCIC from groups like the World Federalists of Canada, Interagency Coalition on AIDS and Development, Partnership Africa Canada, and Inter Church Fund for International Development (1994). For these public interest groups, economic and social indicators of justice and sustainability were at least as important for global peace and stability as military determinants of security. Grassroots pressures drew strength from academic voices like Barry Buzan, Ken Booth, and Thomas Homer-Dixon, who put forward broader conceptions of security, emphasizing their political, economic, social, and environmental dimensions (Buzan, 1983; Booth, 1991; Kaplan, 1994; Werthes and Debiel, 2006).

With political turnover and the election of a majority Liberal government in November 1993, there was a consolidation of these new approaches to security and leadership as viable alternatives on the governmental agenda. The Liberals cultivated a reputation as the 'party with ideas' during the election campaign that unseated the short-lived Conservative government of Kim Campbell, who succeeded Brian Mulroney as prime minister. The end of the Cold War had led to greater political receptiveness for innovative visions of security (Ross, 2001: 84), while fiscal austerity following a period of economic recession made less costly policy alternatives welcome. Controversies in Somalia and Bosnia involving CF *window* personnel, and the perceived failures of wider peacekeeping, added momentum toward new thinking in the conduct of Canadian foreign policy and a move-ment away from traditional international security roles. Democratization of the foreign policy-making process (Nossal, 1995), and the horizontal expansion of security beyond the military protection of territorial integrity (Welch, 1992: 67), became the defining characteristics of the Liberal agenda.

The foreign affairs portfolio was first awarded to André Ouellet, a long-time Liberal MP with previous cabinet experience. Under Ouellet's direction, three broad foreign policy priorities were established: the promotion of prosperity and employment; the protection of security within a stable global framework; and the projection of Canadian values and culture. Among the ideas articulated by *Canada in the World,* the government's 1995 foreign policy statement, was an approach to security recognizing 'a broadening of the focus of security policy from its narrow orientation of managing state-to-state relationships, to one that recognizes the importance of the individual and society for our shared security'.

The first major human security initiative was the campaign to ban land-mines—later dubbed the Ottawa Process. In the early years following the end of the Cold War, landmines came to the attention of publics and officials through the efforts of UN-led security and development initiatives, particularly in Cam-bodia and El Salvador (Ross, 2001: 84). Landmines became a priority of interna-tional NGOs, which by 1992 had combined to pool efforts through the International Campaign to Ban Landmines (ICBL). The NGO campaign alerted the public to the disproportionate and indiscriminate costs for civilian populations resulting from mine use and its hindrance to development. Although 70 per cent of mine victims were men, images of wounded women and children became the faces of the ICBL campaign, helping to convey the message that landmines put innocent civilians at risk (Kitchen, 2002). By the mid-1990s, the Canadian gov-ernment's readings of the national mood from mail, opinion polls, and organ-ized political interest groups, led by Mines Action Canada, indicated widespread support for a change in landmines policy (Tomlin, 1998: 10).

Although countries such as France and the United States had initiated the global campaign to revise landmines policies, Canada had a number of comparative advantages in the political stream that made leadership of the international landmines campaign an attractive proposition. The Canadian military lobby was weak. Canada was not a major user or producer of landmines; opposition from defence stakeholders was less vociferous than in countries like the United States. Moreover, the Canadian Department of Defence was sidelined in the initial stages of the policy-making process and its opposition to a landmines ban undermined by swift changes in the international arena as well as by a domestic crisis of confidence arising from allegations of abuse by CF personnel in Somalia. The mistake made by the UN in 1995, when it included Canada on a list of countries that had implemented export moratoria on landmines, added to the impression in Canada that the policy status quo was inadequate. Canada's international reputation became a motivating political concern: to admit that no moratorium existed was 'unthinkable' (ibid.).

Political turnover generated further impetus to drive the landmines campaign onto the government's decision agenda. Ouellet was succeeded in January 1996 by Axworthy, an ambitious policy innovator eager to make an immediate difference. Under his leadership, the populist character of human security would be reinforced and put to use through the 'new diplomacy':[5] engaging Canadians in the foreign policy-making process. With an active international NGO campaign mobilizing for a ban, Axworthy saw landmines as an opportunity for policy innovation and anticipated that Canada had the right combination of diplomatic resources, multilateral networks, and the international profile to lead a soft-power campaign to ban mines (Howard and Neufeldt, 2000). The minister's staff in the disarmament field was also particularly strong (Kitchen, 2002), moving quickly to elevate landmines from a peripheral item on the arms control and disarmament agenda to a central issue on the human security agenda (Tomlin, 1998: 12).

The Ottawa Process became a model for the soft-power mobilization of ideas as an alternative vehicle for international leadership at a time of depleted morale and diminished capacity at DFAIT. Soft power began at home when the government launched a national effort to encourage Canadians to support the ban, successfully capturing the public imagination. The Liberals enjoyed a safe majority in Parliament, where support for the ban convention was evident among advocates like John English, later appointed Canada's special envoy on landmines, and Keith Martin, who introduced a private member's bill in support of the ban. Domestic political capital was mobilized internationally when the government included Mines Action Canada in its national delegation to the October 1996 strategy conference (Tomlin, 1998). Civil society–government partnerships enabled victims of state policies, and their civil society representatives, to become active players in the Ottawa Process, tipping the political balance away from powerful states and institutional deadlock. The NGO-led 'mobilization of shame' created the political momentum to move past lowest-common-denominator solutions and toward fast-track negotiations for a comprehensive ban on landmines. In his closing remarks to the 1996 strategy conference held in Ottawa, Axworthy issued his groundbreaking challenge for participants to return to the Canadian capital to sign a convention by the end of 1997 (DFAIT, 1996b).

Following the minister's appeal, Canada pursued a two-track approach that combined educating and mobilizing global public opinion, involving maximum civil society participation, with a state-led process to create a formal negotiating forum leading to the conclusion of an internationally recognized treaty (Gwozdecky and Sinclair, 2001: 32). Track one included the strategic use of diplomatic settings to promote, cajole, and entice governments, as well as non-traditional tactics like 'cold-calling' parliamentarians (ibid.). Track two also utilized persuasion, but this time among a 'Core Group' of countries to create common policy positions and legal frameworks for a ban treaty. A series of regional conferences were held to capture media attention, and mobilize local commitment and state support (Gwozdecky and Sinclair, 2001: 33–4). The fruits of a year-long process of bargaining, coalition building, and norms diffusion came in December 1997, when 122 countries formally signed the convention banning landmines, capping the success of a test-case for the soft-power alternative.

The campaign to establish an International Criminal Court (ICC) was another example of the successful political mobilization of soft power to implement human security goals. International outrage stemming from the war crimes committed in the former Yugoslavia and Rwanda led to the establishment of ad hoc criminal tribunals in 1993 and 1994 respectively (Howard and Neufeldt, 2000: 26). The prominent role of Canadian Louise Arbour as the chief prosecutor for the Yugoslavia and Rwanda tribunals (McRae and Hubert, 2001: 267; Howard and Neufeldt, 2000: 27) raised the Canadian profile of issues surrounding impunity and international criminal justice. Feedback indicated, however, that these courts faced substantial difficulties, such as limited jurisdiction (the International Criminal Tribunal for Rwanda [ICTR] was authorized to try only those crimes committed in 1994), overstretched resources, hefty costs, and the difficulties of corralling suspected war criminals. A permanent court was a solution to problems of inefficiency and cost associated with the ad hoc tribunals and was seen as a better deterrent against future crimes.

William Pace, the convenor of the NGO Coalition for an International Criminal Court (CICC), also sought a role. The CICC had been working closely with the Like-Minded Group (LMG) of countries that had formed in 1994 to build support for a conference to establish an international court. Canada assumed the chairmanship of the LMG group (Howard and Neufeldt, 2000: 27) and the ICC became one of the top five human security priorities[6] on the decision agenda. Drawing upon the landmines model, Canada vigorously supported the inclusion of NGOs as participants at the Rome Conference and funded six NGO representatives to attend (ibid.).

At the Rome Diplomatic Conference, held from 15 to 17 July 1998, civil society played an especially significant part in the evolution of negotiations on the powers of the ICC Prosecutor. Many NGOs argued for an independent prosecutor empowered to initiate investigations and prosecutions on the basis of information provided by individuals and citizen organizations, as well as by states. The World Federalists of Canada (WFC) was an active advocate for the ICC campaign, and served as the administrating agency for the Canadian Network for an International Criminal Court (CNICC), an umbrella organization of more than 150 Canadian organizations and individuals (Watt, 1998). Civil society–government partnerships translated into a 'big bang for a relatively small number of bucks'; the ICC campaign enabled Canada to promote its values abroad at 'much lower costs' than through peacekeeping or development assistance (Riddell-Dixon, 2005: 11).

At the main negotiating committee of the Rome Conference, a turnover of personnel offered Canada an opportunity for international influence when Philippe Kirsch replaced the Netherland's Adriaan Bos as chairman. Kirsch's appointment followed from his experience and proven negotiating abilities, but the decision to appoint a Canadian was also based upon the country's reputation as a good neighbour to the US. Media coverage at home projected a positive image of Canadian leadership (Keller, 1998). Kirsch's talent for bargaining, coalition building, and making strategic tradeoffs produced consensus in the political stream for a final draft agreement. The conference overwhelmingly approved the Rome Statute of the ICC on 17 July 1998. Two years later, the *Crimes Against Humanity and War Crimes Act* was enacted on 29 June 2000 and came into force on 23 October 2000, making Canada the first country to adopt domestic legislation to implement obligations under the Rome Statute.[7]

One noteworthy exception to the otherwise favourable political climate for the ICC was American opposition to the world court,[8] despite Canadian efforts to bring the US on board. Although Canada's position on the ICC could potentially alienate the US, its principal international partner, an active domestic constituency and favourable national mood, as well as the opportunity afforded for international leadership, prevailed over bilateral pressures. Canadian efforts to build a strong international coalition, including NGOs and like-minded countries, paid political dividends against the opposition of powerful states like the United States, Russia, and India. Initiatives like the Ottawa Process and the ICC reinforced an impression of independence in the conduct of its foreign policy, long a preoccupation of Canadian political life.

While the landmines ban and the ICC prospered, factors of broader human security, such as the environment, poverty, and underdevelopment, fell off the governmental and decision agendas. The neglect of issues of environmental and economic sustainability was incongruent with public sympathies for principles of environmental protection and sustainable development. The high-profile Rio Summit had put the environment front and centre on the governmental agenda in the early 1990s (Martin and Fortmann, 1995: 376), and the public attention span also had some longevity; a 1997 year-end poll found that an overwhelming majority of Canadians (84 per cent) were willing to change their lifestyle to reduce their footprint on the earth (Evenson, 1997). In 1999, Elizabeth May of the environmental advocacy group The Sierra Club warned of Canada's failing performance and deferral of global environmental leadership. Meanwhile, falling rates of overseas development assistance (ODA) were part of larger trends that challenged both the effectiveness, and economy, of development aid as compared to trade instruments. The public, still reeling from the economic recession of the early 1990s, was relatively indifferent to cuts in ODA—perhaps reflecting an increasingly mainstream vein of criticism that linked ODA with corruption and aid dependency in recipient countries. Pressure groups were largely ineffective in mobilizing general or specialized publics to reverse disinvestment in overseas development.

Feedback from the universities and among some policy practitioners contributed to the national mood and political climate surrounding the decision to narrow Canada's human security agenda to prioritize the protection of civilians during armed conflict. From 'pinchpenny diplomacy' and 'foreign policy on the cheap' to 'pulpit diplomacy' and 'hot air', academics had responded negatively to Axworthy's foreign policy agenda (Nossal, 1998–9; Hampson and Oliver, 1998; Paris, 2001). New diplomacy exercises alerted the government to these dissenting voices, while articles and opinion pieces in national newspapers brought the debate to a wider audience. The 'public intellectual' phenomenon bridged feedback from specialized publics with broader climates of opinion and national mood. A second body of criticism came from a practitioners' perspective. A broad UNDP-style human security agenda was deemed by Andrew Mack, of the University of British Columbia's Human Security Centre, to be analytically unsound while critics noted that it was also fiscally improbable (Owens and Arneil, 1999: 1–12; Mack and Rohlfs, 2003). In an article for the *Ottawa Citizen,* former diplomat Graham N. Green warned that making human security the focus of Canada's two-year term as a non-permanent member of the Security Council, beginning in January 1999, was a 'formula for failure' and, worse, would undermine the country's international credibility and influence (Green, 1999).

The critique of human security frequently included a broader argument that soft power alone could not meet the goals of human security. The merging of soft with hard power, and the drive toward peace enforcement, drew strength from geopolitical developments in the world. Genocide, war crimes, and other crimes against humanity in Somalia, the former Yugoslavia, and Rwanda dominated headlines in the early and mid-1990s. While Somalia and Bosnia precipitated a retreat from UN peacekeeping, Rwanda alerted the international community to the costs of disengagement. Canadian general Romeo Dallaire, who served as commander of the UNAMIR, was particularly vocal about both the scale of atrocity (an estimated eight hundred thousand over one hundred days in the spring and summer of 1994) and the complicity of the international community in refusing to act. Despite Dallaire's repeated pleas for more soldiers, equipment, and a robust mandate, Security Council politics prevented the timely, and strategic, use of force that Dallaire argued could have prevented the genocide (Reuters News Agency, 1998).

The turning point for using hard power to realize human security goals came in March 1999 with the participation of the CF in the NATO air-strike campaign in Kosovo. In early April, a Compas poll found that a sizeable majority of Canadians, 79 per cent, supported NATO actions and that 72 per cent approved of Canadian involvement (Martin and Fortmann, 2001a: 71). Similarly, an Angus Reid survey found that two-thirds of Canadians approved of both NATO's actions and the Canadian part in them (ibid.). Support remained relatively strong over the ensuing weeks, with 57 per cent of respondents to an Environics poll indicating support for the NATO campaign while only 31 per cent were opposed (ibid.).

Leadership was not the determinative factor in mobilizing public support. The government did not hold a parliamentary debate on the decision to deploy troops to Kosovo or go out of its way to engage Canadians (Dewing and McDonald, 2004). Commentators attributed public support for the Kosovo intervention to the importance of values and to the widespread acceptance of new security discourses in which humanitarianism looms large (Martin and Fortmann, 2001a: 71). Other factors in public support were the absence of Canadian casualties and the short duration of the war. Although public opinion did not drive Canadian participation in the NATO intervention, neither was it a constraint to action (ibid.: 70). In addition, defence stakeholders and lobby groups embraced the merging of soft and hard power. After Kosovo, humanitarian roles and peacekeeping-style interventions led by military alliances were perceived as the best way to revive support for the CF (Rigby, 2001).

If the mood among general publics and military stakeholders favoured the NATO alternative, prominent voices in organized interest groups, the universities, and some policy-making circles differed in their estimation of the Kosovo intervention. The Canadian Council of Churches issued an open letter in April 1999, posted by Project Ploughshares on its website, calling for 'an immediate and unilateral moratorium' on the NATO bombing campaign (CCIC, 1999). Diplomat Daryl Copeland responded to this domestic constituency when he wrote of 'rich ambiguities on the home front, where a generation of new Canadians . . . found it difficult to share the enthusiasm of the government for military engagement in the Balkans' (Copeland, 2001: 164). A former Canadian ambassador to Yugoslavia, James Bissett, called the Kosovo intervention a 'tragic blunder', arguing that NATO's actions had worsened, rather than lessened, the humanitarian crisis (Bissett, 2000). Media coverage too, was critical of the campaign, reporting high-profile 'mistakes' such as the bombing of civilian markets. In the months following the end of hostilities, feedback from policy experts and specialized communities indicated growing scepticism that an erstwhile collective defence alliance, serving the strategic interests of a handful of powerful states, could be an appropriate vehicle to enforce human security. Problems of political legitimacy and legality under international law became the major preoccupation of domestic policy debates in and around government about the NATO-led intervention.

Even so, disengagement was a political non-starter. The global reach of media broadcasting made human suffering and atrocities committed far from Canadian shores seem suddenly immediate, creating new domains of responsibility. One indication of this was high levels of support for peacekeeping among the internationally minded public. Despite the increased risks associated with peacekeeping operations since the end of the Cold War, public opinion continued to support peacekeeping over all other military roles for the armed forces[9] (Martin and Fortmann, 1995: 379). Polling results supported the assumption that there remained a sizeable core of Canadians that supported peacekeeping as a matter of principle—regardless of specific events and momentary crises; although support for UN peacekeeping had dropped sharply to approximately 59 per cent by January 1994 (Gallup, 1994), it had rebounded by the following month and levels of support were consistently registered over the next two years to be between 63 and 68 per cent (Martin and Fortmann, 2001b: 47–8). One study of public opinion in Canadian foreign policy making concluded that 'public opinion on peacekeeping tends to be stable over time and reacts in reasonable and predictable ways to external events' (Martin and Fortmann, 2001a: 70). Declining rates of support for Canadian participation in peacekeeping missions during the controversial endeavour in Bosnia, and after the high-profile failures to prevent atrocities in Somalia and Rwanda, were perceived to be indicators of 'mood swing' rather than of an irreversible shift in public opinion.

In the context of the Bosnia and Kosovo crises, and subsequent peace enforcement by NATO, niches in telecommunications, training, and transport seemed increasingly inadequate, even among members of the humanitarian community. One early examination of a new harder-edged solution to humanitarian crises in the post–Cold War was a 1995 report co-authored by Nancy Gordon of CARE Canada, *A Humanitarian Intervention as an Instrument of Human Rights*. The momentum for policy change among specialized publics and pressure groups was also reflected in the general public. An emerging domestic consensus supported the government's determination that traditional peacekeeping tasks, like the monitoring of ceasefires, were not always sufficient to meet contemporary challenges. Sustained public support throughout the complex UN peacekeeping and peace enforcement missions of the 1990s, as well as the initially high levels of support for the NATO intervention in Kosovo, had proven Canadians' commitment to promote and protect human security—including through military means. While human security started its life by bringing attention to the non-military threats to international peace and security, its principles of human protection reduced public tolerance for non-involvement (Regehr and Whelan, 2004: 21).

A congruence of elements in the political stream had created the circumstances for another look at the problem of humanitarian intervention. The global reach of media, or the CNN effect (Heinbecker, 2004), alerted the Canadian public to atrocities committed against civilians within state borders. UN deadlock over the crisis in Kosovo reinforced the organization's diminishing credibility. But the NATO-led intervention, and the shift in alliance mandates from collective defence to 'robust peacekeeping', came under fire from public interest groups, international jurists, academics, and from within government circles. The 'responsibility to protect' responded to domestic and international voices seeking a consensus on how best to reconcile state sovereignty with human rights, while ensuring that the human security of peoples remained at the forefront in defining operational principles for interventions mandated with human protection purposes (Cheung-Gertler, 2006b). Axworthy's leadership and the secretary-general's endorsement provided the remaining political energy to elevate the idea for a commission onto Canadian and international decision agendas. ICISS would publish its seminal report, *The Responsibility to Protect,* in December 2001, initiating international debate on the circumstances governing the use of force for human protection and the necessity to reform the United Nations to better meet its responsibilities to protect.

The impact of political turnover on the human security agenda with the end of Axworthy's term in September 2000 was not immediately obvious. John Manley, the new foreign minister, was much less interested in human security than in 'strong, cooperative relations with the United States' (DFAIT, 2000c). Although human security was mentioned prominently in the Throne Speech of 30 January 2001 (Copeland, 2001: 171), the terrorist attacks in New York on September 11, 2001, shifted government priorities to border security and access.

Notwithstanding security and trade interests, Manley's successor, Bill Graham, was more favourable to human security. At a May 2003 meeting of the Human Security Network (HSN) in Graz, Austria, Graham announced that DFAIT would commit $1.65 million to support the ICC and follow-on efforts to the ICISS report (DFAIT, 2003b). New spending came on the heels of Canada's appointment as chair of the HSN, perhaps reflecting the indirect political pressures resulting from soft-power leadership such as maintaining international credibility before like-minded peers. Nevertheless, Graham reportedly came under pressure to axe Foreign Affairs' $10 million a year Human Security Program first established by the Liberals in 1999 (Mack and Rohlfs, 2003). Manley's 2003 budget statement as finance minister reflected pressures from organized business groups wanting a 'North American Security Perimeter' as part of a 'grand bargain' to protect Canadian access to the American market. The budget allotted significant increases for defence and homeland security (ibid.), but $30 million was subsequently cut in funding for the Department of Foreign Affairs.

Strong domestic support came to the defence of the human security approach to Canadian foreign policy. The majority of Canadians polled in November 2004 endorsed the statement that 'Canada should focus its international efforts on working with non-governmental organizations to build support for specific solutions to key problems, like the ban on land-mines, and not try and do so many other things' (Innovative Research Group [IRG], 2004). From a regional perspective, soft power and humanitarianism has traditionally played well in Quebec, where military roles abroad and defence procurement at home has been met with suspicion (Rioux, 2005: 19–24). In other words, a niche for Canadian foreign policy as a mobilizer of soft power to address problems of human insecurity was overwhelmingly supported by the public over a traditional international security role. One recommendation from April 2005 consultations with academics and civil society was to renew and increase funding for the Human Security

Program (*War to Peace Transitions*, 2005). The Human Security Program was subsequently renewed in the 2005 budget under new funding for Foreign Affairs's peace and security initiatives (Government of Canada, 2005a). Research in human security trends and developments continued and Mack's Human Security Report Project found a new home at Simon Fraser University in June 2007.

Factors of continuity in public institutions and among personnel in and around government were significant. Many of the bureaucrats who had been instrumental in bringing about Axworthy's human security initiatives continued to occupy positions of influence. In 2001, the CCFPD was integrated into the DFAIT's organizational structure as a new division reporting to the Policy Planning Secretariat (DFAIT, 2004). In spite of the portrayal of human security as Axworthy's personal crusade, the staying-power of human security ideas and approaches demonstrates that its principles became a part of Ottawa's bureaucratic institutions and culture.

Human security, however de-glamourized and de-moralized, survived the departure of its leading advocate and the varying commitment of his successors (Cheung-Gertler, 2007). However, the September 11 terrorist attacks in New York and Washington did influence public opinion and government priorities in ways that challenged the human security approach to foreign policy. Although the November poll of the same year (IRG, 2004) indicated continued support among Canadians for human security, an April 2004 poll concluded that the top two foreign policy spending priorities were investments in combatting terrorism at home (at 55 per cent) and national defence in general (at 54 per cent) (POLLARA, 2004). Together, the April and November 2004 polls represented conflicting strains of opinion in Canadian policy communities that pitted economic and national security concerns at home against enduring human security approaches to global governance. A divided domestic policy community causes agenda instability (Kingdon, 2003: 120), reflected in budget cuts and threats to funding pools for government programs. But it also gives the government greater room for discretion in choosing how to read the national mood and frame policy responses.

CHAPTER 11

The Evolution of Human Security Policy

In this chapter, we bring the three streams of public policy making together at critical junctures. Whether in terms of innovation or recombination, enterprising advocates for policy alternatives seized windows of opportunity to move human security policy forward. Progress occurred when policy entrepreneurs attached solutions to problems, overcame constraints by redrafting proposals, or took advantage of fortuitous political developments. In the case of human security, the entrepreneur-in-chief was a policy-oriented, forward-looking, and ambitious minister of foreign affairs, Lloyd Axworthy, who built momentum behind a series of international initiatives—the treaty banning anti-personnel landmines, the establishment of an International Criminal Court (ICC), and development of the responsibility to protect doctrine—that made the most of limited resources at a time of fiscal austerity. Through mobilizing partnerships with civil society and like-minded governments, Axworthy engineered a soft-power approach to foreign policy that placed norms development (or the assertion and institutionalization of guiding principles), effective diplomacy, multilateral cooperation in traditional and non-traditional forums, and universal responsibilities high on the decision agenda. The responsibilities of human security, however, produced its own set of imperatives that transcended soft-power parameters, creating further impetus for policy evolution.

ANTI-PERSONNEL LANDMINES

On 9 November 1995, Canadian foreign affairs minister André Ouellet was engaged in a question-and-answer session at a conference on foreign aid, when he was asked a question about anti-personnel landmines (because Canadian foreign aid was being used in de-mining projects).[1] In his reply, Ouellet said, 'These [mines] should be banned not only in Canada but everywhere in the world.' Ouellet's response was remarkable for two reasons. First, the landmines issue had not even been defined as a problem warranting a place on the government's decision agenda. Second, the idea of banning mines was at odds with existing Canadian policy on the issue: Canada's position on mines had been in place for some time, and was being articulated in the United Nations conference reviewing the Convention on Certain Conventional Weapons (CCW). The mines problem had been identified, a suitable policy had been formulated, and was being implemented, and the government had moved on to other issues. In fact, in the autumn of 1995, the arms control problem on Canada's governmental agenda was nuclear proliferation, not anti-personnel landmines. However, that would all change in a few short months, and Ouellet's statement was evidence of a process that was underway that would move the mines issue to the top of the Canadian government's decision agenda, a movement that would result in the Ottawa Process to ban anti-personnel mines.

Throughout the summer and autumn of 1995, André Ouellet had been pressing Canadian defence minister David Collenette for a change in Canada's policy on anti-personnel mines. Ouellet's awareness of the mines issue came largely from his ministerial responsibility for Canadian development assistance, some of which was allocated for de-mining operations in mine-affected regions of the world. Ouellet was struck by the futility of spending money for de-mining at the same time that new mines were being deployed around the world. In an exchange of letters in the late summer, Ouellet proposed to Collenette that Canada destroy its stocks of mines as a way of taking the lead on the issue. In reply, Collenette presented the standard argument of the Department of National Defence (DND), that landmines could not be eliminated until 'effective and humane alternatives' were found.

Ouellet tried a different tack. The United States was planning to introduce a resolution in the UN General Assembly's First Committee calling for a moratorium on the export of mines, and asked Canada to become a co-sponsor. Earlier, Canada's name had been included, mistakenly, on a list compiled by the UN secretary-general of countries that had in place a moratorium on exports. Ouellet urged Collenette to bring Canada's policy into line with the position portrayed in the secretary-general's report. Again, Collenette's officials advised him to reject Ouellet's request, arguing that the export moratorium was only the thin edge of the wedge in efforts by the Department of Foreign Affairs and International Trade (DFAIT) to control DND weapons policy. The bureaucrats' arguments did not satisfy Ouellet, however, and he was running out of patience with the defence minister. On 11 October 1995, Ouellet again wrote to Collenette, stating that it was time for a change in Canadian policy: he wanted to announce a Canadian moratorium on exports and to co-sponsor the US resolution in the UN, and he wanted to declare Canada's commitment to the eventual elimination of landmines. Reluctantly, DND agreed to the export moratorium, but insisted that this was as far as policy change could go. DFAIT officials agreed that no further changes in Canadian policy, beyond the export moratorium, would be pursued.

While the export moratorium may have satisfied DFAIT bureaucrats, it did not go far enough for their minister. Ouellet was not afraid to set the cat among the pigeons in pursuit of his goals, and this he did on November 9 when, in a follow-up to his statement to the conference on foreign aid, he opined to a CBC (Canadian Broadcasting Corporation) reporter that Canada should destroy its stockpile of landmines and declare a total ban on the production, export, and use of the weapons.[2] The statement took officials in DFAIT's Non-proliferation, Arms Control and Disarmament Division (IDA) by complete surprise. The anti-personnel mines file was being managed by a new officer in the division, Bob Lawson. Upon his arrival in IDA in October 1995, Lawson was told that an outright ban on landmines, however desirable, was not in the cards because DND would not countenance further changes in policy. On November 9, Lawson received a telephone call from the CBC asking for a comment on Ouellet's statement. Begging off, Lawson secured a transcript of the minister's remarks, and immediately took it to Jill Sinclair, the director of IDA, saying, 'You won't believe what just happened.' Sinclair asked if Mines Action Canada (MAC), the principal Canadian non-governmental organization advocating an end to the use of mines, had heard, and suggested that, if MAC was smart, they would arrange to have the minister's office flooded with congratulatory messages on Canada's new policy. Lawson immediately faxed the transcript to MAC, and followed up with a phone call to pass on Sinclair's suggestion, although MAC needed no prompting. They took the statement and ran with it.

Ouellet's statement offered a window of opportunity for policy entrepreneurs inside and outside of government to move the mines issue on to the governmental agenda. In Kingdon's model, policy windows open when the problem, policy, and political streams join, offering policy entrepreneurs an opportunity to advocate particular alternatives. In the problem stream, the chances of a problem securing attention are enhanced by the presence of objective indicators, a focusing event, and feedback about existing policies. There were indicators aplenty on this issue, and statistics on the human costs of anti-personnel mines were used liberally by international and non-governmental organizations, and the latter also provided extensive feedback to Ouellet about the inadequacy of Canada's current mines policy. The focusing event in the problem stream for Ouellet was the dissonance between Canadian de-mining activities and Canada's status quo position on the use of mines, a contradiction that dovetailed with the critique of Canadian policy that mines action groups were presenting to the minister.

These developments in the problem stream were joined with conditions in the political stream to generate pressure in the direction of a change in the policy agenda. By Ouellet's reading, the national mood, reflected in public opinion polls[3] and the heavy flow of mail to the minister's office, was clearly supportive of a ban on landmines, and pressure from organized political interests, led by MAC, was overwhelmingly in this direction. Finally, Ouellet and his advisors had engaged DND in a skirmish over turf on landmines, and while they did not directly challenge the jurisdiction of DND on the issue, Ouellet was determined to keep up the pressure for a change in Canadian policy. Change in the policy stream conspired with events in the other two streams to make change more likely. The UN mistake in placing Canada on a published list of countries with export moratoria in place provided a powerful argument for a change in Canadian policy, and the US request that Canada co-sponsor a UN resolution calling for an export moratorium provided the impetus for change. The alternative, to announce to the world that there had been an error, that Canada did not have such a moratorium in place, was unthinkable, and defence minister Collenette and his officials could not maintain their resistance to the export moratorium alternative. Their initial intransigence provoked Ouellet to act unilaterally, however, so that by the time DND finally gave in and agreed to an export moratorium, the policy window had opened and the mines issue was firmly entrenched on the governmental agenda. Policy entrepreneurs, inside and outside government, would seize the opportunity to begin moving Canada, and the world, in the direction of a complete ban. In the words of one official, 'Ouellet's statement broke the logjam and gave DFAIT the opening it needed.'

Collenette's formal agreement to a Canadian export ban, in a letter to Ouellet on 12 November 1995, was almost immediately overtaken by events in the policy stream. Emboldened by Ouellet's declaration in favour of a ban, mines action groups were pushing for further steps, and IDA officials now knew that they had a minister who would take on DND and fight for policy change. And so, despite their earlier commitment to DND that the export moratorium would be the last step, in that same month of November IDA advised Ouellet to pursue with DND the possibility of declaring a comprehensive Canadian moratorium, not only on exports, but also on the production and use of anti-personnel mines. The DND response to this initiative was, by the normal standards of ministerial correspondence, unusually direct in its acerbity, stating that DND would agree, in principle, to 'acquiesce', but that they did so reluctantly, complaining that this latest policy shift represented 'movement of the goalposts' by DFAIT. In acquiescing, DND lost control of its policy turf on the issue, and soon discovered the extent to which the goalposts had moved. On 17 January 1996, DFAIT announced not only the comprehensive moratorium, but also Canadian support for a complete ban on production, transfer, and use. In the words of one DFAIT official, DND had bought into a ban, and this gave DFAIT the running room it needed on the issue.

January brought change in the political stream as well, when André Ouellet retired and was replaced by Lloyd Axworthy as foreign affairs minister. Whereas Ouellet was a consummate politician whose policy streak did not run deep, Axworthy, a former professor of political science, was a minister genuinely interested in policy innovation who saw politics as a way to advance policy goals. In the transition, Ouellet's senior policy advisor, Michael Pearson, stayed on in the same role for Axworthy. Pearson not only provided important continuity on landmines, but also would soon become Axworthy's alter ego on the issue. Upon his arrival in Foreign Affairs, Axworthy requested the department to provide recommendations on what Canadian foreign policy priorities ought to be. In response, IDA sent two notes up to the minister, one identifying small arms and the other anti-personnel mines. Axworthy, guided by Pearson and seeing an opportunity to run with an issue, picked landmines as an immediate priority. He noted the prominent role played by non-governmental organizations (NGOs) on the issue and, anticipating the process that would unfold subsequently, indicated his interest in a partnership that would link NGO efforts with Canada's ability to champion the issue internationally. Axworthy signalled IDA to move forward on the policy front, extending the moratorium and pressing DND to agree to destroy Canadian stockpiles of mines. Congruent with Kingdon's model, turnover in the political stream elevated the mines issue to the decision agenda, where policy choices would be made. Although we have no way of knowing how the issue would have fared had Ouellet remained in office, officials and advisors agree that Axworthy gave the issue new urgency.

In the policy stream, the US export moratorium resolution in the UN also expanded Canadian policy options, because many of the large number of countries that supported the export moratorium were now prepared to go further. By March 1996, IDA had drafted a Canadian Action Plan to Reduce the Global Use of Land Mines. The plan proposed movement on two tracks. The first was continued Canadian participation in the CCW Review Conference, scheduled to meet in Geneva in April, which the Canadians were convinced would remain deadlocked. The second track consisted of an apparently unremarkable proposal that contained the seeds of the Ottawa Process: IDA proposed that Canada host a small international meeting of officials and NGOs to develop an action work plan on landmines. By April, track two had grown to include a Canadian-sponsored UN resolution on landmines, and the small meeting was now called an 'International Land Mine Strategy Session', to be held in September in Ottawa.[4] It also included a proposal to convert the January moratorium into a permanent ban on production, transfer, and use. Although DND refused the DFAIT request for a ban, Defence was now, effectively, sidelined on the landmines issue; DFAIT would pursue a ban on the international front, while continuing to pressure DND to agree to destroy its stockpiles of landmines.

Change was underway in the problem stream, as well. The CCW Review Conference was winding down in Geneva, and it was clear that no consensus would be achieved. If a ban was Canada's goal, then officials had to deal with the problem of international stalemate. Canada's G7 partners—France, the UK, and the US—wanted to refer the issue to the Conference on Disarmament (CD), but IDA was convinced that the consensus-based decision-making procedures of the CD would only replicate the deadlocked CCW.[5] Policy alternatives would have to take this problem into account. The UN resolution that was being prepared by IDA for introduction by Canada in the General Assembly originally contained a proposal to negotiate in the CD, but that was removed, and officials began to focus their energies on the session planned for 3–5 October in Ottawa. As conceived by IDA in May 1996, the session would include pro-ban states and NGOs from around the world, and its purpose would be to develop a strategic action plan detailing concrete global and regional initiatives for the elimination of anti-personnel mines. In addition, the session would issue a political declaration committing participating states to concrete actions to achieve the elimination of mines.

Although the number of countries that wanted to attend the Ottawa meeting was growing, there was still substantial opposition to the movement to ban mines, and officials in IDA were concerned that opponents might attend the session simply in order to sabotage it. The problem centred on the invitation list. Clearly, they did not want firm opponents in attendance, because, as one official put it in a mixed metaphor, once you let the rats in, they could scuttle the boat. On the other hand, if the goal was to build broad international consensus around a landmines ban, how could one not invite major mines producers and users like France, the UK, and the US? A solution to this dilemma was proposed by IDA Deputy Director Mark Gwozdecky in June 1996, and it was deceptive in its simplicity. The meeting would, in principle, be open to all states, but each would determine for itself whether it should attend. The criterion for such a determination would be the draft political declaration that Canada was preparing for endorsement by the session, which included a reference to countries taking unilateral steps toward a ban. Governments would be given the declaration in advance, and they would decide whether it was something they could endorse and, therefore, whether they should attend the meeting. It was hoped, moreover, that a desire for eligibility might also lead some to change their policy on mines unilaterally in advance of the meeting. This self-selection principle worked like 'magic' (as one official described it): any rats who attended would have to be prepared to face intense scrutiny in the presence of a core group of pro-ban states and NGOs; those who signed the declaration would be held to it by the international coalition of NGOs, determined to make certain that countries would live up to their commitments.

The Canadians were especially keen to bring the US onside, for obvious reasons. In May 1996, US President Clinton announced American support for efforts to conclude an international agreement to ban mines. Coming two weeks after the unsuccessful conclusion of the CCW, Clinton's announcement was very positively received by Canadian officials, especially, as one said, since the meeting planned for Ottawa was now the only show in town. Axworthy responded to Clinton's announcement in a letter to US secretary of state Warren Christopher in which he invited the US to work with Canada to ensure that the planned Ottawa meeting would facilitate progress towards an international agreement. Christopher agreed, and over the spring and summer, Canadian officials travelled to Washington several times to work with their American counterparts in an effort to bring the US into the tent. When, at the conclusion of the CCW, Canada circulated the resolution it was preparing for the UN General Assembly, the US objected that, since they had introduced the export moratorium resolution in the General Assembly the previous autumn, they saw the UN as their show. Canada agreed to withdraw its UN resolution in favour of one sponsored by the US, but only if the Americans would agree not to refer to the CD in their resolution. This the Americans agreed to, even though they eventually decided that the CD was their preferred forum for negotiations. When IDA circulated the political declaration it was drafting for the Ottawa session to the US, the Americans expressed real concerns, objecting that the Canadians were moving too far, too fast. As a result, Canada agreed to remove language referring to 'zero by 2000' (no new mine deployments by the year 2000) from the declaration, and in return the US agreed to consider coming to Ottawa.

The US was also concerned about Canadian plans for extensive participation by NGOs at the Ottawa session. The issue of who should be invited to the Ottawa meeting engaged IDA in extensive consultations with the International Campaign to Ban Land mines (ICBL), particularly with Campaign directors Steve Goose and Jody Williams. ICBL wanted the hurdle for participation to be set very high, in order to keep the rats out, while IDA wanted to engage those states that were wavering on the borderline. IDA officials and ICBL representatives cooperated closely on the resolution of the invitees issue, and in the process forged an alliance that would last throughout the Ottawa Process. Over the course of the summer of 1996, IDA's Lawson conducted weekly conference calls with ICBL members (principally Goose and Williams), and they worked out joint plans for the upcoming meeting. Jill Sinclair, knowing that Axworthy had a history of working with NGOs, reinforced the importance of offering the ICBL, and other NGOs, a central role in the plans DFAIT was formulating. The Canadians went further, deciding that the ICBL should have a seat at the table for the October meeting, a first for the ICBL. In addition, a representative from Mines Action Canada would be a member of Canada's delegation at the session.

It is clear from the written record, and confirmed through interviews, that Canadian officials were not proceeding according to some grand plan, but were feeling their way as policy alternatives were developed over the summer of 1996. The issue was still being managed by IDA, with minimal oversight by senior management, which saw nothing more than a small planning session being organized for the autumn. As one senior manager said, 'We had no idea where the thing was headed.' As plans for the Ottawa strategy session were firmed up, and as more and more countries indicated their desire to participate, however, attention in IDA turned to what should be done in the period following the Ottawa session. Two options were put on the table for presentation to Axworthy, the first a UN resolution, and the second a forum for negotiations. Regarding the latter, Jill Sinclair argued that the CD was unacceptable because of its consensus format, and instead she promoted the idea of a 'stand-alone forum' for 'like-minded' states who would bring pressure to bear on those opposed to a ban; in other words, another version of the Ottawa strategy session, this time constituted as a negotiating forum. At a meeting to discuss options, Mark Gwozdecky raised the prospect of Ottawa hosting such a stand-alone forum. Sinclair's boss, Ralph Lysyshyn, director-general of the International Security Bureau, was also in attendance; drawing on his experience with the 'Open Skies' conference, held in Ottawa in 1990 when he was serving as IDA director, Lysyshyn said that such an initiative would be very expensive, likely in the range of $2 million. In the current fiscal climate, Lysyshyn cautioned that this was simply not possible. The idea was dropped.[6]

While, as the summer progressed, DFAIT energies were increasingly directed to the organization of the Ottawa session, there was nevertheless time available to continue to chip away at DND's turf on the policy front. Although DFAIT had given up its efforts to convince DND to agree to convert the Canadian moratorium into a permanent ban, officials continued to pressure DND to agree to destroy its stockpiles of landmines. Throughout the summer, DND resisted DFAIT pressures on stockpile destruction. DND officials felt they were still being 'nickled and dimed', as Foreign Affairs continued to move the goalposts after each DND policy concession. Finally, in September 1996, Sinclair and Lysyshyn became concerned that the issue was diverting too much energy and generating anxiety among senior people in DFAIT. They asked the Privy Council Office (PCO) to get involved and broker a deal between the two departments so that Canada could announce plans to destroy its stockpiles on the eve of the Ottawa strategy meeting. Jim Bartleman, the PCO foreign policy advisor, presented various options to the prime minister, who opted for compromise language whereby one-third of stocks would be destroyed immediately and the remainder 'in the context of successful negotiations'. That neither party was happy with the tradeoff may be a reflection of its Solomon-like wisdom.

The export moratorium created the opening DFAIT officials needed to move alternatives forward in the policy stream, to a comprehensive moratorium, with the prospect of a complete ban in sight. NGO policy entrepreneurs had softened up the security policy community, as well as the larger public, with continual messages about the need to ban mines, and officials had found an alternative in the policy stream that might address the problem. The problem stream shifted, as well, and the focus became how to engineer agreement on an international ban convention. The requirement for consensus in the CD ruled it out as a forum, and the time was ripe for an alternative forum in which a preponderance of pro-ban states could carry the day. The political transition from Ouellet to Axworthy had moved the landmines issue on to the decision agenda where choices among alternatives would be made. The streams of problem definition, policy alternatives, and political forces had joined again, and policy entrepreneurs had seized the opportunity to organize the October 1996 meeting of like-minded states in Ottawa. The session would provide a test of the effectiveness of an alternative forum as a policy vehicle on the landmines issue.

Near the end of September, the upcoming meeting finally caught the attention of the minister's office, which meant that senior officials in the Foreign Affairs bureaucracy also became interested. And when they saw what was about to happen, they were suddenly very nervous. This was partly because the minister's attention was drawn by the international flak he was starting to get over the structure of the meeting. The Russians, for example, were complaining about the self-selection principle and accusing Canada of behaving outrageously. In addition, the small planning session that had been conceived in the late spring had grown into a major event, and senior managers were concerned that proper arrangements had not been made. These anxieties were transmitted down to Ralph Lysyshyn, who began making adjustments to relieve the heat. In essence, Lysyshyn offered assurances that this was not really a big deal, that there was no need to be concerned. His ministrations ranged from major to minor: the original plan to have the meeting adopt an action plan was dropped in favour of a Chairman's Plan of Action, to which not everyone would have to agree; and plans to have a special logo for the conference were dropped as well, in the interest of keeping the profile low. Effective entrepreneurship was, in this case, a matter of reframing the proposal to make it less visible, without jeopardizing the fundamental innovation that lay at the heart of the Canadian initiative.

Jill Sinclair was also becoming concerned as the conference approached, but for different reasons. The Canadian initiative had attracted a large number of countries, and a very large NGO contingent, and she was convinced that the session had to produce some concrete, and dramatic, result in order to sustain the momentum that had built up in the past month. A week before the scheduled start date, Sinclair met with Ralph Lysyshyn in his office to explain her concern and propose that the meeting issue a call for countries to begin negotiations within a specified period of time, say two years. Lysyshyn rejected the proposal. In the first place, he said, a significant number of countries attending the meeting would be antagonized by even this modest proposal. Lysyshyn noted that an initiative that could capture public attention would be worth their antagonism. However, only bureaucrats could get excited about a commitment to begin to talk in two years; the significance would be lost on the broader public, and Canada would garner no credit. Sinclair left, her problem unresolved, and was swept up in last-minute preparations for, what had originally been billed as, 'a small international meeting of officials and NGOs to develop an action work plan on land mines'.[7]

The Ottawa strategy session that opened at the federal government's Conference Centre in the old Ottawa train station on Wellington Street on 3 October 1996 was attended by 50 governments pledged to support a ban on landmines, as well as 24 observer states. In addition, the ICBL, ICRC (International Committee of the Red Cross), various UN agencies, and a host of other NGOs were in attendance. IDA's self-selection process had worked as hoped. The assembly was dominated by the core group of states that were committed to a ban, supported and guided by the participating NGOs. Any rats in attendance were sure to be subject to intense, and sometimes critical, scrutiny. A defining moment in this regard occurred during a 'Prestige Panel' chaired by Christine Stewart, Canada's secretary of state for Latin America and Africa.[8] The head of the French delegation, Michel Duclos, misjudged the moment badly when he chose to make a statement during the panel. Duclos's statement of the French position, while it may have been perfectly suited to a forum like the CD, was most certainly not suitable for the Ottawa conference, dominated as it was by pro-ban countries and NGOs. Distilled to its essence, the French position boiled down to this: France was prepared to ban landmines—until it needed them. This position was typical of countries that did not want to be seen by their publics to be opposing a ban, but that also did not want an international agreement in the short (or even medium) term.

The French statement was fully anticipated by the Canadians and their NGO allies. As Duclos was speaking, Jill Sinclair gave Jody Williams a high sign, indicating that she should respond to the French statement. A self-described practitioner of what she herself calls in-your-face diplomacy, Williams slammed the French representative in front of the entire assembly. 'Your policy is contradictory,' she told him. 'You are saying that you want to ban land mines, except when you want to use them. I suppose this is better than a stick in the eye, but it is not what we are looking for here.' While some delegates, from both governments and NGOs, were aghast at Williams's public scolding of France, US Senator Patrick Leahy, a leading American proponent of a ban, and others jumped in to echo Williams's condemnation of prevarication on the issue. While this episode confirmed IDA's hopes that any rats who decided to attend would face intense scrutiny in a forum intolerant of equivocation, it also confirmed the worst fears of the US and other doubters that the session would create a bandwagon effect and inexorable pressure to support a ban. It was what foreign minister Axworthy called the mobilization of shame, and it was deliberately intended to move countries in the direction of a ban.

As discussions proceeded, Ralph Lysyshyn, from his position as chair of the meeting,[9] could see a problem emerging, and it related back to the proposal made by Jill Sinclair a week earlier, which he had rejected. During bilateral discussions in the lead up to the conference, the French had insisted that any statement about further negotiations that might emerge from the Ottawa meeting had to include a reference to the CD. As noted earlier, because its consensus format was likely to produce deadlock, the CD was not an acceptable negotiating forum for Canada, and so the Canadians equivocated, replying to the French that negotiations did not necessarily have to occur in the CD, but without having an alternative firmly in mind. Now, as the conference proceeded, first France and then Italy and the United States made their statements to the meeting, with each arguing, in turn, that any follow-up on negotiations should be undertaken in the CD. Listening to these statements, Lysyshyn surveyed his counterparts around the table, international security bureaucrats like himself from the 50 countries formally attending the meeting. He realized that, of the 50, probably 25 or 30 were simply there to ensure that their governments were represented in the meeting; they neither knew, nor cared, a great deal about the mines issue, nor did they believe particularly in the need for a ban. As a result, they could be expected to follow the lead of the major powers and direct the issue to the CD, where it would be buried.

If this was the problem, then Lysyshyn could also see an opportunity unfolding. As noted previously, Lysyshyn had been preoccupied with other international security issues and had left the anti-personnel mines issue largely to Sinclair. Now, at the conference, for the first time he could see how broad the international coalition was on this issue, and he was impressed by the presence of very senior UN officials, there to lend their support to the initiative. He was also aware of the enormous coverage that was being given to the event, and to Canada's leadership role, in the Canadian press. This thing was, Lysyshyn realized, a hell of a lot bigger than he had originally thought. Here was an opportunity for Canada to secure its leadership role on the issue; if it did not do so, chances were that somebody else would. The most likely candidate to usurp Canadian leadership was Belgium. Previously, the Belgians, a founding member of the core group of pro-ban states, had taken a leading role on the issue, and before the Ottawa meeting convened they had declared their intention to host a follow-up meeting. The Belgian foreign affairs minister had a background in international development, and a particular interest in the humanitarian dimension of the mines issue. Just as Lysyshyn could see momentum building in the conference for action following the Ottawa meeting, he could also see the Belgians positioning themselves to take over the lead on the issue.[10]

Between problem and opportunity, Lysyshyn thought he saw an opening. Recall Kingdon's description of the joining of the policy streams where, occasionally, a viable policy alternative is linked to a pressing problem under favourable political conditions and, as a result, a policy window opens. In this circumstance, a policy entrepreneur has to be ready with the alternative, and savvy enough to take advantage of the opening. While sitting in the chair that Friday morning, Lysyshyn came up with an idea, and he decided to move. The idea was drawn from his previous experience as IDA director, the position now occupied by Jill Sinclair, and it concerned a previous negotiation that was initiated by Canada. Recall that earlier in the summer, Mark Gwozdecky had raised the prospect of Ottawa hosting a stand-alone forum to negotiate a ban on land-mines, and Lysyshyn had estimated the costs at $2 million, based on his experience with the 'Open Skies' conference held in Ottawa in 1990. Open Skies held other lessons for Lysyshyn as well.

It was early in 1989, and the US National Security Council staff were conducting a wide-ranging review of American strategic relations with the Soviet Union. While in Washington in April 1989, Lysyshyn met with an NSC staffer who said they were considering all options as part of the review, even a resurrection of the Open Skies concept that had been proposed originally by the Eisenhower Administration in 1955.[11] Back in Ottawa in April 1989, Lysyshyn suggested to his boss, John Noble, director-general of the International Security Bureau, that they should push the US to move forward on the Open Skies idea. Noble secured agreement, and Lysyshyn returned to Washington to meet with NSC officials. Prime Minister Mulroney was scheduled to meet with US President Bush in early May, and Lysyshyn informed the Americans that Mulroney was going to raise the Open Skies idea for discussion with Bush. On 4 May 1989, Mulroney did so in a meeting with Bush at the White House. Urging Bush to move forward with Open Skies, Mulroney also argued that the negotiations should include not just the two superpowers, but the entire membership of NATO and the Warsaw Pact. The negotiations would not take place in Vienna, traditional site of arms control negotiations between the superpowers, but instead would open in Ottawa in February 1990, with plans to reconvene in Budapest, Hungary, only three months later in May 1990, to conclude the final text of a treaty.

Open Skies provided Lysyshyn with the idea for a viable policy alternative that would keep the mines issue from being buried in the CD, and would secure a leadership role for Canada. Open Skies had drawn together an ad hoc collection

of negotiating parties who deliberated outside of the traditional forum for negotiation, according to an unusually short timetable. The same could be done here,
thought Lysyshyn. He also saw a parallel between the political state of play on
the mines issue and that which had prevailed on Open Skies: in each, public
opinion was strongly supportive of action, and political leaders were looking for
something to which they could say yes. At noon on Friday, Lysyshyn phoned his
boss, assistant deputy minister Paul Heinbecker. He said that he thought the
issue was ripe, but that a lot of people were out to kill it. Either way, things could
move quickly, and if Canada did not do something dramatic, the issue would
either be derailed into the CD or it would move forward with somebody else in
the lead. It was obviously an issue that Axworthy liked, and Lysyshyn thought
there was an opportunity here for Canada to do something.

Heinbecker asked what he had in mind, and Lysyshyn laid out his idea that
Canada should offer to host a follow-on negotiation to conclude an international ban treaty before the end of 1997. He told Heinbecker that he had not discussed the idea with anyone in the Canadian group, and that he would not put
the idea to the minister unless he was promised the resources to host the negotiating session. When Heinbecker asked for an amount, Lysyshyn repeated his earlier estimate of $2 million, figuring he could do just about anything with that
amount of money.[12] Three hours later, Heinbecker phoned back to tell Lysyshyn
that he had his $2 million and should proceed, and that in the meantime he and
Gordon Smith, the Foreign Affairs deputy minister, would give Axworthy a preliminary briefing.

With his marching orders in hand, Lysyshyn met with Sinclair and
Gwozdecky to describe his proposal and instruct them as to the content of the
speech they would have to prepare for Axworthy. The speech was ready Saturday
morning. Now, a critical decision for Lysyshyn was whether any other country
delegations should be told about the Canadian plans. Since, by this time, government offices would be closed in Europe and Asia, delegations could do little
but say they disagreed or that they would consult their governments. Lysyshyn
did not want to register either response, and opted instead to let them be surprised. The draft of Axworthy's speech was faxed to Michael Pearson for review
on Saturday morning. Pearson joined the Canadian group, telling them that
Axworthy had some idea of what was being proposed, and had agreed to go
along. At that point, Peter Herby of the ICRC was briefed on the Canadian plan,
and asked to arrange a statement of support from ICRC President Cornelio Sommaruga. In addition, Bob Lawson briefed Jody Williams, and arranged a statement of support from her. When Axworthy arrived, Lysyshyn described the
enthusiasm and momentum that was building in the conference and outlined
the closing statement that had been prepared, in which Axworthy would offer to
host a meeting to sign an international convention before the end of 1997. The
action was risky, said Lysyshyn, particularly the stipulation of an imminent
deadline: it would anger a large number of countries, including the US, UK,
France, Russia, and China; Canada would be accused of grandstanding, failing to
consult, and playing outside the rules; and there was a danger that the initiative

would fail. Nevertheless, Lysyshyn told Axworthy that the issue was ripe for bold action, and that the bandwagon emerging in the conference would be led by somebody else if Canada did not seize the initiative. It was his judgement, Lysyshyn noted to the minister, that the challenge would work, that an international treaty would be achieved. After Lysyshyn had finished his presentation, Axworthy said simply, 'It's the right thing. Let's do it.'

That afternoon, Axworthy invited delegates to gather again in Ottawa no later than December 1997 to sign a ban treaty. As anticipated, his announcement touched off a minor uproar, composed in equal parts of jubilation and consternation. Along with the core group of states, and many NGOs, that were overjoyed with Axworthy's bold initiative, there were a number of allies that thought it foolhardy. To offset the latter view, Sommaruga and Williams made their prearranged statements in support of Axworthy's position, after which Lysyshyn adjourned the meeting. The Ottawa Process was launched. In this final stage of a policy process that began with André Ouellet's declaration of support for a ban almost a year earlier, the three policy streams converged once again, this time to launch a quest for an international ban treaty. And once again, the streams were joined by resourceful entrepreneurs who recognized a window of opportunity and seized the chance to advance an evolving policy alternative. In the problem stream, the NGO policy community stepped up its pressure for a ban and Jill Sinclair identified the need to sustain the momentum that had been generated in the lead up to the Ottawa strategy session. Waiting to be joined with this problem was the alternative that was formulated by Ralph Lysyshyn in the policy stream, namely, extending the idea of a stand-alone forum of self-selected states to apply to an international negotiation, with a deadline for completion attached.

Congruent with Kingdon's model, the consensus around the idea of an alternative forum of like-minded states grew until, in Ottawa, a tipping point was reached when the number of adherents had grown sufficiently that the success of the idea seemed assured. Even with that, it is not difficult to imagine the impediments to such an idea that might arise in the political stream. However, in this case DFAIT had the field to itself, with DND sidelined since the summer, and within DFAIT there was no effective opposition to Lysyshyn and Sinclair on the issue. Most important, when problem, policy, and politics were aligned in Ottawa on 4 October 1996, Lysyshyn played a critically important entrepreneurial role, and was savvy enough to present a *beau risque* to a minister not afraid to take one. Axworthy's announcement launched a year-long multilateral negotiation process that would result in the conclusion of an international ban treaty in Oslo, Norway, in September 1997, and its supporters would reconvene in Ottawa in December 1997 to sign the treaty. The story of that multilateral negotiation is told in Chapter 14.

INTERNATIONAL CRIMINAL COURT

Long-standing Canadian support for the creation of an international criminal court heightened in the early 1990s as a direct consequence of Canada's involvement in the peacekeeping mission in the former Yugoslavia and the activism of Barbara McDougall, Canada's secretary of state for external affairs (1991–3). McDougall's own interest in the issue was motivated, in part, by her tour of refugee camps in Bosnia, where she witnessed the treatment of women in the region. Her personal encounters and profound sense that something had to be done to prevent such abuses in the future led her to 'push the Department of External Affairs on that front and the wide question of setting up a legal mechanism' to investigate and prosecute perpetrators of human rights violations and war crimes. In her speech to the General Assembly on 24 September 1992, in which she expressed Canada's strong support for an international criminal tribunal, 'McDougall challenged the UN to transgress the doctrine of non-intervention' (Gammer, 2001: 149).

Canada was one of the first countries to support the adoption of UN Security Council Resolution 780 of 6 October 1992, providing for the establishment of an impartial commission that would investigate violations of the Geneva Conventions and other human rights abuses in the territories of the former Yugoslavia. The five members of the commission included a Canadian, Commander W.J. Fenrick, who played an important part in its investigations of human rights abuses.

Canada not only provided valuable financial support for the commission, but also, with active support from the foreign minister, agreed to host an international meeting of legal experts in Vancouver in March 1993. The goal of the meeting, which was attended by more than 65 international legal experts from around the globe, was to focus international attention not just on the appalling human rights situation in the disintegrating Yugoslav republics but also to recommend the establishment of an International Criminal Tribunal for the Former Yugoslavia that would pave the way to a more permanent international criminal court. Shortly after the meeting, Canada's Permanent Representative to the United Nations, Louise Frechette, wrote to the secretary-general urging that the war crimes tribunal have as wide a mandate as possible to deal with human rights abuses.

With the passage of Resolution 827, the Security Council formally recognized that those accused of war crimes and other flagrant human rights abuses would have to be tried by an international criminal court. A Canadian, Judge Jules Deschênes, was elected by the General Assembly to be one of 11 serving judges on the court. Canadian officials, however, were quick to point out that the establishment of the tribunal for the former Yugoslavia was merely a stepping stone to a more permanent institution. As Barry Mawhinney, the legal advisor to Canada's UN delegation, stated in a speech he gave to the International Law Commission in October 1993: 'While we [Canada] applauded the Security Council's quick action in creating an ad hoc tribunal . . . Canada still believes that only a permanent criminal court will be able to provide a stable framework necessary to convince those willing to disregard the basic tenets of humanitarian law that the international community is unwilling to tolerate their actions' (quoted in Gammer, 2001: 146).

McDougall's leadership on humanitarian issues had its own impact on Canada's foreign policy bureaucracy: 'Members of the Department of External Affairs were very much attuned to the extraordinary amount of attention McDougall was paying to the transgressions of humanitarian laws, in general, and the plight of women savaged by conflict, in particular. The 3 March 1993 announcement by McDougall and the minister responsible for the status of women that the government was providing $1.5 million in humanitarian assistance for women and children brutalized by sexual abuse was another example of the minister's commitment to bringing to justice those responsible for breaching humanitarian law' (Gammer, 2001: 150).

The adoption by the Security Council of resolutions establishing international criminal tribunals for both Rwanda and the former Yugoslavia effectively extended international humanitarian law and human rights provisions regarding interstate armed conflict into civil conflict situations. As Knight (2001: 124) reports, 'Despite administrative limitations, staffing problems, limited finances, and poor enforcement capabilities, the creation of these two judicial organs became an important step solidifying international criminal law and in moving toward the establishment of a permanent international criminal court. These two tribunals, in addition to showing that a sound mechanism for criminal prosecution could be employed for circumstances that transcended the domestic purview, also spurred on debate about a more permanent tribunal.'

As discussed in the previous chapter, many of the detailed issues and draft treaty provisions for the ICC were thrashed out in the preparatory committee (PrepCom) that was open to all UN members. The PrepCom met six times over the next three years and by early 1998 the main provisions for a treaty setting up the court had been drafted.

In the run-up to the final treaty negotiations in Rome in June 1998, negotiations had coalesced around three distinct groupings: Conservative States; the Restrictive States; and the Like-Minded States (Kaul, 1997; Kirsch and Holmes, 1999). The Conservative States were those countries that were concerned about how the proposed ICC would allow other states to interfere with their sovereignty. In particular, they were wary of creating a court with strong ties to the Security Council, because they felt that this body was incapable of representing their interests. The most active participants among the Conservative States were India, Nigeria, and Mexico. The Restrictive States were also apprehensive about the scope of the ICC, but for different reasons. Consisting mainly of the United States, Russia, and China, this coalition sought to circumscribe the power of the ICC so as to ensure the continued influence of the Security Council, of which they were permanent members. The strength of the Restrictive States was greatly weakened prior to Rome, when the United Kingdom defected from the Restrictive States to join the Like-Minded States after the election of Tony Blair as British prime minister in 1997.

The Like-Minded States (LMS) coalition was characterized by its size and diversity. It included the majority of the European Union nations, the states of the Commonwealth, as well as a large number of African and Caribbean countries.

These states were committed to the creation of a strong court, with independent powers and a wide jurisdiction. Canada became a leader in LMS through its chief delegate, Philippe Kirsch, a distinguished international lawyer and diplomat. Kirsch's assignments had included chairing the Sixth (Legal) Committee of the United Nations; the UN Committee for the Suppression of Nuclear Terrorism; the UN Committee on the Elaboration of a Convention of the Suppression of Terrorist Bombings; and the Drafting Committee of the 12th International Conference of the Red Cross and Red Crescent. Circumstances soon conspired to cast him in a pivotal role in the Rome treaty negotiations.

Civil-society actors were also extremely influential, virtually constituting their own coalition independent of state formations. In addition to being included in various state delegations, approximately 222 non-state actors were accredited to the Rome conference in their own right. Many of these organizations, such as the influential European Student Law Association, made presentations at the plenary sessions, while others worked closely with key countries. The International Committee of the Red Cross, for example, worked closely with the leadership of New Zealand and Switzerland to promote the ICC. The Coalition for the International Criminal Court remained in contact with the British and Canadians, who were increasingly adopting NGO positions as they took leadership roles within the LMS coalition. This brought the coalition of NGOs into the political-bargaining and decision-making processes in the crucial run-up to the Rome conference. Non-state actors also had strong ties with those individuals taking on a leadership role in the UN, such as Adriaan Bos and James Crawford (Kaul, 1997).

US interest in the ICC also gathered momentum, not only with the establishment of special tribunals dealing with the genocide in Rwanda and the former Yugoslavia, but also as a direct consequence of the situation in Cambodia. In 1997 the Khmer Rouge seemed ready to hand over its former leader, Pol Pot, to prosecutors, but Cambodia had neither the legal nor judicial capacities to adjudicate his case (Stork, 1998). In his September 1997 address before the General Assembly, President Clinton formally called for the establishment of an International Criminal Court, a position he reiterated in March 1998 in a speech he gave to the survivors of genocide in Kigali, Rwanda.

The Conference of Plenipotentiaries to review and conclude the terms of the treaty establishing the International Criminal Court took place in Rome, Italy, from June 15 to July 17, 1998. A window of opportunity for Canada opened when Philippe Kirsch, who was supposed to lead the Canadian delegation, was asked to chair the conference because Adriaan Bos, who had previously been elected chair, suddenly fell ill. As Knight reports, 'some commentators have said that Kirsch "played the role of Solomon during the talks" . . . he was unable to persuade the Americans to sign the Rome treaty, [but] he was able to play up the fact that the US was among the first to support the idea of a permanent court and to keep all states' representatives' eyes on the ball' (Knight, 2001: 128).

As opening statements in Rome began, the coalitions were faced with four major unresolved (and highly politicized) issues. The first of these issues was the funding mechanism for the ICC. The US insisted that the ICC be funded solely by contributions from state parties, whereas others argued that the ICC should be funded through the general UN budget. The second issue was how the proposed ICC would handle the sensitive matter of national security information. It was clearly unacceptable for the ICC to compel evidence from states without restriction. The question then became: How would it be determined if the release of information was indeed a threat to the national security of a state? The UK contended that there should be an internal ICC process for determining what constituted information over which the ICC would be disallowed from exercising its jurisdiction. The US rejected this position, arguing that each state must have the individual right to define 'national security information' in each specific instance.

The final two (and most contentious) issues were fundamentally linked. The issue of subject-matter jurisdiction refers to the clarification of exactly what crimes the court has the jurisdiction to prosecute. 'Triggering mechanisms' refers to the determination of when the jurisdiction becomes operative. Thus, a restrictive state may be satisfied by a court with wide subject-matter jurisdiction, if high triggering thresholds were created concurrently. The same state may be satisfied with a narrow subject-matter jurisdiction and low triggering thresholds. Both institutional designs would create a conservative court.

The US advocated a relatively wide subject-matter jurisdiction. However, it now argued adamantly against the inclusion of drugs or terrorism, in line with Kingdon's assertion that policy alternatives evolve as they move through various stages of bargaining in the policy and politics streams. As expected, the US rejected the classification of the use of nuclear weapons as a crime against humanity. The US also joined others in arguing for the assertion of 'chapeaus', which serve to circumscribe the activation of the court's jurisdiction. For example, the US agreed to a broad list of war crimes, but asserted that these crimes must be committed pursuant to a 'plan or policy' if they were to be prosecuted. Similarly, the US was concerned about the scope of the ICC's jurisdiction over crimes against humanity. These positions were justified by the Pentagon's fear that American military personnel would become victims of politically motivated prosecutions. This, in turn, would hamper their ability to establish and maintain peacekeeping operations.

In terms of triggering mechanisms, the US insisted on high thresholds for ICC operation. The US accepted that the ICC should have jurisdiction over aggression, but only as defined by the Security Council. As a permanent member, the US also argued that the Security Council must have a veto over ICC investigations and prosecutions. The American proposal ensured that the US and other permanent Security Council members would, in effect, have a veto over the operation of the ICC. Consistent with such a stance, the US argued against the creation of a prosecutor with *ex officio* powers.

The US proposed an ICC that was triggered mainly by Security Council referral. State party referral was accepted, but, in this respect, ICC jurisdiction could only be activated on a case-by-case basis through a state 'opt-in'. For each crime, both the state of nationality and the territorial state must accept ICC jurisdiction. This would give states an effective veto over the prosecution of their nationals. The US also sought to ensure that the notion of complementarity had teeth; the ICC must not be permitted to supersede the operation of national laws. It was therefore suggested that the ICC would be required to defer to a state that declared a desire to prosecute unilaterally.

Thus as formal negotiations commenced, the American attitude toward the court had become quite conservative. It was unclear how, or if, the US would deviate from its 'wish-list'; the US delegation failed to articulate its 'bottom line' effectively to other states (Wedgwood, 1998). This confusion was largely due to internal divisions, because different departments and agencies articulated divergent opinions on the creation of a court. Although President Clinton, Secretary of State Albright, and Assistant Secretary of State for Human Rights Shuttack were in favour of a strong court, they were not the only domestic actors involved. It has been reported that Clinton, preoccupied with his forthcoming trip to China, allowed Department of Defense views to dominate the negotiations (Neier, 1998). Republican Senator Jesse Helms made it clear that an ICC without a US veto would be 'dead on arrival' at his Senate Foreign Relations Committee (Hall, 1998). Personnel changes also took their toll on policy coherence when US ambassador to the UN, Bill Richardson, was appointed to the US Department of Energy immediately prior to the beginning of negotiations, to be replaced by Richard Holbrooke.

The LMS dominated negotiations. Nevertheless, several important concessions were made in an attempt to satisfy US demands. The strength of the LMS influence was largely a function of its close working relationship with the Bureau of the Committee of the Whole and the Chairman of the Committee of the Whole, Canadian Philippe Kirsch. Chairman Kirsch, displaying creativity and an ability to control and steer formal negotiations (Arsanjanhi, 1999), was instrumental in driving negotiations forward and forging compromise solutions to avoid the pitfalls of a divided policy community. The bureau was designed to aid the chairman in managing and organizing the Working Groups and Drafting Committees. The bureau was largely composed of representatives of the LMS, and therefore served to maximize the coalition's influence in providing bridging policy alternatives. For example, the LMS had championed an ICC with inherent jurisdiction over genocide, war crimes, and crimes against humanity. However, South Korea, a member of the LMS, proposed the adoption of a state consent regime in an attempt to bring the US on board. The ICC would have jurisdiction over the enumerated war crimes and crimes against humanity, but only where the territorial, custodial, or nation-state in question accepted ICC jurisdiction.

The LMS desire for a strong, independent prosecutor was also qualified by the creation of a Pre-Trial Chamber, which would act as a check on politically motivated prosecutions. American concern about the application of crimes against humanity was addressed by a Canadian proposal, which created a 'chapeau' on ICC jurisdiction. The chapeau required that the ICC could only prosecute crimes against humanity committed in the course of 'widespread or systemic attack'. Finally, Singapore continued to assert a compromise position, arguing for the ability of the Security Council to affirmatively vote for the delay or suspension of ICC jurisdiction for 12-month periods. Although these proposals engendered support, it was difficult for delegations to agree to certain elements of the court as they proceeded through the bracketed negotiating text. Indeed, Chairman Kirsch recognized that the bracketed approach was unproductive, given that it was a linear process and because states were not willing to compromise on certain aspects of the court without knowledge of the content of the statute as a whole. Thus, given both time constraints and the interdependence of issues, a 'package deal' was necessary (Kirsch and Holmes, 1999).

Chairman Kirsch and the bureau adopted new procedures. Concerned about time pressure that was being exacerbated by filibustering, Kirsch instituted nighttime negotiating sessions. Further, on July 5, the Canadian Embassy in Rome hosted informal discussions attended by delegates of 30 states. Compromise positions were discussed and sticking points clarified, especially as between the LMS and the US. Based on this information the 'Bureau Paper' was drafted. It outlined the issues that would have to be agreed upon in order to create the ICC. It identified linkages between such issues and proposed a substantive package for the court. This initiative greatly increased the coherence of the negotiations that followed; although the Working Groups continued to function, discussions were increasingly held in private and were centred on the bureau proposal. Subsequently, the bureau refined the paper on July 10. The second bureau paper was substantively tighter as the options for certain issues were narrowed by simply deleting the extreme positions. Negotiations were also aided by discarding contentious but what were judged relatively minor issues, such as drug trafficking.

Response to the bureau's initiative was lukewarm. As the negotiations drew to a close, the members of the bureau and Chairman Kirsch were left with a difficult decision. They could begin preparations for a second session of formal negotiations, or they could put together a final package and force a vote. In choosing to put together the final package, the bureau was aware that a high degree of consensus had to be achieved. Thus, the final package was as broad as possible. It contained a number of 'uneasy technical solutions, awkward formulations and difficult compromises that fully satisfied no one' (Kirsch and Holmes, 1999: 11). Chairman Kirsch, however, gambled that the time was ripe, and that continuing with the negotiations would prove disastrous. In the end, the package resulted in bringing onside the majority of the other conservative states, but not the US. The US insisted on a veto over the court's operation and was extremely wary of an independent prosecutor. As negotiations proceeded, the US became increasingly isolated, and ultimately rejected the court. Canada's pivotal role in the negotiations that culminated in the Rome treaty, which established the International Criminal Court, played out at four levels. First of all, Canada led the coalition of so-called Like-Minded States who were keen to see the court established, working closely as well with the CICC in narrowing policy priorities and setting the agenda. Second, Canada's own lobbying efforts and leadership position helped strengthen this international coalition. Third, Canada made an important financial contribution to a UN Trust Fund, the purpose of which was to enable less-developed countries to participate in ICC negotiations. Canada also funded key non-governmental organizations in developing countries to mobilize public support for the ICC. Finally, Philippe Kirsch played a crucial leadership role as Chair of the Committee as a Whole at the Rome Conference.

The Rome Statute contained many elements of the Canadian vision of an ICC. The court had automatic jurisdiction over crimes, including jurisdiction over internal armed conflicts. The statute incorporated strong provisions related to sexual crimes and crimes against children. It also included the element of complementarity (discussed above), that is, that the court would only take action when national legal systems proved unwilling or unable to do so. Finally, the Statute allowed for the court's jurisdiction to be triggered by an independent prosecutor, states that had ratified the statute, and the UN Security Council.

THE RESPONSIBILITY TO PROTECT

The most controversial addition to the human security agenda has been the concept of the responsibility to protect (R2P). Articulated by the International Commission on Intervention and State Sovereignty (ICISS) in 2001, R2P sought to reconcile state sovereignty with a changing international environment and emerging practices of humanitarian intervention. The solution identified by the commission was to redefine sovereignty as a 'dual responsibility: externally—to respect the sovereignty of other states, and internally, to respect the dignity and basic rights of all people within the state' (ICISS, 2001: 8). Although ICISS reiterated the primary responsibility of states to protect their own peoples, it also invoked a 'residual responsibility' on the part of the international community when states are 'unwilling or unable' to meet their responsibilities to protect their citizens (ICISS, 2001: 17). Where civil war, armed conflict, repression, or state failure pose a compelling threat to the human security of civilian populations, 'the principle of non-intervention yields to the international responsibility to protect' (ICISS, 2001: xi).[13] Canada was instrumental in spearheading the international debate surrounding the limits of absolute sovereignty in a globalized world characterized by interdependence, transnational threats, and respect for basic human rights. As the primary sponsor for ICISS, Canadians played a pivotal role in selecting the commissioners and members of the international advisory board, providing administrative support through a small secretariat housed within DFAIT, and organizing a series of regional roundtables and national consultations to collect feedback and inform public opinion. The responsibility to protect was not simply a policy idea 'whose time had come'. It resulted from a coming together of historical (focusing) events, objective indicators, inspired leadership and pre-existing policy ideas, circulating in policy communities at home and abroad. Human security provided the ideas, processes, and political constituency to guide the evolution in discourse from humanitarian intervention to the responsibility to protect.

With the end of the Cold War, the problem of humanitarian intervention gained prominence on international governmental agendas. Prior to 1989, Cold

War politics, together with the legacy of nineteenth-century colonialism, militated against a general acceptance of the idea of humanitarian intervention, in spite of cases where humanitarian justifications for action were available. The end of superpower confrontation resulted in expectations of a new era of international cooperation and collective security through the United Nations. Between 1988 and 1993, the UN launched 20 peacekeeping operations involving new roles and mandates. Increased muscularity was evident in the greater willingness on the part of the Security Council to authorize interventions in situations of ongoing civil conflict characterized by the absence of, or non-compliance with, peace agreements (Bellamy, Williams, and Griffin, 2004: 76, 129). Peacekeeping could now also include civil functions, such as disarmament, de-mining, elections monitoring, the provision of humanitarian aid, support for public order and postconflict reconstruction, as well as the traditional monitoring of cease-fires and interposition between former belligerents. More than forty-three hundred Canadian Forces (CF) personnel were deployed to UN peacekeeping missions in the early 1990s (Dewing and McDonald, 2004).

In Canada, the tenor of opinion in and around government clearly supported the UN secretary-general's assertion that the age of absolute state sovereignty had been eclipsed. The end of the Cold War's structural bipolarity set the stage for Canada to play a more active role in international security affairs at the same time as new threats and types of conflict were emerging in the international arena. The United Nations, long an important forum for Canadian middle-powered multilateralism, signalled its active engagement with the complex security challenges of resurgent ethnic nationalism and state dissolution (Boutros-Ghali, 1992). Somalia became a symbol of the international security threat posed by failed states. In March 1993, UNOSOM II, a successor force to the United Nations Operation in Somalia (UNOSOM) and US-led (but UN mandated) Unified Task Force (UNITAF), was authorized under chapter VII of the UN *Charter* to establish a secure environment for humanitarian assistance. The Somalia mission was perceived to be the UN's first true humanitarian intervention (Tessier and Fortmann, 2001: 120); all together, CF participation in the East African country involved more than two thousand personnel (Dewing and McDonald, 2004).

The Mulroney government expressed its moral commitment to the new state of affairs and sought to enhance its international standing. Second-generation peacekeeping was part of a wider Conservative-led ideological shift toward more intrusive international policies that favoured liberal-democratic 'good governance' over non-interference in the affairs of sovereign states. With the symbolic defeat of Communism in 1989, the 'new world order' heralded by US President George H.W. Bush envisioned a peaceful world community of liberal-democracies united by values and commerce. The prime minister undoubtedly sought to exploit widespread public support for the UN and peacekeeping to offset the political costs of economic recession, perceived mismanagement of public finances, and divisive constitutional initiatives. Opinion polls conducted between 1991 and 1993 concluded that public support for UN intervention in sovereign countries increased from 58 to 65 per cent, with opposition falling from 39 to 30 per cent (Decima Research, 1992; 1993). There was a 'virtually unanimous backing for peacekeeping at the societal level' (Martin and Fortmann, 2001b: 47) and Canadians voiced support for increasing or maintaining the commitment of the CF to UN peacekeeping (Martin and Fortmann, 2001a: 69). Nor would this jeopardize Mulroney's other major foreign policy preoccupation—the United States. In the early years of the post–Cold War decade, American leaders greeted a strengthened UN capacity to respond to regional crises and civil strife as an alternative to the costly deployment of US forces (Sokolsky, 2000: 17).

Political turnover with the election of a majority Liberal government in November 1993 seemed at first to reinforce the trend of growing support for humanitarian intervention. In an address to Parliament on 15 March 1994, the minister for foreign affairs André Ouellet spoke of a right and a duty of intervention to protect civilians 'being denied their most basic rights' wherever they might be (Dashwood, 2000: 178). Public opinion continued to support the turn toward greater engagement, with a February 1994 poll conducted by Harris determining that 57 per cent of Canadians believed it was 'time the UN took a more active role in working to end conflicts around the world' (Martin and Fortmann, 2001b: 47).

Yet the policy window to advance the robust response to threats posed by the spillover of domestic humanitarian crises would be restricted by difficulties having to do with mission mandates, rules of engagement, resource capacities, and political will, as well as controversies involving Canadian peacekeeping personnel. Between April and July of 1994, an estimated eight hundred thousand ethnic Tutsis and moderate Hutus were massacred by the Hutu-extremist government in Rwanda. The genocide took place under the watch of the United Nations Assistance Mission for Rwanda (UNAMIR) and dampened the spirit of optimism that had greeted second-generation UN peacekeeping. The harrowing personal account of lieutenant-general Romeo Dallaire, the Canadian Force Commander of UNAMIR, raised serious doubts that a principled commitment to the United Nations was sufficient when human lives were at stake. This was added to heavy media coverage beginning in March 1993, and criticism from human rights groups like Amnesty International, regarding the deaths of four Somali civilians in confrontations with Canadian peacekeepers (York, 1993). The withdrawal of US and European personnel in Somalia followed by the termination of UNOSOM II's military enforcement action in February 1994 (Bellamy, Williams, and Griffin, 2004: 159) reinforced a growing sense of failure and controversy.

Media reports of the hostage taking and 'mock executions' of 11 Canadian soldiers in Bosnia in the spring of 1994 (Koring, 1994) amplified public awareness of the dangers involved in complex peacekeeping missions. The incident led to parliamentary debate in May 1995 on the possibility of withdrawing Canadian peacekeepers from the region (Dewing and McDonald, 2004). The humanitarian objectives motivating second-generation peacekeeping were also challenged by the escalating crisis in the former Yugoslavia. In July 1995, the United Nations

Protection Force (UNPROFOR) failed to prevent the massacre of civilians by Bosnian Serbs in Srebenica and Zepa: UN-designated 'safe havens' (Orbinski, 2000: 8). Ethnic cleansing and secessionist conflict between Bosnian Serbs (backed by President Slobodan Milosevic of the Federal Republic of Yugoslavia, FRY) and Bosnian Muslims and Croats demonstrated the disproportionate suffering of civilians resulting from intrastate wars (Hanson, 2001: 89); indicators backed a strong correlation between civil war and assaults on civilians, with some analysts in the mid-1990s arguing that civilian deaths were accounting for up to 90 per cent of total casualties resulting from armed conflict.[14]

Meanwhile, the North Atlantic Treaty Organization (NATO) was undergoing a transformation from primarily a collective defence alliance to a collective security organization operating offensive missions in support of humanitarian and peacekeeping roles. NATO initiated a short air-strike campaign in the summer of 1995, sanctioned by the UN Security Council, to protect UNPROFOR and facilitate the delivery of humanitarian aid. Canada had originally opposed the NATO air campaign, but in the spring of 1995 Minister Ouellet announced in a speech to the NATO Council that Canada was prepared to endorse the use of force to counter violations of resolutions passed by the UN (DFAIT, 1995). The ambiguities inherent in the new peacekeeping precipitated a turn toward peace enforcement as a better alternative in complex security crises where there was no peace to keep.[15] When the Dayton accords were signed in 1995, ending three and a half years of war in the former Yugoslav republic of Bosnia-Herzegovina, NATO backed up diplomacy with a credible military deterrent.

The fall of the UN enclaves, reflected in images of human suffering and exodus (recalling the atrocities of World War II), came to be perceived as the 'diplomatic death-knell' for the UN peacekeeping mission (*The Economist*, 1999b). From a 1993 high of seventy thousand UN peacekeepers deployed around the world, the numbers of personnel working under UN auspices had fallen by 1996 to fewer than twenty thousand (Bellamy, Williams, and Griffin, 2004: 84). Many Canadians seemed to agree with the movement away from UN-led wider peacekeeping. A September 1995 poll found that 58 per cent supported the NATO offensive in Bosnia (Gallup Canada, 1995). Two years later, a Goldfarb survey found that 70 per cent of Canadians believed that Canada should place a very high (24 per cent) or fairly high (46 per cent) priority on its role in NATO (Martin and Fortmann, 2001a: 67).

The Somalia, Rwanda, and Bosnia interventions had set the stage for the military enforcement of human security, breaking the taboo against intervening in the domestic affairs of sovereign states. Among the lessons learned and recommendations from a Canadian Centre for Foreign Policy Development (CCFPD) roundtable in the fall of 1997 was to codify the world's standards, procedures, and laws governing interventions to protect human rights and respond to domestic crimes against humanity (Spencer, 1997: 93).

At the same time, the UN's failure to prevent human rights atrocities challenged its ability to act in an effective and timely manner to protect civilians. Critics noted that intervention and human security were still treated as distinct policy alternatives. Exit strategies were defined militarily and high civilian casualty rates in Somalia, Bosnia, and Rwanda represented a failure to account adequately for the new 'human security equation' (Fortier, 2001: 46). NATO's actions in Bosnia set a precedent for the use of force to halt humanitarian disasters; however, given countervailing objectives including regional stability,[16] human security had not clearly been seen as a *casus belli*.

By the mid-1990s, the costs of second-generation peacekeeping, and the specific problems highlighted by UN missions in Somalia, Rwanda, and the former Yugoslavia, led some members of the Canadian foreign policy community to propose a movement away from hard-powered peace and security roles. Leading policy experts believed that the Somalia mission had 'seriously tarnished the military . . . turning people against foreign engagements involving the military' (Rioux and Hay, 1997: 22). Another critic argued that while the millions of public dollars spent to peacekeep in the former Yugoslavia 'may have satisfied the criterion of identifiable interest', the returns on this investment fell short of 'maximum impact' (Potter, 1996–7: 25) since using soldiers as peacebuilders in situations of ongoing, intrastate conflict was both expensive and highly inefficient. The crisis in peacekeeping also had a negative impact on the national mood, although later polls indicated that the drop in support for UN peacekeeping was relatively short-lived (Martin and Fortmann, 2001a: 69). Nevertheless, among the recommendations of the government's Commission of Inquiry into Somalia was to scale back on international commitments to UN peacekeeping, generating further domestic debate on the need for selectivity through better understanding of mission mandates and the identification of niche roles, such as telecommunications and training (Tessier and Fortmann, 2001: 124).

Niche diplomacy[17] and soft power[18] had already been circulating as policy alternatives on the governmental agenda before human security became the policy framework for Canada's decision agenda (Cooper, 1995–6: 10). When Lloyd Axworthy succeeded Ouellet at the helm of the Department of Foreign Affairs in January 1996, high-profile human security initiatives followed, including the Ottawa Process on landmines and the Rome Treaty for an International Criminal Court (ICC). Networking, norms diffusion, and powers of persuasion were human security's niche tools and tasks. Although a soft-powered human security agenda was not immune from criticism (Hampson and Oliver, 1998; Nossal, 1998), the Ottawa Process demonstrated that soft power could as easily become a successful platform for Canadian leadership as participation in military roles and intervention.

The line between soft power and hard power was challenged by new humanitarian crises, leading again to calls for intervention. The turning point toward a forceful human security came with the 1999 NATO-led intervention in Kosovo, a province in southern Serbia with a majority ethnic-Albanian population. The failure to include the plight of ethnic Albanians in the terms of the Dayton accords had opened the door to abuses in the former Yugoslavia, leading to escalating conflict between FRY Serb forces and the Kosovo Liberation Army (KLA).[19] Beginning in early 1998, the Serbs began a crackdown on the KLA, burning hundreds of homes, emptying villages, and murdering dozens of ethnic Albanians in the Drenica region of Kosovo. UN Security Council Resolution 1160 of 31 March 1998, passed with chapter VII powers under the UN *Charter*, condemned Belgrade's excessive use of force and imposed an arms embargo on Yugoslavia. Violence continued to escalate and culminated in mid-July 1998 in an all-out offensive during which more than two thousand ethnic Albanians were killed, and more than three hundred thousand were displaced from Kosovo (International Crisis Group). On 23 September 1998, the Security Council adopted Resolution 1199, again under chapter VII, which called for an immediate cease-fire and for the negotiation of a political settlement (Axworthy, 2003: 181). As the humanitarian crisis continued to worsen, Axworthy began to articulate a harder-edged version of human security (DFAIT, 1998a).

A diplomatic offensive through the UN and the Contact Group had been ineffectual. At the same time, evidence of human rights abuses were both compelling and increasing. On 15 January 1999, the massacre of 45 ethnic Albanians in the village of Racak heightened the sense that the crisis had reached a critical juncture requiring action. In March 1999, the UN High Commissioner for Refugees reported to the Security Council that 410,000 ethnic Albanians had been pushed out of their villages by Serb forces, while 90,000 were already outside the country as refugees (Heinbecker and McRae, 2001: 124). The media played an instrumental role in bringing international attention to the humanitarian crisis and in mobilizing Canadian public opinion in support of intervention. Paul Heinbecker, who served as Axworthy's assistant deputy minister for global and security policy, explained how the 'CNN effect' persuaded the public that the cause was 'just': 'The steady streaming of refugees . . . evoked the Holocaust . . . [and] persuaded Canadians of the rightness of intervening. No amount of political carping or . . . punditry made a dent in that conviction' (Heinbecker, 1999: 25).

Reflecting the emerging public consensus, in January 1999 Axworthy asserted before the National Forum that 'promoting human security can also involve the use of strong measures including . . . military force' (DFAIT, 1999e). Despite Canada's efforts to gain Security Council endorsement, especially after assuming the presidency of the Security Council in January 1999, Russian and Chinese intransigence blocked UN action. The absence of an explicit UN mandate precipitated an 'agonized debate' within DFAIT, but in the end Ottawa opted to give 'humanitarian concerns priority over the felt need to work through the Security Council'. On 24 March 1999, NATO launched an air-strike campaign against Serbia, conducting its first offensive, out-of-theatre mission. The CF flew 10 per cent of NATO strike sorties in Kosovo (Haglund and Sens, 2000: 193). Absent UN authorization, NATO's actions were justified with reference to the overwhelming necessity to avert humanitarian disaster under the customary, but contested, right of 'humanitarian' intervention[20] (Weller, 1999: 217). As Heinbecker would later reflect, Kosovo proved that 'pragmatically there will sometimes be a necessity to act, Council authorization or not' (Heinbecker, 2004: 13).

If Canadians were not effusive in their support for the NATO intervention, neither was public opinion a major constraint on government policies (Martin and Fortmann, 2001a: 70). Concerns were voiced in Parliament that a combat role under NATO command had not been adequately debated, but the government was able to point to earlier assertions in the House of Commons, taking note 'the dire humanitarian situation' and announcing the government's intention to 'take measures in cooperation with the international community' to resolve the conflict, promote a political settlement, and facilitate the provision of humanitarian aid (Dewing and McDonald, 2004). Axworthy and the minister of defence Art Eggleton consulted with opposition party critics and made successful appearances before the Standing Committee on Foreign Affairs and International Trade (Dashwood, 2000: 296). The invitation extended to Czech President Vaclav Havel to address the House of Commons in April 1999, with his argument that NATO was 'fighting in the name of human interest for the fate of other human beings', also paid political dividends (Hansard, 1999).

Following the beginning of hostilities in March 1999, Axworthy successfully presented the NATO intervention as part of the human security agenda, fostering a positive political climate at home. Kosovo, Axworthy argued, was a 'concrete expression' of the 'human security dynamic at work' (DFAIT, 1999d) and 'a turning point in global affairs, where the security of people figures prominently as an impetus for action' (DFAIT, 1999f). If opinion polls were any indication, the government's message got through. A July 1999 Goldfarb survey found increased support for NATO, with 73 per cent believing that Canada should place a very high (32 per cent) priority on its role in the alliance, and public support remained relatively steady over the course of the campaign. Values, or human security, sustained public support for the Kosovo intervention in spite of the absence of Parliamentary debate, the potential political irritant associated with participation in US-led initiatives, and the lack of UN Security Council authorization (Martin and Fortmann, 2001a: 67, 70). Kosovo became a war for 'human security' (Heinbecker, 2000: 15), proving that Axworthy's foreign policy went far beyond the 'pulpit diplomacy' critics claimed was its basic thrust (Molot and Hillmer, 2002: 3).

Canada's participation in NATO's humanitarian intervention in Kosovo was a product of the convergence of critical events, available policy alternatives, and favourable politics. An existing human security framework enabled the government to circumvent the old problem of non-interference in state sovereignty by employing the ethical imperative of human rights and protection. NATO presented Canadian policy makers with a workable vehicle for an effective response to the humanitarian crises in the absence of a viable alternative from the United Nations. Participation in the alliance's first offensive operation on behalf of human rights was a solution to the problem of domestic criticism of the human security agenda. In the politics stream, images of ravaged refugees and displaced peoples motivated a media-sensitized Canadian public to support the humanitarian military intervention. Kosovo created a policy window for critics and advocates of human security to come together through linking hard-power capabilities with human security goals. By superimposing the pre-existing policy idea of humanitarian intervention onto a human security framework, a bridge was built to the responsibility to protect (Cheung-Gertler, 2006b).

Kosovo would ultimately pose as many new challenges as it solved old problems. The Independent International Commission on Kosovo (IICK) ruled that the Kosovo intervention was 'illegal but legitimate' (IICK, 2000: 4), referring to the absence of a Security Council mandate for a non-defensive use of force coupled with a case of compelling humanitarian need. NATO's actions came under unprecedented scrutiny, not least from the international media. Heinbecker noted that television coverage 'cuts both ways' and that 'NATO behaviour was properly held to a higher standard than that of non-democracies' (Heinbecker, 1999: 25). Canada's former ambassador to Yugoslavia denounced the 'tragic blunder in Kosovo', arguing that more than two thousand civilians had been killed by NATO bombing (Bissett, 2000). Critics complained that the decision to conduct air-strikes rather than use ground troops undermined humanitarian justifications by demonstrating that Western allies were unwilling to put their soldiers at risk to protect civilians. Deployments against civilian targets such as Serbian TV stations and markets also came under fire (Axworthy, 2003: 184). In light of these troubling indicators, NATO actions in Kosovo sparked an intense debate in Canada surrounding the legality and legitimacy of humanitarian military interventions (Hubert and Bonser, 2001: 112).

A series of foreign policy roundtables, academic conferences, and special committees in and around government were held in the aftermath of the Kosovo intervention. The major theme emerging out of these consultations was the need for systematic analysis of the conditions and circumstances when principles of sovereignty could be overridden. An internationally agreed-upon framework for military intervention to protect human security and halt violations of human rights and humanitarian law would be the solution to problems of legitimacy and legality surrounding humanitarian intervention (ibid.).

For Canadian policy makers and in specialized policy communities, the question of right authority (who could legitimately lead humanitarian interventions) became the focus of debate. The Kosovo intervention had challenged the country's commitment to the United Nations as the primary guarantor of human rights and international peace and security. Participants at a fall 1999 roundtable hosted by the CCFPD agreed that the Security Council 'has proven largely ineffective in dealing with humanitarian crises caused by military conflict' (Owens and Arneil, 1999: 8). However, the NATO alternative was fraught with legal and political hazards. In by-passing the Security Council, the alliance—notwithstanding its appeal to humanitarian norms—had flouted both international customary and treaty law (Geislerova, 1999: 14). In practice, it was unclear whether NATO would intervene to protect human security where the strategic interests of the Western allies were not at stake (Heinbecker, 2000: 16). Moreover, following the military intervention in Kosovo, the alliance's military toolbox had been found wanting by the complex peacebuilding tasks undertaken by the UN

Interim Administration in Kosovo (UNMIK), which coordinated the fielding of civilian experts with the provision of physical security (Fortier, 2001: 53). Nor should Kosovo, as Axworthy cautioned in a June 1999 speech to the G8, be 'held up as a precedent justifying intervention anywhere, anytime, or for any reason' (Hubert and Bonser, 2001: 113).

The need to develop an appropriate threshold governing interventions for humanitarian purposes was an important part of the debate. Early policy alternatives included use of the Genocide Convention as the basis for interventions, but members of the policy community disagreed about whether such a definition would be more or less inclusive, with some citing the absence of specific protections for women under the convention (Geislerova, 1999). Another concern was the extent to which Canada would have a seat at the decision-making table. The Senate Standing Committee on Foreign Affairs noted in April 2000 that one lesson gained from the Kosovo intervention was that participation in NATO-led military operations did not guarantee that Canada would be consulted regarding military strategies or political issues.

Government and specialized policy communities focused on the problem for Canada, and for the international community as a whole, of a drastically diminished and weakened United Nations. How could Canada work to maintain the credibility of the UN while at the same time responding effectively to compelling threats to human security? Errol Mendes, a professor at the University of Ottawa and authority on international and human rights law, argued that the only way to resolve the 'tragic flaw' in the UN *Charter* was to place the founding principles of state sovereignty and protection of human rights within the framework of human security (Owens and Arneil, 1999: 8). Participants at an academic round-table hosted by the CCFPD noted that Canada was in an ideal position to act as a 'tipping agent' in guiding the development of new international norms for humanitarian intervention (CCFPD, 2000). What was needed was a human security rationale to conduct interventions for human protection purposes that would also mobilize political will and diffuse harmful divisions playing out in important international forums like the United Nations. Redefining humanitarian intervention, using a human security lens, emerged as the preferred solution to problems of legality, legitimacy, authority—and (through the mobilization of political will) capacity.

In Canada, the lasting policy outcome emerging out of the Kosovo intervention was the renewed attention of policy entrepreneurs in and around government to the problem of UN reform and renewal (Cheung-Gertler, 2006b). Canada was instrumental in the process leading up to the secretary-general's landmark report, *The Protection of Civilians in Armed Conflict*, on 8 September 1999 (DFAIT, 2000). Chairing open debates which included the participation of NGOs like the International Committee of the Red Cross (ICRC), and representatives from the United Nations Children's Fund (UNICEF) and United Nations High Commissioner for Refugees (UNHCR), drove the issue of civilian protection onto the issue agenda (Golberg and Hubert, 2001: 225). The secretary-general's report and the supporting Security Council resolutions (1265 and 1296) condemned attacks on civilian populations, strengthened peacekeeping mandates, and committed the Security Council to take action against crimes against humanity and violations of international humanitarian law (Golberg and Hubert, 2001: 227–8). Canada played a leading role in, to use Kingdon's term, 'softening-up' the international policy community through advocacy at the UN General Assembly, at think-tanks such as the Carnegie Foundation and International Peace Academy, and at high-level meetings of the Human Security Network, as well as at other international and regional forums (DFAIT, 1999a). The secretary-general's opening address to the 54th session of the General Assembly in September 1999, challenging the international community to 'address the prospects of human security and inter-vention in the next century' (ICISS, 2001:15), brought international attention to the issue and support for Canadian efforts. Spearheading the campaign for the principle of the 'responsibility to protect' became as much about keeping the UN *'in'* as it was about creating guidelines for military intervention (Cheung-Gertler, 2006b).

The national mood was conducive to finding UN-led solutions to humanitar-ian crises. The same Goldfarb opinion surveys indicating high and increasing public support for NATO between 1997 and 1999, nevertheless, maintained that Canadians placed the highest priority on the United Nations over all other inter-national organizations (Martin and Fortmann, 2001a: 68). The CNN effect of transnational media networks on public opinion had made acts of omission, as well as commission, equally problematic, and public support for NATO was roughly congruent with Canadians' amplified feelings of international responsi-bility. However, feedback in the aftermath of the Kosovo intervention from media, the universities, and political elites, identified problems with the alliance's record of humanitarianism. Policy entrepreneurs in Canada, respond-ing to the national mood at home, sought to capture an international consensus for the use of force for humanitarian protection purposes under the auspices of the United Nations.

The idea for an international commission of experts to address the problem of reconciling humanitarian intervention with state sovereignty came from the senior ranks of DFAIT. Jill Sinclair, director general of the Global and Human Issues Bureau, and Don Hubert, a senior policy advisor, proposed that Canada sponsor a year-long study by an international commission of experts as a response to the secretary-general's challenge. Sinclair and Hubert drew from a pre-existing policy alternative, the 1987 Brundtland Commission on Environ-ment and Development (bringing economic growth and environmental protec-tion together through 'sustainable development'), as a model for the ICISS commission. Through a process of intellectual and political debate, it was envi-sioned that new perspectives on the problem would emerge that reconciled the 'seemingly irreconcilable notions of intervention and state sovereignty' (ICISS, 2001: 81). Canadian officials were hoping that the commission 'would change the vocabulary, and in changing the vocabulary, it would change the way people think, and if they had consciences, act' (Heinbecker, 2004: 5). The initiative drew upon existing strategies of soft power (persuasion, networking, and norms diffusion) credited with the success of the landmines and ICC campaigns. At the UN Millennium Assembly in September 2000, Prime Minister Jean Chrétien officially launched the International Commission on Intervention and State Sovereignty (ICISS) and proposed that the commission complete its work within one year, enabling the government to announce the commission's recommendations at the 56th session of the United Nations.

The ICISS report was designed to avoid many of the pitfalls associated with humanitarian interventionism. Through changing the discourse from 'humanitarian intervention' to the 'responsibility to protect', ICISS sought to diffuse the opposition expressed by humanitarian agencies and practitioners, like Médecins Sans Frontières (Orbinksi, 2000: 3), to the conflation of humanitarianism with military means (ICISS, 2001: 9). Furthermore, by tilting the terms of the debate from the 'right to intervene' to 'responsibility to protect', the basis for action was focused on those who needed or sought assistance (ICISS, 2001: 18); that is, on the human security of peoples. A spotlight on the protection of civilians, rather than the politically defined objectives of states, was later endorsed by Project Ploughshares in its 2004 recommendations for 'reshaping the security envelope' (Regehr and Whelan, 2004: 22). Significantly, the Liberal government's message to NGOs was that the ICISS report was about more, not fewer, rules for military intervention. The response from civil society was that the 'pro-sovereignty framework' was critical in making the report 'more acceptable to southern governments and NGOs' (WFM, 2003: 9, 12). The cautious balance struck by ICISS's high threshold criteria for intervention was reflected in the rejection of the use of military means to respond to political repression or the overthrow of democratic governments (ICISS, 2001: 34; Ignatieff, 2005: 64). In this respect, the responsibility to protect would not have endorsed the Mulroney government's call for intervention in Haiti following the ouster of democratically elected President Jean-Bertrand Aristide in 1992.

For its Canadian entrepreneurs, the redefinition of humanitarian intervention to focus on human security was politically astute as well as congruent with Canadian values. The human security framework had the added-value of an existing policy community, and bureaucratic infrastructure, to mobilize support for the report. The World Federalist Movement (WFM), a central actor in the ICC and landmines campaigns, supported the ICISS's recommendations, and the Canadian government funded its initiatives to establish NGO networks to promote the report. Large human rights NGOs, most notably Human Rights Watch, also endorsed ICISS (Riddell-Dixon, 2005: 6). Consultations with civil society indicated a 'critical need' for the international community to respond earlier and more effectively to emerging crises (WFM, 2003: 14). At the end of 2005, the minister of foreign affairs noted that the same government–civil society networks that brought about the landmines ban and the ICC could be harnessed 'to grow a broad international public consensus that will take R2P from a concept to concrete action that saves lives' (DFAIT, 2005c).

Implementation and norms-building successes were represented by the inclusion of R2P principles in *A More Secure World*, the 2004 report from the UN's High

Level Panel on Threats, Challenges and Change; *In Larger Freedom*, the secretary-general's 2005 blueprint for UN reform; and, most significantly, the final outcome documents of the September 2005 United Nations World Summit. Achieving consensus around principles for the responsibility to protect was perceived to be a 'ray of hope', and a victory for Canadian diplomacy, at an otherwise lacklustre summit (*Montreal Gazette*, 2005). Success was, however, incomplete. Powerful states such as the United States, Russia, and China refused to entertain any limitations on veto powers, such as in cases of genocide (Trent and Watt, 2005), and discretionary language qualified commitments to R2P as operating on a 'case-by-case basis and in cooperation with relevant regional organizations as appropriate' (Paragraphs 138 and 139). Allan Rock, Canada's ambassador to the UN, explained that compromise language would likely be necessary to meet US resistance to imposing legal obligations on the Security Council as well as to offset the perceived vulnerability of smaller countries to a 'license to intervene' (Edwards, 2005).

Opinion polls continue to find high, and increasing, support for UN missions and peacekeeping tasks that put the rights and security of civilians at the forefront. A November 2004 poll found that 92 per cent of Canadians supported the commitment of troops to assist populations struck by famine, while 79 per cent supported missions to bring peace to civil war (Innovative Research Group [IRG], 2004). According to one high level member of the CF, cited from a 2005 interview, a role for the CF based upon the responsibility to protect 'resonates well with Canadians' (Noble, 2005: 16).

The release of the responsibility to protect report coincided with fundamental changes in the global security landscape following the September 11 terrorist attacks in 2001. The 2003 US-led intervention in Iraq, and counterinsurgency operations in Afghanistan, impeded the drive for an international consensus on R2P. Reflecting a Canadian national mood sceptical of US foreign policy under the Bush administration, Prime Minister Paul Martin asserted at the 2005 World Summit that R2P 'does not bless unilateral action . . . it stands for clear, multilaterally-agreed criteria' to protect civilians at risk (DFAIT, 2005d). Under the government of Stephen Harper that succeeded Martin's in January 2006, the politics of responsibility were further complicated in Canada by the use of humanitarian justifications for military expenditures and interventionist policies in support of the US war on terror (Cheung-Gertler, 2007). But divisive public debate over the extension of the CF mission in Afghanistan to 2009 indicated that the Conservative government faced an uphill battle in characterizing the NATO-led operation as part of a broader responsibility to protect (Decima Research, 2006). In spring 2007, extensive media coverage of an agreement, originally signed in 2005 under the Liberal government, for the Canadian Forces to transfer Afghan detainees to face possible abuse and torture under Afghan authorities, came back to haunt the Conservative government and the Department of National Defence (LeBlanc, 2007: A1, A18). Canadian human rights groups and specialists in international humanitarian law cried foul, asserting that Canada was violating both the Geneva Conventions as well as its own Charter of Rights and Freedoms

(Neve and Gratl, 2007: A19). Events were conspiring to make Canadians cautious in endorsing functional equivalents to the United Nations through coalitions of the willing or unilateral action, particularly where humanitarian objectives were ambiguously supported by events on the ground and allied to other strategic interests.

Canada's International Policies

Ideas matter. So too do interests. But policy change and innovation are about the structure of the policy process as well, and about statecraft and leadership—qualities that rely on specific kinds of entrepreneurial talents and a keen sense of timing. As the review of different issue-areas covered in this book underscores, turning points in the evolution of Canada's international policies in trade and investment, defence and security, and international development have frequently reflected a contest between radically different ideas and interests about the future direction of public policy. In trade and investment policy, for example, the direction shifted in the late 1960s and early 1970s toward a more protectionist, nationalist orientation as Canadian firms found themselves unable to compete successfully. Foreign—largely US—ownership was seen by some as imperilling Canada's industrial development. Policies shifted again toward a much more open market orientation in the 1980s when the Canadian economy experienced its severest recession since the 1930s; Canadian business interests urged a change in investment regulatory regimes and trade policy in order to make Canada more attractive to foreign investors and secure access to US markets. In both instances, however, there was no policy 'consensus' that drove the agenda forward. Champions of free trade and an open market for investment had to contend with vocal and effective champions of nationalism and economic self-determination who warned about the dangers of trade liberalization and excessive levels of foreign ownership in the Canadian economy.

The same is true if we look at turning points in other issue domains. For example, the embrace of neo-liberal, conservative orthodoxy in Canada's development assistance programming in the late 1980s, with ODA cuts and an emphasis on structural adjustment, was diametrically opposed to the views and interests of Canada's NGO community, and even senior officials in the government, who wanted Canada to pay more attention to poverty alleviation and the needs of the world's poorest countries. Similarly, the shift in the 1990s toward a new foreign policy stance that was tethered to the concept of human security also marked a significant and controversial departure from Canada's traditional foreign policy orientation—one based on a preference for formal diplomacy, strong Canada–US ties, and support for traditional negotiating forums and international institutions.

Why did one set of ideas and policy prescriptions win out over the others? And why, in other cases, when there was mounting discontent and debate about the direction of policy—as in the case of Canada's defence and security policies in the late 1980s and early 1990s when many influential foreign policy and defence experts called for a radical overhaul of Canada's armed forces that would see the elimination of Canada's war-fighting capabilities in favour of a smaller, peacekeeping and constabulary-style force—did policy change not occur?

It is too simplistic to portray these different contests of ideas and interests in terms of the relative resources and skills of their proponents—as a battle where the politically or bureaucratically adept prevail over their weaker and fragmented rivals. Many of these debates were long-standing affairs, with effective champions on both sides of the partisan divide, where a standoff prevailed more often than not. Rather, as we have argued repeatedly in this book, important ideas and policies emerge out of the policy primeval soup at critical moments in history, or policy windows, when problems finally capture the attention of key actors and political conditions are right. As discussion of these problems moved to a serious consideration of policy alternatives, leadership—in the sense of policy entrepreneurship—proved a critical element in shaping the debate and direction of public policy.

Policy entrepreneurs offer a special kind of leadership. Not only do they understand the nature of complex public policy problems, but they also have the ability to frame solutions to those problems that resonate with the political circumstances of the times. Policy entrepreneurs understand the importance of timing and the need to link the adoption of new policies to focusing events, such as an actual (or looming) crisis or an election, which, perhaps only for a brief period of time, concentrates wider attention on an issue. Entrepreneurial leadership is about seizing windows of opportunity and shaping political perceptions so that policy agendas can be moved in new directions and decisive action can be taken.

The policy entrepreneurs who drive the agendas forward are also 'couplers' or 'matchmakers' who have the talent to join problems with solutions when they see the streams align and a window of opportunity opening. They also know how to make best use of their political connections and negotiating skills to move agendas forward and get buy-in from political elites. It must also be said that they know how to resist mounting public and political pressure for change and preserve the policy status quo when they believe that proposed solutions are not the right fit for (or corrective to) the problem at hand.

POLICY STREAMS

We used the multiple streams model in our analysis of Canada's international policies to discern pattern and structure in the complicated and fluid events that make up the policy process. The model provides us with a comprehensive representation of the enduring streams in the policy process—problems, alternatives, and politics—and alerts us to the critical ingredients—windows of opportunity and the entrepreneurial initiatives that must couple the streams at the openings—that increase the likelihood of policy change. What can we conclude about these streams in the policy process based on our analysis across five areas of international policy?

First, problems rarely arrive suddenly and fully formed on the government's decision agenda, but more frequently wend their way through the problem stream, as proponents attempt to build a case for their inclusion on the agenda, typically by making the case repeatedly and in a variety of settings. Similarly, policy ideas are rarely created *sui generis* in response to the occurrence of a problem, but instead circulate in the policy stream, their proponents attempting to build receptivity for their adoption in what is often a long softening-up process. Thus, problems and policy alternatives co-exist, frequently for long periods of time without change occurring, until, at times, they are linked by circumstance, and a problem is recognized and a solution adopted. Events in the stream of politics are frequently critical to this linkage, although they are not always related to the electoral and partisan aspects of politics that so preoccupy the chattering classes. Government turnover can lead to a change in policies, but this happens most frequently when proponents of particular agendas and alternatives take advantage of electoral outcomes to make their case, and when other conditions in the stream of politics are supportive.

The pattern of continuity and change in Canada's international policies revealed in the analysis across five policy domains conforms, in many respects, to the punctuated equilibrium conception (Baumgartner and Jones, 1993) of an evolutionary policy process, where policies and agendas, rather than changing gradually over time, actually shift rapidly from one stable point to another. Many ideas about problems and alternatives circulate in policy subsystems, competing for attention, but once a particular idea captures attention, it can expand rapidly, taking over the decision agenda in the problem stream or generating a tipping point among advocacy coalitions in the policy stream. This occurs most frequently in response to either external events, or developments in the stream of politics, that disturb the stable equilibrium. Once it occurs, policy entrepreneurs often step in to exercise the leadership necessary to join problems and alternatives in policy outcomes, and these, in turn, evolve into new stable points of equilibrium.

Our analysis of foreign investment policy described the protracted effort to get investment-related problems on the decision agenda, with ideas about how to deal with foreign investment evolving slowly and unevenly until a middle ground was found between those who argued for unimpeded capital flows and those who argued for controls, and a review process was put in place. That new policy equilibrium lasted for approximately 10 years, but then the investment problem shifted again, and policy moved too, in the direction of more open access secured by international treaties. Thus, over the course of 60 years, Canadian foreign investment policy came nearly full circle, from the open door that prevailed following the Second World War, through the exercise of foreign investment review, and finally to acceptance of the right of establishment and national treatment for foreign investors. Similarly, while the evolutionary path of Canadian trade policy in the 60 years following the end of the Second World War begins and ends with free trade with the United States, the stable equilibrium of multilateral liberalization, accompanied by growing dependence on the American market, prevailed for 20 years before Canada concluded a major sectoral agreement with the US. And it took another 20 years for a new bilateral free trade equilibrium point to be established.

In the realm of Canadian defence policy, factors of continuity—born of history, values, and geopolitics—usually prevailed, in spite of competing domestic agendas, entrepreneurial advocates for change, or the aspirations of politicians. A long-standing defence partnership with the US that began during the Second World War shaped Canadian defence decisions and priorities. Cold War strategic interests, and a desire for international influence, added expeditionary capabilities to domestic and continental defence goals; whenever possible, military operations overseas were conducted in harmony with the UN and as part of multilateral coalitions. All this conspired to prevent defence spending from falling too far, but Canadians' disinterest in (and apathy about) military questions, together with the lack of a perceptible conventional threat to national security, ensured that the subject was seldom at the forefront of the governmental agenda. Military expenditures were characteristically perfunctory in peacetime.

Since the end of the Second World War, four interests and tasks have defined Canada's policy approaches to defence: the protection of Canadian territories and emergency assistance in the event of natural disaster or threats to domestic peace; the defence of North America in cooperation with the United States; the support of like-minded allies through the North Atlantic Treaty Organization (NATO); and contributions to collective security and international stability operations under the auspices of the UN. Over the decades of the Cold War, defence policy in Canada was intimately tied to the interests of the North Atlantic alliance and to the country's powerful continental neighbour, notably through the North American Air (later Aerospace) Defence Agreement (NORAD). Every government after 1945 was committed to the Cold War struggle against international Communism. Pierre Trudeau acted for a while as if he was not, but his government ended as a supporter of NATO and it tested US cruise missiles in the 1980s. The Conservative government of Brian Mulroney that followed sought to advertise itself as a pro-American Cold Warrior in contrast to its predecessor. Like all governments, however, the Conservatives balanced policies that strengthened Canada–US ties with initiatives that promoted international engagement and national sovereignty.

Notwithstanding the basic continuities of Canadian defence policy, aspects of change, rejuvenation, or retrenchment were present in each of the government White Papers discussed in our analysis in Chapters 6 and 7. In the 1960s, armed services waste and mismanagement were addressed by the unification of land, sea, and air forces under a single command headed by a chief of the defence staff (CDS). In 1971, NATO and the UN were supplanted by national unity and sovereignty as the focus of defence policy. In 1987, a radical effort was mounted to bridge the commitment-capability gap, improve Canada's standing with its allies, protect the North, and reassert the country's role in the Cold War. When the Cold War ended, there was a window of opportunity for policy innovation. Common or cooperative security tasks in niche areas of Canadian expertise emerged as possible alternatives to multipurpose, combat-ready forces and traditional international peace and security roles. The new ideas originating in Canadian civil society were ultimately quashed, and the 1994 White Paper reflected the status quo in a leaner form. Policy entrepreneurship in 1994 opposed the winds of change rather than fanned them. Defenders of existing force structuring, training, and capabilities hunkered down to wait for the next policy window to open for advocating increased military expenditures. Spending began to creep up in the late 1990s, and the September 11, 2001, terrorist attacks in the United States moved the Canadian policy community further in the direction of military renewal and reinvestment. *A Role of Pride and Influence in the World,* the title of the 2005 *International Policy Statement,* spoke to a desire to return to a lost time in the 1950s when Canada had valued its military and mattered in the world.

Shifts in policy are frequently short-lived and factors of continuity remain the primary levers of the Canadian defence agenda. The 1971 White Paper only briefly shunted NATO aside, just as domestic constraints and global events crashing down on the 1987 document underlined how quickly inflated expectations could be made to seem unrealistic. Efforts to strike a pragmatic balance between domestic and international imperatives, and cycles of investment and disinvestment, rather than a systematic re-thinking of military priorities, best describes the evolution of defence policy in Canada.

Canada's adoption of a human security agenda under foreign affairs minister Lloyd Axworthy is frequently applauded as a real policy innovation. Our analysis indicated, however, that continuity as well as change defined the origins and evolution of Axworthy's foreign policy 'revolution' (Hillmer and Chapnick, 2001). Human security was preceded by 'niche diplomacy' and 'soft power', which were related to ideas about selective roles and non-coercive influence emerging out of Canadian and international policy communities following the end of the Cold War. With the budget cuts of the mid-1990s, and the perceived failures of wider peacekeeping in the Balkans and Somalia, human security arrived in Canada as a timely and affordable solution to complex post–Cold War problems. Human security, however, was an idea that evolved slowly and different aspects of the paradigm were favoured and adopted at various times to suit particular circumstances.

The Ottawa Process to ban landmines, the International Criminal Court (ICC), and the responsibility to protect (R2P) each employed like-minded coalitions of governments and civil society to build momentum for policy change. Nevertheless, landmines can be placed in the context of long-standing Canadian non-proliferation, arms control, and disarmament (NACD) efforts, and the ICC drew upon the Nuremberg Tribunals and existing bodies of international humanitarian law. Similarly, the responsibility to protect evolved out of controversies surrounding humanitarian intervention and the assertive internationalisms of Prime Ministers Brian Mulroney and Jean Chrétien. In each of these cases, as with the other domains of Canadian international policy, human security policy did not emerge through incremental progress toward well-defined goals, but instead evolved out of a stable equilibrium, and it took external developments or fortuitous political shifts to overcome policy stagnation, institutional deadlock, or apathy.

This finding, that punctuated equilibria characterize the evolutionary development of Canada's international policies, is important in understanding the remarkable continuity manifested by policies over time. However, it is the multiple streams model that helps us to understand change when it occurs, alerting us to the importance of external events and political developments in affecting the stability of agendas and policies, and to the role of entrepreneurs in engineering change. Our multiple streams analysis demonstrates the critical importance of external focusing events in the transformation of existing conditions into policy problems. While indicators of the presence of a problem—high levels of foreign investment, trade concentration, international poverty, threats to security—are rarely sufficient, in themselves, to capture the attention of important people in and around government, policy agendas can be transformed by events that give compelling expression to the conditions reflected in indicators—high-profile foreign takeovers of Canadian firms, threats to Canadian access to American markets and money, wrenching recessions, severe famine, terrorist attacks, and genocide. But this is not always the case, because the decisive influence of events often depends on the ways in which they are manipulated by policy entrepreneurs to secure advantage for particular agendas and alternatives.

The 1971 US threat to reduce access to American markets and capital, while it produced a desire to strengthen economic ties with Europe and Japan, did not lead, as it did in 1982, to a wholesale redefinition of Canada's trade and investment policy agendas; genocide in Rwanda in April 1994 did not elicit a significant Canadian response, but the plight of Rwandan refugees in Zaire's eastern provinces in November 1996 did, and those African events would be instrumental in the development of the G8 Africa Action Plan at the Kananaskis Summit hosted by Canada in 2002. Military disinvestment has been a habitual complaint of the Canadian defence community, but persistent indicators of a commitment-capability gap do not readily or inevitably lead to policy changes or spikes in military spending. The 1987 promise to increase expenditures was jettisoned almost immediately, and a major jump in spending in the early twenty-first century took place because of altered international circumstances, an increased operational tempo in the CF, and direct pressure from the United States that made it difficult to resist action.

POLICY ENTREPRENEURS

The importance of the actions of individuals in changing agendas and promoting policy alternatives shows up time and again across the various policy domains. Entrepreneurs gain access to the policy process because of their official position, their expertise on an issue, or their leadership of organized groups, but their effectiveness depends more on their negotiating skills and ability to influence others, and on their persistence and tenacity in building support for their ideas. Policy entrepreneurs also reside at all levels of the policy hierarchy, both inside and outside government. At times, leadership has come from top elected officials—finance minister Walter Gordon on foreign investment, trade minister Gerald Regan and Alberta Premier Peter Lougheed on free trade with the United States, and foreign affairs minister Lloyd Axworthy on landmines, to name a few. Entrepreneurs also reside at senior levels of the bureaucracy—CIDA President Margaret Catley-Carlson promoting women in development, chief of defence staff Rick Hillier promoting the importance of operations in failed and failing states, and assistant deputy minister Derek Burney at Foreign Affairs and International Trade promoting free trade with the United States. In the middle levels, arms control officials Ralph Lysyshyn, Jill Sinclair, and Bob Lawson are notable examples for their work on landmines. Those outside government can also act as entrepreneurs, exercising their influence on international policies by working in the policy process, as Jody Williams did through the International Campaign to Ban Landmines, and as Business Council on National Issues President Tom d'Aquino did so effectively on free trade.

Among policy entrepreneurs, special mention must be made of Simon Reisman, who stands out for the extent of his continuing influence on policy. Reisman first appeared in our analysis of the evolution of Canadian international economic policy as the assistant director of research for Walter Gordon's royal commission, where he opposed Gordon's trade protectionism and his efforts to promote Canadian ownership, and next as a dissident assistant deputy minister of finance opposing the finance minister's use of tax measures to curb foreign ownership. It was on trade policy, however, where Reisman's influence was decisive, transforming Canada's commercial relationship with the United States over a 20-year period. This began with his instrumental role in the creation of the Auto Pact, continued with his opposition to the Trudeau government's efforts to diversify trade through the Third Option, and concluded with his role in the negotiation of the Canada–US free trade agreement. Reisman had a formidable reputation in Ottawa circles, based in equal measure on his bellicose personal style and his success in the policy game, but there can be no doubt as to the latter, where he exercised a remarkable degree of influence over Canada's international economic policies across four decades.

The evolution of Canadian defence policy was also shaped by the efforts of entrepreneurs from within civilian government and military administration. By the time Paul Hellyer was appointed as Pearson's minister of defence in 1964, the problem of defence policy administration was already recognized in government circles as a pressing concern. Nevertheless, it took Hellyer's personal ambition and firm belief that government, not the military, should make policy decisions to generate real changes aimed at the unification of the Canadian Forces and a re-defined civil–military relationship. Robert Fowler exercised his entrepreneurship not as an elected official but from within the senior ranks of bureaucracy. In 1987, he was the new assistant deputy minister for policy who mobilized the energies of civilian and military experts to produce a document focused on rebuilding the military. When the ambitions of the 1987 White Paper came to nought, and the end of the Cold War challenged the traditional roles of the Canadian Forces, Fowler again demonstrated significant leadership as deputy minister of defence in shaping the ideas and outcomes of the 1994 White Paper. In this case, Fowler proved that entrepreneurs need not be agents of change when he successfully made the case to government that the military status quo of a multipurpose fighting force was also the most affordable solution for the unpredictable threats of the post–Cold War environment. Finally, the military's contribution to Canadian foreign policy goals, and a commensurate need to increase the defence budget in 2005, was the message communicated to government by General Hillier, the chief of the defence staff who made stabilization and reconstruction operations in failed and failing states a benchmark for CF 'transformation' following the September 11 terrorist attacks.

Non-governmental entrepreneurship has seldom been a significant driver of Canadian defence policy. In the early 1990s, after the end of the Cold War, the Canada 21 Council could not compete with the superior bureaucratic resources of the Department of National Defence, nor with the skill and influence of a powerful deputy minister of defence. The 1994 White Paper proved the general rule that, in the case of defence decision-making, entrenched bureaucratic practices and the elliptical nature of military policy make the participation of non-specialists difficult or ineffective. Interest groups like Pugwash and Project Ploughshares on the one hand, and the Conference of Defence Associations (CDA) and the Atlantic Council of Canada on the other, assembled on the sides of the ideological and policy divide. Their impact was explained to us by a senior former defence bureaucrat, who claimed during an interview that advice from one pressure group tended to cancel out the opinions of the other. For him, such interests make 'low-level background noise, signifying nothing'. This supports the contention in our model that organized interests have their greatest effect when all, or most, point in the same direction. All that said, it is clear that, taken together with other factors, the higher profile given to defence at the turn of the twenty-first century owed something to the activities of individuals and organizations such as J.L. Granatstein and the Council for Canadian Security in the 21st Century. The Liberal government's decision to opt out of participation in the American ballistic missile defence (BMD) program in early 2005 was also influenced in some part by dissenting voices in civil society, such as that of Steven Staples and his Polaris Institute.

Finally, international institutions can play a critical role in shaping policy agendas. This has been especially true for Canada's development assistance policies which in recent years have increasingly borne the imprint of international institutions. The Development Assistance Committee of the Organization for Economic Cooperation and Development (OECD) has not only issued reports on 'best development practices' but also contributed to the evolution of Canada's development assistance policies, most notably through its 1996 report that articulated new principles for donor assistance and cooperation. So too has the World Bank, which in recent years has helped shape new partnerships across government and different sectors of society and taken the lead in developing donor requirements for highly indebted poor countries to produce poverty reduction.

POLITICS MATTER

Policy entrepreneurs frequently take advantage of government turnover to promote particular agendas and alternatives, but other conditions in the politics stream must be supportive for change to occur. If politicians, and those who serve them, discern widespread public support for a particular direction in policy—concern over levels of foreign ownership in the early 1970s, for example— then its prospects for adoption are enhanced, just as its prospects for rejection are increased by a perception of substantial public opposition. Similarly, interest groups are important in the policy process, and they ply their trade primarily in the problem and policy streams, pushing some agendas and blocking other ones, and promoting ideas. However, when they present a virtually united front on a particular issue—as Canadian business groups did on the need for secure access to the US market in the early 1980s, for example—their influence in the politics stream can be considerable. Finally, jurisdiction in the politics stream makes a difference, since which unit holds the policy levers can play an important role in policy development, as was the case in the mid-1990s when Foreign Affairs wrested the landmines file away from Defence.

So, while electoral turnover is not always decisive in producing policy change, turnovers have been associated with some significant shifts in Canadian policies. For investment policy, Gordon's 1963 tax measures were proposed by a newly elected minority Liberal government, as was FIRA in 1972, and a new Conservative government dismantled FIRA in 1984, creating Investment Canada in its stead. For trade policy, the Auto Pact was undertaken by that 1963 minority government and the Canada–US free trade agreement by the 1984 Conservative government. NAFTA was negotiated by a Conservative government nearing the end of its term, and looking for an issue to fight an election on, and was implemented by the Liberal victors after the election of 1993, despite their election promises to renegotiate the deal. Successive Liberal and Conservative governments have also placed their own imprint on Canada's development assistance policies. The Liberal political transition from Lester Pearson to Pierre Trudeau saw the institutionalization of Canada's development assistance programs with the creation of the Canadian International Development Agency in 1970. The transition from Trudeau to Brian Mulroney's Conservative leadership marked a thoroughgoing review of Canada's development assistance policies as did the transition in 1993 from a Conservative government to a Liberal one. However, in the 1980s and 1990s fiscal pressures on the ODA budget proved to be a more decisive influence on the diminishing importance of aid to Canadian foreign policy than partisan politics and pressures.

In defence policy making, political turnover preceded all instances of renewal, retrenchment, or innovation represented by defence policy White Papers. The unification of the armed services under the Pearson Liberals followed a contentious election campaign featuring the Conservatives' defence policy mismanagement and a perceived deficit of political control over the military. Trudeau's Canada First defence agenda of the late 1960s and early 1970s was the antidote to his Liberal predecessor's international orientations that, it was claimed, came at the expense of national interests, the national economy, and national unity. Sizeable increases to the defence budget were the Mulroney government's answer to the Trudeau Liberals' legacy of chronic underfunding of the Canadian Forces. In the post–Cold War era, the short-lived Liberal government of Paul Martin used military renewal to differentiate itself from the apparently miserly policies of Jean Chrétien, despite the latter's increases in defence spending once the budget deficit was righted. Partisanship and political rivalry often set the stage for changes on defence policy agendas.

Human security was embraced by a Liberal government in search of new ideas at the dawn of the post–Cold War era. Superpower confrontation had been replaced by an array of transnational threats and disorders linking factors of human development like health, human rights, good governance, and the environment with evolving security dynamics. Economic recovery and growth remained the Liberals' top priority, but Canada's drive for emerging markets seemed to internationally minded Canadians to be a poor replacement for responsible global citizenship and international influence. Meanwhile, organized interest groups had long pushed for inclusion into the foreign policy-making process and innovative approaches to security. When Lloyd Axworthy replaced André Ouellet as foreign minister in January 1996, his 'people-first' agenda struck a chord with the Canadian public. Axworthy was a convert to the principle that there was a direct relationship between conditions of human welfare and security in an interdependent world. Political turnover had set the stage for policy innovation, but it took Axworthy, a populist entrepreneur, to orchestrate solutions to political preoccupations.

THE US PRESENCE

Although we have looked broadly at international policies, Canada's relationship with the United States is at the centre of those policies. Canadian relations with the US are ubiquitous, intimate, and intense, influencing every aspect of international policy. Canadians want and need to be close to the United States, and yet they want and need separation from what often seems an unsubtle giant to the south. Leaders and policy makers are thus caught in the contradiction between the two strong impulses of integration and independence. They choose ever-deepening cooperation with the United States, but wish—always—to underline the importance of national autonomy and difference. The policies and politics of differentiation from the United States have been both positive and negative influences in Canadian national life, sometimes leading to necessary innovations and other times inspiring or encouraging an anti-Americanism that distorts the national interest and devalues the importance of good relations and meaningful cooperation. It is also worth emphasizing, as it seldom is in Canada, the utter interdependence of the relationship. The two countries are, as John Bartlet Brebner memorably put it, the Siamese twins of North America who cannot separate and live (Hillmer, 1989: 5; 2005a: 339–40).

On trade and investment issues, policy makers were preoccupied with the US throughout the period covered in this book. Policies on foreign ownership had their primary effects on American-owned corporations, and trade liberalization initiatives, even when they were undertaken in multilateral fora were, more often than not, concerned with access to the US market. Furthermore, when major shifts occurred in Canadian investment and trade policies, they were usually stimulated by a focusing event that involved a US threat to Canada's economic well-being, most often by limiting Canadian access to American markets and capital. As a result, Canadian policy has been, understandably, preoccupied with this all-important bilateral relationship.

The Canada–US defence relationship has remained a consistent factor throughout the history of Canadian defence policy making. As in the case of the Cuban missile crisis and the downgrading of alliance commitments in the context of détente and the Vietnam War, Canada's relations with the United States could feed nationalist impulses to take independent approaches to national defence and international security. Nevertheless, economic and strategic interests dictated that Canada's primary goal would be to maintain a close partnership with the United States in the defence of North America and Western Europe. The North Atlantic Treaty Organization was a vital aspect of the Canada–US continental partnership and Canada's alignment with the West was obligatory, despite a popular attachment to peacekeeping under UN auspices. Indeed, from Suez onwards, peacekeeping reflected alliance solidarity rather than a uniquely Canadian approach to conflict resolution (Hillmer, 2002: 57).

Canada–US relations cut across both domestic and international decision making in the evolution of Canadian policies. Canadian Forces unification reflected similar efforts undertaken by US secretary of defense Robert McNamara and by NATO's shift to a 'flexible response' doctrine. Despite an experiment in nationalist rhetoric and action, the Trudeau government consolidated ties with the United States through collaboration on peacekeeping missions abroad and, as its time in office wore on, greater attention to NATO. On the continent, the Mulroney Conservatives participated in a modernization program for NORAD in 1985 and, with the end of the Cold War, Canadian Forces took part in the US-led, but United Nations-sanctioned, Persian Gulf War. On September 11, 2001, NORAD was vital in helping to ground civilian air traffic in North America, and Canada subsequently joined with other NATO allies to invoke the collective defence article of the NATO Treaty. Canada opposed the US-led 2003 intervention in Iraq, but the country maintained a substantial military contribution to NATO's stabilization operations in Afghanistan and worked closely with US personnel under Operation Enduring Freedom in that country.

Canada's ODA policies are usually driven by a combination of domestic politics and international memberships, the Commonwealth and *la francophonie* in particular. Canada's Cold War alliance with the United States, however, was central in the early years of Canadian involvement in international development initiatives, such as the Colombo Plan for newly independent Asian countries. After the fall of the Berlin Wall, development assistance was freed from the strategic interests of a bipolar world that was no more, although funds flowed to the transition economies of the former Soviet bloc to support democratic governance. Interventions in countries like Afghanistan, closely tied to American foreign policy in the aftermath of the September 11, 2001, terrorist attacks, also called upon Canadian resources; in the years following the overthrow of the Taliban regime, Afghanistan became the largest recipient of Canadian aid.

In the human security domain, the United States has not been far from the centre of Canadian concerns, and relations with the US informed many human security initiatives including the Ottawa Process, the ICC, and the responsibility to protect. Critics of human security have pointed fingers at 'anti-American' sentiments in foreign policy circles as underlying rationales of Canadian leadership of these campaigns. The United States remained outside of the landmines treaty regime and withdrew its signature from the Rome Statute of the International Criminal Court. American diplomats at the United Nations are steadfast in their opposition to institutionalizing threshold criteria and precautionary principles for the conduct of interventions for human protection purposes and have resisted any limitations on veto powers in the UN Security Council.

Yet Canada–US differences are habitually overstated. American civil society groups like the Vietnam Veterans of America Foundation were early champions of a landmines ban. The issue re-emerged onto the international scene when the United States sponsored a resolution in the First Committee of the UN General Assembly calling for a moratorium on mine exports, and for Canadian co-sponsorship. It is also worth remembering that, up until the mid-1990s, landmines had been part of the arsenal of Canada's defence, just as they were in the US President Bill Clinton and his secretary of state, Madeleine Albright, were principal—and early—supporters of the International Criminal Court, although their advocacy was ultimately limited by a powerful constituency in the American senate that was opposed to the initiative. The report of the 2001 Commission on Intervention and State Sovereignty (ICISS) had little direct American input and US actions in Iraq made the responsibility to protect an even less attractive proposition among many smaller members of the international community.

Nevertheless, the Canadian Forces' combat-heavy operations in the southern Afghan province of Kandahar represent policy convergence between US-led counterinsurgency warfare and the responsibility to rebuild the human securities of a war-torn people. Like all other aspects of Canada's international personality, the interdependent relationship with the United States presents unique challenges as well as opportunities for the human security and other agendas.

THE POLICY PROCESS

We began this book by arguing that the process of making Canada's international policies is inherently messy and unstructured. Although a bird's-eye view of the policy process may see continuities and comparatively little change in foreign policy outlooks and orientations as argued by some, when scrutinized closely there is less method—and direction—to the policy process than first is apparent. Canada's international policies have also been on the move. Like tectonic plates on the earth's surface, they have experienced major shifts over the years with turning points coming almost like earthquakes when change occurs. The challenge for students and observers of the policy scene is to explain why these seismic changes occurred when they did.

The description of the policy process across the five domains covered by this book—investment, trade, development, defence, and human security—has stressed several elements: the competition between ideas and interests, the role of policy entrepreneurs, the importance of windows of opportunity, and the melding of the three policy streams when problem, policy, and politics are in alignment, thus allowing policy entrepreneurs to push forward with their agendas. In offering this description and understanding of the policy process, we naturally stress the importance of certain individuals as actors and agents of policy change. This view may not be fashionable among those who emphasize the importance of institutions or structural factors, such as geography, resources, or military and political power, in shaping Canada's international policies. However, as we have tried to argue, the policy-making process is much more complex and involved than many traditional accounts of Canadian foreign policy acknowledge. At the most general level, such constraints obviously do apply and affect general policy choices. However, within these constraints there are clear choices to be made—choices that sometimes have profound consequences for the government and the nation as a whole. This book has tried to explain how and why policy makers eventually settle on the choices that they do, and why certain ideas get traction in the policy arena while others do not. As we have argued throughout, this is a book about those who made a difference—bureaucrats, politicians, and men and women who stand outside of the governmental arena in the business community or civil society—by shaping policy outcomes through their interventions. We believe it provides important lessons about international policies, not only for students of statecraft, but also for those determined to exercise influence in the public policy arena.

CASE STUDIES

Introduction

The case studies presented in this section were written in 2005 and 2006 by Carleton University students for a graduate seminar in the MA Program of The Norman Paterson School of International Affairs. As an assignment in the course 'Canada in International Affairs', students were asked to prepare a case study on an aspect of Canada's international policies of their choice, using John Kingdon's multiple streams model as a framework for the analysis and presentation of the case. Six of those case studies address Canadian policies on a variety of issues in bilateral relationships and multilateral settings, and we include them here.

In Chapter 13 Lisa Baroldi scrutinizes the tension between Canadian cultural and trade policies, concentrating on Canada's decision to pursue a New International Instrument on Cultural Diversity (NIICD) that would recognize the special role of cultural goods and services and the right of governments to preserve and promote cultural diversity while respecting international trade law. In Chapter 14 John Cadham employs an extension of the multiple streams model to understand the multilateral negotiation process that led to the conclusion of the international treaty to ban landmines. In Chapter 17, Maite Ormaechea examines the changes that occurred in the environmental policy agenda, and in climate change policy, following the election of the Conservative government in 2006. In Chapter 18, Kate Press explores the events that motivated Canada to modify its *Patent Act* to provide developing countries access to pharmaceutical products, as a means of combatting public health crises such as HIV/AIDS, malaria, and tuberculosis.

Anemone Fritzen and Kevin Ma shift the case-study focus from multilateral to bilateral relations. In Chapter 15 Fritzen examines Canada's policies toward China—and by extension Taiwan—in the period since 1949, tracing the long road to Canadian recognition of the People's Republic in 1970 and the re-establishment of trade relations with Taiwan in 1986. In Chapter 16, Ma applies the multiple streams model to both sides of the long-standing transboundary dispute between Canada and the US over Devils Lake, and draws lessons for the effective management of Canada's most important bilateral relationship.

We offer these case studies for their examination of Canadian policies to expand on, or extend beyond, the domains explored in previous chapters. We also believe that they demonstrate the utility of the model as a method of searching for pattern and structure in very complicated, fluid, and apparently unpredictable phenomena. The model provides a comprehensive representation of the enduring streams in the policy process—problems, alternatives, and politics—and alerts its students to the critical ingredients that increase the likelihood of policy change. The six case studies are a further demonstration of the model's relevance for public policy analysis.

At the time of writing, Lisa Baroldi, Anemone Fritzen, Kevin Ma, Maite Ormaechea, and Kate Press were Master's degree candidates at Carleton University, and John Cadham was a special student.

Policy Making and the Culture/Trade Quandary

Lisa Baroldi

'. . . wheat and pork, though useful and necessary, are but dross in comparison with those intellectual products which alone are imperishable.'

– Sir William Osler, 1892 (Ostry, 1978: 113)

On 20 October 2005, 148 countries adopted the United Nations Educational, Scientific and Cultural Organization (UNESCO) Convention on the Protection and Promotion of the Diversity of Cultural Expressions as a tool for fostering cultural diversity[1] within and among states. In addition to differentiating cultural goods and services[2] from regular commercial products and services, the Convention seeks to promote interculturality, reaffirm the importance of the link between culture and development, and reinforce the sovereign right of states 'to maintain, adopt and implement policies and measures that they deem appropriate for the protection and promotion of the diversity of cultural expressions on their territory' (United Nations Educational, Scientific and Cultural Organization [UNESCO], 2005). Although all these objectives were welcomed by an overwhelming majority of the international community,[3] US officials argue that differential treatment for cultural goods and services encourages states to undermine fundamental human rights and guiding principles of free trade (States News Service, 2005). According to US ambassador to UNESCO Louise Oliver (2005b), governments could easily interpret the Convention's vague language to craft policies that would limit consumer choice, disrupt the free flow of ideas, promote a dominant culture, or protect a specific industry.[4] For countries like Canada, however, the Convention is intended to help alleviate the tension between a country's free trade obligations and the desire for domestically produced cultural goods and services that reflect a state's national identity and cultural pluralism. In other words, it is a positive way of dealing with the culture/trade quandary.

The term 'culture/trade quandary' appeared in Canadian policy circles in 1997 following a World Trade Organization (WTO) ruling in favour of US complaints against certain Canadian periodical policies (Browne, 1998). Similarly, the UNESCO Convention has its roots in Canada. In November 1999, the Canadian government decided to address the quandary by pursuing a New International Instrument on Cultural Diversity (NIICD) that would 'recognize the special role of cultural goods and services and the right of governments to preserve and promote cultural diversity' while still respecting international trade law (DFAIT, 1999c). With the collaboration of their counterparts in countries such as France, Sweden, and South Africa, Canadian officials and non-governmental cultural association representatives ensured that the NIICD evolved into the recently adopted UNESCO Convention.

This paper analyzes the domestic pre-decision policy process in Canada between 1997 and 1999. John Kingdon's Multiple Streams Model (MSM), which explains the agenda-setting and policy-formulation stages of policy making, provides a framework for this analysis. The MSM consists of three streams—problem, policy, and politics—that are explored to answer two questions: First, how did the culture/trade quandary become a priority on the policy agenda in 1999? Second, how did the idea for the NIICD emerge as the optimal policy alternative to address this quandary? Before delving first into the problem stream, this paper gives a brief background on Canada's cultural sector. The alternative selection process of the policy stream and politics are then discussed. Although policy making is rarely formulaic, the MSM helps an analyst to structure and make sense of policy making. In this case, the WTO ruling opened a window in the problem stream in 1997. This window was followed two years later by another window opened by parliamentary committee reports. A change in the policy stream in-between these two openings produced a viable alternative to which the problem could be attached. Window one set the governmental agenda, consensus led to the coupling of the NIICD alternative with the culture/trade quandary problem and to the setting of the decision agenda, and window two prompted department of Canadian heritage (DCH) minister Sheila Copps to raise the quandary/NIICD combination on the decision agenda by bringing the three streams together.

The cultural policy sector in Canada consists of individuals and organizations working or volunteering in the arts, cultural heritage, and cultural industries subsectors. In 1951 the Royal Commission on National Development in the Arts, Letters and Sciences (the Massey Commission) 'legitimized the belief that the state must become a major player in the cultural life of the country' (ibid.: 273). The Massey Commission, however, championed policies to promote the arts in Canada while the majority of Canadians actually craved popular culture, especially American pop culture. In reaction to this high demand for and consumption of mass culture, the Pearson government and subsequent Liberal and Conservative federal governments generated policies for mass culture because American cultural influence was, and continues to be, stronger in this subsector than in the arts and heritage (see Figure 13.1).[5]

Figure 13.1: Sphere of American cultural influence in Canada (Mulcahy, 2000)

Strongest			→ Weakest
Movies	Feature Films	'Art-house' Movies	Documentaries
Television	Action, Drama	Comedies, Game Shows	Newscasts, Sports
Music	Rock	Folk/New Age	Classical/Opera
Periodicals	Entertainment	News Magazines	Criticism/Opinion
Visual Arts	Advertising	Design/Galleries	Museum/Heritage

One Pearson-era policy move was to put a customs tariff on split-run maga-zines[6] and restrict tax deductions for advertising expenses to Canadian periodi-cals. *Time* and *Reader's Digest*, two widely circulated American split-runs, were exempted from the new policies. The Trudeau government passed Bill C-58 in 1977 to remove the exemption for the two magazines. The argument in favour of the bill was that the taxation and tariff measures on *Time* and *Reader's Digest* would thwart an influx of split-runs into Canada and lead to an increase in Canadian content (Acheson and Maule, 2001). Despite these measures, a 'Cana-dian' edition of *Sports Illustrated* entered the Canadian market in 1993, and in 1997, 83 per cent of newsstand magazines remained foreign (Rabinovitch, 1998: 30; Acheson and Maule, 1999: 16). Numbers were similar in other cultural indus-tries where foreign content comprised 70 per cent of radio music, 86 per cent and 75 per cent of prime-time drama on English- and French-language television respectively, 70 per cent of books, and 95 per cent of feature films (ibid.).

For DCH, cultural policies are required to provide shelf space for Canadian cul-tural goods and services because they help foster national identity, multicultur-alism, and national unity (Department of Canadian Heritage [DCH], 2003). The belief is that without cultural policies, foreign cultural goods and services would take over the Canadian cultural market.[7] What constitutes a foreign or Canadian cultural good or service is deeply disputed, but DCH remains 'responsible for national policies and programs that promote Canadian content' (see DCH web-site). Arm's-length institutions,[8] sublevel governments, Industry Canada, and the Department of Foreign Affairs and International Trade (DFAIT) also adminis-ter cultural policies in Canada.

Prior to 1997 Canadian foreign cultural policy was largely International Trade Canada's (IT Can's) domain because it is responsible for Canada's trade agree-ments and negotiations. The Canadian government has continually sought spe-cial treatment for or exclusion of culture from various Free Trade Agreements (FTAS) including the General Agreement on Tariffs and Trade (GATT), Canada–US Free Trade Agreement (CUFTA), North American Free Trade Agreement (NAFTA), General Agreement on Trade in Services (GATS), and Multilateral Agreement on Investment (MAI).[9] In 1987, Canadian negotiators, in response to vigorous pres-sure from cultural nationalists at home, insisted on exempting the cultural indus-tries from the CUFTA. Their American counterparts eventually agreed to exclude the cultural industries under Article 2005(1) of the treaty on the condition that the next paragraph allow for retaliatory measures in any sector 'of equivalent commercial effect'. In 1994, the exemption and the retaliatory clause were extended to Article 2106 and Annex 2106 of the NAFTA. Canada also obtained cultural exemptions, and complete exemptions (that is, no retaliatory clauses), in its bilateral agreements with Israel, Chile, and Costa Rica in the late 1990s and early 2000s.

Efforts to achieve cultural exemptions from multilateral agreements were less fruitful. At the end of the Uruguay Round in 1994, Canadian negotiators tried to get a cultural exemption from the GATT with little success.[10] Cultural goods remain subject to the principles of most-favoured-nation (MFN) (Article 1), national treatment (Article III), and prohibition against quantitative restrictions (Article XI) (Bernier, 1998). In terms of cultural services and the GATS, Canada made no commitments related to national treatment and market access (ibid.). With respect to the failed MAI, it is unlikely that Canada could have obtained an exemption, full or partial, because of American opposition (ibid.: 138). The government's overall approach to the culture/trade quandary as demonstrated by various free trade negotiations is traditionally a defensive one. With the decision on the NIICD, however, the federal government embraced a more proactive strategy to deal with the culture/trade quandary. DCH has become the clear lead on the NIICD file.

In the mid-1990s, funding cutbacks for culture, the need for adequate cultural statistics, technological changes such as the Internet, and Canada–US trade disputes over cultural policies were major issues in the cultural sector. The 1995 Quebec Referendum, two-tier healthcare, euthanasia, and many other issues in other policy sectors were also vying for government attention and a spot on the decision agenda. With all of these issues circulating in the problem stream in the mid-1990s, how did the culture/trade quandary become identified as a problem worthy of government attention? For Kingdon (2003), attention is drawn to issues through objective indicators, focusing events, and feedback. When an issue is recognized as a problem that requires serious attention, then it is high on the governmental agenda.

The culture/trade quandary, a high-priority problem under Prime Minister Brian Mulroney, plummeted in importance in the mid-1990s under Prime Minister Jean Chrétien. During the NAFTA negotiations, cultural groups such as the Canadian Conference for the Arts (CCA) and the Film and Television Council of Canada had lobbied the newly elected Liberals to abrogate the CUFTA retaliatory clause and seek a full exemption for culture (Crane, 1993; Harris, 1993). To their disappointment, Prime Minister Jean Chrétien broke his 1993 campaign promise to revisit the contradictory cultural exemption. Instead, Canadian negotiators extended the exemption and clause to the NAFTA and quickly turned their attention to excluding transborder water-diversion agreements from the North American trade pact (Crane, 1993).

Problems such as the culture/trade quandary fall from prominence on policy agendas, when governments consider them resolved and turn toward other issues considered to be more important (Kingdon, 2003: 103–4). When an issue is no longer deemed problematic, it simply becomes another competing issue for a place on policy agendas. For the Canadian government, the culture/trade quandary was perceived to be less pressing than water in the case of the NAFTA and the all-consuming 1995 Québec Referendum at home.

Despite the lack of government attention on the culture/trade quandary at this time, there were indications that the quandary was a problem that deserved more attention. People in and around government assess the nature of an issue through routine monitoring and studies of changes in budgets or number of trade disputes, etc., to determine whether that issue requires government attention (ibid.: 91). An increase in Canada–US trade conflicts in the mid-1990s indicated that the tension between Canada's trade obligations and cultural policies was mounting. Acheson and Maule (1995, 1996a, 1996b, and 1996c) published several papers addressing nine concurrent disputes including Country Music Television (CMT), Sports Illustrated Canada, American direct broadcasting satellite, Borders Books, French-language dubbing, public performing rights for performers and producers, Pay-per-view (Ppv) distribution systems, blank tape levy, and the V Chip (to rate and block certain programs). The authors (1996b) warned that the culture/trade quandary was a serious problem in need of government action and that the cultural exemption policy was perpetuating the problem.

According to Acheson and Maule, Canada incurred high costs each time that it dealt with like cases in a piecemeal fashion. In the Borders Books, Satellite, and CMT cases, American-owned companies were prohibited from Canadian book or television markets. Regulatory agencies determined which companies could have access to Canadian markets. Disputes erupted and were resolved, except in the *Sports Illustrated* case, through negotiations.

This ad hoc resolution process, in Acheson and Maule's view (ibid.: 44–5), lacked consistency and transparency, was costly, and smacked of protectionism. In pursuing cultural exemptions, Canada, argued Acheson and Maule (ibid.: 3) 'opted for resolving cultural disputes through [an] ill-defined political and bureaucratic process depending on vague precedents and procedures rather than a negotiated and relatively transparent [legal] process'. This perception of the cultural exemption policy differs from the equally negative view of exemption held by cultural nationalists[11] from the cultural sector. Cultural nationalists were worried that the CUFTA clause, which has never been invoked, deterred the Canadian government from resisting American domination of the Canadian cultural market (Truehart, 1994).[12] Acheson and Maule (1996a: 44–5), on the other hand, criticized the policy of exemption itself for attempting to insulate protectionist policies.

Problem recognition and definition, as Kingdon points out, are subjective. People in and around government interpret changes in indicators quite differently depending upon their experience, vocation, values, and expertise (2003: 114). DCH minister Michel Dupuy's handling of the CMT case shows that he did not seem to consider the culture/trade quandary as a widespread problem beyond the specifics of each case. Nor did he question the effectiveness of the cultural exemption policy to insulate Canadian cultural policies. In 1994, the Canadian Radio-Television and Telecommunications Commission (CRTC) replaced the American-owned CMT with the Canadian-owned New Country Network (NCN) on the premise that a Canadian company would play more Canadian country music. Owners of CMT petitioned the move and asked United States Trade Representative (USTR) Mickey Kantor to invoke NAFTA's retaliatory clause (Annex 2106) on culture. Before Kantor could retaliate against goods ranging from softwood lumber to maple syrup, a merger between CMT and NCN was finalized, leaving the controversial clause untested (Acheson and Maule, 1995: 3).

In retrospect, the CMT dispute significantly magnified the escalating strain between Canada's free trade obligations and its cultural policies. Dupuy, however, responded by announcing additional controversial cultural measures including a levy on blank tapes sold in Canada and an excise tax on *Sports Illustrated* magazine (Agence France-Presse, 1994). One explanation for Dupuy's actions is that the CMT dispute had ended, like many other Canada–US culture/trade cases, in a backroom deal. The outcome was simply not disastrous enough for Dupuy to see the culture/trade quandary as a problem requiring a priority position on the agenda. Although it drew more media attention, the CMT dispute ended in the same way that other cases had—through negotiated agreement. However, because of Kantor's threat to invoke NAFTA and test the cultural exemption clause, the CMT dispute stands out from other indicators as an 'early warning event'. An early warning event is an indicator that could have been an isolated event or could have led to the recognition of a widespread problem if it had been further investigated (Kingdon, 2003: 98). As an analogy, an early warning event would be bridge deterioration, an indicator of which would be a crack in the bridge, and a focusing event would be bridge collapse. It took a 'collapse' that forced Canada to relinquish its policies toward split-run magazines for the government to consider the quandary as a pressing problem.

Indicators often need a push in the form of a crisis, disaster, or powerful symbol to get people around and, especially, in government to pay attention to a problem. Focusing events are more powerful than indicators because they highlight a crisis situation (ibid.: 94–6). The focusing event in this case that eventually attracted widespread recognition of the culture/trade quandary as a problem and changed the governmental agenda was the unfavourable outcome of the *Sports Illustrated* case. When Time Warner began beaming an electronic copy of its split-run *Sports Illustrated Canada* to a printing press in Ontario in order to circumvent the 1965 import tariff on split-runs, Dupuy reacted by putting a tax on advertising in split-runs in 1995. In March 1996, the United States brought Canada before the WTO on charges that: (1) the 1995 excise tax on advertising and differential mail rates for foreign and domestic magazines violated GATT Article III (national treatment), and (2) an import tariff on split-run magazines and a postal subsidy program contravened GATT Article XI (quantitative restrictions). In January 1997 the WTO Panel found all measures, except the postal subsidy program, in violation of GATT rules. Despite Canada's appeal that GATT rules should not apply in this case because advertising is a service subject to the GATS

(Canada had no obligations for advertising under the GATS), the WTO Appellate Body (1997) upheld the panel's decisions that GATT rules do apply because the advertising is embedded in a product—the magazine. The Appellate Body (ibid.) also concluded that the tax and postal rates violated non-discrimination principles of like products because 'newsmagazines, like *TIME, TIME Canada* and *Maclean's*, are directly competitive or substitutable in spite of the "Canadian" content of *Maclean's*.'

When the WTO panel ruling leaked in January 1997, IT Can minister Art Eggleton, echoing Acheson and Maule's arguments, created controversy by claiming that Canada's cultural industries have never been protected under the NAFTA or any other agreement and do not require protection, but promotion (McCarthy, 1997). Eggleton saw the WTO ruling as an opportunity to push his definition of the problem and proposed solution. He did not, however, get the chance to force his problem-solution combination onto the decision agenda. In June 1997, the same month that the Appellate Body made its final ruling, Eggleton was replaced by Sergio Marchi in a cabinet shuffle. With Marchi's support, Copps began pushing for her own proposal to ban Canadian advertising from split-runs and introduced the proposal as Bill C-55 onto the decision agenda in 1998 (Marchi, 1998).

Bill C-55 addressed the tension between free trade and Canada's periodical policies, but feedback from two committees—the Subcommittee on International Trade, Trade Disputes and Investment of the Standing Committee on Foreign Affairs (SINT) (October 1997 to November 1997) and the Standing Committee on Canadian Heritage (CHER) (October 1997 to June 1999)—indicated that the problem was bigger than just the culture/trade quandary within the context of the magazine industry. According to Kingdon (2003: 31), feedback from the public helps to bring problems to government officials' attention or keeps their attention on certain problems. In the process, feedback also contributes—along with personal experience, values, and goals—to how government officials understand problems.

The message coming from participants in both the SINT and CHER committee hearings was that the NAFTA cultural exemption was problematic because the United States chose to take the *Sports Illustrated* case to the WTO rather than to NAFTA.[13] Cultural nationalists such as the Canadian Council and the CCA saw the move as one that revealed the flawed nature of the international trade regime in which trade obligations, especially those of the WTO, will always trump cultural policies and other FTAs. Those of the open markets persuasion such as the Fraser Institute looked inward, seeing fault, not with free trade, but rather with the government's reluctance to reform protectionist policies. Cultural nationalists had an advantage; their definition had more exposure because of the power of cultural groups and industries, the central position of DCH, and the dominant idea that culture is a public good.[14] Acheson and Maule (1999: 16) point out that in the CHER hearing on 26 November 1997, none of the members expressed an interest in hearing from experts whose views are that 'Canada really doesn't need to protect its culture . . . and that we shouldn't be setting up obstacles to counter the globalization of trade . . . we should not be attempting to thwart this trend through cultural exemptions.'

Despite different perceptions of the problem, both cultural nationalists and those advocating open markets recognized the culture/trade quandary as a problem requiring government action. It was the WTO ruling that incited this recognition, and in effect, solidified the quandary as a serious problem on the governmental agenda. To understand how the quandary appeared on the decision agenda we must look to the policy and politics streams.

In 1997 the culture/trade quandary was not yet on the decision agenda because political receptivity was weak and there was no viable option with which to attach the problem. According to Kingdon (2003: 202), governmental agendas can be set solely by changes in the problem or politics stream, or by a visible actor. In this case, a change in the problem stream set the governmental agenda. A change in the policy stream—the rise of a viable option and subsequent problem/solution coupling—led to the setting of the decision agenda.

The survival of an idea in the policy stream is like biological natural selection. If an idea is technically feasible, is congruent with the values of policy community members, and is politically palatable and financially possible, then it is more likely to rise above other proposals. There were four dominant proposals for addressing the culture/trade quandary before the idea for the NIICD emerged from the combinations of these and other proposals: (1) a NAFTA-like exemption with a retaliatory clause; (2) a full exemption without a retaliatory clause; (3) no exemption; and (4) specific exemptions (country reservation and/or exemption for certain industries/measures). When the WTO panel made its decision, Eggleton began criticizing the exemption policy and argued in favour of revamping Canada's cultural policies to ensure that culture is promoted abroad rather than protected at home.

Other policy proposals surfaced in the wake of the ruling as well. In April 1997 Daniel Schwanen (1997) of the C.D. Howe Institute argued that DCH should take advantage of the renewed focus on cultural policy, brought about by the WTO ruling to update its cultural policies and work with DFAIT to clarify in an international agreement which policies can be used to protect and promote culture. Schwanen's suggestions reflected Acheson and Maule's (1996b: 27) scepticism of cultural policies and recommendation that Canada prevent future disputes by discarding protectionist policies and pursuing an international accord 'establishing reasonable principles of fairness within which national cultural polices can be framed'.

The open view was also expressed by some of the participants of a conference hosted by the Centre for Trade Policy and Law (CTPL) on 9 October 1997 in Ottawa. The conference brought together academics, civil servants, lawyers, economists, and cultural industry representatives to discuss the future of Canadian cultural policy. Sheridan Scott (1998: 83), VP, Multimedia Law and Regulation at Bell Canada, called for a promotional rather than a protectionist approach to encourage the production and consumption of Canadian goods through incentives and marketing support. Law Professor Ivan Bernier (1998:

146) argued that exemption was an ineffective way to address the culture/trade quandary because the United States regards and always will regard 'cultural' goods and services as 'entertainment' products and services requiring no special treatment. Bernier recommended that Canada pursue an agreement within the global trade regime that would help states distinguish between industrial and cultural objectives of state intervention in the event that a culture/trade dispute erupts.

In the cultural nationalist camp, participants such as Victor Rabinovitch (1998: 43), assistant deputy minister for cultural development and heritage at DCH, advised that Canada consider 'marginally adjusting existing instruments and devising new programs based on those that already proved to be successful', but keep culture out of FTAs. While Rabinovitch preferred the status quo (exemption) abroad and an incrementalist approach at home, National director of the CCA Keith Kelly (1998: 191) reckoned Canada ought to look beyond the confines of international trade agreements. In a 2006 interview with the author, Kelly[15] explained his conviction that Canada needed a strategy other than, or in addition to, cultural exemption. After investigating international trade law and meeting with experts to fully understand the details of the WTO ruling and the hierarchy between trade agreements, Kelly presented his case for the coupling of the quandary and an international agreement on culture in several conferences, standing committees, papers, working groups, and meetings with various actors. Many in the cultural community, however, still 'harbored delusions that [Canada] could secure an effective cultural exemption', even from the WTO (ibid.).

In 1997 Kelly's CCA formed the Working Group on Cultural Policy for the 21st Century to help members of the cultural community better understand the constraints that trade agreements impose on cultural policies. According to Kelly, it took a 'long process of collective reflection with different parts of the cultural sector to bring them to an appreciation that the magazine outcome was wholly predicable given the structure of the GATT' (ibid.). He adds that during the process, 'there was a realization that the only way we could really solve [the culture/trade quandary] in a substantive way was to develop an instrument with rules that clearly served Canadian interests' because the Americans would never allow a cultural exemption from the WTO (ibid.). The CCA Working Group's suggestion in January 1998 for an international accord on culture demonstrates that the cultural community had been softened up to the idea of a multilateral agreement to address the culture/trade quandary (Canadian Conference of the Arts [CCA] Working Group, 1998). Kelly helped make this happen by bringing together representatives from the arts and cultural industries for discussion and much-needed consultations with trade specialists. At this initial stage in the policy-making process, Kelly was what Kingdon calls a policy entrepreneur.

Policy entrepreneurs are politically savvy and persistent individuals who invest time and resources to help couple solutions to problems, soften up others to their cause, and harness political forces to pull the three streams together (Kingdon, 2003: 179–80). Softening up or convincing others that your definition of the problem and your proposed solution are best is an essential part of the alternative specification process because 'an idea must both sweep a community and endure' if it is to emerge as the optimal alternative (ibid.: 130). In the policy stream, Kelly worked within the cultural sector to persuade groups to look beyond cultural exemption, while another policy entrepreneur from within government, Copps, worked to convince her counterparts abroad that proactive measures were needed to make cultural diversity thrive globally. Following the WTO ruling, Copps recalled in a 2006 interview with the author[16] that 'it became clear that if we were going to have any success in protecting culture by domestic instruments or protection outside of subsidy we would have to involve a larger consensus than simply Canada'. In 1997 Copps travelled to nine countries to discuss her concerns about the culture/trade quandary with other cultural ministers (DCH, 1998). The following year, she also attended various conferences on culture to push the quandary higher on the international agenda, and more importantly, promote her plans for a cultural ministerial meeting in Ottawa (Scoffield, 1998).

According to a DCH document, the Ottawa ministerial meeting was the first step toward Canada's launching of 'an international initiative similar to that on land mines, to promote the creation of a new instrument to support culture' (ibid.). The 1997 treaty to ban landmines was quickly adopted by 122 countries in 14 months, largely because it was created outside of formal international institutions, and brought civil society to the table (Van Rooy, 2001: 254). Foreign affairs minister Lloyd Axworthy was credited with directly involving civil society in foreign policy deliberations to build international momentum. In the same interview, Copps (2006) confirmed that DCH decided to follow Axworthy's model for meetings to ensure that foreign non-governmental organizations (NGOs) would participate in the discussion and then lobby their own governments to support a movement for the protection and promotion of culture through cultural policies. Kelly (2006), who had suggested that the CCA host the parallel meeting, credits Copps with 'the conviction that a pincer movement would be effective; she could work wonders with her political colleagues but the real push would come from the ground up'.

Copps's goal was to work with civil society to build a global alliance exclusively of cultural ministers (the United States was excluded because it did not have a cultural minister) (Copps, 2004: 160). The next step would be to work toward an international instrument to deal with culture and globalization (Geddes, 1998). On 30 June 1998, the 22 cultural ministers at the conference in Ottawa created the International Network on Cultural Policy (INCP), a network that would meet annually to discuss cultural policy and diversity. After the 1998 meeting, Copps told *Maclean's* magazine that she hoped 'the summit sowed the seeds for cultural institutions that will someday grow to parallel the powerful bodies, such as the World Trade Organization, that hold sway over global commerce' (ibid.). She did not say whether those institutions should be under the auspices of UNESCO. For Copps, however, UNESCO was always the preferred venue for an agreement because 'the WTO has a mandate for trading in goods and services and culture is not a good or service'.

A report presented to IT Can minister Marchi in February 1999 indicated that not everyone thought that an agreement outside of the WTO was the best option. The report by the Cultural Industries Sectoral Advisory Group on International Trade (SAGIT), an advisory committee on culture and trade, did not specify whether an agreement should be outside or within the WTO. It did, however, recommend that the Canadian government pursue a NIICD. The SAGIT report marks what Kingdon calls a tipping point in the policy stream because it incites discussion that indicates an emerging consensus for the idea for an international instrument on culture. The idea for an instrument was 'ideologically friendly' (both cultural nationalists and those of the open view were increasingly sceptical of the cultural exemption policy and sought another approach). The idea was also politically conceivable given the headway that Copps had made by building support abroad and the fact that the Liberals had made culture the third pillar of Canadian foreign policy in 1995. The sticking point, however, was whether an agreement housed outside of the WTO would be technically feasible and effective. The debate at this point shifted as those in the policy community asked whether the international instrument should stand alone or be housed within UNESCO (as Minister Copps envisioned) or be negotiated into the international trade regime. With the release of the SAGIT report cultural nationalists became associated with an agreement outside of the WTO and the open markets camp with an agreement under the auspices of the WTO. Maule (2001: 131), a member of the 1999 SAGIT, reasoned that the WTO was the logical organization to house the instrument because any other body with a dispute-settlement mechanism of its own would be weak compared to the established and powerful trade organization. On the other hand, cultural nationalists questioned whether the WTO could be trusted to appreciate the importance of cultural policies for Canadian culture if it considered *Time* and *Maclean's* to be the same in terms of editorial content (Grant and Wood, 2004: 395).

The debate about whether the agreement should be within or outside of the WTO demonstrates that there was a consensus in the policy stream that Canada ought to change its approach toward the culture/trade quandary, from one based on exemption to the pursuit of some kind of international instrument on culture. There was a problem, although defined differently by the closed and open views, and a clear alternative, a NIICD either within or outside of the WTO. To know how the problem-solution combination climbed the decision agenda, we must look to the politics stream.

The fact that the Canadian government committed itself to pursuing a NIICD is proof that the culture/trade quandary and the solution with which it was coupled became a priority on the decision agenda. In the politics stream, all forces— national mood, interest groups, and top officials—eventually pointed toward a NIICD.

National mood is important in the MSM because 'it has an impact on election results, on party fortunes, and on the receptivity of governmental decision making to interest group lobbying' (Kingdon, 2003: 148). With respect to culture, the national mood from 1997 to 1999 was sympathetic to the cultural nationalists' position. In fact, Baeker (2000: 346) argues that the national mood toward culture in Canada is constant because 'Canadians generally agree that the arts and culture make valuable contributions to their communities, but they are not exactly clear about what those contributions are, or why they are important, because arguments for the importance of the arts have happened almost entirely within the cultural community.' State-funded culture is much like public health care; Canadians become defensive when it appears to be under threat. The dominant perception is that Canadian culture distinguishes Canadians from Americans, and therefore, must be protected. Talk of the Americanization of Canadian culture tends to make Canadians uneasy. In 1998 when asked about the importance of Canadian ownership in the cultural industries, 42 per cent of Canadians said Canadian ownership was 'very important' and 41 per cent said it was 'somewhat important' (Foote, 1998).

Copps did not base her reading of the national mood on polls. Contrary to popular belief, government officials interpret the national mood through information from attentive publics such as interest group representatives, party activists, journalists, and experts (Kingdon, 2003: 149). Media coverage and opposition parties' cooperation were the heritage minister's thermometers for measuring fluctuations in the national mood. According to Copps (2004: 164–5), French-language media sources were generally more supportive of her efforts than the English media because as francophones 'they understood that in order to protect language you have to protect culture'. Unfavourable coverage in the English press was interpreted by Copps as merely the journalists' own 'industrial bosses' lingering concerns that cultural policies and the quest to guarantee the use of such policies would close off foreign markets to their own goods and services. English Canadians, Copps (2004: 164–5) believed, did understand that 'when you're living beside a giant superpower like the US, you have to fight every day for the right to hang on to your identity and culture'. Copps's interpretation of the national mood was that 'there is an appetite for a world market in Hollywood movies, but there is also an appetite to hear our own stories' (Geddes, 1998). Lucky for Copps, Chrétien also argued that Canadians 'want to know more about [themselves]' and publicly defended state-funded Canadian culture (Ferguson, 1995).

Like Copps and the prime minister, opposition parties understood the importance of Canadian cultural content and policies. Copps perceived the country's cultural profile to be characterized by 'virtual unanimity' or 'consensus amongst all members'; she moved to harness a favourable national mood to the government's approach to culture and cultural protection. Indeed, Copps recalled that 'the Alliance critic, Jim Abbott, was well versed in the area [culture] and a pleasure to work with, and Bloc critic Suzanne Tremblay was so supportive that eventually she was removed from the committee [on Bill C-55] because she was deemed by her party to be too uncritical' (Copps, 2004: 153; 2006). Politicians of all stripes accepted culture as an integral part of national identity, even though they disagreed about how to foster that identity.

IT Can minister Eggleton did not agree with the policy of cultural exemption and wanted to see changes to Canada's most protectionist policies. He believed that cultural exemptions would only exacerbate trade disputes and limit cultural export opportunities for Canada because free trade and investment is based upon reciprocity.[17] His position worried the cultural community. Kelly described Eggleton's outspokenness as 'unsettling for everyone because [it] raised the question of who was calling the shots on cultural policy' (Riley, 1997). Eggleton was claiming that the NAFTA exemption was a myth and culture should be on the table in trade negotiations; Copps was defending the exemption and pushing for exemptions from the WTO; and Chrétien did not seem to mind the conflict. Journalist Rosemary Speirs (1997) argued that Chrétien was to blame for the mixed messages coming from cabinet:

> Is this just typical Chrétien absenteeism? Cabinet sources say the Prime Minister concentrates all his attention on two issues—jobs and national unity—and lets his ministers run the rest. When they goof, Chrétien's sidekick Eddie Goldenberg runs around putting out fires. It's too late to avoid the impression of a government that's all over the map, with ministers free to freelance even on sensitive issues affecting Canadian identity.

Speirs (ibid.) predicted that Chrétien's absence would impact the 1997 federal election. The Liberals, however, formed another majority government that year. In a cabinet shuffle following the victory, Chrétien sent Eggleton to the Department of National Defence (DND) and put Sergio Marchi in charge of IT Can. After Eggleton's departure, tension between IT Can and DCH was more acute at the bureaucratic level than at the ministerial level.

While 'senior bureaucrats in the Department of International Trade made no secret of their contempt for [DCH's] approach to globalization', Marchi 'fought shoulder-to-shoulder' with Copps during the magazine wars (Copps, 2004: 162). The ministerial turnover from Eggleton to Marchi was helpful because it reduced barriers for Copps and calmed the cultural community's fears. According to Kingdon (2003: 154), turnover is important because 'new faces mean that new issues will be raised' and new positions taken. Marchi was, as one Globe and Mail journalist described him, 'a new breed of trade minister'; he believed that environmental, social, and human rights should be integral elements of any trade agreement (Eggertson, 1997b). The cultural sector and Copps were thus relieved when Marchi announced upon his appointment that he believed in cultural sovereignty and would 'work with Sheila' to make Washington understand what Ottawa wanted (Toronto Star, 1997). Despite his reservations about US threats to target steel, apparel, plastics, and lumber if Bill C-55 was passed in its original form, Marchi assured Canadians that he fully supported Copps in her quest to get Bill C-55 passed (Marchi, 1998). The bill, which was originally intended to prohibit Canadian advertising in split-runs, was amended in May 1999 after American protests prompted Chrétien to intervene and strike a deal with the Americans that would merely limit Canadian advertising in foreign magazines. The compromise on Bill C-55 was widely reported in the media as a failure for Copps, which likely further motivated her to get the idea for a NIICD to the top of the decision agenda.

The same month that Chrétien made a deal on Bill C-55, Marchi (1999) welcomed the SAGIT report as a basis for informed discussion on how to sustain and promote Canadian culture. He had to tread carefully, however, because IT Can and DCH officials were at odds about what a NIICD should look like. This jurisdictional tension is unsurprising since 'all participants have a stake in preserving current sources of funding and current jurisdictions' (Kingdon, 2003: 157). According to Copps, there was a feud, but 'International Trade was not the lead on the file and they just didn't have Cabinet support.' The friction between IT Can and DCH actually incited, not retarded, government action on the quandary and the NIICD. Seen through the MSM, IT Can and DCH's 'rush to beat each other to the punch', which in this context meant shaping the NIICD, made the culture/trade quandary a more pressing and promising issue than it might have been without the competition (Kingdon, 2003: 157). With the WTO negotiations and the next INCP meeting approaching, both departments were eager to determine Canada's new international culture/trade policy and their role.

In anticipation of the December WTO trade talks, a May 1999 discussion paper from DFAIT asked cultural industry interest groups to reflect upon the nature of the prospective NIICD by presenting their case before the Standing Committee on Foreign Affairs and International Trade (SCFAIT), which was tasked with examining Canada's objectives in the WTO negations (DFAIT, 1999g). The discussion paper did not ask whether or not a NIICD should become government policy, but rather asked what a NIICD would have to look like in order to serve the cultural industries' interests. The language and tone of the May discussion paper indicated that the government planned to make a decision on the NIICD after the release of the SCFAIT report. Meanwhile, the CHER, which had begun in 1997 after the WTO ruling, also turned its attention toward the possibility and nature of a NIICD. In June 1999 both the CHER and SCFAIT released reports agreeing that the government should adopt the SAGIT's recommendation for a NIICD. The difference is that the former report did not specify where the agreement should be housed, while the latter suggested that 'if feasible [it should be] within the WTO framework' (SCFAIT, 1999). While one report reflected DCH's position on the NIICD, the other stemmed from IT Can's preference for a WTO instrument.

With the CHER and SCFAIT paying attention to the NIICD and the government poised to make a decision, interest groups hopped onto the bandwagon for a NIICD to try to influence the characteristics of the agreement. The Council of Canadians' Maude Barlow, who had always been a devotee of exemption, agreed that an international agreement on cultural protection would be worthwhile, as long as it had 'teeth' (Scoffield, 1999). Quebec's minister of culture Agnès Maltais underscored that international agreements must make special allowance for cultural imperatives. In its response to the CHER report, the New Democratic Party (NDP) endorsed the idea of some kind of international agreement on culture. The separatist Bloc Québécois party demanded that the federal government decide whether Canada would seek exemptions from the WTO or pursue a NIICD as the SAGIT proposed. These political parties and cultural nationalists preferred an agreement outside of the WTO that would ensure Canada's cultural sovereignty and protect its current cultural policy apparatus. The Reform Party, however, continued to encourage the development of a 'cultural free market' in its response to the CHER report; it did not make reference to the NIICD.

Actors of the open view were mostly think-tank representatives and academics, who, according to the MSM, have more of an influence on policy formulation than on agenda setting and the politics stream in general. These experts (Jeffrey Schott of the Institute for International Economics, Acheson and Maule, etc.) were proponents of a WTO agreement. The SCFAIT recommendation reflected this view. Debate about whether or not the NIICD should be a WTO agreement continued after the release of the CHER and SCFAIT reports, but Copps chose to act; she recognized and capitalized on strong political receptivity toward the idea for a NIICD. Indeed, Copps appears to have brought the three streams together to push the culture/trade quandary and the idea for a NIICD into a position of enactment on the decision agenda when the SCFAIT and CHER reports opened a window in the politics stream. There were other entrepreneurs. Pierre Pettigrew, who became IT Can minister in August 1999, seemed particularly passionate about the culture portfolio, vowed to be 'very active', and was quoted several times in newspapers following the decision for a NIICD (Scoffield, 1999). Robert Pilon of the Association québécoise de l'industrie du disque created the Coalition for Cultural Diversity (CCD), an umbrella organization for Canadian associations that represented creators, artists, independent producers, broadcasters, distributors, and publishers in publishing, film, television, music, performing, and visual arts. The CCD and the International Network on Cultural Diversity (INCD), a network of artists and cultural groups also established in 1999 in Canada, were fervent advocates for a NIICD. It was Copps, however, who brought the streams together by taking advantage of political momentum in the politics stream.

As the successful entrepreneur in this case, Copps had expertise and experience, an authoritative decision-making position, and, as heritage minister, direct access to cabinet which dictates Canadian foreign policy. Copps also had significant political connections with Axworthy, Chrétien, and new allies in Quebec, such as cultural minister Agnès Maltais and separatist supporter Pierre Curzi, president of l'Union des artistes, a powerful Québécois cultural union. In civil society circles, budding cultural coalitions such as the CCD and the INCD backed Copps and, in return, received funding from DCH. Similarly, Axworthy and Chrétien benefited from Canada's position as a leader on the international stage in cultural matters without having to preoccupy themselves with the cultural portfolio. Québec's Culture and Communications minister was rewarded with invitations to all future INCP and UNESCO meetings after having been excluded from the first international conference of the cultural ministers in June 1998. In addition to smart bargaining, Copps was persistent; she was involved in every meeting at home and abroad to make sure that culture was on the agenda. When the SCFAIT and CHER reports finally opened a policy window, Copps was lying in wait with 'her gun loaded' (Kingdon, 2003: 83). She sensed and capitalized upon political ripeness to ensure that the culture/trade quandary, and the NIICD to which it was attached, ascended to the decision agenda. Copps's entrepreneurship led to the government's decision in November 1999 to pursue a NIICD that would 'recognize the special role of cultural goods and services and the right of governments to preserve and promote cultural diversity' while still respecting international trade law (DFAIT, 1999c).

The process behind the decision to pursue a NIICD occurred under specific conditions. The 1997 WTO ruling against Canada focused government attention on the tension between culture and trade and the precariousness of the policy of exemption. The crisis brought exposure to ideas circulating in the policy stream and led to the formation of new alternatives for addressing the culture/trade quandary. The idea for a NIICD emerged from the policy community as the preferred alternative in 1999. Copps waited for a window of opportunity to push the problem-solution match onto Cabinet's agenda. In the end, it was the appearance of the CHER and SCFAIT recommendations that opened the window. There were many entrepreneurs pushing for a NIICD, but it was Copps who capitalized on political forces to bring the streams together. When the streams aligned, the culture/trade quandary and the idea for an international instrument on culture became a priority on the decision agenda. After 1999 Canada was committed to this problem-solution combination but debate persisted both domestically and internationally about whether the instrument should be under the auspices of the WTO. Following several INCP meetings and the circulation of various convention drafts, 148 UNESCO members finally adopted the UNESCO Convention for the Protection and Promotion of the Diversity of Cultural Expression in October 2005.

Negotiating the Convention on Anti-personnel Landmines

JOHN CADHAM

In the 2000 *Tanner Lecture on Human Values*, Michael Ignatieff, commenting on the growing influence of non-governmental actors in the international human rights debate, observed: 'The advocacy revolution has broken the state's monopoly on the conduct of international affairs, enfranchising what has become known as the global civil society' (Ignatieff, 2000: 291). This same development has been documented by other observers who share the view that NGOs and similar civil society actors have emerged as prominent, and most argue permanent, actors in the international policy arena.[1] Indeed, in their examination of a range of NGO and Middle Power cooperation case studies, Rutherford and colleagues (2003) conclude that 'NGO coalitions are becoming a significant force in world politics on pressing security issues that great powers and familiar international organizations have not been able to address effectively' (Matthew, 2003: 208). Hampson and Reid, in particular, point to the significance of this evolution in multilateral negotiations and argue that it is the growth of coalitions of civil society and middle powers that have the capacity to fundamentally alter the nature of multilateral diplomacy (Hampson and Reid, 2003: 33–7). The conclusion drawn is that the potential strength and breadth of these coalitions can indeed represent an opportunity for non-dominant actors in the multilateral stage, both state and civil society, to exercise leadership in the framing of future international agreements—most especially those in the human security arena.

This evolution has led to considerable debate in the literature about the nature and impact of such coalitions on the form and process of multilateral negotiations prompting suggestions of the need for a reassessment of how 'new multilateralism' or 'democratization' of the foreign policy process affects traditional analytical approaches to multilateral negotiations.[2] Case studies examining different analytic approaches on this topic, generally focusing on either the Ottawa Process leading to the 1997 Ottawa Anti-personnel Landmines Convention or the 1998 Rome Treaty establishing the International Criminal Court (or both), have posited a variety of different approaches.

For an analysis of another international negotiation, Brian Tomlin (2007) has used a multiple streams model based on John Kingdon's *Agendas, Alternatives and Public Policies* as an analytical framework for examining the creation of the Inter-American Democratic Charter. This represents something of an innovative application of the multiple streams model, which is more commonly used to understand the policy formulation and decision-making process within a more purely state-centric context. However, as Tomlin demonstrates, there are many characteristics of the multiple streams model that invite its application to the multilateral setting. The overriding significance of complexity, fluidity, and unpredictability, the relative independence of activities in the problem, policy, and politics streams, the notion that 'the participants and processes can act as an impetus or as a constraint' (Kingdon, 1995: 197), the idea of multiple causation and the focus on questions of why participants deal with certain problems instead of how decisions are made—all of these characteristics are strongly congruent with the multilateral negotiating environment. Yet there is one aspect of the multiple streams model that is, arguably, even more compelling.

In his 2003 examination of the modes of interaction of cross-border institutions, Joachim Blatter asserts that 'we are indeed witnessing a historic transformation of patterns of interaction in which the boundaries between the public and the private spheres, as well as among nation-states, are being rapidly blurred' (2003: 517–20). He goes on to suggest that four important changes are driving this shift:

1. The growing importance of information and communications 'as mechanisms of governance, as well as in the competitive struggle for political power';
2. The growing importance of civil society actors and collaborative relationships—'the paradigmatic shift from government to governance';
3. The importance, especially in multicultural societies, of 'identity politics' based on ethnicity and ethnic group loyalties; and
4. 'The processes of internationalization/globalization and processes of decentralization/devolution undermine the "natural" political ties of citizens to the nation-state and lead to the creation of many supranational, transnational, and subnational political communities and institutions.'

Blatter (2003: 520) concludes that the 'unquestioned monopoly of the nation-state is being challenged as the basis for political community-building and institutional control is being challenged and supplanted by a multiplicity and variety of political communities and institutions.' This is clearly echoed by Richard Matthew who observes:

> Evidence suggests that the end of the Cold War boosted the number and also activities of NGOs, and that the willingness of like-minded middle powers to use the expertise and credibility of NGOs has generally increased. But only in a couple of cases has the cooperation clearly reached the original goals of the boosters. In others, it seems that there is still a long way ahead (2003: 216).

These assessments are entirely consistent with Dolan and Hunt who make the same case in the introduction to their examination of the negotiations of the Ottawa Process. In setting the stage for their review, they emphasize that 'the seductive allure of conceiving the process as heralding new multilateral forms lies, in part, on the middle power/civil society coalition, a partnership seemingly more inclusive, participatory and egalitarian.' However, they go on to warn of ambiguous aspects in the process reflecting the '"schizophrenic" nature of multilateralism in the contemporary era' (Dolan and Hunt, 1998: 396–7).

This leads to the most compelling aspect of the application of the multiple streams model, as conceived by Kingdon, to the analysis of this new multilateralism—its inclusiveness. The Kingdon universe recognizes that no one class of participants has a monopoly on ideas, issues, or agendas, that policy entrepreneurs can conceivably come from anywhere and that civil society, along with any other participant, can play a significant role in all streams. Indeed, if we consider that Kingdon originally conceived his model for application to the complexities of the US political system where the checks and balances of their federal system, referred to by Kingdon as 'general fragmentation', serve to diffuse power and authority and where the influence of actors outside the formal organizations of government is profound, we can readily appreciate the parallels to the new multilateral environment.

This chapter attempts to replicate Tomlin's multilateral application of Kingdon's multiple streams model to see how it can be used as a framework to understand the negotiations that led to the conclusion of the international treaty to ban landmines. We examine this multilateral process, one with significant NGO/civil society and middle-power involvement, to see if the model can help to make sense of the ambiguities highlighted by Dolan and Hunt. We pick up from the historic appeal by Canada's foreign minister Lloyd Axworthy at the conclusion of the International Strategy Conference in Ottawa in October 1996, in which he challenged all governments to return to Ottawa before the end of the following year to sign a treaty banning anti-personnel mines, thereby kicking off what became known as the Ottawa Process. For the purposes of this analysis, the studies by Dolan and Hunt (1998) and Hampson and Reid (2003) will be used as the predominant sources of material for the details of the negotiation. The multiple streams model will be that elaborated by Kingdon and used by Tomlin for his analysis of the Inter-American Democratic Charter.

There are several critical aspects to the events leading up to Axworthy's challenge that are important to consider as initial conditions to our analysis. At a macrolevel, it could be argued that, from a multiple streams perspective, the end of the Cold War in the early 1990s was the focusing event—albeit a rather gradual one—that created the window giving rise to the dramatic realignment of policy agendas and priorities. The result was the introduction of the human security agenda. This, in turn, created much fertile ground for the subsequent dramatic rise in civil society as policy entrepreneurs at the multilateral level. Then, when the First Review Conference of the 1980 UN *Convention on Certain Conventional Weapons* (CCW), held in Vienna in September/October 1995, failed to reach any consensus on effective action to combat the proliferation of anti-personnel land-mines, it led to the mobilization of influential civil society actors, such as the International Committee of the Red Cross (ICRC) and the International Campaign to Ban Landmines (ICBL), who, together with NGOs representing a variety of other rights groups and interests, called for an immediate, outright ban. This wasn't entirely a new idea, the ICRC having originally called for a land-mine ban in the 1970s. However, with a number of states now on board, a pro-ban coalition began 'that had a "rolling snowball effect" of picking up additional supporters over the following months' (Dolan and Hunt, 1998: 401). This 'core-group' momentum was carried forward into the next meetings in Geneva in January and May 1996 that resulted in the so-called CCW *Revised Protocol II.* This Protocol, though it contained certain welcome changes, fell short of an outright prohibition or ban on landmines and was consequently judged a disappoint-ment by the growing core-group coalition that, by this time, included Canada.

In a remarkable about-face, Canada had abandoned its traditional pro-mine policy and become an active pro-ban coalition member.[3] Seeing an opportunity to exercise international leadership, the Canadian delegation announced in Geneva that Canada would host an 'International Strategy Conference: Towards a Global Ban on Anti-Personnel Mines' for pro-ban states in October. This meet-ing subsequently produced the Ottawa Declaration and the Chairman's Agenda for Mine Action and ended with Minister Axworthy's famous challenge—all of which would lay the groundwork for the Ottawa Process.

There are several important aspects to this from a multiple streams perspec-tive. First, the joining of the civil society groups into one policy direction was a significant indicator that the nature of the problem was changing fundamen-tally, becoming more compelling with a nascent sense of urgency. Disappoint-ment caused by the failure of 1995 Vienna meeting prompted important developments in the policy and politics streams. In the politics stream, it fos-tered the initial formation of the pro-ban coalition and the beginning of an aggressive period of coalition building. In the policy stream, the now-joined civil society groups provided important information and feedback to policy makers, and this coalition became fertile ground for the elaboration of ban pol-icy alternatives outside the constraints of the CCW. The subsequent failure of the 1996 CCW meetings to come up with acceptable ban language within the revised protocol was an important tipping point that subsequently created a window of opportunity for the coalition to take the process outside the CCW, leading to the Ottawa Strategy Conference. This marks the start of the process of softening up that would be critical to the success of the Ottawa Process.

Significantly, there is no clear, single source for the ideas and initiative that would become the Ottawa Process. Though the actions of Axworthy, together with key members of his ministry and the NGOs, had particular prominence as entrepreneurs in this phase,[4] it is quite clear that it was a combination of factors across the landmines community that was ultimately responsible for the genesis of the idea for a parallel process. It was the joint effects of several actors coming together under favourable conditions, far more than the impassioned call of one foreign minister, that breathed primordial life into the Ottawa Process.

CD Process / Ottawa process.

There is no question that Minister Axworthy's *beau risque* at the close of the October strategy session briefly threw the windows of opportunity wide open and let loose a virtual flood of activity in the streams of multilateral landmine negotiations. The ICRC had already started convening regional meetings bringing together NGOs, government, and military officials to discuss landmines issues (Hampson and Reid, 2003: 17), and the last quarter of 1996 saw significant activity in both the policy and the political streams. In the policy stream, the Austrians responded quickly to the Axworthy challenge by completing and releasing, as they had been asked, a draft treaty only weeks after the Ottawa strategy session. From the beginning, Austria was playing a prominent entrepreneurial role as keeper of the pen, drafting and re-drafting the treaty as it moved through the process and by organizing and hosting the initial Expert Meeting in February. Indeed, Austria would later be singled out as the 'father of the treaty text' by the ICBL at the close of the Ottawa Conference. Setting, as it did, an important baseline 'single negotiating text' from which the policy discussions and negotiations would begin, it is interesting to note that, true to our model's expectations, this was an evolutionary document combining and refining past discussions 'clearly inspired by the negotiations in the First Review Conference of the CCW and by disarmament law' (Maslen and Herby, 1998: 3) together with a draft treaty originally prepared by the ICBL. There was change, but it largely 'involved the recombination of already-familiar elements' (Kingdon, 1995: 201).[5]

In keeping with the Mine Action Agenda produced by the Ottawa Strategy Conference, the UN General Assembly passed Resolution 51/45S on the 10th of December, which recognized the Ottawa Conference and called on all states to vigorously pursue a complete ban on anti-personnel mines and to conclude a treaty as soon as possible. This motion had originally been drafted for the UN by Canada, but, important from the point of view of symbolism to the problem stream, was subsequently introduced into the Assembly by the US ambassador to the UN, Madeleine Albright.[6] Passage of 51/45S kicked off a flurry of activity in the politics stream as the core-group and the 'non-cores' squared off to haggle over whether to pursue the ban sought by the resolution under the umbrella of the UN Conference on Disarmament (CD) or in the more dynamic, 'free-market' policy forum represented by the Ottawa Process. As Dolan and Hunt describe it:

> The rupture over the landmines issue involved a complex arrangement of states—some who feared that the CD would derail the Ottawa Process some who used the CD to deflect pressure to sign the Ottawa Convention, and yet others who wanted nuclear disarmament to be the top priority for the CD (1998: 405).

Problem

Not surprisingly, prominent in the group pushing for the CD route were all of the permanent members of the Security Council—the P5 'Great Powers'—China, the US, the UK, Russia, and France, who doubtless felt their interests would best be served in the traditional negotiating space that the CD represented. They were joined by Germany, Australia, and a host of other countries in outright opposition to a ban, including India, Pakistan, Iran, South Korea, Libya, Sri Lanka, and others.

A small digression is in order. There appears to be a compelling application of Kingdon to help differentiate between the CD as a negotiating forum and the

Ottawa Process. Kingdon tells us that 'in the political stream, participants build consensus by bargaining—trading provisions for support, adding elected officials to coalitions by giving them concessions that they demand, or compromising from ideal positions that will gain wider acceptance' (Kingdon, 1995: 199). This seems to be an apt description of the CD process, a 'traditional' UN negotiating platform, where the requirement for consensus decision making drives hard bargaining and tradeoffs if an agreement is to be achieved. The Ottawa Process, on the other hand, with the conscious involvement of civil society NGOs, was a considerably more open, public forum seeking to use moral suasion as opposed to bargaining to win support. This is seemingly more akin to Kingdon's description of the policy stream where 'when participants recognize problems or settle on certain proposals . . . , they do so largely by persuasion. They marshal indicators and argue that certain conditions ought to be defined as problems, or they argue that their proposals meet such logical tests as technical feasibility or value acceptability' (Kingdon, 1995: 199). The potential implication of this distinction is interesting. The CD process was a comprehensive but lowest-common-denominator negotiation, while the Ottawa Process, with rules that limited the substance of the debate to those who had already essentially agreed with the outcome,[7] was, in effect, preaching to the converted while trying to persuade spoilers to repent. The former negotiating forum gave natural advantage to the *political* influence of the major powers, while the latter community of the like-minded gave freer reign to the *policy* innovators intent on building a growing coalition of pro-ban adherents. As will be discussed later in this chapter, this tension—underpinning whether the coalition would hold—would become the dominant issue in the politics stream of the Ottawa Process.[8]

The first two meetings of the Ottawa Process, the so-called Expert Meetings, were held in Vienna in February 1997 and in Bonn that April. These meetings were designed to focus primarily on technical issues, verification being the key theme at the Vienna meeting and compliance at Bonn. From the perspective of our analysis, however, these early meetings served as focusing events, drawing participants into the 'soup bowl' mix of problem, policy, and political streams. In the problem stream, the Expert Meetings provided an important venue for feedback, affording an early opportunity to gauge changes in attitudes and reactions since the Axworthy challenge especially with regard to progress and conditions or problems evolving in the CD. As a parallel process to the CD, these meetings served something of a foil, prompting comparison between the two forums and thereby providing important guidance in the policy stream. Also in the policy stream, analysis and consideration of the draft treaty prepared by Austria was underway—Kingdon's communities of specialists working on proposals, alternatives, and solutions comes to mind. In the political stream, the civil society members were actively developing regional initiatives to build awareness and political will. Significantly, in the political stream, the coalition was holding and the size of the participant base was growing—from 75 governments participating in the Ottawa Strategy Conference to 111 in Vienna, to 120 in Bonn. However, at this point, though momentum was clearly building, there was at best only a partial coupling of the streams. The problem—as defined in the UN resolution—was decided, the political mood was favourable, but there was still significant disagreement on the policy aspects of how to proceed— whether in the CD exclusively, in the Ottawa Process, in both, or as some advocated, in neither.

By the middle of 1997, leading up to the Brussels Conference, it was becoming apparent that the CD was deadlocked. The landmines issue had not even made it onto the year's agenda and several countries, Mexico in particular, were determined to see that it did not. General recognition of this deadlock came at an opportune time. Following the UN Resolution, the new secretary-general, Kofi Annan, following the lead of his predecessor, Boutros Boutros-Ghali, had been speaking out strongly in favour of the Ottawa Process. The coalition of states supporting the Ottawa Process had continued to grow and, throughout the year, the regional initiatives to promote public and governmental awareness of the landmines issue had been proceeding in accordance with key elements of the Mine Action Agenda (Dolan and Hunt, 1998: 407). 'A series of regional conferences organized by the ICRC, states, and the ICBL were held around the globe and were essential to building international support for a treaty' (Hampson and Reid, 2003: 19). This concerted pressure from organized groups further tilled the already fertile ground. With the CD stalled, a tipping point was reached, and a window opened as states, the landmines problem now squarely in their decision sights, grasped the alternative solution afforded by the Ottawa Process.

This move away from the CD to the Ottawa Process, especially in the lead up to the Brussels Conference in June, marks a critically important jurisdictional change representing a fundamental shift in authority away from what Dolan and Hunt describe as 'minilateralists' and toward the 'middle powers' and their 'cosmopolitan' coalition partners. As discussed earlier in this chapter, the Ottawa Process represented a different approach with different rules. The 'self-selection' criteria for participation in the Brussels Conference made full participation contingent on agreeing to sign the final declaration that had been circulated in advance, effectively preventing states in opposition to the proposed ban from participating and sabotaging the conference. This arrangement meant that those states supporting a ban would ultimately be able to meet and agree to the terms of a convention without the risk of being vetoed. This arrangement was further enhanced by the voting rules in the Ottawa Process that relied on a two-thirds majority as opposed to the consensus voting in the CD. This jurisdictional shift was the key element in creating the enabling environment that allowed the process to move forward. Indeed, true to Kingdon, the Brussels conference was invigorated by the fresh air of a wide-open policy window because the deadlock in the CD helped to bring the problem, policy, and political streams together. A viable policy alternative was available in answer to a pressing problem under conducive political circumstances with the core-group entrepreneurs primed, ready, and waiting. Of the 75 states that had attended the Ottawa Strategy Conference in October, 50 had signed the final declaration. Just eight months later, 97 states, plus 10 more in the coming weeks, signed the Brussels Declaration, affirming their commitment to negotiate and sign a ban treaty by December. The bandwagon was rolling.

The lead-up to the Oslo Diplomatic Conference in September saw several key developments. Government turnover, always a potent agent of change in the political stream, brought France and the UK into the pro-ban movement. Although the pro-ban coalition appeared to have enough momentum to carry through without them, the addition of the two G7 countries strengthened the coalition immeasurably—'the negotiations no longer looked like David versus Goliath' (Dolan and Hunt, 1998: 408). Oslo also benefited from the emergence of what started as a powerful symbol in the problem stream. Earlier in the year the iconic Diana, the Princess of Wales, had made visits to mine-affected areas in Angola and later to Bosnia and had added her voice to the calls for a ban. This powerful symbol was transformed into a significant external focusing event when, on August 31, her tragic death brought massive and evocative media attention to her activities and to the landmines issue in particular. Coming as it did just weeks before Oslo, this sad event added an important impetus in the political stream. Worldwide awareness was raised, resulting in a discernable shift in the international public mood and calls for a landmine treaty as a memorial to a widely admired public figure.[9]

Certainly, however, the most significant development in the politics stream as Oslo approached was the decision, late in the day, of the US to participate. This was, at once, both a tremendous accomplishment (due, at least in some part, to Canada's entrepreneurial lobbying efforts throughout the summer) and a significant risk. As Dolan and Hunt point out:

> Some ban supporters had very mixed reaction to the last-minute American flip-flop. Quite distinct from Axworthy's comments that the American decision was 'a positive step that further legitimizes the process and makes this into a very significant event,' Steve Goose, who as chair of the US Campaign to Ban Land-mines had laboured to get the US onside, decided that the serious caveats attached to US participation turned wine into vinegar, branding the approach a 'bad-faith position'. Or, as expressed by Cecelia Tuttle, co-ordinator of Mines Action Canada, 'It would be nice to have the US in, but do you kiss every frog, hoping it'll turn into a prince?' (1998: 409).

Also at Oslo, what began as a symbolic decision came to have a crucial impact on entrepreneurship during the proceedings. The election of South Africa's Jacob Selebi as conference president was seen as a simple representation of North/South unity, but it also proved an extremely astute choice because Selebi is acknowledged to have masterfully managed the process of dealing with the divisive American proposals (Dolan and Hunt, 1998: 410–13; Maslen and Herby, 1998). The handling of the negotiations surrounding the proposed American amendments to the Austrian draft treaty has been well covered elsewhere (Dolan and Hunt, 1978: 408–15; Wareham, 1998: 230–4). In brief, the US proposed changes to the draft treaty that would effectively exclude 'smart' mines; US and South Korean landmines on the Korean peninsula; allow states to withdraw from the treaty on short notice in the event of armed conflict; and delay implementation for a period of nine years after the treaty entered into force (Dolan and Hunt, 1998: 410–11). What is significant for our purposes is the fact that Canada drew a line in the sand against 'any open-ended exception' to the proposed treaty;[10] the Process was able to manage the Americans' outright rejection, preserve the coalition, and conclude with an overwhelming momentum that would lead to the treaty signing in Ottawa just three months later.

To explain this, we can turn to Kingdon. If the multiple streams model holds, the US had little, if any, chance of having its proposed changes accepted. The US action in advancing its proposals defied all of the conditions that Kingdon tells us are necessary for a policy to be adopted successfully. There was only the most limited sympathy for the American description of their problem within the conference community. Despite the entrepreneurial efforts of Canada and Germany to find a compromise, the US demonstrated virtually no willingness to make substantive concessions. Their assertive and threatening attitude and 'reject one, reject all' approach to presenting policy alternatives was contrary to Kingdon's understanding of the policy stream in which building support happens through persuasion and diffusion rather than through power and pressure (Kingdon, 1995: Ch. 6). In effect, the US bargaining was an attempt to politicize the process, to break the coalition, and to move Oslo away from a policy refinement exercise preparing the final treaty text (from the third draft prepared by the Austrians) back into the political stream where they could, conceivably, exercise more influence. However, US efforts to create a fertile environment for their proposals fell on deaf ears when up against massive pressure from the civil society groups and, more significantly, the common values that the ban states had come to share. This value issue is important because, as Kingdon tells us, it is a key element in the identification and the common perception of a problem.

With the close of Oslo, despite the menace posed by the late American intervention, the window stayed firmly open. The bandwagon had succeeded in disarming the opposition, and the balance was tipped squarely in favour of the Ottawa Convention. The final draft of the treaty was ready. In December, 122 states signed the *Convention on the Prohibition of the Use, Stockpiling, Production, and Transfer of Anti-Personnel Landmines and on their Destruction*. At the time of writing, this number had grown to 152.

From the moment Canada announced its intention to hold the Strategy Conference in Ottawa, certain of its officials assumed prominent roles as policy entrepreneurs in the Ottawa Process. Throughout the process, Canada worked to expand the coalition by lobbying other states to join the process. Its involvement, most especially through the summer of 1997, in attempting to convince the US to modify its position and wholeheartedly embrace the process was especially active. Indeed, when 'Canada found itself coming under strong pressure from NGOs not to allow the treaty to be watered down by accepting US demands' (Hampson and Reid, 2003: 21) at the Oslo Conference, this implied that Canada exercised some control over the fate of the US proposals. Notwithstanding the difficulties for Canada in navigating the gulf between the interests of its closest neighbour and the expectations of civil society, censure from the ICBL was a compelling tacit acknowledgement of the prominence of Canada's entrepreneurial role. However, it is equally clear that Canada was not working alone. Several other states played lesser, but nonetheless key, entrepreneurial roles: Austria, as already mentioned, Belgium, Germany, South Africa, Norway and Switzerland all played a part. Most notable, though, were the NGOs—including those who were Canada's critics in Oslo—who were essential to the success of the process.

The two key NGOs in the Ottawa Process, the ICRC and the ICBL played different roles. The ICRC was the grandfather of the landmines issue having been the original voice calling for a ban as far back as the early 1970s. The ICRC, as a 'quasi-governmental' organization, enjoys great status and has tremendous depth of expertise and capacity to influence. It was due to this stature that the ICRC was recognized as a full participant in the negotiations at Oslo. On the other hand, the ICBL, which was founded in 1992 by a group of 6 (now over 30) NGOs active on the landmines issue, enjoyed considerably more 'freedom of movement' and was thus in a position to lobby and demonstrate more aggressively than its senior civil society partner.

From the perspective of a multiple streams analysis, Kingdon tells us that entrepreneurs often struggle for years to get their ideas onto the policy agenda and this is certainly true for the ICRC who laboured long and hard on the landmines issue. Perhaps more importantly, though, we recognize that entrepreneurs act in all streams and are more effective the broader the scope of their activities and the greater the depth of their expertise. Kingdon's description fits the *core-group super-coalition* in the Ottawa Process perfectly:

> The appearance of entrepreneurs when windows are open, as well as their more enduring activities of trying to push their problems and proposals into prominence, are central to our story. They bring several key resources into the fray: their claim to a hearing, their political connections and negotiating skills, and their sheer persistence (Kingdon, 1995: 205).

Kingdon also tells us that when the bandwagon effect takes hold, the problems, policy, and political streams converge, and entrepreneurs, with answers in hand, are ready to take advantage, so that events will begin to move very rapidly. This is most certainly the case with the Ottawa Process. Working on a global scale at multiple levels, the coalition of entrepreneurs was able to keep the soup cooking, continually recombining ideas and alternatives in response to their evolving constituency, repeatedly lobbying decision makers and the uncommitted to keep the problem squarely on their agendas, working tirelessly to raise public awareness worldwide, and seizing the initiative when windows presented themselves. A schedule and an outcome that most commentators (and more than a few core participants) pronounced hopelessly optimistic seems, after the fact, to have been an almost foregone conclusion. Yet, were it not for the timely windows of opportunity—most especially in the lead up to the Brussels Conference, coupled with intervention from entrepreneurs at key points throughout the year, the process would most certainly have stalled, perhaps irretrievably.

The multiple streams model is, fundamentally, a non-deterministic analytical framework—it informs but does not answer; it enlightens but does not prescribe. As applied at the multilateral level, it does not build a new storey on an established foundation of tightly structured Kingdon houses representing each of the participant groups; instead, it adds another layer of much greater complexity to an already complex problem. Perhaps the greatest contribution that the multiple streams framework offers to our understanding of the Ottawa Process is its potential for removing some of the ambiguity raised by Dolan and Hunt and cited at the beginning of this chapter. In their conclusion, they point to the inherent difficulties in trying to determine the extent to which the Ottawa Process is truly representative of a new multilateral approach to negotiations:

> [S]tate officials tended to emphasize the uniqueness of the process and the inherent dangers in applying the model in a wider context. NGOs seem to be less circumspect in this regard, highlighting the potential for wider applicability to issues such as child labour (1998: 417).

The very fact that the Ottawa Process seems to lend itself to a multiple streams analysis would certainly be consistent with an argument that the process does indeed represent a departure from traditional 'top-down' negotiations. Perhaps Blatter's (2003) characterization of the transition from government to governance can help if we recast it as roughly analogous to an existential paradigm shift from the world of Westphalia to the world of Multiple Streams. The multiple streams model is, after all, fundamentally a liberal-democratic construct relying on the independence of the individual streams, the freedom and creativity of the entrepreneurs, control that is distributed rather than centralized, and an inherently egalitarian, Darwinian process of consensus building—or what Tomlin refers to as 'public choice models of policy evolution' (2007: 2). In top-down, authoritarian settings, these conditions simply do not pertain. So, if we agree on the applicability of the model, it does seem to indicate a certain *de facto* 'progress', an interesting consequence of which is the seeming limitations this places on the previously unchallenged authority of major powers. As Hampson and Reid argue:

> [T]here appear to be real limits to great power minilateralism in this new diplomacy. In both the landmines and ICC negotiations, the United States was an ambivalent negotiating partner. Although the United States was initially a champion of both treaties, as negotiations advanced and agendas developed, internal divisions within the US government grew, making it increasingly difficult for the US to support either of these ventures. Even so, the United States (and other great powers like Russia and China) were unable to control or block the negotiation process, suggesting that there are observable limits to the exercise of hegemonic or minilateral power and influence (2003: 12).

More fundamentally, though, we must always remember that Kingdon teaches us that variability and complexity in the process make prescriptive generalizations extremely problematic and this is most especially true at the multilateral level. The Ottawa Process was an iterative progression of fortuitous steps with a series of well-timed alignments that allowed some extremely able policy entrepreneurs to advance the agenda to the point that the momentum was sufficient to produce a desired conclusion. This, then, is the 'answer' to the ambiguity question and to the difference of opinion between the officials and the NGOs involved—both groups are right. The civil society model does indeed have application to other issues; indeed, there seems to be almost an inevitability to the 'new multilateralism'—at least insofar as fundamental human security issues are concerned. The role of the 'Middle Powers', such as Canada, Austria, and Belgium, as key policy entrepreneurs in the Ottawa Process, together with their civil-society partners who mobilized communication and information technologies to build influential transnational coalitions, kept the anti-personnel mines issue on the decision agendas of many states—despite the reticence and, in some cases, outright opposition of some major powers. Such empowerment of non-dominant actors can markedly influence future multilateral negotiations.

However, there is no certainty that subsequent attempts to use this model will yield a similar result. As Tomlin (1998: 203) reminds us: 'Recall Kingdon's description of the joining of the policy streams where, occasionally, a viable policy alternative is linked to a pressing problem under favourable political conditions and, as a result, a policy window opens. In this circumstance, a policy entrepreneur has to be ready with the alternative and savvy enough to take advantage of the opening.' This holds true especially at the multilateral level where there can be no guarantee of success because there are simply too many variables to control.

Sino-Canadian Relations, 1949–2005

Anemone Fritzen

Although John Kingdon devised the multiple streams model with the United States in mind, it has also been shown to be relevant to understanding the policy process in Canada.[1] Similarly, though conceived to explain the domestic policy-making process, the multiple streams model is very instructive in tracing the origins of foreign policy. However, additional factors, such as the interests of other nations and the consequent pressures they bring to bear must be taken into account. As Kingdon emphasizes, policy making is not a simple and straightforward process whereby the existence of a problem leads to the consideration of alternatives and selection of a solution. This is especially true with particularly controversial topics: how does an idea that is inconceivable in one year become acceptable in another?

To explore this question, this chapter will examine Canada's policies toward China—and, by extension, Taiwan—over the past 50 years. Using the Kingdon model, this essay will analyze the interplay of problems, politics, and policies in enabling, or in some cases constraining, decisions. The first part of the chapter will focus on the 21-year period—1949 to 1970—during which the People's Republic of China (PRC) was 'a diplomatic problem that seemed to defy solution' for Canada's government (Evans, 1991: 3). The second section will examine factors at play in the years leading up to the re-establishment of trade relations with Taiwan in 1986. Finally, the chapter will look at events that brought the still-controversial issue of Taiwan back into the spotlight, and consider whether the Kingdon analysis of trends in Sino-Canadian relations over the past 50 years can be instructive in predicting how the issue will fare.

The Canadian cabinet had decided, in principle, to accord diplomatic recognition to the PRC in November 1949, but although external affairs minister Lester Pearson expressed enthusiasm for the idea, no formal action was taken.[2] The finance minister, for one, opposed such a move, afraid that such a diplomatic snub would result in significant losses on loans made to the Nationalist government in Taiwan. For another, Prime Minister Louis St Laurent did not want to anger the United States—an important trading partner—which was fundamentally opposed to recognition of the Communist regime. Globally, factors in the politics stream were also wrong: the Soviet Union had recently boycotted the United Nations (UN) over the issue of Chinese recognition, and a Canadian initiative at that point could have tipped the balance in China's favour. Thus, from the beginning, the 'balance of forces' in the politics stream did not favour the policy of recognition (Kingdon, 1995: 163).

Nonetheless, the process moved slowly forward in May of 1950. As Britain had been experiencing 'a humiliating series of procedural delays' at the hands of the PRC in its attempt to establish diplomatic relations, Chester Ronning—Canada's *chargé d'affaires* in China—was instructed to informally survey the Communist authorities on their receptivity to a Canadian initiative (Beecroft, 1991: 51).[3] The PRC expressed interest, but, again, the Canadian cabinet delayed. Ministers continued to express concern about the suitability of the 'climate' (Kingdon, 1995: 146), anticipating negative reactions both from the US and domestically—especially in Quebec.[4] As cabinet was finally set to make a decision in June, the Korean War broke out.

The effect of the Korean War on Canada's foreign policy, particularly with regard to China, was twofold. First, it delayed the possibility of recognition; not only did the UN General Assembly declare the PRC an aggressor, thus effectively blocking its members from recognizing China, but the US also recommitted itself to the defence of Taiwan, casting the island into the centre of Sino-American hostility. As a result, it became clear that any country wishing to establish relations with the PRC would likely have to agree to sever relations with Taiwan—an unacceptable demand according to Canadian public opinion (Beecroft, 1991: 54). Although the Nationalist regime in Taiwan was not popular, Canada's 'national mood' (Kingdon, 1995: 146) was nonetheless strongly sympathetic to Taiwan's right to self-determination. A second effect, however, was that Pearson became even more determined to establish diplomatic relations with China; the Korean War sparked his conviction that bringing China into the world community would be the way to solve the problem of maintaining world peace.[5]

In anticipation of an impending decision on China, Pearson and St Laurent organized a series of speeches that were intended to gradually 'soften up' both domestic and international constituents (Beecroft, 1991: 56; Kingdon, 1995: 129).[6] The softening-up process included private conversations with foreign ministers from Australia and Belgium at the Geneva Conference convened in April 1954 to reach an agreement to end hostilities and restore peace in French Indochina and Korea; encouragingly, these ministers shared Pearson's conviction that the way to lasting peace in the Far East was to recognize China. Although these developments seemed tentatively to point to a Sino-Western rapprochement, hostile Chinese actions in the Taiwan Straits in late 1954 firmly closed the window.

The Taiwan Straits crisis ended in the spring of 1955, and discussions between PRC and US officials were arranged, aimed at finding a peaceful settlement to disputes over the offshore islands. These discussions served as a catalyst—a mild form of focusing event—for the recognition question. In part, there was concern that these discussions would result in the recognition of China by the US ahead of Canada, diminishing the significance of Canada's earlier gestures. Equally important was the fear that any practical advantage to be had in recognizing China would be lost if the US were to move first.[7] Floating another trial balloon, Pearson publicly stated the government's intent to 'have another and searching look at the problem, [and soon]' in August 1955 (Beecroft, 1991: 58, 59). The Canadian press and the Australian and Belgian foreign ministers welcomed a Canadian lead; the US expressed concern, but did not otherwise object.[8]

Forces in the politics stream continued to have a restraining effect, however. For example, many were uneasy that Canadian recognition might reinvigorate Sino-Western tensions at the upcoming UN General Assembly session. There was also the question of optics: while, logistically, action could not be taken on the issue before Pearson was scheduled to visit India and the USSR in late September, moving on the matter too soon after his return would raise questions about who was influencing Canada's policy choices.[9] The American election in early 1956 further stalled action, and the outbreak of crises in Hungary and Suez later that year pushed China off the governmental agenda completely. In 1957, St Laurent had his own election to face; in June of that year, John Diefenbaker came to power. Under Diefenbaker, trade with China was re-established but the question of diplomatic recognition was dropped (Beecroft, 1991: 60), illustrating that turnover, in keeping with Kingdon's model, has a dramatic impact on the policy agenda (Kingdon, 1995: 153).[10] Thus, although potential policies had been developed for the problem, issues largely in the political stream prevented a window of opportunity from opening, at least more than partway.

In 1963, the Liberals were back in power under Pearson, although they were limited by their minority status in Parliament. Whereas, on the one hand, President Kennedy showed signs of wanting to improve Sino-American relations (St Amour, 1991: 106), on the other hand, Diefenbaker, the Opposition Leader, remained staunchly opposed to 'any weakening of support for the Nationalist government in Taiwan' (Head and Trudeau, 1995: 11). This, combined with mounting tensions in Vietnam, caused Canada to move cautiously. A review of Canada's China policy was conducted and it contained recommendations for the adoption of a 'two-Chinas' policy linked to a proposal for both Taiwan and the PRC to hold UN seats. Although minister of external affairs Paul Martin, Sr, felt the proposal would succeed politically if the US were kept fully informed during the process, Pearson was not convinced. The proposal was dropped. This is consistent with Kingdon's model—where civil servants can have an impact on the alternatives, they often have very little influence on the decision agenda (Kingdon, 1995: 43).

Later that year, less than a month after the Kennedy assassination, President Lyndon Johnson was faced with a controversy: his assistant secretary of state for far eastern affairs had publicly conceded that a Communist China would be the reality for the foreseeable future.[11] As Johnson moved to quell speculation that

American policy toward China—and by extension its commitment to Taiwan's security—had changed in any way, the storm in Washington was intensified by France's recognition of the PRC. Pearson attempted to convince Johnson to view this as an opportunity to accept China's right to a seat at the UN while working to preserve Taiwan's seat, but with an election to face in November, Johnson had no intention of revising his policy.[12] Indeed, with 4 of 12 NATO members now recognizing the PRC, the US felt compelled to warn Canada not to follow France's lead.[13] Escalation of the Vietnam conflict cemented the US stance on China, convinced as they were that any moderation would signal acquiescence to Communist hegemony in the Far East. Canada continued to hold the opposite view—that China's isolation was causing its aggression and endangering world peace.

At the suggestion of PRC officials in April 1965, Canada's trade commissioner in Hong Kong floated a trial balloon with Canadian officials regarding the possibility of exchanging permanent trade offices. Though it would have little impact on trade, he felt it would be a promising alternative to the UN as a 'venue in which to work out [a] solution to the problem of our relations with China' (St Amour, 1991: 113). However, as Canada's China policy at that time had become firmly focused on China's accession to the UN—an increasingly contentious subject among UN Members—the suggestion was not followed. Further, anticipating that he would call an election that year to attempt to improve his party's minority status, Pearson was reluctant to make any firm policy commitments on this controversial issue. Once again, despite a wealth of ideas bubbling to the surface in the policy soup, constraints in the politics stream proved too strong.

The PRC was not admitted to the UN in 1965, but the General Assembly was almost divided in two by the question.[14] The precarious balance at the UN also divided officials in the Johnson administration. Sensing a window of opportunity, moderates in the State Department urged President Johnson to authorize support for a 'two-Chinas' approach at the UN. Canada was recruited to the lobbying process, with a promise of 'the opportunity to exert real influence on the [US] administration's China policy' (St Amour, 1991: 117).[15] Encouraged by this, Martin drafted a resolution intended to run counter to the Albanian resolution; whereas the Albanian resolution called for Taiwan's seat to be given to China, the Canadian resolution called for seats for both Taiwan and China in the General Assembly, with the Security Council seat awarded to China (St Amour, 1991: 119).[16] American opposition, however, eroded the support needed to table this resolution. China's Cultural Revolution, which gained momentum in 1967, precluded action for the remainder of Pearson's term, and the Liberal leadership passed to Pierre Trudeau in March of 1968.

As Kingdon notes, 'open windows are small and scarce. . . . Windows do not stay open long. If a chance is missed, another must be awaited' (Kingdon, 1995: 204). Windows of opportunity close if policy entrepreneurs do not recognize them to have opened, or if policy proposals are not ready. Both can be seen to have contributed to the 21-year delay. The first window was in 1949, as attitudes against Communist China did not begin to harden in the US until the spring of

1950; before this time, many believe the US would not have attempted to sway Ottawa's decisions on China. The one-month period between initial discussions with Communist officials and the outbreak of the Korean War represented a second—and last—opportunity for recognition with no conditions about the status of Taiwan attached; in neither case was a policy entrepreneur prepared to take advantage of the open window (Beecroft, 1991: 53).

On another level, a series of constraining focusing events—the Korean War, the Taiwan Straits Crisis, the Vietnam War, and the Cultural Revolution—plagued Pearson. While these events may have served to strengthen Pearson's personal conviction that isolating China was the problem, they had the opposite effect on American convictions. Added to this were focusing events that arose in the mid-1950s—the Suez and Hungary crises—that distracted from the China question completely. Finally, as Kingdon suggests, turnover—or at least the threat of it—was shown to have a 'dramatic effect . . . on policy agendas' (Kingdon, 1995: 153). At key junctures, the timing of elections caused caution on the part of governments, contributing in no small way to the long delay.

'In 1968,' writes Bernie Frolic, 'a new Canadian prime minister set out to put his imprint on Canada's foreign policy' (1991: 189). Indeed, as it turns out, the turnover of federal leadership from Pearson to Trudeau was a crucial development in the recognition question; one of Trudeau's foremost ambitions was to emancipate Canadian foreign policy from American influence, and relations with the PRC were very much a symbol of this desire.[17] But what was different in 1968 that allowed Trudeau to move ahead, where Pearson and St Laurent had been unable? For one thing, it could be said that although windows of opportunity had opened before, there had been no policy entrepreneur ready to recognize or take advantage of it. In 1970, that entrepreneur was found in the person of Trudeau, a man with a 'commitment to do something and the disposition to get on with it' (Holmes, 1970: 13).[18]

In the early 1970s, factors in the politics stream were also coming together. First, the national mood in the US had changed: many were now prepared to accept relations with China as a 'necessary evil', though not at Taiwan's expense. Equally important, and parallel to the shift in mood, was the fact that the US administration's staunch 'One-China' policy was beginning to shift to a possible 'One-China, One-Taiwan' policy.[19] American concerns about the effect recognition would have on the Vietnam negotiations in Paris and domestic Canadian fears of the economic repercussions that American displeasure would bring to Canada were certainly a constraining factor, but Canada's experience with Cuba had served to temper these concerns: although the initial American reaction had been hostile, no sanctions had been placed on Canada (Frolic, 1991: 195, 197). Internationally, China was becoming increasingly open to relations with other countries; where China had humiliated Britain in the early 1950s, it was now actively entertaining recognition proposals. Adding fuel to the fire was concern that Belgium or Italy, which were also in discussions with China, would arrive at an agreement ahead of Canada and thus detract from the significance of a Canadian initiative.

Domestically, the major political parties and a small majority of Canadians now supported recognition while at the same time there was very little organized opposition.[20] Though the Chinese Community Centre (CCC) was certainly a centre of anti-recognition activity, many of its members feared the immediate danger of harassment on immigration issues more than the more remote consequences that Canadian recognition of China might bring (Lum, 1991: 220). Consequently, the efforts of the main interest groups with a stake in the policy ran in opposite directions, having a mutually negating effect. There is also something to the way that the problem was framed. While the objective remained the same—recognizing the PRC—Pearson's reasons for wanting to do so were different from Trudeau's. For Pearson, it had been a question of maintaining the balance of peace in the world: an isolated China was a dangerous China. Trudeau framed the problem in more immediate and emotionally compelling terms: Canadian foreign policy was subservient to the American will.[21]

During the course of the 1968 election campaign, Trudeau floated trial balloons on the China issue in a series of speeches highlighting the China question. This developed into a major policy statement, in which he indicated his desire to recognize the PRC as soon as possible, 'taking into account that there is a separate government in Taiwan.' The issue of China, in addition to being a symbol of emancipation from the US, took the form of a turf war whereby Trudeau sought to reduce the influence of the Department of External Affairs (DEA), which he felt was out of touch with national interests (Frolic, 1991: 190, 192), though he would later come to rely on the department's professionalism and expertise during the negotiations with China.[22] With Mitchell Sharp as the new minister of external Affairs and Ivan Head as his foreign policy advisor, Trudeau had the team he needed to make the statement a reality.

Reality did not come easily, however, and it would be two long years—until 10 October 1970—before the issue was settled. Though Kingdon describes consensus as being built through persuasion in the policy stream and bargaining in the political stream, foreign policy making is not as simple as domestic policy making. It often requires the agreement of outside players (Kingdon, 1995: 159); bargaining with China in order to build a consensus, in this case, was required before a firm policy position could be taken. Though a number of variations on the Canadian approach to this problem had been floated over the years, Canadian policy at the outset of the Stockholm negotiations was familiar but vague: Canada should be allowed to recognize an independent state of Taiwan if possible (Edmonds, 1998: 207). The policy that was ultimately adopted—in which Canada 'took note' of China's position on Taiwan—was seen as the best possible outcome under the circumstances (Frolic, 1991: 211).[23]

According to Robert Edmonds, the Stockholm Negotiations that brought diplomatic recognition to the PRC were 'Canada's second most important negotiation of international significance in the post-war period.'[24] However, the story does not end in 1970; Canada's celebrated solution to the China problem was not without its controversies. First, many charged that Canada abandoned its long-stated support of Taiwan quickly and with little consultation; both Japan and the US eventually found ways to maintain some official ties with Taiwan. Second, the hundreds of millions of dollars worth in claims Canada had against China—the same claims that had been a source of concern from the outset—were eventually settled to Canada's disadvantage (Edmonds, 1998: 201, 211).

Domestically, although many Chinese-Canadians supportive of the Nationalist government in Taiwan had largely remained silent on the issue of PRC recognition out of loyalty to their adoptive country, the favour was not returned (Lum, 1991: 138). Policy toward Taiwan became increasingly dogmatic, despite Edmonds' assertion that Canada intended to retain non-governmental relations with Taiwan. For example, when it became clear that Canada intended to recognize the PRC, Taiwan's Ambassador, Hsueh Yu-Chi, asked to remain in Canada in a 'private' capacity, as had been arranged in Britain and France, but was refused (Andrew, 1991: 246).[25] Later on, amid international controversy, Trudeau prevented Taiwan from participating in the 1976 Olympics under the name 'Republic of China'.[26] Also at this time, Canada Customs refused to admit goods and Canada Post would not process mail marked 'Taiwan, Republic of China'.[27] Travel between the two countries in this period became increasingly difficult; as the *Toronto Star* reported in November 1983, Taiwanese citizens wishing to visit Canada had to apply through a Canadian High Commission in Hong Kong, while Canadians wishing to visit Taiwan were required to apply through the United States. The consequences of the above were twofold: first, it caught the attention of a young new Canadian with roots in Taiwan, and second, the negative consequences on trade with Taiwan helped cultivate sympathetic ears among the ranks of the official opposition.

While Edmonds points to the establishment of the Canadian Trade Office in Taiwan (CTOT) and of the Taipei Cultural and Economic Office in Ottawa (TCEO) as honouring the spirit of Trudeau's policy, establishing unofficial relations with Taiwan was neither as easy as Edmonds seems to suggest, nor was it a Liberal initiative; a 'different government in a different time' was needed to see it through (Edmonds, 1998: 215). Participants around and outside of government can be seen to have contributed to putting the issue on the governmental agenda, but keeping it there and moving it onto the decision agenda is another story. Kingdon stipulates that windows are opened by changes in the politics stream or by the emergence of a new problem that captures the attention of policy makers (Kingdon, 1995: 168). Both conditions arose in the mid-1980s.

When Gabriel Fritzen married a Taiwanese woman in the late 1970s, his efforts to help her integrate into Canadian society put him in touch with the Chinese diaspora, first in Toronto and then in the remote Northwestern Ontario city of Thunder Bay. It is at this time that he learned the extent of the barriers to economic, cultural, and interpersonal exchanges between Canada and Taiwan. When he made no headway even in bringing the issue onto the governmental agenda (let alone the decision agenda) through traditional means, he decided to try a slightly different route in 1983: twinning.[28] The first potential town that came to his mind was the Township of Terrace Bay.[29] When he floated the idea of twinning before both the Government Information Office (GIO) in Taiwan and the Terrace Bay town council, it was warmly received on both ends. By the end of the year both a sister city and a date had been set: Tungkang was to be twinned with Terrace Bay as part of the latter's 25th anniversary celebrations in 1984.

At the same time, the trade opportunities available in Taiwan—'one of the fastest growing economies in the world'—and Canada's inability to take advantage of them were firmly in the sights of Conservative MP Otto Jelinek (Canada, House of Commons Debates, 28 April 1983).[30] Although the Liberal government had affirmed in 1980 that private-sector efforts to promote trade with Taiwan had the government's 'blessing', commentators, and media reports, noted that they were not prepared to facilitate these efforts in any way. To bring attention to this deficiency, Jelinek founded the Canada–Taiwan Parliamentary Friendship Committee (CTPFC). In a highly controversial move, an all-party delegation from this committee accepted an invitation to visit Taiwan in April of 1983.[31] Upon his return, he tabled a private member's bill calling for the establishment of a non-diplomatic presence in Taiwan for the purpose of promoting trade.[32] Nothing came of the bill, but unofficial trade missions continued. In November 1983, a 14-member delegation led by Taiwan's director-general for foreign trade, Victor Siew, visited Canada. Reciprocally, in January 1984, 10 members of the CTPFC visited Taiwan at the invitation of the Taiwanese government. There was some speculation about what China's reaction to this would be, because not only was it financed by a government not recognized by Canada, but it also happened to coincide with Premier Zhao Ziyang's speech before a joint session of the House of Commons—the first by a Communist leader.[33] Interestingly, China's reaction was decidedly mild.

Back in Terrace Bay, arrangements for the twinning ceremony hit a snag: roughly a week before the twinning was to take place, the Canadian High Commission in Hong Kong refused visas to the Taiwanese delegation. As per instructions from the DEA, official visits from Taiwan—which this delegation was considered to be—were not permitted. Speer immediately contacted Keith Penner, his Liberal MP, to inform him that as a result of difficulties with the High Commission, the head table at the 25th anniversary celebrations of the Township of Terrace Bay would have five empty seats—an absence, he warned, that would not go unnoticed by the local media. As luck would have it, unrelated events in the politics stream gave considerable weight to this threat: Trudeau had resigned the leadership in February, and the Liberals were set to face an election that year in which every seat would count. Within 24 hours, the Canadian High Commission contacted Speer, arrangements were made to issue the visas, and the twinning ceremonies were carried out as planned, as part of Terrace Bay's 25th anniversary.[34] The Canada–Taiwan Friendship Association (CTFA) was founded at the ceremony and over the next decade, it campaigned for increased awareness of Canada–Taiwan relations, financing trade missions to Taiwan and ensuring that key individuals in and around government did not lose sight of the issue.

In September 1984, John Turner was swept from power in the worst defeat in Liberal history, winning only 40 of 282 seats. Initially it seemed that the new

prime minister, Brian Mulroney, would concentrate on domestic issues over foreign affairs ones; indeed, he ignored or abandoned much of the complex management system for foreign policy making that had been established under
Trudeau (Kirton, 1985: 24; 1986: 43). Nonetheless, as promised in the Speech
from the Throne, external affairs minister Joe Clark undertook a review of Canadian foreign policy in 1985. Deeply committed to openness and broad public
participation in the foreign policy process, Clark held consultations across
Canada, at which a variety of organizations were invited to make submissions.[35]

With the help of prominent Toronto immigration lawyer Richard Boraks, the
CTFA travelled to Winnipeg to make a presentation to the Standing Joint Committee on Canada's International Relations. Their presentation emphasized the
lack of infrastructure to support trade with Taiwan and recommended support
for establishing a permanent non-diplomatic trade office in Taiwan and encouraging city-to-city ties through twinning. When the committee's final report was
published in May 1986, a number of elements from that presentation, including
the two mentioned above, had been adopted (Fritzen, 2005).[36] In October, the
CTOT opened its doors, and a new period in Canada–Taiwan trade relations
began.[37] China was aware of this development but did not protest it, saying that
'the Taiwan situation [in 1986] is rather different than the one in 1970' (Andrew,
1991: 252).[38]

The idea of reciprocally opening trade offices with Taiwan is certainly in keeping with Kingdon's assertion that, among policy alternatives, there is no new
thing under the sun (Kingdon, 1995: 73). Otto Jelinek proposed a very similar
idea in the bill he tabled in April 1983. He indicated in an interview to the
Toronto Star (15 November 1983) that a non-diplomatic Canadian office in Taiwan would be opened, 'possibly by next year'. Thus, the alternatives put forward
by the CTFA had been considered before, and may also have been put forward by
others during the consultation period. The important thing to consider, however, is why it took hold when it did (Kingdon, 1995: 72).

Several factors conceivably contributed to the eventual establishment of trade
relations with Taiwan. Externally, China had established an Open Door policy in
1978 to improve its flagging economy. In Canada, a number of forces can be seen
to have been at play. First was the existence of an organized interest group, the
CTFA, whose efforts were largely pointing in the same direction as many participants around government; at the same time there were no strongly organized
forces running in the opposite direction. Second was the election of new government in 1984; the Opposition MPs who had been most vocal about potential
trade opportunities with Taiwan now held the power of a majority government.

Another important factor may have been the problem to which the solution
was attached: a prolonged and serious economic recession.[39] Trudeau, toward the
end of his term, had chosen to focus largely on peace initiatives; Turner in his
short tenure did the same. This despite the fact that, in Canada, unemployment
in 1984 stood at 11 per cent and the economic environment was uncertain
(though largely on its way to recovery). Consequently, there had been growing
disenchantment with Liberal economic policies; Turner was, in many ways, a

casualty of this sentiment. The economic climate may also help explain a lack of resistance to promoting trade with Taiwan; in a speech before the House of Commons in April 1983, Otto Jelinek asserted, 'For every $1 billion spend on trade, approximately 25,000 new Canadian jobs are created' (Canada, House of Commons Debates, 28 April 1983). If one can assume that this statistic was fairly widely accepted, the emphasis on trade diversification in the 1986 Joint Committee Report—with a special mention of Taiwan—can be seen as a result of this belief.

Prior to the dissolution of Parliament on 29 November 2005, a private member's bill submitted by Conservative MP Jim Abbott had made it past second reading and was under review by the Standing Committee on Foreign Affairs and International Trade (SCFAIT). This bill, *The Taiwan Affairs Act* (Bill C-357), stirred up considerable controversy in Canada and overseas, but also enjoyed support from all parties in the House of Commons when it was tabled (Canada: House of Commons Debates, 16 May 2005). Modelled after the American *Taiwan Relations Act*, Bill C-357 was intended to provide an improved framework for Canada–Taiwan relations. Those opposed, mostly business lobbies such as the Canadian Council of Chief Executives (CCCE), feared that the bill would have a negative impact on Canada's important trade relations with China (d'Aquino, 2005).[40] Those in favour applauded its emphasis on Taiwan's positive democratic record, and the protection it would afford Canada in managing bilateral relations.

Although Taiwan had been on Abbott's mind since the 2003 SARS crisis, two factors can be seen as important in his decision to table the bill in April 2005: the existence of a minority government, and new procedures for private members' bills. The first factor was important in that Abbott's bill had support from all parties in the House of Commons, and was thus more likely to pass when it came to a vote at each stage of the process. Second was the new procedure for handling private members' bills: where in the past private members' bills were votable only by exception, they now automatically came to a vote.[41] When his name was drawn in the random lottery that determines which private members can table bills, it was mainly the second factor that convinced Abbott that the time was right to act.

The dissolution of Parliament at the end of 2005 put an end to the issue, for the time being. Nonetheless, the exercise may eventually prove to have been a valuable one for the issue. According to Kingdon, tabling a bill can be considered part of the 'softening-up' process; even if a politician doesn't think it will pass that year, the very act 'gauge[s] the receptivity to an idea' (Kingdon, 1995: 129). And even if that particular effort did not get very far, the problem itself will have gained exposure—perhaps enough for other policies and participants to come along and attempt to couple the streams.

Can any lessons from the Kingdon analysis of the process that shaped Canada's Taiwan policy over the last 50-plus years be applied to the future of a bill like the *Taiwan Affairs Act*? Though the multiple streams model is probabilistic rather than deterministic, some tentative predictions can arguably be generated. First, any movement on this issue will require a policy entrepreneur with the determination to do something and the ability to do it. Although Abbott has indicated his intent to resubmit the bill in the next Parliament regardless of who forms the next government, he will likely have more luck if his own party forms the government, and if they hold a majority of seats—and certainly even more luck if Abbott becomes a minister with a relevant portfolio. Even then, it would be helpful to have a prime minister with Trudeau's forceful and unapologetic personality with a personal interest in the subject—particularly in Canada, where a prime minister with the right inclination has almost no checks on his power.[42]

Second, the problem will have to be framed correctly. As was seen in the period leading up to the recognition of the PRC, framing the problem as one of sovereignty rather than world peace was key to the coupling of the streams; the former had much more of a sense of immediacy than the latter. In 1986, trade diversification attached to the serious unemployment problem helped re-open unofficial relations with Taiwan. The most recent bill's focus seems to have been on security issues—the lack of protection for Canada in its relations with Taiwan under current statutes (Canada, House of Commons Standing Committee on Foreign Affairs and International Trade, 15 November 1983). Given the current preoccupation with issues of national security, this would seem to be an ideal problem to use. Since many feel the status quo is adequate, however, it will likely take some sort of focusing event—a serious breach of national security in dealings with Taiwan—to prove that change is needed.

Third, lacking a convincing focusing event, the concerns of powerful interest groups will need to be addressed; by default, this will also require convincing China that Canada's intent is not to change its official relationship to Taiwan in any way. This, in turn, will likely depend on how China–Taiwan relations continue to unfold. Alternatively, as Trudeau did, one could take the stand that foreign policy should be set within Canada, not by other countries like the US in 1970 or like China in the 1980s and today. In other words, just as in the previous two eras, movement on the issue this time will depend largely on unpredictable developments in the politics stream, though there might also be some room for the right policy entrepreneur to take the lead.

John Holmes observes that Canadian recognition of China was merely 'the correction of an acknowledged error of twenty years ago' (Holmes, 1970: 12). Though perhaps longer than the average 'Softening-up' period, the long process seems to have been necessary in preparing domestic and foreign constituents to accept such a controversial change. St Laurent and Pearson, in speeches, made it clear that the recognition of China was delayed, not postponed indefinitely. Diefenbaker, for his part, was uninterested in the recognition question, but his open attitude on trade with China inadvertently also helped soften Canadian public opinion toward eventual recognition (English, 1991: 138). But as the above analysis has shown, in a manner consistent with the Kingdon model, the 'error' was not ready to be corrected until 1970, due to the complex interplay of problems, policies, politics, and, of course, participants.

As the analysis on the establishment of an unofficial mission in Taiwan showed, the idea for doing so surfaced in the early 1980s, but required a new administration and the right problem to become reality. Similarly, the time does not appear to be right for movement on the *Taiwan Affairs Act*: there has been little softening up, and the problem to which it is currently attached does not appear immediately pressing.[43] It may well be, to paraphrase Mitchell Sharp, that the question of the future of Taiwan is still for the future to decide.

CHAPTER 16

Canada–US Relations
and the Devils Lake Dispute

KEVIN MA

*'This is a triumph for democracy. It is a wonderful example of how our two
countries can work together for the benefit of our shared environmental interests.'*

– US Ambassador David Wilkins on the Devils Lake settlement,
5 August 2005

One cannot help but feel sceptical about this statement's portrayal of historical
events. True, Canadian and US federal officials did issue a joint press release in
2005 that ostensibly ended one of the longest transboundary environmental
disputes in the history of their nations: the Devils Lake dispute.[1] But if Devils
Lake was a 'triumph for democracy', then only the Americans had reasons to cel-
ebrate it. For Canada, Devils Lake was a bitter defeat in a 12-year war over water,
one that involved little, if any, cooperation for the benefit of shared environmental interests. It is a loss we can understand if we remember one of the key
conclusions of the Kingdon model: when the policy, problem, and political
streams unite, there is little anyone can do to stop the resulting flood of action.

Devils Lake is a water-filled Prairie pothole in North Dakota. It has no natural
outlets, so any water that enters it has to leave by evaporation. In a 2005 interview with the author, Joe Belford, the commissioner for Ramsey County (which
contains Devils Lake)[2] noted that the lake had risen some 26 feet as a result of
record amounts of precipitation over the past 12 years, flooding 75,000 acres of
land and costing US state and federal authorities about $600 million in emer-
gency repairs. The Devils Lake dispute centres on North Dakota's proposed solution for the flooding: an outlet to drain the lake into the Sheyenne River. Canada
opposed this solution, since the Sheyenne River leads to the Red River and Lake
Winnipeg in Canada, meaning that the outlet could dump foreign pathogens
and pollutants into Canadian waters and threaten Manitoba's fisheries. Canada
said this would violate Article IV of the *Boundary Waters Treaty* (signed in 1909 to

regulate Canada–US water flows), which says waters flowing across the Canada–US border should not be polluted on either side to the injury of health or property on the other (International Joint Commission, 1998: 8). The outlet was also said to be part of a broader plan by North Dakota to add an inlet to the lake, one that stabilized its water levels when it was dry and worsened the environmental threat to Canada. Canada wanted the administrators of the treaty, the Canadian-American International Joint Commission (IJC), to settle the dispute. North Dakota refused, claiming that the flood was an emergency in need of immediate action, and that there was no time to bring in the IJC.

After 10 years of bitter struggle, North Dakota got its way. The August 2005 Canada–US press release allowed the state to build and open an outlet to the lake. In exchange, it made non-binding promises to refrain from building an inlet to the lake and to add a biota-stopping sand filter to the outlet sometime in the future.[3] Where North Dakota won, Canada lost. It had no IJC settlement, no guarantee that an inlet would not materialize, and no assurance that its waters would be protected from pollution. In terms of scientific and political support, Canada should have won this battle. Canada had the support of Minnesota, Missouri, the Great Lakes states, several Aboriginal and environmental groups, the US Army Corps of Engineers, Congress and the US State Department on its side. In contrast, North Dakota had virtually no one in its corner.[4] From a balance-of-power perspective, North Dakota should have lost. How, then, did Canada lose? In terms of issue complexity, Devils Lake should not have taken this long to resolve. Canada and the US somehow took about 40 years to settle a fight over a pipe sticking out of a lake. The infinitely more complex Canada–US free trade agreement, in comparison, was negotiated in two years, and the Smart Border Accord was negotiated in about five months. Even the acid rain dispute had a shorter run-time at 20 years, and it was once considered to be utterly intractable. Why, then, did this dispute last so long?

Don Munton's examination of the acid rain problem might hold an answer to these questions. Munton's studies of the Canada–United States acid rain dispute suggest that it is domestic political factors, not lobby groups or scientific evidence, that decide when and how nations tackle ecological issues (Munton, 1997). A given problem might be particularly severe, and a policy solution for it particularly effective, but problem and solution will not meet unless the right political conditions exist. This same thesis holds true for Devils Lake: it was a political shift that led to the August 2005 settlement of the dispute, not some new policy initiative or change in the lake's condition. Kingdon's multiple streams model can help us understand why. According to Kingdon, political change happens when the three streams of problems, policies, and politics come together at a fortuitous moment of time, a policy window, to create a flood of action. Canada lost the Devils Lake dispute when it did and how it did because of the interaction of these three streams and its inability to stop them from coming together.

We will divide our examination of the Devils Lake dispute into three phases, each corresponding to one of Kingdon's streams. Phase one, problem definition, covers 1995 to 1997. Here, North Dakota catapults Devils Lake onto the governmental agenda by redefining the lake's problem so that it demands immediate action. Phase two, policy jockeying, covers 1997 to 2003. Here, Canada and North Dakota struggle to create a feasible and politically acceptable solution to the Devils Lake flood, but cannot, resulting in deadlock. Phase three, political change, covers 2003 to 2005. Here, two shifts in the US political climate, specifically the ascendancy of North Dakota's two senators to key committee positions and the appointment of secretary of state Condoleezza Rice, radically change North Dakota's policy toward Devils Lake and render Canadian opposition to an outlet ineffective, resulting in the August 2005 settlement.

There were a vast number of groups opposed to the Devils Lake outlet, including the governments of Canada, Manitoba, Missouri, Minnesota, and others. For the sake of simplicity, all forces opposed to the Devils Lake outlet will collectively be referred to as 'Canada', because the Canadians were the most active members of the opposition, and the members mostly shared the same positions and arguments. We should also explain the biota transfer issue. Ecologists divide lands into regions called watersheds, which include all lands that drain into a specific water body. When you transfer biota between watersheds, you can create fox-in-the-henhouse-type disasters where the introduced species runs rampant due to a lack of natural predators.[5] Devils Lake is part of the same watershed as the Sheyenne and Red Rivers, but has been isolated from them for thousands of years. Canada's concern was that either the lake itself or water pumped into it via an inlet from another watershed would have foreign biota in them that would be pumped into Manitoba's Red River, home of many fisheries, through an outlet. Further to be noted, the Devils Lake dispute actually involves two outlets. The first was designed by the US Army Corps, and will be referred to as the Corps outlet. This outlet would take water from Pelican Lake (which feeds south into Devils Lake), run it through a sand filter, and move it to the Sheyenne River. If it's ever built, it will cost about $200 million. The second outlet is the one currently in operation, hereafter called the state outlet. This outlet is about half as long as the Corps outlet, cheaper (at $25 million), in part because it does not include environmental measures like a sand filter, smaller, since it drains about a third as much water from the lake, and temporary, designed to go offline once the Corps outlet comes in.[6]

Kingdon says problem definition is crucial in determining an issue's placement on the governmental agenda and the kinds of policy solutions that can be attached to it (Kingdon, 2003: 109–10). How you define a problem often means the difference between immediate response and permanent ignorance of it. Devils Lake demonstrates this well.

North Dakota has wanted to do something about Devils Lake for over a century. Broadly speaking, the lake's problem is that its water level is unstable. The lake has fluctuated some 65 feet over the last ten thousand years, overflowing into the Sheyenne River in one century and vanishing completely in another, which wreaks havoc on any roads, homes, and industries in the area (Pearson and Conrad, 2003: 4). Since at least 1902, local residents have variously called for an outlet or an inlet to the lake to stabilize it, depending on whether it was rising or falling at the time.[7] North Dakota took its first stab at building an inlet in the 1960s with the federally funded Garrison Diversion Unit, a multimillion-dollar scheme to pipe water to the lake and the rest of the state from the Missouri River to reinvigorate North Dakota's agricultural industry.

Canada and other American states (particularly Missouri) attacked the project. They argued that the diversion would transfer foreign biota from the Missouri to the Red River and violate Article IV of the *Boundary Waters Treaty*. Canada and the US referred the matter to the IJC in 1975, and the commission advised both parties to put Garrison on hold until they either eliminated the risk of biota transfer or decided the question of biota transfer was no longer a matter of concern (IJC, 1977: 121). North Dakota tried to revive interest in Devils Lake over the next 20 years, but to no avail; the US federal government refused to touch it. The inlet was very expensive, both financially and politically (due to Canada's opposition to Garrison and anything like it), which discouraged the federal government from getting involved. Since Devils Lake was not seen as an urgent problem (it was drying up very slowly, and the North Dakota economy was not at risk of collapse), the huge financial and political cost of Garrison could not be justified.

The flood changed everything. Starting in 1993, torrential rain and snowfall sent the lake shooting up five feet in two years, flooding thousands of acres of farmland and hundreds of homes. Suddenly, the region was 'one thunderstorm away from disaster', and there were only two ways to prevent it: 'an outlet or three or four years of severe drought' (Walsh, 1995; Wheeler, 1995).[8] The problem stream had shifted; what was once a minor inconvenience to North Dakota was now a major crisis. The flood was a focusing event, a crisis or disaster that demands an immediate response from policy makers. North Dakota now had a window of opportunity to get Devils Lake on the governmental agenda by re-imaging it from an economic inconvenience to a humanitarian disaster (Kingdon, 2003: 95).

That task fell to a small group of people known as 'The Doughnut Club'. The Doughnut Club was a loose-knit collection of city, state, and federal officials designed to address wetland issues in North Dakota, typically while meeting over coffee and doughnuts. At the time of the flood, they had been floating ideas on how to get federal support for an inlet to the lake (Sprynczynatyk, 2005). Through its members, the group had direct access to a diverse array of government departments, including the state engineer (Dave Sprynczynatyk, at the time), state governor (Ed Schafer [1992–2000] and John Hoeven [2000–5]), and Congressional representatives (Democratic senators Kent Conrad and Byron Dorgan), giving it considerable influence over the state's policy.

Its most active member was the county commissioner, Joe Belford. Kingdon would call him a policy entrepreneur, or a leadership figure that invests time and energy into a particular cause in order to create the political conditions needed for its realization (Kingdon, 2003: 122). Belford took the lead in softening up people to the idea of an outlet, promoting it through public talks, interviews, and his membership in some 12 local water boards (including the Canada–US Red River Basin Commission). Belford subsequently explained that he was the main media contact in the area, arranging and appearing in most of the articles written on the lake in Canada and the United States, and spending much of 1995–2005 travelling around North Dakota, Manitoba, and Washington talking about Devils Lake.[9]

Belford and other Doughnut Club members shaped the Devils Lake problem two ways. First, they said that this was a problem that would only get worse over time. Belford and others emphasized this point through frequent use of an analogy: 'The lake is like a cancer—it just grows and grows.'[10] This analogy acted as a powerful symbol that invoked an emotional response in others (by linking the disaster to a hot-button disease), helping the flood get a prominent place on the governmental agenda (Kingdon, 2003: 97). Second, club members framed Devils Lake as an emergency requiring immediate action. Belford and others argued that the sudden upswing in lake levels was the result of a 'wet cycle', a sudden, once-in-a-millennium spike in the region's precipitation. They argued that geologic records showed similar spikes had happened before, each time causing catastrophic overflows of the lake into the Sheyenne River that were capable of destroying cities. An outlet, they said, was the only way to prevent this from happening.

Canada and its allies did not do much to challenge North Dakota's attempts to redefine the Devils Lake problem, both because the problem actually had changed due to the sudden flood and because they got a late start. The main US opponent to the Devils Lake outlet, the North Dakotan civilian group, People To Save The Sheyenne, did not start operations until 1997.[11] Likewise, Canada voiced its concern about the environmental impact of the outlet a couple of times prior to 1997, but didn't kick its protests into high gear until after March of that year, when the Red River flood made the idea of anything adding more water to the Sheyenne–Red River system abhorrent.[12] All told, North Dakota basically had a two-year headstart on its opponents when it came to convincing others to see the Devils Lake problem in a new way.

North Dakota's redefinition of the Devils Lake problem worked. The Doughnut Club's message caught the ear of the Federal Emergency Management Agency and President Clinton, and in March 1997, Clinton asked Congress to give the US Army Corps $32 million in emergency funds to construct an inlet and outlet to the lake (Wheeler, 1995; Rebuffoni, 1997). By recognizing the focusing potential of the 1995 floods, North Dakota had redefined the Devils Lake problem and got it on the US federal government's agenda.

Kingdon argues that a policy must be technically feasible and politically acceptable before a government will implement it (Kingdon, 2003: 131–9). Those qualifications eluded the policy alternatives of Canada and North Dakota for many years, preventing a resolution to the lake dispute.

North Dakota's initial policy solution for the Devils Lake flood had five flaws in it, flaws Canada used to keep the Devils Lake outlet at bay for almost a decade. The state proposed a three-part solution to lower Devils Lake: more upstream water storage, more dikes, and the construction of an outlet *and an inlet* to the lake built with federal funds. That was the first flaw: a mismatch between policy and problem. The North Dakotans had gone to great lengths to redefine the Devils Lake problem as a humanitarian crisis (a flood) rather than an economic one (a lake that ruins local farms, fisheries, etc., when it floods or dries up), but their policy solution made no sense unless Devils Lake was, in fact, an economic crisis; why build an inlet when what you needed was an outlet?

Canada leapt on this contradiction, saying that the North Dakotans were using the flood as an excuse to revive the Garrison project. Rising lake levels had reinvigorated the fish-tourism industry in the region, it argued, and the state wanted an inlet to the lake to top it up with water once dry conditions returned (Lokkesmoe, 1999: 4). This would be a core argument against the outlet throughout the rest of the dispute: the idea that the North Dakotans had secret plans to build an inlet after they built the outlet. Around 2000, according to Belford and Sprynczynatyk, North Dakota gave up on the inlet when it determined that environmental concerns over the transfer of water from the Missouri River to Devils Lake made it a political impossibility. All mention of an inlet dropped from the lexicon of North Dakotan politicians, and, via the 2000 *Dakota Water Resources Act*, the state removed authorization for the inlet from the Garrison Diversion Unit.[13] Despite this apparent abandonment of the inlet, Canada continued to argue that the state was still pursuing it, noting that there was nothing stopping the state from re-authorizing it in the future, that the North Dakota Century Code (the state's collected record of laws) still listed it as a goal of Garrison, and that a 2003 map of future projects by the State Water Commission included a 'Devils Lake Inlet/Outlet' (Pearson and Conrad, 2003: 4, 11).[14]

The second problem with the North Dakotan solution was simple: it wouldn't work. Policy proposals usually need to be technically feasible in order to be accepted, and Canada argued that the Corps outlet was not. The federal outlet would cut about three feet of water from the lake's maximum predicted future height, and the state outlet less (as it had less capacity). Since the lake had risen about 26 feet, neither outlet would stop the flood or undo its effects. What's more, under certain climate scenarios, the lake would continue to rise and burst its banks even with an outlet in place (United States Army Corps of Engineers, 2003: S-5). Canada and its allies repeatedly emphasized these facts in their opposition to the outlet.

Third, the outlet was economically inefficient. Calculations by the Corps found that since the outlet would not take more than a few inches of water off the lake a year, it would save North Dakota just 19 to 55 cents in flood damages for every dollar spent on it (United States Army Corps of Engineers, 2003: S-5).[15] According to the Corps, the most cost-effective way for North Dakota to deal with the flood was to simply build more dikes and levees. Their studies suggested there was a 50 per cent chance that the lake would soon stop rising, rendering the outlet useless, and a 94 per cent chance that the lake would not rise enough to make building the outlet worthwhile (United States Army Corps of Engineers, 2003: S-5, S-6). It was cheaper overall to spend money on infrastructure as needed, they found, than to spend a lot of cash on an outlet that might never be needed.

Fourth, Canada argued that the North Dakotans did not need an outlet. The state's recent spike in precipitation, it said, was a freak event, not part of a 'wet cycle' as North Dakota had claimed (Kellow, 2003).[16] The rains would soon level off, there would be no catastrophic overflow into the Sheyenne, and Devils Lake would recede—there was no emergency, and no need for Clinton's emergency funds.

Lastly, Canada insisted that the state could not legally build an outlet without the approval of the IJC. The *Boundary Waters Treaty* forbids Canada or the US from doing anything that would harm their shared waters, and Canada argued that the outlet would cause tremendous harm. The lake, Canada and company said, had been isolated from the Sheyenne River for ten thousand years, and was believed to contain several parasites and fish species foreign to the river, as well as a large amount of phosphorous, a nutrient that can cause rampant algae growth. Releasing these substances could devastate Manitoba's fishing industry, Canada argued, and seriously compromise water quality. The US Army Corps provided evidence that supported these arguments. It noted that the outlet would cause levels of total dissolved solids in the Red River to exceed standards set by North Dakota and the IJC, and could cause excessive nutrients (such as phosphorous) to build up in it. They also found that the outlet could also worsen flooding in the Sheyenne and Red Rivers, reduce crop yields, alter shoreline vegetation, increase erosion, affect fish habitat, and would cost downstream users about $1.7 to $3.3 million a year in additional water treatment costs (United States Army Corps of Engineers, 2003: S-15, 6-5, 6-46, 6-47, 6-51, 6-79).

Canada used these policy criticisms to influence Congress and freeze federal funds for the Corps outlet. Allied senators added several restrictions to Clinton's 1997 funding authorization. First, none of the funds could be used to build an inlet to Devils Lake. Second, the outlet itself could not be built until the Corps proved it was economically viable, conducted a complete environmental impact assessment, and had the assurances of both the secretary of state and the IJC that it would not violate Article IV of the *Boundary Waters Treaty* by causing transboundary pollution (Guttormson, 1997). Since the Corps had already determined that the outlet wasn't worth the money, and the IJC had yet to evaluate the outlet, these restrictions meant that the funds would never be released, and North Dakota's policy solution would never be implemented. Canada had effectively closed the state's window of opportunity to have its way.

Unfortunately, Canada didn't have a viable alternative to the outlet. The actual Devils Lake problem was still on the governmental agenda, unsolved. Canada argued that North Dakota should build more levees and restore more wetlands instead of building an outlet. As mentioned, Canada and the Corps argued that it was more efficient for North Dakota to flood-proof its roads and bridges as needed instead of dropping a bunch of cash on an outlet. Canada also argued that most of the flooding at Devils Lake was due to North Dakota's own agricultural practices. The state had drained about 189,000 acres of wetland and installed 22,700 irrigation drains upstream of the lake over the years, actions that funnelled vast amounts of precipitation into Devils Lake and could be adding up to two feet of water to it (Pearson and Conrad, 2003: 37). The state could solve its problems if it shut those upstream taps and convinced farmers to flood their lands.

Unfortunately, the idea of stopping a flood by flooding land met with little enthusiasm in North Dakota. Interviews and this researcher's media survey suggest that the majority of North Dakotans emphatically believed that they needed an outlet to solve the Devils Lake flood, with the majority of local editorials and politicians strongly in favour of its construction.[17] State officials also argued that they had already taken infrastructure protection and upland storage as far as they could go. For example, a 1996 state plan to store 75,000 acre-feet of water by flooding fields resulted in less than a third of that amount of storage being made because farmers weren't willing to sell their property, and legislators weren't willing to annex their land (*Bismarck Tribune*, 1996). Follow-up plans in 2000 and 2003 added just 835 acre-feet to this capacity. As for infrastructure protection, the state argued that despite spending some $200 million on it (at the time), the lake was still rising and the state was still losing valuable land and homes to the waters (United States Congress, 1997). Politically, the mood in North Dakota was dead set in favour of building an outlet, making Canada's solution a non-starter. Meanwhile, the Doughnut Club's activities kept Devils Lake squarely in the public eye. As a result, the problem of Devils Lake remained on the governmental agenda, unsolved.

Kingdon notes that shifts in administration and the national mood can create policy windows through which savvy people can pass policy solutions (Kingdon, 2003: 146–9, 153–4). The resolution of the Devils Lake dispute involved both of these, and was helped along by a critical strategic error by the Canadians.

Belford and Sprynczynatyk say North Dakota started thinking about building a state-funded outlet soon after 1997. Canada and its allies had made federal funding for an outlet effectively impossible. The state was convinced that the Corps was all talk and no action; they had declared Devils Lake an emergency in need of a response, but did not appear willing to do anything about it (Schafer, 2005). The state also believed it could build its outlet faster and cheaper than the Corps, since they would exclude certain elements (such as the sand filter) they felt were unnecessary. North Dakota got its chance to get the state outlet moving in 1999. On June 10, the Corps released their draft plan for the outlet. The Corps said building the outlet was not economically feasible at the time since the water level was not yet high enough. They recommended that the lake be allowed to rise six feet more before starting construction, which would push construction back to about 2005 and inundate about 80,000 acres of land (Brasher, 1999). Schafer pointed to this announcement as a clear sign that the Corps did not care about Devils Lake. Declaring that the state could 'no longer afford to sit back and let the Corps dictate our fate in those areas that they clearly don't care about,' he said on June 22 that North Dakota would study and possibly build its own temporary outlet to Devils Lake (Wetzel, 1999). However, North Dakota did not immediately commit itself to building the outlet since it still hoped the Corps outlet would eventually go through.

The state outlet got another boost when senators Conrad and Dorgan became chairs of the Senate Budget committee and Appropriations and Commerce sub-committee (respectively) in 2001, effectively giving them control over all government spending.[18] The two used their new positions of power to push for progress on both the Corps and state outlets. Recall that the Corps outlet had to undergo a complete environmental assessment and be approved by the IJC before the federal government could release funds for it. Normally, Canada and the US prefer not to have the IJC examining an issue at the same time their domestic agencies are doing so; it creates needless duplication, and potential embarrassment if the IJC's findings differ from those of their own agencies. Since the Corps was in the middle of its environmental impact statement in 2002, the US was not interested in starting an IJC referral anytime soon (Heisler, 2005). To speed things up, Conrad and Dorgan went to secretary of state Colin Powell and asked for the IJC reference and the Corps assessment to happen at the same time. The two used their powers of office to hold back funds for the Afghanistan war and delay many government appointments until Powell agreed. In May 2002, Powell officially asked Canada if it wanted to refer the Corps outlet to the IJC (Donovan, 2002; Pearson and Conrad, 2003: 8). Surprisingly, Canada said no, a decision it would later regret.

In August 2002, the Corps decided to push back the release of its environmental assessment to January 2003 (Kuxhaus, 2002). This delay, combined with Canada's decision not to refer the Corps outlet to the IJC, convinced North Dakota that the Corps outlet was a dead end. On 28 August 2002 state officials threw open for bids the contract to build the state outlet. Actual construction started on 21 October 2003 (Nicholson, 2003). Although they mostly gave up on the Corps outlet after 2003, Conrad and Dorgan continued to use their influence to speed along the state and Corps outlet over the next few years. On 20 February 2003 the two senators managed to change the law governing the funds for the Corps outlet. The revised *Public Law 108–7* removed the stipulation that the outlet be approved by the IJC and economically justified by the Corps before being built; now, all the Corps had to do was 'fully describe' the justification for the outlet, including their analysis of the costs and benefits, and get the approval of the State Department that it would not break the *Boundary Waters Treaty*.[19] As a result, on February 25, the Corps, after saying for some six years that the outlet should not be built since it was not economically justified, suddenly announced that they had agreed to build it (*Winnipeg Free Press*, 2003). Although the Corps still believed the outlet was not economically justified, they also noted that *Public Law 108–7* 'removed the traditional requirements regarding economic justification' for the outlet. As a result, the Corps was able to justify the outlet as 'an insurance policy' against the admittedly unlikely chance of a catastrophic overflow event (United States Army Corps of Engineers, 2003: S-1, S-3). The Corps' environmental assessment also found little to no risk of foreign biota being transferred from Devils Lake to the Hudson Bay basin, debunking one of

Canada's key policy points against the outlet (Kuxhaus, 22 April 2003).[20] However, the assessment also doubled the price of the Corps outlet to $180 million, which put it out of fiscal reach of the North Dakotans for the foreseeable future (Associated Press, 2004). Powell, following *Public Law 108–7*, gave his assent that the outlet would not violate the *Boundary Waters Treaty* on 20 January 2004, but this meant little, as the North Dakotans had abandoned the Corps outlet due to its cost (Powell, 2004).

Conrad and Dorgan's influence on the state outlet (beyond promoting it whenever they could) was indirect. In 2004 a Republican candidate defeated Senate Democratic leader Tom Daschle in South Dakota. President Bush was a close friend of North Dakota's governor at the time, John Hoeven, and wanted him to run for senator in 2006 to unseat either Conrad or Dorgan. Hoeven had to look like a strong leader able to influence the president if he was to have a shot at the senate, so Bush had an incentive to let Hoeven have his way when it came to high-profile projects like the state outlet (Ibbitson, 2005; Jacobs, 2005). This, combined with Conrad and Dorgan's own influence over the federal government, appears to have dissuaded the Bush administration from strongly opposing the state outlet.

This would explain the curiously diplomatic letter sent by the State Department to North Dakota on the subject of the outlet on 10 March 2004. The letter urged the state 'in the spirit of trans-boundary co-operation and to avoid unnecessary conflicts between the United States and Canada or its concerned provinces' to consult Canada 'at the earliest opportunity' before building the state outlet—not exactly a stinging rebuke (Kelly, 2004). Curiously, North Dakota had been digging the outlet for six months at the time of the letter, and Canada and its American allies were just days away from filing what would be a bitter lawsuit against the outlet (MacAfee, 2004). Since the State Department would also have known how Canada and its allies felt about the state outlet (they had been protesting it since 1999), this letter suggests the US federal government was either reluctant or unable to oppose the outlet in 2004.

Canada's decision to decline North Dakota's offer of an IJC reference proved fatal. It gave North Dakota an excuse to give the state outlet the go-ahead. This effectively took Congress out of the picture (since it could not directly affect how North Dakota spent its own money), meaning that Canada could no longer use its Congressional allies to stop the outlet. It also gave North Dakota the home-field advantage. First, it had rock-solid political support for the state outlet. Its media campaigns and high-level leadership from the governor's office had overpowered any opposition Save the Sheyenne could muster, making it nearly impossible for Canada to get political support for solutions it proposed. Second, it gave North Dakota a political stick with which to beat off Canada's insistence on an IJC reference. When Canada later requested a reference on the state outlet, North Dakota erroneously and repeatedly said they had offered Canada a reference in 2002, and Canada refused it. The state would also argue that any such reference would take too long (saying that the average reference time was 8.5 years), despite Canada's claim that it could be done in one year (Wattie, 2005).[21]

Canada's decision to turn down the 2002 reference effectively robbed it of its ability to stop the outlet.

It seems curious that Canada would decline an IJC reference when one of its key policy objectives was obtaining one. Before we examine Canada's decision, we should clarify why it wanted an IJC referral. The IJC had a strong reputation for making fair, impartial rulings based on scientific fact, and was generally considered to be isolated from political influence (Willoughby, 1981: 31). Getting the IJC to review the outlet would remove North Dakota's congressional influence from the picture (or at least counterbalance it with Canada's influence), start a detailed environmental review of the outlet, and possibly block the outlet altogether (provided the commission accounted for its 1977 ruling on biota transfer). There was also a good chance that the US would obey any ruling that came out of the IJC since the IJC operates via consensus; by the time the IJC issues a ruling, Canada and the US have usually agreed to follow it (Heisler, 2005). The IJC was a classic bilateral bond with which to tie down American unilateralism.

Officially, Canada declined the reference for two reasons. First, it argued that the reference was premature since the Corps had not yet finalized their design for the outlet (Kergin, 2002). Technically, this would not have prevented Canada and the US from referring the issue to the IJC (the commission will review whatever issue it's given, regardless of the circumstances), but Canada and the US prefer to avoid having their domestic agencies working on the same issues as the IJC to prevent needless duplication and embarrassment (Heisler, 2005). Second, Canada wanted any such reference to include other projects related to the Garrison diversion, namely the Northwest Area Water Supply project (designed to funnel drinking water from the Missouri to North Dakota) and the proposed state outlet.[22] The US reference excluded both projects.

Canada knew that the Corps outlet was no longer a threat to its interests. According to a Canadian foreign affairs official close to the Devils Lake dispute, Canada was heavily involved in the Corps environmental assessment of the Corps outlet, and was reasonably satisfied it could use the process to ensure the outlet was nature-safe.[23] As a result, the federal official said, Canada saw North Dakota's offer as a non-starter: since the reference did not include the state outlet (the real threat) and the threat of the Corps outlet was already under control, agreeing to a reference on the Corps outlet would do nothing but waste Canada's time. In retrospect, say Canadian observers, Canada should have gone for the reference, as it could have answered crucial scientific questions on the environmental state of Devils Lake, given Canada an equal say in what was done about it, and possibly neutralized the environmental threat of the outlet altogether (Olivastri, 2006). However, it seems unlikely that Canada could have predicted back in 2002 how the North Dakotans would respond to its decline of a reference.

Canada probably would have won the Devils Lake dispute had it recognized and exploited a policy window, one that closed after 2003 due to a shift in the American political climate. Canada could not stop the state outlet through legislation; it had no allies in the North Dakotan legislature and little public support inside North Dakota. It could try challenging the outlet's legal authorization (which it did in March 2004) but this would involve proving that North Dakota had violated its own laws—not an easy task. Canada's best hope in stopping the outlet (or at least neutralizing its harm) was to refer it to the IJC. Unfortunately, the American political climate turned against Canada in 2004, slamming the door for this option shut.

There were several reasons for the turn. The events of 9/11 focused America's attention on security almost to the exclusion of everything else. In 2004, the US governmental agenda included two wars, climate change, trade liberalization, terrorism, missile defence, border security, and many other issues. In the words of former state governor Ed Schafer, the US State had 'bigger fish to fry' than Devils Lake, like the Iraq war (Schafer, 2005). The lake outlet was a huge issue for Canada, but a minor one for the US. The Chrétien and Martin governments also had poor relations with the Bush administration. Americans were 'disappointed and upset' about Canada's decisions to stay out of the Iraq war and missile defence, as US ambassador Paul Cellucci put it, making them less predisposed to doing Canadians any favours (Brean and Alberts, 2003). President Bush's political leanings and pressure from Conrad and Dorgan also dissuaded the US from intervening in Devils Lake on Canada's behalf.

Another factor crystallized these shifts: the appointment of Condoleezza Rice as secretary of state in January 2005. As the former national security advisor, Rice was not pleased by Canada's Iraq and missile defence decisions, and had cancelled her March 2005 visit to Canada as a result of the latter (Blanchfield, 2005). Canada was also asking the US for a lot of favours in 2005: it wanted action on softwood lumber, Alberta beef, the Kyoto Protocol, and Devils Lake, effectively everything but the Americans' main interest, security. Rice's appointment catalyzed the shift in America's mood, turning the administration against Canada. Since the IJC will usually not review an issue unless both Canada and the US ask it to, Canada needed to convince the US to agree to a referral if it wanted the state outlet reviewed—not an easy task, given the political climate.[24]

Canada officially requested that the state outlet be referred to the IJC on 7 April 2004, and thereafter tried everything it could think of to convince the US to make the reference. Canada tried diplomacy. In addition to having Prime Minister Martin talk about the issue with Rice and Bush, Canada also gathered political support from across the continent. On 14 April Canada sent an open letter to the IJC directed at the US calling for a reference, and attached letters from 15 American senators, congresspersons, and governors in support of one (DFAIT, 2005b). Later, the Great Lakes and St Lawrence Cities Initiative, representing Toronto, Chicago, and other major area cities, spoke out in favour of an IJC reference, noting the important role the commission played in protecting the Great Lakes against diversion projects (Samyn, 2005e). Canada tried the media. Manitoba water stewardship minister Steve Ashton wrote an editorial in the *Winnipeg Free Press* warning of ecological disaster if the outlet opened (Ashton, 2005). Ambassador Frank McKenna handled the American front with his 'Hell From

High Water', warning *New York Times* readers that the outlet would spell ruin for the *Boundary Waters Treaty* (McKenna, 2005). Canada tried breaking the law. On 2 February 2005, Manitoba unilaterally terminated a 2002 deal to build culverts under a road that was blocking the flow of water south to North Dakota farmers, saying they did so in protest over Devils Lake (Johnson, 2005).[25]

Canada even tried name calling. Alluding to a popular expression in Alberta during Trudeau's National Energy Program, Manitoba MP Pat Martin said Canada should 'let the (North Dakotan) bastards freeze in the dark' by cutting off American oil supplies in retaliation for the Devils Lake dispute. He later apologized for the tone, but not the meaning, of his words (Samyn, 15 June 2005). By 5 June 2005 it was clear that nothing would have any influence on Rice. Fourteen months had passed and she had not even acknowledged the request for a reference; the policy window Canada needed (a receptive American political climate) was firmly shut. On June 5th, Manitoba lost its case against the state outlet's health permit, removing the last legal obstacle to its operation. The outlet was complete, and could essentially open at any time. Canada realized it was time to deal.

Most policy advocates will stick to their positions until the very last minute of any dispute and then suddenly compromise so as not to be locked out of the final settlement, and this was certainly true of Canada (Kingdon, 2003: 168). On June 21, in a stunning policy reversal, Canadian officials suggested that the dispute might not have to be referred to the IJC after all; it could instead negotiate the issue bilaterally with the US and have the commission supervise implementation of the settlement (Samyn, 2005a). McKenna and Hoeven began formal talks on the state outlet soon after. On July 30, Canada and the US agreed to conduct a joint environmental assessment of Devils Lake to address Canada's concerns about pollution (Samyn, 30 July 2005). Interestingly, this agreement was foreshadowed by Powell's 2004 approval of the Corps outlet, which advised the Corps to invite Canada to participate in a joint biota survey of Devils Lake (Powell, 2004). On August 3, North Dakota agreed to add a gravel filter to the outlet and build a sand filter in the future (Samyn, 2005c). This, recalling the 1977 Garrison ruling by the IJC, was apparently enough to make the issue of biota transfer 'no longer a matter of concern' to Canada and the US. To address Canada's fears of the Garrison diversion, North Dakota agreed to state publicly that it had no current plans to build an inlet to Devils Lake. Canada and the US published their joint press release on the outlet on August 5. North Dakota opened the outlet on August 15, two weeks before Canada and the US finished their joint environmental assessment of the lake (Rabson, 2005b). It closed the outlet on August 25 after detecting excessive levels of sulphates (a pollutant) in the water it pumped. The outlet is expected to remain shut until spring 2006 (Samyn, 2005b).

Canada would do well to learn from Devils Lake, if only to avoid similar defeats in the future. One thing that was very clear was the importance of science. During the acid rain dispute, like-minded scientists backed by impeccable research were instrumental in getting acid rain onto the governmental agenda, changing public opinion, and propelling both sides to a compromise. Science was Canada's greatest ally in convincing the US to act; the undeniable scientific proof that the acid rain problem existed forced the Americans to do something about it (Munton, 1980; 1997). At Devils Lake, there was no scientific consensus, and no indisputable evidence. Canada and North Dakota squabbled about almost every bit of science in Devils Lake, including what creatures were in it, how high it would rise and how to best deal with that rise. Both claimed to have science on their side, but, in truth, neither did: prior to the 2003 Corps environmental assessment, no one had done a comprehensive environmental assessment of the lake, and to this day, no one has done a complete (i.e., spring-to-fall) study of the lake's biota (Heisler, 2005; Olivastri, 2006). Canada and the US argued about the environmental impact of the Devils Lake outlet for 15 years, yet neither made a concerted effort to find out exactly what that impact was. Partially, this was the fault of the North Dakotans, who often insisted they hadn't the time for a detailed study. But Canada was also at fault: Manitoba turned down a North-Dakotan offer to do a joint study of the lake in 2000 (Premier Gary Doer said it would not be thorough enough), and Canada declined an IJC reference in 2002. In future disputes, Canada should make every effort to get its science straight by promoting joint studies with the Americans, with or without the IJC's supervision. Had Canada agreed to do a joint study of Devils Lake prior to 2005, it's likely that the outlet dispute could have been resolved much sooner, and (at the very least) more scientifically.

Canada also needs to pay more attention to how politics interact with policy. Canada should not have expected the North Dakotans to accept a policy that involved flooding land to stop a flood, as doing so was bad politics. Yet it offered no alternative plans that the state might have accepted. Canada or its American allies could have offered to help pay for the wetland restoration, for example, or for the additional flood measures that the state would build in lieu of an outlet, or for the installation of the sand filter proposed for the current outlet. Whatever Canada does in the future, it needs to remember that it cannot block an American policy solution without providing an alternative to it, one that is just as effective and politically acceptable. If it does, it should expect the Americans to turn to unilateral action, as North Dakota did.

Canada should also re-examine the interaction of problem definition and politics. Policy entrepreneurs like Belford and Schafer firmly framed Devils Lake as an emergency in need of immediate action. Canada could not affect this definition of the problem because, to a large extent, Belford and Schafer were right: they needed only to point over their shoulders at the hundreds of flooded homes and thousands of angry people as evidence. Despite this, Canada decided to assume a position of total opposition to an outlet and slow, careful review, an untenable position given how North Dakota had defined the problem. So long as North Dakotans believed they were under threat, they would take any and all actions they believed necessary to eliminate that threat, including the construction of an outlet, as quickly as possible. Had Canada realized this, they may have been more willing to work with North Dakota earlier in the dispute.

Most importantly, Devils Lake emphasizes the importance of politics in dispute resolution. Politics and the politics stream determined the course of the Devils Lake conflict. Canada's fierce opposition to the Garrison project made an outlet a political impossibility for some 10 years. It took a sudden shift in the American political mood and the timely intervention of Schafer and the North Dakotan senators to negate Canada's influence and make the outlet happen. What's more, had it not been for the significant influence of Manitoba and North Dakota over their respective federal governments, it is unlikely that the Devils Lake dispute would have been as protracted as it was.

CHAPTER 17

Turning the Corner on the Kyoto Protocol

MAITE ORMAECHEA

In the autumn of 2006, with the Vancouver Harbour as his backdrop and the glare of media cameras within sight, Prime Minister Stephen Harper walked onto a hotel balcony to deliver his government's new policy on climate change. The issue had been a feature in Canadian policy circles for years; since coming to power 10 months earlier, an announcement by the Conservative government was not only anticipated but, in many respects, also long overdue. In opposition, the Tories had been constant critics of the then-Liberal government's environmental record, particularly its ability to make good on its Kyoto commitment. The Kyoto Protocol, an international agreement signed in 1997 and ratified by Canada in 2002, committed the country to cutting greenhouse gas emissions (primarily caused by burning fossil fuels) to 6 per cent below 1990 levels. Meeting the reduction target by 2012 would be Canada's contribution to the worldwide war against global warming.

The Tories denounced the Kyoto pledge as too much, too soon, and warned that efforts to meet the emissions target would destroy the economy and hurt Canadian families (Sallot, 2005). At their 2004 policy convention, the Conservatives announced they would rethink the international commitment. By the following year, their leader was calling for a 'new approach' to climate change. 'Our plan is to reduce our emissions,' Harper said, 'not just carbon dioxide, but a range of pollutants' (Galloway, 2005). Once elected, however, the Conservative's rollout of the so-called made-in-Canada environmental plan would take months (Mills, 2005).

Meanwhile, Kyoto signals were crossed. The budget made no mention of the accord; instead, existing climate change programs were slashed (Canadian Press, 2006). The prime minister announced Canada would not meet its emissions target under Kyoto and even seemed to question the science behind global warming (Curry, 2006e). At the same time, efforts to curb greenhouse gases—through

subsidies for transit users and federal–provincial talks on boosting ethanol production—began (Laghi, 2006; Reguly, 2006).

It was only on that crisp autumn day in Vancouver that Harper finally cleared
the air on his government's environmental way forward. *Green Plan II*, with its
proposed *Clean Air Act*, promised to fight *both* climate change and air pollution.
Greenhouse gases would be cut and a host of pollutants, primarily those causing
smog, were to be targeted. But as a Kyoto alternative, the initiative offered only
distant timelines, promises of further consultations, and a proposal for basing
future greenhouse gas reductions on production 'intensity'—instead of the
immediate cap on total emissions required under the international treaty. It all
but guaranteed greenhouse gas levels would continue to rise in Canada and that
the Kyoto Protocol was, for all intents and purposes, dead (Simpson, 2005). In
the end, Harper's green alternative amounted to nothing less than an attempt to
'change the channel on environmental policy from Kyoto to smog' (Sears, 2006:
10). It didn't work.

The Conservative plan—what the prime minister called the 'centrepiece' of his
environmental agenda—was widely panned as a non-plan; it was a retreat from
Kyoto without a credible alternative to replace it (Dion, 2006; Leblanc et al.,
2006; Simpson, 2006b). Under attack and politically outmanoeuvred by the
opposition parties who executed a parliamentary rewrite of the *Clean Air Act* to
recommit Canada to Kyoto's objectives, the Harper government was forced back
to the environmental drawing board (Reguly, 2007). In April 2007, the government unveiled a new strategy for reducing greenhouse gases and air pollution,
which it heralded as 'turning the corner' (Government of Canada, 2007).

The government's latest climate change plan sets mandatory emissions reduction targets on industry: short-term cuts of 18 per cent starting as early as 2010
and going up as high as 26 per cent per unit of production by 2015, with 2006 as
the baseline. Companies that fail to meet the targets can compensate for excess
production by either buying credits on a domestic carbon-trading market or by
paying into a technology fund. Further reductions are expected to come from
higher efficiency standards for cars and trucks, household appliances, and even
light bulbs. In total, the government forecasts greenhouse gas production will
fall in Canada to 6 per cent below 1990 levels by 2025—13 years past the Kyoto
deadline. Whether it can deliver on the environmental promise is, depending on
who's asked, a matter of fact, faith, or outright fantasy (Galloway and Curry,
2007; Simpson, 2007c).

Regardless, a dramatic shift occurred in Canada's governmental agenda and in
its international position with respect to global warming in a span of a year-and-
a-half. Beyond the change in government, how to account for the change in
political priorities, and the Tories evolution from denial and indifference to
action on the environment?

This chapter will analyze the rise and fall of Canada's commitment to the Kyoto
Protocol and the recently emerged alternative for combatting climate change. To
do so, it will rely on the analytic framework provided by John Kingdon.

Kingdon's policy process model conceives of three independent streams—of problems, policy alternatives, and politics—that when converged through a series of circumstances, increase the probability of changes to policy. Kyoto's fall from agenda prominence and the switch to less ambitious strategies will, therefore, be examined in terms of how problem definition, policy proposals, and political forces combined to enable the focus change from Kyoto, to the *Clean Air Act*, to the government's April 2007 attempt to 'turn [. . .] the corner' on climate change (Government of Canada, 2007). In so doing, the chapter will also identify those policy entrepreneurs, who, according to Kingdon, use the alignment of the three streams—the point at which a window of opportunity opens—to try to push their particular policy problems and prescriptions to the top of the government's agenda. We begin with the problem stream.

The significance of the prime minister's policy 'u-turn' on climate change in the autumn of 2006 and again in April 2007 is best understood in the context of the country's early leadership role in putting global warming onto the international agenda. Canada figured prominently, for example, in the World Commission on Environment and Development (known as the Brundtland Commission) and its seminal 1987 report, *Our Common Future*. The report focused on global warming and called for an international summit to address the threat posed to the planet. The following year—the hottest on record—Canada joined the UN's World Meteorological Organization and the United Nations Environment Programme in hosting a major scientific gathering on climate change. Both the Brundtland report and the conference in Toronto brought global warming to world attention (May, 2002–3; Doyle, 2007). They also paved the way for the 1992 Rio Earth Summit, where the Framework Convention on Climate Change was negotiated, a treaty that set off the process toward Kyoto. In the run-up to the international summit, Canada, under the Conservative government of Brian Mulroney, pledged to hold its greenhouse gas emissions to 1990 levels by 2000.

The problem then was planet-warming gases and their impact on the environment. Rising sea levels, sweltering heatwaves, droughts, floods, and ice storms— were all events laid at the doorstep of climate change (McBean, 2006). Beginning with Mulroney and followed by the Liberals' Jean Chrétien and Paul Martin, Canadian prime ministers publicly accepted the international problem. Doing something about it would prove more difficult.

Indeed, there were signs everywhere that the country was not living up to its global promises: Canada took five years to ratify the Kyoto Protocol, programs created to curb greenhouse gases failed to meet their stated goals, and the costs of action spiralled ever upwards without a greener outcome in sight. The difficulties in matching Kyoto rhetoric with reality created new opportunities for policy entrepreneurs to redefine the problem. Together, these elements conspired to help push a new problem onto the policy agenda—one that focused on the feasibility of the Kyoto commitment—and eventually led to the prime minister's Vancouver announcement. Other forces would cause his government to redouble its efforts in the global warming fight but, before looking at these, the chapter will examine how Canada's difficulties meeting its Kyoto obligations under the Liberals resulted in the problem being reframed by the incoming Conservatives.

As early as 1997, reports confirmed that Canada's pledge to freeze greenhouse gas emissions to 1990 levels by the turn of century had failed 'spectacularly' (Knox, 1997). Despite the environmental tough talk, little action was taken to satisfy the target set leading up to the Rio Summit (McIlroy and Laghi, 1997). However, Canada's inability to honour the commitment would, remarkably, not prevent it from agreeing to even deeper cuts under Kyoto. A year and a half after the ink had dried on that agreement, carbon emissions were up in Canada (*Globe and Mail* editorial, 5 January 2000). By 2004, a growing economy fuelled by a booming oil industry would see them rise higher still. The UN confirmed that emissions were out of control in Canada the following year, up 24 per cent over 1990 (Mittlestaedt, 2005). And by 2006, the Kyoto gap had widened another 3 percentage points to 27 (Curry, 2006e). The trend was not in Kyoto's favour.

However, under the protocol, the then-Liberal government had until 2008 to start making reductions and, for whatever reason, chose not to interpret these developments as indicators of a problem on Canada's way to Kyoto. The incoming Conservative government did—a conclusion compounded by years of costly delays and policy disappointments or, as one analyst put it, by the 'Kyoto implementation fiasco' (Sears, 2006: 6).

Even after the Liberal government ratified the protocol, it had no implementation strategy and no cost/benefit analysis of alternatives available for tackling greenhouse gas emissions (Sears, 2006). Kyoto seemed to have 'no priority at the cabinet table' (Ibbitson, 2004). Attention began to focus on efforts to come up with a workable emissions reduction strategy. The government announced three between 2000 and 2005: the 2000 Action Plan on Climate Change, the 2002 Climate Change Plan for Canada, and 2005 Project Green. With few exceptions, they focused on information campaigns and federal subsidies to encourage Canadians to do their part for Kyoto. The strategies failed. A senate committee concluded 'concerns about energy efficiency and climate change are not the primary drivers when it comes to consumers' decisions' and should not drive Canadian policy (Simpson, 2004). An internal government report, *Project Green: Overview and Summary Analysis*, agreed: relying on advertising to get people to change behaviour produced 'poor and sometimes "terribly disappointing" results' (Chase, 2005). Soon after, in the federal budget, the government proposed mandatory targets for industry and changes to the *Environmental Protection Act* to make the cuts stick. But, the opposition stymied progress (May, 2007). Meanwhile, by 2005, the cost of Liberal efforts to make good on Kyoto totalled nearly $4 billion and a report to senior cabinet ministers warned that achieving the promised results could cost the government more than $10 billion. According to one official, Kyoto was becoming a 'political horror show' (Sallot and Chase, 2005).

The Kingdon model anticipates that budget considerations can constrain costly initiatives, particularly in tight times. But times were not tight in Canada during the Kyoto years. The economy grew an impressive 40 per cent between

1990 and 2002 (Chase, 2005b). And while it could be argued that with no comprehensive strategy, the Liberals may not have fully anticipated the cost of meeting the protocol's commitment, it is more likely that the government chose not to pay the short-term price, as Eddie Goldenberg, former advisor to then-Prime Minister Jean Chrétien, confirmed.

Regardless, Kyoto remained on the agenda as policy entrepreneurs monitored the rollout of one government strategy after another. With greenhouse gas emissions continuing to surge, programs failing, and costs ballooning, interest groups on either side of the Kyoto divide began to push for change. Some called for more credible efforts to achieve the treaty's target, others for Kyoto to be abandoned altogether.

In opposition, Ottawa's problem meeting its international promises reinforced Stephen Harper's less-than-enthusiastic view of the accord. As Canadian Alliance leader, he had called Kyoto the 'worst international treaty' Canada had ever signed, insisting compliance would cost billions of dollars and hurt business (Brethour, 2002). When his party failed to prevent the accord from being ratified, he urged the provinces to block Ottawa's climate change efforts (Chase, Mackie, and Brethour, 2002). Following the merger of the Canadian Alliance and the Progressive Conservative parties, Harper would unveil his own 'made-in-Canada' alternative during the 2004 election, although few details were available. By the following year and back on the campaign trail, the Conservative leader would again attack Kyoto timelines as 'unrealistic', 'unattainable', and devastating for Canada (Sallot, 2005).

The Conservatives' attempts at problem redefinition were echoed by interest groups and individuals, such as former Alberta Premier Peter Lougheed who helped lead a provincial campaign against Kyoto and likened the accord to the Liberals' much-despised National Energy Program in Western Canada (CTV.ca, 2002). Together with business groups, such as the Canadian Council of Chief Executives, the Canadian Chamber of Commerce, and the Canadian Manufacturers and Exporters (CME), these opponents shared the view that Kyoto would make Canada uncompetitive against its US neighbour and plunge the country into 'an economic hell of lost jobs, soaring taxes and European-style energy prices' (McKenna, 2002: B10). To emphasize the point, the CME released a report warning Kyoto could cost Canada four hundred and fifty thousand manufacturing jobs—one in five—in less than a decade (Chase, 2002). Another study underwritten by the American Petroleum Industry and American Automobile Manufacturers Association stated Canada had assumed a greater economic risk than any other signatory to the deal (*Globe and Mail* editorial, 5 January 2000). It predicted the ensuing economic disruption and expense would do little to prevent global warming because both the US and China—the world's largest and world's fastest-growing producers of greenhouse gases, respectively—were not part of the deal (Anderson, 2005).

In response to the gloomy public forecasts, the then-Liberal government commissioned its own report, *Costs of Kyoto—What We Know*, to try to reassure Canadians the country was not on the road to economic ruin (Environment Canada,

2002). Policy entrepreneurs in the environmental movement, among others, bolstered this position. Like Ottawa, they argued opponents overstated Kyoto's costs and overlooked its benefits. The David Suzuki Foundation, for example, released a study claiming Canada could halve its greenhouse gas emissions using available technology, without upsetting the economy (MacKinnon, 2002). Others foresaw a boost to 'innovation, investment and job-creation' resulting from the country's efforts to meet the targets (Stanford, 2002–3: 53).

However, the Conservatives' rise to power in January 2006 coincided with the fall of global warming as a government concern. Citing the previous administration's failure to make inroads on greenhouse gas reductions and questioning the negotiated treaty on economic and social grounds, the new government perceived an opportunity to change the nature of the problem: from meeting the Kyoto target to the problem with Kyoto. Over the protests of environmentalists, the international community, even Canada's former environment commissioner who was calling for a 'massive scale-up of efforts' to meet the country's international obligations, Kyoto dropped from agenda prominence (CBC, 2006a; Curry, 2006e).

In its place, came the *Clean Air Act*. Defending the revised commitment to fighting global warming, the then-environment minister Rona Ambrose touted the government's bill as a 'realistic compromise' to Kyoto, a deal whose target was now out of reach—'technically [un]feasible'—due to years of Liberal neglect (Mittelstaedt and Galloway, 2006; Simpson, 2006a). The case for the accord's exit from the government's agenda was reinforced in public statements by the prime minister and others who argued Kyoto had failed and that further efforts to try to meet Canada's international commitment would result in devastation. Just eight days into the new year, for example, Stephen Harper warned that the country was 'headed to be 50 per cent above its Kyoto target in 2012' (Curry, 2007b). A month later, he dismissed claims that Canada could still meet the terms of the treaty as a 'fantasy' (Curry, Elash, and Mittelstaedt, 2007). John Baird, who replaced Ambrose as environment minister, even likened the impact of Kyoto on Canada to the collapse of Russia after the Communist fall.

The Kingdon model suggests issues drop from agenda prominence when the government decides they have adequately addressed them or when the financial or social price of action proves prohibitive (Kingdon, 2003: 103–4). The government seemed to make the case for both. Yet, questions persisted over the adequacy of its response to climate change and, one could argue, Kyoto never entirely faded from view. By early spring, the government was forced to unveil a new, tougher plan in the hopes of getting out from under the shadow of Canada's international obligations. This policy correction was in no small part due to the emerging consensus in the policy community about the science behind global warming and the need for credible action. That, and the prevailing political conditions in Canada, set the stage for yet another change in environmental direction. To understand that change, we shift to an examination of proposals circulating in the stream of policy alternatives.

The international negotiations that culminated in the Kyoto Protocol, in effect, worked the Kingdon model in reverse. The agreement imposed a problem onto Canada's domestic agenda and created opportunities for policy entrepreneurs to draw attention to their ideas on global warming. When the prime minister redefined the issue, from combatting climate change by way of Kyoto to the problem of Kyoto itself, a re-examination of alternative proposals took place, and with it, renewed attempts by policy entrepreneurs to influence the government's environmental direction.

Both the *Clean Air Act* and the April 2007 revised action plan on regulating greenhouse gases mirrored ideas promoted by some policy entrepreneurs, in large part, those in the oil-and-gas and auto industries, most likely to feel the brunt of Kyoto. While companies such as Imperial Oil, Talisman, Petro-Canada, Syncrude, and EnCana led the anti-Kyoto charge (Simpson, 2007a), other business groups, think-tanks, and even some economists helped soften resistance to less ambitious proposals. For all but the economists, it was a two-pronged strategy: first, attack Kyoto as unworkable—'cleaning up the environment is not a one-year fix' argued Marcel Coutu, CEO of Canadian Oil Sands Trust, the largest owner of Syncrude Canada—and threaten to shut down whole sections of industry, as energy companies did in 2002 and the Automobile Parts Manufacturers' Association's Gerry Fedchun repeated in May 2007 (Ebner, 2007; Walton, 2007). Second, promote intensity-based targets for greenhouse gas cuts and focus on future environment-friendly technologies to help save the planet.

The proposal for intensity-based rather than absolute cuts was supported by Tom d'Aquino of the Canadian Council of Chief Executives (CCCE) and Joseph Doucet, writing for the C.D. Howe Institute (Urquhart, 2002–3; Doucet, 2004). Like Harper, d'Aquino called for a made-in-Canada solution and favoured a fund for green technologies. Both also agreed that air pollution should be slated for environmental action (d'Aquino, 2002–3). Gwyn Morgan, founder and former CEO of EnCana, brought up the rear in a series of articles published by the *Globe and Mail*. In them, Morgan argued that pursuing Kyoto would be economic suicide and that the *Clean Air Act*, while not 'perfect' struck a better balance between the economy and the environment (Morgan, 2007a and b).

The anti-Kyoto momentum was helped by what columnist Jeffrey Simpson calls 'the dirty truth' about the treaty, that 'there is absolutely no chance Canada will meet its emission-reduction targets by 2012', and policy entrepreneurs who came to the same conclusion (Simpson, 2005). The government's so-called validators, five expert economists who supported the view Kyoto was bad for Canada, also contributed to the sense that policy change was needed (Chase, 2007). Winning agenda status, then, was facilitated by policy entrepreneurs who, through published articles, reports, interviews, public campaigns, and appearances before parliamentary committees (Urquhart, 2002–3: 24), built acceptance for their preferred course of action.

Even after the government toughened its climate change plan in April 2007, the basic elements behind the two policies remained the same, save for the tighter deadlines in bringing in mandatory targets for industry. Like the *Clean Air Act* before it, the revised plan was technically feasible and allowed the government to back away from Kyoto without appearing to abandon the climate change fight. It was also flexible enough to permit industry targets to be satisfied even as greenhouse gas emissions climb. Nevertheless, the evolution from the initial proposal to the more ambitious plan was, in part, the result of efforts by opposing policy entrepreneurs pushing to keep Kyoto (or something close to it) alive.

As far back as 1987, Canadian elites, scientists, and environmentalists helped raise the planetary alarm over global warming. Canadians such as businessman Maurice Strong and the former head of environment at the OECD (Organization for Economic Cooperation and Development) Jim MacNeill both sat on the Brundtland Commission and were party to its groundbreaking report. Another Canadian, Walter Ferguson, former assistant deputy minister at Environment Canada and head of the World Meteorological Organization, helped organize the meeting of climate change experts where another Canadian, scientist Ken Hare, became the first to make the link between the unseasonably hot weather and global warming (May, 2002–3: 52). Their early efforts led to Kyoto and some, like Strong, continue to advocate in both domestic and international forums against Canada's abandoning of the treaty (Strong, 2006).

They are joined by environmentalists such as David Suzuki, Matthew Bramley of the Pembina Institute, the Climate Change Action Network's John Bennett, and Beatrice Olivastri of Friends of the Earth. Through protests, cross-country speaking tours, reports, and interviews, even a staged ambush of the prime minister or languishing on the lawns of Parliament Hill dressed up as a sunbathing polar bear, these and other policy entrepreneurs drew attention to their preference for Kyoto (Curry, 2007d and h; Gray, 2007; Laghi and Howlett, 2007). Friends of the Earth went as far as taking the government to court to force Ottawa to make good on its international promise (Mittelstaedt, 2007).

As the country struggled to abide by Kyoto and the Conservatives began looking to other alternatives, this segment of the environment policy community argued the problem was not the treaty, but Canada's failure to comply with it. They recommended tougher action on cutting greenhouse gases, specifically, mandatory rules and penalties for industrial offenders and a hike in gasoline taxes to get the country back on track by Kyoto's 2012 deadline (Bramley, 2005; Curry, 2007h; Pembina Institute, n.d.; Menzies, 2007). In a widely cited paper, academic Mark Jaccard came to the same conclusion: industry should foot the bill for the planet-warming gases it emits (Jaccard, 2006). And in late 2006, Canada's former environment commissioner agreed in her report, urging government to 'take on' the oil-and-gas and auto industries (Curry, 2006e; Office of the Auditor General, 2006). Proposals to find greater energy efficiencies and establish a carbon emissions trading market were also circulating (Macdonald and VanNijnatten, 2005).

A breakaway group emerged, too, as the deadline for Kyoto got closer, and compliance further away. Climatologist Andrew Weaver, Canada research chair in climate modelling and analysis and lead author on two reports for the UN International Panel on Climate Change (IPCC), Glen Murray, head of the federally funded Roundtable on the Environment, and conservationist Ken Ogilvie of Pollution Probe argued (as did the Tories) that Kyoto was no longer feasible, but they urged deeper cuts to greenhouse gas emissions to get Canada as close to the Kyoto target as possible.

Competing views on feasibility aside, a consensus on the fact of climate change and the need for action was growing. As a colleague of Weaver's stated after the release of the latest IPCC report: 'the debate on the science is effectively over. Climate change has unequivocally been detected' (Scott, 2007). Suddenly, *The Weather Makers* and *Heat*, books warning about the perils of global warming, were on the bestseller lists. Al Gore, former US vice-president and star of *An Inconvenient Truth*, the Oscar-winning documentary about the impending 'crisis' and what to do to reverse the damage, was touted as 'the world's best-known environmental activist'. When Gore called on Canada to show 'moral leadership' on climate change, it mattered; as it did when former Tory Prime Minister Brian Mulroney suggested the government's lacklustre *Clean Air Act* was a 'work in progress' (Simpson, 2006c; Galloway, 2007c). And inside some Canadian and US boardrooms there was a small but perceptible shift from delay and denial to acceptance that more needed to be done (Associated Press, 2006: B9; Ball, 2007; Simpson, 2007b).

Kingdon describes the moment at which an idea catches on in the policy community as a tipping point. The idea that credible action was needed to combat climate change seems to have reached that critical juncture. Indeed, although pro-Kyoto entrepreneurs were unable to move Kyoto back onto the government's agenda, the April 2007 announcement of mandatory targets for industry suggested a response to pressure from the policy community: if the revised plan did not go as far as some would like, it went much further than government originally had intended to go.

Meanwhile, competing proposals continue to stir in Kingdon's so-called policy primeval soup, from joining a rival pact (Curry, 2006a; Reguly, 2006) to taking no action—this last from a dwindling group of climate change deniers (Jang, 1997; Struck, 2006; *Financial Post*, 2007). Policy entrepreneurs behind these and other less successful propositions continue to search for windows of opportunity even as the Harper government insists it is 'turning the corner'.

That policy announcement in spring 2007, like the *Clean Air Act* that preceded it, represents the rise of a new problem and corresponding solution to the top of the decision agenda. For the Conservatives, it was clear Canada could not meet its greenhouse gas emission reductions under Kyoto without damaging the economy. The *Clean Air Act* became the government's short-lived alternative of choice. But after being attacked for offering little of substance to combat climate change, a more environment-friendly option emerged. The spring strategy combines elements of the original plan with beefed-up emission benchmarks for industry, a key condition in several pro-Kyoto proposals.

However much that compromise solution indicates that the Harper government has firmly climbed onto the climate change bandwagon depends on what happens next, because the domestic carbon trading market and technology fund only exist on paper for now. What is clear, though, is that two policy windows opened in autumn 2006 and spring 2007, respectively; and while new problems and alternative solutions were necessary to effect agenda changes, they would have been impossible if not for the right political conditions. Attention will now turn to these last, from turnover and national mood to interest group and juris-dictional issues, to analyze forces in the political stream from 2006 to spring 2007, and how these shaped resulting policies. Among the most significant were the changes in government and in national mood.

The Conservatives rose to power on 23 January 2006, following four consecutive Liberal mandates. As the ballots were counted, Canada began to experience a westward shift in its political centre of gravity. The Tories would win every seat in Alberta, including the prime minister's and that of his soon-to-be environment minister, Rona Ambrose. Their Liberal counterparts had hailed from Kyoto-friendly Quebec but, unlike that province, much of the West, particularly Alberta, remained allergic to the international agreement. The province is home to the country's largest fossil-fuel reserves, and it is also its fastest-growing source of greenhouse gas emissions (Simpson, 2006b).

Stephen Harper was first elected to Parliament in 1987 as a Reform Party candidate from resource-rich Alberta. His campaign against Canada's practice of federalism was neatly captured by the party's 'West wants in' rallying cry and through his own earlier appeal to build a 'firewall' around the province to protect it from Ottawa. Today, his party's Western base (inherited from Reform), coupled with the prime minister's own ideological preference for smaller, less intrusive government, continue to influence his political calculus on Kyoto.

According to Kingdon (1995: 153), administrative turnover has a powerful effect on the agenda. The Conservatives' election win and Kyoto's defeat as a policy option seem to make a persuasive case for the model. In fact, any pretense Canada would abide by the previous government's promise to cut greenhouse gas emissions by 6 per cent below 1990 levels, as Kyoto required, was effectively abandoned when the *Clean Air Act* was announced. And yet, the legislation's focus on intensity-based targets and deadlines that stretched over several elections to 2050 would turn it into one of the government's greatest political liabilities. The policy's fortunes were compounded by other political factors and turnover by other actors, including leadership changes at the rival Liberal Party in December 2006 and the precarious hold the Conservatives had on power since being elected a minority government.

The 2006 upset Liberal leadership win by Stephane Dion is credited with 'touch[ing] off a political chain reaction' and helping breathe new life into Kyoto (Duffy, 2007). The former Liberal environment minister and Kyoto crusader pledged to put climate change front-and-centre and was given 'a ready credibility on [the] issue, despite the Liberal record' (Murphy, 2007). With criticism mounting over the Harper government's less-than-impressive efforts, and up against a political opponent who even named his dog Kyoto, the ruling Tories were suddenly vulnerable.

To make matters worse, Canada's opposition parties—the Liberals, New

Democrats, and Bloc Québécois—were united in their support for the accord, complicating the prime minister's ability to act (Macdonald and VanNijnatten, 2005). In late 2006, the New Democrats threatened to topple the government over its proposed legislation (Galloway, 2007a). Instead, the *Clean Air Act* was sent to an all-party committee where, outnumbered by the opposition, it was completely made over. Originally intended to put Kyoto to rest, the legislation, as now written, recommits the county to implementing its goals. Meanwhile, a non-binding motion and a private member's bill were introduced by the Liberals in the winter session of Parliament in 2007. Both called on Canada to abide by its international obligations and both passed over the objections of the Harper government (Bueckert, 2007).

Early on in the legislative showdown, the prime minister responded to the political heat: he reversed previous cuts to climate change programs, criss-crossed the country making one green announcement after another, and created a special cabinet committee on climate change. Moreover, to convincingly 'smash his reputation as a reluctant friend of the planet', he engineered another administrative change, by shuffling his cabinet (Hume, 2007; Murphy, 2007; Priest, 2007). Rona Ambrose, the rookie environment minister whose star, along with her proposed environmental policy, was fading fast, lost her portfolio to the more experienced John Baird. That her *Clean Air Act* likely reflected the prime minister's, and his party's, views on climate change did not matter (May, 2007: 46). That she underperformed as minister—routinely botching her environmental message—probably did not help (Curry, 2006g). But more importantly, the cabinet shuffle offered the government a fresh start: 'a new face to deliver a revamped environmental policy', and a signal it would do better (Laghi, Taber, and Clark, 2007).

This from a party that less than two years earlier was elected to office touting five top priorities, none of which included environmental action. The policy push toward the *Clean Air Act*, whose rhetoric exceeded its substance, to para-phrase one critic, reflected the new administration's changing preferences (May, 2007). But if government turnover ushered in a Kyoto-less agenda, other forces would complicate the perfect alignment of the problem, policy, and politics streams. April 2007's 'turning the corner', made possible by the cabinet turnover, was the government's attempt to force open a window of opportunity in order to make a much-needed policy correction. That a critical mass of people seemed to be demanding it, only accelerated the process, as the national mood on the environment seemed to undergo a fundamental shift.

Canadians care about the environment. It has ranked among their top con-cerns in public opinion polls for years. But while Kyoto may be popular with vot-ers in principle, few seem to understand what it means in practice (Wente, 2005). As one analyst put it, 'it is a mystery to most opinion researchers [how] "Kyoto" acquired such powerful if meaningless "brand equity." Few Canadians have a clue about what the Kyoto agreement required [and] how it would impact their lives' (Sears, 2006: 10). In other words, while respected, Kyoto was also vulnera-ble. When Alberta mounted a campaign against the accord in 1992, for instance, support for Kyoto plummeted 45 percentage points to 27 (Urquhart, 2002–3). The deal also temporarily lost favour in Ontario (Ibbitson, 2002). The Harper government counted on this perceived vulnerability when it changed course on climate change. It also relied on the previous government having done so much damage to the 'brand' by failing to curb greenhouse gases that resistance to the policy u-turn would be manageable. However, the government underestimated Kyoto's hold on the public imagination.

In the summer of 2006, nearly 60 per cent of those polled said they did not want to abandon the treaty, although one in three supported a different strategy for cutting greenhouse gases (Angus Reid, 2006). While Kyoto typically garnered respectable numbers, they would take on a new importance by January 2007 when the environment surged to the top of the polls, trumping healthcare, terrorism, the Afghanistan war, and every other major issue for the public's attention (Galloway, 2007b; Galloway and Moore, 2007). Climate change had 'developed a top-of-mind salience the likes of which we've never seen before,' one pollster marvelled—a sign that Kingdon's critical tipping point had arrived. Ratcheting up the political stakes were reports that Canadians felt the Harper government was not doing enough to save the planet: two out of three wanted the country to stick with Kyoto; an almost equal number said they did not believe the environment minister when he claimed that meeting the terms of the treaty would cost hundreds of thousands of jobs (Laghi, 2007).

Meanwhile, Kyoto champion and Green Party leader Elizabeth May made headlines when she placed second in a federal by-election, outperforming the Conservatives and winning twice as many votes as the NDP in late 2006 (MacGregor, 2007). In Canada, a quarter-million people flocked to movie theatres to watch a documentary about climate change and Arctic activist Sheila Watt-Cloutier was nominated for a Nobel prize for her efforts on global warming (Mellgren, 2007). The environment had taken centre stage—even long-time resister, US President George Bush, was now calling climate change a 'serious problem'—and in Canada, everywhere the talk was about how the issue could decide the next election (Duffy, 2007; Mittelstaedt, 2007).

In describing the policy implications of shifts in national mood, Kingdon notes that they can bear on political fortunes and result in 'some proposals [being made] viable that would not have been viable before' (1995: 149). Evidence suggests the Harper government misjudged the popular mood when it made the policy switch from Kyoto to the *Clean Air Act*, helping to secure for itself the lowest approval ratings ever for a government at the one-year mark (Martin, 2007). To borrow from one policy watcher, the government had 'diminish[ed] climate change as a widely popular concern' (Sears, 2006: 8). The ensuing political crisis renewed attention on the environmental challenge and alternatives available for shifting to a greener gear. The April 2007 announcement was the outcome. As one British MP understood the conversion: when the 'Canadian government was elected . . . [its] intention was to kick the whole climate-change issue into the long grass. . . . I think they underestimated Canadian public opinion [and have] now come to the conclusion that they've really got to do something' (Curry, 2007c). While not enough to resurrect Kyoto, the climate change compromise moved the government past the *Clean Air Act* into a more environmentally credible position—an attempt to better navigate the national mood, and proof that the changing politics of global warming had had an influence. Whether the compromise will succeed in painting the Harper government a dark-enough-shade-of-green to permit it to turn its attention away from the climate change file remains unclear. A lot depends on other political forces and the people aligned around them.

The groups organized both for and against Kyoto are formidable. Scientists, environmentalists, former politicians, and other elites—both nationally and internationally—are committed to Canada meeting its treaty responsibilities. Judging by the polls, so is a majority of Canadians. With some exceptions, business groups, industry (especially large greenhouse gas producers), some former politicians, economists, and academics, among others, are on the other side. They too have global counterparts.

Predictably, the first group rejects both shifts in the current government's environmental direction as representing retreats from Kyoto, while the latter supports the changing policies (Galloway and Curry, 2007). Motivated and well resourced, each has been able to make its voice heard around climate change. But the group opposed to Kyoto, with the most to lose under the international agreement, has arguably had more influence, in part because it forms the Conservative government's natural constituency. The group's relative power would be tested, however, when the politics behind global warming turned into a red-hot agenda issue. But before that transformation, even before the *Clean Air Act*, there was Kyoto and groups on either side.

When the Harper Conservatives were elected, the interest groups organized against Kyoto won a powerful spokesperson to their cause. Like them, the prime minister worried aloud about the economic cost of Kyoto compliance; and like them, his preference was to push the treaty aside in favour of a made-in-Canada alternative. That proposal appealed to the prime minister's domestic interests and possibly his own ideological preferences. Together, it made for a seemingly perfect policy window from which the *Clean Air Act* could emerge.

Still, condemnation from opposing interest groups was quick and unequivocal. Many environmentalists urged Canada to respect its international undertakings (Laghi, 2006); others, simply that the country do more to combat climate change. 'For the first time . . . [a] Canadian government will repudiate an international treaty,' wrote one columnist (Ibbitson, 2006). From France came threats of an import tax on Canadian goods; from the rest of Europe the label, 'environmental laggard' (Curry, 2006f). And yet, as a political columnist observed, 'the Harper government could have withstood international embarrassment and Suzukite criticisms, since core Harper supporters would be unimpressed by both,' but, 'when prototypical "ordinary" Canadians began to signal unhappiness . . . the Harper party began moving' (Simpson, 2007c). It announced its revised policy commitment to fighting global warming six months later.

Kingdon (1995: 150) suggests the notion of conflict or consensus among interest groups is central to understanding how they affect policy change. If the groups are in conflict, the model predicts governments will seek out solutions they perceive satisfies the balance of support. Leading up to the introduction of the *Clean Air Act*, the political calculus favoured those interests organized against Kyoto. But when the national mood shifted and a critical mass of people began to care about global warming and the lack of government effort in addressing it, that began to change. Reports that the green movement was 'getting a blue-chip hue' would provide further momentum (Blackwell, 2007a).

Leaders of corporate America began pressing the US president for environmental action (McKenna, 2007). The CEO of Royal Dutch Shell declared 'the debate . . . over' (Associated Press, 2006). And Exxon Mobil, head of worldwide resistance to climate change, suddenly began talking about what legislation to curb greenhouse gases might look like (Ball, 2007). In Canada, there was a similar softening; if not for Kyoto, for something closer to it. Surveys showed the country's top executives worried about global warming. Nearly 40 per cent said they were less likely to vote Tory in the next election because of the government's policy position. But, if business leaders were warming to the problem, it was by no means a full embrace. Regional divides existed—the West was notably less enthusiastic—and there was no consensus about what should be done (Blackwell, 2007b).

Kingdon refers to the moment when organized groups seemed to begin pointing in the same direction as a 'powerful impetus' for change. That Canada's emerging consensus was less than perfect did not prevent the government's revised environmental plan from being introduced. 'Swings of national mood,' says Kingdon (1995: 152), 'can be sufficient to overcome [remaining] opposition.' Despite that, the resulting policy revision only came about after significant consultation with the oil patch and even now, some organized interests continue to lobby to get the government to do more.

Whatever the policy position or base of political support, both the Conservative and Liberal governments have been forced to take jurisdictional factors into account. In the case of climate change, the most notable among them is the need for federal/provincial cooperation. This governmental fact of life, according to Kingdon (1995: 158), can either stall or speed agenda progress. For the Liberals, it retarded action on Kyoto; for the Conservatives, it revved it up, partly because Alberta, a politically significant holdout, preferred the Tories' alternative plans, but mostly because of the sudden surge in popularity of climate change.

To understand the federal/provincial dynamic on the issue is to know that even though the federal Liberals were authorized to sign Kyoto, the provinces were, by and large, responsible for implementing it. For example, under the Constitution, they are charged with regulating the energy industry. Provincial resistance began long before the accord was signed, fuelled by concerns over the economic harm Kyoto might do, and in Quebec, by the role the federal government should play in achieving greenhouse gas reductions. By the time Ottawa ratified the deal, the then-Conservative governments of Alberta and Ontario were already pressing for a 'made-in-Canada' alternative (Stilborn, 2002: 2).

To complicate matters, fossil-fuel reserves, and, as such, the costs of compliance, are regionally concentrated. Not surprisingly, Alberta, Saskatchewan, and British Columbia, flush with oil, were ground zero for resistance. Newfoundland and Labrador and Nova Scotia, with offshore reserves to protect, were also unenthusiastic (Mittelstaedt, 2002). And in vote-rich Ontario, Kyoto would send shivers down the province's economic back by threatening the auto industry. When then-Liberal leader Paul Martin placated the province by excluding Ontario car companies from Kyoto, this further strained relations between the West and Ottawa. That Martin led a minority government only made the intergovernmental constraints more acute.

It is unclear what reception the Conservative government's *Clean Air Act* would have received from the provinces, given that consultations on the proposed law never began. However, while the prime minister's preference for intensity-based targets reflected in the *Act* was shared by Alberta, it did not satisfy the demands of Quebec and Manitoba. Those provinces, originally united in opposing the Liberals' plans, were awash in relatively clean hydroelectric power and poised to benefit from Kyoto-like efforts. So, when the *Clean Air Act* was unveiled, they pressured for more. Together, with recent Kyoto-convert Newfoundland and Labrador, they vowed to meet the protocol's greenhouse gas target regardless of what Ottawa did (Séguin, 2006). That certain provinces chose to act more forcefully should not have impeded the *Clean Air Act*'s progress, even if Quebec was particularly significant to the Harper government's re-election fortunes. But, the climate change one-upmanship took on a new significance when combined with the growing popularity of going green.

By January 2007, at least seven provinces had signed climate change pacts with their neighbouring US states. British Columbia and Ontario promised to do more, and BC announced some of the toughest targets in the country, second only to Quebec (Howlett, 2007). Even Toronto had a plan. It was all a seemingly remarkable reversal given that, as one observer remembers, most 'premiers were never exactly what you would call enthusiastic of the Kyoto accord', or anything close to it (Spector, 2007). While few plans matched Kyoto in ambition, clearly, going green—or at least, appearing to—had turned into political gold. In comparison, the federal government's efforts paled, highlighting what environmentalists characterized as 'a leadership vacuum' and leaving the prime minister in the provinces' climate change wake (Curry, 2007f and a). A few weeks after BC and Ontario's announcements, however, Ottawa moved on its own revised plan to curb greenhouse gas emissions.

Kingdon (1995: 158) describes how jurisdictional competition, instead of stalling policy action can sometimes accelerate it, if each attempts to best the other in initiating politically popular proposals. He adds, this competition, 'simply reinforces the political and policy forces . . . already at work.' The jurisdictional jockeying over climate change coupled with the changing national mood seems to be a case in point. Together, these elements increased the likelihood that a more ambitious proposal would emerge from Ottawa. That the proposal took the form that it did reflects the mix of political elements and how they combined with a newly defined problem—that the *Clean Air Act* was no longer viable and more needed to be done. A newly identified course of action was the strategy announced by the environment minister in April 2007.

This chapter began by proposing to analyze the Kyoto Protocol's rise and fall from the Canadian agenda using John Kingdon's policy process model. The former Liberal government's inability to make inroads on their commitment to Kyoto, despite spending years and billions of dollars trying, was examined. Consistent with the model, the incoming Conservatives recognized a new problem: it was the Kyoto accord. Coupled with the election of a Western-based party protective of the oil patch and a feasible policy alternative, conditions were ripe for a change to Canada's domestic and international agenda. But even as the government introduced its *Clean Air Act*, political constraints challenged its resolve. The opposition exercised its majority in the House, eviscerating the Conservatives' environmental legislation, while the Conservatives watched their electoral hopes melt as global warming became a red-hot public worry. Pressured and vulnerable, the Harper government made a policy correction, unveiling a revised climate change plan to help it turn the corner. It was, arguably, an incremental shift in direction, as the new policy, like the original *Clean Air Act*, backed Canada away from hard, fast caps on greenhouse gas emissions. Even so, the new policy is more ambitious than its predecessor, and takes the government further than it intended to go on climate change. If the Harper government is now on the environmental bandwagon, it was forced there by political circumstances. And if it is sitting a little uneasily, it is because the pressure continues to go further.

International Assistance to Secure Access to Essential Medicines

KATE PRESS

In 2001 Canada signed the *United Nations General Assembly Special Session on HIV/AIDS (UNGASS) Declaration of Commitment*, pledging to take action against the global HIV/AIDS crisis (Canadian Aids Society [CAS] and Canadian Treatment Action Council [CTAC], 2003). In the same year members of the World Trade Organization (WTO) issued the *Declaration on the Trade Related Intellectual Property . . . (TRIPS) Agreement and Public Health*, stating that TRIPS 'can and should be interpreted and implemented in a manner supportive of WTO Members' right to protect public health and, in particular, to promote access to medicines for all' (Elliott, Bonin, and Devine, 2003). Despite this statement, Article 31(f) of the TRIPS Agreement stated that generic drugs produced under compulsory licensing had to be 'predominantly for the supply of the domestic market'. For countries unable to manufacture medicines and therefore wanting to import generics, this Article posed a significant constraint (World Trade Organization [WTO], 2003).

Frustration began to build among developing countries and within the NGO community. By August 2003, no WTO decision facilitating access to essential medicine beyond the domestic market had been made, and the issue was at the forefront of the international trade agenda. On the eve of the Fifth WTO Ministerial in Cancun, fearing that an impasse on this issue would result in its failure, negotiators finally agreed to relax international rules on patent protection allowing for the export of drugs to countries in need (Foster, 2005b: 92).

In late September 2003, at a pan-African conference on HIV/AIDS in Nairobi, Kenya, the United Nations chief AIDS envoy, Stephen Lewis, challenged Canada to take the lead in combatting the global AIDS pandemic by amending or overriding its *Patent Act* to permit the large-scale production of generic drugs for export to countries in need (Nolen, 2003: A1). Accepting this challenge, Allan Rock, then minister of industry, committed Canada to action (Canadian HIV/AIDS Legal Network [CLN] & AIDS Law Project [ALP], 2003). The ensuing *Jean*

Chrétien Pledge to Africa Act (Bill C-9) modified Canada's *Patent Act*, with the aim 'to facilitate access to pharmaceutical products to address public health problems afflicting many developing and least-developed countries, especially those resulting from HIV/AIDS, malaria, tuberculosis and other epidemics' (House of Commons, 2004). This bill sets the criteria under which a compulsory licence can be issued to a generic producer for the manufacturing and export of a patented drug to a developing country.

The decision to be the first 'developed' country to implement the August 2003 WTO General Council Decision was a major policy shift on the part of the Canadian government.[1] This shift had been largely unanticipated by most observers as underscored in a 2002 review of Canada's response to the AIDS crisis, which stated that Canada—in terms of access to critically needed drugs— remained 'firmly anchored in the trade docket and to the interests of the multinationals' (Foster, 2002: 202).

From the time of Rock's original September 2003 proclamation, it took almost two years for Canada to implement Bill C-9. First tabled as Bill C-56 in November 2003, it was reinstated unchanged as Bill C-9 in February 2004. After undergoing substantial amendments, Bill C-9 was passed unanimously by the House of Commons in May 2004. The adoption of enabling regulations delayed enforcement by another year (Reddon and Dipchand, 2004). A finalized Bill C-9 came into force on 14 May 2005.

Section one of this chapter focuses on how accessibility to essential medicines became a critical piece of the Canadian government's decision agenda. Section two looks at the evolution of Bill C-56 into Bill C-9, the *Jean Chrétien Pledge to Africa Act*. To better understand both agenda setting and the formulation of policy alternatives, John Kingdon's multiple streams policy model is used. In the first section, the Kingdon model is applied to an analysis of the initial conception of Bill C-56. Kingdon suggests two explanatory factors to account for the emergence of an issue on the government's decision agenda: objective indicators of the presence of a problem and focusing events (Kingdon, 2003: 94).

The decision to address the problem of access to essential medicines for the disadvantaged peoples of the world occurred in the context of the global AIDS crisis. By 2003, more than 42 million people worldwide had HIV, 95 per cent of them living in the 'developing' world.[2] AIDS had already killed more than 28 million people and these numbers were continuing to grow daily. In developing countries only 5 per cent of people with HIV/AIDS had access to anti-retroviral treatment; in Africa, this figure was only 1 per cent (Elliott, Bonin, and Devine, 2003). While these objective indicators were indeed devastating, they were not new, and thus cannot alone explain the sudden government reassessment of its generic drug policy. This is where the second prong of Kingdon's analysis comes into play: a focusing event.

Activist Stephen Lewis's public demand that Ottawa lead the way in amending its legislation guaranteed that access to critically needed drugs would be defined as a critical problem on Canada's policy agenda. The challenge was directed at Rock because, as Lewis reasoned, Rock was 'prepared in a snap, to waive patent law for low-cost drugs when there was the anthrax scare. If [he could] do that for Canadians why not for Africans?' (Nolen, 2003: A1). During the 2001 anthrax scare, Rock, then minister of health, issued an 'illegal' order for the patent-breaking production of Bayer's product Cipro, an order later withdrawn as an 'error' (Corcoran, 2003: FP13). Rock's earlier experience with gun and tobacco regulation demonstrated his willingness to take on substantial initiatives that he felt reflected 'Canadian values' (Rock, 2002). Lewis presented the minister of industry with an opportunity to vindicate himself in a *legal* manner while simultaneously promoting Canada as the champion of the developing world. Rock's public statement resulted in both global and domestic acclaim for Canada.

Kingdon argues that viable alternatives must exist before a problematical issue is given a fixed position on the government's decision agenda (Kingdon, 2003: 142). An October 2003 article in the *Globe and Mail* claimed that federal ministers were not coordinated on the drug issue and 'seemed to be assembling their plan on the fly' (Scoffield and Chase, 2003: A1). This apparent off-the-cuff perspective does not take into account the many policy alternatives circulating in communities of specialists and advocates, inside and outside government.

Immediately following the 2003 WTO Decision, a team of ministers—trade minister Pierre Pettigrew, foreign affairs minister Bill Graham, health minister Anne McLellan, international cooperation minister Susan Whelan, and industry minister Allan Rock—jointly pressed Prime Minister Chrétien on the initiative (Foster, 2005a). In response, Chrétien authorized these ministers to put together a cabinet committee to look into different viable options. McLellan, at the request of Graham, directed the Ministerial Council on HIV/AIDS, an advisory council to the minister of health, to act as a counselling body to the Ministry of Foreign Affairs regarding Canada's approach to HIV/AIDS on the international stage. In its submission, one of the key foreign policy directions promoted was access to treatment (Foster and Garmaise, 2003: 7).

Furthermore, stakeholders from both the public and private spheres voiced their support for a government policy to promote access to essential drugs. On the first day of the WTO Cancun Summit, Pettigrew received a letter from the Canadian Generic Pharmaceutical Association (CGPA) demanding that Ottawa override the *Patent Act* and permit the CGPA to manufacture for export, patented HIV/AIDS pharmaceuticals (Chase, 2003a: B1). The Canadian HIV/AIDS Legal Network, a national, community-based, charitable organization working exclusively in the area of HIV/AIDS-related policy and legal issues, published a high-profile op-ed in the *Globe and Mail* arguing that 'We can change our laws so that generic drugs made in Canada can be exported to countries in need. It's a simple step, easily done' (Elliot, 2003: A23). Finally, a coalition of NGOs had written a joint letter demanding that Ottawa 'amend Canada's *Patent Act* to facilitate the export of Canadian-made generic medicines to developing countries in need' (CLN & ALP, 2003).

Although Rock's announcement to change Canada's *Patent Act* came 'out of the blue' for industry officials, the minister had already been exposed to the notion that a modification to the *Patent Act* was feasible, and would substantially address the problem of access. In response to Rock's announcement, Canada's Research-Based Pharmaceutical Companies (Rx&D), a lobby group for the brand-name firms, argued that the pressing need in developing countries is not going to be resolved by changing Canadian law but rather through 'more cash from rich nations to fund more clinics and infrastructure to diagnose diseases: contributions to the UN's Global Fund to Fight AIDS, Tuberculosis and Malaria, [and] to lift up health-care standards in Africa and elsewhere' (Chase and Fagan, 2003: A1). Lewis, however, had *not* urged Canada to lead the struggle against HIV/AIDS but rather to 'undertake the simple legislative amendment allowing for the production and export of generic antiretrovirals' (Nolen, 2003: A1). While Lewis generally agreed that increased funding for medical infrastructure represented an important policy step in the long run, it would not be capable of replacing legislative changes that improve access to medicine.

The WTO ruling to relax patent rules for developing countries had paved the way for Canada to become a supplier of lower-cost medicine (CLN & ALP, 2003). Rock seemed to understand the international prestige that Canada could gain from being the first country in the world to adopt enabling legislation in order to implement the WTO Decision. A policy window had opened, providing Canada with the opportunity to shine internationally with little financial cost to the government. All other policy alternatives were immediately voided, leaving no other options.

A second key element of Kingdon's policy stream is the need for an entrepreneur to be willing to invest him/herself in promoting a certain solution. Despite 'uncertain legal status' surrounding the changes made at Doha, Qatar, and calls from Industry to abstain from action, Rock was 'gung-ho' and 'didn't want to hear any of that'. He decided that the advantages of the initiative were worth the risks.[3] Having informally ensured that other key ministers were onside, Rock became the principal government advocate in demanding amendments to Canada's *Patent Act* (Fagan, 2003: A4). Industry became the department in charge of the initiative with Rock at the helm. Powlick argued that media coverage is one of the most reliable sources of information used by policy officials to measure public opinion (1995: 427). Most media sources heralded Canada's leadership role, demonstrating broad support for the initiative. Dissent, however, was voiced in a 2 October 2003, *National Post* editorial that described Rock as 'running over other people's rights . . .' by 'throwing around the patent rights of HIV-AIDS drugs owned by pharmaceutical firms' (Corcoran, 2003: FP13).

Despite this isolated negative response, advocates banked on the moral authority inherent in the new initiative to drum up support; as one political aide asked, 'Who in their right mind is going to say this is a bad idea?' (Fagan, Scoffield, and Chase, 2003: A20). Indeed, national polls showed that 60 per cent of Canadians perceived HIV/AIDS as a 'worldwide epidemic best described as an international emergency' (Ipsos Reid, 2005). Lewis, speaking in part as a Canadian, echoed this view: 'Canadians would love to do this . . . Canadians are desperately looking for ways to help' (Nolen, 2003: A1).

Policy proposals for amending the *Patent Act* had been circulating since the 2003 WTO Decision. The CGPA had consistently declared that its member companies wished to produce generic formulations of patented medicines for export to developing countries (CLN & ALP, 2003). Beyond the CGPA was an industrious network of Canadian NGOs, which came together under the already formed Global Treatment Action Group (GTAG), a group created in 2001 to raise public awareness and coordinate NGO efforts to lobby the Canadian government. Led by the HIV/AIDS Legal Network and Médecins Sans Frontières (MSF), an international medical relief organization, GTAG rallied the government to revise legislation. MSF had already launched its Access to Essential Medicines campaign in 1999 in an effort to lower the cost of life-saving medicines in the poor regions of the world (Morley, 2004: A11).

Despite initial protest and continuous lobbying to weaken the legislation (Elliot, 2006), Rx&D publicly supported the initiative stating in a news release that it recognized that Canada 'ha[d] an opportunity to show international leadership' (Scoffield and Knox, 2003: A1). The unprecedented speed at which the bill was taking form may have shocked the brand-name firms. The bill's moral weight and public backing ensured that it would pass. Accepting the new bill meant Rx&D would have a say in formulating its specific details; contesting it may have blackened the industry's reputation and lessened their credibility in negotiations.

Another stakeholder in the Canadian initiative was the United States. Refuting a broader definition, the US had fought to ensure that the reference to 'public health problems' in the Doha Declaration,[4] adopted at the November 2001 WTO ministerial conference in Doha (WTO, 2001), was limited to HIV/AIDS, tuberculosis, malaria, and other epidemics. Despite this restriction, the US government initially walked away from the WTO Decision. Months later, facing condemnation from all sides, the US grudgingly acquiesced (Elliot, 2003a: A23; 2003b: 9).

The North American free trade agreement (NAFTA) allows member governments to override critical drug patents if the drugs are 'predominantly' for domestic use. Allowances, however, are not made for the export of these drugs to other countries. Given that the US had conceded to the WTO agreement, it realized that any reversion to the NAFTA provisions would act as a lightning rod for criticism (Klein, 2003). This decision was made despite opposition from Harvey Bale, the director-general for the International Federation of Pharmaceutical Manufacturers Associations (IFPMA), the US-based drug lobby for the brand-name firms, who, days after the public announcement by Rock, argued that the plan was 'window-dressing' and a 'negative black eye' that would drive investment away from Canada (Scoffield and Knox, 2003: A1). In July 2004, an agreement was made to exempt the Canadian bill from NAFTA. In a statement, US trade representative Robert Zoellick said, 'I'm pleased that we've reached an agreement to clarify that NAFTA's provisions will not stand in the way of Canada's implementation of its new law on pharmaceuticals' (Reuters News Agency, 2004).

A change in jurisdiction or a turnover in government can strengthen, weaken, or force a policy's demise (Kingdon, 2003: 154–5). Although Chrétien had authorized the creation of a cabinet committee to look into viable policy alternatives, Rock had not consulted with the prime minister about publicly committing Canada to action. Rock's self-directed public response demonstrates Chrétien's decreased control at the end of his 10-year reign (Fagan, Scoffield, and Chase, 2003: A20). In spite of this, the political centre still had enough control so that only a PM-approved policy would have staying power. While Rock moved the issue onto the government agenda, only Chrétien's support could ensure that it would stay at the forefront.

Chrétien's personal experience with Africa—he had already ensured that Africa was the focus of the 2002 G8 Summit in Kananaskis, Alberta—made him sympathetic to the initiative. Moreover, enacting such a pioneering resolution presented the soon-to-be retired prime minister with 'legacy legislation' (Bourrie, 2003). Finally, there was speculation that he was interested in joining the United Nations in the future as an advisor on Africa (Chase, 2003b: A10). Forty-eight hours after Rock had promised action, the prime minister called to declare his support (Fagan, Scoffield, and Chase, 2003: A20). As one of his last acts in the House of Commons, Chrétien personally introduced Bill C-56. His efforts were rewarded with a laudatory letter from U2 singer and AIDS activist Bono: 'From the perspective of a pesky Irish rockster, your leadership in Africa will be a legacy that lives on and flourishes way beyond your time in office' (Dimitrakopoulos, 2003).

During the Liberal leadership race to succeed Chrétien, Paul Martin drew on his connection with the singer Bono as part of his campaign. Bono is head of the Debt AIDS Trade Africa (DATA) NGO and, in his speech at the Liberal leadership convention, he warned Martin that his support came at a price: 'While he might come to regret it, I am here for Paul Martin and I am honoured' (Bono, 2003). The rocker statesman further asserted that he was pleased that Martin was throwing his weight behind the government's plan to change patent laws to make cheaper generic AIDS drugs available for Africa. The appearance of Bono at the convention may have drawn attention to Martin in the leadership race, but it also had the effect of committing Martin to get generic AIDS drugs to Africa (Dimitrakopoulos, 2003).

The evolution from the 2001 WTO *Declaration on the* TRIPS *Agreement and Public Health* to the 2003 WTO Decision drew attention to the issue of the provision of generic drugs. Any international obligation that would have prevented a member state from taking action was removed (Elliot, 2003a: A23). In this way the opportunity arose for Canada to amend its domestic *Patent Act* without being brought in front of the WTO Dispute Settlement Body. The Canadian government could balance Canada's humanitarian intentions with its international intellectual property obligations (Reddon and Dipchand, 2004). Thus, a change in international law opened a policy window to change domestic law. A second window opened when Stephen Lewis explicitly connected the problem of access to drugs with the solution of amending domestic legislation. Lewis was not speaking simply about AIDS, but about access. Although Canada had already been looking into responding to the 2003 WTO Decision, 'Lewis was a reminder' and helped draw public attention to the initiative. The publicized conjunction of a specific problem with a specific policy solution opened the window for a political shift.

In the second section of this paper, the Kingdon model will be reapplied to an analysis of the transition from Bill C-56 to the *Jean Chrétien Pledge to Africa Act*, the final and preferred policy alternative of the Canadian government. Kingdon's third explanatory factor for moving an item up on the government agenda is feedback received about the inadequacy of existing policies and programs already in place (Kingdon, 2003: 100).

Chrétien wanted Bill-C56 introduced under his leadership as part of his legacy (Kiddell-Monroe, 2006). Bureaucrats scrambled to get the legislation into Parliament before the change in Liberal leadership (Bourrie, 2003). From the moment Rock had opened his mouth 'a fast timeline was set. It was full steam ahead.' The bill had to be fit into the fall agenda that was only weeks away (Fagan, Scoffield, and Chase, 2003: A20). On its first introduction, Pettigrew described Bill C-56 as 'broad, flexible and faithful to what WTO [m]embers have spent so long negotiating' (Government of Canada, 2003). In actuality, Bill C-56 was much more limiting than the WTO decision on TRIPS (Esmail, 2004: 9). Several flaws, which will be discussed later in this chapter, rendered the bill meaningless.

While the House Leader of the Liberal Party had secured an all-party agreement to pass the legislation through all three required readings before prorogation, last-minute interventions by the Legal Network, The Canadian Council for International Cooperation (CCIC), and Stephen Lewis ensured that the bill would be referred to committee for further public discussion (Elliot, 2006). Rock, among others, became convinced that consultations with stakeholders needed to be conducted. The House of Commons Standing Committee on Industry, Science and Technology, held hearings. In its attempt to rally the government, GTAG engaged a wide range of organizations from across the country, including human rights advocates, development NGOs, humanitarian organizations, faith-based groups, labour unions, student groups, and thousands of individual Canadians. As GTAG lobbying intensified, core members began to meet on a daily basis (Kiddell-Monroe, 2006b).

Despite the efforts of civil society, on 12 February 2004, after a change in government leadership, the bill was reinstated without revision as Bill C-9. Jim Keon, president of the CGPA, complained: 'The government has allowed this landmark initiative to be hijacked by the multinational brand-name pharmaceutical industry' (Canadian Generic Pharmaceutical Association [CGPA], 2004a). The reintroduction of the unchanged bill led to an increase in lobbying intensity, thus, ensuring that the bill remained on the decision agenda.

Throughout the period in which Bill C-56 evolved into the final version of Bill C-9, the government held informal consultations with the brand name and generic pharmaceutical manufacturing industries, as well as with a number of

NGOs. Interested parties prepared numerous policy briefings, hoping to sway the government to adopt their alternative. The majority of the alternatives put forth responded to four aspects of the original version of Bill C-56:

1. Right of Refusal provision;
2. Limited list of eligible importing countries;
3. Limited list of pharmaceutical products; and
4. No provision for NGOs or international organizations to negotiate contracts (Esmail, 2004: 9–10).

Bill C-56 had been criticized for providing brand-name companies with a chance to scoop up an already finalized contract between a generic producer and an importing agent. In other words, under the right of refusal provision, a generic producer would foot the bill of negotiating a contract and have no guarantee that it would reap the associated benefits. The NGO coalition and the CGPA supported the most evident alternative to the right of refusal: to eliminate it altogether (CLN & ALP, 2003). CGPA President Jim Keon explained, 'The very existence of the right of first refusal will dissuade Canadian generic companies from pursuing agreements or bidding on contracts under this initiative. Generic drug companies will not invest time and millions of dollars if it could all be taken away' (CGPA, 2004). Aware of this dissatisfaction, Rx&D proposed the 'Equal Opportunity to Supply Countries in Need' proposal as an alternative (Rx&D, 2004a). Under this alternative, the generic company would notify the patent holder of its intent to begin negotiating a contract with an importer. The rationale for this design is that the patentee can take over a contract pre-negotiation, thus, the generic producer can avoid negotiation incurred costs (Rx&D, 2004c).

The Intellectual Property Institute of Canada (IPIC) put forth a third alternative to the right of refusal provision. IPIC suggested that the generic manufacturer must inform the patent holder of its *final* negotiated contract with the purchasing agent. The patent holder can then either offer a voluntary licence or attempt to take over the contract. If the patent holder chooses the latter, it must bid a lower price than that put forward by the generic producer (in sharp contrast to the original right of refusal in which the price is matched). 'Price-matching' tactics of big suppliers are thus avoided, and an incentive is provided to the generic company to put in its best offer. Under IPIC's plan, if the brand company scoops the contract, it must compensate the generic company for costs incurred from negotiating the contract. The intent is to avoid penalizing the generic company for negotiating a contract by rewarding its efforts with a 'finder's fee' (Intellectual Property Institute of Canada [IPIC], 2004).

Schedule III of Bill C-56 provided for developing countries that were members of the WTO to import generic pharmaceuticals. GTAG, with the support of the CGPA, demanded that non-WTO developing countries be included: 'People in all developing countries should have access to affordable medicines regardless of whether their country belongs to the WTO. Countries such as Viet Nam, East Timor, Lebanon, Uzbekistan, and many others struggle with poverty, low per capita income, and many public health needs, but do not belong to the WTO. Patients in those countries should also benefit from this important legislation' (CLN & ALP, 2003). The Canadian International Development Agency (CIDA) supported this move and Rx&D accepted this new provision but stipulated that WTO regulations had to be followed by both exporter and importer, regardless of membership status.

The NGO coalition, along with the CGPA, called for the elimination of the restrictive pharmaceutical product list, claiming 'developing countries, as sovereign decision-makers, can determine for themselves the pharmaceutical products they need to protect public health in their context' (CLN & ALP, 2003). This time, however, Rx&D agitated for the retention of the restricting list. Another CGPA concern was the restriction that the buyer must be a government, to the exclusion of NGOs that deliver health services in developing countries. The generic industry called for the elimination or modification of the provision to 'allow NGOs to participate in this initiative' (CGPA, 2004b). The NGO coalition called for even further measures to add to the list any 'purchaser legally entitled to import and distribute the product in the country' (CLN & ALP, 2003). This alternative would allow international organizations, and other legally entitled importers, as well as NGOs, to negotiate a contract with a generic manufacturer. Rx&D (2004b) argued that NGOs must have 'permission from the government of the importing country' in order to participate.

Although all stakeholders had accepted that the *Patent Act* would be amended, intense wrangling occurred over the exact wording. The consultative process used by government to prepare the finalized bill drew out these amendment battles. For example, the government held separate consultations with civil society, the CGPA, and Rx&D ostensibly to avoid 'catfights'. However, this 'manipulative' tactic prevented any one group from knowing what the other groups were demanding (Kiddell-Monroe, 2006). The 'Liberals played a double or triple strategy' and 'tried to please everyone rather than [lead] on an expeditious approach' (Foster, 2005a). The decision was characterized by intense intragovernmental negotiations with outside interests being represented by different departments; the bill inched forward at a snail's pace (Foster, 2005b: 93).

Although responsibility for the *Patent Act* fell under Rock's portfolio and, notwithstanding his willingness and 'bullish' desire to 'act expeditiously', the minister of industry was told by Chrétien that it was Pettigrew, the minister of trade, who would be in charge of the initiative (Fagan, 2003: A4). Chrétien thought that the 2001 Cipro 'error' had tarnished Rock's relationship with the brand-name companies. Pettigrew, in comparison, had good relations with the multinational drug manufacturers—many of which are headquartered in Quebec, his home province (Fagan, 2003: A4). The Prime Minister's Office believed that transferring the file 'would be the most prudent way to proceed' (Chase and Scoffield, 2003: A9). Initially, Pettigrew did not want the responsibility of leading the initiative and actually impeded the amendment process, slowing it down substantially. His obstructionism was short-lived, however, when Rock unofficially reclaimed his position at the helm. Industry, and not

Trade, continued to chair the daily consultations with outside stakeholders. As one Industry official stated, 'but for Rock, nothing would have happened. In early 2004 Rock became Canada's ambassador to the United Nations and could no longer be involved in the amendment of Bill C-56. The task to amend the *Patent Act* was transferred back from zealous advocate Rock to a 'risk-averse' administrator, Pettigrew.

Although government experienced a policy entrepreneur loss, on the civil society front, Richard Elliot, the head of the Canadian HIV/AIDS Legal Network, and Rachel Kiddell-Monroe, a lead officer in MSF's Access to Essential Medicines Campaign, became major forces in propelling forward the movement to amend the unchanged bill. Not only did they write numerous newspaper editorials and press releases to ensure that the public remained aware of the issue, they were also key players in preparing an information package on behalf of GTAG that was distributed to every Member of Parliament (Elliot, 2004). In comparing the lobbying efforts of the stakeholders, one Industry official said that Rx&D was a 'walk in the park' compared to the 'non-compromising idealism' of Richard Elliot who 'made our lives hell'. On the international level, both Lewis and Bono remained involved. Lewis participated in the Standing Committee Hearings and Bono wrote a personal letter to Martin to protest the right of first refusal and the restricted list of medicines included in the bill (Kiddell-Monroe, 2006b).

The initial euphoria surrounding Canada's role in the groundbreaking initiative had died down. Canadians remained supportive of the bill but had become less engaged in the issue as a whole. While national newspapers continued to report on the progress of the initiative, details of the exact amendments were scarce. Despite the fact that anyone could have access to the proposed amendments as well as to the different stages of the bill—both published in *The Canada Gazette*, the government's official paper—one reporter for Canadian Press wrote, 'Any serious attempt to explore the bill's potential has been impossible because its regulations, the detailed rules on what is and isn't allowed, have not yet been published' (Bueckert, 2005). Most criticisms of the bill lacked explanatory details, and no specific issues were presented over which to mobilize. For example, Steven Chase wrote in a *Globe and Mail* article that the 'government's much-touted plan to get discount medicine to poor nations is flawed and may never succeed in sending a significant amount of drugs overseas' (Chase, 2004). Instead of passing Bill C-56 immediately, opening up the bill to consultations resulted in an immediate increase in public participation. However, the consultation process was 'lugubrious' (Foster, 2005a) and public interest waned. Relative to its whirlwind conception, the details of the bill were being hammered out at a crawl.

As seen in the policy stream, there were many well-organized political interests advancing various viable alternatives. The Canadian HIV/AIDS Legal Network, under the leadership of Elliot and MSF represented by Kiddell-Monroe, led Canadian civil-society organizations involved in advocacy on Bill C-9. Included in this group were the Canadian Council for International Co-operation, World

Vision, the Interagency Coalition on AIDS and Development, the United Church of Canada, the Canadian Labour Congress, RESULTS Canada, KAIROS: Canadian Ecumenical Justice Initiatives, McGill International Health Initiative, Students Against Global AIDS, CAP/AIDS Network Inc., Action Canada for Population and Development, The Canadian Council For Reform Judaism, and BC Persons With AIDS Society, among many others (CLN & ALP, 2004b).

Joining ranks with the civil society movement was the CGPA. Many of the amendments proposed by the civil society movement favoured the generic industry and, together, the political leverage of the group was substantial.

Still attempting to restrict generic industry access, Rx&D remained a staunch opponent to certain amendments. Not only did the multinational pharmaceutical producers have an extremely powerful lobby, but also being based in Quebec meant that issues of Quebec autonomy were linked to the preparation of the bill. Thus, two extremely powerful blocs were created, with civil society and the CGPA on one side, and Rx&D on the other.

Divisions between political parties—not to mention divisions between MPs within parties—were along coalition lines. The Conservatives were pro-brand even though they were genuinely interested in implementing a bill and the NDP was staunchly on the generic side of the debate. Liberal MP Dan McTeague, a known critic of 'Big Pharma' (what he likes to call the brand-name companies) was sceptical about the restrictive pharmaceutical list (Politics Watch, 2004). Before the new election laws had come into play, Apotex, a large Toronto-based generic drug company, had funded his campaign. On the other hand, Liberal MP Marlene Jennings—representing the 'Pharma sensitive' riding of Notre-Dame-de-Grâce-Lachine and one of the members on the Standing Committee on Industry, Science and Technology—was able to add a number of pro-brand amendments late in the process (House of Commons, Standing Committee on Industry, Science and Technology [SCIST], 2004).

Heeding the recommendations of the civil society and generic industry bloc, the government removed the *Right of Refusal* completely from the final bill. In addition, the list of eligible importing countries was expanded to include non-WTO member countries. However, many critics argued that the terms for non-WTO members to be included were 'unjustifiably strict'. To the dismay of the coalition, the new bill retained the restricted list of pharmaceuticals, although seven, single, anti-retroviral drugs and two fixed-dose combination drugs were added (CLN & ALP, 2004). Theoretically, cabinet has the power to amend the list and remove or add a drug that 'may be used to address public health problems afflicting many developing and least-developed countries, especially those resulting from HIV/AIDS, tuberculosis, malaria and other epidemics' (House of Commons, 2004). However, an attempt by NDP MP Brian Masse to add the drug Moxifloxacin to the list was not supported by Health Canada, largely due to lobbying by Bayer Corporation (Kiddell-Monroe, 2006b).

The scope of the provision concerning who could or could not negotiate contracts was subsequently broadened to include any person or entity, thereby giving individuals or organizations, such as NGOs, the right to contract directly with generic exporters. However, as requested by Rx&D, in situations where neither the government nor an agent of the government is responsible for the importation, the contracting party is required to obtain the permission of that government (Reddon and Dipchand, 2004). Even the bill's name was disputed. The Prime Minister's Office under Martin had chosen the name in an attempt to salvage the reputation of former Prime Minister Chrétien, who faced allegations of corruption stemming from the so-called sponsorship scandal. The *Jean Chrétien Pledge to Africa Act* was almost defeated by the Conservatives and Bloc Québécois because they were disaffected by its name. The *Act* had become more of a 'sum of trade-offs between the interests at play than a signal initiative dominated by the single objective of assuring speedy and affordable access to medicines for the seriously affected' (Foster, 2005b: 93). As Elliot noted, 'the devil is in the details—and the details [got] lost in the congratulatory rhetoric' (Elliot, 2003c: 14).

The application of the Kingdon model to the analysis of the conception and transformation of Bill C-9 demonstrates the importance of each stream in ensuring a successful policy outcome. The ample feedback on Bill C-56 came from select interests and not from public engagement. The lengthy time required to amend Bill C-9 resulted in a 'CNN effect' and there was no focusing event to mitigate public apathy. Moreover, the policy window began to close as the bill crept through Parliament; the 2003 WTO General Council Decision was old news by the time Bill C-9 was reinstated. The international agenda had changed. Therefore, while Bill C-9 remained on the government decision agenda, it had lost its prominence. Even though many viable policy alternatives existed, Pettigrew, a 'cautious' career politician did not position himself in any camp (Fagan, Scoffield, and Chase, 2003: A20). When Rock became Canada's ambassador to the United Nations, a policy-entrepreneur vacuum was created. The other ministers chose not to fill this vacuum and simply administered the trade-off between interests.

Since Bill C-9 came into force on 14 May 2005, at the time of writing not one pill has been exported to developing countries and their needy citizens. The health minister in the Harper government, Tony Clement, blamed the generic drug companies for not taking advantage of the new rules: 'We haven't had any applicants as far as I'm aware on the AIDS drugs side of things for this act. So my operators are standing by . . . if anyone wants to call and set up a meeting and discuss how we can get more HIV anti-retrovirals to more people to meet our international commitments, I'm ready' (Perry, 2006). In contrast to Clement's assertion, MSF has agreed to purchase the first competitively priced batch of drugs from Apotex (Médecins Sans Frontières [MSF], 2006). In turn, Apotex had applied to Health Canada to produce an AIDS drug for sale overseas.

Critics assert that significant barriers remain that prevent the export of generic drugs to the developing world. Jack Kay, president of Apotex, complained about the difficulty of the legislation: 'it was just ill conceived legislation by the prior administration who made it unbelievably cumbersome for us to be able to provide these products at affordable prices.' It can take up to two and half years for a generic company to get regulatory approval of the drug. For Apotex to proceed, it needs Health Canada approval and permission from three name-brand drug companies that hold 10 patents on the various elements of the medication (Perry, 2006). A major complaint made by MSF is that a developing country must notify the WTO of its negotiating intentions. However, developing countries are under pressure from the United States Government not to take advantage of the August 30th WTO Decision and Bill C-9 (Kiddell-Monroe, 2006).

At the XVI International AIDS Conference, held 13–19 August 2006 in Toronto, the Canadian government was asked to answer for this inaction. At the conference MSF alone conducted 64 media interviews with the Press regarding Bill C-9. The conference as a focusing event, coupled with feedback and increased lobbying, has moved the bill back onto the government's decision agenda. As expected under Kingdon's model, the Conservative government agreed to revisit the legislation (Kiddell-Monroe, 2006).

Notes

Chapter 1

1. For a critical assessment of the research program associated with the Cohen, March, and Olsen model, see Bendor, Moe, and Shotts, 2001; for a response, see Olsen, 2001.
2. Mucciaroni (1992: 466) suggests that Kingdon's model may be more useful for describing policy making in the United States, 'where the institutional structure is fragmented and permeable, participation is pluralistic and fluid, and coalitions are often temporary and ad hoc. By contrast, policy making in other countries takes place among institutions that are more centralized and integrated, where the number of participants is limited and their participation is highly structured and predictable.' Obviously, these are matters of degree, and the model's applicability must be established in each case. It has been successfully applied in the Canadian (Hart and Tomlin, 2002, 2004; Tomlin, 1998, 2001) and European (Cherry, 2000; Lord and Winn, 2000; Richardson, 2001) settings, where policy making is sufficiently open, fluid, unpredictable, and ad hoc to reflect the model's central dynamics.
3. Cohen, March, and Olsen, 1972: 2, as quoted in Kingdon, 1995: 85.
4. For a critique of the Kingdon model, see Mucciaroni, 1992; for a response, albeit indirect, see Kingdon, 1995: 222–30. Bendor, Moe, and Shotts note that Kingdon's work 'is one of the most highly regarded treatments of policymaking in the last two decades' (2001: 169).

Chapter 2

1. Foreign direct investment is made to acquire an interest in an enterprise, and a degree of control, whereas portfolio investment involves the purchase of securities (such as bonds and debentures), but conveys no control over the enterprise. This book deals only with foreign direct investment.
2. Howe immigrated to Canada from Massachusetts in 1908 when he was in his early twenties. After a brief stint as an academic, he founded a highly successful engineering and construction firm before entering Parliament in 1935.

3. Quoted in Wolfe, 1978: 13.

4. See Azzi (1999: 38–40) for a description of the commissioners and staff members. Gordon's draft article was never published.

5. Press Release, Prime Minster's Office, 2 March 1970 (cited in Smythe, 1994: 185).

6. Foreign ownership was restricted in certain key sectors, such as finance and communications media (Smith, 1973: 94; Fayerweather, 1974: 10, 169–72; Beckman, 1984: 14; Smythe, 1994: 262).

7. Azzi (1999: 59) makes the point that Gordon wrote the investment recommendations himself, largely ignoring the work of the commission researchers, whose conclusions suggested that tax laws to discourage foreign investment were unnecessary.

8. Azzi (1999: 97) describes Conway as a doctoral student in business administration. Either way, Conway was a tax specialist.

9. Smith (1973: 380) notes that Conway went on in his April letter to state: 'A better solution would be to pass legislation requiring government approval of any sale of equity stock to a non-resident.' He added that small sales could be exempt, and approval could be granted where Canadian capital was not available or the Canadian economy would benefit from the sale. This is an interesting footnote in the story of the evolution of alternative ideas about foreign investment policy because Conway was ahead of his time, and while this 'better solution' was not pursued by Gordon, it would become the foundation of Canadian policy toward investment, as we show below.

10. Smith (1973: 19) indicates that Gordon's idea originated in 1938, when he set out to raise capital for a private, rather than public, holding company to buy up Canadian companies, instead of seeing them sold to American corporations. His efforts were undone by the prospect of a European war. Azzi (1999: 25) doubts the idea stemmed from a desire to prevent American takeovers, arguing instead that Gordon was more concerned with capital accumulation. In his memoirs, Gordon (1977: 25) indicates that the tendency for Canadian owners to sell out to Americans was just beginning in the 1930s, and notes that many companies were sold at very low prices while holding large cash balances, suggesting he saw a good business opportunity. What is important in our effort to trace the evolution of ideas is Gordon's notion of creating a pool of domestic capital to buy up Canadian assets, and its subsequent adaptation into a national public fund.

11. Bliss (1984: 7) notes that the Watkins Report had identified the foreign investment screening practices that were in place in many countries, including Britain, France, and Japan, but did not include screening in their policy recommendations.

12. The functional equivalent of Conway's 1963 'better solution' (see note 9), this was along the lines of Wahn's Canadian Ownership and Control Bureau (Azzi, 1999: 181).

13. Edited by Abraham Rotstein, who had been a member of the Watkins task force.

14. Foster (1982: 140) maintains that the EMR proposals were transmitted to the incoming Liberals by Joel Bell, Trudeau's former economic advisor who was then a senior vice-president at Petro-Canada.

15. In addition, the practice of restricting foreign ownership in certain key sectors was continued with special rules concerning takeovers in the Canadian publishing field (Smythe, 1994: 251).

16. The agreement also gave Mexico the right to review direct acquisitions by foreign investors; the Mexican threshold for review was set at $25 million (US) for a 10-year period, and Mexico retained restrictions on foreign ownership in its petrochemical sector.

17. The OECD consists of 30 democratic countries with market economies, including major industrialized, industrializing, and transitional economies. The organization provides a forum to analyze and coordinate domestic and international policies.

18. Canada was still engaged in negotiations with China and India in 2006, and with Peru as well.

19. Smith (1973: 257–62), who also cites Newman (1968: 373–5) on this point. See also Azzi (1999: 109).

20. According to a study for the Economic Council of Canada, officials in the department believed that the 'only problem with foreign investment is that there isn't enough of it' (Schultz, Swedlove, and Swinton, 1980: 19, cited in Saccomani, 1987: 47).

CHAPTER 3

1. In 1900, the US accounted for 13.6 per cent of foreign investment in Canada, and by 1950, that figure was 75.5 per cent (Bliss, 1984: 2). In 1939, 65 per cent of foreign investment was still in the form of portfolio flows, but by 1952 direct investment accounted for more than one-half of total capital flows, and grew to 64 per cent by 1974 (Beckman, 1984: 10).

2. The other people considered for chair were Graham Towers, who had recently retired after 20 years as governor of the Bank of Canada, and W.A. Mackintosh, a prominent economist and principal of Queen's University (Azzi, 1999: 38). It is unlikely that foreign ownership would have emerged as a central issue in a report drafted by either of these men.

3. The commission study on Canada–United States Economic Relations was prepared by Simon Reisman, the commission's assistant director of research, and economist Irving Brecher. A similar disagreement over a staff study on tariffs, also involving Reisman, generated even more controversy (Azzi, 1999: 59–62).

4. Simon Reisman was one of the dissident assistant deputy ministers, and he had a history with Gordon, having previously crossed swords with him on the foreign investment issue while assistant director of research on Gordon's royal commission.

5. Parliamentary critics initially concentrated their fire on Gordon's use of outside advisors in the preparation of the budget (Smith, 1973: 155); when the budget measures themselves encountered a storm of opposition, both process and content were discredited, causing Gordon to withdraw the provisions.

6. On condition that Canada would not increase its foreign exchange reserves through borrowing in the US.

7. Azzi (1999: 113) cites Wright (1974: 142) on this point.

8. In fact, Sharp's position may have been changing on the issue as well. In 1972, as minister of external affairs, Sharp put his name on an article on Canada–US relations which advocated a policy 'to lessen the vulnerability of the Canadian economy to external factors, including, in particular, the impact of the United States and, in the process, to strengthen our capacity to advance basic Canadian goals and develop a more confident sense of national identity.' (Quoted in Fayerweather, 1974: 37). This initiative is discussed in Chapter 4. The conversion was not complete, however, since Sharp would argue in cabinet in favour of a narrow scope for investment screening (Saccomani, 1988: 47).

9. The CIC supported the new legislation, as did the New Democrats.

10. Their entrpreneurial skills were also transferable. When the Conservative government was elected in 1984, both would leave government, Cohen eventually becoming CEO

of Olympia & York, one of the world's largest property development firms, and Clark CEO of Toronto-Dominion Bank.

11. Marc Lalonde (1990: 70) noted in retrospect that the greatest flaw in the NEP was the scenario of rising oil prices on which it was based, and 'winces' at how wrong that forecast was.

12. This examination of bilateral negotiations on investment is drawn from Doern and Tomlin, 1991.

13. Baker got an opportunity to repay the Canadians in kind on the issue of culture. Canada's request to exempt cultural industries from the agreement had been matched by an American demand for a notwithstanding clause on culture, permitting the US to retaliate against Canadian actions to protect cultural industries with measures of equivalent commercial effect. The Canadians were concerned because the clause would permit American retaliation in areas unrelated to culture, making Canadian action in the cultural sector more difficult. Baker cared little about the cultural issue, but when the Canadians pressed him to drop the retaliatory clause, he refused because he was angry over their recalcitrance on investment.

14. This examination of the trilateral negotiations on investment is drawn from Cameron and Tomlin, 2000.

15. In any case, the government was of the view that Canada should no longer bargain with investors over access to the Canadian market (Smythe, 1998: 255).

CHAPTER 4

1. Quoted in Hart, 2002: 363.

2. Nixon also announced a wage and price freeze to control inflation and economic measures to stimulate American industry; as well, he suspended the convertibility of the dollar into gold (Granatstein and Bothwell, 1990: 61).

3. This examination of agenda change in the early 1980s is drawn from Tomlin, 2001.

4. This is described in Chapter 2.

5. The hub-and-spoke problem had been demonstrated in C.D. Howe Institute studies (Lipsey, 1990; Wonnacott, 1990).

6. This examination of agenda change following the 9/11 attacks is drawn from Hart and Tomlin, 2004.

7. Canada subsequently used duty remission programs to attract Japanese automotive firms to locate some of their North American production facilities in Canada. However, when the Auto Pact was subsequently brought within the ambit of the Canada–US free trade agreement, Canada agreed to phase out the duty remission programs to stave off pressures from American interests to end the Auto Pact altogether.

8. The article was published in *International Perspectives*, the house organ of the Department of External Affairs (Sharp, 1972).

9. The report actually ranked multilateral free trade and free trade with any combination of the European Community, Japan, and the US ahead of Canada–US free trade, but judged that attainment of the latter was most likely (Hart, 2002: 363).

10. This examination of the evolution of policy ideas in the early 1980s is drawn from Tomlin, 2001. In September 1981, the Priorities and Planning Committee of the federal cabinet initiated a wide-ranging review of government policies. Coming at the peak of the conflict with the United States, the mandate included a trade policy review, as well as a separate assessment of Canadian–American relations.

11. Government of Canada, 1983.

12. The commission was established by the Liberal government in 1982.

13. The remaining chapter in the agreement deals with an ad hoc list of trade irritants.

14. Subsequently, Canada persuaded Chile to seek accession to NAFTA rather than pursue a separate bilateral deal with the US (Bailey, 1995).

15. This examination of political change in the early 1980s is drawn from Tomlin, 2001.

16. Anti-dumping duties averaging 12.6 per cent were imposed on 31 Oct. 2001.

CHAPTER 5

1. This overview of Canadian trade policy from the late nineteenth century to the Second World War is drawn from Doern and Tomlin, 1991.

2. Firms included the Big Three plus American Motors, Studebaker, and International Harvester (Dawson, 2005: 242).

3. While Canada was negotiating the Auto Pact in 1964, Canadian negotiators were also in Geneva participating in the opening of the Kennedy Round of multilateral trade negotiations. As mentioned previously, earlier multilateral negotiating rounds had failed to produce a significant opening of international markets for Canada. However, the Kennedy Round, which concluded in 1967, brought about substantial cuts in industrial tariffs, although little progress was made on agriculture.

4. This had been done as well in 1963 when the US imposed a tax on purchases of foreign securities by Americans.

5. The Canadians also learned that Connally originally had intended to cancel the Auto Pact as part of the August measures, and only a last-minute intervention by the State Department saved it. For details, see Granatstein and Bothwell, 1990: 65.

6. For a more general assessment of the Third Option, see von Riekhoff, 1978. The balance of payments measures taken by the US in August 1971 also triggered a new round of multilateral trade negotiations. The Tokyo Round, first broached in 1972, concluded in 1979, and, in addition to the usual focus on tariffs, addressed a number of non-tariff issues. For present purposes, it is interesting to note that the results of the round provided more Canadian export opportunities in the US than the EC, making the success of the Third Option even less likely.

7. This analysis of Canada's free trade decision is drawn from Tomlin, 2001.

8. Lipsey is co-author of the 1985 C.D. Howe Institute study recommending negotiation of a bilateral free trade agreement.

9. *Globe and Mail*, 19 Nov. 1984

10. For a comprehensive analysis of the negotiations, see Doern and Tomlin, 1991, and Hart, 1994; this examination of the trade remedies negotiations is drawn from the former.

11. The deadline for concluding an agreement was midnight on 3 Oct. 1987.

12. For a comprehensive analysis of the negotiations, see Cameron and Tomlin, 2000, from which this examination of the trade remedies negotiations is drawn.

13. Bilateral discussions over a substitute system had been halted by 1991, after it became clear that there was no basis for an agreement between the two countries.

14. This Congressional authorization enables the US administration to negotiate international trade agreements.

15. At the time, Legault was senior assistant deputy minister for the US and coordinator of the Canada–US agreement in DEAIT.

16. These included the Dominican Republic, the Republic of Korea, Singapore, the CA4 (El Salvador, Guatemala, Honduras, and Nicaragua), and members of the European Free

Trade Association (Iceland, Norway, Switzerland, and Liechtenstein), the Andean Community (Bolivia, Colombia, Ecuador, Peru, and Venezuela), and CARICOM (the 13-member Caribbean Community).

17. This description of ideas is drawn from Hart and Tomlin, 2004.

18. Despite these changes in the politics stream, proponents of deeper integration continued to promote their cause. In May 2005, the Council on Foreign Relations (2005) published a task force report recommending both a security perimeter and a customs union, among other things.

CHAPTER 6

1. Chapters 6 and 7 are based primarily on 26 interviews with persons closely involved with the making of Canadian defence policy, including a former prime minister and ministers of national defence, chiefs of the defence staff, deputy ministers of defence, senior policy analysts, and members of interest groups. The interviews were carried out between the spring of 2005 and June 2007 by Norman Hillmer and Philippe Lagassé. Mr. Lagassé prepared an account of the interviews and other materials, and Daniel Bon, a retired Department of National Defence director general of policy planning, extensively annotated it. We are also grateful to the Royal Military College's Joel Sokolsky and to Kenneth Calder, who was the DND assistant deputy minister (policy) from 1991–2006, for their careful comments on the chapters themselves. Copies of the White Papers on national defence, 1964–94, are reproduced in Douglas L. Bland, *Canada's National Defence*, vol. 1: *Defence Policy*. Kingston, ON: School of Policy Studies, Queen's University, 1997. The 2005 defence policy document forms part of *Canada's International Policy Statement: A Role of Pride and Influence in the World*, 5 vols. Ottawa: Government of Canada.

2 Joe Clark, Mulroney's foreign minister, served for two weeks as acting minister of national defence after Coates resigned in February 1985.

3. Erik Nielson vehemently denies this account in his memoirs *The House Is Not a Home* (Nielson, 1989: 251).

CHAPTER 10

1. Established by the United Nations General Assembly in 1947, the International Law Commission is responsible for promoting the progressive development of international law and its codification. The commission meets annually and its membership is composed of 34 individuals who are elected for five-year terms by the General Assembly. They serve in their individual capacity and not as government representatives.

2. The NGO Coalition for the International Criminal Court (CICC) is comprised of over one thousand NGOs, international law experts, and other civil society groups. According to the CICC website, 'The multi-track approach of the Coalition involves: promoting education and awareness of the ICC and the Rome Statute at the national, regional, and global level; supporting the successful completion of the mandate of the Preparatory Commission and facilitating NGO involvement in the process; promoting the universal acceptance and ratification of the Rome Statute, including the adoption of comprehensive national implementing legislation following ratification; and expanding and strengthening the Coalition's global network' (www.iccnow.org/html/coalition.htm). Key NGO members of the Steering Committee include Amnesty

International, Asociacion Pro Derechos Humanos, ELSA International, Federation Internationale des Ligues des Droits de L'Homme, Human Rights Watch, International Commission of Jurists, Lawyers Committee for Human Rights, No Peace Without Justice, Parliamentarians for Global Action, Right and Democracy, Women's Caucus, and the World Federalist Movement.

3. Human security found a home in the newly established Global Issues Bureau within the Department of Foreign Affairs and International Trade (DFAIT). Conceived and championed by Gordon Smith, deputy minister of foreign affairs (1994–7), the bureau was formed in 1994 to deal with non-traditional factors of insecurity including the environment, human rights, gender rights, health, population issues, migration and refugees, and the 'drugs and thugs' problems of terrorism, crime, and narcotics. See David M. Malone, 'The Global Issues Biz: What Gives?' in Fen O. Hampson, Michael Hart, and Martin Rudner, eds, *Canada Among Nations 1999: A Big League Player?* Toronto: Oxford University Press, 1999, 197.

4. This section of Chapter 10, and the responsibility to protect portion of Chapter 11, were developed as part of a Carleton University Centre for Security and Defence Studies (CSDS) project on human security, carried out by Norman Hillmer and Jasmin Cheung-Gertler in 2006–7. We are grateful to the CSDS and its director David Mendeloff for their financial support of this research.

5. Hosted by the Canadian Centre for Foreign Policy Development (CCFPD), the National Public Forum Initiative, beginning in September 1996, institutionalized the 'new diplomacy' approach. New diplomacy was the domestic face of soft power: public constituencies were mobilized to exert influence on governments and decision makers through the forming of 'coalitions of the willing to move difficult issues forward'. Meanwhile, governments benefited from increased feedback, and opportunities to gauge changes in national mood, as well as from innovative vehicles to foster support for their policies. See Rob McRae and Don Hubert, eds, *Human Security and the New Diplomacy*. Montreal and Kingston: McGill-Queen's University Press, 2001.

6. The government's top five priorities on the human security ('Freedom from Fear') agenda since the late 1990s (DFAIT, 1999; 2006a) included: the responsibility to protect; landmines; the International Criminal Court; protection of civilians; and war-affected children (DFAIT, 2006a). These issues have also accounted for the greatest proportion of resources from DFAIT's Human Security Program: a $50 million funding mechanism over five years established by the Liberals in 1999.

7. For details of Canada's first trial, in the Quebec Superior Court, under the *Crimes Against Humanity and War Crimes Act*, see Andy Blatchford, 'Montreal War Crimes Trial Captures International Attention', *Montreal Gazette*, 2 Apr. 2007. Available at: <www.canada.com/montrealgazette>.

8. Fearing the vulnerability of US personnel to politically motivated prosecutions, the US threatened to veto every peacekeeping operation until blanket immunity was achieved for US and other military servicemen. See Alex J. Bellamy, Paul Williams, and Stuart Griffin, *Understanding Peacekeeping*. Cambridge, UK: Polity, 2004, 91.

9. Three opinion polls taken in 1990, 1991, and 1992 registered peacekeeping as the top priority for the Canadian Armed Forces.

CHAPTER 11

1. This analysis of the Ottawa Process to ban landmines is drawn from Tomlin (1998).
2. As reported in the *Toronto Star*, 10 Nov. 1995, A12.

3. A Gallup International review of national public opinion in the spring of 1996 showed 73 per cent of Canadians in favour of an international agreement to ban the use of mines (with only 8 per cent opposed). In comparison, 22 per cent of Americans opposed a ban (with 60 per cent in favour).

4. September would become October. Originally, IDA planned to have this meeting in June 1996, expecting it to be very small and informal. However, initial soundings with other countries revealed substantial interest, indicating that it would be a bigger meeting than expected, requiring more time for planning.

5. Several developing countries, Mexico and Indonesia prominent among them, maintained that the first priority of the CD should be nuclear weapons, not landmines. Neither could Canada count on support from the major powers. The UK, for example, bitterly opposed Canada on the landmines issue prior to the change to a Labour government in Britain.

6. But not permanently—in October, Lysyshyn would draw again on his experience with Open Skies to considerable effect, as described below.

7. As described in the *Canadian Action Plan* prepared in March 1996.

8. The panel included prominent ban proponents such as US Senator Patrick Leahy, UNICEF Deputy Director Stephen Lewis, and ICRC President Cornelio Sommaruga.

9. Lysyshyn was in the chair because Canada was hosting the meeting.

10. Belgian leadership would also make the CD track more likely, especially since the head of the Belgian delegation in Ottawa was scheduled to take up a position as Belgium's ambassador to the CD, where he might be tempted to take the issue.

11. The Open Skies regime provided for the US and the Soviet Union to monitor each other's strategic arsenals, although the agreement was not ratified by the US until 3 Nov. 1993 and the treaty did not come into force until 1 Jan. 2002.

12. The figure was truly invented, since Lysyshyn had no idea what the Open Skies conference in 1990 had actually cost.

13. While the report articulated three domains of responsibility—prevention, reaction, and postconflict peacebuilding—ICISS's guidelines for military intervention attracted the most attention and controversy. Interventions in Somalia, Haiti, the former Yugoslavia, and Rwanda, carried out in response to humanitarian crises during the 1990s, challenged traditional assumptions about the inviolability of borders and sovereign state control over civilian populations.

14. For more recent analysis and statistics, see Chapter 2, 'Deadly Assaults on Civilians', *Human Security Brief 2006*. Human Security Centre, University of British Columbia.

15. UNPROFOR's paradoxical mandate was to protect safe areas and secure provision of humanitarian aid, on the one hand, while operating on the basis of consent and minimal force.

16. According to one line of thinking, using humanitarian justifications for the Kosovo intervention offset the concern that Kosovo might be regarded as setting a precedent for an expanded application of the right to self-determination at the expense of the doctrine of territorial unity.

17. Associated with an attitude of greater selectivity in the conduct of foreign policy to maximize influence in the context of the rise in the numbers and complexity of foreign policy issues at the same time as resources available to manage them were decreasing.

18. Non-coercive approaches to leadership were premised on powers of persuasion, creating like-minded networks, mobilizing and empowering civil society, utilizing information technologies, and leading the development of new international norms.

Frequently, they were juxtaposed with 'hard power', or military or economic instruments of influence and leadership.

19. In the late 1980s, Serbian President Slobodan Milosevic began to push for constitutional changes that would amount to the suspension of autonomy for Kosovo. Reports by the UN Special Rapporteur on Human Rights in the former Yugoslavia condemned discriminatory actions designed to disenfranchise Kosovar Albanians. On 2 July 1992, an unofficial Kosovo Parliament declared Kosovo to be an independent country. After the Dayton agreements in 1995, the KLA was formed and began to carry out guerrilla-style tactics against Serbian police forces.

20. A controversial doctrine, it supported the legitimate use of force in cases of extreme humanitarian need. See Marc Weller, 'The Rambouillet Conference on Kosovo', *International Affairs* 75, 2 (1999).

CHAPTER 13

1. The term 'cultural diversity' first appeared in the 1982 *World Conference on Cultural Policies* (MONDIACULT), but was popularized in 1995 when the World Commission on Culture and Development (WCCD) released its report 'Our Creative Diversity'. The basic premise of the 1995 report is that 'the diversity and plurality of cultures has benefits comparable to those of bio-diversity' (Pérez de Cuéllar, 1995: 54).

2. The Convention defines these goods and services as those that embody or convey 'cultural expressions', which in turn have 'cultural content' or symbolic meaning and expressions of identity. Cultural goods and services are more clearly characterized in the North American Free Trade Agreement (NAFTA) as books, audio, or video recordings, etc. and the publication, distribution, sale, or exhibition of such goods (see Section 2107 for details).

3. The United States and Israel voted against the Convention; Australia, Nicaragua, Honduras, and Liberia abstained.

4. Examples include censorship and the construal of agricultural goods (e.g., French wine) as cultural goods.

5. In 2003, Canada imported C$1.1 billion worth of newspapers, journals, and periodicals, with more than 91 per cent of them coming from the United States. In the same year, 95 per cent of the films shown in Canadian cinema were foreign (mostly American) productions (Mergent Industry Reports, 2005).

6. A split-run magazine has primarily foreign articles and editorial content, but advertising aimed at a domestic market.

7. The US entertainment industry enjoys an economy of scale, meaning that the mass production of a product decreases the cost of producing one unit of that good. An industry with an economy of scale can export goods that are relatively less expensive than similar goods produced in a country without an economy of scale in the same industry. One study noted that 'it can cost about $1 million to produce an hour of prime-time television drama in Canada, and only one-tenth of that amount to purchase an hour of an American drama' (Cultural Industries Sectoral Advisory Group on International Trade [SAGIT], 1999).

8. The government funds arm's-length councils and organizations, which in turn distribute grants to individuals and other organizations in the cultural sector. The political advantage of such a system is that politicians do not appear to be dictating what creators should produce by deciding who receives funding.

9. The MAI, which developed countries negotiated from 1995 to 1998, would have limited government control of foreign direct investment (FDI), but the negotiating parties failed to reach an agreement.

10. Only two articles of the 1947 GATT refer to cultural goods: Article IV exempts screen quotas and Article XX(f) exempts 'national treasures of artistic, historic, or archeological value' (Bernier, 1998).

11. Acheson and Maule (1996b; 1999) put all those who favour government intervention in the cultural sector in the 'cultural nationalist' or 'closed view' camp of the culture/trade debate, and those who argue for freer trade in the 'open view' camp. There are obviously those who are more 'open or closed' than others, but this broad distinction is done to facilitate discussion of the debate.

12. In 1993, Paul Audley of the Director's Guild complained that the government failed to deliver on policy initiatives such as the 1987 film distribution law because of the CUFTA retaliatory clause (Harris, 1993).

13. Azzi and Feick (2003: 103–4) point out that the United States government could have retaliated through the NAFTA, but decided that the WTO provided 'an opportunity for a quick and binding resolution'. It was also an opportunity to make an example of Canada to the rest of the world.

14. Murray (2002: 342) argues that cultural groups actually dictate cultural policy in Canada: 'it is not in the law courts, government corridors, or academic halls where cultural politics are made. It is frequently in the circles of the cultural practitioners–those pragmatists who try to influence policy direction.' Madger (1998: 47) adds that DCH is the clear winner of the governmental actors involved in the creation and implementation of cultural policy. DCH and representatives from the cultural community work together to create cultural policies in Canada that 'muddy the marketplace transparency so much in vogue'.

15. All references to Keith Kelly, with the exception of the 1998 and 2004 references, are taken from a 2006 interview conducted by the author.

16. All references to the Honourable Sheila Copps, with the exception of the 1998 and 2004 references, are taken from a 2006 interview conducted by the author.

17. In 1996 CanWest Global, a large Canadian private television network, considered expanding internationally. The company claimed it was hindered from doing so because a 20 per cent foreign ownership restriction in Canada put a cap on the level of reciprocity CanWest could offer potential partners (Acheson and Maule, 1996c: 23).

CHAPTER 14

1. See, e.g., Anderson (2000), Cameron (1998), Dolan and Hunt (1998), Hampson and Reid (2003), Rutherford, Brem, and Matthew (2003), and Hubert (2000), to name but a few.

2. Ibid.

3. See Chapter 11 for an analysis of the remarkable sequence of events that led to this conversion.

4. Including, notably, the initiative of Canada's Ralph Lysyshyn in proposing the idea of the parallel process in the first place—as described in detail in Chapter 11.

5. There is an interesting and important parallel here between Kingdon and negotiation theory—Fisher and Ury's (1991) 'one-text procedure' in particular. Kingdon's concept of the recombination of familiar key themes, as captured in this instance in the provisional treaty prepared by the Austrians, is essentially synonymous with the concept

of a single negotiating text where the initial working document reflects interests and values commonly held by the participants and thereby 'greatly simplifies the process both of inventing options and of deciding jointly on one' (Fisher and Ury, 1991: 121).

6. See Chapter 11 for a discussion of the background of the negotiations between Canada and the US leading to this move and to the significance of the US agreement to remove a reference to the CD from their resolution. Had the US not conceded this point, the pro-CD forces could have seen to it that the Ottawa Process would never have got off the ground.

7. See Chapter 11 for a more complete description of the evolution of the Ottawa Process 'self-selection' criteria.

8. See Hampson and Reid (2003: 16–17), Wareham (1998: 226–8), and Dolan and Hunt (1998: 399–408) for different perspectives on the 'contest' between the CD and the Ottawa Process and the fragility of the entire process.

9. The measurable impact of this is, admittedly, somewhat speculative. However, there is considerable 'after-the-fact' media analysis asserting a significant role for the Princess's activities. Leading NGOs in the campaign, including the Landmine Survivors Network and the ICBL, were unanimous in their acknowledgement of the significance of her efforts. Also notable, the UK government symbolically passed second reading of the bill enacting the APM treaty on the 10 July 1998, just days after what would have been Diana's 37th birthday, with the foreign minister Robin Cook proclaiming: 'All hon. Members will be aware from their postbags of the immense contribution made by Diana, Princess of Wales to bringing home to many of our constituents the human costs of landmines. The best way in which to record our appreciation of her work, and the work of NGOs that have campaigned against landmines, is to pass the Bill, and to pave the way towards a global ban on landmines' (<www.parliament.the-stationery-office.co.uk/>).

10. See letter from the prime minister to the US president, 8 Sept. 1997, in Dolan and Hunt (1998: 408, note 59).

CHAPTER 15

1. See Kingdon, 1995. For an example of the multiple streams model for Canadian policy making, see Brian W. Tomlin, 'Leaving the Past Behind: The Free Trade Initiative Assessed', in *Diplomatic Departures: The Conservative Era in Foreign Policy, 1984–93*. Vancouver: UBC, 2001, 45–58.

2. Pearson is quoted as writing to St Laurent in January 1950, 'If we are to get any advantages out of recognition, I think we should avoid being the last to do so. My present inclination, therefore, is to recommend on my return to Ottawa that we should, without further delay, recognize the new Government' (Beecroft, 1991: 50). As an early demonstration of this resolve, Canada had instructed its ambassador to remain in Nanking when the Nationalist government fled to the South. Despite these statements and gestures of intent, a change did not come about until 1970 (pp. 43–8).

3. Britain did not in fact succeed in establishing missions even at the *chargé d'affaires* level until 1955, and ambassadors were not exchanged until 1972. From the website of the British Embassy, Beijing, www.uk.cn/ bj/, accessed Dec. 2005.

4. Quebec under Maurice Duplessis was staunchly anti-Communist. Even Paul Martin, Sr, opposed recognition at the time, though later, as minister of external affairs, he became one of its key advocates (Beecroft, 1991: 52).

5. Following the resumption of truce talks in 1953, the Department of External Affairs (DEA) issued a memorandum to that effect. However, it was decided that no action should be taken until the spring of 1954 at the earliest, lest it be misconstrued as 'a reward for ending aggression' (Beecroft, 1991: 55).

6. The speeches were fairly non-committal, stressing that recognition was contingent on China's goodwill in Korea and its willingness to remain at peace. Incidentally, St Laurent's office was flooded with angry letters following his statement that Canada 'would eventually have to recognize the government that the Chinese people wanted' (Beecroft, 1991: 56). To be fair, letters supportive of this stance were also received, but not in the same volume.

7. The DEA was also concerned that Canada would be portrayed, once again, as obediently following the United States (Beecroft, 1991: 58).

8. Beecroft notes that Canada's perception of America softening its China policy was mistaken, a fact reaffirmed by the consistently hard line the US took at the Geneva talks. This was a further factor contributing to Canadian caution on the China question (1991: 60).

9. At the time, India was a strong proponent of Communist representation in the United Nations (Page, 1991: 85).

10. Diefenbaker was 'philosophically disposed against recognition and never seriously considered moving in that direction'. Also during his administration, however, Canadian public opinion began to swing in favour of PRC presence at the UN. There were signs of movement on the hard line in the US as well (Page, 1991: 87).

11. The assistant secretary of state, Roger Hilsman, stated that this idea had been taking hold in the State Department for a number of years already, and that the US would keep the door to better relations with China open when 'a more pragmatic second echelon of Chinese leaders someday assumed power' (St Amour, 1991: 108).

12. St Amour notes that American policy at this time was increasingly viewed as 'stubbornly perverse', and Pearson's actions were in part an attempt to avoid the isolation of the US from the world community (1991: 109).

13. Denmark had recognized China shortly after Britain, in 1950, and Norway had done so in 1954.

14. The PRC's failure to gain a seat at the UN can largely be attributed to the US's success in having it deemed an 'important question', requiring a two-thirds majority vote (Lumbers, 2004: 68–114).

15. Over the year, there had been several signs that movement on the part of a third country, such as Canada, toward recognition, could tip the scales of the debate in the US.

16. Just as Kingdon points out that policy options are rarely new ideas (1995: 73), this one was a modification of a Canadian proposal that had been floated, but not tabled, during the 1965 General Assembly, and that had been approved by cabinet in October 1966. The rationale Canada offered the US was that it could no longer justify opposition to the Albanian resolution without offering its own proposal. However, having Taiwan relinquish its Security Council seat was unacceptable to both the US and Nationalist governments (Lumbers, 2004: 109).

17. Trudeau had spent time travelling in China prior to his political career, and was fully familiar with the political situation. Interestingly—and perhaps tellingly—Trudeau had been part of the 1966 UN delegation and was instrumental in convincing Pearson that abstention on the Albanian resolution was the proper course of action.

18. As Trudeau's policy advisor, Ivan Head may also have played a significant role, but no direct written evidence of this was found.

19. China, on the other hand, shifted firmly from a relative lack of concern about the status of Taiwan in Western foreign policy to a firm 'One-China' policy. This was to have a significant impact on the policy ultimately adopted.

20. Previously, Diefenbaker had been staunchly opposed. It is also interesting to note that, in Canada, opposition to recognition of the PRC was never negligible in the period before 1970 (see Evans, 1985).

21. Pearson had been strongly criticized for 'humiliating subservience' to the US during his tenure (St Amour, 1991: 107), which may have helped strengthen Trudeau's campaign to emancipate Canadian foreign policy.

22. The DEA had not been informed of his intentions ahead of time. Had they been, Frolic states, they would have advised against it (Frolic, 1991: 193). With regard to the comment on the professionalism of the foreign service, this is certainly consistent with Kingdon's assertion that, while elected officials are central to agenda setting, civil servants are very influential when it comes to the definition of alternatives and to policy implementation (Kingdon, 1995: 43).

23. This is the formula that other Western nations would later use in establishing relations with the PRC, and the Canadian accomplishment was seen as a watershed in that regard.

24. This is because, Canada had not only managed to avoid alienating the US, but it also 'occupied the centre stage of world diplomacy' for nearly two years (Frolic, 1991: 210).

25. The governments of Britain and France were aware of this arrangement; they did not sanction it, but it was allowed. Ultimately, the Taiwanese ambassador, Hsueh Yu-Chi, quietly left Ottawa, following his government's instructions to take the initiative in breaking off relations with Canada.

26. See, e.g., CBC Archives, 'The Taiwan Controversy', available from http://archives.cbc.ca/IDC-1-41-1316-7921/sports/montreal_olympic_games/clip5, accessed Dec. 2005. In the clip, Diefenbaker states that Trudeau's actions were 'giving Canada a black eye internationally'.

27. This was significant not only from a symbolic perspective, but also in terms of trade practicalities; Taiwanese manufacturers had to segregate shipments to Canada in order to manually remove references to the 'Republic of China' (Fritzen, 1983b).

28. Though at the time, Canadian cities largely regarded twinning as a public relations gesture, it also often led to a significant increase in trade links 'at the level where agreements to do business can be concluded' (Government of Canada, 1986: 77).

29. In a conversation with township reeve Dave Speer the previous summer, Fritzen had commented that Taiwan means 'Terrace Bay' in English (Fritzen, 1983a).

30. Jelinek argues that Canada is virtually the only Western country without trade offices in Taiwan, putting it at a disadvantage in this regard.

31. See David Vienneau, 'MPs Visit Taiwan, But Trip's Purpose, Financing Unknown', *Toronto Star*, 19 April 1983, A04 and David Vienneau, 'Taiwan Trip "No Junket" But to Aid Trade: Jelinek', *Toronto Star*, 29 Apr. 1983, A11.

32. At the time, private members' bills were not votable unless deemed so by the Standing Committee on Procedure and House Affairs. Jelinek's bill was not, and expired when the time allotted for debate came to an end (Jelinek, 1984).

33. See Allen Abel, 'MP Delegation Tests Peking in Exploring Taiwan Trade', *Toronto Star*, 12 Jan. 1984, A14 and Martin Cohn, 'Tory MP Refuses to Stand or Clap for Visiting Premier', *Toronto Star*, 18 Jan. 1984, A10.

34. It is worth noting that, although this was not the first twinning ceremony to have taken place between Canadian and Taiwanese cities, it appears to have been the first

to be allowed to take place on Canadian soil. An attempt to hold a signing ceremony for the twinning of Winnipeg, Manitoba, with Taichung, Taiwan, in 1975 was delayed by 'an unfortunate incident', and the ceremony was ultimately held in Taiwan in 1982 (Norrie, 1984).

35. Clark was convinced that the foreign-policy process to date had been too closed, and that Canadians should be given the opportunity to contribute to policy decisions (Molot and Tomlin, 1986: 9).

36. See also Government of Canada, 1986: 77–80.

37. The office does not perform consular functions and does not represent the Canadian government; it does, however, receive considerable funding from government sources.

38. A Taipei Economic and Cultural Office opened in Ottawa in October 1991 to handle travel visa and information exchange services as well as trade promotion services.

39. Tomlin and Molot describe this as 'the most severe recession since the 1930s' (1985: 9).

40. These concerns may not have been unfounded, as China did warn Canada against any redefinition of relations with Taiwan following the introduction of this bill. See 'Embassy Spokesperson's Remarks on the *Taiwan Affairs Act* Being Debated by the Canadian House of Commons', 21 June 2005, <http://ca.chineseembassy.org/>, accessed Dec. 2005.

41. This is important because it was this particular provision that had 'defeated' Otto Jelinek's bill on trade with Taiwan in 1983.

42. The 'personal interest' refers to the time Trudeau spent in China as a young man, which he described in a co-authored book, *Two Innocents in Red China*; for the latest edition of this book, see Pierre Elliott Trudeau and Jacques Hebert, *Two Innocents in Red China* (new introduction by Alexandre Trudeau), Vancouver: Douglas & McIntyre, 2007.

43. National security is certainly a pressing concern, but Taiwan appears to be among the least of Canada's worries.

CHAPTER 16

1. The press release was not a binding legal document, so it did not officially settle the dispute. Indeed, as of spring 2006, Canada and the US were still bickering over the outlet.

2. From an interview with Joe Belford, Ramsey County Commissioner, on 24 November 2005.

3. According to Belford and Sprynczynatyk, North Dakota abandoned all hope of ever getting an inlet to Devils Lake after 2000. North Dakota officials have repeatedly stated that they do not believe the filter is necessary; the Canadians and the US federal government can add one if they wish, but they should not expect North Dakota to pay for it.

4. The US Army Corps officially supported the construction of an outlet as of 2003, but their studies of it listed so many environmental and economic problems with the outlet that that they are effectively in the anti-outlet camp. The Corps only supported the outlet after North Dakota changed a law to waive their requirement that any project they undertake be economically feasible. Most of Congress and the Senate opposed the outlet or favoured a reference to the IJC. The State Department's support of the outlet wavered over the years. Both Madeleine Albright and Colin Powell urged North Dakota to work closely with Canada in constructing the outlet, but both were under

constant pressure from the state to build the outlet as fast as possible. President Clinton appears to have been an enthusiastic supporter of the outlet. President Bush's position is more complex, and will be explained later in this chapter.

5. The classic example of this are the zebra muscles, which have devastated native clam species in the Great Lakes and caused billions of dollars damage to marine infrastructure (Reeves, 1999).

6. The Corps outlet has a maximum output of 300 cubic feet per second. The state outlet can handle 100.

7. The *Grand Forks Plaindealer* described North Dakota's concerns about the drying up of Devils Lake on 30 July 1902 (*Grand Forks Herald*, 30 July 2002). Former state engineer Dave Sprynczynatyk said in an interview that he once read a government engineering report on the problem written in 1912.

8. Both quotes attributed to Joe Belford, Ramsay County commissioner.

9. One high-profile tour of Manitoba happened in January 2002 when Belford was invited by the provincial Progressive Conservative party to talk about the lake. Belford testified before the senate committee on environment and public works on the outlet on 23 October 1997.

10. There were several variations on this phrase used from 1995 to 2005. After 1997, this evolved into 'If the Red River flood was a heart attack, then Devils Lake is like a cancer.'

11. For further information on People To Save The Sheyenne, see the organization's website at: http://savethesheyenne.org/. Accessed on 13 July 2007.

12. The first publicized meeting between premier Gary Filmon and governor Ed Schafer after the start of the flood at Devils Lake was in October 1995. Filmon said he would be leery of any outlet unless it was approved by the IJC (Samyn, 10 October 1995). A Canadian diplomat reiterated these concerns in March 1997 (Wetzel, 5 March 1997). Filmon's rhetoric cranked up considerably during the Red River flood when he argued that the outlet would add more water to the Red River and worsen the flood's devastation, and called for federal support to stop the outlet. Manitoba-based MP Lloyd Axworthy, then minister of foreign affairs, responded that he was already voicing his concerns to US officials, and vowed to make a full-court press on the issue (Samyn, 1997; Lett, 1997).

13. Section 5(a)(2) of the *Dakota Water Resources Act*, which lays out the Garrison unit, reads, 'None of the irrigation authorized by this section may be developed in the Hudson Bay/Devils Lake Basin.'

14. The author is somewhat sceptical of the map argument, as it could have been left in accidentally.

15. Under North Dakota's 'wet scenario', the outlet would save $1.50 per dollar spent. The Corps found that the outlet would not be cost-effective unless the lake rose higher than 1,458 feet above sea level, and there was only a 6.5 per cent chance of that happening. In other words, there was a 93.5 per cent chance the outlet would not be economically viable.

16. One memorable criticism of the cycle came from Missouri that said it 'would make the rains experienced by (the Biblical) Noah look like a passing shower' if the amount of precipitation it required were to actually fall (Mahfood, 2003).

17. Gleaned from interviews with Sprynczynatyk, Belford, former *Devils Lake Journal* editor Gordon Weixel, former governor Ed Schaefer, Betting, and coverage in the *Bismarck Tribune* and *Grand Forks Herald*.

18. Dorgan had been a member of the appropriations subcommittee since 1996, which may have influenced Clinton's support of the outlet as well.

19. *Public Law 106–60*, passed in 2000, states that, before any funds for the construction of the Corps outlet were to be released, it must be proven that it is 'economically justified', 'the economic justification shall be prepared in accordance with the principles and guidelines for economic evaluation as required by the regulations and procedures of the Army Corps of Engineers for all flood control projects and that the economic justification be fully described including the analysis of the benefits and costs', and 'that the plans for the emergency outlet shall be reviewed and, to be effective, shall contain assurances provided by the Secretary of State, after consultation with the International Joint Commission' that they do not violate the Boundary Waters Treaty. *Public Law 108–7*, passed 20 February 2003, does not include the words 'economically justified' and deletes almost all the second phrase, leaving the words 'the justification for the emergency outlet shall be fully described, including the analysis of the benefits and costs.' The statement describing compliance with the *Boundary Waters Treaty* now reads, 'That the plans for the emergency outlet shall be reviewed and, to be effective, contain assurances provided by the Secretary of State' that the project won't violate that treaty.

20. Canadian officials interviewed by the author criticized the Corps biota assessment as incomplete, as it did not (among other things) study how the lake's biota changed from spring to fall.

21. Congressional researcher Pervaze Sheikh says Hoeven was technically correct, but that IJC references actually vary from as short as six weeks to as long as 73 years. Heisler adds that the 8.5-year average also includes several references suspended because of the World Wars and at least one that was designed never to be resolved (the IJC was directed to issue biennial reports on it indefinitely). He says a one-year review would be possible, but that the commission would need at least a full season (start of spring to end of fall) to do a proper environmental assessment of the outlet.

22. Kergin's letter does not specifically mention the state outlet, but it does refer to 'other Garrison and inter-basin water transfer proposals', which would include the state outlet. Heisler said Canada wanted any IJC reference to look at all projects in Devils Lake on a watershed basis instead of examining each piecemeal. The author is not sure why the letter did not mention the state outlet, as it was clearly on Canada's mind at the time.

23. The official has been granted anonymity in order to protect his or her job.

24. Technically, Canada and the US can unilaterally refer any matter to the IJC without the support of the other, Heisler says. However, this almost never happens for practical reasons: the IJC operates on consensus and requires an equal number of American and Canadian participants in its negotiations, meaning it's nearly impossible for it to operate if Canada or the US refuses to cooperate.

25. As part of the August 2005 settlement, Manitoba was ordered to complete work on the culverts by the end of the month.

CHAPTER 18

1. This term refers to the OECD definition of any high-income country (see <www.oecd.org>).

2. For this paper, a developing country is any country that is on the OECD DAC List of ODA Recipients (see <www.oecd.org>).

3. An Industry official from the Patent Policy Directorate stated in an interview that the statement made by Minister Rock was "Unilateral and uninformed."

4. The Doha Declaration on the TRIPS Agreement and Public Health affirms that the implementation and interpretation of the TRIPS Agreement should be carried out in a way that supports public health—by promoting both access to existing medicines and the creation of new medicines. The ministers agreed that the TRIPS Agreement does not and should not prevent member governments from acting to protect public health. The declaration also affirms governments' right to use the agreement's flexibilities in order to avoid any reticence the governments may feel. For further explanation of the Doha Declaration, see the website of the WTO, available at: <http://www.wto.org/English/tratop_e/dda_e/dohaexplained_e.htm>.

References

Acheson, Keith, and Christopher Maule. 1995. *Trade Disputes and Canadian Cultural Policies*. Ottawa: Carleton University.

———. 1996a. *Canada's Cultural Exemption: Insulator or Lightning Rod?* Ottawa: Carleton University.

———. 1996b. *Canada's Cultural Policies—You Can't Have It Both Ways*. Ottawa: Carleton University.

———. 1996c. *International Agreements and the Cultural Industries*. Ottawa: Carleton University.

———. 1999. *Much Ado About Culture: North American Trade Disputes*. Ann Arbor: University of Michigan Press.

———. 2001. 'No Bite, No Bark: The Mystery of Magazine Policy', *American Review of Canadian Studies* 31, 3 (Autumn): 467–81.

Agence France-Presse (AFP). 1994. 'Canada's Move to Protect "Culture" May Spark New Trade War with US', 23 Dec.

Alexander, Rajani E. 1995. 'Evaluating Experiences: CIDA's Women in Development Policy, 1984–94', *Canadian Journal of Development Studies* 16: 79–87.

Anderson, David. 2005. 'Kyoto: A Win or a Loss? A Win, Says David Anderson, Former Environment Minister. It Is Not Perfect, But It's a Good First Step', *Globe and Mail*, 16 Feb., A17.

Anderson, John B. 1991. 'An International Criminal Court—An Emerging Idea', *Nova Law Review* 15: 433–47.

Anderson, Kenneth. 2000. 'The Ottawa Convention Banning Landmines, the Role of International Non-Governmental Organizations and the Idea of International Civil Society', *European Journal of International Law* 11, 1: 91–120.

Andrew, Arthur. 1991. 'A Reasonable Period of Time: Canada's De-Recognition of Nationalist China', in Paul M. Evans and B. Michael Frolic, eds, *Reluctant Adversaries: Canada and the People's Republic of China 1949–1970*. Toronto: University of Toronto Press, 241–52.

Angus Reid Global Monitor. 2006. 'Canadians Reject Harper on Kyoto Accord', public opinion poll, 7 June. <http://www.angusreid.com/polls/index.cfm/fuseaction/view Item/itemID/12141>.

Annan, Kofi. 2000. *We the Peoples: The Role of the United Nations in the 21st Century.* Millennium Report of the Secretary General of the United Nations. New York: United Nations, Department of Public Information. <http://www.un.org/millennium/sg/report/>.

Appellate Body. 1997. 'Certain Measures Concerning Periodicals', 30 June. Geneva: World Trade Organization. <http://www.wto.org/english/tratop_e/dispu_e/cases_e/ds31_e.htm>.

Arsanjani, Mahnoush. 1999. 'The Rome Statute of the International Criminal Court', *American Journal of International Law* 93, 1: 22–43.

Ashton, Steve. 2005. 'IJC should Settle Devils Lake', *Winnipeg Free Press*, 13 May, A15.

Associated Press. 2004. 'Devils Lake Outlet Gets Powell's Approval', *Winnipeg Free Press*, 23 Jan., B12.

———. 2006. 'Shell Chief Berates US for Snub of Kyoto Accord', *Globe and Mail*, 5 Dec., B9.

Axworthy, Lloyd. 1997. 'Canada and Human Security: The Need for Leadership', *International Journal* 52, 2 (Spring): 183–96.

———. 1998. 'Lessons from the Ottawa Process', *Canadian Foreign Policy* 5, 3: 1–2.

———. 2001. 'Human Security and Global Governance: Putting People First', *Global Governance* 7, 1 (Jan.–Mar.: 19–23).

———. 2003. *Navigating a New World: Canada's Global Future.* Toronto: Vintage Canada.

——— and Sarah Taylor. 1998. 'A Ban for All Seasons—The Landmines Convention and Its Implications for Canadian Diplomacy', *International Journal* 53, 2 (Spring): 189–203.

Azzi, Stephen. 1999. *Walter Gordon and the Rise of Canadian Nationalism.* Montreal and Kingston: McGill-Queen's University Press.

———. 2007. 'Foreign Investment and the Paradox of Economic Nationalism', in Norman Hillmer and Adam Chapnick, eds, *Canadas of the Mind: The Making and Unmaking of Canadian Nationalisms in the Twentieth Century.* Montreal and Kingston: McGill-Queen's University Press, 63–88.

——— and Tamara Feick. 2003. 'Coping with the Cultural Colossus: Canada and the International Instrument on Cultural Diversity', in David Carment et al., eds, *Canada Among Nations 2003: Coping with the American Colossus.* Toronto: Oxford University Press, 100–20.

Bailey, Glen. 1995. 'Canadian Diplomacy as Advocacy: The Case of Chile and the NAFTA', *Canadian Foreign Policy* 3, 3: 97–112.

Ball, Jeffrey. 2007. 'Exxon Softens Climate Change Stance—Hoping to Shape Policy, Oil Giant Joins Dialogue on Curbing of Emissions', *Wall Street Journal*, 11 Jan., A2.

Bassiouni, M. Cherif, and Christopher L. Blakesley. 1992. 'The Need for an International Criminal Court in the New International World Order', *Vanderbilt Journal of Transnational Law* 25, 9: 151–82.

Baumgartner, Frank, and Bryan Jones. 1993. *Agendas and Instability in American Politics.* Chicago: University of Chicago Press.

Beckman, Christopher. 1984. *The Foreign Investment Review Agency: Images and Realities.* Study No. 84. Ottawa: The Conference Board of Canada.

Beecroft, Stephen. 1991. 'Canadian Policy Towards China, 1949–1957: The Recognition Problem', in Paul M. Evans and B. Michael Frolic, eds, *Reluctant Adversaries: Canada and the People's Republic of China 1949–1970.* Toronto: University of Toronto Press, 43–72.

Behringer, Ronald M. 2003. 'Middle Power Leadership on Human Security', paper presented at the meeting of the Canadian Political Science Association, Halifax, Nova Scotia, 30 May–1 June.

Bellamy, Alex J., Paul Williams, and Stuart Griffin. 2004. *Understanding Peacekeeping*. Cambridge, UK: Polity Press.

Bendor, Jonathan, Terry Moe, and Kenneth Shotts. 2001. 'Recycling the Garbage Can', *American Political Science Review* 95: 169–90.

Bernier, Ivan. 1998. 'Cultural Goods and Services in International Trade Law', in Dennis Browne, ed, *The Culture/Trade Quandary: Canada's Policy Options*. Ottawa: Centre for Trade Policy and Law, 108–48.

———. 1999. *Cultural Issues: What Canadians Are Saying*. Report of the Standing Committee on Foreign Affairs and International Trade. Ottawa: House of Commons. <http://www.parl.gc.ca/InfoComDoc/36/1/FAIT/Studies/Reports/faitrp09/20.htm>.

Bismarck Tribune. 1996. 'Flood Plan Endangered', 29 Feb., 5A.

Bissett, James. 2000. 'The Tragic Blunder in Kosovo', *Globe and Mail*, 10 Jan.

Blackwell, Richard. 2007a. 'Green Movement Getting a Blue-chip Hue', *Globe and Mail*, 8 Jan., B10.

———. 2007b. 'The Greening of the Corner Office', *Globe and Mail*, 26 Mar., B1.

Blanchfield, Mike. 2005. 'Wars, Softwood, Border Irritants Top Meeting Agenda for Rice, Martin', *Ottawa Citizen*, 25 Oct., A2.

Bland, Douglas L. 1993. 'Controlling the Defence Policy Process in Canada: White Papers on Defence and Bureaucratic Politics in the Department of National Defence', in B.D. Hunt and R.G. Haycock, eds, *Canada's Defence: Perspectives on Policy in the Twentieth Century*. Toronto: Copp Clark Pitman, 211–41.

———. 1995. *Chiefs of Defence: Government and the Unified Command of the Canadian Armed Forces*. Toronto: Brown Book Company.

———. 1997. *Canada's National Defence*, vol. 1: *Defence Policy*. Kingston: School of Policy Studies, Queen's University.

Blatter, Joacim. 2003. 'Beyond Hierarchies and Networks: Institutional Logics and Change in Transboundary Spaces', *Governance, An International Journal of Policy, Administration and Institutions* 16, 4: 503–26.

Bliss, Michael. 1984. 'Founding FIRA: The Historical Background', in James Spence and William Rosenfeld, eds, *Foreign Investment Review Law in Canada*. Toronto: Butterworths, 1–11.

Bono. 2003. Notes for a speech at the Liberal Convention, Ottawa, 14 Nov. <http://www.data.org/archives/CanadaSpeech.pdf>.

Booth, Ken. 1991. 'Security and Emancipation', *Review of International Studies* 17, 4 (Oct.): 313–27.

Bourrie, Mark. 2003. 'Cheap HIV Drugs for Africa Threatened by Domestic Politics', *Inter Press News Service*, 4 Nov. <http://www.globalpolicy.org/socecon/develop/aids/2003/1104canada.htm>.

Boutros-Ghali, Boutros. 1992. *An Agenda for Peace: Preventive Diplomacy, Peacemaking, and Peace-keeping*. New York: United Nations.

Bramley, Matthew. 2005. 'Ottawa Lacks Credibility on Kyoto', *Globe and Mail*, 15 Apr., A19.

Brasher, Philip. 1999. 'Corps Proposes Waiting for Devils Lake to Rise', *Bismarck Tribune*, 11 June 3A.

Brean, Joseph, and Sheldon Alberts. 2003. 'US Loses Faith in Canada', *National Post*, 26 Mar., A1.

Brethour, Patrick. 2002. 'Alliance to Fight Kyoto Ratification: Parliament to Hear Party's Warnings that Deal Would Cost Billions of Dollars', *Globe and Mail*, 30 Sept., A4.

Brewster, Murray. 2006. '$15B Military Boost on Way', <ChronicleHerald.ca>, 26 June.

Brodhead, Tim, and Cranford Pratt. 1996. 'Paying the Piper: CIDA and Canadian NGOs', in Cranford Pratt, ed, *Canadian International Development Assistance Policies: An Appraisal*, 2nd edn. Montreal and Kingston: McGill-Queen's University Press.

Browne, Dennis, ed. 1998. *The Culture/Trade Quandary: Canada's Policy Options*. Ottawa: Centre for Trade Policy and Law.

Browne, Stephen. 1999. *Beyond Aid: From Patronage to Partnership*. Aldershot, UK: Ashgate.

Brundtland, Gro Harlem. 1987. *Our Common Future: World Commission on Environment and Development*. Oxford: Oxford University Press.

Brunnee, Jutta, and Stephen J. Toope. 2006. 'Norms, Institutions and UN Reform: The Responsibility to Protect', Canadian Institute of International Affairs, *Behind the Head-lines* 63, 3 (July). <http://www.igloo.org/ciia/Library/ciialibr/behindth>.

Bueckert, Dennis. 2005. 'Drug Aid for Africa Political Illusion', *Canadian Press*, 1 May.

———. 2007. 'Opposition MPs Pass Pro-Kyoto Motion', *Globe and Mail*, 6 Feb., A10.

Burney, Derek. 2004. *Getting It Done: A Memoir*. Montreal and Kingston: McGill-Queen's University Press.

Buzan, Barry. 1983. *People, States and Fear*. Brighton: Wheatsheaf Books.

Byers, Michael. 2005. 'This Round in the Cultural Protection Fight Goes to Canada', *Globe and Mail*, 21 Oct.

Cameron, Maxwell A. 1998. 'Democratization of Foreign Policy: The Ottawa Process As a Model', *Canadian Foreign Policy* 5, 3: 147–65.

——— and Brian Tomlin. 2000. *The Making of NAFTA: How the Deal Was Done*. Ithaca: Cornell University Press.

———, Bob Lawson, and Brian Tomlin, eds. 1998. *To Walk Without Fear: The Global Movement to Ban Landmines*. Toronto: Oxford University Press.

Canada 21: Canada and Common Security in the Twenty-First Century. 1994. Toronto: Centre for International Studies, University of Toronto.

Canada. House of Commons. 1983. *Debates*, 28 Apr.

———. 2005. Standing Committee on Foreign Affairs and International Trade. *Evidence*. Meeting no. 72, 15 Nov., 38th Parliament, 1st Session. <http://www.parl.gc.ca/Info Com/ CommitteeMinute.asp?Language=E& Parliament=1&Joint=0& CommitteeID= 110>.

Canada's Research-Based Pharmaceutical Companies (Rx&D). 2004a. 'Providing Affordable Medicines to Patients in the Developing World', submission to the House of Commons Standing Committee on Industry, Science and Technology. <http://www. canada pharma.org/meds_e.htm>.

———. 2004b. 'Remarks by Canada's Research-Based Pharmaceutical Companies', submission to the Senate Foreign Affairs Committee on Bill C-9. <http://www. canada pharma.org/Media_Centre/News_Releases/2004/English_Speaking_Remarks. pdf>.

———. 2004c. 'Remarks by Canada's Research-Based Pharmaceutical Companies', submission to the House of Commons Standing Committee on Industry, Science and Technology. <http://www.canadapharma.org/Media_Centre/Speeches/WTO_Speech.pdf>.

Canadian Aids Society (CAS) and Canadian Treatment Action Council (CTAC). 2003. 'National AIDS Organizations Salute Government of Canada—Federal Government to Amend the Patent Act', press release, 26 Sept. <http://www.aidslaw.ca/Maincontent/ issues/cts/patent-amend/e-press-CAS-CTAC-sept2603.htm>.

Canadian Centre for Foreign Policy Development (CCFPD). 2000. *Academia and Foreign Policy: Ahead or Behind the Curve?* Report from the Second Annual Academic Roundtable, Ottawa, 5 May.

Canadian Conference of the Arts (CCA) Working Group on Cultural Policy for the 21st Century. 1998. *Preliminary Findings of the Working Group on Cultural Policy for the 21st Century: Executive Summary and Key Recommendations*. Ottawa: Canadian Conference of the Arts. <http://www.ccarts.ca/en/advocacy/publications/policy/workinggroup.htm>.

Canadian Council for International Cooperation (CCIC). 1994a. *Economic Justice: Toward a Just and Sustainable Canadian Foreign Policy*. Ottawa: CCIC.

———. 1994b. *Towards a Common Future*. Ottawa: CCIC.

———. 1994c. *Human Rights and Democratic Development in Canadian Foreign Policy*. Ottawa: CCIC.

———. 1994d. *Fighting Poverty First: The Development Challenge*. Ottawa: CCIC.

———. 1998. Canada, Development Cooperation Review Series, No. 26, Development Assistance Committee, OECD.

———. 2001. 'Looking to the Future: Issues in CIDA's Long Term Strategy: A CCIC/CIDA Roundtable and Consultation', Feb. <http://www.ccic.ca/e/docs/002_aid_20001-0>.

———. 2004a. 'Recent Trends in Canadian Aid to Sub-Saharan Africa', A Briefing Note. October 2004. <http://www.ccic.ca/e/docs/003_acf_2004-10_subsaharan_africa_aid_trends.pdf>.

———. 2004b. '"At the Table or in the Kitchen?" CIDA's New Aid Strategies, Developing Country Ownership and Donor Conditionality', CCIC Briefing Paper, Halifax, Sept. <http://www.ccic.ca/e/docs/002_aid_2004-09_at_the_table.pdf >.

Canadian Council of Chief Executives. 2002. 'The Kyoto Alternative Revisited: A Responsible and Dynamic Alternative for Canada', strategy paper, June. <http://www.ceocouncil.ca/publications/pdf/01964417efe20dbbe1a2b1ace8e7db94/presentations_2002_06_21.pdf >.

Canadian Council of Churches. 1999. Canadian Church Leaders' Letter to the Prime Minister on the NATO Bombing of Kosovo and Yugoslavia. 13 Apr. <http://www.plough shares.ca/libraries/Build/CanChLeadLet.html>.

Canadian Generic Pharmaceutical Association (CGPA). 2004a. *Access to Medicines Bill Needs Major Changes to be Effective: Generic Drug Industry*. 12 Feb. <http://www.cdma-acfpp.org/en/news/feb_12_04.shtml>.

———. 2004b. *Bill C-9 an Act to Amend the Patent Act and the Food and Drugs Act Comments from Canada's Generic Pharmaceutical Industry*. 26 Feb. <http://www.cdma-acfpp.org/en/docs/CGPA_ind_com_feb26.pdf>.

Canadian HIV/AIDS Legal Network (CLN) and AIDS Law Project (ALP). 2003. *Global Access to Medicines: Will Canada Meet the Challenge?*, brief to Members of Parliament on Bill C-9. <http://www.aidslaw.ca>.

———. 2004a. 'Canada Proceeds with Bill C-9 on Cheaper Medicine Exports: NGOs Say Initiative Is Important, and Urge Other Countries to Avoid the Flaws in the Canadian Model', news release, 28 Apr. <http://www.aidslaw.ca/Media/press-releases/e-press-apr2804.pdf>.

———. 2004b. *Canada's Patent Act Amendment: Allowing Compulsory Licensing for the Export of Generic Pharmaceutical Products*. Toronto: Canadian HIV/AIDS Legal Network. <http://www.aidslaw.ca/Maincontent/issues/cts/patent-amend.htm>.

———, Médecins Sans Frontières Canada, Oxfam Canada and the Interagency Coalition on AIDS and Development. 2003. Letter to Honourable Allan Rock, Minister of Industry, 23 Sept. <http://www.aidslaw.ca/Maincontent/issues/cts/Generic_exports_letter_23Sept2003.pdf>.

Canadian Institute for International Peace and Security (CIIPS). 1989. 'The Federal Budget: Defence and Foreign Policy. A Media Roundtable', *Peace and Security* 4, 2 (Summer): 6–9.

Canadian Institute of International Affairs (CIIA). 2000. *Culture Sans Frontière: Culture and Canadian Foreign Policy.* Report of the CIIA Foreign Policy Conference, Nov. Toronto: Canadian Institute of International Affairs.

———. 2003. 'Canada Now: Fading Power or Future Power?' prepared for the Department of Foreign Affairs and International Trade, National Foreign Policy Conference, Toronto, 28–30 Mar.

Canadian International Development Agency (CIDA). 1971. *Annual Review, 1970–71.*

———. 1983. 'Managing the Process of Change: Women in Development', Women in Development Policy Branch.

———. 1986. *Women in Development Action Plan.* Hull: CIDA.

———. 1987. *Sharing Our Future.* Hull: Minister of Supply and Services.

———. 1989. *Women: A Vital Force in Development: Report on CIDA's Progress on Implementing Its WID Action Plan,* Ottawa: Public Affairs Branch.

———. 1995. *CIDA's Policy on Women in Development and Gender Equity.* Ottawa: CIDA.

———. 1996a. *Policy of Canada for CIDA on Human Rights, Democratization, and Good Governance.* Hull: CIDA.

———. 1996b. *Policy on Poverty Reduction.* Jan. <http://www.acdi-cida.gc.ca/ publications-e.htm>.

———. 1997. *Sustainable Development Strategy for 1997–2000.* Hull: Minister of Public Works and Government Services Canada.

———. 1999. *Policy on Gender Equality.* Ottawa: Minister of Public Works and Government Services Canada.

———. 2000a. *CIDA's Social Development Priorities: A Framework for Action.* Hull: Minister of Public Works and Government Services Canada.

———. 2000b. *Accelerating Change: Resources for Gender Mainstreaming* (ed. Melissa Innes). Hull: Minister of Public Works and Government Services Canada.

———. 2001a. *Sustainable Development Strategy 2001–2003.* Hull: Minister of Public Works and Government Services Canada.

———. 2001b. *CIDA's Action Plan on Health and Nutrition.* Hull: Minister of Public Works and Government Services Canada.

———. 2001c. *CIDA's Action Plan on Child Protection: Promoting the Rights of Children Who Need Special Protection Measures.* Hull: Minister of Public Works and Government Services Canada.

———. 2002a. *Canada Making a Difference in the World: A Policy Statement on Strengthening Aid Effectiveness.* (Sept.). Hull: Minister of Public Works and Government Services Canada.

———. 2002b. *CIDA Takes Action against HIV/AIDS around the World.* Hull: Minister of Public Works and Government Services Canada.

———. 2003a. *Promoting Sustainable Rural Development through Agriculture.* Hull: Minister of Public Works and Government Services Canada.

———. 2003b. *Expanding Opportunities for Private Sector Investment.* Hull: Minister of Public Works and Government Services Canada.

———. 2004. *Sustainable Development Strategy 2004–2006.* Ottawa: CIDA. <http://www.acdi-cida.gc.ca/INET/IMAGES.NSF/vLUImages/Sustainable_development/$file/SDS-E.pdf>.

Canadian Peace Alliance. 1992. *Transformation Moment—A Canadian Vision of Common Security.* Report of the Citizen's Inquiry into Peace and Security. Waterloo, Toronto: Project Ploughshares and The Canadian Peace Alliance.

Canadian Press. 2006. 'Ottawa Axes Another Kyoto Program', 6 May, A7.

Cardoso, Fernando Enrique, and Faletto Enzo. 1979. *Dependency and Development in Latin America*. Berkeley: University of California Press.

Carment, David. 2005. *Effective Defence Policy for Responding to Failed and Failing States*. Calgary: Canadian Defence and Foreign Affairs Institute.

Carnegie Commission on Preventing Deadly Conflict. 1997. *Preventing Deadly Conflict: Final Report*. Washington, DC: The Commission.

Carrington, D. Owen, ed. 1968. *Canadian Party Platforms 1867–1968*. Toronto: Copp Clark.

Cavell, Nick. 1954–5. 'Canada and Colombo', *Queen's Quarterly* 61 (Autumn): 319–44.

CBC.ca. 2006a. 'Hundreds of Protesters Demand PM Act on Kyoto'. 4 Nov. <http://www.cbc.ca/canada/story/2006/11/04/kyoto-protest.html>.

———. 2006b. 'French Minister Slams Canada's Kyoto Retreat'. 16 Nov. <http://www.cbc.ca/world/story/2006/11/16/kyoto-ambrose.html>.

Cellucci, Paul. 2005. *Unquiet Diplomacy*. Toronto: Key Porter Books.

Centre de Recherche sur l'Opinion Publique (CROP). 1991. Public Opinion Poll, Dec.

———. 1992. Public Opinion Poll, Oct.

Centre for Research and Information on Canada (CRIC). 2005. *Portraits of Canada 2004*. Montreal: Centre for Research and Information on Canada.

Charlton, Mark. 1992. *The Making of Canadian Food Aid Policy*. Montreal and Kingston: McGill-Queen's University Press.

Chase, Steven. 2002. 'Ratifying Kyoto Estimated to Cost Up to 450,000 Jobs. Manufacturers Warn Curbing Emissions Will Boost Costs', *Globe and Mail*, 27 Feb., B6.

———. 2003a. 'Canadian Generic Drug Makers Seek Export Rights: Association Wants Change to Canadian Law', *Globe and Mail*, 11 Sept., B1.

———. 2003b. 'Chrétien's Anniversary: Chrétien Sets Sights on Drug Legislation for Legacy', *Globe and Mail*, 5 Nov., A10.

———. 2004. 'Liberals' Discount Medicine Plan Panned', *Globe and Mail*, 19 Nov. <http://www.theglobeandmail.com/servlet/story/RTGAM.20041119.wxdrug19/BNStory/National/>.

———. 2005a. 'Debate Swirls over Kyoto Failures; Government Looks to Spend Billions, Offer Incentives to Reach Targets', *Globe and Mail*, 14 Jan., A4.

———. 2005b. 'As Economy Revs Up, Kyoto Obligations Mount', *Globe and Mail*, 17 Jan., A1.

———. 2007. 'Ottawa Rolls Out "Validators" to Boost Anti-Kyoto Stand', *Globe and Mail*, 19 Apr., A1.

——— et al. 2002. 'Divulge Plan for Kyoto Deal Eves Demands', *Globe and Mail*, 2 Oct., A5.

——— and Drew Fagan. 2003. 'Drug Companies Balk at Ottawa's AIDS Plan', *Globe and Mail*, 27 Sept., A1.

——— and Heather Scoffield. 2003. 'Ottawa Leans Toward Limits on Cheap-Drug Distribution: Export of Generics to Poor Countries Likely to Target Only AIDS, Malaria, TB for Now', *Globe and Mail*, 16 Oct., A9.

Cherry, Barbara. 2000. 'The Irony of Telecommunications Deregulation: Assessing the Role Reversal in US and EU Policy', in Ingo Vogelsang and Benjamin Compaine, eds, *The Internet Upheaval: Raising Questions, Seeking Answers in Communications Policy*. Cambridge: MIT Press, 355–85.

Cheung-Gertler, Jasmin H. 2006a. 'The Politics of Human Security and Humanitarian Intervention as Human Security', brief prepared for *Canada's International Policies*, unpublished.

———. 2006b. 'Postcards from a Middle Power: Liberal Internationalism in the Post-Cold War Era', Ottawa: Carleton University, unpublished.

———. 2007. 'A Model Power for a Troubled World? Canadian National Interests and Human Security in the 21st Century', *International Journal* 62, 3.

Clarke, Robert E. 1990. 'Overseas Development Assistance: The Neo-Conservative Challenge', in Maureen Appel Molot and Fen Osler Hampson, eds, *Canada Among Nations 1989: The Challenge of Change*. Ottawa: Carleton University Press, 193–206.

Clarkson, Stephen. 1968. *An Independent Foreign Policy for Canada?* Toronto: McClelland and Stewart.

———. 1982. *Canada and the Reagan Challenge: Crisis in the Canadian-American Relationship*. Toronto: James Lorimer.

———. 2002. *Uncle Sam and Us: Globalization, Neoconservatism, and the Canadian State*. Toronto: University of Toronto Press.

——— and Christina McCall. 1990. *Trudeau and Our Times*, vol. 1: *The Magnificent Obsession*. Toronto: McClelland and Stewart.

Cohen, Andrew. 2002. 'Seize the Day', *International Journal* 58, 1 (Winter): 139–53.

———. 2003. *While Canada Slept: How We Lost Our Place in the World*. Toronto: McClelland and Stewart.

Cohen, Michael, James March, and Johan Olsen. 1972. 'A Garbage Can Model of Organizational Choice', *Administrative Science Quarterly* 17: 1–25.

Collard-Wexler, Simon, Thomas Graham Jr., Wade Huntley, Ram Jakhu, William Marshall, John Siebert, and Sarah Estabrooks. 2006. *Space Security 2006*. Waterloo: Project Ploughshares. <http://www.spacesecurity.org/SSI2006.pdf>.

Collings-Rohozinska, Deirdre. 2005. *War to Peace Transitions*. Conference Report of the 8th Peacebuilding and Human Security Consultations, Ottawa, Apr.

Cooper, Andrew F. 1995–6. 'In Search of Niches: Saying "Yes" and Saying "No" in Canada's International Relations', *Canadian Foreign Policy* 3, 3 (Winter): 1–13.

———. 1997. *Canadian Foreign Policy: Old Habits and New Directions*. Scarborough: Prentice-Hall Allyn and Bacon Canada.

———, Richard A. Higgott, and Kim R. Nossal. 1993. *Relocating Middle Powers: Australia and Canada in a Changing World Order*. Vancouver: UBC Press.

Copeland, Daryl. 2001. 'The Axworthy Years: Canadian Foreign Policy in the Era of Diminished Capability', in Fen O. Hampson, Norman Hillmer, and Maureen Appel Molot, eds, *Canada Among Nations 2001: The Axworthy Legacy*. Toronto: Oxford University Press, 152–72.

Copps, Sheila. 1998. 'Speaking Notes for the Honourable Sheila Copps, Minister of Canadian Heritage, UNESCO Canadian Delegation Plenary Intervention', Intergovernmental Conference on Cultural Policies for Development, 31 Mar. <http://www.pch.gc.ca/progs/ac-ca/discours-speeches/sc971411_e.cfin>.

———. 2004. *Worth Fighting For*. Toronto: McClelland and Stewart.

Corcoran, Terence. 2003. 'Allan Apotex's New Drug Fiasco', *National Post*, 2 Oct., FP13.

Coulon, Jocelyn. 1987. 'Another Path for Canada? The Politics of Neutralism', *Peace and Security* 2, 1 (Spring): 8–9.

Council on Foreign Relations. 2005. *Building a North American Community*. New York: Council on Foreign Relations.

Craig, David, and Doug Porter. 2006. *Development Beyond Neoliberalism*. London: Taylor & Francis.

Crane, David. 1993. 'Cultural Coalition Criticizes Trade Talks', *Toronto Star*, 27 Nov.

Crawford, James. 1994. 'The ILC's Draft Statute for an International Criminal Tribunal', *American Journal of International Law* 88: 140–52.

CTV.ca. 2002. 'Peter Lougheed Joins Alberta's Fight on Kyoto', 1 Oct. <http://www.ctv.ca/servlet/ArticleNews/story/CTVNews/20021001/lougheed_kyoto021001?s_name=&no_ads=>.

Cultural Industries Sectoral Advisory Group on International Trade (SAGIT). 1999. *New Strategies for Culture and Trade: Canadian Culture in a Global World*. Ottawa: International Trade Canada. <http://dfait-maeci.gc.ca/tna-nac/canculture-en.asp?format=print>.

Curry, Bill. 2006a. 'Ottawa Considers Joining Rival to Kyoto Protocol', *Globe and Mail*, 26 Apr., A1.

———. 2006b. 'Ottawa Wants Kyoto Softened: In Report to UN, Tories Argue Second Phase of Climate Pact Should Be More Lenient', *Globe and Mail*, 12 May, A1.

———. 2006c. 'Door Left Ajar for Canada to Join Kyoto Alternative', *Globe and Mail*, 19 May, A5.

———. 2006d. 'Ottawa Now Wants Kyoto Deal Scrapped: Voluntary Climate Change Pact Preferred with Easier Targets, Leaked Paper Reveals', *Globe and Mail*, 20 May, A1.

———. 2006e. 'Tories Mum as Environment Report Calls for Push on Global Warming', *Globe and Mail*, 29 Sept., A8.

———. 2006f. 'French PM Wants to Hit Canada with Carbon Tax', *Globe and Mail*, 15 Nov., A1.

———. 2006g. 'Ambrose Feels the Heat as Blunders Pile Up: Critics Heap Scorn on Rookie Minister Leading Sensitive Climate-Change File', *Globe and Mail*, 12 Dec., A3.

———. 2007a. 'Provinces Signing Climate Deals With States; Premiers, Governors Joining Forces in Agreements to Reduce Greenhouse Gases', *Globe and Mail*, 1 Jan., A7.

———. 2007b. 'Green Plan Limited, PM Warns; Canada Will Be Off Kyoto Targets by 50% in 2012, Harper Says', *Globe and Mail*, 8 Jan., A1.

———. 2007c. 'British MP Puts Ottawa on Climate Change Hot Seat; Blair's Envoy Urges Canada to Help Craft Post-Kyoto Plan in Time for G8 Meeting', *Globe and Mail*, 25 Jan., A1.

———. 2007d, 'Tories Cut a Deal with NDP on Climate Legislation', *Globe and Mail*, 30 Jan., A1.

———. 2007e. 'Kyoto Would Ruin Economy, Baird Warns; Environment Minister Compares Fallout of Compliance to Post-Communist Russia', *Globe and Mail*, 9 Feb., A4.

———. 2007f. 'Forces of Green Pressuring Tories', *Globe and Mail*, 15 Feb., A6.

———. 2007g. 'Canada to Ban Traditional Light Bulbs; By 2012, Retailers Will Be Required to Stock More Efficient Lighting Such as Compact Fluorescent and Halogen Bulbs', *Globe and Mail*, 26 Apr., A11.

———. 2007h. 'Opposition Calls for Vote on Tory Clean Air Bill: NDP Wants United Front in Pushing Ottawa on Carbon Emissions', *Globe and Mail*, 28 Apr., A4.

——— et al. 2007. 'Harper Vows to "Stabilize" Emissions: But Critics Contend Ottawa Not Dealing Fast Enough on Greenhouse Gases', *Globe and Mail*, 3 Feb., A4.

d'Aquino, Thomas. 2005. Letter from Ottawa to Paul Martin and Stephen Harper, Ottawa, 20 June. <http://www.ceocouncil.ca/publications/pdf/a38ef0e5178dc1ffed859844a19b7244/Letter_to_Prime_Minister_Martin_and_Stephen_Harper_re_Bill_C357_June_20_2005.pdf>.

Dashwood, Hevina A. 2000. 'The NATO-Led Intervention in Kosovo', in Maureen Appel Molot and Fen O. Hampson, eds, *Canada Among Nations 2000: Vanishing Borders*. Toronto: Oxford University Press, 275–302.

Davey, William. 1996. *Pine and Swine: Canada-United States Trade Dispute Settlement–The FTA Experience and NAFTA Prospects*. Ottawa: Centre for Trade Policy and Law.

Dawson, Laura. 2004. 'Nationalism Versus Interdependence in the Evolution of Canada's Post-War Investment Policies', paper presented at the Centre for Trade Policy and Law Investment Conference, Ottawa, Ontario, Nov.

———. 2005. *Making Canadian Trade Policy: Domestic Decision Making and the Negotiation of the Auto Pact and the CUFTA*. PhD diss. Ottawa: Carleton University.

Debiel, Tobias, and Sascha Werthes. 2006. 'Human Security on Foreign Policy Agendas: Introduction to Changes, Concepts and Cases', in Tobias Debiel and Sascha Werthes, eds, *Human Security on Foreign Policy Agendas: Changes, Concepts and Cases*, INEF report 80, Duisberg: Institute for Development and Peace, University of Duisburg-Essen, 7-17. < http://inef.uni-due.de/page/documents/Report80.pdf>.

Decima Research. 1992. *Perspectives of a Changing World: What Canadians Think and Feel About International Affairs*, Oct.

———. 1993. *A Decima Research Report to the Department of External Affairs and International Trade: Public Opinion on Peacekeeping; Update 1993*, May.

———. 2006. 'More Oppose Than Support Extension of Mission in Afghanistan', 2 June. <http://www.decima.com/en/pdf/news_releases/060605CE.pdf>.

Department of Canadian Heritage (DCH). 1998. 'Ministers from 22 Countries Expected at Ottawa Meeting on Culture', news release, 24 June. <http://www.pch.gc.ca/newsroom/index_e.cfm?fuseaction=displayDocument&DocIDCd=8NR039>.

———. 2003. *Connecting Canadians Through Canada's Stories*. Ottawa: Public Works and Government Services Canada. <http://www.pch.gc.ca/pc-ch/mindep/misc/culture/htm/1.htm>.

Department of External Affairs. 1985. *Competitiveness and Security: Directions for Canada's International Relations*. Ottawa: Supply and Services Canada.

Department of Foreign Affairs and International Trade (DFAIT). 1994. Address by André Ouellet at the Parliamentary Debate on Peacekeeping, 94/2, Ottawa, 25 Jan.

———. 1995a. Address by André Ouellet to the NATO Council: The Situation in the Former Yugoslavia, Noordwijk, 30 May.

———. 1995b. *Canada in the World. Canadian Foreign Policy Review*. Ottawa: Department of Foreign Affairs and International Trade. <http://www.international.gc.ca/foreign_policy/cnd-world/menu-en.asp>.

———. 1996a. 'Axworthy Addresses United Nations', notes for an address by Lloyd Axworthy, Minister of Foreign Affairs, to the 51st General Assembly, New York, 24 Sept. <http://w01.international.gc.ca/minpub/Publication.aspx?isRedirect=True&publication_id=376763&Language=E&docnumber=172>.

———. 1996b. 'Canada Offers to Host Treaty Conference to Sign Ban on Anti-Personnel Landmines', notes for an address by Lloyd Axworthy, Minister of Foreign Affairs, 5 Oct. <http://w01.international.gc.ca/minpub/Publication.aspx?isRedirect=True&publication_id=376785&Language=E&docnumber=183>.

———. 1998a. Address by Lloyd Axworthy to the 53rd Session of the United Nations General Assembly, 98/59, New York, 25 Sept.

———. 1998b. 'The New Diplomacy: The UN, the International Criminal Court and the Human Security Agenda', notes for an address by the Honourable Lloyd Axworthy, Minister of Foreign Affairs, to a conference on UN reform at the Kennedy School, Harvard University, Cambridge, 25 Apr.

———. 1999a. 'Axworthy to Advocate Protection of Civilians in Armed Conflict at UN General Assembly', news release, no. 207, 17 Sept. <http://w01.international.gc.ca/

MinPub/Publication.aspx?isRedirect=True&publication_id=377198&Language=E&doc-number=207>.

———. 1999b. *Human Security: Safety for People in a Changing World.* Ottawa: Department of Foreign Affairs and International Trade, 14 May.

———. 1999c. *It's Your Turn: Canada and the Future of the World Trade Organization. Government Response to the Report of the Standing Committee on Foreign Affairs and International Trade.* Ottawa: Department of Foreign Affairs and International Trade. <http://www.dfait-maeci.gc.ca/tna-nac/canwto-en.asp#Culture>.

———. 1999d. 'Kosovo and the Human Security Agenda', notes for an address by the Honourable Lloyd Axworthy, Minister of Foreign Affairs, to the Woodrow Wilson School of Public and International Relations, Princeton University, Princeton, 7 Apr.

———. 1999e. Notes for an address by the Honourable Lloyd Axworthy, Minister of Foreign Affairs, to the National Forum, Montreal, 22 Jan.

———. 1999f. Notes for an address by the Honourable Lloyd Axworthy, Minister of Foreign Affairs, to the G8 Foreign Ministers' Meeting, 9 June. <http://w01.international.gc.ca/minpub/Publication.aspx?isRedirect=True&publication_id=377168&Language=E&docnumber=99/40>.

———. 1999g. 'Consultations on FTAA and WTO Negotiations: Sectoral Consultations – Intellectual Property', discussion paper (May). <http://maeci-dfait.gc.ca/tna-nac/discussion/ip-en.asp#1>.

———. 2000a. 'Axworthy Launches International Commission on Intervention and State Sovereignty', news release, no. 233, 14 Sept. <http://w01.international.gc.ca/MinPub/Publication.aspx?isRedirect=True&publication_id=378044&Language=E&docnumber=233>.

———. 2000b. 'Protecting People from War—Canada's Human Security Priority in 2000', *Canada World View* 7 (Spring). <http://www.dfait-maeci.gc.ca/canada-magazine/issue07/7t3-en.asp>.

———. 2000c. 'Canada's Foreign Policy Agenda and Priorities', notes for an address by the Honourable John Manley, Minister of Foreign Affairs, to the Third Annual Diplomatic Forum, Winnipeg, Manitoba, 20 Oct. <http://w01.international.gc.ca/minpub/PublicationContentOnly.asp?publication_id=378123&Language=E&MODE=CONTENTONLY&Local=False>.

———. 2003a. 'Canadian Elected Judge of International Criminal Court', news release, no. 17, 6 Feb.

———. 2003b. 'Graham Announces New Human Security Initiatives', news release, no. 55, 9 May. <http://w01.international.gc.ca/MinPub/Publication.aspx?isRedirect=True&publication_id=380069&Language=E&docnumber=55>.

———. 2004. *Final Audit of the Canadian Centre for Foreign Policy Development.* Ottawa: Office of the Inspector General. <http://www.international.gc.ca/department/auditreports/2004/ccfpd04-en.asp>.

———. 2005a. 'Canada Contributes $500,000 to International Criminal Court for Darfur Investigations', news release, no. 58, 4 Apr. <http://w01.international.gc.ca/MinPub/Publication.aspx?isRedirect=True&publication_id=382368&Language=E&docnumber=58>.

———. 2005b. 'Canada's Statement to the International Joint Commission'. <http://www.dfait-maeci.gc.ca/can-m/washington/shared_env/statementtoIJC-en.asp>.

———. 2005c. 'Coherence and Commitment: Implementing the New International Policy Statement', notes for an address by the Honourable Pierre Pettigrew, Minister of Foreign Affairs, to the Canadian Institute of International Affairs (CIIA), Toronto, 12 Oct.

———. 2005d. 'The Responsibility to Protect and UN Reform', address by Prime Minister Paul Martin at the United Nations General Assembly, New York, 16 Sept.

———. 2006a. *Official Responses to eDiscussion on Failed and Fragile States*. Policy Research Division, 22 Feb. Ottawa: Department of Foreign Affairs and International Trade. <http://geo.international.gc.ca/cip-pic/current_discussions/fragilesummary-en.asp>.

———. 2006b. *Global Partnership Program-Making a Difference*. Ottawa: Department of Foreign Affairs and International Trade. <http://www.globalpartnership.gc.ca>.

Department of National Defence. 2006. 'Canada First Defence Procurement', media advisory, 25 June.

Dewing, Michael, and Corrinne McDonald. 2004. *International Deployments of Canadian Forces: Parliament's Role*. Ottawa: Library of Parliament, Parliamentary Research Branch.

Dewitt, David, and John Kirton. 1983. *Canada as a Principal Power: A Study in International Politics and Foreign Policy*. Toronto: John Wiley.

Dimitrakopoulos, Sandra. 2003. 'Bono and Martin Join Forces on Aid to Africa', *CTV News Online*, 14 Nov. <http://www.ctv.ca/servlet/ArticleNews/story/CTVNews/1068842746991_64251946?s_name=&no_ads>.

Dion, Stephane. 2006. 'Canada's Climate Change Dilemma and How to Solve It', *Policy Options* (Oct.): 25–30.

Dobell, Peter C. 1985. *Canada in World Affairs*, vol. 17: *1971–1973*. Toronto: Canadian Institute of International Affairs.

Dobrota, Alex. 2007. 'Critics Assail Ottawa's Dire Kyoto Predictions: Tories Accused of Ignoring Economic Gains in Report Warning of Major Recession', *Globe and Mail*, 20 Apr., A4.

Doern, Bruce. 1982. 'Liberal Priorities 1982: The Limits of Scheming Virtuously', in Bruce Doern, ed, *How Ottawa Spends Your Tax Dollars: National Policy and Economic Development*. Toronto: James Lorimer, 1–36.

———. 1984. 'Energy Expenditures and the NEP: Controlling the Energy Leviathan', in Allan Maslove, ed, *How Ottawa Spends 1984: The New Agenda*. Toronto: Methuen, 31–78.

——— and Brian Tomlin. 1991. *Faith and Fear: The Free Trade Story*. Toronto: Stoddart.

———, Leslie Pal, and Brian Tomlin. 1996. *Border Crossings: The Internationalization of Canadian Public Policy*. Toronto: Oxford University Press.

Dolan, Michael, and Chris Hunt. 1998. 'Negotiating in the Ottawa Process: The New Multilateralism', *Canadian Foreign Policy* 5, 3: 25–50.

Donaghy, Greg. 1998. 'A Continental Philosophy: Canada, the United States and the Negotiation of the Autopact, 1963–1965', *International Journal* 53, 3: 441–64.

———. 2002. *Tolerant Allies: Canada and the United States 1963–1968*. Montreal and Kingston: McGill-Queen's University Press.

———. 2003. 'All God's Children: Lloyd Axworthy, Human Security and Canadian Foreign Policy, 1996–2000', *Canadian Foreign Policy* 10, 2 (Winter): 39–58.

Donaldson, Robert. 1984. 'Canadianization', in James Spence and William Rosenfeld, eds, *Foreign Investment Review Law in Canada*. Toronto: Butterworths, 93–119.

Donovan, Lauren. 2002. 'N.D. Senators Increasingly Powerful', *Bismarck Tribune*, 2 June, 1A.

Doran, Charles F. 1987. 'Sovereignty Does Not Equal Security', *Peace and Security* 2, 3 (Autumn): 8–9.

Dosman, Edgar J. 1988. 'The Department of National Defence: The Steady Drummer', in Katherine A. Graham, ed, *How Ottawa Spends, 1988–89: The Conservatives Heading into the Stretch*. Ottawa: Carleton University Press, 165–94.

Doucet, Joseph A. 2004. 'The Kyoto Conundrum: Why Abandoning the Protocol's Targets in Favour of a More Sustainable Plan May Be Best for Canada and the World', C.D. Howe Institute—*Backgrounder* No. 83 (May): 1–9.

Doxey, Margaret. 1989. 'Constructive Internationalism: A Continuing Theme in Canadian Foreign Policy', *The Round Table* 311 (1989): 288–304.

Doyle, John. 2007. 'Global Warming: Frontline Places the Blame Squarely on the US', *Globe and Mail*, 24 Apr., R3.

Draimin, Tim, and Brian Tomlinson. 1998. 'Is There a Future for Canadian Aid in the Twenty-First Century?' in Fen Osler Hampson and Maureen Appel Molot, eds, *Canada Among Nations 1998: Leadership and Dialogue*. Toronto: Oxford University Press, 143–68.

Drummond, Ian M., and Norman Hillmer. 1989. *Negotiating Freer Trade: The United Kingdom, the United States, Canada, and the Trade Agreements of 1938*. Waterloo, ON: Wilfrid Laurier University Press.

Duffield, Mark R. 2001. *Global Governance and the New Wars: The Merging of Development and Security*. London: Zed Books.

Duffy, John. 2007. 'Green Politics: Close to the Tipping Point: Globally, Politicians are Acting, Says Liberal Strategist John Duffy. Here's How Canada Rates', *Globe and Mail*, 5 Feb., A15.

Dymond, William. 1999. 'The MAI: A Sad and Melancholy Tale', in Fen Hampson, Michael Hart, and Martin Rudner, eds, *Canada Among Nations 1999: A Big League Player?* Toronto: Oxford University Press, 25–53.

Eayrs, James. 1987. 'Assessing the Ice-Pack Rationale', *Peace and Security* 2, 3 (Autumn): 10–11.

Ebner, David. 2007. 'The Greening of the Oil Sands: Global Warming Is Concentrating Minds, David Ebner Writes, in a Sector That Has Come Far, and Has Farther to Go', *Globe and Mail*, 6 Jan., B4.

Economic Council of Canada. 1975. *Looking Outward: A New Trade Strategy for Canada*. Ottawa: Supply and Services.

Economist, The. 1999a. 'Not so Caring', 350, 8101, 9 Jan.

———. 1999b. 'Balkan Wars', 351, 8116, 24 Apr.

Edmonds, Robert. 1998. 'Canada's Recognition of the People's Republic of China: The Stockholm Negotiations 1968–1970', *Canadian Foreign Policy* 5, 2 (Winter): 201–17.

Edmonton Journal. 2006. 'Why So Low Key on Defence Boost?' 29 June.

Edwards, Michael, David Hulme, and Tina Wallace. 1999. 'NGOs in a Global Future: Marrying Local Delivery to Worldwide Leverage', *Public Administration and Development* 19, 2: 117–36.

Edwards, Steven. 2005. 'Canada Floats Responsibility to Protect Proposal', *Regina Leader Post*, 10 Sept.

Eggertson, Laura. 1997a. 'Culture Not Safe Under NAFTA: Eggleton Could Stir Fight With Copps', *Globe and Mail*, 29 Jan.

———. 1997b. 'Marchi A New Breed of Trade Minister: The Former Environment Minister Says Putting Social Concerns Alongside Business Matters Will Be His Trademark', *Globe and Mail*, 8 July.

Elliot, Richard. 2003a. 'Op-Ed: Canada Can Carry Much More', *Globe and Mail*, 23 Sept., A23.

———. 2003b. 'TRIPS from Doha to Cancún . . . to Ottawa: Global Developments in Access to Treatment and Canada's Bill C-56', *HIV/AIDS Policy and Law Review* 8, 3: 7–18.

———. 2003c. 'Will Canada Join the Global Effort to Fight HIV/AIDS? Government Risks Sabotaging Its Own Initiative That It Announced with Much Fanfare a Few Weeks Ago', *Hill Times*, 15 Dec., 14.

———. 2004. 'Steps Forward, Backward and Sideways: Canada's Bill on Exporting Generic Pharmaceuticals', *HIV/AIDS Policy and Law Review* 9, 3 (Dec.).

———. 2006. 'E-mail re: clarification on Bill C-9 formulation', 5 June.

———, Marie-Hélène Bonin, and Carol Devine. 2003. *Patents, International Trade Law and Access to Essential Medicines*, 3rd edn. Toronto: The Canadian HIV/AIDS Legal Network and Médecins Sans Frontières Canada. <http://www.aidslaw.ca/Maincontent/issues/cts/Patents-international-trade-law-and-access.pdf>.

Emmerij, Louis, Richard Jolly, and Thomas G. Weiss. 2005. 'Economic and Social Thinking at the UN in Historical Perspective', *Development and Change* 63, 2: 211–35.

English, John. 1991. 'Lester Pearson and China', in Paul M. Evans and B. Michael Frolic, eds, *Reluctant Adversaries: Canada and the People's Republic of China 1949–1970*. Toronto: University of Toronto Press, 133–47.

———. 1998. 'The Ottawa Process: Paths Followed, Paths Ahead', *Australian Journal of International Affairs* 52, 2: 121–32.

———. 2001. 'In the Liberal Tradition: Lloyd Axworthy and Canadian Foreign Policy', in Fen Osler Hampson, Norman Hillmer, and Maureen Molot, eds, *Canada Among Nations 2001: The Axworthy Legacy*. Toronto: Oxford University Press, 89–107.

——— and Norman Hillmer. 1989. 'Canada's American Alliance', in Norman Hillmer, ed, *Partners Nevertheless: Canadian-American Relations in the Twentieth Century*. Toronto: Copp Clark Pitman, 32–42.

———, eds. 1992. *Making a Difference? Canadian Foreign Policy in a Changing World*. Toronto: Lester Publishing.

Environment Canada. 2002. *Costs of Kyoto—What We Know*, report. <http://www.ec.gc.ca/minister/speeches/2002/020318_t_e.htm>.

Escobar, Arturo. 1994. *Encountering Development: The Making and Unmaking of the Third World*. Princeton: Princeton University Press.

Esmail, Laura C. 2004. *An Analysis of Bill C-9: An Act to Amend the Patent Act and the Food and Drugs Act, the Right of Refusal and Alternative Mechanisms*, Working Paper. Toronto: University of Toronto. <http://www.law.utoronto.ca/healthlaw/docs/student_Esmail-TRIPS.pdf>.

European Information e-technologies. 2005. 'Universal Delight at Convention on Cultural Diversity except in the United States', 28 Oct.

Evans, Paul. 1985. *Canadian Public Opinion on Relations with China: An Analysis of the Existing Survey Research*. Toronto: York University.

———. 1991. 'Introduction: Solving Our Cold War China Problem', in Paul M. Evans and B. Michael Frolic, eds, *Reluctant Adversaries: Canada and the People's Republic of China 1949–1970*. Toronto: University of Toronto Press, 3–16.

Evenson, Brad. 1997. 'What Is a Canadian? Poll Provides Clue', *Ottawa Citizen*, 24 Dec. <http://www.pollara.ca/Library/News/dec_24.html>.

Fagan, Drew. 2003. 'Ottawa's AIDS Drug Plan Caught Up in Debate', *Globe and Mail*, 24 Oct., A4.

———, Heather Scoffield, and Steven Chase. 2003. 'Ottawa Scrambles to Meet AIDS-Drug Pledge', *Globe and Mail*, 4 Oct., A20.

Farr, David. 1989. 'Prime Minister Trudeau's Opening to the Soviet Union, 1971', in J.L. Black and Norman Hillmer, eds, *Nearly Neighbours. Canada and the Soviet Union: From Cold War to Détente and Beyond*. Kingston: Ronald P. Frye and Company, 102–18.

Faveri, Christine M. 1992. *The Evolution of* CIDA*'s Women in Development Discourse: Shaping Knowledge of Southern Women*. MA thesis, Norman Paterson School of International Affairs. Ottawa: Carleton University.

Fayerweather, John. 1974. *Foreign Investment in Canada: Prospects for National Policy*. Toronto: Oxford University Press.

Ferencz, Benjamin B. 1992. 'An International Criminal Code and Court: Where They Stand and Where They Are Going', *Columbia Journal of Transnational Law* 30: 375–99.

Ferguson, Derek. 1995. 'Canada Will Guard Culture, PM Vows', *Toronto Star*, 7 Apr.

Financial Post. 2007. 'Financial Post Business: Climate Change Power List', 28 Mar. <http://communities.canada.com/financialpost/blogs/fpbmagazine/archive/2007/03/289-ross-mckitrick-economist-university-of-guelph.aspx>.

Fisher, Roger, and William Ury. 1991. *Getting to Yes: Negotiating Agreement Without Giving In*, 2nd edn. New York: Penguin Books.

Fisher, William F. 1997. 'Doing Good? The Politics and Antipolitics of NGO Practices', *Annual Review of Anthropology* 26: 440–64.

Foote, John A. 1998. 'Canada's Cultural Policy: A Model of Diversity', Canadian Cultural Research Network (CCRN) Colloquium, Ottawa, 4 June. <http://www.arts.uwaterloo.ca/ccm/ccrn/documents/colloq98_foote.html>.

Fortier, Patricia. 2001. 'The Evolution of Peacekeeping', in Rob McRae and Don Hubert, eds, *Human Security and the New Diplomacy*. Montreal and Kingston: McGill-Queen's University Press, 41–64.

Foster, John. 2002. 'Canada and International Health: A Time of Testing on AIDS', in Norman Hillmer and Maureen Molot, eds, *Canada Among Nations 2002: A Fading Power*. Toronto: Oxford University Press, 191–208.

———. 2005a. 'E-mail re: interview regarding the formulation and implementation of Bill C-9', 12 Dec.

———. 2005b. 'The MDGs and Infectious Diseases: Focus on HIV/AIDS', in The North-South Institute, *Canadian Development Report 2005—Towards 2015: Meeting our Millennium Commitments*. Ottawa: Renouf Publishing, 89–102.

——— and David Garmaise. 2003. 'Meeting the Challenge: Canada's Foreign Policy on HIV/AIDS with a Particular Focus on Africa', submission to the Ministerial Council on HIV/AIDS. <http://www.nsi-ins.ca/english/pdf/challenge_full_report.pdf>.

Foster, Peter. 1982. *The Sorcerer's Apprentices: Canada's Super-Bureaucrats and the Energy Mess*. Toronto: Collins.

Fowler, Robert. 2003. 'Canadian Leadership and the Kananaskis G-8 Summit: Towards a Less Self-Centered Foreign Policy', *Canada Among Nations 2003: Coping with the American Colossus*. Toronto: Oxford University Press, 219–41.

Franck, Thomas. 2006. 'The Use of Force and International Law after Iraq', an address given at the Department of Foreign Affairs and International Trade, Ottawa, 2 June.

Frank, Andre Gunder. 1969. *Latin America: Underdevelopment of Revolution*. New York: Monthly Review Press.

Fraser, Graham. 2005. 'Cultural Diversity Policy Voted In: Protection for National Cultures Only Israel, US Oppose Convention', *Toronto Star*, 18 Oct.

Fredenburg, Major Paul W. 1997. 'The Banning of the Anti-Personnel Landmines', *Canadian Defence Quarterly* 27, 2: 5–9.

Fritzen, Gabriel. 1983a. Letter from Thunder Bay to Dave Speer, Reeve, Terrace Bay, 31 Mar.

———. 1983b. Letter from Thunder Bay to Jack Masters, MP for Nipigon, Ottawa, 17 May.

———. 2005. Telephone interview, 27 Nov.

Frolic, B. Michael. 1991. 'The Trudeau Initiative', in Paul M. Evans and B. Michael Frolic, eds, *Reluctant Adversaries: Canada and the People's Republic of China 1949–1970*. Toronto: University of Toronto Press, 189–216.

Fukushima, Akiko. 2004. *Human Security: Comparing Japanese and Canadian Governmental Thinking and Practice*. Canadian Consortium on Human Security (CCHS) Visiting Fellow Paper, Aug. <http://www.humansecurity.info/sites/cchs/files/pdfs/Research/cchs_fukushima_research_paper.pdf>.

Galloway, Gloria. 2005. 'Harper Heaps Scorn on Kyoto; Conservative Leader Offers Alternative on Climate Change: Tax Deductible Transit Passes', *Globe and Mail*, 5 Aug., A7.

———. 2007a. 'Layton Draws a Line in the Sand on Climate: NDP Leader Says He Told Baird Action Is Needed Before Budget', *Globe and Mail*, 11 Jan., A7.

———. 2007b. 'NDP Plotting Strategy to Out-Green Its Rivals: Layton Says He'll Expect Robust Action From the Conservatives on Climate Change', *Globe and Mail*, 12 Jan., A6.

———. 2007c. 'Tories Twisted My Words, Gore Says: Encouragement on Climate Change Should Not be Taken as Praise for Party, He Says in a Statement', *Globe and Mail*, 13 Feb., A4.

——— and Bill Curry. 2007. 'Green Plan's Pegged at $8-Billion a Year: Environment Minister Defends Price Hike on Cars and Appliances as Necessary', *Globe and Mail*, 27 Apr., A1.

——— and Oliver Moore. 2007. 'Make Industry Pay for Emissions, Climate-Change Activists Argue', *Globe and Mail*, 10 Jan., A4.

Gallup Canada, Inc. 1992. 'Majority Support UN Intervention in Former Yugoslavia', 26 Oct.

———. 1994. 'Canada's Peacekeeping Role Assessed', *Gallup Poll*, 27 Jan.

———. 1995. '58% Agree with NATO Offensive in Bosnia', *Gallup Poll*, 18 Sept.

Gammer, Nicholas. 2001. *From Peacekeeping to Peacemaking: Canada's Response to the Yugoslav Crisis*. Montreal and Kingston: McGill-Queen's University Press.

Gecelovsky, Paul, and Tom Keating. 2001. 'Liberal Internationalism for Conservatives: The Good Governance Initiative', in Nelson Michaud and Kim R. Nossal, eds, *Diplomatic Departures: The Conservative Era in Canadian Foreign Policy, 1984–93*. Vancouver: UBC Press, 194–207.

Geddes, John. 1998. 'Canada's Culture Clash', *Maclean's* 111, 28 (13 July): 26–8.

Geislerova, Marketa. 1999. 'Report from the Roundtable on Canada, NATO and the UN: Lessons Learned from the Kosovo Crisis', *Canadian Foreign Policy* 7, 1 (Fall): 13–18.

Gérin-Lajoie, Paul. 1976. *The Path We Have Come*. CIDA. Ottawa, Supply and Services Canada.

Gilmore, William C. 1995. 'The Proposed International Criminal Court: Recent Developments', *Transnational Law and Contemporary Problems* 5: 264–85.

Girard, Charlotte S.M. 1980. *Canada in World Affairs*, vol. 13: *1963–1965*. Toronto: Canadian Institute of International Affairs.

Globe and Mail. 2002. 'Thoughtful Strategies for a Warmer World: The Commitment Canada Made in Kyoto May Need Some Adjustment', 5 Jan., A14.

Golberg, Elissa, and Don Hubert. 2001. 'Case Study: The Security Council and the Protection of Civilians', in Rob McRae and Don Hubert, eds, *Human Security and the New Diplomacy*. Montreal and Kingston: McGill-Queen's University Press, 223–30.

Goldenberg, Eddie. 2006. *The Way It Works: Inside Ottawa*. Toronto: McClelland and Stewart.

Gordon, Nancy. 2005–6. 'Canada's Position on the Use of Force Internationally', *International Journal* 61, 1 (Winter): 129–34.

——— and Gregory Wirick. 1995. 'Humanitarian Intervention as an Instrument of Human Rights', paper presented to the Seminar on 'States without Law: The Role of Multilateral Intervention to Restore Local Justice Systems', University of British Columbia, Dec.

Gordon, Walter. 1961. *Troubled Canada*. Toronto: McClelland and Stewart.

———. 1966. *A Choice for Canada*. Toronto: McClelland and Stewart.

———. 1977. *A Political Memoir*. Toronto: McClelland and Stewart.

Gotlieb, Allan. 2006. *The Washington Diaries 1981–1989*. Toronto: McClelland and Stewart.

Government of Canada. 1970. *Foreign Policy for Canadians*. Ottawa.

———. 1972. *Foreign Direct Investment in Canada*. Ottawa: Information Canada.

———. 1975. *Strategy for International Development Cooperation, 1975–1980*. Ottawa: Information Canada.

———. 1983. *Canadian Trade Policy for the 1980s: A Discussion Paper*. Ottawa: Department of External Affairs.

———. 1984. *A New Direction for Canada: An Agenda for Economic Renewal*. Ottawa: Department of Finance.

———. 1985. *How to Secure and Enhance Access to Export Markets*. Ottawa: Department of External Affairs.

———. 1986. *Independence and Internationalism: Final Report of the Special Joint Committee of the Senate and the House of Commons on Canada's International Relations*. Ottawa.

———. 1987. *To Benefit a Better World*. Hull: Minister of Supply and Services.

———. 1995a. *Towards a Rapid Reaction Capability for the United Nations*. Ottawa.

———. 1995b. *Government Response to the Recommendations of the Special Joint Parliamentary Committee Reviewing Canadian Foreign Policy*. Ottawa.

———. 1999. *Canada and the Future of the World Trade Organization: Advancing a Millennium Agenda in the Public Interest*. Report of the Standing Committee on Foreign Affairs and International Trade (SCFAIT), June. Ottawa: Standing Committee on Foreign Affairs and International Trade. <http://www.parl.gc.ca/infocomdoc/36/1/fait/studies/reports/faitrp09-e.htm>.

———. 2000. *The New NATO and the Evolution of Peacekeeping: Implications for Canada*. Report of the Standing Senate Committee on Foreign Affairs, seventh report, Apr. Ottawa: Standing Committee on Foreign Affairs.

———. 2003. 'Government of Canada Introduces Legislative Changes to Enable Export of Much Needed, Low Cost Pharmaceutical Products to Developing Countries', press release, 6 Nov. <http://www.cptech.org/ip/health/c/canada/canada11062003.html>.

———. 2005a. *Canada's International Policy Statement: A Role of Pride and Influence in the World*, 5 volumes. Ottawa. < http://geo.international.gc.ca/cip-pic/current_discussions/ips-archive-en.aspx>.

———. 2005b. Subcommittee for International Development. Notes on Minutes from 5 May 2005 (IPS Development Review). <http://www.parl.gc.ca/committee/Committee List.aspx?Lang=17PAR.SES=381&JNT-0&SELID=e22_.27STAC=1249042>.

———. 2007. 'Turning the Corner: An Action Plan to Reduce Greenhouse Gases and Air Pollution'. <http://www.ecoaction.gc.ca/turning-virage/index-eng.cfm>.

Gow, James Ian. 1970. 'Les Québéquois, La Guerre et La Paix 1945–1960', *Revue canadienne de science politique* 3, 1: 88–122.

Granatstein, J.L. 1981. *A Man of Influence: Norman A. Robertson and Canadian Statecraft, 1929–68*. Ottawa: Deneau Publishers.

———. 1986. *Canada 1957–1967: The Years of Uncertainty and Innovation*. Toronto: McClelland and Stewart.

———. 1991. 'Preparing for the Millennium: The Trudeau and Mulroney Defence and Foreign Policy Reviews', in C.H.W. Remie and J.M. Lacroix, eds, *Canada on the Threshold of the Twenty-First Century*. Amsterdam and Philadelphia: John Benjamins.

——— and Robert Bothwell. 1990. *Pirouette: Pierre Trudeau and Canadian Foreign Policy*. Toronto: University of Toronto Press.

Grand Forks Herald. 2002. 'Coping With a Drying Up Devils Lake, 100 Years Ago', 30 July.

Grant, Peter, and Chris Wood. 2004. *Blockbusters and Trade Wars: Popular Culture in a Globalized World*. Toronto: Douglas & McIntyre.

Gray, Jeff. 2007. 'Suzuki Urges Mayor to Out City's Worst Polluters; Web-base Registry Aims to Embarrass Firms into Reducing Harmful Emissions', *Globe and Mail*, 16 Feb., A11.

Grayson, Kyle. 2004. 'Branding "Transformation" in Canadian Foreign Policy: Human Security', *Canadian Foreign Policy* 11, 2 (Winter): 41–68.

Green, Graham N. 1999. 'Canada's Formula for Failure', *Ottawa Citizen*, 2 Jan.

Greenhill, Robert. 2005. *Making a Difference? External Views on Canada's International Impact*. Toronto: Canadian Institute of International Affairs, Jan.

Guttormson, Kim. 1997. 'Wary Eye on N.D. Diversion', *Winnipeg Free Press*, 28 Sept., A4.

Gwozdecky, Mark, and Jill Sinclair. 2001. 'Case Study: Landmines and Human Security', in Rob McRae and Don Hubert, eds, *Human Security and the New Diplomacy*. Montreal and Kingston: McGill-Queen's University Press, 28–40.

Gwyn, Richard. 1985. *The 49th Paradox: Canada in North America*. Toronto: McClelland and Stewart.

Haglund, David G., and Allen Sens. 2000. 'Kosovo and the Case of the (Not So) Free Riders: Portugal, Belgium, Canada, and Spain', in Albrecht Schnabel and Ramesh Thakur, eds, *Kosovo and the Challenge of Humanitarian Intervention: Selective Indignation, Collective Action, and International Citizenship*. Tokyo, New York, and Paris: United Nations University Press.

Haggart, Blayne. 2005. *Cooperation, Not Harmonization: Explaining Canada's Support for the December 2001 Smart Border Accord*. MA research essay. Ottawa: Carleton University.

Hall, Christopher Keith. 1997. 'The First Two Sessions of the UN Preparatory Committee on the Establishment of an International Criminal Court', *American Journal of International Law* 91, 1 (Jan.): 177–87.

———. 1998a. 'The Fifth Session of the UN Preparatory Committee on the Establishment of an International Criminal Court', *American Journal of International Law* 92, 2 (Apr.): 331–9.

———. 1998b. 'The Sixth Session of the UN Preparatory Committee on the Establishment of an International Criminal Court', *American Journal of International Law* 92, 3 (July): 548–56.

———. 1998c. 'The Third and Fourth Session of the UN Preparatory Committee on the Establishment of an International Criminal Court', *American Journal of International Law* 92, 1 (Jan.): 124–33.

Halperin, Morton H., Joseph T. Siegle, and Michael M. Weinstein. 2005. *The Democratic Advantage: How Democracies Promote Prosperity and Peace*. New York: Routledge.

Hampson, Fen Osler. 1988. 'Call to Arms: Canadian National Security Policy', in Maureen Appel Molot and Brian W. Tomlin, eds, *Canada Among Nations 1987: A World of Conflict*. Toronto: James Lorimer and Company, 68–91.

——— and Dean F. Oliver. 1998. 'Pulpit Diplomacy: A Critical Assessment of the Axworthy Doctrine', *International Journal* 53, 3 (Summer): 379–406.

——— with Jean Daudelin, John B. Hay, Todd Martin, and Holly Reid. 2002. *Madness in the Multitude: Human Security and World Disorder*. Toronto: Oxford University Press.

———— and H. Reid. 2003. 'Coalition Diversity and Normative Legitimacy in Human Security Negotiations', *International Negotiation* 8, 1: 7–42.

———— and John B. Hay. 2004. 'The Canadian Policy Context', paper prepared for the IDRC Corporate Strategy and Program Framework 2005–2010. Ottawa: International Development Research Centre.

Hansard. 1999. Address of Vaclav Havel, President of the Czech Republic, before the Houses of Parliament, vol. 218, 29 Apr.

Hanson, Sam. 2001. 'Case Study: Bosnia and Herzegovina', in Rob McRae and Don Hubert, eds, *Human Security and the New Diplomacy*. Montreal and Kingston: McGill-Queen's University Press, 88–95.

Harris, Christopher. 1993. 'Group Issues Cultural Blueprint', *Globe and Mail,* 7 Oct.

Hart, Michael. 2000. 'The Role of Dispute Settlement in Managing Canada–US Trade and Investment Relations', in Maureen Molot and Fen Hampson, eds, *Canada Among Nations 2000: Vanishing Borders*. Toronto: Oxford University Press, 93–116.

————. 2002. *A Trading Nation: Canadian Trade Policy from Colonialism to Globalization*. Vancouver: UBC Press.

———— and Brian Tomlin. 2002. 'Inside the Perimeter: The US Policy Agenda and Its Implications for Canada', in Bruce Doern, ed, *How Ottawa Spends 2002–2003: The Security Aftermath and National Priorities*. Toronto: Oxford University Press, 48–68.

————. 2004. 'The Emerging Policy Shift in Canada–US Relations', in Bruce Doern, ed, *How Ottawa Spends 2004–2005: Mandate Change in the Paul Martin Era*. Montreal and Kingston: McGill-Queen's University Press, 46–69.

———— (with Bill Dymond and Colin Robertson). 1994. *Decision at Midnight: Inside the Canada–US Free Trade Negotiations*. Vancouver: UBC Press.

Hataley, T.S., and Kim R. Nossal. 2004. 'The Limits of the Human Security Agenda: The Case of Canada's Response to the Timor Crisis', *Global Change, Peace & Security* 16, 1 (Feb.): 5–17.

Hay, Robin Jeffrey. 1999. 'Present at the Creation? Human Security and Canadian Foreign Policy in the Twenty–First Century', in Fen Osler Hampson, Michael Hart, and Martin Rudner, eds, *Canada Among Nations 1999: A Big League Player?* Toronto: Oxford University Press, 215–32.

———— and Jean-François Rioux. 1999. *Human Security and National Defence*. Project Report No. 99916, Sept.

Head, Ivan L., and Pierre Elliott Trudeau. 1995. *The Canadian Way: Shaping Canada's Foreign Policy 1968–1984*. Toronto: McClelland and Stewart.

Heinbecker, Paul. 1999. 'Human Security', from an address delivered to the Human Rights Centre of the University of Ottawa, *Canadian Foreign Policy* 7, 1 (Fall): 19–25.

————. 2000. 'Human Security: The Hard Edge', *Canadian Military Journal* 1, 1 (Spring): 11–16.

————. 2004. 'The UN and Never Again: the Responsibility to Protect'. Conference on the Media and the Rwanda Genocide, Carleton University, Ottawa, 13 Mar.

———— and Rob McRae. 2001. 'Case Study: The Kosovo Air Campaign', in Rob McRae and Don Hubert, eds, *Human Security and the New Diplomacy*. Montreal and Kingston: McGill-Queen's University Press, 122–33.

Heisler, Nick. 2005. 'Interview with Nick Heisler, International Joint Commission Spokesperson', 29 Nov.

Hellyer, Paul. 1990. *Damn the Torpedoes: My Fight to Unify Canada's Armed Forces*. Toronto: McClelland and Stewart.

Hillmer, Norman, ed. 1989. *Partners Nevertheless: Canadian-American Relations in the Twentieth Century.* Copp Clark Pitman.

Hillmer, Norman. 2002. 'Canada, the North Atlantic Treaty Organization and the Boundaries of Alignment', in Ann-Sofie Dahl and Norman Hillmer, eds, *Activism and (Non)Alignment.* Stockholm: The Swedish Institute of International Affairs, 55–71.

———. 2003. 'Peacekeeping: The Inevitability of Canada's Role', in Michael A. Hennessy and B.J.C. McKercher, eds, *War in the Twentieth Century: Reflections at Century's End.* Westport, CT and London: Praeger, 145–65.

———. 2005a. 'Reflections on the Unequal Border', *International Journal* 60, 2 (Spring): 331–40.

———. 2005b. 'The Secret Life of Canadian Foreign Policy', *Policy Options*, Feb.: 32–3.

———. 2006. 'Are Canadians Anti-American?' *Policy Options*, July–Aug.: 63–5.

——— and Adam Chapnick. 2001. 'The Axworthy Revolution', in Fen O. Hampson, Norman Hillmer, and Maureen Appel Molot, eds, *Canada Among Nations 2001: The Axworthy Legacy.* Toronto: Oxford University Press, 65–88.

——— and J.L. Granatstein. 1994. *Empire to Umpire: Canada and the World to the 1990s.* Toronto: Copp Clark Longman.

———. 2007. *For Better or For Worse: Canada and the United States into the Twenty-First Century.* Toronto: Thomson Nelson.

Hockin, Tom, and Simard, Jean-Maurice. 1986. *Independence and Internationalism: Report of the Special Joint Committee on Canada's International Relations.* Ottawa: Queen's Printer.

Hoffman, Kerstin, ed. 1999. *Framework for a Mine-Free World*, Disarmament Forum No. 4. Geneva: United Nations Institute for Disarmament Research. <http://www.unog.ch/unidir/e-df4.htm>.

Holmes, John. 1970. *The Better Part of Valour: Essays on Canadian Diplomacy.* Toronto: McClelland and Stewart.

House of Commons. 2004. 'Bill C-9: An Act to Amend the Patent Act and the Food and Drugs Act', first reading.

House of Commons, Standing Committee on External Affairs and International Trade (SCEAIT) (Winegard Report). 1987. *For Whose Benefit? Report of the Standing Committee on External Affairs and International Trade on Canada's Official Development Assistance.* Ottawa: Queen's Printer.

———, on Industry, Science and Technology (SCIST). 2004. Minutes of proceedings of meeting no. 11, 22 Apr. <http://www.parl.gc.ca/committee/CommitteePublication.aspx?SourceId=80260>.

Howard, Peter, and Reina Neufeldt. 2000. 'Canada's Constructivist Foreign Policy: Building Norms for Peace', *Canadian Foreign Policy* 8, 1 (Fall): 11–38.

Howlett, Karen. 2007. 'Ontario on Target to Meet Kyoto Goals, Government Says: Coal-plant Emissions Drop Below 1990 Levels', *Globe and Mail*, 16 Feb., A11.

Howlett, Michael, and M. Ramesh. 2003. *Studying Public Policy: Policy Cycles and Policy Subsystems.* Toronto: Oxford University Press.

Hubert, Don. 2000. *The Landmine Ban: A Case Study in Humanitarian Advocacy.* Occasional Paper 42. Providence, RI: Thomas J. Watson Jr. Institute for International Studies, Brown University.

——— and Michael Bonser. 2001. 'Humanitarian Military Intervention', in Rob McRae and Don Hubert, eds, *Human Security and the New Diplomacy.* Montreal and Kingston: McGill-Queen's University Press, 111–21.

Huebert, Rob. 2001. 'A Northern Foreign Policy: The Politics of Ad Hocery', in Nelson Michaud and Kim Richard Nossal, eds, *Diplomatic Departures: The Conservative Era in Canadian Foreign Policy, 1984–93.* Vancouver: UBC Press, 84–99.

Human Security Centre. 2005. *Human Security Report 2005: War and Peace in the 21st Century.* Oxford: Oxford University Press. <http://www.humansecurityreport.info>.

Hume, Mark. 2007. 'Tories Lead "Green Rush" to B.C.', *Globe and Mail*, 25 Jan., S1.

Ibbitson, John. 2002. 'With Friends Like Mr. Chrétien, Who Needs Enemies?' *Globe and Mail*, 4 Nov., A13.

———. 2004. 'Awaiting Martin on Kyoto', *Globe and Mail*, 24 Aug., A4.

———. 2005. 'Who'll Stop Draining of Devils Lake?' *Globe and Mail*, 12 July, A3.

———. 2006. 'Clean Air Act Delivers Rude Awakening: Real Environmental Changes Aren't Coming in our Lifetime', *Globe and Mail*, 20 Oct., A4.

Ignatieff, Michael. 2000. 'Human Rights as Politics, Human Rights as Idolatry'. Tanner Lecture on Human Values, Princeton, 4–7 Apr. <http://www.tannerlectures.utah.edu/-lectures/ Ignatieff_01.pdf>.

———. 2005. 'Human Rights, Power and the State', in Simon Chesterman, Michael Ignatieff, and Ramesh Thakur, eds, *Making States Work—State Failure and the Crisis of Governance.* Tokyo: United Nations University Press.

Independent International Commission on Kosovo (IICK). 2000. *Kosovo Report: Conflict, International Response, Lessons Learned.* Oxford: Oxford University Press.

Industry Official. 2006. 'Interview re: the Formulation and Implementation of Bill C-9', 27 Jan.

Innovative Research Group (IRG). 2004. *Visions of Canadian Foreign Policy.* Public Opinion Poll, Nov.

Intellectual Property Institute of Canada (IPIC). 2004. 'Testimony by the Intellectual Property Institute of Canada', submission to the House of Commons Standing Committee on Industry, Science and Technology. <http://www.parl.gc.ca/InfoCom/PubDocument. asp?DocumentID=1232502&Language=E>.

Interchurch Fund for International Development, Churches' Committee on International Affairs, Canadian Council of Churches. 1991. *Diminishing Our Future: CIDA: Four Years After Winegard.* A Report on Recent Developments in Canadian Development Assistance Policies and Practices. Oct.

International Commission on Intervention and State Sovereignty (ICISS). 2001. *The Responsibility to Protect.* Report of the International Commission on Intervention and State Sovereignty. Ottawa: International Development Research Centre.

International Committee to Ban Landmines-Landmine Monitor Core Group. 2000. *Landmine Monitor Report 2000: Toward a Mine-Free World.* Washington, DC: Human Rights Watch.

International Crisis Group. 1999. 'War in the Balkans: Consequences of the Kosovo Conflict and Future Options for Kosovo and the Region', Europe Report 61, 19 Apr. <http://www.crisisgroup.org/home/index.cfm?l=1&id=1592>.

International Joint Commission. 1977. *Transboundary Implications of the Garrison Diversion Unit.* Ottawa and Washington, DC: International Joint Commission.

———. 1998. *The International Joint Commission and the Boundary Waters Treaty of 1909.* Ottawa: International Joint Commission.

International Labor Organization (ILO). 1976. *Employment, Growth and Basic Needs: A One World Problem.* Director-General's report to the World Employment Conference. Geneva: ILO.

Ipsos-Reid. 2005. *Canadians, Views on HIV/AIDS: A New World Vision Canada Survey.* 14 June. <http://www.ipsos.ca>.

Jaccard, Mark et al. 2006. 'Burning Our Money to Warm the Planet: Canada's Ineffective Efforts to Reduce Greenhouse Gas Emissions', *C.D. Howe Institute: Commentary,* No. 234 (May): 1–31.

Jackson, Andrew. 2003. *Why the 'Big Idea' Is a Bad Idea—A Critical Perspective on Deeper Economic Integration with the United States.* Ottawa: Canadian Centre for Policy Alternatives.

Jacobs, Mike. 2005. 'Devils Lake Deal Looks Possible', *Winnipeg Free Press,* 22 June, A14.

Jang, Brent. 1997. 'Oil Firms Split on Global Warming/Arguments Over Emission Controls Are Fuelling Resentment Over Alliance with Ottawa and Disagreement on Impacts', *Globe and Mail,* 5 Dec., A22.

Jelinek, Otto (MP for Halton). 1984. Letter from Ottawa to Gabriel Fritzen, Thunder Bay, 22 Feb.

John, Peter. 2003. 'Is There Life After Policy Streams, Advocacy Coalitions, and Punctuations: Using Evolutionary Theory to Explain Policy Change?' *Policy Studies Journal* 31: 481–97.

Johnson, Rona K. 2005. 'Manitoba Pulls Plug on Project', *Grand Forks Herald,* 3 Feb.

Kaplan, Robert D. 1994. 'The Coming Anarchy', *Atlantic Monthly* 273, 2 (Feb.).

Kapoor, Ilan. 2002. 'Capitalism, Culture, Agency: Dependency Versus Postcolonial Theory', *Third World Quarterly* 23, 4: 647–64.

Kaul, Hans-Peter. 1997. 'Towards a Permanent International Criminal Tribunal, Some Observations of Negotiator', *Human Rights Law Journal* 18: 169–74.

Kaul, Inge, Isabelle Grunberg, and Marc A. Stern, eds. 1999. *Global Public Goods: International Cooperation in the 21st Century.* New York: Oxford University Press.

———— Pedro Conceição, Katell Le Goulven, and Ronald U. Mendoza, eds. 2003. *Providing Global Public Goods: Managing Globalization.* New York: Oxford University Press.

Keating, Thomas. 1993. *Canada and World Order: The Multilateralist Tradition in Canadian Foreign Policy.* Toronto: McClelland and Stewart.

Keck, Margaret E., and Kathryn Sikkink. 1998. *Activists Beyond Borders: Advocacy Networks in International Politics.* Ithaca: Cornell University Press.

Keller, Tony. 1998. 'Canada Steps to the Fore on World Court', *Globe and Mail,* 13 July.

Kellow, Richard. 2003. Letter to US Army Corps of Engineers regarding the Devils Lake Outlet Final Integrated Planning Report and Environmental Impact Statement, 19 June. <http://www.gov.mb.ca/waterstewardship/water_info/transboundary/pdf/canadian-comments-eis-jun19-2003.pdf>.

Kelly, Keith. 1998. 'Commentary and Discussion', in Dennis Browne, ed., *The Culture/ Trade Quandary: Canada's Policy Options.* Ottawa: Centre for Trade Policy and Law, 189–91.

Kelly, Paul V. 2004. Letter to John Hoeven, Governor of North Dakota, regarding a water outlet project for Devils Lake, 10 Mar. <http://savethesheyenne.org/Kelly%20letter%20to%20Hoeven%2010Mar04.pdf>.

Kergin, Michael. 2002. Letter to Marc Grossman, Undersecretary for Political Affairs, US Department of State, regarding a referral of the Corps outlet to the IJC, 21 May. <http://www.swc.state.nd.us/projects/newdevilslake/pdfs/IJC_Referral_MB_Response.pdf>.

Kiddell-Monroe, Rachel. 2006a. 'Telephone interview re: the formulation and implementation of Bill C-9', 19 Sept.

————. 2006b. 'E-mail re: chronology of MSF involvement', 19 Sept.

Kingdon, John. 1995. *Agendas, Alternatives, and Public Policies*. New York: HarperCollins.

————. 2003. *Agendas, Alternatives, and Public Policies*, 2nd edn. New York: HarperCollins.

Kirsch, Phillippe, and J.T. Holmes. 1999. 'The Rome Conference on an International Criminal Court: The Negotiation Process', *American Journal of International Law* 93, 1: 2–12.

Kirton, John. 1985. 'Managing Foreign Policy', in Brian W. Tomlin and Maureen Appel Molot, eds, *Canada Among Nations 1984: A Time of Transition*. Toronto: James Lorimer, 14–28.

————. 1986. 'The Foreign Policy Decision Process', in Brian W. Tomlin and Maureen Appel Molot, eds, *Canada Among Nations 1985: The Conservative Agenda*. Toronto: James Lorimer, 25–46.

————. 1994. 'Sustainable Development as a Focus for Canadian Foreign Policy', Working Paper No. 25. Ottawa: National Round Table on the Environment and the Economy, Sept.

————. 2007. *Canadian Foreign Policy in a Changing World*. Toronto: Thomson Nelson.

Kitchen, Veronica. 2002. 'From Rhetoric to Reality: Canada, the United States, and the Ottawa Process to Ban Landmines', *International Journal* 57, 1 (Winter): 37–55.

Klare, Michael, and Robert I. Rotberg. 1999. *The Scourge of Small Arms*. Cambridge: World Peace Foundation.

Klein, Naomi. 2003. 'Bush's Aids "Gift" Has Been Seized By Industry Giants', *The Guardian*, 13 Oct. <http://www.guardian.co.uk/Columnists/Column/0,,1061636,00.html>.

Knight, Andy W. 2001. 'Soft Power, Moral Suasion, and Establishing the International Criminal Court: Canadian Contributions', in Rosalind Irwin, ed, *Ethics and Security in Canadian Foreign Policy*. Vancouver: UBC Press, 113–37.

Knox, Paul. 1997. 'Canada Limps into Kyoto Arena: Former Environmental Leader Spent Five Years Fiddling While Everyone Else Moved On', *Globe and Mail*, 28 Nov., A1.

Korey, William. 1998. *NGOs and the Universal Declaration of Human Rights*. New York: St Martin's Press.

Koring, Paul. 1994. 'Serbs Hold Canadians Hostage—17 Soldiers Under Detention As UN Peacekeepers Become Targets', *Globe and Mail*, 15 Apr.

Kuxhaus, David. 2002. 'North Dakota Moves Ahead on Water Diversion Project', *Winnipeg Free Press*, 29 Aug., A7.

————. 2003. 'Devils Lake Report Sees No Major Impact', *Winnipeg Free Press*, 22 Apr., B4.

Lagassé, Philippe. 2006. 'Canada's Post-1945 Defence Policies', brief prepared for *Canada's International Policies*, unpublished.

Laghi, Brian. 2006. 'Ottawa Seeks Help Developing Alternative to Kyoto: Ethanol Initiative Targets Emissions', *Globe and Mail*, 23 May, A1.

————. 2007. 'Climate Concern Now Tops Security and Health: One in Four Label Environmental Issues as Most Important', *Globe and Mail*, 26 Jan., A1.

———— et al. 2007. 'Harper to Unveil New-Look Cabinet: With an Election Likely Looming, PM Shifts Responsibilities of a Quarter of His Cabinet Ministers', *Globe and Mail*, 4 Jan., A1.

———— and Karen Howlett. 2007. 'PM Under Fire for Backing US Version of Climate Plan; Harper Yet to Give Commitment to Support German Plan to Control Carbon Emissions', *Globe and Mail*, 29 May, A1.

Lalonde, Marc. 1990. 'Riding the Storm: Energy Policy, 1968–1984', in Thomas Axworthy and Pierre Trudeau, eds, *Towards a Just Society: The Trudeau Years*. Toronto: Viking, 49–77.

Lawson, Robert J. 1995. 'Construction of Consensus: The 1994 Canadian Defence Review', in Maxwell A. Cameron and Maureen Appel Molot, eds, *Canada Among Nations 1995: Democracy and Foreign Policy*. Ottawa: Carleton University Press, 99–117.

LeBlanc, Daniel. 2007. 'O'Connor Left Hung Out to Dry on Detainee File, Official Says', *Globe and Mail*, 28 Apr.

———— et al. 2006. 'Liberals Poised to Block Tory Budget: Dion Joins Duceppe Saying He Is Willing to Topple Minority', *Globe and Mail*, 15 Dec., A1.

Lee, Steven. 1998. 'Beyond Consultations: Public Contributions to Making Foreign Policy', in Fen Osler Hampson and Maureen Appel Molot, eds, *Canada Among Nations 1998: Leadership and Dialogue*. Toronto: Oxford University Press, 55–68.

Leys, Colin. 1996. *The Rise and Fall of Development Theory*. Bloomington: Indiana University Press.

Leyton-Brown, David. 1986. 'Canada–US Relations: Towards a Closer Relationship', in Maureen Molot and Brian Tomlin, eds, *Canada Among Nations 1985: The Conservative Agenda*. Toronto: James Lorimer, 177–95.

Lipsey, Richard. 1990. 'Canada at the US–Mexico Free Trade Dance: Wallflower or Partner?' *C.D. Howe Institute Commentary*. Toronto: C.D. Howe Institute.

———— and Murray Smith. 1985. *Taking the Initiative: Canada's Trade Options in a Turbulent World*. Toronto: C.D. Howe Institute.

Lloyd, Trevor. 1960. *Canada in World Affairs, 1957–1959*. Toronto: Oxford.

Lokkesmoe, Kent. 1999. 'Minnesota DNR Comment on Public Notice, Devils Lake/Stump Lake Emergency Outlet', 10 Sept. <http://www.savethesheyenne.org/minnesot.htm>.

Long, David, and Laird Hindle. 1998. 'Europe and the Ottawa Process: An Overview', *Canadian Foreign Policy* 5, 3: 69–83.

Longwoods Research Group. 1990. Public Opinion Poll, Sept.

Lord, Christopher, and Neil Winn. 2000. 'Garbage Cans or Rational Decision? Member Governments, Supranational Actors and the Shaping of the Agenda for the IGC', *Current Politics and Economics of Europe* 9: 237–56.

Lougheed, Peter. 2001. 'Only Ottawa Can Lose the West: Western Separatism Isn't the Issue. Western Alienation Is, Says Former Alberta Premier Peter Lougheed', *Globe and Mail*, 16 Feb., A13.

Lum, Janet. 1991. 'Recognition and the Toronto Chinese Community', in Paul M. Evans and B. Michael Frolic, eds, *Reluctant Adversaries: Canada and the People's Republic of China 1949–1970*. Toronto: University of Toronto Press, 217–40.

Lumbers, Michael. 2004. 'The Irony of Vietnam: The Johnson Administration's Tentative Bridge-Building to China, 1965–1966', *Journal of Cold War Studies* 6, 3 (Summer): 68–114.

Lyon, Peyton. 1964. *Canada in World Affairs, 1961–1963*. Toronto: Oxford University Press.

MacAfee, Michelle. 2004. 'Manitoba Files Lawsuit to Block North Dakota Water Diversion', *Montreal Gazette*, 30 Mar., A14.

McBean, Gordon. 2006. 'An Integrated Approach to Air Pollution, Climate and Weather Hazards', *Policy Options* (Oct.): 18–24.

McCarthy, Shawn. 1997. 'Copps and Eggleton Battle Over Culture', *Toronto Star*, 30 Jan.

Macdonald, Douglas, and Debora VanNijnatten. 2005. 'Sustainable Development and Kyoto Implementation in Canada: The Road Not Taken', *Policy Options* (July–Aug.): 13–19.

MacFarlane, Neil S., and Yuen Foong Khong. 2006. *Human Security and the UN: A Critical History*. Bloomington: Indiana University Press.

MacGregor, Roy. 2007. 'Green Party's Showing in London's By-election Hints at Something Big', *Globe and Mail*, 29 Nov., A2.

McIlroy, Anne, and Brian Laghi. 1997. 'Ottawa Changes Gas Target: Emissions Pledge Angers Provinces', *Globe and Mail*, 2 Dec., A1.

Mack, Andrew. 2005. 'Peace on Earth? Increasingly, Yes', *Washington Post*, 28 Dec. <http://www.washingtonpost.com/wpdyn/content/article/2005/12/27/AR2005122700 732.html>.

———— and Oliver Rohlfs. 2003. 'The Great Canadian Divide', *Globe and Mail*, 28 Mar.

McKenna, Barrie. 2002. 'Despite the Hazy Debate, Kyoto May Be Just What Canada Needs', *Globe and Mail*, 20 Sept., B10.

————. 2007. 'US CEOs Want Action on Climate Change: Bush Faces Pressure for Tougher Rules', *Globe and Mail*, 23 Jan., B1.

McKenna, Frank. 2005. 'Hell from High Water', *New York Times*, 12 May, 27.

MacKenzie, Lewis. 2006. 'United Nations—Forget a UN Army', *Globe and Mail*, 26 June.

MacKinnon, Mark. 2002. 'Halve Greenhouse Gases Soon, Easily: Suzuki Says Reduction Does Not Mean Economic Disruption, Study Argues', *Globe and Mail*, 18 Apr., A2.

MacLean, George. 2000. 'Instituting and Projecting Human Security: A Canadian Perspective', *Australian Journal of International Affairs* 54, 3 (Nov.): 269–75.

MacPherson, Bryan F. 1998. 'Building an International Criminal Court for the 21st Century', *Connecticut Journal of International Law* 13, 1: 1–60.

Madger, Ted. 1998. *Franchising the Candy Store: Split-Run Magazines and A New International Regime for Trade in Culture*. Orono, ME: Canadian-American Center, University of Maine.

Mahfood, Stephen. 2003. Letter to the US Army Corps of Engineers Regarding the Devils Lake Outlet Final Integrated Planning Report and Environmental Impact Statement, 18 June. <http://www.gov.mb.ca/waterstewardship/water_info/transboundary/pdf/devils-06-18-03-final.pdf>.

Malone, David M. 1999. 'The Global Issues Biz: What Gives?' in Fen O. Hampson, Michael Hart, and Martin Rudner, eds, *Canada Among Nations 1999: A Big League Player?* Toronto: Oxford University Press, 197–214.

Marchi, Sergio. 1998. 'Marchi Supports Copps on Culture', *Toronto Star*, 6 Dec.

————. 1999. Notes for an address by the Honorable Sergio Marchi, Minister for International Trade to the Standing Committee on Transport and Communications on Bill C-55', 25 May. <http://w01.international.gc.ca/minipub/Publication.asp?publication_id= 375025&Language=E>.

Martin, Erica. 2005. 'The Impact of the News Media in Shaping Canadian Development Assistance Policy', *Undercurrent* 2, 2: 28–40.

Martin, Lawrence. 2006. 'Are We Better Off Today Than a Year Ago? Just Ask the People', *Globe and Mail*, 21 Dec., A21.

Martin, Pierre, and Michel Fortmann. 1995. 'Canadian Public Opinion and Peacekeeping in a Turbulent World', *International Journal* 30, 2 (Spring): 370–400.

————. 2001a. 'Public Opinion: Obstacle, Partner or Scapegoat?' *Policy Options* (Jan.–Feb.): 66–72.

————. 2001b. 'Support for International Involvement in Canadian Public Opinion after The Cold War', *Canadian Military Journal* (Autumn): 43–52. <http://www.journal.dnd.ca/engraph/vol2/no3/pdf/43-52_e.pdf>.

Maslen, Stuart, and Peter Herby. 1998. 'An International Ban on Anti-Personnel Mines: History and Negotiation of the "Ottawa Treaty"', *International Review of the Red Cross* 325: 693–713.

Matthew, Richard. 2003. 'Middle Power–NGO Coalitions: A Significant Force in World Politics', in Ken Rutherford, Stefan Brem, and Richard Matthew, eds, *Reframing the Agenda: The Impact of NGO and Middle Power Cooperation in International Security Policy*. Westport, CT: Praeger, 202–9.

Maule, Christopher. 2001. 'State of the Canada–US Relationship: Culture', *The American Review of Canadian Studies* 30, 1 (Spring): 121–42.

May, Elizabeth. 2002–3. 'From Montreal to Kyoto, How We Got from Here to There—Or Not', *Policy Options* (Dec.–Jan.): 14–18.

———. 2007. 'The Saga of Bill C-30: From Clean Air to Climate Change or Not', *Policy Options* (May): 42–7.

Mayer, Frederick. 1998. *Interpreting NAFTA: The Science and Art of Political Analysis*. New York: Columbia University Press.

Médecins Sans Frontières (MSF). 2006. *Neither Expeditious, Nor a Solution: The WTO August 30th Decision is Unworkable*. XVI International AIDS Conference Pamphlet. Geneva/Montreal: Médecins Sans Frontières.

Mellgren, Doug. 2007. 'Inuit Leader Nominated for Nobel: Along With Al Gore, Sheila Watt-Cloutier Recognised for Efforts on Global Warming', *Globe and Mail*, 2 Feb., A5.

Menzies, Peter. 2007. 'Give Us a Break—Last Thing We Need is Another Gas Tax', *Globe and Mail*, 11 May, A23.

Mergent Media Reports. 2005. 'Media—North America', Jan.

Michaud, Nelson. 2001. 'Bureaucratic Politics and the Making of the 1987 Defence White Paper', in Nelson Michaud and Kim Richard Nossal, eds, *Diplomatic Departures: The Conservative Era in Canadian Foreign Policy, 1984–93*. Vancouver: UBC Press, 260–75.

——— and Kim Richard Nossal. 2001. 'The Conservative Era in Canadian Foreign Policy, 1984–93', in Nelson Michaud and Kim Richard Nossal, eds, *Diplomatic Departures: The Conservative Era in Canadian Foreign Policy, 1984–93*. Vancouver: UBC Press, 3–24.

Milner, Marc. 1999. *Canada's Navy: The First Century*. Toronto: University of Toronto Press.

Mittelstaedt, Martin. 2002. 'Fossil Fuel Producers Main Foes of Treaty', *Globe and Mail*, 16 Feb., A4.

———. 2005. 'Canada's Greenhouse-gas Emissions Rise: UN Report Shows Lack of Progress on Kyoto, Reveals 24-per-cent Increase in 1990–2003', *Globe and Mail*, 28 Nov., A8.

———. 2007. 'Why It's Peak Time to Hit the Brakes: From Blue-chip Reports to Red-carpet Documentaries, a Critical Mass of People Around the World—and Especially in Canada—Want to Shift into Greener Gear', *Globe and Mail*, 27 Jan., A8.

——— and Gloria Galloway. 2006. 'PM Unveils Chemical Crackdown: Seeking to Keep Green Agenda from Liberals, Tories Get Tough with Hazardous Substances', *Globe and Mail*, 9 Dec., A1.

Molot, Maureen Appel. 1984. 'The Political Implications of North American Capital Flows', in Jon Pammett and Brian Tomlin, eds, *The Integration Question: Political Economy and Public Policy in Canada and North America*. Toronto: Addison-Wesley, 163–81.

——— and Norman Hillmer. 2002. 'The Diplomacy of Decline', in Norman Hillmer and Maureen Appel Molot, eds, *Canada Among Nations 2002: A Fading Power*. Toronto: Oxford University Press, 1–33.

——— and Brian W. Tomlin. 1986. 'The Conservative Agenda', in Brian W. Tomlin and Maureen Appel Molot, eds, *Canada Among Nations 1985: The Conservative Agenda*. Toronto: James Lorimer, 3–24.

Montreal Gazette. 2005. 'Ray of Hope at the UN', editorial/op-ed, 18 Sept.

Morgan, Gwyn. 2007a. 'Effective Green Policies Must be Rooted in Facts', *Globe and Mail*, 22 Jan., B2.

————. 2007b. 'Life after the Fog of Kyoto Accord Must Cut Through China's Smog', *Globe and Mail*, 5 Feb., B2.

Morley, David. 2004. 'Drug Companies Focus on Profits, Not People', *Times Colonist*, 20 Apr., A11.

Morrison, David. 1998. *Aid and Ebb Tide: A History of* CIDA *and Canadian Development Assistance*. Waterloo, ON: Wilfrid Laurier Press.

Mucciaroni, Gary. 1992. 'The Garbage Can Model & the Study of Policy Making: A Critique', *Polity* 24: 460–82.

Muirhead, Bruce. 1992. *The Development of Postwar Canadian Trade Policy: The Failure of the Anglo–European Option*. Montreal and Kingston: McGill-Queen's University Press.

Munton, Don. 1980. 'Dependence and Interdependence in Trans–Boundary Environmental Relations', *International Journal* 36, 1: 139–84.

————. 1988–9. 'Canadians and their Defence', *Peace and Security* 3, 4 (Winter): 2–5.

————. 1989–90. 'Uncommon Threats and Common Security', *Peace and Security* 4, 4 (Winter): 2–5.

————. 1997. 'Acid Rain and Trans–Boundary Air Quality in Canadian–American Relations', *American Review of Canadian Studies* 27, 3: 327–58.

————. 2002–3. 'Whither Internationalism?' *International Journal* 58, 1: 155–80.

———— and Tom Keating. 2001. 'Internationalism and the Canadian Public', *Canadian Journal of Political Science* 34, 3 (Sept.): 517–49.

Murphy, Rex. 2007. 'Green's Not Mr. Harper's Best Colour', *Globe and Mail*, 6 Jan., A19.

Neier, Arey. 1998. 'Waiting for Justice: The United States and the International Court', *World Policy Journal* 15, 3: 33–7.

Neufeld, Mark. 2004. 'Pitfalls of Emancipation and Discourses of Security: Reflections on Canada's "Security with a Human Face,"' *International Relations* 18, 1: 109–23.

Neve, Alex, and Jason Gratl. 2007. 'Responsibility Doesn't End with the Torturer—Until Canada Receives Greater Assurances, the Transfer of Detainees Has to Stop', comment, *Globe and Mail*, 3 May.

Newman, Peter. 1963. *Renegade in Power: The Diefenbaker Years*. Toronto: McClelland and Stewart.

————. 1968. *The Distemper of Our Times*. Toronto: McClelland and Stewart.

Nicholson, Blake. 2003. 'County, State Haggle Over Lake Definition', *Bismarck Tribune*, 22 Oct., 2B.

Nielson, Erik. 1989. *The House Is Not a Home: An Autobiography*. Toronto: Macmillan.

Noble, Sarah. 2005. 'Talking to Canadians about Defence: Giving to Whom you Trust', in Conference of Defence Associations Institute, *Understanding the Crisis in Canadian Security and Defence*. Ottawa: Conference of Defence Associations Institute, 9–18.

Noël, Alain, Jean-Philippe Thérien, and Sébastien Dallaire. 2004. 'Divided Over Internationalism: The Canadian Public and Development Assistance', *Canadian Public Policy* 30, 1: 29–46.

Nolen, Stephanie. 2003. 'Spearhead AIDS Fight, UN Envoy Tells Canada', *Globe and Mail*, 25 Sept., A1.

Norrie, William. 1984. Letter from Winnipeg to Gabriel Fritzen, Thunder Bay, 28 Mar.

North-South Institute. 2004. *Canadian Development Report: Investing in Poor Countries: Who Benefits?* Ottawa: The North-South Institute.

Nossal, Kim Richard. 1989. 'All in Favour, Say Aye', *Peace and Security* 4, 1 (Spring): 4–5.

————. 1995. 'The Democratization of Canadian Foreign Policy: The Elusive Ideal', in Maxwell A. Cameron and Maureen Appel Molot, eds, *Canada Among Nations 1995: Democracy and Foreign Policy*. Ottawa: Carleton University, 29–43.

———. 1997. *The Politics of Canadian Foreign Policy,* 3rd edn. Scarborough: Prentice-Hall Canada.

———. 1998. 'Foreign Policy for Wimps', *Ottawa Citizen,* 23 Apr., A19.

———. 1998–9. 'Pinchpenny Diplomacy: The Decline of "Good International Citizenship" in Canadian Foreign Policy', *International Journal* 54, 1 (Winter): 88–105.

———. 2003. *The World We Want—The Purposeful Confusion of Values, Goals, and Interests in Canadian Foreign Policy.* Calgary: Canadian Defence and Foreign Affairs Institute.

Nowak, Manfred, ed. 1994. *World Conference on Human Rights, Vienna, June 1993: The Contributions of NGOs: Reports and Documents.* Vienna: Manzche Verlags.

Nye, Joseph S., Jr. 2004. *Soft Power: The Means to Success in World Politics.* New York: Public Affairs.

——— and John D. Donahue, eds. 2000. *Governance in a Globalizing World.* Washington, DC: Brookings Institution.

OECD/DAC. 1996. *Shaping the 21st Century: The Contribution of Development Co-operation.* Paris: OECD.

———. 2000. *Development Cooperation 1999 Report.* Paris: OECD.

———. 2003. *Development Cooperation Review: Canada.* Paris: OECD.

Office of the Auditor General. 2006. 'Opening Statement to the Standing Senate Committee on Energy, Environment and Natural Resources', 3 Oct. <http://www.oag-bvg.gc.ca/domino/other.nsf/html/06nr02_e.html>.

Olivastri, Beatrice. 2006. CEO Friends of the Earth Canada. Telephone interview, Ottawa, 14 Feb.

Olsen, Johan. 2001. 'Garbage Cans, New Institutionalism, and the Study of Politics', *American Political Science Review* 95: 191–8.

O'Neil, Maureen, and Andrew Clarke. 1992. 'Canada and International Developments: New Agendas', in Fen Osler Hampson and Christopher J. Maule, eds, *Canada Among Nations 1992–93: A New World Order?* Ottawa: Carleton University Press, 219–34.

Orbinski, James. 2000. 'There Is No Such Thing as Military Humanitarianism', Nobel Peace Prize 1999 acceptance speech, *Peace Magazine* 16 (Winter).

———. 2003. 'Rock Is Right on AIDS Patent Plan', Letter to the editor, *National Post,* 14 Oct., FP11.

Ostry, Bernard. 1978. *The Cultural Connection: An Essay on Culture and Government Policy in Canada.* Toronto: McClelland and Stewart.

Owens, Heather, and Barbara Arneil. 1999. 'The Human Security Paradigm Shift: A New Lens on Canadian Foreign Policy', *Canadian Foreign Policy* 7, 1 (Fall): 1–12.

Pace, William R., and Jennifer Schense. 2001. 'Coalition for the International Criminal Court at the Preparatory Commission', in Roy S. Lee, ed, *The International Criminal Court: Elements of Crimes and Rules of Procedure and Evidence.* New York: Transnational Publishers.

Page, Don. 1991. 'The Representation of China in the United Nations: Canadian Perspectives and Initiatives, 1949–1971', in Paul M. Evans and B. Michael Frolic, eds, *Reluctant Adversaries: Canada and the People's Republic of China 1949–1970.* Toronto: University of Toronto Press, 73–105.

Paris, Roland. 2001. 'Human Security: Paradigm Shift or Hot Air?' *International Security* 26, 2: 87–102.

Parkinson, Rhonda. 2005. 'Canada Pledges to Fight HIV/AIDS in Africa', *Maple Leaf Web.* <http://www.mapleleafweb.com/features/general/aids-africa/pledges.html>.

Pammett, Jon, and Brian Tomlin. 1984. 'Integration in Canada and North America', in Jon Pammett and Brian Tomlin, eds, *The Integration Question: Political Economy and Public Policy in Canada and North America.* Toronto: Addison-Wesley, 1–9.

Parliament of Canada. 1994. *Security in a Changing World: The Report of the Special Joint Committee of the Senate and of the House of Commons on Canada's Defence Policy*. Ottawa: Public Works and Government Services Canada.

Peacebuilding and Human Security after September 11. 2002. Report from the sixth annual consultations by DFAIT and the Canadian Peacebuilding Coordinating Committee (CPCC), 24–6 Apr.

———. 1973. *Mike: Memoirs of the Right Honourable Lester B. Pearson*, vol. 2. Toronto: University of Toronto Press.

Pearson, Gary L., and David R. Conrad. 2003. *Comments of the National Wildlife Federation on the U.S. Army Corps of Engineers' April 2003 Final Devils Lake, North Dakota Integrated Planning Report and Environmental Impact Statement*. Washington: National Wildlife Federation.

Pearson, Geoffrey. 1993. *Seize the Day: Lester B. Pearson and the Crisis Diplomacy*. Ottawa: Carleton University Press.

Pearson, Lester B. 1969. *Partners in Development: Report of the Commission on International Development*. London: Pall Mall.

Pembina Institute. 'Our Work: Regulated Emission Targets for Large Industrial Emitters'. <http://www.pembina.org/climate-change/work-lfe.php>.

Penson, Charlie. 1999. 36th Parliament, 1st Session. House Publications, 10 June. <http:www2.parl.ca.ca/HousePublications/Publication>.

Pérez de Cuéllar, Javier. 1995. *Our Creative Diversity*. Report of the World Commission on Culture and Development. Paris: UNESCO Publishing.

Perreaux, Les. 2001. 'North Dakota Threatens to Drain Lake over Canada's Protests', *National Post*, 18 July, A2.

Perry, Tom. 2006. *The House*, CBC Radio program, 10 June.

Peters, Stuart S. 1969. 'A Canadian Search for New Development Imperatives', paper presented at the 7th Annual Banff Conference on World Affairs, Aug.

Pfister, Lisa. 1989. *CIDA, WID, and GAD: A Critical Examination of CIDA's Women in Development Policies*, MA thesis, University of Guelph.

Plumptre, A.F.W. 1977. *Three Decades of Decision: Canada and the World Monetary System, 1944–75*. Toronto: McClelland and Stewart.

Politics Watch. 2004. *Access to Generic Drugs*, 4 May. <http://72.14.205.104/search?q=cache:3QAti-PuZLgJ:lists.essential.org/pipermail/ip-health/2004-May/006363.html+%22dan+mcteague%22+big+pharma+bill+c-9&hl=en&gl=ca&ct=clnk&cd=6>.

POLLARA. 2004. *Domestic Terrorism and National Defence Top Canadians' Foreign Policy Spending Priorities*, 20 Apr. Toronto: POLLARA (report prepared for the Canadian Institute of International Affairs, CIIA). <http://www.pollara.com/Library/News/POLLARA-CIIA.pdf>.

Potter, Evan H. 1996. 'Canada Must Become an Expert in Niche Diplomacy', *Ottawa Citizen*, 15 Apr.

———. 1996–7. 'Niche Diplomacy as Canadian Foreign Policy', *International Journal* 52, 1 (Winter): 25–38.

Powell, Colin. 2004. Letter to General Robert Flowers, US Army Corps of Engineers, regarding plans for an outlet project at Devils Lake, 20 Jan. <http://savethesheyenne.org/SecPowelltoGenFlowers.pdf>.

Powlick, Philip J. 1995. 'The Sources of Public Opinion for American Foreign Policy Officials', *International Studies Quarterly* 39, 4: 427–51.

Pratt, Cranford. 1993–4. 'Canada's Development Assistance: Some Lessons from the Last Review', *International Journal* 49, 1 (Winter): 93–125.

————. 1994–5. 'Development Assistance and Canadian Foreign Policy: Where Are We Now?' *Canadian Foreign Policy* 3 (Winter): 77–85.

————. 1996. 'Canadian Development Assistance: A Profile', in Cranford Pratt, ed, *Canadian International Development Assistance Policies: An Appraisal*, 2nd edn. Montreal and Kingston: McGill-Queen's University Press, 334–70.

————. 1999. 'Competing Rationales for Canadian Development Assistance', *International Journal* 54, 2 (Spring): 306–23.

Priest, Lisa. 'Ottawa Unveils Plan for Energy Rebates; Minister Announces $300-million to Be Used to Retrofit Homes, Buildings', *Globe and Mail*, 22 Jan., A4.

Rabinovitch, Victor. 1998. 'The Social and Economic Rationales for Canada's Domestic Cultural Policies', in Dennis Browne, ed, *The Culture/Trade Quandary: Canada's Policy Options*. Ottawa: Centre for Trade Policy and Law, 25–45.

Rabson, Mia. 2005a. 'Doer Rejects Offer of Meet On Devils Lake', *Winnipeg Free Press*, 26 Mar., B7.

————. 2005b. 'Doer Rages as Water Flows', *Winnipeg Free Press*, 16 Aug., A1.

Rankin, L. Pauline, and Jill Vickers. 2001. 'Women's Movements and State Feminism: Integrating Diversity into Public Policy', Research Directorate, Status of Women Canada. Ottawa: Carleton University.

Razavi, Shahra, and Carol Miller. 1995. 'Gender Mainstreaming: A Study of Efforts by the UNDP, the World Bank, and the ILO to Institutionalize Gender Issues', Geneva: United Nations Research Institute for Social Development.

Rebuffoni, Dean. 1997. 'North Dakota Flood-Control Plan Is under Fire', *Star Tribune*, 9 May, 22A.

Reddon, Andrew J., and Elizabeth S. Dipchand. 2004. 'The African Act and Canadian Compulsory Licensing: From the Perspective of the Innovators', paper given at the 3rd Annual Forum of Pharma Patents, Toronto, 9 Nov.

Reeves, Eric. 1999. 'Exotic Policy: An IJC White Paper on Policies for the Prevention of The Invasion of The Great Lakes By Exotic Organisms', Great Lakes Water Forum, Milwaukee.

Regehr, Ernie. 1994. Project Ploughshares, quoted in the *Toronto Star*, 2 Jan.

———— and Peter Whelan. 2004. *Reshaping the Security Envelope: Defence Policy in a Human Security Context*. Project Ploughshares Working Papers, Nov. Waterloo, ON: Project Ploughshares.

Reguly, Eric. 2007. 'Baird Is Tough, But Meeting His Deadlines Is Next to Impossible', *Globe and Mail*, 9 Jan., B2.

————. 2006. 'Kyoto Protocol No One-Night Stand', *Globe and Mail*, 4 May, B2.

Report of the Independent Commission on International Development Issues (Brandt Commission). 1980. *North–South: A Programme for Survival*. Cambridge, MA: MIT Press.

Reuters News Agency. 1998. 'UN Erred Over Rwandan Genocide Warning: Official', *Globe and Mail*, 8 Dec.

————. 2004. 'US, Canada Agree to Exempt AIDS Law from NAFTA', 16 Jul. <http://lists.essential.org/pipermail/ip-health/2004-July/006753.html>.

Richardson, Jeremy. 2001. 'Policy-Making in the EU: Interests, Ideas and Garbage Cans of Primeval Soup', in Jeremy Richardson, ed, *European Union: Power and Policy-Making*. New York: Routledge, 4–24.

Riddell-Dixon, Elizabeth. 2005. 'Canada's Human Security Agenda: Walking the Talk?' *International Journal* 60, 4 (Autumn): 1067–92.

Rigby, Vincent. 2001. 'The Canadian Forces and Human Security: A Redundant or Relevant Military?' in Fen O. Hampson, Norman Hillmer, and Maureen Appel Molot, eds,

Canada Among Nations 2001: The Axworthy Legacy. Toronto: Oxford University Press, 39–63.

Riley, Susan. 1997. 'No Magic Bullet to Preserve Culture, Copps Tells Cabinet', *Ottawa Citizen*, 10 Feb.

Rioux, Jean-François, and Robin Hay. 1997. 'Canadian Foreign Policy: From Internationalism to Isolationism?' discussion paper no. 16. Ottawa: Norman Paterson School of International Affairs.

Rioux, Jean-Sebastian. 2005. *Two Solitudes: Quebecers' Attitudes Regarding Canadian Security and Defence Policy.* Calgary: Canadian Defence and Foreign Affairs Institute. <http://www.cdfai.org/PDF/Two%20Solitudes.pdf>.

Ripsman, Norrin M. 2001. 'Big Eyes and Empty Pockets: The Two Phases of Conservative Defence Policy', in Nelson Michaud and Kim Richard Nossal, eds, *Diplomatic Departures: The Conservative Era in Canadian Foreign Policy, 1984–93.* Vancouver: UBC Press, 100–12.

Risse, Thomas, Stephen C. Ropp, and Kathryn Sikkinnk, eds. 1999. *The Power of Human Rights: International Norms and Domestic Change.* Cambridge, UK: Cambridge University Press.

Rock, Allan. 2002. 'Interview with Christopher Thomas re: the gun registry, Newsworld Television Clip', 5 Dec. <http://www.cbc.ca/story/news/national/2002/12/06/gun registry021206.html>.

———. 2005. Telephone interview re: the formulation and implementation of Bill C-9, 14 Dec.

Rodrik, Dani. 1999. *The New Global Economy: Making Openness Work.* Washington, DC: Overseas Development Council.

Ross, Jennifer. 2001. 'Is Canada's Human Security Policy Really the "Axworthy Doctrine"?' *Canadian Foreign Policy* 8, 2 (Winter): 75–93.

Ross, Val. 1997. 'Copps Plans "Private" Culture Session, Invitations Snub Large Lobby Groups', *Globe and Mail*, 23 Jan.

Rostow, Walt Whitman. 1971. *The Stages of Economic Growth: A Non-Communist Manifesto*, 2nd edn. Cambridge, UK: Cambridge University Press.

Rothschild, Emma. 1995. 'What is Security?' *Daedalus* (Summer).

Rudner, Martin. 1987. 'Trade Cum Aid in Canada's Official Development Assistance Strategy', in *Canada Among Nations 1986: Talking Trade.* Toronto: James Lorimer, 127–46.

———. 1991. 'Canada, the Gulf Crisis and Collective Security', in Fen Osler Hampson and Christopher J. Maule, eds, *Canada Among Nations 1990–91: After the Cold War.* Ottawa: Carleton University Press, 241–80.

Russett, Bruce. 1993. *Grasping the Democratic Peace: Principles for a Post–Cold War World.* Princeton: Princeton University Press.

Rutherford, K., S. Brem, and R. Matthew, eds. 2003. *Reframing the Agenda: The Impact of NGO and Middle Power Cooperation in International Security Policy.* Westport: Praeger.

Sabatier, Paul, and Hank Jenkins-Smith. 1993. *Policy Change and Learning: An Advocacy Coalition Approach.* Boulder, CO: Westview Press.

Sabourin, Louis. 1976. 'Canada and Francophone Africa', in Peyton Lyon and Tareq Ismael, eds, *Canada and the Third World.* Toronto: Macmillan, 134–61.

Saccomani, Silvana. 1987. *The State, the Society and the Making of Canadian Foreign Investment Policy: The Foreign Investment Review Act and the Investment Canada Act.* MA research essay. Ottawa: Carleton University.

Sallot, Jeff. 1994. 'Defence Trimmers Target Brass', *Globe and Mail*, 1 Nov., A1.

———. 1999. 'Gag Order Silenced Military Crisis', *Globe and Mail*, 18 Feb.

———. 2005. 'Farmers Could Receive $1-billion Under Kyoto Plan, Dion Says', *Globe and Mail*. 15 Apr., A4.

——— and Edward Greenspon. 1994. 'Defence Shopping for Copters, Vehicles', *Globe and Mail*, 1 Dec., A1–2.

——— and Steven Chase. 2005. 'Kyoto Costs Ballooning, Cabinet Ministers Warned', *Globe and Mail*. 14 Mar., A1.

Samyn, Paul. 1995. 'North Dakota Is Holding Its Water', *Winnipeg Free Press,* 10 Oct., A10.

———. 1997. 'US Plan Alarms Filmon', *Winnipeg Free Press*, 20 Mar., A1, A2.

———. 2005a. 'Canada Appears to Give Up Hope for IJC Review', *Winnipeg Free Press,* 21 June, A7.

———. 2005b. 'Devils Lake Outlet Shut Until Spring?' *Winnipeg Free Press*, 15 Sept., A1.

———. 2005c. 'Devils Lake Pact in Sight', *Winnipeg Free Press*, 4 Aug., A1.

———. 2005d. 'Devils Lake Tested At Last', *Winnipeg Free Press*, 30 July, A1.

———. 2005e. 'Great Lakes Mayors Back Manitoba in Devils Lake', *Winnipeg Free Press*, 27 May, A1.

———. 2005f. 'Let the Bastards Freeze in the Dark', *Winnipeg Free Press*, 15 June, A1.

Sarty, Leigh. 1993. 'A Handshake Across the Pole: Canadian–Soviet Relations in the Era of Detente', in David Davies, ed, *Canada and the Soviet Experiment: Essays on Canadian Encounters with Russia and the Soviet Union, 1900-1991*. Toronto: Canadian Scholars' Press, 117–35.

Saywell, J.T., ed. 1963. *Canadian Annual Review of Politics and Public Affairs, 1963 (CAR)*. Toronto: University of Toronto Press.

———, ed. 1964. *Canadian Annual Review of Politics and Public Affairs, 1964 (CAR)*. Toronto: University of Toronto Press.

———, ed. 1970. *Canadian Annual Review of Politics and Public Affairs, 1970 (CAR)*. Toronto: University of Toronto Press.

———, ed. 1971. *Canadian Annual Review of Politics and Public Affairs, 1971 (CAR)*. Toronto: University of Toronto Press.

———, ed. 1987. *Canadian Annual Review of Politics and Public Affairs, 1987 (CAR)*. Toronto: University of Toronto Press.

Schafer, Ed. 2005. Telephone interview, 7 Dec.

Schwanen, Daniel. 1997. *A Matter of Choice: Toward a More Creative Canadian Foreign Policy on Culture*. Toronto: C.D. Howe Institute. <http://www.cdhowe.org/pdf/sch-02.pdf>.

Scoffield, Heather. 1998. 'Copps Takes Fight Against Hollywood to World Stage; UNESCO Speech to Push Cultural Policies', *Globe and Mail*, 23 Mar.

———. 1999. 'Global Culture Pact Needed, Reports Say House Committees Find Current Exemption in Trade Agreement Ineffective', *Globe and Mail,* 11 June.

——— and Steven Chase. 2003. 'Ottawa Heeds Call on AIDS; Ministers Respond to Lewis with Pledge to Relax Generic-Drug Laws in a Hurry', *Globe and Mail*, 26 Sept., A1.

——— and Paul Knox. 2003. 'Big Drug Companies Embrace AIDS Plan; Decision by Brand–Name Firms Lifts Major Barrier to Generic–Drug Blitz', *Globe and Mail*, 2 Oct., A1.

Scott, Norval. 2007. 'Global Warming Will Hit Poor Countries Harder, Report Says', *Globe and Mail*, 2 Apr., A8.

Scott, Sheridan. 1998. 'The Impact of Technological Change on Canada's Cultural Industries', in Dennis Browne, ed, *The Culture/Trade Quandary: Canada's Policy Options*. Ottawa: Centre for Trade Policy and Law, 54–93.

Sears, Robin V. 2006. 'The Politics of Climate Change: From One Government to the Next', *Policy Options,* Oct.: 6–11.

Seguin, Rhéal. 2006. 'Quebec Unveils Carbon Tax; Province Hopes Levy on Oil and Gas Firms Will Put $1.2-billion Toward Its Kyoto Goals', *Globe and Mail*, 16 June, A1.

Sharp, Mitchell. 1972. 'Canada–US Relations: Options for the Future', *International Perspectives* , Special Issue (Autumn): 1–24.

Sheikh, Pervaze, and Julie Jennings. 2005. Letter to Kent Conrad, Senator for North Dakota, regarding references to the IJC, 25 Apr. <http://www.swc.state.nd.us/projects/newdevilslake/pdfs/IJC_Referrals_Summary_Memo.pdf>.

Sierra Club. 2004. 'Kyoto Report Card 2004', <http://www.sierraclub.ca/national/kyoto/executive-summary-2004.html>.

Simpson, Jeffrey. 2004. 'Here's a Shocker: We're Flunking the One-Tonne Challenge', *Globe and Mail*, 7 Dec., A19.

———. 2005. 'The Dirty Lowdown about Canada's Commitment to Kyoto', *Globe and Mail*, 2 Dec., A23.

———. 2006a. 'Still Looking For Bold (Or Anything) On Climate Change', *Globe and Mail*, 29 Sept., A17.

———. 2006b. 'The Prime Minister Is Blowing a Lot of Hot Air', *Globe and Mail*, 11 Oct., A21.

———. 2006c. 'Rona Ambrose Has Been Left to Smile Pretty for the Cameras', *Globe and Mail*, 15 Dec., A23.

———. 2007a. 'The Silence of Big Business on Climate Change is Deafening', *Globe and Mail*, 23 Jan., A17.

———. 2007b. 'It's Official: The Climate is Warming. Now What?' *Globe and Mail*, 3 Feb., A25.

———. 2007c. 'Kyoto Was Too Ambitious; This Latest Plan Not Ambitious Enough', *Globe and Mail*, 28 Apr., A23.

Sjolander, Claire Turenne. 1996. 'Cashing In on the 'Peace Dividend': National Defence in the Post–Cold War World', in Gene Swimmer, ed, *How Ottawa Spends, 1996–97: Life under the Knife*. Ottawa: Carleton University Press, 253–81.

——— and Miguel De Larrinaga. 1998. '(Re)Presenting Landmines From Protector to Enemy: The Discursive Framing of a New Multilateralism', *Canadian Foreign Policy* 5, 3: 125–46.

Slaughter, Anne-Marie. 2005. 'Security, Solidarity and Sovereignty: The Grand Themes of UN Reform', *American Journal of International Law* 99, 619.

Smith, Denis. 1973. *Gentle Patriot: A Political Biography of Walter Gordon*. Edmonton: Hurtig.

Smith, Gordon. 2007. 'Canada in Afghanistan: Is It Working?' Canadian Defence and Foreign Affairs Institute.

——— and John B. Hay. 1999. 'Canada and the Crisis in Eastern Zaire', in Chester A. Crocker, Fen Osler Hampson, and Pamela Aall, eds, *Herding Cats: Multiparty Mediation in a Complex World*. Washington, DC: United States Institute of Peace, 85–106.

Smith, Jackie, Ron Pagnuco, and George A. Lopez. 1998. 'Globalizing Human Rights: The Work of Transnational Human Rights NGOs in the 1990s', *Human Rights Quarterly* 20: 378–9.

Smith-Windsor, Brooke A. 2000. 'Hard Power, Soft Power Reconsidered', *Canadian Military Journal* 1, 3 (Autumn): 51–6.

Smythe, Elizabeth. 1994. *Free to Choose? Globalization, Dependence and Canada's Changing Foreign Investment Regime, 1957–1987*. PhD diss. Ottawa: Carleton University.

———. 1996. 'Investment Policy', in Bruce Doern, Leslie Pal, and Brian Tomlin, eds, *Border Crossings: The Internationalization of Canadian Public Policy*. Toronto: Oxford University Press, 188–208.

————. 1998. 'The Multilateral Agreement on Investment: A Charter of Rights for Global Investors or Just Another Agreement?' in Fen Hampson and Maureen Molot, eds, *Canada Among Nations 1998: Leadership and Dialogue.* Toronto: Oxford University Press, 239–66.

Sokolsky, Joel J. 2000. 'Over There with Uncle Sam: Peacekeeping, the Trans–European Bargain and the Canadian Forces', in David Haglund, ed, *What NATO for Canada?* Kingston: Centre for International Relations, Queen's University, 15–36.

————. 2002. 'Clausewitz Canadian Style?' *Canadian Military Journal* 3, 3 (Autumn): 3–8.

————. 2004. *Realism Canadian Style: The Chrétien Legacy in National Security Policy.* Montreal: Institute for Research on Public Policy.

South China Morning Press. 2005. 'One for the Little Guys', 26 Oct.

Special Joint Committee of the Senate and House of Commons Reviewing Canadian Foreign Policy (SJC-CFP). 1994. *Canada's Foreign Policy: Principles and Priorities for the Future.* Ottawa: Parliamentary Publications Directorate.

Spector, Norman. 2007. 'Schwarzenegger's Visit Muddied the Waters on Climate Change', *Globe and Mail*, 4 June, S2.

Speirs, Rosemary. 1997. 'Who's In Charge of Cabinet?' *Toronto Star,* 1 Feb.

Spencer, Metta. 1997. 'Science for Peace Roundtable on the Lessons of Yugoslavia', *Canadian Foreign Policy* 5, 1 (Fall): 73–94.

Spicer, Keith. 1966. *A Samaritan State? External Aid in Canada's Foreign Policy.* Toronto: University of Toronto Press.

Sprynczynatyk, Dave. 2005. Telephone interview, 24 Nov.

St Amour, Norman. 1991. 'Sino–Canadian Relations, 1963-1968: The American Factor', in Paul M. Evans and B. Michael Frolic, eds, *Reluctant Adversaries: Canada and the People's Republic of China 1949–1970.* Toronto: University of Toronto Press, 106–32.

Stairs, Denis. 1972. 'The Military as an Instrument of Canadian Foreign Policy', in Hector J. Massey, ed, *The Canadian Military: A Profile.* Toronto: Copp Clark, 86–118.

————. 1995. 'The Public Politics of the Canadian Defence and Foreign Policy Reviews', *Canadian Foreign Policy* 3, 1 (Spring): 91–116.

————. 2003. 'Myths, Morals, and Reality in Canadian Foreign Policy', *International Journal* 58 (Spring): 239–56.

Stanford, Jim. 2002–3. 'Two Roads to Kyoto: More or Less', *Policy Options*, Dec.–Jan.: 53–6.

Status of Women Canada. 1996. 'Canada's International Activities to Promote the Advancement of Women: Highlights 1990–1997', Ottawa: Status of Women Canada.

Stein, Janice Gross. 1994. 'Canada 21: A Moment and a Model', *Canadian Foreign Policy* 2, 1 (Spring): 9–13.

Steinstra, Deborah. 2003. 'Gendered Dissonance: Feminists, FAFIA, and Canadian Foreign Policy', in Claire Turenne Sjolander, Heather Smith, and Deborah Stienstra, eds, *Feminist Perspectives on Canadian Foreign Policy.* Toronto: Oxford University Press, 198–215.

Stiglitz, Joseph. 1998. *Towards a New Paradigm for Development: Strategies, Policies, Processes.* Washington, DC: The World Bank.

————. 1999. *Participation and Development: Perspectives from the Comprehensive Development Paradigm.* Washington, DC: The World Bank.

Stilborn, Jack. 2002. 'The Kyoto Protocol: Intergovernmental Issues', *Library of Parliament—Political and Social Affairs Division.* (1 Nov.): 1–13.

Stork, Joe. 1998. 'International Criminal Court', *Human Rights Watch* 3, 4 (Apr.). <http://www.fpif.org/briefs/vol3/v3n4icc_body.html>.

Strong, Maurice. 2007. 'A Super Agency? Yes, Canada Should Propose One, Says Maurice Strong, Who First Put Global Warming on the World Agenda', *Globe and Mail*, 7 Mar., A15.

Struck, Doug. 2006. 'Canada Alters Course on Kyoto: Budget Slashes Funding Devoted to Goals of Emissions Pact', *Washington Post*, 3 May, A16.

Tessier, Manon, and Michel Fortmann. 2001. 'The Conservative Approach to International Peacekeeping', in Nelson Michaud and Kim Richard Nossal, eds, *Diplomatic Departures—The Conservative Era in Canadian Foreign Policy, 1984–93*. Vancouver: UBC Press, 113–27.

Tiessen, Rebecca. 2003. 'Masculinities, Femininities, and Sustainable Development: A Gender Analysis of DFAIT's Sustainable Development Strategy', in Claire Turenne Sjolander, Heather Smith, and Deborah Stienstra, eds, *Feminist Perspectives on Canadian Foreign Policy*. Toronto: Oxford University Press, 108–23.

Tomlin, Brian W. 1998. 'On a Fast Track to a Ban: The Canadian Policy Process', *Canadian Foreign Policy* 5: 3–23.

———. 2001. 'Leaving the Past Behind: The Free Trade Initiative Assessed', in Nelson Michaud and Kim Nossal, eds, *Diplomatic Departures: The Conservative Era in Foreign Policy*, 1984–93. Vancouver: UBC Press, 45–58.

———. 2007. *A Garbage Can Model of Multilateral Negotiation: Creating the Inter-American Democratic Charter*. Occasional Papers in International Trade Law and Policy. No. 59. Ottawa: Centre for Trade Policy and Law.

——— and Maureen Molot. 1985. 'A Time of Transition: Issues, Environment and Government', in Brian Tomlin and Maureen Molot, eds, *Canada Among Nations 1984: A Time of Transition*. Toronto: Lorimer, 3–13.

Tomlinson, Brian. 2000–1. 'Tracking Change in Canadian ODA', *International Journal* 56, 1 (Winter): 54–72.

Toner, Glen. 1984. 'Oil, Gas, and Integration', in Jon Pammett and Brian Tomlin, eds, *The Integration Question: Political Economy and Public Policy in Canada and North America*. Toronto: Addison-Wesley, 226–47.

Toronto Star. 1997. 'Sheila and Sergio', 14 June, B2.

Transformation Moment: A Canadian Vision of Common Security. 1992. The report of the Citizen's Inquiry into Peace and Security.

Treasury Board of Canada. 2007. *RPP 2007–2008: Canadian International Development Agency–Section I: Departmental Overview*. Ottawa: Treasury Board of Canada.

Treasury Board Secretariat, Government of Canada. 2003. <www.tbs-sct.gc.ca/est-pre/20022004/cida-acdi/cida-acdir34_e.asp>.

Trent, John, and Fergus Watt. 2005. *United Nations World Summit-Major Achievements, Postponements, Failures*. 30 Sept. Ottawa: World Federalist Movement. <http://www.world federalistscanada.org/summitassessment.pdf>.

Trudeau, Pierre Elliott, and Jacques Hebert. 2007. *Two Innocents in Red China*. Vancouver: Douglas & McIntyre.

Truehart, Charles. 1994. 'Culture Clash: Canadian Nationalists Decry American Infiltration', *Washington Post Foreign Service*, 2 Dec.

United Nations. 1997. *The World Conferences: Developing Priorities for the 21st Century*. New York: United Nations.

———. 2000. 'United Nations Millennium Declaration', General Assembly Resolution A/RES/55/2. New York: United Nations.

———. 2005. *World Summit 2005: Outcome Documents*. United Nations General Assembly, 60th Session, (A/60/L.1) 31, paragraphs 138 and 139. 20 Sept.

United Nations Development Programme (UNDP). 1994. *Human Development Report 1994—New Dimensions of Development*. New York: Oxford University Press.

United Nations Educational, Scientific and Cultural Organization (UNESCO). 2005. *Convention on the Protection and Promotion of the Diversity of Cultural Expressions*. Paris: UNESCO. <http://portal.unesco.org/culture/en/ev.php-URL_ID=29123&URL_DO=DO_TOPIC&URL_SECTION=201.html>.

United Nations General Assembly. 1975. 'Thirtieth Session of the General Assembly: Resolutions'. New York: United Nations.

——. 1993. A/RES/48/75, 81st Plenary Meeting, 16 Dec.

United States Army Corps of Engineers. 2003. *Final Devils Lake, North Dakota Integrated Planning Report and Environmental Impact Study*, vol. 1. St Paul: US Army Corps of Engineers.

United States Congress. Senate. 1997. 'Statement of Senator Kent Conrad', *Devils Lake Flood Control Project*. 105th Congress, 1st Session, 23 Oct. <http://epw.senate.gov/105th/con10-23.htm>.

United States Department of State. 1994. *Hidden Killers: The Global Problem with Uncleared Landmines*. Washington, DC: US Department of State.

——. 2005a. 'Joint Press Statement on Devils Lake Flooding and Ecological Protection by The United States and Canada, North Dakota, Minnesota and Manitoba', press release, 5 Aug. <http://www.state.gov/r/pa/prs/ps/2005/50831.htm>.

——. 2005b. 'United States Opposes Draft UN Cultural Diversity Convention—Ambassador Louise Oliver Tells UNESCO the Draft Is Defective', press release, 19 Oct.

Urquhart, Ian. 2002–3. 'Kyoto and the Absence of Leadership in Canada's Capitals', *Policy Options*, Dec.–Jan.: 23–6.

Van Rooy, Alison. 2001. 'Civil Society and the Axworthy Touch', in Fen Osler Hampson, Norman Hillmer, and Maureen Molot, eds, *Canada Among Nations 2001: The Axworthy Legacy*. Toronto: Oxford University Press, 253–69.

Velin, Jo-Anne. 1997. 'Verification Issue Cleaves Landmine Ban Supporters', *Disarmament Diplomacy* 14 Apr. <http://www.acronym.org.uk/dd/dd14/14land.htm>.

von Riekhoff, Harald. 1978. 'The Third Option in Canadian Foreign Policy', in Brian Tomlin, ed, *Canada's Foreign Policy: Analysis and Trends*. Toronto: Methuen, 87–109.

—— John Sigler, and Brian Tomlin. 1979. *Canadian–U.S. Relations: Policy Environments, Issues, and Prospects*. Montreal: C.D. Howe Research Institute.

Waddell, Christopher. 2003. 'Erasing the Line: Rebuilding Economic and Trade Relations After 11 September', in David Carment, Fen Hampson, and Norman Hillmer, eds, *Canada Among Nations 2003: Coping with the American Colossus*. Toronto: Oxford University Press, 54–76.

Walsh, Edward. 1995. 'Once a Puddle, Lake Knows No Bounds As It Grows and Grows', *Washington Post*, 5 July, A3.

Walton, Dawn. 2007. 'PM Not Addressing Problem, Critics Charge', *Globe and Mail*, 7 Apr., A3.

Waltz, Kenneth N. 1959. *Man, the State, and War: A Theoretical Analysis*. New York: Columbia University Press.

——. 1979. *Theory of International Politics*. Toronto: Addison-Wesley.

Wareham, Mary. 1998. 'Rhetoric and Policy Realities in the United States', in Brian Tomlin, Max Cameron, and Bob Lawson, eds, *To Walk Without Fear: The Global Movement to Ban Landmines*. Toronto: Oxford University Press, 212–43.

War to Peace Transitions. 2005. A Conference Report of the 8th Peacebuilding and Human Security Consultations. Ottawa, Apr. <http://www.humansecurity.info/sites/cchs/files/pdfs/Consultation%20Papers/8th/8th_peacebuilding_consult_finalreport.pdf>.

Watt, Fergus. 1998. *Campaign for the International Criminal Court—An Independent and Effective International Criminal Court*. Ottawa: World Federalist Movement.

———. 2005. '*A Time for UN Reform?*' remarks presented to the 8th Annual Peacebuilding and Human Security Consultations. Ottawa, 19–20 Jan.

Wattie, Chris. 2005. 'US Senators Reject "Devils" Compromise', *National Post*, 28 Apr., A11.

Wedgwood, Ruth. 1998. 'Fiddling in Rome: America and the International Criminal Court', *Foreign Affairs* 77, 6: 20–4.

Welch, David A. 1992. 'The New Multilateralism and Evolving Security Systems', in Fen O. Hampson and Christopher J. Maule, eds, *Canada Among Nations 1992–93: A New World Order?* Ottawa: Carleton University Press, 67–93.

———. 2005. *Painful Choices: A Theory of Foreign Policy Change*. Princeton: Princeton University Press.

Weller, Marc. 1999. 'The Rambouillet Conference on Kosovo', *International Affairs* 75, 2: 211–51.

Welsh, Jennifer. 2004. *At Home in the World: Canada's Global Vision for the 21st Century*. Toronto: HarperCollins.

Wente, Margaret. 2005. 'Kyoto Always Was a Fantasy', *Globe and Mail*, 29 Nov. A21.

Werthes, Sascha, and David Bosold. 2006. 'Caught between Pretension and Substantiveness—Ambiguities of Human Security as Political Leitmotif', in Tobias Debiel and Sascha Werthes, eds, *Human Security on Foreign Policy Agendas: Changes, Concepts and Cases*. INEF report 80, Duisberg: Institute for Development and Peace, University of Duisburg-Essen, 21-38. < http://inef.uni-due.de/page/documents/Report80.pdf>.

Wetzel, Dale. 1997. 'Canadian Officials Want a Look at Plans for Devils Lake Outlet', *Bismarck Tribune*, 5 Mar., 2B.

———. 1999. 'N.D. Will Do Study on Outlet', *Bismarck Tribune*, 22 June, 1A.

Wheeler, Marilyn. 1995. 'Aptly Named Slow-Motion Flood on Devils Lake Maroons Homes', *Chicago Tribune*, 11 June, 7A.

Willoughby, William R. 1981. 'Expectations and Experience', in Robert Spencer, John Kirton, and Kim Richard Nossal, eds, *The International Joint Commission Seventy Years On*. Toronto: University of Toronto Press, 24–42.

Winham, Gilbert. 1994. 'NAFTA and the Trade Policy Revolution of the 1980s: A Canadian Perspective', *International Journal* 49, 3: 472–508.

Winnipeg Free Press. 2003. 'Devils Lake Channel Gets OK', 26 Feb., B1.

Wise, Carol. 1998. *The Post-NAFTA Political Economy: Mexico and the Western Hemisphere*. University Park: Pennsylvania State University Press.

Wolfe, David. 1978. 'Economic Growth and Foreign Investment: A Perspective on Canadian Economic Policy, 1945–57', *Journal of Canadian Studies* 13, 1: 3–20.

Wonnacott, Ronald. 1990. 'US Hub-and-Spoke Bilaterals and the Multilateral Trading System', *C.D. Howe Institute Commentary*. Toronto: C.D. Howe Institute.

Wood, Bernard. 1990. *Peace in Our Time? A Canadian Agenda into the 1990s*. Ottawa: Canadian Institute for International Peace and Security.

World Bank. 2000. *World Bank Development Report 2000/1: Attacking Poverty*. Washington, DC: The World Bank.

———. 2006. Comprehensive Development Framework. <http://web.worldbank.org>

World Federalist Movement Civil Society—Institute for Global Policy. 2003. *Perspectives on the Responsibility to Protect—Final Report*, 30 Apr. New York: World Federalist Movement Civil Society—Institute for Global Policy. <http://www.wfm.org>.

World Trade Organization (WTO). 2001. 'The Doha Declaration Explained', ministerial declaration, adopted on 14 Nov. <http://www.wto.org/English/tratop_e/dda_e/dohaexplained_e.htm>.

————. 2003. 'Decision Removes Final Patent Obstacle to Cheap Drug Imports', press release, 30 Aug. <http://www.wto.org/english/news_e/pres03_e/pr350_e.htm>.

Wright, Gerald. 1974. 'Persuasive Influence: The Case of the Interest Equalization Tax', in Andrew Axline, James Hyndman, Peyton Lyon, and Maureen Molot, eds, *Continental Community? Independence and Integration in North America.* Toronto: McClelland and Stewart, 137–62.

York, Geoffrey. 1993. 'Military's Image Badly Tarnished', *Globe and Mail*, 20 May.

Index